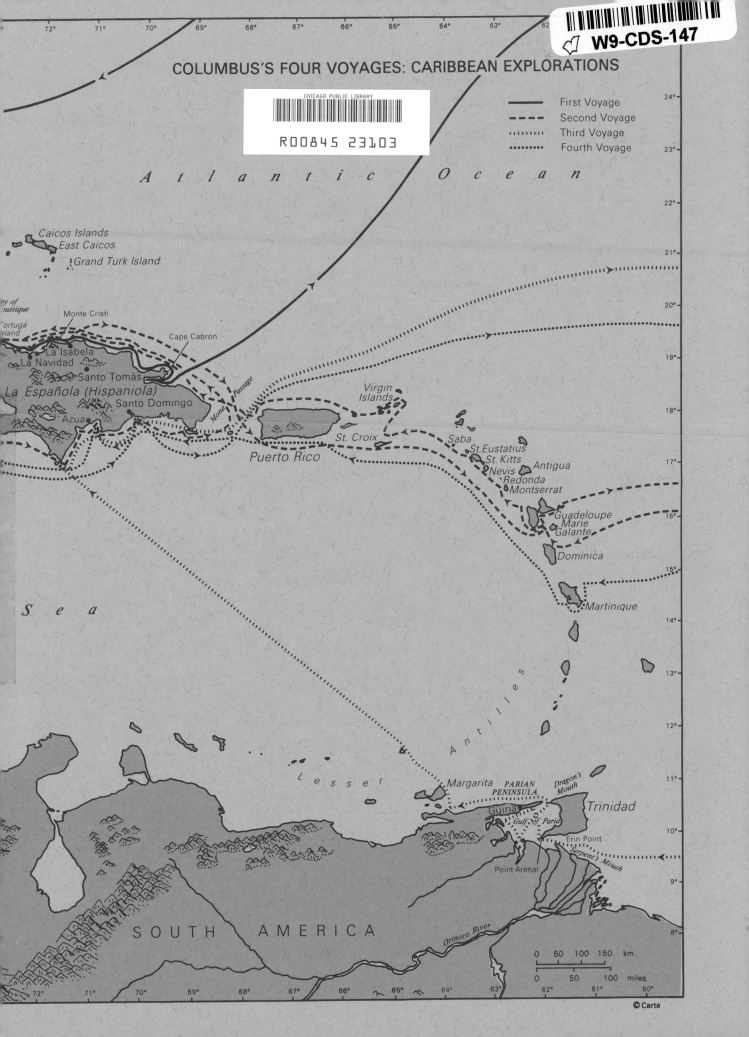

COLUMBUS'S FOUR VOYAGES: CARIBBEAN EXPLORATIONS

First Voyage
Second Voyage
Third Voyage
Fourth Voyage

A t l a n t i c   O c e a n

Caicos Islands
East Caicos
Grand Turk Island

y of
ustique

ortuga
sland

Monte Cristi

Cape Cabron

La Isabela
La Navidad
Santo Tomás

La Española (Hispaniola)

Santo Domingo

Azua

Mona Passage

Virgin Islands

St. Croix

Saba
St. Eustatius
St. Kitts
Nevis   Antigua
Redonda
Montserrat

Puerto Rico

Guadeloupe
Marie
Galante

Dominica

Martinique

S e a

L e s s e r

A n t i l l e s

Margarita   *PARIAN PENINSULA*   Dragon's Mouth

Guiria   Trinidad
Gulf of Paria

Erin Point

Serpent's Mouth

Point Arenal

S O U T H   A M E R I C A

Orinoco River

| 0 | 50 | 100 | 150 | km. |

| 0 | 50 | 100 | miles |

© Carta

The
Christopher Columbus
Encyclopedia

The Christopher Columbus Encyclopedia

SILVIO A. BEDINI, Editor
Emeritus, The Smithsonian Institution

Editorial Board

DAVID BUISSERET
The Newberry Library

HELEN NADER
Indiana University

WILCOMB E. WASHBURN
The Smithsonian Institution

PAULINE MOFFIT WATTS
Sarah Lawrence College

Volume 2

SIMON & SCHUSTER

A Paramount Communications Company

New York   London   Toronto   Sydney   Tokyo   Singapore

Academic Reference Division
Simon and Schuster
15 Columbus Circle
New York, New York 10023

Printed in the United States of America

printing number
2 3 4 5 6 7 8 9 10

Library of Congress Cataloging-in-Publication Data

The Christopher Columbus Encyclopedia

Silvio A. Bedini, Editor in Chief

Includes bibliographies and index.
1. Columbus, Christopher—Encyclopedias.
2. America—Discovery and exploration—Encyclopedias.

E111.0774 1992   970.01′5′03—dc20   90-29253

ISBN 0-13-142662-1 (set)
ISBN 0-13-142688-5 (v. 2)

*Acknowledgments of sources, copyrights, and
permissions to use previously printed materials
are made throughout the work.*

Abbreviations and Symbols Used in This Work

A.D. *anno Domini,* in the year of (our) Lord
A.H. *anno Hegirae,* in the year of the Hijrah
Ala. Alabama
A.M. *ante meridiem,* before noon
Ariz. Arizona
Ark. Arkansas
b. born
B.C. before Christ
B.C.E. before the common era
c. *circa,* about, approximately
Calif. California
C.E. of the common era
cf. *confer,* compare
chap. chapter (pl., **chaps.**)
cm centimeters
Colo. Colorado
Conn. Connecticut
d. died
D.C. District of Columbia
Del. Delaware
diss. dissertation
ed. editor (pl., **eds.**); edition; edited by
e.g. *exempli gratia,* for example

Eng. England
enl. enlarged
esp. especially
et al. *et alii,* and others
etc. *et cetera,* and so forth
exp. expanded
f. and following (pl., **ff.**)
fl. *floruit,* flourished
Fla. Florida
frag. fragment
ft. feet
Ga. Georgia
ibid. *ibidem,* in the same place (as the one immediately preceding)
i.e. *id est,* that is
Ill. Illinois
Ind. Indiana
Kans. Kansas
km kilometers
Ky. Kentucky
La. Louisiana
m meters
M.A. Master of Arts
Mass. Massachusetts
mi. miles
Mich. Michigan
Minn. Minnesota
Miss. Mississippi
Mo. Missouri

Mont. Montana
n. note
N.C. North Carolina
n.d. no date
N.Dak. North Dakota
Neb. Nebraska
Nev. Nevada
N.H. New Hampshire
N.J. New Jersey
N.Mex. New Mexico
no. number (pl., **nos.**)
n.p. no place
n.s. new series
N.Y. New York
Okla. Oklahoma
Oreg. Oregon
p. page (pl., **pp.**)
Pa. Pennsylvania
pl. plural, plate (pl., **pls.**)
P.M. *post meridiem,* after noon
Port. Portuguese
pt. part (pl., **pts.**)
r. reigned; ruled
rev. revised
R.I. Rhode Island
sc. *scilicet,* namely
S.C. South Carolina
S.Dak. South Dakota
sec. section (pl., **secs.**)

ser. series
sing. singular
sq. square
supp. supplement; supplementary
Tenn. Tennessee
Tex. Texas
trans. translator, translators; translated by; translation
U.S. United States
USNR. United States Naval Reserve
U.S.S.R. Union of Soviet Socialist Republics
v. verse (pl., **vv.**)
Va. Virginia
var. variant; variation
vol. volume (pl., **vols.**)
Vt. Vermont
Wash. Washington
Wis. Wisconsin
W.Va. West Virginia
Wyo. Wyoming
? uncertain; possibly; perhaps
° degrees

A Note on Monetary Systems

Various monetary systems were in use in the Columbian era. The maravedi was a unit of account only, used to record salaries and payments. The Spanish and Genoese maravedi were roughly equal in value and related to different forms of currency as follows:

375 maravedis to 1 gold ducat,
435 maravedis to 1 gold castellano (or peso d'oro),
870 maravedis to 1 gold excelente.

L

LA COSA, JUAN DE. See *Cosa, Juan de la.*

LANDFALL CONTROVERSY. "In 1492, Columbus sailed the ocean blue." Despite the appalling geographical ignorance of schoolchildren, many would recognize these words. But just where did Columbus land? Virtually every island in the Bahamas chain, from the Berry Islands on the north to Grand Turk on the south, a distance of more than three hundred miles, has been suggested as the landfall site. This lack of knowledge of where Columbus first landed can be traced, first, to the fact that Columbus was searching for something else: densely populated lands and vast stores of wealth. These islands were mere way stations on the way to his prime objective. That objective, as he noted in his journal at the time, was the noble island of Cipangu (Japan) or, if he overshot that island, the mainland of China. Instead he found Cuba and some of the other great islands of the Caribbean. Second, the limited wealth of the islands, such as it was, consisted primarily of the bodies of their inhabitants, and this wealth was quickly exhausted by slave-raiding expeditions, at which point the islands ceased to be of any real interest to the Spaniards.

The cartography of the period following the discoveries does not help us much in solving the mystery. San Salvador, as Columbus named the landfall island, or Guanahani, as he reported the island was called by its inhabitants, was often placed by cartographers at differing and widely separated islands in the Bahamas. Charting the earth's surface was plagued by uncertainty, the result of the limited scientific methods available to establish latitude and longitude and the often conflicting and confused reports of navigators.

Nor do the early Spanish histories of the discoveries help in solving the mystery. Gonzalo Fernández de Oviedo's *Historia general y natural de las Indias* (1535) states that the first lands discovered were called the "white islands" (*islas blancas*) because these sandy isles seemed to be white, that Columbus named them "the princesses," and that Guanahani was adjacent to them and to another island called "Caicos." This passage—late though it is—gives support to proponents of the Grand Turk as the landfall island since that island is surrounded by small sandy islets (of exceptional whiteness) and is adjacent to the Caicos Islands. But other histories, such as Antonio de Herrera y Tordesillas's four-volume *Historia general de los hechos de los castellanos en las Islas, y Tierra Firme de el Mar Océano* (1601–1615), in discussing Juan Ponce de León's 1513 discovery of Florida while sailing from San Juan, Puerto Rico, through the Bahamas from south to north, locates the island of San Salvador, "the first that Admiral Don Christóval Colón discovered," in the central or northern Bahamas.

Although the islands first sighted by Columbus rapidly declined in importance, their significance at the time is evident from the names he bestowed upon them and the order in which he did so. The first island, which served to validate the lifetime of faith and reason that Columbus had invested in his great enterprise, he named San Salvador in honor of the Savior Jesus Christ; the second, Santa María de la Concepción, in honor of the Virgin Mary; the third, La Fernandina, in honor of King Fernando; and the fourth, La Isabela, in honor of Queen Isabel.

Eighteenth- and Nineteenth-Century Theories

Although the location of Columbus's landfall was not a matter of great concern in the first century after his

Columbus's Landfalls in the Bahamas in 1492

EARLY THEORIES						
Columbus's Name (Indian Name)	M. Fernández de Navarrete	Washington Irving	A. B. Becher	J. B. Murdock	G. V. Fox	George Gibbs
1. San Salvador (Guanahani)	Grand Turk	Cat Island	San Salvador (Watlings)	San Salvador (Watlings)	Samana Cay	Grank Turk
2. Santa María	Caicos	Conception Island	Long Island	Rum Cay	Crooked Island	Caicos
3. Fernandina (Yuma)	Little Inagua	Great Exuma	Great Exuma	Long Island	Long Island	Little Inagua
4. Isabela (Saometo)	Great Inagua	Long Island	Crooked Island	Crooked Island Fortune Island	Fortune Island	Great Inagua
5. Islas Arenas or Cuban Coast		Mucarras	Ragged Islands Port Nipe	Ragged Islands Bay of Gibara	Ragged Islands Port Padre	

TWENTIETH-CENTURY THEORIES						
Columbus's Name (Indian Name)	Northern Landfall		Central Landfall			Southern Landfall
	Arne Molander	John Hathaway Winslow	S. E. Morison M. Obregon	Pedro Grau y Triana	Joseph Judge	Robert Power
1. San Salvador (Guanahani)	Egg Island	Great Harbor Cay	San Salvador (Watlings)	San Salvador (Watlings)	Samana Cay	Grand Turk
2. Santa María	New Providence	New Providence	Rum Cay	Rum Cay	Crooked Island Acklins Island	Providenciales
3. Fernandina (Yuma)	Andros	Andros	Long Island	Long Island	Long Island	Mayaguana Acklins Island
4. Isabela (Saometo)	Long Island (Southern)	Hurricane Flats	Crooked Island	Crooked Island	Fortune Island	Great Inagua
5. Islas Arenas or Cuban Coast	Ragged Islands	Fragoso Cay	Ragged Islands	Ragged Islands	Ragged Islands	Ragged Islands

SOURCE: Joseph M. Laufer, *Discovery 500,* Spring, 1990.

voyage, in the eighteenth century scholars became interested as they began to study the history and character of the area. The first to comment on the location of the landfall was Mark Catesby, in the first volume of his *Natural History of Carolina* (1731), in which he identified Cat Island ("formerly called Salvador, or Guanahani") in the northern Bahamas as the landfall site. His choice was given added luster when Washington Irving, in his *Life and Voyages of Christopher Columbus* (1828), supported this designation. In the meantime, however, Juan Bautista Muñoz, commissioned by the Spanish king to write *Historia del Nuevo Mundo* (1793), concluded that the island Columbus named San Salvador was Watlings Island in the central portion of the Bahamas chain. And, in 1825, Martín Fernández de Navarrete, in his five-volume *Colección de los viages y descubrimientos que hicieron por mar los españoles desde fines del siglo XV con varios documentos inéditos* (1825–1837), came to the conclusion that Columbus's landfall must have been the Grand Turk, the southernmost island of the Bahamas chain, now under

separate political jurisdiction as part of the Turks and Caicos Islands.

Subsequent historians, naval officers, geographers, journalists, and amateurs with a wide variety of professional or nonprofessional skills offered other candidates for the landfall, including Mayaguana, Samana, South Caicos, Concepción (Conception Island), Eleuthera, Lignum Vitae Cay (Great Harbour Cay in the Berry Islands), Egg and Royal islands, and Plana Cays, or reiterated the choice of Cat, Watlings, or Grand Turk. On the four-hundredth anniversary of the discovery of America, the World's Columbian Exposition sent a special commissioner, Frederick A. Ober, to the Bahamas to determine the site of the first landfall. Ober published his report, *In the Wake of Columbus* (1893), noting that "no two investigators agree as to the first landfall without disagreeing as to the second; and if they happen to coincide on the first, it is only to fall out over the fourth." Ober concluded, however, that the weight of opinion favored Watlings Island.

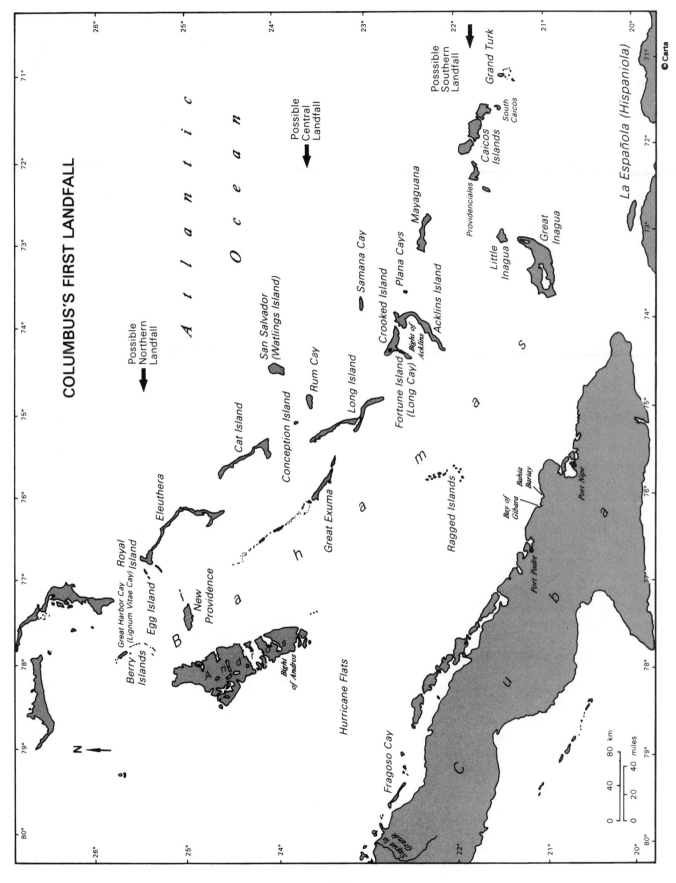

COLUMBUS'S FIRST LANDFALL

Possible Northern Landfall

Possible Central Landfall

Possssible Southern Landfall

A t l a n t i c   O c e a n

Royal (Lignum Vitae Cay) Island
Great Harbor Cay
Berry Islands
Egg Island
New Providence
Eleuthera
Cat Island
San Salvador (Watlings Island)
Conception Island
Rum Cay
Long Island
Samana Cay
Crooked Island
Plana Cays
Fortune Island (Long Cay)
Bight of Acklins
Acklins Island
Mayaguana
Providenciales
Caicos Islands
South Caicos
Grand Turk
Little Inagua
Great Inagua

B a h a m a s

A n d r o s
Bight of Andros
Hurricane Flats
Great Exuma
Ragged Islands
Fragoso Cay

Bay of Gibara
Bahia Bariay
Port Nipe
Port Padre
Puerto Padre
C u b a
Sagua la Grande

La Española (Hispaniola)

© Carta

N

0   40   80 km
0   20   40 miles

The Twentieth-Century Debate

The debate over the Columbus landfall intensified as the five-hundredth anniversary of the landing approached and popular interest in the question mounted. The intensity of the debate rose to a particular peak with the publication in 1986 in *National Geographic* of the results of an extensive examination of the question by Joseph Judge, the senior associate editor of the magazine. Judge's candidate for the landfall was Samana Cay, a judgment that was supported by a high-tech attempt to duplicate the voyage across the Atlantic and the subsequent route to Cuba, by an attempt to match Columbus's description of the landfall island with Samana, and by a quick archaeological investigation on the now uninhabited island itself.

Too often the protagonists in the landfall debate, who met in conferences and debates in the late 1980s and early 1990s, tended to dismiss the claims of their opponents with ill-concealed contempt, turning what might have been well-mannered scholarly debate into a series of undignified squabbles. The participants occasionally approached the question in the spirit of religion, relying on faith and inferences, rather than in the spirit of scientific caution.

Columbus's Journal. Few of the modern participants in the landfall debate have recognized the wisdom of Justin Winsor, editor of the eight-volume *Narrative and Critical History of America* (1884–1889), who wrote that "the main, or rather the only source for the decision of this question is the Journal of Columbus; and it is to be regretted that Las Casas did not leave unabridged the parts preceding the landfall, as he did those immediately following, down to October 29. Not a word outside of this Journal is helpful."

All arguments on the question of the landfall, as Winsor pointed out, ultimately depend upon the journal of Columbus, the original of which was presented to Queen Isabel, who had scribes make a copy for Columbus. Both are lost. The friar and historian Bartolomé de las Casas made an abstract of Columbus's journal from the returned copy (sometimes quoting, as Winsor noted, Columbus's exact words) for use in his *Historia de las Indias*. Fernando Colón, the Admiral's son, seems also to have had access to this copy (or possibly to another) of the original log and made use of it in preparing his book on the life of his father, which has come down to us in the form of his 1571 *Historie del S. D. Fernando Colombo*. Whether Las Casas worked from the first copy or even a copy of the copy, the possibility of transcription errors makes all estimates of Columbus's course and distances covered problematic. In the Las Casas transcription of Columbus's journal, numerous words and numbers have been crossed out and corrected; moreover, Las Casas himself noted the difficulty of determining the original meaning of some of the passages of the journal. No one can know how many words of the original log (or of the second copy) were wrongly transcribed and left uncorrected.

Las Casas has been accused not only of distortions, conscious or unconscious, in his rendition of the Columbus log but even of falsifying its contents to support his own views. Most such attacks on his honesty, however, are now discounted and his commitment to recording Columbus's journal with accuracy and goodwill conceded.

Samuel Eliot Morison. The debates of the 1980s and 1990s, starting with papers presented at the 1981 meeting of the Society for the History of Discoveries, took as the accepted wisdom (or principal target) the conclusion of the American scholar Samuel Eliot Morison. He had concluded in 1942, in his *Admiral of the Ocean Sea*, a Pulitzer Prize–winning biography of Columbus, that "there is no longer any doubt that the island called Guanahani, which Columbus renamed after Our Lord and Saviour, was the present San Salvador or Watlings." Morison went on to assert that "that alone of any island in the Bahamas, Turks or Caicos groups, fits Columbus's description. The position of San Salvador and of no other island fits the course laid down in his Journal, if we work it backward from Cuba."

The assumed landing in Cuba was, in Morison's opinion, Bahia Bariay, a wide harbor backed by several mountain peaks, one of which Columbus described as having on its summit "another little peak like a pretty little mosque," which later Spanish settlers named "La Teta de Bariay." Virtually all the theorists of the landfall island concede Bahia Bariay to be Columbus's Cuban terminus. One theorist, however, John Hathaway Winslow, has postulated a landing point in Cuba west of Bahia Bariay, at the river Sagua la Grande, which he feels is a better match than Bahia Bariay with Columbus's log and which supports his own candidate for the landfall island, Lignum Vitae (Great Harbour Cay) in the Berry Islands, the farthest north and west of the proposed landfall islands.

Despite the assurance with which Morison stated his conclusion, his argument depended (as he himself noted) on drawing a number of conclusions from frequently contradictory or at least confusing evidence. Nowhere is this more evident than in Morison's adjustment of Las Casas's report of Columbus's calculation of distances sailed between the landfall island and Cuba. Morison postulates that Columbus used a smaller "league" to describe along-shore distances in comparison with overwater distances, a hypothesis that seems to be derived more from the need to make the distances reported in the log conform to the postulated route than from any logical theory. The alternate league (a league of about 1.5 nautical miles instead of 3.18 nautical miles) is proposed first to explain why Columbus described the second island, Rum Cay, a small island with a five-mile north-south coast and a ten-mile east-west coast, as ten leagues long and five leagues wide. The choice of Rum Cay for the second island forces Morison to make another significant assumption. That is that Rum Cay could be initially perceived as a string of six islands that upon closer observation turns out to be a single island with six hillocks. The difficulty in Morison's reasoning to explain the lack of a proper fit between the Columbus log and the course reported between the first and second islands is matched by all the other proposed landfall theorists, though the major difficulty for each appears at different stages in the course between the landfall and the arrival in Cuba.

Mauricio Obregon, a participant in some of the landfall debates and an accomplished pilot and yachtsman, had flown over and sailed through the islands with Morison and others. Obregon defended Morison's judgment concerning the Watlings Island landfall, though he made some modifications in the subsequent route laid down by Morison.

The fatal weakness of all landfall theories, it is important to remember, rests on the absence of the original log. All the theories necessitate arbitrary assumptions about the direction of Columbus's movement, the distances sailed, and the length of the league or mile he used. Since the Spanish words for *east* and *west* are susceptible to mistranscription, since it is not always clear whether Columbus was referring to a mile or the much longer league, and since distances, particularly when recorded in roman numerals, can be easily confused, it is little wonder that all participants in the landfall debate require the reader's indulgence to explain some gap in the route and accept a reality on sea or land that cannot be derived from the text of Columbus's journal. None of the participants in the debate lacks ingenuity, however, in explaining why the anomalies in his route should be accepted while those of his opponents should not.

Physical Descriptions. The evidence least capable of distortion in transmission is the physical description of the island in the log. In what Las Casas recorded as the actual words (*palabras formales*) of the Admiral, Columbus described the first island as quite large (*bien grande*), level, without mountains, and with a large lake or lagoon in the middle (*una laguna en medio*) and *muchas aguas* (which might mean bodies of water or possibly sources of drinking water). Columbus also described the island as having at least one coast running north-northeast, a harbor that would hold all the ships in Christendom, reefs surrounding much of the island, and a peninsula that could be cut through to make a site for a fortress. In addition, it was green with many trees and heavily

populated. This physical description, in words that are Columbus's own, is less capable of mistranscription than the directions and distances of his prior and subsequent sailing. More difficult to deduce from the journal than the physical description of the island is its exact size. The size can be estimated by calculating the time Columbus may have taken in surveying the island by longboat, though it is unclear from the account in his log exactly what route was followed, whether the longboat could have been assisted by sails, and whether it returned to the precise spot from which it departed.

Assuming that the physical description of the island in Las Casas's transcription of the log is the most reliable of all the evidence of the landfall, the two suggested islands that most closely fit the description are Watlings and Grand Turk. The absence of any archaeological evidence of native habitation on Grand Turk was, until the discovery by William Keegan in December 1989 of a Lucayan site on the southern end of the island, a near-fatal flaw in the Grand Turk candidacy. With that discovery, the island's claim was enhanced. More difficult to reconcile with the physical description of the island in Columbus's log is Samana Cay, the candidate of Capt. Gustavus Vasa Fox of the U.S. Navy in 1882 and, more than a hundred years later, of Joseph Judge of *National Geographic*. Judge has argued long and forcefully that there are "many waters" and a lake or lagoon in the middle of "his" island and has found other parallels to the description of the island and the course to and from it in the Columbus log. But, despite the prestige of the National Geographic Society sponsorship, few scholars have been converted to the Samana Cay solution. Judge bitterly attacked Mauricio Obregon for his presumed role in encouraging the 5th Ibero-American Quincentenary Conference, meeting in Puerto Rico in May 1987, to declare that San Salvador/Watlings Island would be considered the landfall of Columbus for purposes of the celebration of the Quincentenary, even though the declaration did not imply that the issue was definitely settled.

Cartographic Evidence. It might be assumed that the geographical location of the landfall island could be most easily determined from the cartographic evidence. But the maps on which the landfall island and surrounding islands are recorded form an unreliable guide. In part this was because, as the *Atlas Maritimus and Commercialis*, published in London in 1728, put it, "there is not any of these Islands worth naming, any more than they have been worth possessing: And Columbus, first Discoverer, soon found Places of more Importance to him." Guanahani, as the island was called by the inhabitants who greeted Columbus, appears on many of the maps that were drawn in the several centuries following the discovery, but as one student of the cartographic evidence has said, "this island, at least at first glance, appears to float about the central Bahamas." The earliest map on which Guanahani is found is the world map of Juan de la Cosa, of about 1500, which also records an island named Samana to the south. Unfortunately, on the Cosa map and later ones, both islands lack a precise outline and a consistent location. Alonso Cháves's *Espejo de navegantes*, the earliest set of sailing directions for the Bahamas (c. 1530), describes Samana as east-southeast of Guanahani at a distance of eight leagues, both islands being at twenty-five degrees north latitude.

Although identification must be speculative, Kim Dian Gainer believes that the Samana island on Juan de la Cosa's map represents Rum Cay, and "therefore the first cartographic evidence we have is consistent with a landfall on Watling rather than Samana Cay." "One thing is certain," Gainer adds: "this Samana is not today's Samana Cay." After an exhaustive study of all the relevant maps, Gainer concluded that the preponderance of evidence for the location and relationship of the various islands of the Bahamas on early maps "appears to favor a Watling landfall rather than one on Samana Cay. . . . The only maps that do not seem to favor a Watling landfall are those that fall outside the Spanish tradition." Nevertheless, the cartographic evidence is sufficiently uncertain that other candidates for the landfall should not be ruled out on that evidence alone.

The Latitude Question. The latitude of the landfall island has also been a persistent subject of debate. Columbus asserted in his journal entry for October 13 that he was not surprised by the color of the natives of San Salvador because their complexion resembled that of the natives of the Canary Islands and were located on an east-west line directly west of Hierro (Ferro) in the Canaries. San Salvador is at twenty-four degrees, six minutes; Ferro, twenty-seven degrees, forty-six minutes. Was Columbus navigating by latitude sailing rather than dead reckoning? The former method, by which the navigator maintains a constant elevation angle to the solar and stellar meridians, is far more accurate than sailing by dead reckoning, which relies on compass headings and estimates of the ship's speed, both subject to great errors. Samuel Eliot Morison argued that Columbus used dead reckoning as his navigational method, but this is not inconsistent with trying to "run down" a latitude that would carry him from the Canaries directly to Cipangu and which could be done by taking nightly observations of Polaris—the North Star—as well as by dead reckoning. It is clear that Columbus did not attempt to plot his course by celestial navigation, though he admired those men of learning, like the astronomer Josephus Vizinho, adviser to the Portuguese king João II, who were experts in such matters. It is also clear that he was wildly off in many of his estimates of his latitude in the New World. But so were most navigators of his time.

In fact, the latitude of Hierro is several degrees north of the latitude of San Salvador and even farther north of Samana and Grand Turk. Arne B. Molander, one of the participants in the landfall debate, uses Columbus's attempted latitude sailing and his belief that he was at twenty-eight degrees north latitude to support his candidate for the landfall: Egg and Royal islands off the northern end of Eleuthera in the northern Bahamas. On the other hand, Robert Power and Josiah Marvel, proponents of the southern landfall at Grand Turk, cite the fact that Grand Turk and Hierro on the Juan de la Cosa map and other early maps are on the same latitude to support their conclusion, on the theory that Columbus, as will be noted below, was deceived by the magnetic variation of the compass in the Western Hemisphere into thinking he was sailing due west when in fact he was being diverted toward the south.

National Geographic sought to trace Columbus's route from the Canary Islands utilizing computers to calculate the effect of ocean currents or leeway (the sideways slip of a sailing vessel owing to the force of the wind). The expedition, under the direction of Luis Marden, sought to check the accuracy of the 1941 attempt of Lt. John W. McElroy, USNR, Morison's collaborator, to follow Columbus's log day by day. McElroy made no allowance for leeway or ocean currents on the assumption that they were negligible or canceled out, and his route ended near Watlings Island. Marden's ended near Samana Cay. Marden's work was challenged by Philip L. Richardson and Roger A. Goldsmith of the Woods Hole Oceanographic Institution, using historical wind and current data assembled as part of their ongoing investigations into the currents and circulation of the world's oceans. Applying this data to the track of *Santa María*, and correcting flaws in the Marden study, Richardson and Goldsmith brought Columbus's ships to within twenty-five kilometers of Watlings Island.

Despite the learned debate about current, leeway, the length of a league, and the magnetic variation of the compass (all continuing matters of debate over Columbus's route), the attempt to replicate the course of a voyage across three thousand miles of ocean to the exact site of a tiny landfall island is fraught with difficulties. It is little wonder that doubts about the exact course of Columbus's route across the ocean continue to puzzle students of the voyage.

Proponents of the Grand Turk landfall, several degrees of latitude farther to the south, face an even greater difficulty in explaining why Columbus landed so much farther south of the latitude he assumed he was following. The explanation given by advocates of Grand Turk is framed in terms of Columbus's misunderstanding of the effects of magnetic declination of the compass as his ships sailed across the Atlantic. Marvel and Power assert that if Columbus's compass was, as was customary, calibrated for local magnetic variation at its place of manufacture, presumably Seville, at 5⅝ degrees east, then the contrary westerly magnetic variation in the western Atlantic would cause a vessel "sailing across the Ocean by dead reckoning to veer imperceptibly to the south." They are encouraged by the fact that Richardson and Goldsmith concede that with a different assumption of the extent of westerly magnetic variation as it may have existed in 1492—a matter about which no one can speak with certainty—Grand Turk becomes "a reasonable candidate" for the landfall.

The presumption of the magnetic variation theory is that while assuming he was sailing due west, Columbus would increasingly be headed farther south than he realized. "A northward displacement of the lands of the New World near the Tropic of Cancer of at least six degrees," Marvel notes, "is consistently found on Discovery Period charts." The inference is drawn by supporters of the southern route that navigators, including Columbus, were unable to recognize the true direction they were following because of the magnetic shift in the compass as the ships moved across the Atlantic. This assumption, however, can be questioned for a number of reasons, not the least of which is that Columbus was the first to notice (on September 13, 1492) the shift from easterly to westerly variation in the compass. He observed and commented on the shift in the course of his first three voyages. Although he was not, as his son Fernando claimed, the discoverer of westerly variation, Columbus recognized the diurnal rotation of Polaris and the necessity to make the appropriate adjustments in determining one's latitude. On his third voyage, on the night of August 15–16, 1498, when sailing from Margarita Island to La Española, he noticed that the compass needles were suddenly showing a westerly variation of about seventeen degrees. As Morison noted, "If he had not discovered this variation, and altered his course accordingly, he would have missed Hispaniola [La Española]." Although Columbus often misjudged his latitude, such inaccuracies, whether caused by irregularities in Columbus's compass needle or other factors, seem unlikely to be determinative of the true landfall site.

Archaeological Evidence. Archaeological excavations undertaken in the Bahamas in recent years give us evidence that may confirm some of the observations found in Columbus's log. Charles A. Hoffman has found Spanish objects in an otherwise undisturbed pre-contact site on Watlings Island. William F. Keegan has located the densest concentration of Lucayan habitations in the Bahamas (including a settlement stretching along the shore for more than three miles) in the Acklins Island area, bordering on the shallow lagoon made up of Fortune, Crooked, and Acklins islands. In addition he unearthed a leg bone of a crocodile (hitherto unknown in the Bahamas) on a site near the northwestern cape of Crooked Island, which may represent the creature described as a "serpent" that Columbus and his men killed after it slithered into a shallow pond where Columbus was collecting fresh water for his ships. The archaeological evidence, which is sparse on Samana and Grand Turk, tends to support those who point to Watlings as the landfall island.

Northern or Southern Bahamas? A significant weakness of the southern landfall theory is the fact that Columbus records that he understood from the Indians on San Salvador that if he went to the south, or around the island to the south, he would find a king who had much gold, including "large vessels of it." Columbus, in his log, recorded his intention to go to the southwest in search of gold and precious stones, a direction he presumably followed although he did not specifically record his course when he left San Salvador. It is the horseshoe-shaped group of islands made up of Fortune, Crooked, and Acklins, surrounding a shallow lagoon, that Keegan concludes is the best match for the fourth island, named by Columbus "Isabella," an island identified by the Indians Columbus took with him from San Salvador as "Samonet, where the gold is." Columbus was unable to reach the king of the island because of the shallowness of the bay or bight that lay between his ships and the reported site of the king's village. Because he was eager to continue his voyage of exploration, and because he was somewhat doubtful about the reports he had received from the Indians "from not understanding them well and also from recognizing that they are so poor in gold that any little bit that the king may wear seems so much to them," Columbus decided to push on. If Columbus's communication with the Indians of San Salvador was free of error, in both its initial transmission and its notation in the log used by Las Casas, and if it referred to a king in the islands of the Bahamas rather than on the larger island of Cuba farther south, and if Columbus sailed in the direction he said he intended to, then the landfall island would more likely be in the northern rather than the southern portion of the Bahamas. But, like much of the evidence set forth in the landfall debate, such facts and inferences are always subject to error or misinterpretation.

Two participants in the landfall debate, Christopher C. Larimore and John Hathaway Winslow, have argued that Columbus would have been able to sail through, in the one case the Bight of Acklins, and in the other the Bight of Andros, because of changes in the sea depths in those areas since 1492. But such changes seem doubtful in the light of the work of Keegan and the geologist Neil Sealey.

The Historical Perspective. It would be futile to recount all the arguments and reasoning behind each of the candidates for the landfall. All are ingenious, but they all depend upon a fragile superstructure of evidence. From the historian's point of view, the question of which island was Columbus's landfall is of minor interest. Just as Columbus soon left the island behind in his memory, so the historian is more concerned about what followed than with the famous first sighting and landing in the New World. For the historian, these moments comprise less a series of firsts or events than a complex process of the movement of Europeans into a world inhabited by people of whom they had no knowledge.

The fact and location of the landfall is an important historical datum and a subject worthy of careful scrutiny, but it is more interesting to the public than to the historian. Part of this interest is commercial. The public is fascinated by the historical past and willing to pay much to "see" it. The island on which Columbus landed is expected to be heavily visited well beyond the quincentennial year. Hotels and resorts will be built in proximity to the presumed site of the landing. The government of the Bahamas is well aware of the attraction of San Salvador to a world of tourists to whom "The Past is a Foreign Country," to quote the title of David Lowenthal's book on the subject of our pervasive and nostalgic attempt to recapture the past. For the same reason, the government of the Turks and Caicos Islands is also aware of the advantage of having the Grand Turk designated the landfall island of Columbus. Indeed, all the islands that have a claim to be the site where Columbus first set foot in the New World stand to benefit monetarily from the public's fascination with historical firsts. From a scholarly as well as a touristic point of view the question of the landfall of Columbus might more profitably remain open rather than closed.

[See also *Compass,* article on *Declination of the Compass; Navigation; Tides and Currents.*]

BIBLIOGRAPHY

De Vorsey, Louis, Jr., and John Parker. *In the Wake of Columbus: Islands and Controversy.* Detroit, 1985.

Discovery Five Hundred (Newsletter of the International Columbian Quincentenary Alliance) 5, no. 2 (Spring 1990). Special issue: Columbus Landfall.

Gainer, Kim Dian. "The Cartographic Evidence for Columbus Landfall." *Terrae Incognitae* 20 (1988): 43–68.

Jane, Cecil, trans. *The Journal of Christopher Columbus.* With an appendix by R. A. Skelton on "The Cartography of Columbus's First Voyage." New York, 1960.

Judge, Joseph. "Our Search for the True Columbus Landfall." *National Geographic* 170, no. 5 (1986): 564–605.

Keegan, William F. "The Columbus Chronicles." *The Sciences* (New York Academy of Sciences) (January–February 1989): 46–55.

Keen, Benjamin, trans. and ed. *The Life of the Admiral Christopher Columbus by His Son Ferdinand.* New Brunswick, N.J., 1959.

Marvel, Josiah. "On the First Landfall of Christopher Columbus in the New World: Textual and Cartographic Evidence Supporting the Hypothesis That It Took Place on Grand Turk Island." Typescript. 1990.

Morison, Samuel Eliot. *Admiral of the Ocean Sea: A Life of Christopher Columbus.* Boston, 1942.

Morison, Samuel Eliot. "Columbus and Polaris." *American Neptune* 1, no. 1 (1941): 6–25; 1, no. 2 (1941): 123–137.

Morison, Samuel Eliot, and Mauricio Obregon. *The Caribbean as Columbus Saw It.* Boston, 1964.

Ober, Frederick A. *In the Wake of Columbus.* Boston, 1893.

Peck, Douglas T. "Reconstruction and Analysis of the 1492 Columbus Log from a Sailor-Navigator Viewpoint," Rev. ed. Multilith. 1988.

Richardson, Philip L., and Roger A. Goldsmith. "The Columbus Landfall: Voyage Track Corrected for Winds and Currents." *Oceanus* 30 (1987): 2–10.

Sealey, Neil E. "An Examination of the Geography of Three Major Contenders for Columbus's First Landfall in 1492." Mimeograph. 1990.

Winsor, Justin. "Columbus and His Discoveries." In vol. 2 of *Narrative and Critical History of America.* 8 vols. Boston, 1884–1889.

Wilcomb E. Washburn

LAS CASAS, BARTOLOMÉ DE

LAS CASAS, BARTOLOMÉ DE (1484–1566), Spanish defender of the Indians, theologian, and historian. The son of a merchant, Las Casas was born and raised in Seville, then a great Spanish commercial and cultural center. He was eight when Columbus returned from his first voyage, and in his *Historia de las Indias* (History of the Indies), recalled how he and his father watched a solemn procession led by Columbus and his crew, followed by the first Indians to set foot in the Old World, as it passed through the streets of Seville on Palm Sunday, 1493. His father, Pedro de las Casas, and three uncles accompanied Columbus on his second voyage of 1493 that brought some two thousand colonists to La Española (Hispaniola). In 1502, Bartolomé, aged eighteen, himself went over to manage the land and Indians that Columbus had granted his father. Although troubled by the disastrous situation of the Taino Indians, whose numbers were rapidly dwindling as a result of the ruthless exploitation and slavehunting expeditions initiated by Columbus, the young Las Casas was concerned above all with bettering his fortunes and even appears to have taken part in a military campaign organized by Governor Nicolás de Ovando against the Indians in the eastern part of the island.

BARTOLOMÉ DE LAS CASAS. Engraving from *Retratos de los Españoles illustratres con un epitome de sus vidos*, 1791.

LIBRARY OF CONGRESS, RARE BOOK DIVISION

In 1506 Las Casas returned to Europe where he remained for several years. His close, friendly ties with the Columbus family are suggested by the fact that in 1506 he accompanied the Admiral's older brother, Bartolomé Colón, to Rome to inform Pope Julius II of the opportunities for the spread of the faith created by the discovery of the New World. In Rome, too, in 1507, Las Casas was ordained to the priesthood (he had already taken the tonsure, probably in 1501). Meanwhile Columbus had died, and in 1507 Las Casas returned to La Española with Columbus's son and heir, Diego Colón, second Admiral and Viceroy of the Indies. Las Casas undoubtedly hoped that the condition of the Indians would improve under Diego's milder rule, but the viceroy, hampered by his disputes with the Crown over the extent of his rights and with royal officials on the island, proved unable to achieve reform.

Favored, like his father, by the Columbus family, Las Casas received a good piece of land and a grant of Indians from Diego and combined the profitable activities of agriculture, stockraising, mining, and trade with the office of *doctrinero*, a parish priest who provided religious instruction to the Indians. In 1510 a group of Dominican friars arrived in the island. Horrified by the barbarous treatment of the Indians, they delegated one of their number, Antonio Montesino, to preach a sermon that would drive home to the settlers the wickedness of their deeds. The angry colonists responded by calling on the friars to retract their sentiments or pack up and sail for home. In reply, Montesino mounted the pulpit the following Sunday and let loose an even more terrific blast against mistreatment of the Indians. Although Las Casas sympathized with the Dominicans, he did not agree with their denunciation as mortal sin of the encomienda system of forced Indian labor. He was still a priest-colonist, a man of good will who treated his own Indians kindly but was interested above all in promoting his *granjerías*, or enterprises. In 1513–1514 he served as military chaplain in the conquest of Cuba—a conquest whose atrocities he vainly tried to prevent—and was again rewarded for his services with a large grant of Indians. His Cuban agricultural and stockraising enterprises prospered, and he coldly rebuffed a Dominican friar who reproached him for neglecting the religious instruction of the natives.

In 1514, however, he experienced a conversion, apparently the awakening of a dormant sensitivity as a result of the horrors he had seen about him. He renounced his own encomienda of Indians and, in 1515, accompanied by Antonio Montesino, set sail from Santo Domingo, determined to inform King Fernando and his ministers that the encomienda system was destroying the Indians and must be abolished.

Las Casas arrived in Spain at a propitious time, for in late 1516 Fernando, who had been indifferent or hostile to reform, died and was succeeded as regent by the aged Cardinal Francisco Jiménez de Cisneros. Las Casas presented the cardinal with a plan, supported by Diego Colón, for the removal of the Indians from individual encomiendas and their resettlement in self-sustaining villages with Spanish administrators. These villages would pay tribute to the Crown and contribute a limited number of workers for mining, and the encomenderos would be compensated for their loss of workers. Las Casas envisaged a parallel colonization by Spanish peasants who would live and work side by side with the Indians, teach them to live in a civilized way, and gradually bring into being an ideal Christian community. Cisneros authorized the experiment, but assigned its supervision to a group of Jeronymite friars (known for their successful management of large estates), with Las Casas to accompany them as "Protector of the Indians." The Jeronymites, lukewarm toward the project from the first and swayed by the hostile attitude of the settlers, soon gave as their opinion that the

Indians were unfit to live by themselves in a civilized way; they also complained of Las Casas's interference with the new trade in Bahaman slaves.

Fleeing La Española to escape arrest for disobeying the Jeronymites, Las Casas returned to Spain and resumed his struggle in defense of the Indians. Cisneros died in 1517, and the arrival in Spain of the young King Carlos I (the future Emperor Charles V), surrounded by Flemish courtiers who took a broader view of the royal interest in the Indies than the late King Fernando or his ministers, favored Las Casas's reformist projects. He won approval for a new scheme that combined a program of peasant colonization of Tierra Firme (Venezuela) and of Indian conversion with exploitation of the pearl and gold resources of the region by a company based in Santo Domingo. But the project ended in a complete fiasco, for the peasants recruited by Las Casas abandoned him on reaching the islands to join in the profitable slave trade, and his mission outpost of Cumaná was destroyed by Indians provoked by slavehunting raids organized by the very same Caribbean interests on whose support Las Casas had naively counted.

The disastrous failure of the Venezuelan colonization project produced what the French scholar Marcel Bataillon called Las Casas's "second conversion." Las Casas himself tells that after the fiasco of Cumaná in 1521 he felt he was dead and buried—perhaps meaning that he was buried in the Dominican convent in Santo Domingo, which he entered in 1522, and became dead to the world that he had known. The Las Casas who "died" in 1521 was the priest-reformer who proposed to reconcile Spanish private interests and Indian welfare and himself did not scruple to share in the profits of colonial enterprise; the Dominican friar who emerged from the convent in 1531 after almost ten years of immersion in juridical-theological study advanced a revolutionary creed based on solid doctrinal foundations. Henceforth Las Casas's ideology centered on the right of the Indians to their land, on the principle of self-determination, and on the subordination of all Spanish interests (including those of the Crown) to Indian interests, material and spiritual. Las Casas argued that the papal grant of America to the Crown of Castile had been made solely for the purpose of conversion and gave the Spanish Crown no temporal power or possession in the Indies. The Indians had rightful possession of their lands by natural law and the law of nations. All Spanish wars and conquests in the New World were illegal. Spain must bring Christianity to the Indians by the only method "that is proper and natural to men . . . namely, love and gentleness and kindness."

With the passage of time, Las Casas's thought became progressively more radical. His final program called for the suppression of all encomiendas, liberation of the Indians from all forms of servitude except a small voluntary tribute to the Crown in recompense for its gift of Christianity, and the restoration of the ancient Indian states and rulers, the rightful owners of those lands. Over these states the Spanish king would preside as "Emperor over many kings" in order to fulfill his sacred mission of bringing the Indians to the Catholic faith and the Christian way of life. The instruments of that mission should be friars, who would enjoy special jurisdiction over the Indians and protect them from the corrupting influence of lay Spaniards. These elements of Las Casas's final program may be called truly utopian and were never taken seriously by the Crown. But the main thrust of his program after his "second conversion"—the demand that the encomienda be abolished and the colonists be denied control over Indian tribute and labor—fully coincided with the royal interest in curbing the power of the conquistadores and preventing the rise of a powerful colonial feudalism in the New World. This coincidence explains the official support that Las Casas's reform efforts received in the reign of Carlos I (Charles V of the Holy Roman Empire), 1516–1556.

The common view of Las Casas as waging a lonely struggle to convince a reluctant Crown to accept colonial reform could not be more mistaken. The most elementary interests of the Crown demanded that the catastrophe of the West Indies, where the Indians had become an extinct race, should not be repeated in the newly conquered rich and populous empires of Mexico and Peru. But the Crown had to move cautiously, for it feared a revolt by the aggressive conquistadores. As early as 1523, when Las Casas was still secluded in his monastery, King Carlos sent Hernando Cortés an order forbidding the establishment of encomiendas in New Spain (the former Aztec Empire), because "God had created the Indians free and not subject." But in the face of Cortés's disobedience, backed by his hard-bitten followers, the Crown chose to retreat.

Far from waging a lonely struggle in defense of the Indians, then, Las Casas enjoyed the support of powerful political and social forces including the Crown, royal officials, and important members of the clergy, all of whom had an obvious interest in the preservation of the Indian population. Even the Cortes (parliament) of Castile intervened in the Indian question; summoned by Charles V in 1541, it asked that the abuses committed by the Spaniards in the Indies be ended lest the native population disappear.

Las Casas owed his leadership of this broadly based struggle in defense of the Indians to his militant, combative spirit; his mastery of scholastic philosophy and Church doctrine, which he displayed with telling effect in his famous debate in 1551–1552 with the humanist Juan Gimés de Sepúlveda over the justice of wars against the

Indians; his gifts as a propagandist, illustrated by the simple yet profoundly moving style of his *Brevíssima relación de la destruición de las Indias* (Very brief account of the destruction of the Indies); and his great political talent, his ability to negotiate, maneuver, and even compromise without sacrificing essential principles.

Las Casas and his followers won a major victory with the issuance of the New Laws of the Indies (1542). These laws appeared to doom the encomienda. They forbade the enslavement of Indians, ordered the release of slaves to whom legal title could not be proved, barred compulsory personal service by the Indians, and proclaimed that existing encomiendas were to lapse on the death of the holder. Las Casas himself, named Bishop of Chiapas, then a province of Guatemala, went out in 1545 to ensure compliance with the New Laws in a region that was a hotbed of slavehunting and other abuses against the natives. Received with hostility by the settlers who rejected his authority and even threatened him with death, and denied support by the audiencia (high court) for the region, Las Casas had to return to Spain. Meanwhile, faced with a storm of protest by the colonists throughout the Indies and a great revolt in Peru, the Crown had yielded to pressure and agreed to a compromise that recognized the right of inheritance by the heir of an encomendero; this right was gradually extended for a number of generations.

Under pressure, Charles V had made a partial retreat from his own pro-Indian policy; his son, Philip II, in effect abandoned that policy on his accession to the throne in 1556. Faced with a desperate financial crisis, Philip increased the burden on Indians paying tribute to the Crown and moved toward a rapprochement with the colonial oligarchies, allowing them greater control over the Indians on their estates and encomiendas. Simultaneously the influence of Las Casas and his Indianist movement virtually disappeared from the Spanish court. What Marcel Bataillon calls "the anti-Lascasian reaction" of Philip's reign was reflected, among other ways, in decrees forbidding colonial clergy to use the spiritual arms of the church: excommunication, interdict, and denial of absolution—weapons that Las Casas and his followers had systematically employed to secure compliance with Indian protective legislation. Despite the collapse of his Indian policy, Las Casas continued to the end of his life his struggle for justice for the Indians. One of his last actions was to send a letter to Pope Pius V asking the pontiff to order, on pain of excommunication, an end to the unjust wars against the Indians and the violent expropriation of their lands on the pretext of their conversion. The depth of Las Casas's disillusionment with Spain's Indian policy is suggested by his testament, notarized on March 5, 1564, in which he affirmed that on

account of the "great sins and injustices" committed by the Spaniards in the Indies, and "the robberies and murders and usurpations of the states and lordships of the natural kings and lords," God must vent upon Spain "His force and wrath."

An integral part of Las Casas's campaign in defense of the Indians was his authorship of a large body of works that made important contributions to anthropology, political theory, and history. In his debate with Sepúlveda, a spokesman for the encomenderos who invoked Aristotle to prove that the Indians were slaves by nature and that their conquest was a just war, Las Casas eloquently affirmed the equality of all races and the essential unity of mankind. He elaborated these arguments in his great *Apologética historia sumaria* (Apologetical history), not published until 1909, an immense accumulation of ethnographic data used to demonstrate that the Indians met all the requirements laid down by Aristotle for the good life. In this work he also developed a rudimentary theory of cultural evolution, applied to all Indian societies, that enabled him to examine the customs and beliefs of an Indian people dispassionately and within the framework of its own culture. This relativist approach even led him to develop the daring argument that Indian human sacrifice was not proof of depravity but evidence of a profound religious feeling. The theory also suggested comparison of Indian cultures with civilizations of other times and places that appeared to represent about the same state of development. Las Casas may justly be called the father of anthropology.

In his tract *De regia potestate* (Concerning the royal power), written in opposition to the encomenderos' proposal for a grant of the perpetual encomienda, which would convert their Indian tributaries into hereditary serfs, Las Casas advanced what his modern Spanish editors call three "democratic dogmas." First, all power derives from the people; second, power is delegated to rulers in order that they may serve the people; third, all important governmental acts require popular consultation and approval. These democratic ideas had medieval antecedents, but in their new context, challenging the right of the king to dispose of his Indian subjects, those old ideas acquired a subversive, revolutionary tinge.

For students of Columbus and his voyages, Las Casas's monumental *History of the Indies*, written between 1527 and 1562 but not published until 1875, has a special interest and value, for it is in considerable part a biography of Columbus and incorporates the single best source of information on the Discovery: Las Casas's abstract—part summary and part direct quotations—of Columbus's lost Diario, the journal of his first voyage to America.

Las Casas passionately admires the Admiral, chosen "among all the sons of Adam" for the providential task of opening "the doors of the Ocean Sea." He sees a divine design in the pattern of his life until his arrival in Castile, endows him with great virtues, and bitterly criticizes the injustice and ingratitude with which the Spanish monarchs treated him and his family. But when Las Casas turns to discuss Columbus's arbitrary, exploitive conduct with the Indians, his tone changes. The hero Columbus becomes flawed, and Las Casas charges him with "inexcusable ignorance" of the rights of the Indians. Viewed from this perspective, the sufferings of the Admiral—his imprisonment, the loss of part of his privileges, and other injustices—are explained by Las Casas as divine punishment for Columbus's offenses against the Indians, a punishment meant to purge him of his sins and save him from eternal damnation. Despite this alternation between praise and blame, Las Casas leaves no doubt of his overwhelmingly favorable opinion of Columbus.

In the aftermath of World War II, which led to the collapse of regimes and colonial systems based on racism and the right of the strong to dominate the weak, Las Casas's teachings concerning the unity of mankind, the principle of self-determination, and the right of all people to the satisfaction of their elementary material and cultural needs have acquired a new relevance. The influence of his ideas is particularly evident in the growing acceptance by many clergy, especially in Latin America, of the so-called theology of liberation. This doctrine teaches that the church, returning to its roots, must again become the church of the poor. In Latin America today, the poorest of the poor are precisely the Indians who were the principal objects of Las Casas's care and compassion. The theology of liberation also teaches that the church must cease to be an ally of the rich and powerful and commit itself to the struggle for social justice, to "the preferential option for the poor." Clearly, these doctrines have much in common with Las Casas's own teachings.

[See also *Black Legend*; *Encomienda*; *Exploitation of Indians*; *Indian America*; *Missionary Movement*.]

BIBLIOGRAPHY

Friede, Juan, and Benjamin Keen, eds. *Bartolomé de las Casas in History: Toward an Understanding of the Man and His Work.* De Kalb, Ill., 1971.
Hanke, Lewis. *Aristotle and the American Indians.* London, 1959.
Hanke, Lewis. *The Spanish Struggle for Justice.* Philadelphia, 1949.
Wagner, Henry R. *The Life and Writings of Bartolomé de las Casas.* Albuquerque, 1967.

Benjamin Keen

LAST WILL AND TESTAMENT OF COLUMBUS.

See *Writings*, article on *Last Will and Testament*.

LATITUDE. Terrestrial latitude is the angular distance from the equator measured north or south on an arc of ninety degrees extending from the equator to either one of the poles. The linear distance of a degree of latitude on the earth's surface, its length, will depend, of course, on the figure of the earth adopted. The first known measurement of the circumference of the earth was made by Eratosthenes in the second century B.C., a calculation of extraordinary accuracy if the value of the somewhat flexible Greek stade is taken as 159 meters. Two centuries before, the latitude of Marseilles had been measured by Pytheas to within fifteen minutes of arc of its true value by using the gnomon to measure the sun's noonday shadow at the equinox. The gnomon could also be used to establish the terrestrial meridian, from the bisection of shadows of equal length either side of noon. And once latitude had been established, it could also be used to find the sun's declination. A table could then be drawn for other dates that would enable latitude to be calculated on any day in any locality by measuring the height of the sun at local apparent noon. Historically, then, the measurement of latitude, at least in principle, presented no difficulty.

During the fifteenth and sixteenth centuries latitude at sea was determined by observations of the North Star according to the Regiment (rule) of the North Star, a formula given in early Portuguese and Spanish navigation manuals. The rule gave the correction to the altitude of the North Star for its position in relation to the pole of the sky using the Guard Stars to trace its counterclockwise movement round the axis of the earth's rotation. Alternatively, latitude at sea could be obtained by measuring the meridian altitude of the sun using tables of the sun's declination or by measuring the altitude of any star at its culmination, which could be judged either by the relative positions of other stars or, less satisfactorily, from its compass bearing.

Despite the enormous impact on the scholarly world of the rediscovery of Ptolemy, whose *Geography* defined positions on the globe by their angular distance north or south of the equator and east and west of a chosen meridian, the fifteenth-century seaman still thought of observations of sun or star altitudes simply in terms of *altura* (height). Although parallels and meridians were starting to appear on maps, it was not until 1502 that a scale of latitude appeared on a sea chart.

The earliest altitude observations of the sun, as of the North Star, had been made to check the linear distance traveled in a north-south direction between a first observation, at the port of departure (typically Lisbon), and subsequent observations; the difference between readings was multiplied by 16⅔ (later 17½) to give the distance in leagues, corresponding to the accepted length of a degree of the meridian. Once the Portuguese in their explorations had reached the Gulf of Guinea, however, and a major part of the voyage was in an east-west direction, such a procedure became navigationally meaningless. Also, once the equator had been crossed, and the North Star lost, it became essential to develop techniques that would enable the navigator to use the sun to define latitude. This was the task undertaken by the mathematical commission appointed by King João II of Portugal, and the commission's findings were tested by José Vizinho in Guinea in 1485 and encapsulated in the new "Regiment of the Sun." A table of the sun's declination simplified by Vizinho from the tables of the astronomer Abraham Zacuto allowed the navigator to calculate his latitude at local apparent noon anywhere in the world. The procedures laid down in the Regiment of the Sun were far from simple. The sun's maximum altitude would first be observed, generally by the mariner's astrolabe, and the sun's declination for the day extracted from the table. The rules for applying the declination differed according to whether the observer was north or south of the equator (a difficulty in itself in equatorial latitudes), whether the declination was north or south, and whether, when both latitude and declination were either north or south, the declination was greater or less than the latitude.

In integrating the new methods, standard navigational practice now came to include observing the latitude each day, recording the courses made good and the estimated distances sailed, and, from the resulting position (the dead-reckoning position) and the observed latitude, determining the distance traveled east or west. The objective was to sail to a position one hundred leagues east or west of the destination and sail down the latitude to it. When in due course a latitude scale was added to the charts, the procedures laid down in the Regiment of the North Star would be used to derive latitude directly in degrees and fractions (or minutes). Latitude navigation in substantially this form was to endure well beyond the time when longitude observations became possible with the aid of a timekeeper, for the determination of latitude from the sun's meridian altitude is relatively simple, in terms of both observation and calculation.

[See also *Altura Sailing; Circumference; Longitude; Navigation.*]

BIBLIOGRAPHY

Albuquerque, Luís de. *Astronomical Navigation.* Lisbon, 1988.
Cotter, Charles A. *A History of Nautical Astronomy.* London, 1968.
Taylor, E. G. R. *The Haven Finding Art: A History of Navigation from Odysseus to Captain Cook.* London, 1956.

M. W. RICHEY

LAWSUITS (PLEITOS COLOMBINOS).

The Pleitos Colombinos are the texts of litigation between the heirs of Christopher Columbus and the Spanish Crown. The initial litigation stretched from 1508 to 1536 and then was continued by the family to 1790. The various legal suits of the Pleitos are filed in six *legajos* (batches of collected documents) on deposit in the Archivo General de Indias (Seville), dated 1508 to 1536. They concern the interpretation of Christopher Columbus's privileges as the circumstances of discovery and conquest drastically changed a risky venture into an unprecedented enterprise. Currently being published, this litigation will fill eight printed volumes.

The conflict with the Crown arose over the definitions of privileges, governmental and judicial powers, territorial extent, and economic rights and obligations. The privileges and contractual rights of Columbus, amended by confirmations and changes, are the substance of the litigation.

The judgments and compromises of the litigation drew the map of the Spanish enterprise in the Indies. Moreover, one can trace in the Pleitos the participation of bankers, merchants, entrepreneurs, soldiers, settlers, and professionals in the economy. The Pleitos Colombinos also shed light on the way the Spanish legal system functioned.

The inheritance litigation waged over ten generations is a separate series of lawsuits initiated after the extinction of the direct line of Columbus's descendants. It is briefly mentioned at the end of this discussion.

The Substance of the Conflict: The Capitulations of Santa Fe. An original agreement, comprising "capitulations" between the Spanish monarchs, Isabel and Fernando, and Columbus, was signed in two parts at the encampment of the Spanish army before the city of Santa Fe de la Vega de Granada on April 17 and 30, 1492. The opening reads: "The things supplicated and which your Highnesses give and declare to Christopher Columbus in some satisfaction for what he will discover [*ha de descubrir*] in the ocean-seas, and for the voyage which now, with the aid of God, he is about to make therein, are as follows." In the main points of the agreement, Columbus was given the following:

1. The position of viceroy and governor "over all the islands and mainland which by his hand and industry may be discovered or acquired in the said oceans," with the right to propose to the Crown a list of three names for every governmental post from which an appointee was to be selected by the sovereigns.
2. The position of admiral of the said islands and mainland, with the salaries, prerogatives, and privileges enjoyed by the high admiral of Castile, and with the right in person or by his representative to adjudge controversies regarding merchandise and commerce.
3. One-tenth of the net profits of the Crown in all the

articles and merchandise, whether pearls, precious stones, gold, silver, spices, or others, which might be bought, exchanged, found, acquired, or obtained within the limits of his jurisdiction.

4. The right to contribute and enjoy a participation of one-eighth in every expedition.

According to a memorial by Columbus, each of the articles was notarized separately, the whole being registered and signed "I, the King, and I, the Queen."

The so-called *título*, dated April 30, in Granada, contained the formal appointment to the office of Admiral of the Ocean Sea and to the titles and privileges of viceroy and governor. This document indicated the royal intention of making all three appointments hereditary, whereas the assumption of the first document was that only the admiralty would be hereditary. The prolix text also reads: "You may have the power to punish and chastise delinquents and may exercise the powers of Admiral, Viceroy and Governor, you and your lieutenants, over all that concerns and appertains to the said office and to each of them; and that you shall have and levy the fees and salaries annexed, belonging and pertaining to the said offices."

These were provisions written in anticipation of realizations of Alexandrian proportions on the part of Columbus and simultaneously with no intention to abdicate any privileges of sovereignty on the part of the Crown, no matter what the result of Columbus's venture. Although these clauses were prolix and judged by posterity as badly drawn, with blame liberally apportioned by litigants and historians, it is unrealistic to expect that an airtight legal agreement would have been produced under the complex historical circumstances—the siege of Granada, the recent victory over the Muslim foe of centuries, and the unanticipated discovery of a hemisphere.

Anticipation and Reality. The formula suggested by Columbus for his profit was unsustainable: one-tenth of the royal profit from the enterprise; one-eighth return on one-eighth of investment by him in the trade as it would develop; and one-third of any profit due him by virtue of his title of Admiral of the Ocean Sea. This would have added up to about 55 percent of the income from the enterprise of the Indies, a sum greater than that set aside for the Crown. The issue of the one-third of royal profit that was claimed by the admiral of Castile (from seizures at sea), a clause Columbus copied when he demanded the privileges of admiral, does not appear in the capitulations as such, but it had a phantom existence through the demands that Columbus lodged with the Crown subsequently and throughout his life. It should be understood that the income of the admiral of Castile from raids at sea was utterly distinct from Columbus's license to carry on

legitimate trade. It should also be noted that the admiralty of the Ocean Sea of the *título* did not include hereditary privileges in the Spanish ports.

Upon first landing on an unknown island, Columbus was rudely disappointed not to find himself in Cathay or even to be able to obtain local information about his legendary goal. But on his return to Spain, he persuaded the Crown of the vast potential of his discovery, especially as a source of gold. Columbus lost no time after his triumphant return in obtaining a confirmation of the agreements. A document of May 28, 1493, stated that the capitulations and the offices of admiral, viceroy, and governor covered lands in the same area granted to Spain in the papal bull of May 4, 1493, by Alexander VI that drew the famous Line of Demarcation between the spheres of influence of Spain and Portugal.

Reconfirmation of the capitulations was again obtained four years later, in Burgos on April 23 and 30, 1497. This document repeats the capitulations, with an added clause

DECREE OF ISABEL AND FERNANDO. Confirming the favors bestowed on Admiral Christopher Columbus before the Discovery. Barcelona, May 28, 1493. First page.

ARCHIVO GENERAL DE INDIAS, SEVILLE

stating that it was the royal will that they "be valid and be observed in favor of him and his children and descendants, now and hereafter forever, in entirety, and if it were necessary [the king and queen] make the said grant anew."

Anticipation that Columbus might indeed discover more lands, peoples, treasure, products, and markets led to greater care in the preparations for the following voyages. The admiral's monopoly on discovery of what was beginning to appear to be a vast region was the first privilege infringed upon by the man put in charge of the Indies fleets, Juan Rodríguez de Fonseca. In April 1495, he allowed Spaniards free navigation to the recently discovered lands, with the exception of lands protected under treaty with Portugal and those actually touched by Columbus. This order was retracted, however, on June 2, 1497, when Columbus received a confirmation of his rights from the Crown.

It is at this point that Columbus began to feel threatened and began to collect the documents of his privileges, honors, rights, claims to possession, and income. Questions about the extent of his jurisdiction, his monetary rights, the appointment of judges and officials, and other colonial initiatives, such as the granting of Indian labor, were cleared up only gradually before courts of law and through successive appeals.

On February 22, 1498, Columbus received royal permission to establish a *mayorazgo,* or entailed estate, including all his titles, privileges, and possessions. This document established the line of succession to the next of kin and repeated the entitlements given in perpetuity.

Events and Claims. Christopher Columbus never instituted a lawsuit during his lifetime. Instead, his complaints about the infringement of his rights by the treasury officials were lodged directly with the *fiscal,* or government solicitor. These concerned the method of determining his share of the royal profits. He insisted that his part of the profit be calculated on the gross receipts and that costs and expenses be taken from the portion that was left. He pleaded directly for the enforcement of his rights by the Crown. But royal officials insisted that costs and expenses be deducted before any distribution could be made. An agreement to this effect, to last for three years, was signed on June 12, 1497. The officials accused Columbus of taking more than his share, an accusation supported by the growing disaffection of the unruly colonists in La Española (Hispaniola), who presented their own case against Columbus and his brother Bartolomé in Spain.

Complaints about the abuse of his judicial powers, financial claims, administrative irregularities, and violations of agreements with settlers resulted in the suspension of the Admiral's governmental prerogatives, and the sequestration of his properties. Sent by the Crown to investigate Christopher's and Bartolomé's administration of the colony of La Española, Francisco de Bobadilla, as *juez pesquisidor* (investigative judge), forced the return of the brothers to Spain in October 1500. These facts, and the alleged infringement of Columbus's privileges, became the basis for the disputes with the Crown recorded in the Pleitos.

Columbus undertook a third and a fourth voyage, and the territorial extent of his claims was built on all four voyages. Doubts about where he had been and whether he had exercised the act of possession became one focus for conflict between the Admiral and the Crown; the actual contacts he made with the new lands during his voyages were the issue. On the first voyage he touched the Bahama Islands and discovered the north coasts of Cuba and of La Española. The second voyage took him through the Lesser Antilles. He then added the south coasts of La Española and Cuba and the island of Jamaica to the map. His third voyage made a landfall at Trinidad. He discovered the Dragon's Mouth (Boca del Dragón, the Gulf of Paria between Venezuela and Trinidad) and sailed along the mainland coast of the Paria Peninsula. After sighting the island of Margarita, he returned to the town of Santo Domingo and to Spain. His last exploration was along the coast of Central America from Honduras (Isla de Piños) to Darién. Since his having been at the coasts of South and Central America was a certainty, conflict arose over the extent of his claims to this mainland in terms of the capitulations of Santa Fe.

A parallel controversy arose over the scope of his governmental powers. One reading of the capitulations and confirmatory documents—granting the posts of viceroy and governor-general of all the lands discovered, with the right to submit three names for appointments to office, and with no restrictions specified—would have created a greater and more powerful monarchy than Spain, with rights to hang Spaniards, enslave Indians, and reap enormous profits. At what point could the Spanish kings interfere when their viceroy proved incapable of orderly government and was faced with the rebellion of Spanish subjects? Was Columbus to be allowed to appoint his own men and to dominate the administration of justice?

Precedent in Spain gave the viceroy of a region (for instance Naples) the full confidence of the king. Since viceroys were chosen on the basis of their demonstrated competence, Columbus's own failure at government in Santo Domingo led to a revocation of his rights, as interpreted by the *fiscal.* The reports of a royal agent, Juan de Aguado (1495), and Bobadilla's commission precipitated the first infringements on Columbus's privileges of government. Although the titles and privileges of the admiralty were restored to him before the third voyage, no mention was made of the governorship or the viceroyalty. In 1501, Nicolás de Ovando was appointed governor of La Española explicitly because of the failure of Columbus, "who had made ill use of his grant [*merced*], and had indulged in excesses of the administration of justice." Thus Columbus was relieved of his offices of viceroy and governor.

In 1504, after the death of the queen, King Fernando tried a novel solution by offering Columbus the fiefdom of Carrión de los Condes, near Valladolid, in return for relinquishing his claim to the Indies. Columbus declined the offer and continued his complaints until his death in 1506, when his son Diego Colón, called "the second Admiral," inherited his rights and added new complaints.

Beginning of the Litigation and Its Procedures. In 1508 Diego instituted the first suit of the Pleitos Colombinos with the branch of the Council of Castile, which eventually became the Council of the Indies (Consejo de Indias). Demanding recognition of succession to his father's rights, he claimed the viceroyalty of all the lands discovered and to be discovered, including Puerto Rico and especially Veragua. This was the "Tierra Firme" stretching along the mainland Caribbean coast. Columbus discovered and reconnoitered the area in 1503 when he landed at the mouth of the Veragua River, a stream that flows into the Caribbean Sea about seventy-five miles west of the present Canal Zone. Diego insisted on his right to appoint officers and he claimed one-tenth of all royal revenues, including customs taxes.

On economic matters, the *fiscal* generally conceded the rights of Diego to profits from his father's discoveries, subject to an agreed-upon distribution. He referred to a law of 1480 (Toledo) that prohibited the grant of the administration of justice in perpetuity and thus left the door open to appeal on grounds of both economic claims and governmental powers.

A positive change in Diego's fortunes came with his marriage to María de Toledo, who was a niece of the powerful house of the duke of Alba. In a decisive turn of events, Diego, who was personally well-received at court, was appointed governor-general of the Indies without prejudice to the rights of the parties to the pending suit and "for such period as it may be the royal pleasure and will" in royal orders dated August 9 and December 9, 1508.

A conflict then arose over the extent of his grant, which rested upon the clause "all the islands and mainland which . . . he [Columbus] discovered or acquired in the said oceans." While the contract may have been intended literally to cover all the lands discovered, it eventually would have included the hemisphere from Florida to Mexico and Peru, to which he opened the way. This was the interpretation taken up by the heirs of Columbus. The government contended that only those parts actually discovered by Columbus or by someone commissioned by him were to be included under the contract.

According to the Crown, the Andalusian voyages sponsored by Fonseca established other claims to the South American coasts. There were about eleven such voyages before 1506, directed to various stretches of the coasts of South and Central America. The settlements of Puerto Rico and Cuba became bases for explorations toward the north. (Four voyages eventually entered the lawsuit.) Once the American hemisphere was revealed in a magnitude not predicted by anyone, the royal councils acted to limit the title of the Columbus family to the Caribbean area. Diego continued his suit and made a request to the king in a letter of September 7, 1509, to participate in certain royal revenues. The response, dated November 14, 1509 states: "To the claim that you are entitled, [the answer is] no, concerning participation in the tithes, fines imposed, and income from our lands—no, concerning the tithes and fines; as to the gold found, there is doubt. The matter will be considered by our Council to your satisfaction and justice will be done you."

After Diego married María de Toledo, the duke of Alba helped to expedite his son-in-law's legal proceedings by writing letters to the king, to Fonseca, and to Fernando Vega, president both of the Military Order of Santiago and of the royal council (not yet the Council of the Indies) with jurisdiction over the suit.

The Judgment of Seville. On May 5, 1511, the judges rendered the judgment of Seville, the first stock-taking of the relationship of the Columbus claims to the reality of America. Successive judgments were each to be limited to specific issues under litigation. The decision confirmed Diego's privileges as perpetual viceroy and governor-general of the islands discovered by his father, in accordance with the capitulations made with Fernando and Isabel. These privileges, however, were circumscribed so as to uphold the sovereignty of the Crown, allow supervision of the viceroy's acts, and protect the rights of colonists. The viceroy's powers were further limited by the establishment of a royal audiencia, or high court, on August 5, 1511. A royal order of November 15, 1511, confirmed the judgment, which satisfied neither side and led to new appeals.

Diego Colón announced his appeal from his palace in Santo Domingo on December 29, 1512. He accompanied it with an extended list of claims and grievances. This provoked the *fiscal*, who also challenged the judgment. The claims and counterclaims, all officially certified, were then exchanged between the lawyers of the parties and made available to the members of the Council of the Indies.

Diego Colón, his uncle Bartolomé, María de Toledo, and others were meanwhile also negotiating directly with the king and later the emperor. Attempts to circumvent restrictions, for instance, by claims to governorships of Puerto Rico, later extended to New Spain, and Peru had their roots in ill-defined clauses. The lack of geographic knowledge, the unreliability of agents, and other such uncertainties increased rather than decreased during the first decades of expansion. Extralegal issues must be kept in mind when considering the sequence of filings, appeals, and judgments, which do not follow a consistent sequence of demand and response.

The Pleito del Darién. The major issues of contention can be summarized as follows:

1. Diego's claim to the right to appoint judges and exercise judicial powers as viceroy and governor over all the lands discovered. The reply by the *fiscal* restated the illegality of hereditary granting of judicial powers because of the impossibility of knowing the qualifications of the successors to the person first designated.
2. The demand for the salaries of all three offices of admiral, viceroy, and governor, plus a grant for a guard of honor. According to Fonseca, the latter was an exclusive right of kings. The *fiscal* argued that these privileges were only granted to Christopher Columbus and did not descend to his son; also, the salary of an admiral was only paid while on duty at sea.
3. Diego claimed the right of appointment to all offices, whether of civil or criminal jurisdiction, and exemption from *residencia* (account of his administration) for himself. Again, according to the *fiscal*, these privileges were granted to Columbus only and not to his heirs.
4. The right, deriving from the office of admiral, to judicial powers in the Casa de la Contratación (House of Trade/Colonial Office) in Seville on matters relating to the Indies. This was denied by the *fiscal* as not included in the contract.
5. The right to appoint officials to the Casa de la Contratación. The *fiscal* alleged that only Christopher Columbus, by special grant, enjoyed rights of this kind and that they could not go to his heirs.
6. Diego's claim to one-tenth of all royal profits and revenues from the islands and mainland discovered and to be discovered. The *fiscal* denied this reading of the contract.
7. A claim to one-tenth of the customs duties *(almorifazgo)*. Since trade with the Indies was now open to all Spaniards who paid this tax, Diego's right to a one-eighth share in all expeditions had been rendered valueless and should be compensated by a share in the customs duties. The *fiscal* maintained that this tax was royal revenue and neither Columbus nor his son had a right to any part of it. In fact, if they had received any monies from this source, they would have to be repaid.

These issues were the substance of the second lawsuit. The arguments presented by the *fiscal* answered the claim by Diego that he should be appointed governor of the province of Darién (Panama) now being settled, as the land had been discovered by his father. It was also declared that Urabá and Veragua were on one and the same coast. Moreover, in order to exploit his properties, Diego insisted that he should receive grants of Indian labor *(repartimientos)*. The Pleito del Darién introduced the new feature of depositions from witnesses produced by both sides. This is the very heart of legal procedure, and such documents make up the volumes of *probanzas* (testimonies) collected in the Pleitos. Questions were formulated by lawyers for both sides and posed to witnesses gathered in localities where statements could be notarized. Each witness had to declare his origin, age, and profession and that he was beholden to neither party. Ranging widely in social rank and age (from twenty-three to eighty-five years), a host of seamen, pilots, companions of Columbus, rivals, experts, lawyers, supporters, and adversaries testified. Each side also produced copies of texts, royal letters, provisions, and other previous documents.

The representative for Diego Colón, the attorney Juan de la Peña, submitted his petition of appeal of the judgment of Seville on January 3, 1512. The Crown responded in 1512 with the "lawsuit between the *fiscal* of their Majesties against the Admiral of the Indies concerning the island of Darién [Panama]."

The critical issue that ensued in the flow of claims and counterclaims was the contention of the opponents of Columbus that the discovery of the South American coast had not been made by him. They alleged that Columbus had only touched at the Dragon's Mouth, near Trinidad, and Paria and had then returned, leaving the exploration of Veragua to others. Among the witnesses interrogated in Santo Domingo was Bartolomé Colón. He provided testimony on the fifth question that dealt with this issue. He supported the claim of Columbus's discovery of Veragua by testifying that, due to indisposition of the Admiral, he himself had taken possession in the name of the king and queen. He also stated that the Andalusian discoveries had only been possible because the Admiral had first brought news of the coast.

The *fiscal* likewise rounded up witnesses in Santo Domingo to prove that other pilots had discovered Darién. Information was exchanged and depositions continued to be taken in Santo Domingo (November 10, 1513) and in Puerto Rico, Cuba, Jamaica, and Spain (1514–1515). Frequent mention of certain places in Spain—Moguer, Palos, Huelva and Seville—show the Andalusian involvement in the ventures. A deposition in favor of Diego was taken in Salamanca from the oldest witness, Rodrígo Maldonado, eighty-five years old, a member of the city council and of the board of churchmen, lawyers, and seamen who examined Columbus before the discoveries.

According to Maldonado, that group agreed that "it was impossible that what the Admiral said could be true, and against the opinion of the majority the said Admiral argued." Witnesses in Palos had stated that Columbus had been mocked on account of his plan. Here was testimony to Columbus's heroic foresight and steadfastness.

In the spring of 1515 Diego Colón thought he had proved his case, only to suffer the setback of another request by the *fiscal* for more depositions and postponements. The *fiscal* gathered thirteen friends of the Pinzón brothers; three of the brothers had been on the first voyage as partners of Columbus and were later his rivals. In Palos, on October 1, 1515, a member of Martín Alonso Pinzón's crew swore that Pinzón discovered America and that if not for Captain Pinzón the voyage would have been a failure. By October 11, 1516, Diego had decided to address himself directly to King Carlos I, who was in the Low Countries, and he succeeded in obtaining an order from Brussels directing the Council to speed the decision. This was followed shortly by an order to suspend the matter (Mechelen; April 15, 1517) until the king's arrival in Spain, "because we are now informed that many of the questions touch our prerogative and sovereignty and should not be decided without consulting the King."

Diego pursued his interests at court in 1511 and again in 1513. He remained there from 1515 to 1520, with time out in 1517 to look after his government in La Española. Diego was able to befriend Carlos I, and in 1520, when the king became Holy Roman Emperor Charles V, Diego lent him 10,000 ducats, a sum greater than the cost of his father's first voyage.

The Judgment of La Coruña. A judgment considered very favorable to Diego Colón was rendered at La Coruña on May 22, 1520. The forty-two clauses of the judgment are a definition of intent and procedure by the Spanish government with respect to the Columbian privileges. A new feature is an evident concern for the Indians: "Inasmuch as God created the Indians free, the laws relating to them shall be observed. . . . Investigators of Indian affairs shall have the right only to question whether the Indians have committed misdeeds, or actions against the faith, and report their findings, but shall have no right to give orders in connection therewith." There is also an order to the treasurer to pay Diego the sum of 365,000 maravedis per annum from that time forward, which is granted "as a contribution to his costs."

Still, Diego was dissatisfied with any limitation put upon him, especially with regard to the geographical extent of his authority. He had to contend especially with the claims based on the Andalusian expeditions to the South American coasts by (1) Alonso de Ojeda, Amerigo Vespucci, and Juan de la Cosa; (2) Pedro Alonso Niño and Cristóbal Guerra; (3) Vicente Yañez Pinzón; and (4) Diego de Lepe (all dating from 1499 to 1500); and the exploration of

Panama and discovery of the "South Sea" by Vasco Núñez de Balboa in 1513. Diego took up another strategy; he advocated before the Council of the Indies an extension of the privileges granted to his father, to include Panama and Mexico. All administrative offices would be appointed from lists submitted by him. Diego considered himself entitled to consideration for the governorships held by Hernando Cortés and Pedro Arias de Ávila. Diego died on February 23, 1526, worn out by his labors (according to Oviedo).

Decision at Valladolid. The appeal of the judgment of La Coruña, which led to a case of eight *capítulos*, was initiated when Diego was recalled from La Española in 1524. It was continued by María de Toledo and was closed in Valladolid on June 25, 1527. The suit was not only an appeal of the judgment of La Coruña but also contained new claims by both sides based on interpretations of the original capitulations of Santa Fe. The briefs submitted by the attorneys for the Colón interests and those of the *fiscal* moved the Council of the Indies to nullify the judgments of Seville (1511) and of La Coruña (1520) and to propose a completely new case to be heard by the Council. An interlocutory appeal by both parties led to a confirmation of that decision. The litigation with the government started afresh under the guiding hand of María de Toledo on behalf of her children, four girls and three boys. The eldest, Luis, was the successor to the *mayorazgo*.

The Judgment of Dueñas. The appeal against the decision of Valladolid resulted in a suit that was terminated by the judgment of Dueñas, containing an elaborate settlement of thirty clauses (August 27, 1534). It left both sides unsatisfied and left unanswered three questions: (1) whether the Admiral should be put in possession of the viceroyalty and governorship; (2) whether he was entitled to the one-tenth of all income from his admiralty; and (3) whether he was entitled to one-tenth of the income from the importation of brazilwood.

The Final Arbitration, 1536. In the last suit (1535–1536) of the Pleitos Colombinos proper, the twenty-eight questions of the interrogatory solicited information on the most extreme claims by the *fiscal* and the Pinzón party: that Columbus had not discovered America at all, but that Pinzón had. The Pinzóns had challenged Diego in a lawsuit of 1513, the arguments of which were incorporated by the *fiscal*. Luis Colón, in his turn, claimed that he was entitled to all the Indies from Florida to Peru. At this point a number of factors, including the rapid growth of Spain's enterprise in the Indies, the unthinkable prospect of validating the exact wording of the original capitulations, and the unworkable interim decisions, prompted a compromise decision that brought an end to the Pleitos Colombinos. Cardinal Garcia de Loayza, president of the Council of the Indies, and Gaspar de Montoya of the Council of Castile reached the decision on June 28, 1536.

This arbitration was extended somewhat by an order of July 7 and confirmed by the emperor on September 8, 1536, and March 24, 1537.

In this judgment Luis Colón renounced the following privileges granted to Columbus by Fernando and Isabel:

1. The claim to one-tenth of the revenue of the Indies.
2. The title of viceroy (the viceroyalty in this case being defined as the islands of La Española, Puerto Rico, Cuba, and Jamaica and parts of Veragua and Paria).
3. The claims to the right to appoint officials in the New World.

He was granted:

1. A perpetual annuity of ten thousand ducats payable on the revenues of La Española.
2. The island of Jamaica in fief, with full rights of government, subject only to the supreme sovereignty of the Spanish king.
3. A fief of a tract of land of twenty-five square leagues (which was larger than Jamaica) in the province of Veragua.
4. The titles of duke of Veragua and marquis of Jamaica.
5. The title of admiral of the Indies, with the privileges of office.
6. The right of appointment to the office of *alguacil mayor* (chief constable) of La Española. This was a fee-paying position that Luis Colón soon assigned to his brother Cristóbal.
7. The right to found a town on his sugar estate in La Española and to appoint municipal officers for it.

Life pensions were also granted for the daughters. Diego, the youngest child, still a minor, was made a member of the Order of Santiago, with the income therefrom. María de Toledo was awarded a sum of four thousand ducats payable over a period of four years in partial payment for the sums she had spent in the pursuit of the litigation. The sisters of Luis Colón were given noble names.

Further Litigation. But this was not the end of the litigation or of Luis Colón's attempts to sustain his claims. Two matters of continuing dissension were the designation of the ports where duties were owed the admiralty (with documents dating from 1537 to 1541) and the extent of the admiralty's jurisdiction there (1554). Next came the disastrous expedition mounted by María de Toledo and Luis Colón to settle Veragua. To this was added the effect of Spanish inflation on the sums of money settled upon in 1536. Luis's candidacy for the governorship of Peru came to nothing. María de Toledo died in 1549, but Luis Colón pursued his claims until the compromise of 1556, which was the ultimate settlement between the last direct descendant of Columbus and the Crown. The following are the terms of this compromise:

1. Luis renounced his fief in Veragua but was allowed to establish a *señorio* (hereditary estate) and received the titles of duke of Veragua and marquis of Jamaica.
2. Luis retained only the title of admiral, without income and authority.
3. Luis retained the right to appoint the chief constable in La Española. (There was no mention of a town on the sugar estate, the economy of the island having collapsed.)
4. He received the title of duke de la Vega.
5. The estate was awarded an increase in the annuity to seventeen thousand ducats, drawn on the account of La Española, except during the lifetime of Luis Colón, when it was to come from customs receipts in Seville.

During the following years, new litigation involved missing or diminished payments of Luis Colón's pension. When Luis, the last in the direct line of succession, died in 1572, his nephew Diego inherited the pension.

On balance the Pleitos are a remarkable illustration of the rise of monarchical sovereignty over private lordship. The individual judgments did not furnish broad resolutions of the issues but were rendered piecemeal as a consequence of the enormous growth of the royal enterprise of the Indies.

The Columbus Legacy. The rivalries that endured for ten generations after the extinction of the direct line reveal the wide-ranging social world of the family. They are not properly part of the Pleitos, but they tell the story of the Columbus legacy, of the connections among the family in the colonies, for instance. The Columbus clan in Europe contains names of the highest nobility. The family's quarrels with the Crown included, of course, conflicts over the order of descent as well as claims that continued to arise from reconsideration of the capitulations of Santa Fe and subsequent suits. A late eighteenth-century lawsuit brought by Mariano Colón de Larreátegui y Embrún, eleventh admiral and ninth duke of Veragua, was decided on June 16, 1790. He traced his claim to the *mayorazgo* to its descent from Luis Colón to his nephew Diego. This question of genealogy, first brought by the Larreátegui family in 1650, was thus finally brought to a successful conclusion by the famous statesman of the Spanish Enlightenment and chief justice of the king's court, Gaspar Melchor de Jovellanos. From this settlement emerged today's line of bearers of the titles of Columbus and the claimants of his income, converted to a fixed pension.

[See also *Book of Privileges; Santa Fe Capitulations.*]

BIBLIOGRAPHY

Duro, Cesareo Fernandez, ed. *Colección de documentos inéditos relativos al descubrimiento, conquista y organización de las antiguas posesiones Españolas de ultramar.* Vols. 7–8. Madrid, 1885–1932.

Garcia-Gallo, Alfonso. "El título jurídico de los reyes de España sobre las Indias en los Pleitos Colombinos." *Revista de la Faculdad de Derecho de México* 26, nos. 101–102 (1976): 129–155.

Gil, Juan. "Pleitos y clientelas colombinas." *Annali della Facolta di Scienze Politiche* (Genoa) 3 (1983–1986): 182–199.

Muro Orejón, Antonio. "Cristóbal Colón: El original de la capitulación de 1492 y sus cópias contemporaneas." *Annuario de Estudios Americanos* (Seville) 7 (1950): 505ff.

Pleitos Colombinos. 8 vols. Edited by Antonio Muro Orejón et al. Seville, 1964–1984. Vol. 1, *Proceso hasta la sentencia de Sevilla* (1967); vol. 2, *Pleito sobre el Darién* (1983); vol. 3, *Probanzas del Almirante de las Indias* (1984); vol. 8, *Rollo del proceso sobre la apelación de la sentencia de dueñas y probanzas del fiscal y del Almirante (1534–1536)* (1964).

Ramos Pérez, Demetrio. *Los Colón y sus pretensiones continentales.* Casa Museo de Colón, Seminario de la Universidad de Valladolid. Valladolid, 1977.

Schoenrich, Otto. *The Legacy of Columbus: The Historic Litigation Involving His Discoveries, His Will, His Family and His Descendants.* 2 vols. Glendale, Calif., 1949.

Vigneras, Louis André. *The Discovery of South America and the Andalusian Voyages.* Chicago, 1976.

URSULA LAMB

LEAD AND LINE. Essentially a plumb bob on the end of a long line, the lead and line (also called sounding-line) is used to determine the depth below the surface of the sea of the seabed and also to take samples of the seabed. Such a simple instrument, fulfilling an obvious need, no doubt had a long history dating back to ancient times. Possibly the earliest illustration of a lead and line is in an English manuscript of sailing directions, which dates from around 1460 to 1480. A lead and line appears on the engraved title page of Lucas Janszoon Wagenaar's *Spieghel der Zeevaerdt* (Leyden, 1584). From the similarity of the earliest illustrations and descriptions of the lead and line to those of the present time, David W. Waters has argued that the early sixteenth-century English predecessors were similar, and no doubt this is equally true of the late medieval period. An example from a seventeenth-century English seaman's manual gives a lead weight of 14 pounds (6.3 kilograms) on a thin line of 200 fathoms (370 meters) for use in deep water, and a weight of 7 pounds (3.2 kilograms) on a thicker line for use in depths of less than 20 fathoms (37 meters). The shorter line was marked at intervals by leather or cloth; for example, at 2 fathoms and 3 fathoms with black leather or at 7 fathoms with red cloth. Another contemporary manual notes that the deep-water line is marked first at 20 fathoms and then at every 10 fathoms with small knots in short strings attached to the line and says that the weight is hollow, so that hard tallow or a white woolen cloth with a little tallow can be placed

inside it to bring up a sample of the seabed, for example, fine black sand or "white soft woormes." The lead and line was especially useful in those waters over a continental shelf, where depths change abruptly, but was also valuable for avoiding shoals and dangerous rocks in shallow and tidal coastal waters. An experienced mariner was able to "locate himself by the contours, colour, smell, taste, and texture of the seabed." In *The Art of Navigation in England in Elizabethan and Early Stuart Times*, Waters quotes a fifteenth-century traveler in the Baltic who said that in that sea navigators used lead and line, but not chart or compass.

BIBLIOGRAPHY

Taylor, E. G. R. *The Haven-Finding Art: A History of Navigation from Odysseus to Captain Cook.* Rev. ed. London, 1971.

Waters, David W. *The Art of Navigation in England in Elizabethan and Early Stuart Times.* London, 1958.

Waters, David W. *The Rutters of the Sea: The Sailing Directions of Pierre Garcie. A Study of the First English and French Sailing Directions.* New Haven, Conn., and London, 1967.

FRANCIS MADDISON

LEIF ERICSSON. See *Ericsson, Leif.*

LEÓN, JUAN PONCE DE. See *Ponce de León, Juan.*

LIBRARY OF COLUMBUS. Only ten extant items remain from Christopher Columbus's personal library, and there is no record of how large it might have been during the discoverer's lifetime. After the Admiral died, his library was eventually incorporated into the extensive book collection of his son, Fernando Colón, who spent much of his life browsing bookstalls all over Europe, becoming one of the greatest bibliophiles of the sixteenth century. In the back of most of his books, Fernando carefully recorded the date and place of purchase of each; he left an unfinished catalog of all the books he owned. Thus, those books owned by his father are clearly distinguished by autograph and marginal notes. When Fernando died in 1539, he willed his library (known as the Libreria Fernandina) to his nephew, Luis Colón, the son of Diego Colón and the grandson of Christopher. The will stipulated that if Luis renounced the legacy, the library would go first to the cathedral chapter at Seville, and, if rejected by the cathedral, to San Pablo Monastery in Seville. Numerous legal delays in processing the will and in Luis's renunciation of the books kept the library in storage at Fernando's residence (although Bartolomé de las Casas probably held some of the books) until 1544. In that year, it was moved to San Pablo Monastery, and in 1552 the library was transferred to the cathedral.

Estimates of the size of the Libreria Fernandina range from twelve thousand to twenty thousand books and manuscripts. Care for the library varied for the next three centuries. By royal command, some items were removed to the national archives in the 1560s. No list of the removed items exists, and they seem to have disappeared. The books were stored and abandoned in the cathedral until the period from 1684 to 1709, when a cathedral librarian was named who shelved the library, repaired some damage, and drew up a new inventory. The collection at that point had shrunk to around four thousand books. After 1709, the library was again neglected. Until 1832 children were allowed to run freely through the library and sad tales are recorded of the destruction of books by their unsupervised play.

In 1832 a new librarian was named who again preserved the books and actually added to the collection by buying contemporary volumes for the library. But, even with this renewed care, many of the volumes were stolen and resold in the bookstalls of Paris, London, and Amsterdam in the nineteenth century. The great Columbus scholar Henri Harrisse brought a halt to the thefts by writing exposés in the 1880s. Since then, the Biblioteca Colombina, as the library is now called, has been made into a professionally run library filling four rooms of the cathedral buildings. Centuries of neglect and plunder have reduced the core collection owned by Fernando and his father today to about two thousand items.

The surviving items identified as once owned by Christopher Columbus are now stored in a special bookcase. They include seven books, two notebooks, and a palimpsest:

1. Pierre d'Ailly. *Imago mundi.* Louvain, 1480–1483 (date uncertain). Columbus's copy also contained a small collection of treatises on various topics such as astronomy and geography.
2. Enea Silvio Piccolomini (Pope Pius II). *Historia rerum ubique gestarum.* Venice, 1477.
3. Marco Polo. *De consuetudanibus et conditionibus orientalium regionum.* A Latin summary by Francesco Pipino of *Il milione.* Antwerp, 1485.
4. Pliny the Elder. *Historia naturalis.* An Italian translation by Cristoforo Landino. Venice, 1489.
5. Plutarch. *Las vidas de los ilustres Varones.* A Castilian translation by Alfonso de Palencia. Seville, 1491.
6. Anonymous. *Concordantiae Bibliae Cardinalis S.P.* No publisher, no date (probably fifteenth century).
7. Saint Antoninus of Florence. *Summa confessionis.* No publisher, 1476.
8. A "notebook" of folios copied by Christopher Columbus and others now titled *Libro de las profecías* (Book of Prophecies) containing lengthy passages from scripture and the pseudepigrapha; the church fathers; ancient, medieval, and contemporary Christian theologians; and Jewish and Muslim writers.
9. A loose-leaf "notebook" copied by Christopher Columbus and others containing selections from Abraham Zacuto's *Almanach perpetuum coelestium motium.*
10. A fifteenth-century palimpsest containing Seneca's *Tragedies.*

Other books suspected to have been owned by the Admiral are a copy of John Mandeville's *Travels,* Julius Capitolinus's *De locis habitabilibus,* a copy of the *Alfonsine Tables* (astrological calculations), Albertus Magnus's *Philosophia naturalis,* and a Bible including pseudepigraphical texts. If Columbus made a living in Castile as a book dealer in the 1480s (as recorded by Andrés Bernáldez and Bartolomé de las Casas in their histories), his private library may have been very fluid as he bought and sold books.

How many books Columbus personally owned is unknown. In his own writings, Columbus cited, referenced, or quoted over sixty ancient, medieval, and contemporary writers from Christian, Jewish, and Muslim cultures. He read voraciously in his own collection, in other private book collections, and in the great monastery libraries at Santa Maria de La Rábida and Nuestra Señora Santa Maria de Las Cuevas. Although these two libraries were destroyed and no catalogs remain, it has been estimated that each contained around ten to twelve thousand books and manuscripts.

Columbus was mostly a self-taught reader. It is likely that as a boy in Genoa he attended a school established for the children of the cloth guild, where he learned some elementary Latin. As a young man, he and his brother Bartolomé learned to read and write Latin, Spanish, and Portuguese well enough to enable them to study difficult scientific and theological books, achieving a level of intellectual refinement to make mathematical calculations and analyze sophisticated scientific, historical, and theological arguments. Reflecting on his intellectual life in 1501, Columbus stated, "During this time, I have searched out and studied all kinds of texts: geographies, histories, chronologies, philosophies, and other subjects" (from the cover letter to the Book of Prophecies).

The importance of the Columbus Library, of course, is that it gives us some idea about his intellectual preparation for his "Enterprise of the Indies," and it testifies to the breadth of his interests. Explorers rarely go forth and probe; they have preconceived notions that cause them to envision the unknown environment of terrae incognitae.

They search for definite objects that they believe to exist based on both empirical and nonempirical information available to them. Further, it became evident to Columbus that he would have to debate leading intellectuals to gain support for his enterprise; thus, he read everything that he could in his effort to present his case effectively before learned councils. He intensified his studies while waiting in Spain for backing from the monarchs.

Columbus's book collecting and study enabled him to impress his contemporaries with his deportment, confidence, and knowledge before learned commissions. Before these groups, he presented maps drawn by himself and his brother, Bartolomé, and quoted frequently from ancient and contemporary texts as well as the Bible. His manner was that of a man well prepared and well versed in his subject to argue his theses with numerous citations from respected sources at his fingertips.

Although he was well read when he presented his case before commissions and monarchs, it is likely that only two of the books that survive from his personal library were read by him before the first voyage, Enea Silvio Piccolomini's *Historia rerum ubique gestarum* and Pierre d'Ailly's *Imago mundi*. These two books and the scriptures were the most powerful influence upon him and his ideas. He collected, or read, his other books at a later date.

Controversy surrounds the dates at which he began accumulating scholarly data to support his dream of crossing the Ocean Sea. The evidence suggests that he was reading his copy of Piccolomini's *Historia* as early as 1481, although this date is strongly disputed by G. Caraci and P. Taviani. Columbus had undoubtedly read d'Ailly's *Imago mundi* by 1488, for an early marginal note refers to Bartolomeu Días's return to Portugal.

The *Historia* by Piccolomini gave Columbus a solid background in fifteenth-century historical geography and its lore. It aided him immeasurably in imagining the world and its features. The book so stimulated him that he made copious marginal notes throughout the text with extensive summaries of information on the flyleaves.

D'Ailly's *Imago mundi* was undoubtedly his best-loved book other than the Bible. He annotated it with more marginal notes than any other book that survives of his library. D'Ailly was a diligent encyclopedist who opened authoritative and influential ancient and medieval authors to Columbus. The *Imago mundi* led him to understand a working interrelationship between science and theology. It was a key document for forming an image of the Ocean Sea in his mind and the relationship of land masses to that sea and to each other. The *Imago mundi* supported Columbus's calculations (actually miscalculations) about the circumference of the earth and the distance from Europe to Asia.

COPY OF THE LETTER FROM PAOLO DAL POZZO TOSCANELLI TO CANON MARTINS. Transcribed by Columbus on a blank page in his copy of Enea Silvio Piccolomini's *Historia rerum*. The letter is Toscanelli's response to an inquiry by Martins (writing for King Afonso V of Portugal) concerning the possibility of sailing west to Asia. Toscanelli replied on June 25, 1474, with a detailed letter and a map, the originals of which are lost. Columbus would have found in Toscanelli's letter support for his ideas as to the circumference of the earth.   BIBLIOTECA COLOMBINA, SEVILLE

Columbus probably did not read the other books in his personal library until after the first voyage. The most controversial issue is the date at which he read Marco Polo's book of travels to Asia. Juan Gil in his *El libro de Marco Polo* (1986) has made definitive studies of this text that suggest that it was not read or annotated until the mid-1490s. There is no evidence as to when Columbus read Pliny, and he may not have read the Plutarch book at all (the marginal notations in it are in the hand of his son Fernando). The Bible concordance has no notes in it, but it is well larded with highlighting marks commonly used by Columbus and others (hands with fingers and other symbols pointing to key texts).

Both the palimpsest, on which is copied Seneca's *Tragedies*, and the copy of Saint Antoninus's *Summa confessionis*, may or may not have belonged to Columbus. Ownership of the two items remains in doubt, and whether either was read by Columbus is also a guess, as neither contains marginal notes. He did quote a passage from Seneca in the Book of Prophecies, however.

The notebooks pose their own problems. According to the marginal notations in the books of Columbus that survive, and according to Fernando in his biography of his father, Columbus collected important information in notebooks. Most of these notebooks have disappeared. Columbus used and referred to the material collected from Zacuto's almanac over the years. The notebook of prophecies is a collection of biblical and nonbiblical sources (with marginal notations) which Columbus planned to use in writing a lengthy apocalyptic poem to the monarchs (a genre common to the fifteenth century).

There has been little reason to reproduce the books owned by Columbus. Césare de Lollis reproduced all the marginal notes with brief text to which they referred (1892–1894). In 1930, E. Buron reproduced and translated into French the *Imago mundi* by Pierre d'Ailly with Columbus's notes. A study and translation of the Book of Prophecies has been completed by Delno C. West and August Kling.

The most impressive reproduction of the Columbus Library is the Colección Tabula Americae (Madrid, 1983–). Under the general editorship of Francisco Morales Padron, several Columbian documents, including key books from Columbus's personal library, are being printed in exact facsimile from the original. Accompanying each volume is a modern translation in Spanish and a commentary on each book.

[See also *Museums and Archives*; *Writings*, especially the articles on *Book of Prophecies* and *Marginalia*.]

BIBLIOGRAPHY

Caraci, G. "Quando cominciò Colombo a scrivere le sue postille?" In *Scritti geografici in honore di Carmelo Colamonico*. Naples, 1963.

Harrisse, Henri. *La Colombine et Clément Marot*. Paris, 1886.

Harrisse, Henri. *Grandeur et décadence de la Colombine*. Paris, 1885. Spanish translation, *Grandeza y decadencia de la Colombina*. Seville, 1886.

Huntington, Archer. *Catalogue of the Library of Ferdinand Columbus*. New York, 1905.

Lollis, Césare de, ed. *I scritti di Cristoforo Colombo. Raccolta di documenti e studi pubblicati dalla R. Commissione Colombiana per quarto centenario dalla scoperta dell'America*, part 1. Rome, 1892–1894.

María Martínez, T. *Obras y libros de Hernando Colón*. Madrid, 1970.

Streicher, Fritz. *Die Kolumbus-originale: Eine paleographische Studie*. Spanische Forschungen der Gorresgesellschaft, vol. 1. Munich, 1928.

Taviani, Paolo E. *Christopher Columbus: The Grand Design*. London, 1985.

West, Delno C., and August Kling. *The "Libro de las profecías" of Christopher Columbus*. Gainesville, Fla., 1991.

DELNO C. WEST

LINE OF DEMARCATION. The Line of Demarcation refers to an imaginary line set in the Atlantic Ocean separating the zones of exploration and colonization reserved to Spain and Portugal, respectively. The circumstances that brought this about were the following. While the Portuguese, under the direction of Prince Henry the Navigator (d. 1460), were exploring the west coast of Africa and beginning to settle Madeira and the Azores, Portugal and Castile were disputing control over the Canary Islands. These issues were resolved when Afonso V of Portugal (r. 1438–1481) concluded the Treaty of Alcáçovas with Fernando of Aragón (r. 1479–1516) and Isabel of Castile (r. 1474–1504) on September 4, 1479. The treaty reserved to Portugal the west coast of Africa, Madeira, the Azores, and the Cape Verde Islands, while the Canaries fell to Castile.

When Columbus sailed westward across the Atlantic, he was under strict instructions from Fernando and Isabel not to intrude on any of the places reserved for Portugal. Nevertheless, in the Castilian interpretation of the Treaty of Alcáçovas, the Portuguese were limited to the waters adjacent to West Africa and the western Atlantic was open to anyone. Columbus gave Spain claim to the vast reaches of the New World, a circumstance unforeseen when the Treaty of Alcáçovas was drawn up. When he stopped in Lisbon on his return, João II (r. 1481–1495) received him warmly on March 9, 1493. Referring to the treaty, the king made the point that "according to the capitulation between the Catholic Kings and himself that conquest belonged to him." In the king's judgment, whatever lands might be discovered south of the Canaries and west of Guinea would belong to Portugal. Columbus responded that he had not seen the capitulation, but the king and queen had forbidden him to go to any part of the west coast of Africa, reserved for Portuguese exploitation. The Portuguese historian Rui de Pina reported that João II, annoyed by Columbus's tendency to exaggerate and probably regretting that he had not sponsored his voyage (Columbus had approached him before he turned to Castile), held that whatever he had discovered fell within his own lordship of Guinea or West Africa. João II's claim in effect challenged whatever rights Spain might have as a result of Columbus's voyage. The Spanish ambassador in Lisbon informed Fernando and Isabel that Portuguese preparations for a voyage of discovery might jeopardize their rights.

Unlike the Portuguese, the Spanish sovereigns had not previously sought papal authorization for the work of exploration, but now, in order to secure an undisputed title to the newly discovered lands, they appealed to Pope Alexander VI. Exercising the plenitude of papal power, the pope issued four bulls relating to this matter in 1493. In

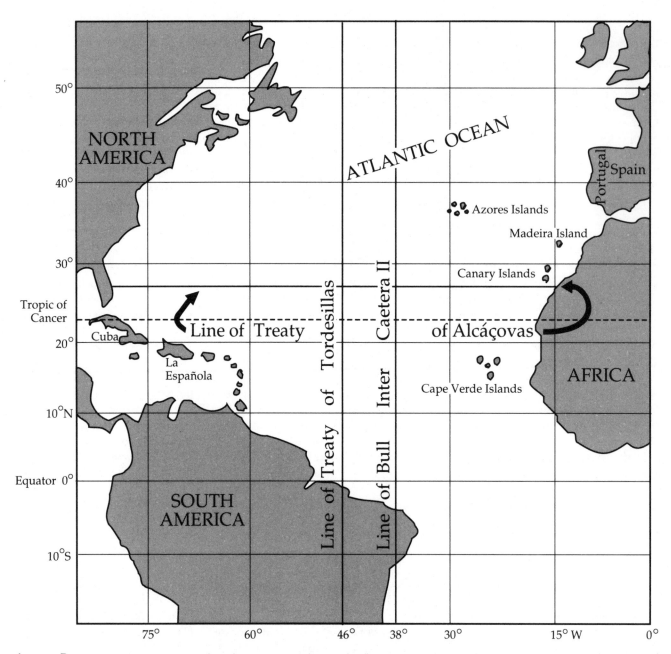

LINES OF DEMARCATION. Between Spanish and Portuguese spheres of influence, according to the Treaty of Alcáçovas, the Treaty of Tordesillas and the papal bull *Inter caetera II*.   AFTER SAMUEL ELIOT MORISON, *ADMIRAL OF THE OCEAN SEA*, LITTLE, BROWN AND CO., 1942.

the bull *Inter caetera* of May 3, after applauding the desire of the king and queen to spread the Catholic faith, he confirmed their dominion over the islands and lands already discovered and those that might be discovered, provided they were not already held by another Christian ruler.

Recognizing that the language of this document left open the possibility of conflict with Portugal, Fernando and Isabel approached the pope once again. This time he

drew up two additional bulls in June, though predating them to May 3–4. *Eximiae devotionis*, dated May 3, conferred on the Spanish rulers the same rights in the lands they discovered as the Portuguese had in theirs. The third bull, also called *Inter caetera* and dated May 4, clarified the grant to Spain by drawing "a line from the Arctic or North Pole to the Antarctic or South Pole." The line was "distant one hundred leagues to the west and the south of any of the islands commonly called the Azores

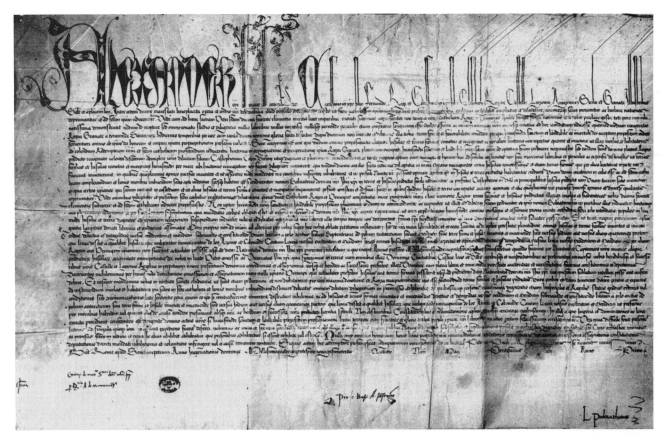

Papal bull *Inter caetera*. Issued by Alexander VI and dated May 4, 1493.

Archivo General de Indias, Seville

and Cape Verde." The pope, asserting his authority as the successor of Saint Peter and the vicar of Jesus Christ on earth, granted to Spain all the islands and mainlands discovered to the west and south of that line that were not subject to another Christian ruler.

Columbus may very well have suggested the idea of a line of demarcation to the king and queen. In their letter to him of September 5, 1493, they referred to "the line that you said ought to be in the papal bull." The line was probably set one hundred leagues west of the Azores because Columbus encountered milder temperatures west of that line, as he noted in the journal of his third voyage and in his letter to the king and queen concerning it. In any case, the Portuguese expressed their objections to this bull, prompting Fernando and Isabel to ask the pope for a further emendation.

In the fourth bull (*Dudum siquidem*), dated September 26, 1493, and sometimes called "the bull of extension," the pope took into account the fact that Columbus was ready to sail on his second journey to the New World (he sailed on September 25 from Cádiz). Alexander VI now amplified his previous gift by giving Spain title to all islands and mainlands to be discovered by sailing west-ward or southward toward the Orient and India. All previous grants to kings, princes, infantes, or military orders (an obvious reference to Henry the Navigator and the Order of Christ) were nullified.

The Portuguese were greatly disturbed by this latest papal bull because it gave Spain a right to the eastern route to the Indies and to lands off the West African coast. Though willing to accept the principle of demarcation, João II decided to negotiate directly with Fernando and Isabel. The ensuing negotiations between Spain and Portugal resulted in the Treaty of Tordesillas signed on June 7, 1494, settling the Line of Demarcation 370 leagues west of the Cape Verde Islands, where the king of Portugal suggested. All lands discovered (even if by Spaniards) east of this line would belong to Portugal, while those to the west would be reserved for Spain. That proved to be a great boon to Portugal because it subsequently guaranteed its rights to Brazil.

[See also *Treaty of Alcáçovas; Treaty of Tordesillas.*]

BIBLIOGRAPHY

Batllori, Miguel. "The Papal Division of the World and Its Consequences." In vol. 1 of *First Images of America: The*

Impact of the New World on the Old. Edited by Fredi Chiappelli. 2 vols. Berkeley, 1976.

Morison, Samuel Eliot. *Admiral of the Ocean Sea: A Life of Christopher Columbus.* Boston, 1942.

Pérez Embid, Florentino. *Los descubrimientos en el Atlántico y la rivalidad castellano-portuguesa hasta el tratado de Tordesillas.* Seville, 1948.

Weckmann, Luis. *Las bulas alejandrinas de 1493 y la teoría política del papado medieval: Estudio de la supremacia papal sobre islas, 1091–1493.* Mexico City, 1949.

JOSEPH F. O'CALLAGHAN

LISBON. The capital of Portugal is situated on the Tagus River. Conquered by various peoples, Lisbon was called Olissippo by the Romans (205 B.C.) and Ashbouna by the Moors (A.D. 716). In 1147 it was seized by Afonso Henriques (1111?–1185), the founder of the Portuguese monarchy, and in 1255 it was raised to the status of capital of the kingdom. Lisbon was a strategic port on the Atlantic, and the great discoveries and the expansion of maritime commerce in the fifteenth century turned it into one of the largest and richest European capitals. At the end of the century its population was about 60,000 and a century later, 120,000.

Two factors turned Lisbon into a renowned capital: nautical science and the development of the bourgeoisie. Prince Henry the Navigator surrounded himself with cosmographers, cartographers, and navigators and was responsible for greatly developing nautical science. Naval building improved, leading to the appearance of the caravel, a light type of ship. The Portuguese made numerous advances in navigation. In the fifteenth century they discovered the Madeira archipelago, the Azores, Cap Vert, and the coast of Guinea, from which came African slaves, gold, rubber, ivory, pepper, and pimenta longa. Sugar, rye, honey, dyes, and cattle were transported from the Atlantic islands through merchants from Genoa, Biscay, and Seville as well as by Arab and Jewish merchants. In its role as mediator between the Mediterranean populations and the centers of production in northern Europe, Lisbon became a formidable cosmopolitan bazaar. But in spite of Portugal's superiority in navigation and naval construction, it did not have its own capital for investment or easy access to great markets; thus, it relied on German and Italian capital and Spanish money.

Enormous privileges were granted to foreign merchants; the role of the Italians, especially the Genoese, after the fourteenth century, was essential to commerce in the metropolis. Flemish, German, and French ships also cast anchor frequently in the port, and in 1478 taxation was reduced and legal protection was extended to them. The discovery of America enlarged the economy; in Lisbon there began to arrive dyes, parrots, and, most important, after the middle of the sixteenth century, sugar from Brazil.

The society had an ambiguous character: an ecclesiastical class of nobles was based in a mercantile economy whose power was concentrated in the hands of a dynamic bourgeoisie, devoted to trade. Many were Jews who converted to Catholicism after 1497 and were called new Christians. A small bourgeoisie of tradesmen and craftsmen was also involved in commerce. In the fourteenth century the society was divided into distinct groups: clergy, nobility, and the general population, each with its own juridical differences and behavioral values. The third group was composed of farmers, merchants, craftsmen, and servants.

Economic prosperity enhanced artistic creativity, which in Lisbon was reflected by such masterpieces as the Jeronimos monastery and the Belém Tower, built in 1515 to celebrate overseas discoveries. In the 1460s Nuno Gonçalves painted Saint Vicente's altar in the cathedral of Lisbon. In the sixteenth century various masterpieces reflecting Italian influence were produced.

The Portuguese intelligentsia, concentrated in Lisbon, focused on scientific and experimental studies; two remarkable examples are those of García d'Orta in the field of botany and Pedro Nunes in cosmology. The expulsion of the Jews from Spain brought 120,000 immigrants to Portugal, including scientists, philosophers, and other professionals; some played an important role in the intellectual life of the metropolis. Among them, for example, was Abraham Zacuto, whose work was used by Christopher Columbus.

The seven or eight years that Columbus spent in Portugal are surrounded by shadows, and many facts and dates are uncertain. He apparently arrived in Lisbon after 1477. At that time Italian merchants controlled 78 percent of the sugar trade; the Genoese company Centurione, which Columbus represented, probably sent him to the Azores and Madeira. The experience acquired in Lisbon through his contacts with Portuguese navigation experts was decisive for his future life course. He married Felipa Moniz y Perestrelo, the daughter of the governor of Porto Santo; this is where he lived, according to some authors, for a number of years and where his son Diego was born. He had access to his father-in-law's documents and maps concerning navigation in the Atlantic and lived among men of the sea who stimulated his imagination with their stories. He went to Lisbon in 1481 and presented his project to King João II, who refused it when a committee of nautical scientists branded Columbus a "dreamer." After his wife's death he was in debt and burdened by his little son, and he left Lisbon.

Portuguese society offered a model of cultural and

PORT OF LISBON. Engraving from Théodor de Bry's *Americae*. Frankfurt, 1594.

religious coexistence that had no equal beyond the Pyrenees. But after the establishment of the Inquisition and the beginning of discriminatory and exterminative policies by the state and the church, the creative bourgeoisie was debilitated or expatriated, and Lisbon went into a decline.

BIBLIOGRAPHY

Castelo Branco, Fernando. *Museus de Lisboa.* Lisbon, 1961.
Freire, Eduardo de Oliveira. *Elementos para a história do municipio de Lisboa.* 17 vols. Lisbon, 1882–1911.
Godinho, Vitorino Magalhães. *Estrutura da antiga sociedade portuguesa.* 2d ed. Lisbon, 1975.
Godinho, Vitorino Magalhães. *Os descobrimentos e a ecônomia mundial.* 2d ed. 4 vols. Lisbon, 1983.
Heers, Jacques. *L'occident au XIV et XV siècles: Aspects économiques et sociaux.* 3d ed. Paris, 1970.
Marques, A. H. Oliveira. *História de Portugal.* Vol. 1. Lisbon, 1972.
Mauro, Fréderic. *O porto de Lisboa, estudo de história econômica seguido de um catalogo bibliográfico e iconográfico.* Lisbon, 1960.

ANITA WAINGORT NOVINSKY
Translated from Portuguese by Paola Carù

LITERATURE. [This entry includes three articles that survey the appearance of Christopher Columbus as a figure in literature:

Columbus in European Literature
Columbus in Hispanic Literature
Columbus in American Literature
For discussion of Columbus's own literary output, see *Writings*. For discussion of scholarly research on Columbus and his times, see *Bibliography.*]

Columbus in European Literature

Christopher Columbus enters French literature through the interest shown his discovery by François Rabelais (c. 1483–1553) and Michel de Montaigne (1533–1592). Rabelais was inspired by Pietro Martire d'Anghiera's *De orbe novo* (1530) to write the fourth and fifth books of *Pantagruel* (1533). The protagonist's navigations are viewed ironically, but Rabelais's admiration for Columbus leads him to place the oracle sought by Panurge in Cathay, the happy land dreamed of by the discoverer. Besides having written a letter to Etienne de La Boétie in which he speaks admiringly of the discovery of the New World, Montaigne devotes several paragraphs of his *Essais* (1588) to the American Indians. Montaigne's benevolence toward the "savages" in the chapter "Des cannibales" was later shared by Rousseau and Montesquieu.

Many French poets showed respect for Columbus in their work, among them Marie Anne du Boccage who wrote a didactic epic poem, *La Colombiade, ou la foi porté au Nouveau Monde* (1756). Blaise Pascal (1623–1662) cites Columbus in the eighteenth letter of the *Provinciales* (1657), written to a Jesuit priest, declaring that the king of Spain had done well to believe Columbus rather than those who denied the existence of the antipodes. Voltaire (1694–1778) also admired Columbus and went so far as to state that all that had occurred before the discovery of America seemed of no consequence compared to this great event. The New World and its inhabitants appeared in many of Voltaire's volumes, including *Candide* (1759). His tragedy, *Alzire* (1736), is set in the city of Los Reyes. Jean-Jacques Rousseau (1712–1778) wrote *Christophe Colombe, ou la découverte du Nouveau Monde* as a piece to be put to music. The three acts in verse portray Columbus as a sort of deus ex machina, whose friendship toward the natives is distinctly modern.

Columbus is the subject of two fictionalized biographies of this period: Lamartine's (1790–1869) *Christophe Colomb* and a chapter in Jules Verne's (1828–1905) *Histoire des grands voyages et des grands voyageurs*. According to Verne, Columbus's genius lay in his perseverance and audacity: his greatness stemmed not from his arrival in the New World, but from his having left the Old. During this same period Fernand Denis's *Ismael Ben Kaizar, ou la découvert du Nouveau Monde* (1829) was published. The novel presents an almost entirely fictionalized Columbus, who is conceived as a romantic character. Commissioned by Pope Pius IX, Count Roselly de Lorgues published *Christophe Colomb* (1856), intended to encourage the beatification of the discoverer. In 1881 Gustave Flaubert's *Bouvard et Pécuchet* appeared posthumously. Bouvard reproaches Bossuet for not having spoken of America, while Vacombeil declares the necessity of exalting the discovery. Bouvard and Pécuchet feel weighed down by the world's stupidity upon learning that the inconsistent chatter they hear is repeated on the other side of the globe. Hence, Flaubert demonstrates that stupidity spares no one.

During the 1900s Columbus's almost mad audacity is conjured up in André Breton's *Manifeste du surréalisme* (1924). The most salient drama written on the navigator is Paul Claudel's (1868–1955) *Le livre de Christophe Colomb* (1928). Ferdinando Taviani in his *La parabola teatrale: Un saggio sulteatro di Paul Claudel* (1969) has pointed out that Claudel's play releases the spectator from traditional space and time, permitting a view from above, as God might view the world. Similar to the way in which Dante viewed a world that was structurally Ptolemaic and morally hierarchical, Claudel sees a tired multitude seeking to build a destiny for itself on a lost planet.

Guillaume Apollinaire (1880–1918) invokes in the poem *Toujours* (from *Calligrammes*) a Columbus who brings about the oblivion of the Old World. A clear quote from the Admiral can be found in *Le maître de Santiago* (1947) by Henri-Marie-Joseph Millon de Montherlant, in which it is said that the enterprise of the Genoese "is the most sublime thing that has ever happened to the World." The French-speaking Swiss writer Blaise Cendrars (Frédéric Sauser, 1887–1961) in his poem *Christophe Colomb* speaks of the Admiral falsifying for the crew the calculation of the miles covered. The Belgian writer Michel de Ghelderode (1898–1962) was moved to write his baroque

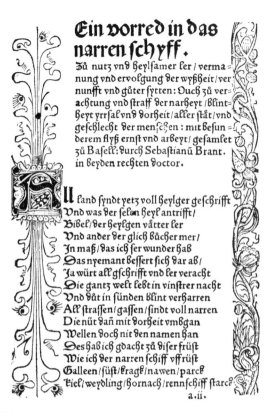

Das Narrenschiff. Basel, 1494. First page of the work containing the first literary reference in German to the islands discovered by Columbus. LIBRARY OF CONGRESS, RARE BOOK DIVISION

play *Christophe Colombe* (1929), after reading Baudelaire's poem *Le voyage*. Despite its numerous historical errors, the text is interesting for its portrayal of Columbus trying to redeem himself of his own transitoriness by "doing," thus seeking self-perpetuation through action. The Belgian Charles Bertin's *Christophe Colomb* presents Columbus as burdened with a sense of absolute solitude, just as the New World and his own personal victory are within reach.

An examination of Columbus as he appears in German literature should begin with the poem *Das Narrenschiff* (1494) by Sebastian Grant, which vaguely recalls Columbus's first voyage in a cutting satire on stupidity. In the following years, Jakob Ayrer (1540–1605) wrote *Die Schöne Sidea,* whose similarity with Shakespeare's *Tempest* is remarkable. In his preface to the *Mantissa codicis jurus gentium diplomatici,* Gottfried Wilhelm Leibnitz (1646–1716) characterizes Columbus as a great Genoese of even greater fame.

Although he did not refer directly to Columbus, Friedrich Maximilian von Klinger (1752–1831) chose America as the setting for his drama *Der Wirrwarr, oder Sturm und Drang* (1776), which was staged in 1777 and whose title would later become the name of the first movement of German romanticism. In his poem *Columbus*, Friedrich von Schiller (1759–1805) enthusiastically praises Columbus's courage, in which he discerns the human ability to create reality out of nothingness.

As Johan Peter Eckermann writes in *Gespräche mit Goethe in den letzten Jahren seines Lebens* (1836–1848), Johann Wolfgang von Goethe (1749–1832) claimed that Columbus's groping was of a person who already knew what he had to find. References to America are found in both *Wilhelm Meisters Lehrjahre* and in the lyric poem *Glückliche Fahrt*. In the former, America is portrayed as a space open to the future and is praised for not having a past made of ruins.

The playwright August Friedrich Ferdinand von Kotzebue (1761–1819) also treated American themes in his work. In *La Colombona*, the Swiss author Johann Jakob Bodmer (1698–1783) perceives Columbus as a sort of prophet inspired by God. Joachim Heinrich Campe's (1746–1818) *The Discovery of America*, a didactic and moralistic dialogue addressed to the youth of the period, portrays Columbus as an intelligent man determined to reach his goal. In *Kolomb*, Friedrich Hölderlin (1770–1843) declares that had he, the poet, wished to lead a heroic life, he would have wanted to be a hero of the seas, adding that he would have enjoyed going to Genoa to visit the house in which Columbus spent his youth. In 1818, August Platen (1796–1835) wrote the ballad *Columbus Geist* in which Columbus appears as a shadow hovering over the ocean who pessimistically predicts Europe's downfall to Napoleon, who is locked in the prison of Saint Helena.

Heinrich Heine (1797–1856) devoted his long poem, *Vitlipuzli*, to the tragedy of the Aztec civilization destroyed by Hernando Cortés. He writes that Columbus was a true hero and compares his generous, luminous soul to the sun. He asserts that it would have been better for Columbus never to have been born, or at least to have retained his anonymity, than have his pure, great name linked with that of a criminal.

Although many German thinkers (including Kant, Hegel, and Marx) wrote on the discovery of the New World, it was Friedrich Wilhelm Nietzsche (1844–1900) who acutely rendered Columbus's yearning for immortality. Besides likening himself to Columbus in *Die fröhliche Wissenschaft*, Nietzsche in his poem *Colombus novus* (published as *Yorik-Colombo* in 1884) imagines Columbus as a navigator holding the helm of his ship as space and time shimmer in the distance.

Sigmund Freud's (1856–1939) antipathy toward Columbus is quite singular, especially since he believed that he shared many traits with the discoverer—whom he did not consider to be a great man. During the 1900s, Hans Joachim Haecker interpreted Columbus as a Strindberg-

esque figure; Walter Hasenclaver and Kurt Tucholsky portrayed him as an expressionist; and Hans Kyser, as a progressive. In Peter Hack's first book, *Die Eröffnung des indischen Zeiltalter*, Columbus can be compared to Brecht's Galileo. This brief overview of the treatment of Columbus in German literature concludes with Thomas Mann's (1875–1955) little-known work *Meerfahrt mit Quichote* (1934), in which Columbus is specifically mentioned and the sea is seen as a metaphor for infinity.

There are a few other texts in European literature that are worthy of note: the ambitious *Kolombus* by the Czech author Jaroslav Hilbert and the Dutch author G. Gorris's *Christoffel Columbus, laatste Kruisvaarder*. Two important dramas must also be noted: *Cristoval Colon* by the Yugoslavian Mirolsva Krleza and Nikos Kazantzàkis's *Cristoforo Colombo*. Krleza treats Columbus as a man whose future reputation has yet to be determined, a man crucified by his shipmates, who do not understand him. In Kazantzàkis's text Columbus becomes a sinner through God's will—obeying a higher plan that transcends his individual fate.

The expression *Novyk Mir* (New world)—which later became the title of an important Russian literary magazine founded in the 1920s—was first used by Maksim Grek, a Greek monk who moved to Russia in 1518 with the intention of revising liturgical texts. The first direct reference to Columbus in Russian is made by the monk Simeon Polckij (1629–1680) in a semiserious poem contained in his *Carmina Varia*. The discovery of America is given the same importance as that of vodka and hair dye. Columbus is said to have sailed around the globe, to have fought against sea monsters, and to have found the new lands for his lord, the king of Spain.

In 1761, Mikhail Vasilyevich Lomonosov called the explorers of the Bering Strait "Russian Columbuses." The Ukrainian poet and philosopher Grigory Skovorada wrote *Americus Colombus* in 1772, drawing inspiration from the episode of the dove sent by Noah, following the Flood, to search for land. In his *Scena iz Fausta* (1825), Aleksandr Pushkin (1799–1837) scolds the Spanish for having brought syphilis to Europe. Nevertheless, he was benevolent toward Columbus, whom he cites twice in his *Istorija Petra–Istorija Pugačeva* (1832–1834), stating that Karamzin discovered Russia, just as Columbus discovered America.

In 1925, on a ship bound for New York, the poet Vladimir Majakovskij (1893–1930) wrote a piece entitled *Christofor Kolomb*, in support of an article from a Madrid newspaper that claimed that Columbus was a Spanish Jew. But in previous poems Columbus is described as a sturdy noose of Genoese rope, an allusion to the insults hurled by his shipmates just as land was coming into view. Other Russian texts that should be mentioned are Ilia Ilf and Evgenij Petrov's play *Kolumb*, a satirical piece written in

1928, and Joseph Brodsky's *Less than One: Selected Essays* (1986) in which Columbus is quoted as discoverer of the West Indies.

Although Columbus is the subject of much Italian literature, its quality, ironically, is inferior to works published in other languages. The Florentine writer Giuliano Dati's poem *La historia della inventione delle diese isole Canaria indiane, extracta d'una epistola di Cristoforo Colombo* is essentially a translation from the Castilian of the letter Columbus wrote to Luis de Santángel describing his first journey.

Columbus receives better treatment in the works of Giordano Bruno (1548–1600) and Tommaso Campanella (1568–1639). In *La cena delle ceneri*, Bruno compares the Genoese navigator to the mythical Tifi, although he expresses serious reservations about the impact of the Old World on the New. In Campanella's *La città del sole*, a Genoese ship's captain describes a utopian island that is reminiscent of Thomas More's *Utopia;* other works of his also mention Columbus. Francesco Guicciardini (1483–1540) exalts the discoverer's audacity in his *Storia d'Italia*.

Fortune foretells a Ligurian's passing through the Pillars of Hercules in Torquato Tasso's (1544–1595) *Gerusalemme liberata*. Giacomo Leopardi (1798–1837) treated Columbus with a sophisticated aesthetic—albeit from a peculiar psychological angle. In *Diario di Cristoforo Colombo e Pietro Gutierrez*, Leopardi imagines Columbus on the night before his discovery of the New World; he is seen as a man whose sense of anticipation and risk seems to be the only means of battling against the tedium of existence and the gray ambitions of a mediocre life.

Few Italian dramas inspired by Columbus are worthy of note, although two nineteenth-century dramas by Paolo Giacometti—*Cristoforo Colombo alla scoperta dell'America* and *La morte di Cristoforo Colombo*—received vast public acclaim, and Antonio Gazzoletti's monologue *Le ultime ore di Cristoforo Colombo* reduced at least two generations to tears. Among the plays on Columbus published during the 1900s, two are of interest: *L'Ammiraglio degli oceani e delle anime* by Rosso di San Secondo (1887–1956), which portrays Columbus in a lyrical form as a "Bearer of Christ" (not only for the inhabitants of the New World, but also for a ship boy of his crew) and *Isabella, tre caravelle e un cacciaballe* by Dario Fo, which, while mocking the great Navigator, reluctantly recognizes his glory.

A good example of narrative works on Columbus published during the 1800s is Anton Giulio Barrili's cycle: *Le due Beatrici, Terra vergine, I figli del cielo, Fior d'oro,* and *Raggio di Dio*. The humorous tone used by Cesare Pascarella (1858–1940) in *La scoperta dell'America* is taken up in the second half of the twentieth century in works by Achille Campanile, Massimo Simili, and Umberto Eco,

who render Columbus the protagonist of quite amusing short stories.

Cristoforo Colombo nella leggenda e nella storia (1923) by Cesare de Lollis and *Il Genovese* (1951) by Paolo Revelli have a lively narrative style. Though lacking in historical fact, these stories have contributed enormously to making the Admiral a sentimental hero.

The most important Italian prose on Columbus remains Paolo Emilio Taviani's *La meravigliosa avventura di Cristoforo Colombo*, in which he summarizes his preceding fundamental books on Columbus and his achievement in a more popular style while retaining the scrupulous accuracy of his earlier books.

BIBLIOGRAPHY

Bedarida, H. "Christophe Colomb dans la littérature française." In *Genova municipale*. Vol. 10. Genoa, 1930.

Conti, S. *Un secolo di bibliografia colombiana 1880–1985*. Genoa, 1986.

Gerbi, A. *La disputa del Nuovo Mondo: Storia di una polemica.* Milan and Naples, 1975.

Marcialis, N., ed. *E i russi scoprirono l'America*. Rome, 1989.

Martini, D. G. *Cristoforo Colombo tra ragione e fantasia*. Genoa, 1986.

Martini, D. G. *Cristoforo Colombo, l'America e il teatro*. Genoa, 1988.

Pike, R. "The Image of the Genoese Age of Literature." In *Hispania*. Madrid, 1963.

Spina, Giorgio. *Cristoforo Colombo e la poesia*. Genoa, 1988.

Taviani, P. E. *La meravigliosa avventura di Cristoforo Colombo.* Novara, 1989.

Wetzel, E. *Der Kolumbus: Stoff im Deutschen Geistesleben*. Breslau, 1935.

DARIO G. MARTINI
Translated from Italian by Francesca Giusti

Columbus in Hispanic Literature

The figure of Columbus in Hispanic literature is part of Iberoamerican cultural history as well as of the world vision of its peoples and cultures. Although a figure blurred and modified by myth, legend, and folktale, Columbus has not always been blindly revered in the Hispanic world. The historical character, the legendary discoverer, the navigator par excellence, the visionary and persevering man who, against all odds, ultimately achieved his dreams, has been a rich source of creative inspiration, but he has been a problematic figure as well. Although among the Spanish of his time, Columbus may have been admired as an instrument of imperial expansion, he has, for many Hispanic Americans in the twentieth century, become the symbol of a legacy of colonialism, exploitation, and destruction. Nevertheless, in Iberian literature, his historical reputation never exceeded the proportions of his real accomplishments as recorded in his Letter of Discovery (1493) and in the chronicles and historical narratives. And in Hispanic America, the letter and his journal, published in the nineteenth century, have attained the status of foundational texts of Hispanic American letters. In Spain and in Hispanic America, then, both documents occupy privileged places, but for different reasons.

For the Spanish, Columbus's letter substantiated and legitimized the Castilian Crown's exclusive right to commercial, religious, and political enterprises in other lands. The fact that a new continent had indeed been discovered was realized and confirmed only after Columbus's death in 1508. But by then, the discoveries, explorations, conquests, and settlements had been realistically described by Spanish writers for what they were: a collective Spanish or Portuguese enterprise.

The first literary reference to Columbus by a Spanish writer is attributed to Ambrosio Montesinos, Queen Isabel's favorite poet, who during the time of the first voyage wrote a short poem (published in 1508) that captures the anxiety felt over the fate of those who had departed with Columbus. Juan Sobriano Segundo, an erudite author, wrote a poem in Latin, dedicated to King Fernando, which includes a few verses devoted to the "Discovery of New Islands" and credits the king with the propagation of Christianity. There are, on the one hand, references to mistreatment of the Indians in such plays as Micael de Carvajal's *Las cortes de la muerte* (Death's courts, 1552–1557) and, on the other, praises of the conquistadores' prowess as in Francisco de Herrera's *Elegies VII and XI* (1582). The poet Juan de Castellanos, a soldier and conquistador and later a priest who died in Colombia, was the first to devote a lengthy poem to Columbus in his biographical sketches of conquistadores, *Elegías de varones ilustres de Indias* (Elegies of illustrious men of the Indies), written between 1570 and 1592. Here Columbus is depicted as a "renowned navigator" whose mission—the fulfillment of the prophecy of completion of the world—justifies the nobility, titles, and wealth he has earned. King Fernando is portrayed as the most likely person to have supported the enterprise. Castellanos was the first one to include in a literary work the sixteenth-century popular versions of the genesis of Columbus's enterprise: that it was the outcome of practical experience rather than intellectual speculation; that his certainty about its feasibility depended on his knowledge of a prior discovery; and that he possessed Paolo dal Pozzo Toscanelli's letter and map concerning a westward route to the Indies.

Few writers of Spain's literary golden age (1500–1680) paid attention to Columbus, although Francisco de Quevedo wrote a poem, "Túmulo de Colón" (Tumulus for Columbus), in which a fragment of the sunken *Santa María* "speaks" of him as "venerable and saint." It was Lope de Vega, however, the creator of Spanish national drama, who wrote the first important European work devoted to Columbus. Written between 1595 and 1605, *El Nuevo Mundo descubierto por Cristóbal Colón* (The New World discovered by Columbus) was published in 1614. Structurally and thematically a problematic play, it nevertheless stands as the first effort to dramatize crucial scenes in the Admiral's life: from his requests for support from the monarchs of Portugal, England, and Spain to his triumphant return to Spain in 1493. Columbus is portrayed as a man divinely inspired to carry out the important mission of disseminating Christianity (although his honor is shared by King Fernando). He stands above all other humans, while his companions represent the lust for gold, a characterization that was to become paradigmatic in subsequent treatments of Columbus and the conquistadores. Using allegorical characters, Lope de Vega examines the controversial political, ethical, and moral issues related to the new lands and their inhabitants. Scenes of Indian dances, songs, and love affairs and their first reactions to the men who come from the sea, even when articulated within the dramatic conventions popular in the seventeenth century, capture the wonder and the surprise of both groups at that encounter. The play portrays the Indians' "distinctiveness" and stresses their response to accepting Christianity as their new religion.

The texts after Lope de Vega's play enunciated, reformulated, and transformed the various biographical episodes in Columbus's life to form a mythic version, beginning with the hero's birth and first wanderings along the Mediterranean and extending through his quest for support for his enterprise, the perilous voyage, his discoveries in the New World, his first triumphant return, and his ultimate ruin and death in obscurity and poverty.

During the Enlightenment, only a few authors dealt with Columbus's story, and their portrayals reflect the negative nuances of the Black Legend. In the early nineteenth century, Spanish writers subscribed to the neoclassic tradition as seen in the odes "Al Mar" (To the sea) and "Juan Padilla" by Manuel José Quintana and "El Oro" (Gold) by Catalan poet Manuel Cabanyes. *Cristóbal Colón* (1790), a play by Luciano Comella, portrays Columbus's tragic return to Spain in chains and depicts him as a man who is condemned to imprisonment by the intrigues of his enemies but is finally saved by the queen's intervention.

The figure of Columbus underwent further metamorphosis under the influence of romanticism and realism. The narrative of his life was strongly shaped by Sir Walter Scott's and Alphonse de Lamartine's works, Washington Irving's biography of Columbus, and, most important, by James Fenimore Cooper's *Mercedes of Castile; or The*

Voyage to Cathay, dealing with the first voyage. Francisco José Orellana, Cooper's most fervent Spanish follower, popularized Columbus in his best historical novel, *Cristóbal Colón* (1868). Some plays, seeking to portray an adventurous, dramatic, and sentimental Columbus, concern themselves with love affairs and duels, as in Patricio de Escosura's *La aurora de Colón* (1838). In other works he was identified with Spain's glorious past: Antonio Ribot y Fonserré's *Cristóbal Colón o las glorias de España* (1840), Tomás Rodriguez Rubí's *Isabel la Católica* (1863), Cabanyes's poem "Colombo," Duque de Rivas's "Oda a Cristóbal Colón," Ramón de Campoamor's dramatic poem *Recuerdos de un gran hombre* (1853), and Angel Lasso de la Vega's "Colón y España" (1859). In still other works Columbus was identified with the Wandering Jew, as in Eugenio Sánchez de la Fuente's *Colón y el judío errante* (1843), or was the object of romantic attraction, as in Juan de Dios de la Rada's *Cristóbal Colón* (1860) in which Beatriz out of passionate love tries everything possible to persuade him not to follow his mission.

With the coming of the four hundredth anniversary of 1492 the literary production increased. Several Columbian romances were published such as V. García-Escobar's *Romancero de Cristóbal Colón* (1866) and *Romancero General* (1873), José Velarde's *Romancero de Colón* (1887), and Narciso Campillo's five romances about Columbus at La Rábida in *Nuevas poesías* (1867). Catalan Jacinto Verdaguer portrayed Columbus as Christ-bearer in his well-known *La Atlántida* (1877), and several authors presented him on the verge of death reminiscing about his past misfortunes, as in Luis M. de Larra y Wetoret's play *La agonía* (1861), Vicente W. Querol's poem "Colón" (1890), and Victor Balaguer's play *La última hora de Colón* (1868).

In the twentieth century Columbus caught the attention of hundreds of writers. Novelist Vicente Blasco Ibáñez, in *En busca del Gran Khan* (In search of the Grand Khan, 1938), authored one of the best novels about Columbus ever written in Spain. The latest versions of the Columbus story, for example, Alberto Miralles's plays *Cataro Colón* (1969) and its revised version, *Colón* (1981), portray the nation and Columbus as more concerned with commercial and trade profits than with spiritual matters.

To Hispanic Americans Columbus's letter and journal marked the first step toward the integration of the New World into the Old, starting a transformation that is still in progress. They generated a dialogical relationship between historical and literary texts that goes back to the nineteenth century and is present in the historical reformulations of contemporary writers. For Colombian Nobel laureate Gabriel García Márquez—as for many Hispanic Americans—Columbus's letter is the first masterpiece of magical realism as literary narrative, and Columbus's journal, surrounded by "mysteries which he himself propitiated," constitutes the second work of Caribbean literature.

Washington Irving's biography (1828) influenced many early portraits of Columbus in Hispanic American literature. In "Los compañeros de Colón" (1832), a neoclassic poem by Cuban José María Heredia, Columbus is envisioned as "a prophetic inspired genius." Another Cuban poet, Gertrudis Gómez de Avellaneda, devoted a hymn to a statue of Columbus in 1863. For other writers, under the influence of Victor Hugo, Columbus represents the human race, which had conquered the New World and bestowed upon it liberty and progress—an outlook seen in Olegario V. Andrade's *La Atlántida* (1881) and José Joaquín Ortiz's *Colón y Bolívar, Colombia y España,* and *Los colonos.* A wide variety of other themes were sounded in the literature: for Rafael Pombo, in *Isaac y Colón,* Columbus was the evangelist bent on a messianic mission; for Peruvian José Santos Chocano, America, in *Alma América* (1906), was the outcome of the energy and dream of a woman (Queen Isabel) and a man (Columbus); for Nicaraguan Rubén Darío, Columbus was both the bringer of the Spanish language and the "unfortunate discoverer" who left a legacy of misery in the Americas; for Mexican Amado Nervo, he was the symbol of the ultimate voyager; for Chilean Vicente Huidobro, he was the son or god of the sea.

Later in the twentieth century Columbus became less a symbol of spiritual conquest, of Hispanism (Gabriela Mistral, Blanco Fombona), and was portrayed more critically, as in the work of Nobel Prize laureate Pablo Neruda of Chile, to whom he represents all the evils of colonialism. Possibly the most technically and ideologically innovative literary representations have been written in the last few decades. Nicaraguan poet Ernesto Cardenal in *El estrecho dudoso* (1966) re-creates the discovery of Central America, emphasizing the themes of disillusionment and the beginning of the loss of identity for American communities. Columbus's presence in García Marquéz's novel *El otoño del patriarca* (Autumn of the patriarch, 1975), a text interpolated by other fictional texts, recasts Columbus's traditional image as discoverer of the New World with that of Columbus as modern positivist. In 1976 Venezuelan playwright José I. Cabrujas staged *Acto cultural o Colón, Cristóbal, el Genovés alucinado* (Cultural act or Columbus, Christopher, the Genoese hallucinated) an iconoclastic treatment in which Columbus's voyage of discovery becomes a metaphor for the characters' psychological voyage to the discovery of their intimate frustrations and fears.

In 1979 Cuban novelist Alejo Carpentier published *El arpa y la sombra* (The harp and the shadow), a powerful novel in which the author orchestrates a chorus of voices through a mixture of genres (confession, travelogue, letter, history, drama), anachronism, and various historical perspectives to provide a complex, but human image of Columbus. He is not a saint or a genius or a victim or a scoundrel but rather a convincing schemer who at the end complains that during the last four hundred years no one has been able to portray him adequately because "having come from mystery, I returned to mystery." Argentinian writer Abel Possé in *Los perros del paraíso* (The dogs of paradise, 1983) reelaborates Columbus's voyage, emphasizing through the image of dogs the legacy of violence bequeathed by that "infamous" 1492 voyage. And in Mexican novelist Carlos Fuentes's *Cristóbal Nonato* (Christopher unborn, 1987), Columbus is an unborn fetus who discovers in the Mexico of 1992 a grotesque country with such an enormous national debt that hope and optimism are impossible to sustain.

BIBLIOGRAPHY

Bierstadt, A. O. "Columbus in Romance." *Magazine of American History* 28 (1982): 272–279.

Dille, Glen F. "El descubrimiento y la conquista de América en la comedia del Siglo de Oro." *Hispania* 71 (1983): 422–502.

Flint, Weston. "Colón en el teatro español." *Estudios Americanos* 22 (1961): 165–186.

Flint, Weston. "The Figure of Christopher Columbus in French, Italian and Spanish Drama." Ph.D. diss., University of North Carolina, 1957.

Gárate Córdoba, José María. *La poesía del Descubrimiento.* Madrid, 1977.

Lasso de la Vega, Angel. "Colón y el descubrimiento en la antigua poesía castellana." *La Ilustración Española y Americana* (Madrid) 19 (May 12, 1890): 322.

Moríñigo, Marcos A. *América en el teatro de Lope de Vega.* Buenos Aires, 1954.

Oyuela, Calixto. "Colón y la poesía." Vol. 2 of *Estudios literarios.* Buenos Aires, 1943.

Palencia-Roth, Michael. "Prisms of Consciousness: 'The Worlds' of Columbus and García Márquez." In *Critical Perspectives on Gabriel García Márquez.* Edited by Bradley A. Shaw and Nora Vera-Golwin. Lincoln, Neb., 1986.

Regazzoni, Susanna. *Cristoforo Colombo nella letteratura spagnola dell' ottocento.* Milano, 1988.

Regazzoni, Susanna. "La historia de Cristóbal Colón en el siglo decimonónico: ¿Biografías o novelas?" *Rassegna Iberistica* 29 (Sept. 1987): 15–23.

Shannon, Robert M. *Visions of the New World in the Drama of Lope de Vega.* New York, 1989.

ASELA R. LAGUNA

Columbus in American Literature

Not until after the American Revolution did writers in the United States look to Christopher Columbus as a figure of significance. Indentured to religion and (increasingly) to politics, prerevolutionary poetry and prose had little concern for matters of exploration, even less for an Italian who had sailed for the Spanish Crown. As all forms of colonial writing attest, Americans had no doubt that they had come to a New World. But only after the founding of the nation did poets and orators connect the New World to Columbus and begin to fashion images of the Admiral according to American specifications.

Among the formative expressions of praise from the early years of the Republic were the ceremonies at the first Columbus Day festivities in Boston in 1792, Philip Freneau's poem "Pictures of Columbus, the Genoese" (1788), and Joel Barlow's epic *The Columbiad* (1807), first written as *The Vision of Columbus* in 1787. Together with Washington Irving's *History of the Life and Voyages of Christopher Columbus* (1828), these works shaped images of Columbus that prevailed throughout the nineteenth century.

Boston's tricentennial celebration of Columbus's landing featured an address by Jeremy Belknap and an ode sung by a select choir. According to Belknap, Columbus discovered America and opened to European commerce "a new world." According to the choir, Columbus uncovered a land—"fair Columbia"—hidden since creation until at the appointed time she opened her arms to embrace "her adopted children." Ideas of regeneration thus joined with those of self-reliance to define a nation that looked to the past with designs on the future: while Columbia could nourish and harbor, Columbus could serve as a symbol of ongoing exploration.

Freneau's "Pictures of Columbus" and Barlow's *Columbiad* contemplate the future from radically different perspectives, one deeply personal, the other resolutely political. Freneau presents Columbus as a dreamer with practical resolve who sails on a voyage of discovery because he sees "blunders" on the existing maps. Frustrated by an arrangement of land he cannot accept, he designs his own globe, places "a new world" far to the west, and then embarks in search of what he has already envisioned. Barlow's poem begins at a tragic end with an imprisoned Columbus bemoaning "a world explored in vain" and then salutes the value of republican institutions in a series of visions offered by Hesper, the guardian genius of the "western continent."

Although Barlow's *Columbiad* celebrates an event in which Columbus played the principal role, its emphasis celebrates consequences in which he has no part. The burden of the poem is to link event and consequence, to bring Columbus and the reader to see the continuity of New World experience. And despite the patches of tedium in this curious epic, Barlow's characterization of an unnamed and largely uninhabited continent links a fifteenth-century "discovery" to a nation celebrating its uniqueness at the beginning of the nineteenth century.

LIFE AND VOYAGES OF CHRISTOPHER COLUMBUS
BY WASHINGTON IRVING.

1492

COPYRIGHT, 1892, BY F. E. WRIGHT.

(51)

TITLE PAGE OF WASHINGTON IRVING'S *LIFE AND VOYAGES OF CHRISTOPHER COLUMBUS*. From a four-hundredth-anniversary issue published in New York in 1892.

Washington Irving's *History of the Life and Voyages of Christopher Columbus* (1828) comes at its subject from a different perspective. Under reproach for his lengthy stay in Europe when American literature was struggling to find a voice of its own, Irving hoped that a biography of Columbus would silence his critics. After two years he completed a study that added nothing significant to existing accounts. But his biography did validate the dual image of the Admiral that had been defined in the late years of the eighteenth century and added disquieting thoughts on the consequences of Europeans coming to the hemisphere. Repeatedly during his first voyage Irving's Columbus calms the superstitious fears of his mariners. He is not only a courageous leader but a "visionary," both "practical and poetical," concerned with knowledge rather than exploitation. Yet Columbus is implicated in a darker drama of history: Irving concludes that the arrival of Europeans in the New World was fatal to

"the indolent paradise of the Indian." His study posits a fall from Eden in a New World, with European avarice embodying the evil. As the representative of Europe and its civilization, Columbus bears a responsibility for destroying innocence; as the hero of a biography written to demonstrate Irving's commitment to an American literary agenda, Columbus is magnanimous, misjudged in his aspirations. Irving's genuine and complex ambivalence brings him to add one romantic perspective to another, to glorify Columbus and then to mourn paradise defiled.

By 1830, the figure of Columbus had been praised, split into male and female components (Columbus and Columbia), and given romantic dimensions that served a variety of expressive purposes. Irving's misgivings did not express the majority view. More indicative of popular feeling were the words of James Kirke Paulding in a letter to President James K. Polk in 1845: the moment at which Columbus first glimpsed "this Continent" yielded consequences "greater and more lasting, than ever emanated from any human being since the fall of Adam." The consequences were dependent on self-approbation: the better Americans felt about themselves, the more they praised Columbus.

Few novels were devoted to Columbus. Typically, they were flimsy attempts at narrative, unsure of their historical ground. Susanna Rowson's *Reuben and Rachel; or, Tales of Old Times* (1798) and James Fenimore Cooper's *Mercedes of Castile* (1840), for example, are labored efforts that subordinate the Admiral to formulaic concerns. But markedly different poets found Columbus and the idea of discovery useful to their purposes—among them James Russell Lowell, a Boston Brahmin; Sidney Lanier, a Confederate soldier and accomplished musician; Emma Lazarus, a spokeswoman for Jewish causes whose sonnet "The New Colossus" (1883) is carved on the Statue of Liberty; Paul Laurence Dunbar, a midwestern African American trained as a lawyer; and Joaquin Miller, a self-promoting Far Western adventurer from Liberty, Indiana. Lowell's "Columbus" (1844) portrays the explorer on his first voyage, solitary in his dreams, convinced that Europe no longer nourishes the human spirit. Lazarus's "1492" (1883) describes a year saddened by the persecution of Jews in Spain but joyful at the unveiling of a "virgin" world that will nourish the downtrodden. Dunbar's "Columbian Ode" (written in 1893, the year of the Columbian Exposition) contrasts Old World scholars blinded by superstition and Columbus whose vision fathoms the unknown. Lanier's brooding "Centennial Meditation of Columbia" (1876) and Miller's declamatory "Columbus" (1896) reveal still other ways in which Columbus served as a source for poetic expression. More profound in achievement are Walt Whitman's "Passage to India" (1871) and "Prayer of Columbus" (1874): the first yearns for a spiritual passage to truth; the second dramatizes Whitman's identification of himself with the discouraged dreamer Columbus became. Along with the more conventional work of other writers, Whitman's poems bring us to see the pervasive and sometimes eloquent romanticism that surrounded the figure of Columbus in the nineteenth century.

Although writers in the twentieth century have devoted less attention to Columbus, William Carlos Williams's study *In the American Grain* (1925) and Hart Crane's poem *The Bridge* (1930) attend to the Admiral's voyages in strikingly modern ways. The idea that the American image of Columbus reflects the American view of America is borne out again in Williams's impressionist meditations on the explorers who came early to the North American continent—Columbus, Hernando Cortés, and Hernando de Soto, among them. Williams portrays Columbus as someone who found a New World of purity and left a legacy of poison that claimed him as well as others. But Williams does not cast specific blame for what became a lethal encounter; rather, his explorers are helpless in their destructiveness, beset with an instinctive evil that haunts both conquerors and victims. Likewise an ensemble piece, though far more mystical in its vision, Crane's *The Bridge* renders a symbolic portrait of Columbus returning from his initial voyage with the supposed gift of Cathay, the first of the unifiers or "bridgers" who set the conditions for integrating past and present. Whereas Williams plunges Columbus into the plot of a fallen world, Crane presents his mistaken navigator as a prophet lifted above the mundane, ennobled by his consciousness.

Brief but salient allusions likewise suggest the diverse ways in which writers have assimilated the idea of Columbus. In her book-length study, *Woman in the Nineteenth Century* (1845), Margaret Fuller praises Isabel of Castile for giving Columbus the means of voyaging to the "New World." "This land," she continues, "must pay back its debt to Woman, without whose aid it would not have been brought into alliance with the civilized world." Henry David Thoreau enjoins in the concluding chapter of *Walden* (1853), "Be a Columbus to whole new continents and worlds within you." If Tom Sawyer landed on a wrecked riverboat, Huckleberry Finn remarks in Mark Twain's *Adventures of Huckleberry Finn* (1884), "you'd think it was Christopher C'lumbus discovering Kingdom Come." The invocation of the New World at the end of F. Scott Fitzgerald's *The Great Gatsby* (1925), the reference to Columbus standing an egg on end in the swirling conversations of William Faulkner's *Go Down, Moses* (1942), the mention of the Admiral taking native Americans back to Spain in the double-edged dialogue of Alice Walker's *The Color Purple* (1982)—such allusions testify to the continued presence of this explorer in the American literary imagination, no matter the debate over what he found or encountered, no matter the perspective on the consequences of his landing.

BIBLIOGRAPHY

Elliott, Emory. *Revolutionary Writers: Literature and Authority in the New Republic, 1725–1810.* New York, 1982.

Franklin, Wayne. *Discoverers, Explorers, Settlers: The Diligent Writers of Early America.* Chicago, 1979.

Kolodny, Annette. *The Lay of the Land: Metaphor as Experience and History in American Life and Letters.* Chapel Hill, N.C., 1975.

Mitchell, Lee Clark. *Witnesses to a Vanishing America: The Nineteenth-Century Response.* Princeton, 1981.

Pearce, Roy Harvey. *The Continuity of American Poetry.* Princeton, 1961.

Spengemann, William. *The Adventurous Muse: The Poetics of American Fiction, 1789–1900.* New Haven, 1977.

Tichi, Cecelia. *New World, New Earth: Environmental Reform in American Literature from the Puritans through Whitman.* New Haven, 1979.

Terence Martin

LODESTONE. Widely distributed in the composition of volcanic rocks, lodestone (or loadstone; the first component of the word derives from an Old English word for way or journey; French, *aimant naturel;* Italian, *calamita*), or magnetite, is a mineral consisting mainly of black oxide of iron (Fe^3O^4). The attractive properties of lodestone were known in ancient Greece and Rome and in the Muslim world. It is supposed that the earliest western compasses consisted of a lodestone placed on a piece of wood and floated on water, but the Chinese used, for divination, a spoon-shaped piece of lodestone on a polished surface *(sinan)*. Lodestones were used to magnetize, or remagnetize, floating compass needles and pivoted compass needles. Lodestones are listed in ships' inventories of the late thirteenth and fifteenth centuries: in 1294 an Italian ship had two lodestones with two charts and a pair of dividers; in 1410–1412, two English ships had, respectively, "1 sailing piece [sc. lodestone]" and "12 stones, called adamants, called sailstones . . ."; the latter were bought in Flanders. Columbus's son Fernando Colón in a passage referring to the observed "northwesting" of the compass needles in July 1496, on the third voyage, says that he believes that each piece of lodestone has points that, when applied to the needle, can make it point east, west, or south, and that this is why "he who makes the compass-needle covers the lodestone with a cloth, all but the north point of it. . . ."

In the sixteenth century the foundations were laid for the science of terrestrial magnetism, which was to have

ARMED LODESTONE. Circa 1700. A copper mounting holds the roughly shaped lodestone and its steel pole-pieces.

MUSEUM OF THE HISTORY OF SCIENCE, OXFORD

far-reaching effects on the design of the marine compass. Following the publication at London in 1600 of William Gilbert's *De magnete*, the lodestone with polished poles and mounted with pole pieces or ground to a sphere (*terella*, little earth) to simulate the earth's magnetic system became important items in the apparatus used for "philosophical" experiments.

[See also *Compass*.]

BIBLIOGRAPHY

Balmer, Heinz. *Beiträge zur Geschichte der Erkenntnis des Erdmagnetismus*. Veröffentlichungen des schweizerischen Gesellschaft für Geschichte der Medezin und der Naturwissenschaften, vol. 20. Aarau, Switzerland, 1956.

Mitchell, A. Crichton. "Chapters in the History of Terrestrial Magnetism. Chapter II—The Discovery of the Magnetic Declination." *Terrestrial Magnetism and Atmospheric Electricity* 42 (1937): 241–280.

Needham, Joseph, Wang Ling, and Kenneth Girdwood Robinson. "Physics." Part 1 of vol. 4 of *Science and Civilisation in China*. Cambridge, 1962.

Radelet de Grave, P., and D. Speiser. "Le *De Magnete* de Pierre de Maricourt. Traduction et commentaire." *Revue d'histoire des sciences et de leurs applications* 28, pt. 3 (1975): 193–234.

Waters, David W. *The Art of Navigation in England in Elizabethan and Early Stuart Times*. London, 1958.

Wiedemann, Eilhard. "Über Magnetismus." *Aufsätze zur arabischen Wissenschaftsgeschichte*. Edited by Wolfdietrich Fischer. Vol. 1, pp. 28–37. Hildesheim and New York, 1970.

FRANCIS MADDISON

LONGITUDE. The idea of defining position on the earth's surface in circular measure goes back to Ptolemy (A.D. 100–165), although Hipparchus (fl. 146–127 B.C.) before him had already proposed a geographical grid of latitude and longitude. Terrestrial longitude is the angle at the pole between a prime meridian (Ptolemy's went through the Fortunate Isles) and the meridian of the place in question (in the modern system measured through 180 degrees east and west from the prime meridian). The measurement of latitude from the altitude of the sun or a circumpolar star at meridian altitude was developed without great difficulty. But the accurate calculation of longitude, because the earth's rotation is synonymous with time, proved virtually impossible at sea until the advent of the marine chronometer in the eighteenth century. The idea that differences of longitude could be measured by timing an astronomical event, such as an eclipse or the conjunction of planets, that could be seen simultaneously by observers in different places was familiar to both the ancient Greeks and medieval astronomers, and Arab mathematicians had drawn up time differences for ephemerides compiled for Toledo so that they could be used in other places. The rate of the earth's rotation, however, is such that one degree of longitude corresponds to four minutes of time, and by the year 1500 the best mechanical clocks were subject to an error of about ten minutes a day. The Flemish astronomer Gemma Frisius proposed the use of a mechanical clock to find longitude and, had a sufficiently accurate one been available, the time of a celestial event (say an eclipse) could have been predicted for one meridian and timed at another and in this way the difference of time, and thus of longitude, established.

The lunar-distance method of determining longitude was proposed by Regiomontanus (Johann Müller) in 1474; it relies on the fact that whereas the stars appear to revolve from east to west at just over fifteen degrees every hour, the moon lags behind at a rate of about one-half degree every hour. In 1514 Johann Werner suggested measuring the lunar distance, the angle between the moon and the sun or a zodiacal star, to determine longitude at sea. However, because of its proximity to the earth, the moon will be seen at different positions in the sky by observers in different geographical locations, a parallax error that could amount to two degrees. The method was theoretically sound but only became practicable toward the end of the eighteenth century, when sufficiently precise instruments were available for the observations and the precise positions of the fixed stars, and of the moon against that background for years to come, were published in the nautical almanac. Fixing longitude by the eclipses of Jupiter's satellites had to await the invention of the telescope. For some time attempts were made to link longitude with magnetic variation, an idea finally discredited by João de Castro in 1538.

So long as it could not be determined at sea, longitude was of little consequence to the pilot, who continued to keep a careful account of the distance traveled east-west with reference to the observed latitude and the position derived from the courses made good and the estimated distances run. However, determination of longitude became a crucial issue when Pope Alexander VI decreed a meridian one hundred leagues west of the Azores as the dividing line between the Portuguese and Spanish discoveries in the Western Hemisphere. Spain would own all that lay west of the meridian, Portugal all that lay east. Adjustments were made and agreement reached with the Treaty of Tordesillas (1494), but the determination of longitude became increasingly important as transatlantic commerce grew and the question of the anti-meridian in the Eastern Hemisphere was raised concerning rival claims to the Spice Islands. Distances in leagues were sometimes converted into degrees of longitude and compared with Ptolemy's *Geography* to establish the position of newly discovered lands within that framework. In *Portuguese and Spanish Attempts to Measure Longitude in the 16th Century*, W. G. L. Randles cites the example of Giovanni da Verrazano, who in 1524, having sailed 1,200 leagues to an undiscovered land in the west, converted the distance into degrees of longitude, allowing for the convergence of the meridians in the latitude sailed, in order to see how close he had come to China, which was the objective of the voyage. Columbus probably had similar considerations when he sought to determine longitude by observation of eclipses while at anchor in the Caribbean in 1494 and 1504. He used the tables of Regiomontanus and Abraham Zacuto. He miscalculated the true longitude on the earlier occasion by 22° 30', on the later by 38'. Randles gives little credence to Amerigo Vespucci's claim to have observed lunar distances off the Venezuelan coast in 1499.

Ruy Faleiro, the Portuguese astronomer who was engaged for the preparations for Ferdinand Magellan's expedition (1519–1522) and was to have accompanied it, drew up detailed instructions for determination of longitude from observations of the latitude of the moon, lunar distances, and magnetic variation. Faleiro was unable to undertake the voyage and was replaced by Andres de San Martín who, using the tables of Regiomontanus and Zacuto, made a series of five observations along the eastern coast of South America. Of the two results that survived, one is wildly inaccurate, the other uncannily close. In the sixteenth century, the precision of both tables and instruments was wholly inadequate to the needs of navigation, let alone cartography. Randles quotes a letter from the cartographer Lopo Homem to the king of Portugal that refers to a master chart of the route to India drawn up by Pedro Nunes on which longitudes had been determined by lunar and solar eclipses. Portuguese pilots had been ordered to use the new chart, and, according to Homem, it had been the cause of shipwrecks. Portuguese pilots were thus reduced to having their charts made secretly in Spain by traditional methods.

[See also *Latitude; Line of Demarcation; Navigation; Treaty of Tordesillas.*]

BIBLIOGRAPHY

Randles, W. G. L. *Portuguese and Spanish Attempts to Measure Longitude in the 16th Century.* Coimbra, 1985.

Taylor, E. G. R. *The Haven Finding Art: A History of Navigation from Odysseus to Captain Cook.* London, 1956.

M. W. RICHEY

LOUIS XI (1423–1483), king of France. The elder son of Charles VII, Louis was on bad terms with his father from early on. He joined a revolt of the nobility in 1440 and was sent off to govern Dauphiné in 1446. Louis never again saw his father, who, angered by his independence, dispatched an army to Dauphiné in 1456. Louis sought refuge with Duke Philip of Burgundy until his father died in 1461 and he ascended the throne.

As king, Louis alienated the nobility by his tight-fisted fiscal policy and use of non-noble officials. In 1465 the nobles organized the League of the Public Weal to oppose him. With the skillful use of force and duplicity, which earned him the tag "Universal Spider," Louis defeated the nobles but was forced to concede to them a permanent exemption from the major tax, the taille.

One who refused to submit was Charles the Bold of Burgundy (r. 1467–1477). Determined to unite his separated domains of Burgundy and the Low Countries, Charles formed alliances with the kings of England and Aragón and the Holy Roman Emperor. The major issue with Aragón involved Cerdagne and Roussillon on the north slope of the Pyrenees, which Louis had invaded in 1462. Aragonese efforts to regain them failed, and France annexed them in 1475. Louis convinced the Swiss, the best soldiers of the day, that Charles's pretensions were a threat to them. In 1477 the Swiss smashed Charles's forces in the Battle of Nancy and killed him.

Louis immediately moved to take control of those of Charles's lands that were French fiefs—Burgundy, Picardy, Artois, and Flanders. Charles's daughter Mary held on to Flanders, the Low Countries, and the Franche-Comté. Ignoring Louis's demand that she wed his son, she married Maximilian of Habsburg. In 1482 Maximilian and Louis signed a treaty by which Louis's gains of 1477 were confirmed. The death of René of Anjou in 1480 passed Provence to Louis, giving France ports on the Mediterra-

LOUIS XI.   ELSEVIER PUBLISHING PROJECTS, AMSTERDAM

nean and making the French a factor in Mediterranean naval wars.

Louis's relentless efforts to force the nobility into submission and to raise taxes resulted in a dramatic increase in royal authority but also made him feared and despised. When the Spider King died in 1483, passing the throne to his son Charles VIII, few mourned him.

BIBLIOGRAPHY

Champion, Pierre. *Louis XI.* 2 vols. Paris, 1911.

Commynes, Philippe de. *Memoirs.* Edited by Samuel Kinser. Translated by Isabelle Cazeaux. 2 vols. Columbia, S.C., 1969.

Kendall, Paul. *Louis XI, the Universal Spider.* New York, 1971.

FREDERIC J. BAUMGARTNER

LOUIS XII (1462–1515), king of France. A second cousin to Charles VIII, Louis was a member of the Orléans branch of the Valois dynasty. As a youth Louis was forced to marry Louis XI's deformed daughter Jeanne. His resentment was a factor in his rebellion against the government of Anne of Beaujeu, who was governing France for her brother Charles. Captured in battle in 1488, Louis spent three years in prison. But in April 1498 Charles died childless, and Louis gained the throne. He quickly secured an annulment of his marriage to Jeanne and married Anne of Brittany, Charles's widow, attaching her duchy permanently to the Crown.

Louis had inherited the Visconti claim to the duchy of Milan, and in 1499 he led the second French invasion of Italy and occupied Milan. He then negotiated a treaty with Fernando of Aragón in 1500, dividing the Kingdom of

Naples between them. But Fernando quickly moved to control all of Naples, and by 1503 it was securely in Spanish control.

The election of Julius II in 1503 put a strongly anti-French partisan in the papacy. After manipulating Louis into crushing Venice at Agnadello in 1509, the pope turned his Holy League into an anti-French alliance. Louis's response was to call a general council at Pisa in 1511, but its only result was Louis's excommunication as a schismatic. Julius's anti-French policy culminated in the French defeat at Novara in 1513 and eviction from Milan. More trouble for France followed when Henry VIII of England invaded Artois in 1513 and occupied Tournai. Louis was forced to conclude peace with his enemies.

In hopes of having a son, Louis agreed to marry Henry's sister Mary, Queen Anne having died in January 1514. His young bride's disruption of his life weakened his already poor health, and the "Father of the People," so called for his enlightened domestic policy, died on January 1, 1515, passing the throne to his cousin and son-in-law, Francis I.

BIBLIOGRAPHY

Bridge, John. *A History of France from the Death of Louis XI.* 5 vols. New York, 1929.

Febvre, Lucien. *Life in Renaissance France.* Translated by Marian Rothstein. Cambridge, Mass., 1977.

Quilliet, Bernard. *Louis XII, Père du peuple.* Paris, 1986.

FREDERIC J. BAUMGARTNER

LUNAR PHENOMENA. To sailors in the time of Columbus the moon was important because of its effect on tides and because lunar eclipses could be used to determine longitude. The exact influence of the moon on tides, however, was imperfectly comprehended before Isaac Newton described the law of universal gravitation, and the relation of the sun and the moon was not understood.

Observers tried to determine the recurring cycles (saros cycles) of eclipses since antiquity. The exact hour of the beginning or the end of an eclipse could not be determined correctly since a satisfactory theory of lunar movements did not exist. From the beginning of the sixteenth century, the time of a lunar eclipse was used to determine the geographic longitude of a place. It was also thought that longitude could be determined by observing the stars during occultation by the moon, by observing the opposition of the moon and Venus, and by using other equally fallible methods. Because of insufficient knowledge of the perturbations of the orbit of the moon, however, sixteenth-century methods were inherently imprecise.

Determining longitude and latitude—and therefore the exact position of a ship—was a crucial problem for

1298	1400	1401
Eclipfis Solis	Eclipfis Lune	Eclipfis Lune
29 3 2	9 18 2	2 18 29
Iulii	Nouembris	Maii
Dimidia duratio	Dimidia duratio	Dimidia duratio
0 36	1 38	1 92
Puncta tria	Puncta decem	

1402	1402	1408
Eclipfis Solis	Eclipfis Lune	Eclipfis Lune
30 19 89	19 12 20	29 13 36
Septembris	Octobris	Februarii
Dimidia duratio	Dimidia duratio	Dimidia duratio
1 8	1 1	1 86
Puncta decem	Puncta tria	

FIFTEENTH-CENTURY STUDY OF LUNAR ECLIPSES. Regiomontanus's *Ephemeria*, a page showing lunar and solar eclipses. Nürnberg, 1475. LIBRARY OF CONGRESS, RARE BOOK DIVISION

navigators. The first half of the fifteenth century saw the beginning of fairly accurate findings of latitude and longitude, that is, with insignificant errors of observation, on board caravels and other ships.

The most common way to determine longitude during navigation was based on the lunar eclipse. The process, although certain in principle, had the drawback of infrequent occurrence, since to be useful, the determination of longitude had to be done often in the progress of a voyage. Furthermore, the moment of eclipse or reappearance of the moon was always estimated imprecisely; because of this, the process almost always involved enormous errors. Columbus, whose navigational abilities are unquestioned today, determined longitudes with errors of twenty degrees.

Navigators in the seventeenth century finally understood that the solution of the problem of determining longitude lay in the construction of an accurate timepiece. This enterprise engaged various scientists, Christiaan Huyghens in particular. It was John Harrison (1693–1776) who succeeded in finding the solution in the second half of the eighteenth century by developing the marine chronometer.

BIBLIOGRAPHY

Albuquerque, Luís de. *Astronomical Navigation*. Lisbon, 1988.

Costa, A. Fontoura da. *A marinharia dos descobrimentos*. 2d ed. Lisbon, 1939.

Cotter, Charles A. *A History of Nautical Astronomy*. London, 1968.

Randles, W. G. L. *Portuguese and Spanish Attempts to Measure Longitude in the 16th Century*. Coimbra, 1985.

Taylor, E. G. R. *The Haven-Finding Art: A History of Navigation from Odysseus to Captain Cook*. Rev. ed. London, 1971.

LUÍS DE ALBUQUERQUE
Translated from Portuguese by Paola Carù

M

MADEIRA. The archipelago of Madeira lies in the Atlantic Ocean about 560 kilometers (350 miles) from Morocco and 800 kilometers (500 miles) from continental Portugal. Known to the Romans as the Purple Islands, they were rediscovered by João Gonçalves Zarco and Tristão Vaz Teixeira in 1418 and 1420. Under the orders of Prince Henry the Navigator the two largest islands of the group, Madeira and Porto Santo, were settled rapidly; two of the island groups, the Selvagens and the Desertas, are uninhabited. Together, the two inhabited islands, which boast one of the finest climates in the world, comprise the Funchal district of Portugal.

Some fifty years after colonization had begun, Columbus established important connections with Madeira. In the summer of 1478, Paolo di Negro, an associate of the wealthy Genoese merchant, Luigi Centurione, engaged him in Lisbon to go to Madeira to purchase Madeiran sugar for Centurione's account. Di Negro had been paid 1,290 ducats in advance to make this purchase, but he failed to provide Columbus with the required amount of cash to pay for the sugar he had sent him to buy; it appears that he intended to pay for part of the sugar with woolen goods. However, these found no takers and Columbus was unable to meet his obligations with the scanty sum of 103 ducats that di Negro had sent him and was forced to proceed to Genoa with a short consignment of sugar.

Not long after his return from the sugar-buying voyage to Madeira and Genoa, in 1479, Columbus established an even firmer connection with Madeira as a result of his marriage to a young noblewoman, Felipa Perestrelo y Moniz, the daughter of Bartolomeu Perestrelo, the first governor and *donatário* (grant holder) of the island of Porto Santo, and of Isabel Moniz, his second, or third, wife.

It was at Prince Henry's instigation that, within a few years of the settlement of Madeira, the hardy malvasia grape vine was imported from Crete and the sugarcane from Sicily. Both were in due course to play their part in making Madeira a great wine exporter. Several sugar mills had been built in the island by Genoese merchants. The Genoese also shipped out of the islands large quantities of valuable products, such as orchilla, pastel, cotton, and hides.

Porto Santo, the island that Bartolomeu Perestrelo had governed and where his son succeeded him never prospered like Madeira. It was only natural, however, that, with his brother-in-law established in Porto Santo, Columbus should settle on the island that, coupled with Madeira, was the advance headquarters of the exploration of the Atlantic. For the next two or three years, from 1480 to 1483, Columbus made his home first in Porto Santo, where his first son was born, and then at Funchal, the small but thriving capital of Madeira, where his curiosity was constantly being whetted by meeting with sailors and ship captains who had been to the edge of the unknown world and by the fact that he himself was living on the frontiers of the Atlantic.

Columbus's third and last known contact with Madeira took place in 1498, on his third voyage to America. At that time Spain was at war with France, and a French fleet was said to be lying off Cape St. Vincent, waiting to despoil Columbus's fleet. Accordingly, he made a wide sweep to the south, passing near the African coast, instead of taking the straight course to Porto Santo, which was his first objective. On June 7, the fleet arrived at Porto Santo, after a journey of at least 1,050 kilometers (650 miles). The inhabitants, believing his fleet to be French corsairs, took to the hills with their flocks and herds. That same night he set sail for Madeira. On June 10 he anchored in Funchal roads. In his *Historia de las Indias,* Bartolomé de las Casas writes that the local inhabitants outdid themselves in their welcome: "in the town [Funchal] he was given a very fine reception and much entertainment, for he was very well known there, having been a resident thereof for some time. He stayed there six days, completing his lading of water, wood, and other things necessary for his voyage."

In the opinion of many experts, the greatest part of Columbus's education in the sea belongs to Madeira, and his own son was supposed to have said that the fact that his father had lived in Madeira "was the beginning of the discovery of the New World."

BIBLIOGRAPHY

Albuquerque, Luís de, and Alberto Vieira. *The Archipelago of Madeira in the XV Century.* Translated by Martin A. Kayman and M. Filomena Mesquita. Funchal, 1988.

Cruz, Visconde do Porto da. "A Estada de Cristovam Colombo na Madeira." *Revista de Arqueologia* 2 (1936): 283–288.

Pereira, Eduardo C. N. "Cristóvão Colombo no Porto Santo e na Madeira." *Das Artes e da História da Madeira.* 22 (1956): 20–27.

Treen, Maria de Freitas. "Columbus in Madeira and Porto Santo." *Bulletin of the American Portuguese Society* (Fall 1976): 1–3.

Vieira, Alberto. "Colombo: A Ilha, os homens e a história." *Diário de Notícias* (Madeira). May 30, 1987.

REBECCA CATZ

MADRID. Madrid, a comparatively minor town in twelfth-century Castile, was growing steadily at the close of the Middle Ages and came into its own when Philip II decided to establish his court there in 1561. Situated on the Manzanares River more than two thousand feet above sea level and bounded on the north by the Sierra de Guadarrama, Madrid is surrounded by productive and fertile agricultural lands. Though evidence of settlement dates back to prehistoric times, Madrid first gained notoriety in 932 when Ramiro II of León knocked down its walls. After the fall of Toledo in 1085 it passed into Christian hands along with other towns in the Tagus valley. In the twelfth century the town received various royal privileges that were incorporated in the *fuero,* or municipal charter, granted by Fernando III in 1222. The town itself was divided into parishes (*colaciones*) and the municipal district into four *seismos,* or regions. The determination of the boundaries of the municipal district was the source of frequent conflict with neighboring Segovia.

From the thirteenth century onward municipal law was largely shaped by royal actions as the Crown intensified its efforts to control town government more effectively. In 1346 Alfonso XI replaced the open municipal council with a council composed of a limited number of regidores chosen by the king. In the fifteenth century the regidores nominated several persons for the offices of alcalde, or judge, and alguacil, or police inspector, and the king made his appointments from these nominees, who usually came from the principal families of the city. The king also named a corregidor to supervise the administration of justice and to maintain law and order. Taken together all these officials constituted the ayuntamiento, a governing body with responsibility for revenues, public works, and other matters affecting the municipality. The *Libros de acuerdos del concejo de Madrid* (Books of agreements of the council of Madrid) contain acts relating to municipal government from 1464 onward. As the town continued to grow in importance, the Cortes was convened there on several occasions in the fourteenth and fifteenth centuries. Madrid was one of the eighteen towns with representation in the Cortes in the reign of Fernando and Isabel. Sessions of the audiencia, or royal tribunal, were occasionally held there in accordance with a decree of Juan I in 1387.

At the end of the fifteenth century Madrid was still a comparatively small town. According to data from 1530, the city had a population of four thousand, in contrast to Segovia, with fifteen thousand, and Medina del Campo with twenty thousand. On the other hand, Madrid's location in the geographic center of the peninsula made it more and more attractive in the economic development of the Kingdom of Castile. When Philip II decided to make it his capital in 1561, Madrid also had the advantage of being close to the new royal palace of El Escorial. The establishment of Madrid as the capital aided the growth of population, which rose to thirty-seven thousand in 1594. Not until after 1606, however, did Madrid achieve permanent status as the political and financial capital of the realm.

BIBLIOGRAPHY

Domingo Palacio, Timoteo. *Documentos del archivo general de la villa de Madrid.* 6 vols. Edited by Agustín Millares Carló and Eulogio Varela Hervías. Madrid, 1888–1943.

Gibert, Rafael. *El Concejo de Madrid: Su organización en los siglos XII a XV.* Madrid, 1949.

MacKay, Angus. *Spain in the Middle Ages: From Frontier to Empire, 1000–1500.* New York, 1977.

O'Callaghan, Joseph F. *A History of Medieval Spain.* Ithaca, 1975.

JOSEPH F. O'CALLAGHAN

MAGELLAN, FERDINAND (1480?–1521), Portuguese navigator. Although Magellan (Fernão de Magalhães, in Portuguese; Magallanes, in Spanish) was a Portuguese, his great journey across the Pacific was purely Spanish in its impact: it reached the Orient via a westward passage and thus completed the work Columbus had undertaken but had to abandon when the American landmasses blocked his way. Magellan himself technically did not circumnavigate the globe, for he died on Mactan Island, near Cebu, in the Philippines. Rather, his officer Juan Sebastián de Elcano finished the circuit, although along a return passage already well established by the Portuguese. Much of this return distance Magellan probably had himself sailed earlier in his career while in the service of Portugal; if so, he himself had also traveled effectively around the globe, though not all upon the same voyage or in consecutive years.

Magellan was born into petty nobility, probably in the village of Sabrosa, near Vila Real in the province of Tras-os-Montes. The date, never established with certainty, was around 1480, which made him of prime age to seek social and economic advancement in the great Indies enterprise that followed the return of Vasco da Gama from Calicut in 1500. In fact, he enlisted in the service of Francisco de Almeida, the first Portuguese viceroy, and sailed for the Orient in 1505. He filled minor positions there for the next eight years—in Goa, Cochin, Quilon, and possibly Mozambique. Then he accompanied Diogo Lopes de Sequeira on his ill-fated voyage to Malacca in

FERDINAND MAGELLAN.   ELSEVIER PUBLISHING PROJECTS, AMSTERDAM

1508–1509. Returning to India, he was shipwrecked on some shoals near the Maldive Islands. Here he first came to the attention of the chroniclers for bravely refusing to abandon his subordinates.

It is also known that even before the fall of Malacca to the Portuguese in 1511, he had become a close friend of Francisco Serrão, one of the first European visitors to the Moluccas, or Spice Islands, and manager of the Portuguese Crown factory at Ternate. Magellan himself may have sailed as far as Ambon, at 128 degrees east longitude, before returning to India. From Serrão it would seem he obtained detailed information about the islands' location and their products. Magellan returned to Portugal in 1513, though it is far from certain that he maintained further correspondence with Serrão, as has been claimed, or that this played a part in the subsequent maturation of his daring plans for a voyage to the islands from the Americas.

One of the principal Portuguese military operations closer to home (and one that certainly diverted men and matériel from further adventures in Asia) was devoted to empire building in Morocco. Soon after his return from India, Magellan took part in a campaign under the duke of Braganza at Azamour, where he appears to have distinguished himself in battles and skirmishes; he was appointed quartermaster of war spoils. After his return to Portugal, he petitioned King Manuel I for modest recompense of his services. At the same time, however, rumors spread that he had sold captured cattle back to the enemy, whereupon the monarch obliged him to return to Africa to clear his name—which he succeeded in doing. Nonetheless, Manuel refused to increase his yearly stipend, as Magellan requested. This soured him and seems to have been instrumental in his decision to leave Portugal.

Exactly when Magellan conceived his plan of sailing to the Moluccas via a passage around or through the American continents is not known. He may well have had the idea before returning to Portugal from India, though he seems to have worked out the final details in Lisbon with a Portuguese cartographer, Rui Faleiro—including the idea that the Moluccas actually lay on the Spanish side of the 1494 Line of Demarcation as extended around to the Eastern Hemisphere. By then he was in disfavor, and though seemingly he tried to present it to Manuel as a more efficient way of reaching the islands, after his unhappy treatment he resolved to take it to Manuel's rival, Carlos I of Spain, or actually to Bishop Juan Rodríguez de Fonseca, head of the Spanish Consejo de Indias.

Magellan's contract and the arrangements for his voyage were much like those of Columbus in that the voyage was sponsored by commercial sources such as merchants of Seville and Antwerp, and the capitulación he received made him and his cocaptain, Faleiro, adelantados and gave them a share of the profits. (Faleiro, however, demurred to go at the last moment.) In September 1519, five small vessels, none in good condition, *Santo Antonio, Trinidad, Concepción, Santiago,* and *Victoria* (the heaviest at 120 *toneladas*), passed the bar at Sanlúcar de Barrameda. Their crews were even more international than most of the age. Besides Spaniards and Basques, they included Genoese, Sicilians, Neapolitans, Germans, Greeks, Flemings, an Englishman, and even some Malays and Africans. The largest foreign contingent, however, was thirty-seven Portuguese. Also with the expedition were Magellan's brother-in-law, the Portuguese Duarte Barbosa, author of an early description of the East, and Antonio Pigafetta, a gentleman of Vicenza, who went as a passenger and later became the expedition's most famous chronicler.

Magellan expected rightly to find a passage to the south, though certainly not so southerly as it proved to be. From the easternmost part of Brazil, the ships coasted on the lookout for a westerly passage, exploring the bay of Rio de Janeiro and the Rio de la Plata before wintering in Patagonia from March to August 1520. During this time Magellan effectively dealt with a serious mutiny, and subsequently, *Santo Antonio* deserted the fleet. When a strait was finally found to the Pacific, Magellan skillfully navigated it at the cost of *Santiago,* which foundered on a

reef, though with the loss of only one life. Next, after coasting northward along Chile for a thousand miles or so, he effected an arduous Pacific crossing of ninety-eight days. His starting point had the effect of aligning the remaining three ships with a belt of easterly trade winds, but it also caused them to bypass all the great archipelagoes to the south, which might have provided refreshment; in the whole passage only two islands were sighted—seemingly one in the Tuamotu group and one in the Line Islands. Thereafter, Magellan steered to a still more northerly course in hopes of reaching the coast of China for surer relief than the Moluccas might have provided. This took the expedition to Guam, whose thieving natives prompted them to call the group the Ladrones. Finally, on April 7, the little fleet reached Cebu in the Philippines. Less than three weeks later, Magellan was dead, killed in a skirmish on Mactan Island after the Spaniards became involved in a brawl between indigenes.

Command was then assumed by the Portuguese captain, João Serrão, but he, too, was slain by natives within a short time, along with Duarte Barbosa. Command then devolved upon Elcano, a capable Basque who had been involved in the Patagonian rebellion earlier in the voyage. Of his three remaining vessels, *Concepción* had to be abandoned, but after calling at Brunei in Borneo and

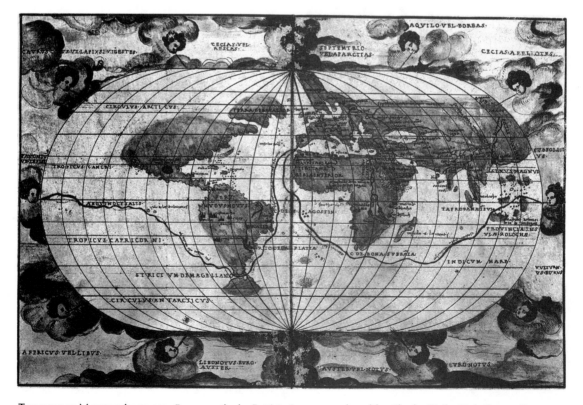

THE ROUTE OF MAGELLAN'S VOYAGE. From an atlas by Battista Agnese produced for Charles V, the Holy Roman Emperor, in Venice in 1552.

NEW YORK PUBLIC LIBRARY, WALLACH DIVISION

returning to the Philippines, Elcano reached the Moluccas at Tidore. Thereafter, the rotting *Trinidad*'s captain elected to try to recross the Pacific. Elcano, however, returned via India and the Cape of Good Hope, arriving home in September 1522, three years after the expedition had departed. Needless to say, Elcano was happy to assume credit for what belonged nearly in full to the expedition's fallen leader. It was only the testimonies of others, among them Pigafetta's, that eventually provided a true picture of what had ensued and restored to Magellan his place as perhaps the greatest pilot and navigator of the early discovery era.

The triumphal return of Elcano in *Victoria* might have obscured the achievement of Magellan temporarily—but hardly the implications of his journey. The Spanish had signed the Treaty of Tordesillas in 1494, but at the time, no one could ascertain longitude with any certainty—nor did either the papal bull *Inter caetera* or the treaty itself specifically say that Portuguese or Spanish influence must end exactly at the edge of the hemispheres where the Atlantic line cut around on the opposite side of the globe. Worried that Spain might try to claim bits of the Orient as on the other side of the line, Manuel in 1514 obtained the bull *Praecelsae devotionis*, limiting the demarcation line to the Atlantic and awarding all the Asian Indies to Portugal—something the Spanish Crown scorned, however.

Armed with Elcano's reports, the Emperor Charles V weighed upon the Portuguese monarch, João III, for a binational commission composed of distinguished seamen and representatives to negotiate an agreement on the issue. It met on the bridge over the tiny Caia River, which formed the border of Spain and Portugal between Elvas and Badajoz. Among those present were Elcano himself, Fernando Colón, Diogo Lopes de Sequeira, and Sebastian Cabot. The Spanish delegation at first maintained that the Moluccas were on their side of the line. Then, when the Portuguese vehemently denied this, the Spanish even called for a papal investigative commission to visit the Far East and decide the question.

Debate dragged on for years until in 1529, by the Treaty of Zaragoza, João agreed to buy from Spain for 350,000 gold dobras all rights to exclusive access and usufruct of the islands. Under a clause of the treaty, the Spanish were supposed to pay back the sum should the islands be shown by future science to lie within the Portuguese sphere. That they did indeed lie within the purview of the Portuguese was subsequently shown by modern methods of determining longitude—but not until the eighteenth century. By then the Portuguese had long since been expelled from the islands by the Dutch and the issue forgotten.

Magellan had both "discovered" and died in the Philippines (named in honor of Prince Philip, later Philip II).

The archipelago actually lay to the west of the Moluccas, but even though the Spanish had given up their rights to those Spice Islands, they had no intention of yielding what they considered rightfully theirs, no matter what the location might ultimately prove to be. Thereafter, Portuguese protests over the repeated Spanish incursions into the area went unheeded—and the issue was effectively settled only by the Union of Crowns in 1580.

In modern times, the sole aspect of the voyage that remains universal knowledge is that of Magellan's great circumnavigation. But his achievement in fact was his discovery and skillful passage of the straits named for him and his successful crossing of the unknown Pacific Ocean to Asia, thus fulfilling the great objective that had eluded Columbus.

BIBLIOGRAPHY

Albo, Francisco. "Diário o derrotero del viaje de Magellanes." In vol. 4 of *Colección de los viajes y descubrimientos.* Edited by Martin Fernández de Navarrete. 5 vols. Madrid, 1835–1837.

Denucé, Jan. *Magellan, la question des Moluques et la première navigation du globe.* Brussels, 1911.

Guillemard, F. H. H. *The Life of Ferdinand Magellan and the First Circumnavigation of the Globe.* London, 1890.

Jong, Marcus de, ed. *Um roteiro inédito . . . [de Vazquito Gomes Gallego (?)].* Coimbra, 1937.

Medina, José Toribio de. *El descubrimiento del Océano Pacífico: Vasco Nuñez de Balboa, Hernando de Magallanes y sus compañeros.* 3 vols. Santiago de Chile, 1914–1920.

Nowell, Charles E., ed. *Magellan's Voyage around the World: Three Contemporary Accounts.* Evanston, Ill., 1962.

Queiroz Velloso, José Maria de. *Fernão de Magalhães, a vida e a viagem.* Lisbon, 1941.

GEORGE D. WINIUS

MALINCHE (fl. 1519), native American princess, known also as Doña Marina; interpreter for Hernando Cortés during the Spanish conquest. Malinche was the daughter of a high-ranking lord of the region of Coatzacoalcos, on the southeastern fringe of the Aztec empire. Her father died while she was still young, and her mother, protecting the inheritance for Malinche's half-brother, later passed her on to coastal merchants. She was then sold by these traders to the ruler of Tabasco and was presented by him to the Spanish newcomers along with nineteen other women in 1519. Her native name, perhaps Malinalli (twisted grass) or some variant, was changed by the Spaniards to Marina when she was baptized. Because the reverential *-tzin* was added to her native name to yield Malintzin, so *doña* was appended to Marina in recognition of her high native status.

Marina became Cortés's most important ally in the Spanish conquest of Mexico, although he barely mentions her in his letters to the Spanish king. She served Cortés as interpreter, adviser, confidante, and mistress. As interpreter, Marina demonstrated considerable linguistic skills, being conversant in Nahuatl and a coastal Maya dialect.

Marina was not only a translator of words, but an interpreter of native customs and intentions. She was intensely loyal to Cortés and guided his path through the political maneuverings and cultural confusions that faced him on his trek to the Aztec capital. She was not only responsive to Cortés's needs and goals, but on occasion took the initiative in achieving those goals. She endured many hardships, including the frantic Noche Triste (the "sad night" of the Spaniards' retreat from the Aztec capital in early July 1520) and Cortés's arduous march to Honduras following his capture of Tenochtitlan (Spanish, Tenochtitlán).

Marina was also Cortés's mistress; she bore him a son, Don Martín Cortés, who should not be confused with Cortés's legitimate son by his second wife, also named Martín. Once Marina's usefulness had ceased, Cortés married her to one of his men, Juan de Jaramillo. She was given estates in her native province, but little is known of her later life.

Marina is a symbol of cultural contact and blending; she is also considered by Mexicans as a traitor to the native way of life. Early on, the Mexica ruler Motecuhzoma II recognized her pivotal role in the fall of his empire and transformation of his culture; the news that she was accompanying the newcomers "pierced Motecuhzoma's heart."

BIBLIOGRAPHY

Anderson, Arthur J. O., and Charles E. Dibble. *The War of Conquest: How It Was Waged Here in Mexico*. Salt Lake City, 1978.

Díaz del Castillo, Bernal. *The Conquest of New Spain*. Baltimore, 1963.

Orozco y Berra, Manuel. *Historia antigua y de la conquista de Mexico*. Vol. 4. Mexico City, 1960.

Rodríguez, Gustavo A. *Doña Marina*. Mexico City, 1935.

FRANCES F. BERDAN

MANDEVILLE, JOHN. Mandeville's *Travels*, composed most likely in French around the mid-fourteenth century, was the most widely read European book about the world during the late Middle Ages. Its unknown author represents himself as a far-traveling English knight, Sir John Mandeville of St. Albans, who has written this narrative upon returning home after thirty-four years of travels. The book was soon translated into nearly every European language as well as Latin and survives in more than 250 manuscripts (almost three times the number that Marco Polo's travel account engendered). As one of the earliest printed books, it enjoyed special popularity in the two decades from 1480 to 1500. The book presents a first-person account of supposed travels based on the eyewitness authority of a narrator who is at once pious, curious, skeptical, and tolerant.

The first part of the book (a prologue and fifteen chapters) portrays the world that European pilgrims would encounter in taking one of the several land or sea routes to the Holy Land. Mandeville describes the possible itineraries; informs readers of distances, local history, customs, marvels, relics, and foreign alphabets; and explains at some length the pilgrimage sites in and around the Holy Land. Chapter 15 is a summary of Islamic customs and beliefs and includes a lecture by the sultan about the sinfulness of Western Christians and their consequent crusading failures.

The second part of the book recounts Mandeville's exploration of the wonders of the little known, non-Christian world farther east. He discovers there fantastic animals and humans of surprising shapes, powers, and behaviors (some of which are parodies or reminders of Christian practices). He discourses on the roundness of the earth and the possibility of its circumnavigation. He describes journeys to the home of the Amazons, the Well of Youth (at which he drank), the land of the pygmies (whose laborers are giants), the dominion of the great Chan of Cathay, the region of the Tartars, the realm of the legendary Prester John, the bastion of the Muslim terrorists known as the Assassins, the Vale Perilous (which Mandeville but not all his companions survived), the Isle of Bragman (a utopia where people live in preternatural harmony), and at the easternmost edge of the world the earthly paradise, about which Mandeville says (in a Middle English manuscript version), "ne can I not speken propurly, for I was not there." Near the end of the book he states his conviction that "wee knowe not whom God loueth ne whom God hateth" and that most of these non-Christian peoples seem to know the "God of Nature" through their "naturelle wytt."

Although no copy of the *Travels* known to have been read by Columbus has yet come to light, there is direct and indirect evidence that the Admiral knew Mandeville's account. Three of his contemporaries—his son Fernando Colón, Bartolomé de las Casas, and Andrés Bernáldez—indicate he read Mandeville. It is also apparent from Columbus's writings that the book was an influential source or confirmation for several of his fundamental ideas and motivations.

First, Columbus would have been struck by the chapter in which Mandeville asserts that the earth is circumnavigable and that it is both inhabitable and inhabited worldwide. Mandeville's conviction about these matters is based on his alleged authority as a world traveler, his calculations with an astrolabe, and the experience of an unnamed northern European who, he says in a lengthy anecdote, sailed around the world twice—once in each direction.

Second, Columbus's assumptions about the Caribbean peoples he met would have been shaped by Mandeville's depiction of the world east of Jerusalem as a series of increasingly marvelous societies, each one older, more advanced, and ethically superior to the one before. At the eastern edge of Asia—where Columbus thought he had arrived—Mandeville encounters the perfect natives of the Isle of Bragman, then the near-Edenic island of Taprobane with its Bahamas-like two seasons and shallow seas, and at last Eden itself.

Finally, Columbus would have found in Mandeville's book an emphasis on the centrality of Jerusalem that matched his own abiding crusader's concern to rescue the Holy Land for Christianity. The Jerusalem pilgrimage that occupies the first half of the *Travels* balances the exotic Asian journeying of the rest of the book and emphasizes the spiritual objective that ought to motivate every Christian voyager. From the Book of Prophecies and other of his writings it is apparent that Columbus understood his worldly explorations as a form of pilgrimage and that the attainment of Jerusalem, literally or allegorically, was his ultimate goal.

BIBLIOGRAPHY

Bennett, Josephine W. *The Rediscovery of Sir John Mandeville.* New York, 1954. Reprint, New York, 1971.

Campbell, Mary B. *The Witness and the Other World: Exotic European Travel Writing, 400–1600.* Ithaca and London, 1988.

Seymour, M. C., ed. *Mandeville's Travels.* Oxford, 1967.

Zacher, Christian K. *Curiosity and Pilgrimage: The Literature of Discovery in Fourteenth-Century England.* Baltimore and London, 1976.

CHRISTIAN K. ZACHER

MANUEL I (1469–1521), king of Portugal. Manuel the Fortunate inherited the Kingdom of Portugal in 1495 when his cousin King João II died without a legitimate heir. Manuel strengthened the monarchy, enacted legal reform, and supervised the political organization of Portuguese claims in the New World.

Manuel carried out João II's plan for the exploration of India and presided over the global expansion of Portugal. During Manuel's reign, Vasco da Gama sailed around the Cape of Good Hope to India (1498), and by 1505 the Portuguese had begun the territorial organization of India. In 1500 Pedro Álvares Cabral claimed Brazil for Portugal, and in 1502 present-day Uruguay and Argentina were explored. In 1511 the first large-scale Portuguese expedi-

tions were sent to chart the Pacific via Da Gama's route. By 1521 the fleet of the Portuguese navigator Ferdinand Magellan, sailing in the service of Emperor Charles V, had circumnavigated the globe.

In 1497 Manuel married Isabel, daughter of Fernando and Isabel, and at her insistence he expelled the Jews from Portugal. When the Castilian prince Juan died in 1498, Isabel and Manuel were named heirs to Castile. But Castile slipped out of Manuel's grasp when Isabel died in childbirth (1498), followed two years later by their son, Miguel. In 1500 Manuel married Isabel's sister María who bore him eight children, among them his heir, João III, and Isabel, future wife of Emperor Charles V. In 1518, a

MANUEL I. From an illuminated manuscript, 1521.

ARQUIVO NACIONAL DA TORRE DO TOMBO

year after the death of María, he married Leonor, the sister of Emperor Charles V, who bore him two children. Manuel died in 1521 and is buried in the abbey of the Hieronymite monastery in Lisbon.

BIBLIOGRAPHY

Domingues, Mário. *D. Manuel e a epopeia dos descubrimentos: Evocação histórica.* Lisbon, 1960.

Goes, Damião de. *Crónica do felicissimo Rei D. Manuel.* 4 vols. Coimbra, 1926.

Oliveira Marquês, A. H. de. *History of Portugal.* 2 vols. New York, 1972.

Sanceau, Elaine. *The Reign of the Fortunate King, 1495–1521.* Hamden, Conn., 1969.

THERESA EARENFIGHT

MAPPAMUNDI. In the Middle Ages, *mappamundi* (from Latin *mappa,* napkin; and *mundus,* world; pl., *mappaemundi*) designated a world map whatever its form or purpose. In modern terminology, the word is restricted to images of the world determined by religious or ideological considerations executed in a more or less schematic manner. Although such images were known in Asia and the Islamic world, the expression refers to a body of documents specific to the West. Originating in the monasteries, *mappaemundi* combined in one representation a few scientific elements (derived from classical antiquity) with ideas taken from biblical and patristic texts. Usually oval or circular in form, *mappaemundi* primarily accompanied texts and had essentially didactic and moral functions, illustrating the narratives of traditional Christianity.

The commonest maps give a tripartite representation of the inhabited world *(oikoumene)* within a T-O *(orbis terrarum)* scheme. The three continents, Europe, Asia, and Africa, are encircled by the ocean and are separated by the Mediterranean (the vertical element of the T) and by the Don and the Nile (the horizontal elements of the T). Jerusalem, placed at the intersection of the two elements, is thus at the center of the world, at least on maps dating from after the Crusades. The whole is oriented toward the east, from which flow the rivers of the terrestrial paradise. A second type of *mappamundi,* which derived from the Greeks, represents the whole world in parallel zones or "climates," the habitable temperate zones of the two hemispheres being symmetrically arranged on either side of the central torrid zone which, like the two polar zones, was considered uninhabitable. Quadripartite *mappaemundi* include elements from the first two types. The tripartite *oikoumene* of the northern hemisphere is flanked in the southern hemisphere by a fourth continent, inhabited or not, called the Antipodes.

As *mappaemundi* gradually became dissociated from texts, taking on increasingly imposing dimensions, their contents and appearance evolved under the double influence of nautical cartography (from the fourteenth century) and the revival of Ptolemaic geography (from the beginning of the fifteenth century). From nautical cartography, exemplified by portolan charts, *mappaemundi* borrowed the network of rhumb lines and scale (though here not functional); a good delineation of the Mediterranean and Black sea areas, contrasting with a dramatically less accurate depiction elsewhere; and an interest in the geographical knowledge produced by recent voyages such as those of Marco Polo in Asia in the thirteenth century and the Portuguese navigators along the African coast in the fifteenth century. Ptolemy's *Geography,* translated into Latin in 1406–1407 and widely diffused in printed editions after 1475, offered on the other hand a learned cartographic model that simultaneously revived some archaic geographical concepts (such as the closed Indian Ocean and a Mediterranean Sea twenty degrees too long) and reintroduced the idea of the rigorous location of places on a grid marked in latitude and longitude produced by projection. One of the best-known *mappaemundi* of the late Middle Ages, that drawn by Fra Mauro in 1459, is a compendium of geographical sources that uses the Marco Polo narratives, the Portuguese exploration of Africa, the portolan charts, and Ptolemy's *Geography.*

From among these "transitional" *mappaemundi,* historians have sought to identify first, any that could have aided the development of Columbus's project or illustrate the presuppositions behind it, and second, any that mark the stages of the establishment of the idea of a new continent. Among the first, the most important is the map that Paolo dal Pozzo Toscanelli presented to the Portuguese court in 1474 in defense of the idea that the western route to India across the Atlantic was shorter than the eastern route around the southern tip of Africa, toward which Portuguese colonial policy was oriented. In 1483, when this project was examined by a committee of cosmographers in the service of João II, Columbus had not yet annotated the works that would eventually help him to transform his intuition into a full theory; the Toscanelli map, of which he obtained a copy, was doubtless his most important scientific support. He had moreover himself copied the letter that accompanied the map, thus demonstrating the interest that it had for him. Unfortunately, the map is lost, and the fairly precise description given by the written sources do not allow it to be identified certainly among surviving *mappaemundi* (the suggestion that it was similar to the Genoese world map of 1457 is open to many objections), nor to come to unanimity of opinion about a reconstruction. It may be

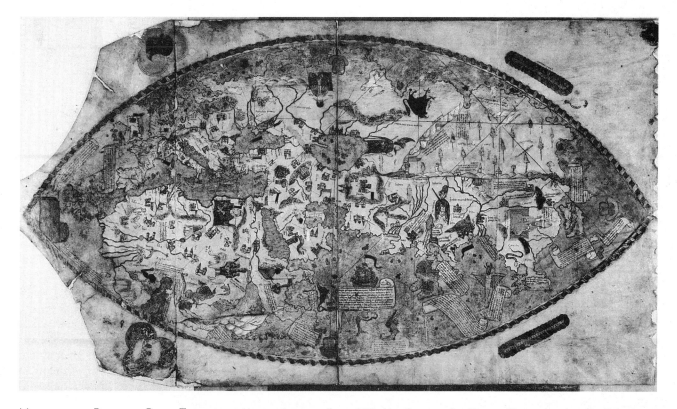

supposed that the map was graduated in latitude and longitude, but historians are divided about what system of projection might have been used. In the end, we know nothing of Columbus's practice in the drawing of his maps.

The classic sources of Columbus biography, particularly Andrés Bernáldez, suggest that Columbus presented to the Spanish sovereigns and their specialist advisers at Salamanca (1486–1487) and at Santa Fé (1491) a map on which he, or his brother Bartolomé, had drawn "the lands and seas to discover." This map was probably also shown by Bartolomé to Henry VII of England during his mission of 1488. But the ambivalence of the term *mappamundi* conceals whether it was actually a *mappamundi* or a nautical chart, and no document of either type can be certainly identified as drawn by the brothers. The geographical vestiges that best correspond with Columbus's vision of the world are those found on the globe of Martin Behaim, which derived from a prototype common to several late-fifteenth- and early-sixteenth-century *mappaemundi*. This prototype was developed by the German cartographer Henricus Martellus, who worked in collaboration with the Florentine engraver Francesco Rosselli,

and it underlies several surviving manuscript and printed *mappaemundi* from the 1490s.

One of these was acquired in 1961 by Yale University Library. It has a latitude scale and is also the only non-Ptolemaic *mappamundi* of the fifteenth century to be divided for longitude. There is no direct proof that this map was known to Columbus, but it illustrates several of his leading ideas. The very large east-west extent of the *oikoumene* (270 degrees) and the reduced distance to be sailed between the Canaries and Cipangu (90 degrees) are measures that correspond to those that Toscanelli had deduced from Marinus of Tyre and Marco Polo, and were known to Columbus. Converted into marine leagues on the median line of the map, the 90 degrees correspond approximatively with the 1,142 leagues that Columbus reckoned he had sailed when he arrived in the Caribbean Islands that he took to be Cipangu. The same world map, which shows Bartolomeu Dias's voyage of 1488, depicts Africa with a prolongation into the southern hemisphere and therefore even more difficult to circumnavigate than supposed because it is also extended to the east by a cape, called a *promontorium passum* in Ptolemy's *Geography,* that enclosed the Indian Ocean.

The eastern route to India pursued by the Portuguese for so many years thus seemed extremely difficult. Such a picture of the world at this date could well have influenced the Spanish authorities to give support to Columbus.

Such *mappaemundi*, in which "the beginning of the Indies" faced the West across an ocean of no great width, dominated cartographic production until about 1506. Such a presentation appears in the Contarini map engraved by Rosselli in 1506, and the texts it carries indicate clearly that the author believed that Columbus had reached the coast of Asia. In the map by Johan Ruysch that accompanied the 1508 Rome edition of Ptolemy's *Geography*, the North American lands explored by the Côrte-Reals and the Cabots are parts of Asia, but the coast visited by Columbus belongs to a continent separated from Asia by a stretch of open sea. This may indicate a direct influence from Bartolomé Colón, the presumed author of three anonymous and undated sketches, sections of a world map drawn to illustrate the voyage along the central coast of America during Columbus's fourth voyage. These sketches, found as marginal drawings in a copy of Columbus's letter from Jamaica (July 7, 1503), give the first general picture of the lands discovered by Columbus. The route across the narrow ocean is marked by the Spanish islands, with the exception of Cuba. Asia, with the *serici montes*, is next to Honduras and extends as far as Venezuela. A tiny strait separates this continent from the South American coast, where the hinterland is labeled "Mondo Novo." Columbus, if these sketches are authentic, was thus convinced that he had discovered, at least in South America, a New World. Nonetheless it is in the large world map of Martin Waldseemüller, published at Strasbourg in 1507, that the first cartographic expression of South America appears.

BIBLIOGRAPHY

Almagia, Roberto. "I mappamondi di Enrico Martello e alcuni concetti geografici di Cristoforo Colombo." *La Bibliofilia* 42 (1940): 288–311.

Destombes, Marcel, ed. *Mappemondes A.D. 1200–1500: Catalogue préparé par la commission des cartes anciennes de l'Union géographique internationale.* Amsterdam, 1964.

Liethäuser, Joachim C. *Mappaemundi: Die geistige Eroberung der Welt.* Berlin, 1958.

Randles, William G. L. "The Evaluation of Columbus' 'India' Project by Portuguese and Spanish Cosmographers in the Light of the Geographical Science of the Period." *Imago Mundi* 42 (1990).

Skelton, R. A. "The Cartography of Columbus' First Voyage." Appendix to *The Journal of Christopher Columbus.* Translated by Cecil Jane, annotated by L. A. Vigneras. London, 1960.

Woodward, David. "Medieval Mappaemundi." In vol. 1 of *The History of Cartography,* edited by J. B. Harley and David Woodward. Chicago and London, 1987.

ISABELLE RAYNAUD-NGUYEN
Translated from French by Anthony Turner

MAPS. For discussion of the history of mapmaking through the Age of Exploration, see *Cartography.*

MARGARET OF AUSTRIA

MARGARET OF AUSTRIA (1480–1530), daughter of Maximilian I; princess of Spain (1497); regent of the Netherlands (1507–1530). As daughter of Emperor Maximilian I and his first wife, Mary of Burgundy, Margaret played an important role in the diplomatic marriages that linked the Austrian Habsburg family with the kingdoms of Castile and Aragón. As an infant Margaret was betrothed to the French dauphin Charles VIII (1482), but Charles repudiated her to marry Anne of Brittany. To offset the power of France, a double marriage was negotiated in 1495 by Maximilian and Fernando of Aragón. Margaret was betrothed to Juan, prince of Asturias and heir to the throne of Castile and Aragón, and her brother, Philip the Handsome, to Juan's sister, Juana of Castile. Juan and Margaret were married in Burgos on April 3, 1497, but the marriage was tragically brief, ending only months later with Juan's sudden death on October 6 in Salamanca.

Margaret returned to Flanders in 1499, and in 1501 she married Duke Philip of Savoy. When Philip died in 1504, she was briefly under consideration as a possible bride for Henry VIII of England. The death of her brother, Philip, in 1506 and the madness of his wife, Juana, forced Maximilian to appoint Margaret to the regency of the Netherlands for her young nephew, Charles. Her competent governance of the Netherlands, notably her mediation of alliances between Maximilian, England, Spain, and the papacy in 1513, prompted Charles to retain her as regent after the death of Maximilian in 1519 until her death in 1530.

BIBLIOGRAPHY

Boom, Ghislaine. *Marguerite d'Autriche.* Brussels, 1946.

Bruchet, Max Pierre Marie. *Marguerite d'Autriche, duchesse de Savoie.* Lille, 1927.

Iongh, Jane de. *Margaret of Austria, Regent of the Netherlands.* Translated by M. D. Herter Norton. New York, 1953.

Winker, Elsa. *Margarete von Österreich: Grande Dame der Renaissance.* Munich, 1966.

THERESA EARENFIGHT

MARÍA

MARÍA (1482–1517), princess of Castile; queen of Portugal. María, daughter of Fernando and Isabel of Castile, was the second wife of King Manuel I of Portugal. They were married in Alcácer do Sal on October 30, 1500. By marrying María, Manuel hoped to revive his plan to unite Portugal and Castile under his personal rule, a goal that had suffered a setback with the deaths of his first wife, María's older sister Isabel, in 1498 and their two-year-old son, Miguel, in 1500. The Castilian succession, however, eventually passed not to María but to her sister Juana and Philip the Handsome of Austria. Nevertheless, by all accounts, María and Manuel had a happy marriage, overseeing the expansion of Portugal from a continental kingdom to an overseas empire.

María was born in Granada in 1482; her twin sister was stillborn. Little is known of María's childhood, but of all the children of Fernando and Isabel, she appears to have led the most peaceful life. Like her brothers and sisters, she was educated by the court tutors, the Italian humanists Antonio and Alessandro Geraldino and Lucio Marineo Siculo. She traveled frequently with her mother and the peripatetic court, taking part in the momentous events of fifteenth-century Castile—the Inquisition, the conquest of Granada, and Columbus's return from his voyages to the New World.

María had eight children who lived to adulthood: João (1502), the future king João III; Isabel (1503), future wife of Emperor Charles V; Beatriz (1504); Luis (1506); Fernando (1507); Afonso (1509); Enrique (1512); and Duarte (1515). María died in March 1517, two months after giving birth to a stillborn boy christened Antonio.

BIBLIOGRAPHY

Azcona, Tarsicio de. *Isabel la Católica: Estudi crítico de su vida y su reinado*. Madrid, 1964.

Miller, Townsend. *The Castles and the Crown: Spain 1451–1555*. New York, 1963.

Prescott, William H. *History of the Reign of Ferdinand and Isabella the Catholic*. Boston, 1838.

Sanceau, Elaine. *The Reign of the Fortunate King, 1495–1521*. Hamden, Conn., 1969.

THERESA EARENFIGHT

MARINE COMPASS. See *Compass*, article on *Marine Compass*.

MARINUS OF TYRE (fl. c. A.D. 100–135), geographer. Almost all our knowledge of Marinus is derived from Ptolemy's *Geography* (about A.D. 148), which calls him the most recent contemporary geographer. Marinus's lost work, written in Greek and referred to by Ptolemy as "the *diorthosis* [rectification] of the map," went through several editions, and as Ptolemy implies, aimed at improving the tradition of world mapping, long connected with Greek mathematical geographers.

The impetus for scientific world cartography came primarily from Eratosthenes of Cyrene (c. 275–194 B.C.), who, assuming that the earth is a sphere, determined its circumference by comparing the angle of the sun at Alexandria at midday on the summer solstice with the angle 5000 stades (about 890 kilometers) south at Syene (Aswan). From these measurements he calculated the angle of the arc of a circle between Alexandria and Syene subtended at the earth's center as one-fiftieth of 360 degrees, thus reaching a fairly close approximation to the circumference of the earth. Eratosthenes's map of the world (c. 225 B.C.) was later criticized by Hipparchus (fl. 162–126 B.C.) and others.

By the second century more detailed knowledge had resulted from the expansion of the Roman Empire. Ptolemy criticized Marinus because of the way he claimed to rectify the geographical *pinax* (world map, presumably of Eratosthenes). Marinus proposed an orthogonal system for a map of the world based on the latitude-longitude ratio of Rhodes, whose latitude was reckoned as 36° N. But his assumption that a degree of longitude equaled 400 stades and a degree of latitude equaled 500 meant that his approximations decreased in accuracy as one moved away from the latitude of Rhodes. Marinus estimated the north-south extent of the *oikumene* (known world) as 87 degrees or 43,500 stades; this placed Thule (probably Shetland) at 63° N instead of 66° N as reckoned by Pytheas of Marseilles and Eratosthenes. Marinus reckoned the longitude of the known world on the latitude of Rhodes as 225 degrees; the difference in longitude between the Canary Islands and Weihai, China, is in fact about 140 degrees. Marinus's calculation relied on exaggerated figures of travel times; he accepted seven months as the west-to-east traveling time from Kashgar (in western China) or thereabouts to Luoyang (on Hwang Ho River) and four months as the north-to-south traveling time from the territory of the Garamantes (in the Fezzan) to Agisymba (Lake Chad area). Marinus claimed to determine the extent of *klimata* (belts of latitude, literally "inclinations" to the earth's axis) and one-hour belts of longitude, though it seems that he did so by putting lists of places together, not by mapping. Although Ptolemy considered the use of *klimata* inexact, the concept of *klimata* persisted until the Renaissance. Marinus's work was rediscovered by the Arab geographer al-Mas'udi (d. A.D. 956/957), who mentions a colored map attributed to Marinus showing the seven *klimata*. No "Marinus" maps are known to have survived the Middle Ages in western Europe.

The information available on Marinus in the Renaissance was to be found in Greek, Latin, or Arabic manuscripts or in Greek or Latin editions and, later, vernacular editions, of Ptolemy's *Geography*. Columbus read about Marinus in Pierre d'Ailly's *Imago mundi* (1410), a book printed around 1483. Of particular interest in the time of Columbus was Marinus's estimate of 225 degrees longitude for the whole *oikumene* on the parallel of Rhodes; if this estimate was right, there would be only 135 degrees of unknown territory between the Canaries and the east coast of China. This assumption led Columbus to believe that a westward voyage from Europe to China was possible.

BIBLIOGRAPHY

Dilke, O. A. W. *Greek and Roman Maps*. Ithaca, N.Y., 1985.

Dilke, O. A. W., and the editors, "Updating the Map: Ptolemy's Criticism of Marinus of Tyre." In vol. 1 of *The History of Cartography*, edited by J. B. Harley and David Woodward. Chicago, 1987.

Ptolemy, Claudius. *Geography of Claudius Ptolemy*. Edited by E. L. Stevenson. New York, 1932.

Temporini, Hildegard, ed. *Aufstieg und Niedergang der römischen Welt*. Berlin, 1978.

O. A. W. DILKE

MARTELLUS, HENRICUS (fl. late fifteenth century), cartographer. Among the geographic charts of the fifteenth century that were based on Portuguese originals that have since disappeared, one stands out from the rest. It is the *mappamundi* designed by a German cartographer who worked in Italy and became known by his Latin name, Henricus Martellus Germanus. The map, four manuscript copies of which are included in the *Insularium illustratum Henrici Martelli Germani*, was later engraved and can be dated around 1490. Martellus worked in Florence in the last quarter of the fifteenth century in association with the engraver Francesco Roselli, who probably engraved not only this chart but also at the beginning of the next century, those of Contarini and others.

This map is the first to record the places reached in the voyage to the southern tip of Africa. Recorded are the results of the second voyage of the Portuguese navigator Diogo Cão, who sailed as far as Cape Padrão, and the voyage of Bartolomeu Dias, who rounded the Cape of Good Hope and reached the Indian Ocean.

The previous absence of these southern regions in Portuguese cartography can certainly be attributed to the policy of secrecy of the Portuguese king João II. Martellus must nonetheless have had access to information from Portugal. In his new toponymy, twelve of the place names derive from the voyage of Cão and twenty-one from the voyage of Dias.

Among the chart's various legends is the following:

"Hec est vera forma moderna affrice secundum descriptione Portugalensium inter mare Mediterraneum et oceanum meredionalem" (This is the true modern shape of Africa, according to the description of the Portuguese, between the Mediterranean Sea and the Southern Ocean). Another has given rise to much debate among scholars:

"Ad hunc usque montem qui vocatur niger per venit classis secûdi regis portugalie cuius classis p[er]fectus erat diegus canus qui in memoriam rei erexit colûnam marmorea cum crucis in signe et ultra processit usque ad serram pardam que distat ab môte nigro mille miliaria et. hic moritur" (The armada of the king of Portugal sailed as far as this mountain, which they call Negro. It was commanded by Diogo Cão, who erected stone pillars with crosses in memory of the king, and proceeded on his way until he got as far as the Serra Parda, which is located at a distance of one thousand miles from Mount Negro, and ends there).

Some scholars have interpreted "hic moritur" as "there he ended [his days]" or "there he died," asserting that the phrase refers to Diogo Cão, who may have died there, which would explain why he is undocumented after the return of this expedition. Others, however, think the phrase refers to the mountain, and thus means that the Serra Parda "ends there." (Evidence for the second interpretation may be a document found very recently that seems to indicate that Diogo Cão indeed survived the voyage.)

But the *mappamundi*'s real importance lies elsewhere. It is the first that shows the southern tip of Africa, which is depicted, so to speak, experimentally. Its workmanship is extremely modern in relation to its date, which we know from another legend referring to Dias's last voyage: "Hunc usq ad ilhe de fonti p[er]venit ultima navegatio portugalesium, ano dm. 1489" (The last Portuguese navigation reached as far as the Island of the Fountain in the year of the Lord 1489). The chart was certainly made a few months after Dias returned to Lisbon in December of 1488. This would mean that the Portuguese prototype on which Martellus based his map was made immediately after the return of the navigator, which was the usual practice. No known Portuguese chart represents the results of Dias's voyage, and though Martellus's map was certainly based on some chart, it is not extant.

Various references to these Portuguese charts, on which were methodically and progressively recorded the latest advances in navigation, attest to their existence. Some have been found in modern times—namely, the chart of Pedro Reinel, dated around 1485, and that of Jorge de Aguiar, dated 1492. These charts, and their very perfection, which presupposes antecedents, are proof of the development of Portuguese cartography in the fif-

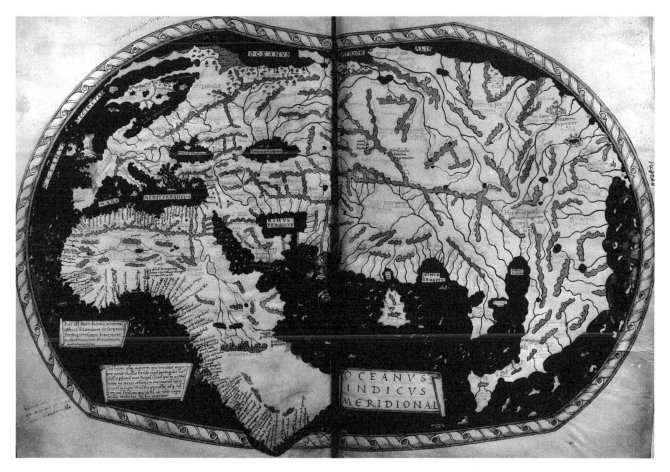

WORLD MAP OF HENRICUS MARTELLUS, 1489.

teenth century. Although Martellus must have based his map on such a chart, it contains an error that is not found in the Portuguese models that are known. His coordinates are incorrect; the African continent is unduly extended about six degrees to the south and dislocated by about twenty degrees to the east.

According to the Portuguese historian Jaime Cortesão, and as corroborated by Armando Cortesão, the errors could have been the result of misinformation circulated by King João II in an effort to make people believe that the African route was far longer than it actually is; Martellus was probably provided with this erroneous information. King João's policy of secrecy explains his showing Christopher Columbus (or his brother Bartolomé) a chart on which the voyage of Dias was represented with false latitudes. The king's objective was to discourage Portugal's rivals from following the southeastern route. It is probably not by chance that the first known Portuguese map to represent the southern tip of Africa—the so-called Cantino planisphere of 1502—was a clandestine chart secretly obtained by bribing a cartographer.

Aside from its representation of Africa, Martellus's *mappamundi* is a typical chart drawn according to Ptolemaic conceptions. It represents the Indian Ocean in a characteristically Ptolemaic form and, of course, it does not show any continent between western Europe and the extremity of Asia. It allows us to see the world as it was conceived on the eve of the first voyage of Christopher Columbus.

BIBLIOGRAPHY

Almagiá, Roberto. "I mappamondi di Enrico Martello e alcuni concetti geografici di Cristoforo Colombo." *La Bibliofilia* (Florence) 42 (1940): 288–311.

Castro, Augusto César da Silva, Jr. "Diogo Cão e a legenda de Henrique Martellus." In vol. 2 of *Actas do Congresso Internacional de história dos descobrimentos (1960)*. Lisbon, 1961.

Cortesão, Armando, and Avelino Teixeira da Mota. *Portugaliae Monumenta Cartographica*. 6 vols. Lisbon, 1960. Vols. 1, p. 10, and 5, p. 170.

Crone, G. R. *Maps and Their Makers: An Introduction to the History of Cartography*. 2d ed. London, 1962.

Nunn, George Emra. *The Geographical Conceptions of Columbus*. American Geographical Society, research series no. 14. New York.

Ravenstein, Ernest George. *Martin Behaim: His Life and His Globe.* London, 1908.

Vietor, Alexander O. "A Pre-Columbian Map of the World, Circa 1489." *Yale University Library Gazette* 37 (July 1962): 8–13.

ALFREDO PINHEIRO MARQUES
Translated from Portuguese by Rebecca Catz

MARTÍNEZ DE IRALA, DOMINGO (1509–1557),

Spanish conquistador; known as the Father of Paraguay. Born in Vergara, Guipúzcoa, in Spain, Martínez de Irala was the second son of Martín Perez and Marina de Albisúa Toledo. Following his older brother's death, he received an entailed estate from his parents, but in 1534 he transferred it to a brother-in-law and sailed for the Río de la Plata with Pedro de Mendoza, the newly appointed adelantado for the region.

Mendoza founded Buenos Aires in February 1536 but failed to find the great wealth he had hoped for. Soon under seige at Buenos Aires, he sent Juan de Ayolas to scout farther up the river in search of a way to Peru. During the second of these trips, Irala was left in charge of the ships and men posted at Candelaria (modern Corumbá?) while Ayolas marched westward. According to some accounts, Irala participated in the founding of Asunción, Paraguay, on August 15, 1537. (The city's government was created in 1541.) Following Mendoza's return to Spain and Ayolas's disappearance, Martínez de Irala emerged as a popular leader among the remaining colonists. In June 1539, he was elected governor of Paraguay. He continued to search for Ayolas until early in 1540 when news of Ayolas's death reached the governor. A year later, Irala withdrew the garrison at Buenos Aires.

The arrival on March 9, 1542, of the royally appointed replacement for Mendoza as governor and adelantado, Alvar Núñez Cabeza de Vaca, began the most controversial years of Martínez de Irala's life. Cabeza de Vaca claimed that Irala was plotting against him, but other sources indicate that Irala played the obedient subordinate until April 25, 1544, when failure of Cabeza de Vaca's efforts to reach El Dorado (or Peru) led the royal treasury officials and ordinary soldiers to overthrow him. Irala again was elected governor.

As governor between 1544 and 1556, Irala oversaw the solidification of the Spanish presence in Paraguay. He was unable to make peace with all the Indian groups antagonized during the previous decade, although most were pacified. Among the many explorations he authorized to the north and west of Asunción, his own in 1548 to the foothills of Bolivia was the most spectacular. Beginning in 1554, he sent explorers east to find routes to the Brazilian coast. His rule was challenged on a number of occasions; the Crown had even appointed a new governor, Diego de

Sanabría, in 1547, but the new governor and his son of the same name died before reaching Asunción. Martínez de Irala's own royal appointment as governor finally occurred in 1554. In 1556 he oversaw the granting of encomiendas, a measure he had previously resisted. He died on October 2, 1556, at the age of forty-seven.

BIBLIOGRAPHY

Morison, Samuel Eliot. *The European Discovery of America: The Southern Voyages, A.D. 1492–1616.* New York, 1971.

Warren, Harris G. *Paraguay: An Informal History.* Norman, Okla., 1949.

PAUL E. HOFFMAN

MARTYR, PETER. See *Anghiera, Pietro Martire d'.*

MAXIMILIAN I (1459–1519),

German king from 1486 and Holy Roman Emperor-elect in 1493. Maximilian, son of Emperor Frederick III (1415–1493) and Leonor of Portugal, never formally received papal confirmation of his title of emperor. According to the terms of an agreement signed in Trent (1508), he declared that he would use the title of Holy Roman Emperor-elect until his coronation in Rome, which never took place.

Maximilian used his matrimonial alliances and military skill to bring the Austrian House of Habsburg to prominence in European affairs, especially in the west. His marriage in 1482 to Mary of Burgundy, daughter of Duke Charles the Bold, brought with it the wealth and territory of Flanders and the Franche-Comté. Maximilian increased his influence in 1495 through a double marriage alliance with Fernando of Spain. According to the terms of this diplomatic coup, Maximilian's only surviving legitimate son, Philip the Handsome, was betrothed to Juana of Castile, and his daughter Margaret was to marry Juan, prince of Asturias and heir to the thrones of Aragón, Castile, and Granada. Prince Juan died in 1497, followed by Philip in 1506, leaving Juana's son and Maximilian's grandson, the future Emperor Charles V, heir to the Castilian Crown as well as the territories in the Low Countries. Maximilian paved the way for the addition of Hungary and Bohemia to his territories by negotiating the marriages of his granddaughter Mary to King Louis II of Hungary and his grandson Ferdinand to Anne of Bohemia.

Until the death of his father in 1493, Maximilian had little German territory or political power and was preoccupied with his territories in the Low Countries. He was named co-regent of the Netherlands in 1477, and he became the ruling duke of Burgundy at the death of his wife, Mary (1482), and titular co-regent for his son, Philip, in 1488. Although Maximilian derived his political power from

MAXIMILIAN I. Engraving by Albrecht Dürer.

ELSEVIER PUBLISHING PROJECTS, AMSTERDAM

rial princes, who claimed to be the representatives of the popular will. In his dealings with the German princes, Maximilian was at a disadvantage because he constantly needed revenue for his campaigns against the French in Italy and northern France and the Ottoman Turks in eastern Europe. His financial difficulties were exacerbated by his desire to establish a permanent army. Maximilian was forced to bargain for his much-needed funds by promising administrative reforms of the imperial government. The reform movement was initiated by Berthold of Henneberg, the powerful archbishop of Mainz, but the reforms were stymied by the chaotic nature of German territorialism. His most lasting reforms were the creation of an imperial chamber court and imperial "circles" designed to maintain the peace. The Diet of Worms (1495) was a turning point in the constitutional history of the empire, but the reform movement ultimately failed because the princes and the emperor were unable to work together.

Maximilian had wide-ranging interests and was well read and reasonably intelligent. He furthered the humanist program of the Renaissance through his patronage of the University of Vienna and the University of Freiburg. He cultivated the fine arts, especially the work of artists such as Albrecht Dürer and the composers Heinrich Isaac and Ludwig Senfl. Maximilian did much to advance military organization and the newer technologies of warfare. His use of improved weapons such as lightweight lances and firearms made his foot soldiers, the Landsknecht, feared throughout Europe.

By the time of his death in 1519 Maximilian had established the foundations for the enduring dominance of the Habsburg family in European politics. He is buried not in his monumental tomb in Innsbruck but in the Chapel of St. George in Wiener Neustadt.

BIBLIOGRAPHY

Benecke, Gerhard. *Maximilian I (1469–1519): An Analytical Biography.* London, 1982.

Seton Watson, Robert William. *Maximilian I: Holy Roman Emperor.* Westminster, 1902.

Waas, Glenn Elwood. *The Legendary Character of Kaiser Maximilian.* New York, 1941.

Wiesflecker, Hermann. *Kaiser Maximilian I: Das Reich, Österreich und Europa an der Wende zur Neuzeit.* 4 vols. Vienna, 1971–1986.

THERESA EARENFIGHT

MAYAS. See *Indian America*, article on *Mayas*.

MEDICI FAMILY. Members of the Medici family, which originated in the Mugello region north of Florence,

Flanders, it was the source of many of his thorniest problems. The strength of the Flemish townspeople and their reluctance to be ruled by a foreign prince clashed violently with Maximilian's autocratic style. His policy of appointing officials from his Habsburg realms rather than from local territories was especially unpopular. He became embroiled in uprisings in Flanders in 1482 and 1488, and the Flemish burghers held him captive for several months during the latter rebellion. In addition, the acquisition of Flanders and the advent of Habsburg influence in western Europe inevitably led to conflict with the French kings Louis XI and Charles VIII.

Within his German realms he fared little better. Despite his personal popularity among the German people, Maximilian was considered an outsider, interested only in establishing the Habsburg family as a ruling dynasty. His territorial expansion, which began with his Burgundian marriage, raised Maximilian and the Habsburg family far above the competing German princes, thus making it nearly impossible for the imperial electors to refuse the Habsburgs the title of emperor without risking civil war. A deep rift developed between Maximilian and the territo-

migrated to that city in the early thirteenth century. They established themselves in the district around the church of San Lorenzo, investing in urban real estate and engaging in moneylending and cloth manufacture while still maintaining property in the Mugello. In the turbulent 1200s and 1300s, the family played a modest role in Florentine politics, filling some offices and participating in the factional conflicts that were so typical of the age. In 1400, the family was one of dozens of prominent Florentine lineages who controlled the city's economy and political life and constituted an urban elite. Giovanni di Bicci de' Medici (1360–1429) laid the foundation for the family's prominence in the fifteenth century by building a vast fortune from his banking operations in the Roman Curia. His son Cosimo (1389–1464) expanded his father's business operations, developing a network of branches in Rome, London, Bruges, Geneva, and Venice. In 1458, Cosimo's tax returns revealed that he was the richest citizen in Florence; he may well have been the wealthiest European of his time.

A factional conflict erupted in Florence in the late 1420s and early 1430s, which resulted in the exile of Cosimo and his cousin Averardo in 1433. But a year later, the two returned to Florence in triumph and established a regime of their partisans, which governed Florence for the next

LORENZO DE'MEDICI. Bust by Andrea del Verrocchio.

NATIONAL GALLERY OF ART, WASHINGTON, D.C.

sixty years. The foundations of this Medicean hegemony were (1) the family's vast wealth, which enabled Cosimo to build a large network of dependent clients; (2) constitutional reforms, which guaranteed that only Medici partisans filled the key offices of the state; and (3) the political astuteness of Cosimo and his successors. Cosimo projected an image of himself and his family as civic benefactors by maintaining peace and prosperity and by embellishing the city with palaces, villas, and restored churches and monasteries, most notably, San Lorenzo and San Marco. Even with these formidable assets, however, the Medici regime encountered opposition from disgruntled citizens: some who deplored the erosion of republican institutions and values, and others who wished to replace the Medici with their own faction. The most serious challenge to the regime was the Pazzi conspiracy (April 1478), in which Lorenzo de' Medici was wounded and his brother Giuliano was killed by assassins in the cathedral. The Pazzi conspirators failed to rouse the citizenry to their cause, and many were hunted down and executed.

Lorenzo (1449–1492) had succeeded to his father Piero's position as the leading citizen of Florence in 1469 when he was only seventeen. During his short life, he achieved an extraordinary reputation as statesman, patron of the arts, scholar, and poet. No other European of his time could match Lorenzo's versatility, which was a rare combination of political acumen, scholarly expertise, and poetic sensibility. He maintained close personal ties with the rulers of Italian states and was given credit for maintaining a fragile peace in the peninsula. He was particularly intimate with Pope Innocent VIII (r. 1484–1492), who bestowed a cardinal's hat on Lorenzo's son Giovanni. This was an important aspect of Lorenzo's strategy to build an Italian context for his family's power and influence.

After Lorenzo's death in 1492, Medici fortunes experienced a dramatic decline. His son Piero (1471–1503) was a less skillful politician than his father, and he alienated a number of influential citizens. He had initially opposed the efforts of King Charles VIII of France to claim the Kingdom of Naples as his inheritance. When a French army moved across the Alps in the summer of 1494 and threatened Florence, Piero abandoned the city. Opponents of the Medici established a republican regime, which was strongly influenced by the Dominican friar Girolamo Savonarola. This regime controlled Florence for fourteen years before it was overthrown and replaced by a pro-Medici party. From 1512 to 1527, the Medici dominated Florentine politics, while maintaining a republican form of government. After a brief interlude (1527–1530), when the city was governed by anti-Mediceans, the family again reasserted its control over the city. After a brief period of instability, Medici control of the Florentine state was solidified in 1537 under Cosimo (1517–1574), the first grand duke of Tuscany. His descendants ruled Florence for two hundred years before the family died out in 1737.

After Lorenzo's death, the most prominent members of the Medici family were two of its popes, Leo X (r. 1513–1521) and Clement VII (r. 1523–1534). Although they provided critical support for the family's control of Florence, they were unsuccessful in suppressing the Protestant revolt, and both failed in their attempts to limit the expansion of Spanish power in Italy. Clement VII supported the efforts of the Dominicans and Franciscans to convert the Indians in the New World, and he established a diocesan organization for the Roman Catholic church in the Caribbean and in Central and South America.

BIBLIOGRAPHY

DeRoover, Raymond. *The Rise and Decline of the Medici Bank, 1394–1494.* Cambridge, Mass., 1963.

Hale, John R. *Florence and the Medici: The Pattern of Control.* London, 1977.

Kent, Dale. *The Rise of the Medici: Faction in Florence, 1426–34.* Oxford, 1978.

Rubinstein, Nicolai. *The Government of Florence under the Medici (1434–94).* Oxford, 1966.

Stephens, John. *The Fall of the Florentine Republic, 1512–1530.* Oxford, 1983.

GENE A. BRUCKER

MEDICINE AND HEALTH. On the eve of the great voyages of the late fifteenth century, the practice of medicine in western Europe was in a transitional stage. Medieval Christianity discouraged all investigation of natural causes and this, in turn, retarded the development of medical inquiry. The scholastic dedication to rationalism, buttressed by new readings of Aristotle, did not penetrate deeply into the fabric of medieval society. For the vast majority of the population, disease was viewed as a punishment for sins or the result of some commerce with the devil. While individual illness could be cured by divine intervention encouraged simply by the ministrations of prayer, epidemic disease had to be countered by more public religious expressions such as mass processions, the building of churches, and the erection of inspiring religious statues. Medical practice was thus more a function of culture than of biology.

A powerful agent of change presented itself in a totally unanticipated form. The Black Death (most likely bubonic plague) arrived in western Europe between 1347 and 1351 with devastating results and was followed by other epidemics in 1361–1363, 1371, 1375, and 1396–1397. The bubonic plague had originated in Asia. It was carried to Europe by black rats (*Rattus rattus*) aboard sailing vessels to Mediterranean ports. The black rats quickly infected local rodents with the deadly bacillus, *Pasteurella pestis,* and before the urban rats died the infection was carried from the rodent population to human hosts by fleas that shared the rodents' burrows. The sudden presence of thousands of dead rats in a community was an unmistakable sign of impending disaster.

The arrival of *Pasteurella pestis* in western Europe could not have come at a worse time. The famine years of 1345 to 1347 had left a weakened and highly susceptible population. Those persons living in crowded and dirty medieval cities were obvious targets since the accumulation of garbage and sewage attracted rodents and the flying vectors they harbored. Once *Pasteurella pestis* reached the human population, it was passed on not only by fleas but occasionally from person to person, generally from the mucus sprayed by the coughing or sneezing of someone already infected. High fevers, abscesses, and carbuncles brought death to about half of those infected within four or five days; in some parts of Europe, entire towns were virtually wiped out. Those who managed to survive were left in such a frail condition that they were easy prey to secondary infections. Besides bubonic plague, smallpox, tuberculosis, scabies, erysipelas, leprosy, and trachoma all reached epidemic proportions and wreaked demographic havoc in western Europe in the fourteenth and fifteenth centuries.

There is no general agreement on the average life span in western Europe on the eve of the great discoveries. It was certainly less than twenty-nine years of age, probably closer to twenty-eight. This low average figure reflects a very high infant and young-child mortality rate. It is believed that over one-third of the population died before reaching the age of five. Though the epidemics commanded most attention, poor diet, horrible hygienic practices, and the general lack of competent medical care all contributed to low life expectancy.

The heavy toll exacted by the recurring epidemics in western Europe for the first time prompted genuine public concern with medical education, the regulation of medical practice, the construction of hospitals, the need for hygiene, and the elusive search for effective therapy. There were few large advances in medical knowledge, but social pressure rather than religious discourse clearly began to affect the direction of medical inquiry. Spain affords one good example of the European response to epidemic disease, and in Spain it was the Black Death especially that encouraged the medical effort.

The rapid spread of the Black Death throughout Iberia left some cities with less than half of their original populations. The kingdoms of Aragón and Catalonia were hit as hard as any regions of Europe. The city of Barcelona, for example, had a population of about 50,000 in 1340. Ten years later the number had been reduced to 38,000 and by 1377 to 20,000. This demographic devastation alerted the Iberian medical community to the matter of contagiousness. The institution of quarantine emerged as the first response. Ships calling at Spanish ports were sometimes required to remain at anchor in the harbor for forty days (thus the word quarantine) before anyone could disembark. Concern with prophylaxis prompted the construction of elementary sewage systems, the cleaning of public latrines, and a more systematic regulation of public market places and slaughter houses.

In the century that followed the cataclysm of the plague, many uneducated Spaniards turned to religious practices in their search for solace, but an increasing number of educated Spaniards began to free themselves from the bondage of superstition, alchemy, and astrology to search for rational explanations of disease. A new emphasis was placed on medical education at the leading Spanish universities. Anatomy was at the core of the curriculum and grave robbers began to provide corpses for classroom dissection. The propriety of dissection of the human body occasioned much anxious wrangling but the process was fundamental to the new questions addressed by Spanish physicians. Without it medical science simply could not exist.

The University of Salamanca, founded by King Fernando III of Castile in 1243, had offered medical training on a regular basis since 1252; by the fifteenth century Valencia, Seville, Barcelona, Valladolid, Lerida, and Alcalá de Henares were making major contributions as well. If not yet ready to compete with Salerno and Padua in Italy and Montepellier in France, they were improving rapidly. By attending lectures and listening to the explication of texts,

BLOODLETTING. A standard treatment. From a fifteenth-century illuminated manuscript.   ELSEVIER PUBLISHING PROJECTS, AMSTERDAM

medical students sought to master Hippocrates, Galen, Ibn Sina (Avicenna), and Ibn Rushd (Averroës) during their four-year course of study; they were expected to question these venerable authorities as well. Responsibility for the systematic acquisition and transmission of medical knowledge was institutionalized rather than passed on casually from a "practitioner" to any interested party. Institutionalization made certain elements of control possible.

With the establishment of an environment for academic medicine, the quest for better teaching materials took on new meaning. In the hope of providing more appropriate tools for disciplined inference, Jewish scholars in Toledo, especially Alvaro de Castro and Diego Sobrino, began the arduous task of translating medical treatises from Greek and Arabic. By the late fifteenth century Spanish presses had begun to accelerate their diffusion of medical treatises and in the classroom, as well as the clinic, these scholarly works were taken seriously for the first time. The medical literature used in Spanish universities in the fifteenth and sixteenth centuries was heavily indebted to the Greeks, especially Galen and Hippocrates. It is not surprising that Spanish physicians embraced a modified humoral theory of medicine, according to which disease resulted from a disequilibrium of the body's four basic qualities: hot, cold, wet, and dry. Therapy, as a result, was designed to restore that equilibrium through the use of foods and medicines that harbored the appropriate hot or cold, wet or dry therapeutic properties. It was one of those theories not quickly killed by fact.

At approximately the same time that medical education was institutionalized, hospitals were established throughout the Iberian kingdoms. During the second half of the fifteenth century, general hospitals could be found in Madrid, Zaragoza, Burgos, Toledo, Salamanca, Barcelona, and Seville, and more specialized institutions for the mentally impaired in Barcelona, for women in Madrid (Hospital de la Pasión), and for lepers in Seville (Hospital de San Lázaro). A special military hospital was established in Granada to care for Christian soldiers wounded during the wars of the Reconquista. By the time that Columbus began his first voyage to America the practice of medicine to a large extent had been taken out of the monasteries and much of the Spanish medical community had rejected the deductive method in favor of the experimental.

Equally important were the early steps to regulate medical practice. During the earlier Middle Ages, the regulation of medicine seemed designed more to guard morals than to promote public health or medical competence. The *fueros* (bodies of regional laws) were concerned that male doctors might use their influential positions to corrupt their female patients and therefore prohibited all treatment of women unless parents or husbands ordered the treatment or were present during the specific procedures. But gradually regulatory control directed itself to the charlatan, the quack, and the medical incompetent. The *Siete partidas* provided that a false doctor who caused a person's death be banished for five years and provided that a pharmacist who dispensed medicine without a doctor's order could be tried for murder if the patient died. But it was not until the second half of the fifteenth century that comprehensive laws for the licensing of physicians were ordered by the Spanish monarchs.

On March 30, 1477, nine years before they met Columbus for the first time, King Fernando and Queen Isabel signed a significant *pragmática* (a royal edict) in Madrid establishing a special council known as the *protomedicato*. Designed to safeguard the public interest, the *protomedicato* was charged with examining all doctors, surgeons, curers, apothecaries, and sellers of herbs to determine their competence in their respective fields. If they were judged to be competent they were given a formal letter of approval and a license to practice. Those who continued their activities without the license were subject to stiff fines; a special prosecutor, the *promotor fiscal,* was attached to the council to bring charges against violators. In addition to licensing doctors, the *protomedicato* also heard all complaints brought by the public against the medical profession. Its decision in these cases was final as the enabling act provided that there would be no appeal to any other royal tribunal. It is significant that the decree establishing the *protomedicato* was made applicable to all existing Spanish kingdoms and possessions and all future possessions that the Crown might acquire. Following the voyages of Columbus, the *pragmática* of 1477 would be applied in the New World.

The royal decree establishing the *protomedicato* was supplemented by a series of other regulatory measures in the decades that followed its promulgation. The most important of these was a statute that provided that all practicing physicians have a medical degree from an approved university in addition to two years of internship with a certified doctor. Evidence of compliance had to be presented to the *protomedicato.* All these regulatory measures were hesitant steps in the right direction but in and of themselves they were insufficient to make a major impact on health care, much less to establish the dominion of humanity over disease.

A new round of epidemics swept through the Iberian kingdoms in the two decades prior to the voyages of Columbus. Though not as severe as the Black Death of the fourteenth century they took a heavy toll. The plague visited Barcelona in 1478, 1483, 1489, and 1490; Mallorca in 1475; Zaragoza in 1486 and 1490; and Valencia in 1489. Typhus apparently made its European debut in Spain when it struck Granada in 1489 and 1490; it reportedly caused over 17,000 deaths in the Spanish army, making it a much more effective killer than the Moors the Spanish were attempting to drive off Iberian soil. Some of the Spanish adventurers, servants, and slaves would carry these deadly pathogens, along with others, to the New World on the Atlantic voyages that began in 1492.

The first European travelers to the New World crossed the Atlantic on small, crowded ships that lacked proper sanitary facilities. These vessels were designed to carry freight, not passengers, and the travelers often shared their space with animals. They had the choice of finding a niche in the stench of the hold, surrounded by seasick passengers, or sitting on a cluttered deck exposed to the elements and the epithets of hardened sailors. Seldom would they encounter a doctor aboard. When all went well, the time between landfalls was only about a month and a half, but ocean calms often lengthened the journey. The diet for the trip (primarily salted meat, salted flour, biscuit, lard that quickly became rancid, dried grains, peas, and beans, and about a quart of water per day) was barely tolerable even when the ration was not attacked by rats or fouled by seawater. The absence of fresh fruit, vegetables, and meat left the travelers weak and vulnerable to scurvy, especially if poor dietary practices prior to the initial boarding had lowered their resistance. Scurvy seemed to attack the whole body, causing swelling of the joints, excruciating pain in the back and kidneys, hemorrhaging from the mucous membranes, general weakness, and the swelling of gums and loss of teeth. Shipboard deaths were not uncommon in the late fifteenth and early sixteenth centuries, especially when climatic conditions, improper navigation, or malfunctioning of the vessels unexpectedly lengthened the duration of the journey. Short trips in the Caribbean were less prone to the ravages of scurvy but the disease was the chief cause of mortality among Spanish seamen.

For native Americans the most dramatic impact of the European contact was the introduction of new epidemic diseases. Isolated for millennia from the gene pools of the Old World, the Indian populations of the Americas had few immunological defenses against Old World diseases. Smallpox, typhus, measles, pertussis, tuberculosis, and pneumonia, once turned loose, devastated the Indians of the New World and in time left only remnants of once vibrant preconquest societies. Some of Columbus's sailors returned to Europe with a new disease thought to be of American origin, syphilis, which spread through Europe with a vengeance during the last few years of the fifteenth century.

The early Spanish chroniclers offered Europe tantalizing descriptions of the botanical bounty of the New World at a time when medicinal plants were in great demand. Samples of jalap, sarsaparilla, sneezewort, sassafras, wormwood, creosote, chinchona bark (from which quinine is extracted), peyote, and countless other plants found their way back to Europe and worked their way into the *Materia medica*. The Spanish physician Nicolás Bautista de Monardis collected these specimens in Seville and in 1565 published his *Dos libros, el uno que trata de todas las cosas que traen de nuestras Indias Occidentales que sirven al uso de medicina*. It soon inspired an English translation under the overly optimistic title *Joyfull Newes out of the Newe Worlde* (London, 1577). Many of the plants did not live up to expectations, but the medical syncretism of the Old World and the New World had begun.

[For further discussion of disease in the New World, see *Disease and Demography*. See also *Syphilis* for further discussion of its origins and spread.]

BIBLIOGRAPHY

Crosby, Alfred W. *The Columbian Exchange: Biological and Cultural Consequences of 1492*. Westport, Conn., 1972.

Entralgo, Laín. *Historia universal de la medicina*. Barcelona, 1981.

Granjel, Luis S. *La medicina española renacentista*. Salamanca, 1980.

McNeill, William H. *Plagues and Peoples*. Garden City, N.Y., 1976.

Twigg, Graham. *The Black Death: A Biological Reappraisal*. London, 1984.

Zinsser, Hans. *Rats, Lice, and History*. Boston, 1934.

MICHAEL C. MEYER

MEDINACELI, DUKE OF. The fifth duke of Medinaceli, Luis de la Cerda (d. 1501), played a critical role in introducing Christopher Columbus into the royal court of Spain. The duke of Medinaceli was the most logical Spanish nobleman for Columbus to ask for help with his enterprise of the Indies because he was one of the great sea lords of Spain. His ancestors had been among the first conquerors of the Canary Islands, and he was lord of the strategic port of Puerto de Santa María.

When Columbus approached him in late 1485, the duke was in Puerto de Santa María, where he had married his third wife, Catalina Bique de Orejón, a local citizen. He was eager to expand his shipping business and considered outfitting three or four ships for Columbus. But he decided that Columbus's plan would more appropriately be sponsored by the monarchs. So from his village of Rota, he wrote to the queen recommending Columbus.

Columbus could not have chosen a better patron in the merchant and shipping world of Spain's southern coast. The duke was descended from Castilian kings and was closely related to the most powerful member of the royal court, Cardinal Pedro González de Mendoza. The duke

was the cardinal's nephew, and the duke's granddaughter was married to the cardinal's son. The connections worked marvelously well. By early 1486, Columbus was at the royal court presenting his plan to Fernando and Isabel. The queen placed her chief accountant, Alonso de Quintanilla, in charge of the project, and Quintanilla wrote to the duke that the proposal was risky but if it succeeded Her Highness would give him a share of it.

We can reconstruct this story from a letter that the duke wrote to Cardinal Mendoza on March 19, 1493. At the time, the duke was in his town of Cogolludo north of the city of Guadalajara, supervising the building of a palace. On the recommendation of the cardinal, he had hired the Italian-trained architect, Lorenzo Vázquez, to design a Renaissance building for him. In the midst of this building project, he received word that Columbus had returned safely from his first voyage.

The duke of Medinaceli wrote to tell his uncle about the great event and asked for two favors. Since he had supported and recommended Columbus, he wanted a share of the new shipping business. He asked that all the cargoes in this new trade should be loaded and unloaded in Puerto de Santa María.

He did not get this, but he did receive his second request, that he be permitted to send some of his own caravels every year. One of the ships that participated in Columbus's second voyage was captained by an employee of the duke, Alonso de Ojeda. And the duke may have been the principal investor in Ojeda's later voyages of exploration to the coast of South America.

Meanwhile, the duke's palace in Cogolludo lagged. By the time he died in 1501, only the facade had been built, and the structure remains in the same incomplete state today.

BIBLIOGRAPHY

Gutiérrez Coronel, Diego. *Historia genealógica de la casa de Mendoza*. Edited by Angel González Palencia. 2 vols. Cuenca, 1946.

Layna Serrano, Francisco. *Castillos de Guadalajara*. Madrid, 1962.

Medinaceli, Duke of. "Letter to the Grand Cardinal of Spain, about the Duke's early support of Columbus." In *The Conquerors and the Conquered*. Vol. 1 of *New Iberian World: A Documentary History of the Discovery and Settlement of Latin America to the Early 17th Century*. Edited by John H. Parry and Robert G. Keith. 5 vols. New York, 1984.

HELEN NADER

MEDINA SIDONIA, DUKE OF. Hereditary noble titles were a new invention in Castile during Christopher Columbus's lifetime, and one of the richest of these new titles was duke of Medina Sidonia, which King Juan II bestowed on the count of Niebla, Juan Alfonso de Guzmán, in 1445. The dukes of Medina Sidonia were exceptionally wealthy because they were lords of the important port of Sanlúcar de Barrameda and because the king gave them as a hereditary property the royal taxes on the annual tuna catch in the Straits of Gibraltar. The second duke, Enrique de Guzmán (duke from 1468 until his death in 1492), was an important commander in the war against Granada. Some historians believe that Christopher Columbus asked the duke of Medina Sidonia to finance his project to sail west to the Indies because the duke was one of the patrons of the monastery of La Rábida and owned property around Huelva, where Columbus's sister-in-law and her husband lived. If Columbus did so, it would have been sometime between 1485, when Columbus came to Castile, and 1492, when Fernando and Isabel agreed to sponsor the project. No documentary evidence exists that Columbus approached the duke of Medina Sidonia, however, and there is some reason to believe that authors have confused this nobleman with the duke of Medinaceli, whose early support for Columbus is well documented.

BIBLIOGRAPHY

Manzano Manzano, Juan. *Cristóbal Colón: Siete años decisivos de su vida, 1485–1492.* 2d ed. Madrid, 1964.
Pierson, Peter. *Commander of the Armada.* New Haven, 1989.
Rumeu de Armas, Antonio. *La Rábida y el descubrimiento de América.* Madrid, 1968.

HELEN NADER

MEMORIAL ARCHITECTURE. See *Monuments and Memorials.*

MÉNDEZ, DIEGO (c. 1472–c. 1536), captain of *La Capitana.* Méndez, by all accounts, emerges as the true hero of Columbus's disaster-plagued fourth voyage to America, for which he enlisted as *escudero,* "gentleman volunteer." Little is known of his early life except that he came from the Segura region of Spain and had served for a time as majordomo for Columbus. The recorded history of his heroic exploits begins in Veragua, a gold-rich area in the western part of present-day Panama, where Columbus was attempting to establish a settlement.

The apparent permanence of the settlement was causing a rapid deterioration in the once-friendly relations with the local Indians. Méndez, who had become a trusted aide of the Admiral, observed the increase in the numbers and hostility of the natives and undertook a bold reconnoitering expedition. He returned with the warning that the area's principal chieftain, the cacique El Quibián,

had assembled thousands of warriors and was clearly planning an attack. Méndez advised the Admiral and his brother Bartolomé Colón, who was to remain in charge of the new settlement as adelantado (military and political leader), that the only safe course was to seize El Quibián and his principal subordinates and outlined a plan to do so. The daring plan was approved and carried out with great skill by Colón, Méndez, and a force of about eighty men. The cacique was taken prisoner, together with several key subordinates and their families. Through the laxness of guards, El Quibián was able to escape, enabling him to continue his campaign against the Spaniards.

On April 6, 1503, the day the Admiral was to depart the area with three of his four ships, a force of about four hundred armed natives attacked the settlement. Seven of the Spanish force were killed and several others wounded, including the adelantado. As Méndez later recorded, "This fight lasted three full hours, and Our Lord miraculously gave us the victory, we being so few and they so numerous." When the fight was over, the captain of the Admiral's flagship, Diego Tristán, who had been sent ashore in a ship's boat to take on a final supply of water, ignored the advice of Méndez and proceeded up the river to find good sweet water. The regrouped natives attacked and killed Tristán and all his men but one, who managed to escape and report the disaster. Remembering the loss of the entire force left at La Navidad in La Española on the first voyage, Columbus realized that the situation ashore had become untenable, and he reluctantly decided it would be prudent to abandon the settlement. Méndez constructed a raft out of two dugout canoes and cross timbers and in two days transported to the ships all the garrison, together with the food and gear that had been stored ashore. The worm-eaten hulk of the caravel *Gallego* was abandoned. When Méndez came aboard with the last load, the Admiral embraced him and promoted him to captain of the flagship *La Capitana,* to replace Tristán. On Easter Sunday, April 16, 1503, the three remaining ships departed for La Española.

Of this voyage Méndez wrote, "as the ships were all pierced and worm-eaten . . . we soon had to abandon one of them . . . for not even the entire crew with pumps, kettles and pots were able to keep ahead of the water which leaked in through the worm holes." After seventy torturous days of fighting head winds and strong adverse currents, the two remaining ships, barely afloat, finally were able to reach Puerto Santa Gloria in Jamaica where the Admiral found it necessary to run them aground to keep them from sinking.

Although they were now in fact marooned, the immediate problem was food. Méndez gave out the last rations of hardtack and wine and took off into the interior of the island with three men to bargain with the caciques for food. He found the natives to be friendly and eager to trade food for beads, bits of lace, hawkbells, and other such trinkets he had to offer. One important cacique named Huareo agreed to furnish provisions regularly, to be paid for when delivered. At the eastern end of the island, Méndez established a friendship with a cacique named Ameyro from whom he purchased a "splendid canoe in exchange for a fine chamber pot, a coat and a shirt." The cacique also provided six natives to paddle. Loading the canoe with provisions, Méndez proceeded westerly along the coast until he reached Puerto Santa Gloria.

Columbus then requested that Méndez go to La Española in the canoe to arrange with Governor Nicolás de Ovando for their rescue. He was afterward to proceed to Spain at the first opportunity to deliver to the sovereigns a report of the voyage. (That letter, dated July 7, 1503, which eventually was delivered by Méndez, has become known as the "Lettera Rarissima" from an Italian transcript.) Méndez's first attempt was thwarted by hostile natives, but he escaped and returned to the stranded ships. Another attempt was made at once, with more thorough preparations. A second canoe was added to the expedition under the charge of Bartolomeo Fieschi, a Genoese who had commanded the abandoned *Vizcaína*. The second attempt, with an armed party under the adelantado following them along the shore to the eastern end of the island, was successful, but all suffered from the intense heat. Their supply of water gave out, and one of the Indians died of thirst and exhaustion. After four trying days, they arrived at Cape Tiburon, the southwestern peninsula of La Española.

After much difficulty, Méndez finally located the governor in Jaraguá. Ovando received him cordially but made excuse after excuse for not sending relief to Columbus. He detained Méndez for seven long months before granting him permission to go to Santo Domingo. There Méndez was able to purchase on the Admiral's account one of a fleet of three caravels just then arrived from Spain. Having appropriately supplied the caravel and seen it depart for Jamaica, Méndez, in the other ships of this opportune fleet, sailed directly for Spain to carry out the further instructions of the Admiral.

After proceeding with the letter to court, Méndez remained there for some time with the Admiral's son Diego to work for the restitution of promised titles and privileges that had been stripped from Columbus and his heirs. When the Admiral finally returned to Spain, Méndez continued to serve him and was present at his deathbed.

BIBLIOGRAPHY

Irving, Washington. *The Life and Voyages of Christopher Columbus and His Companions.* 3 vols. New York, 1849.

Morison, Samuel Eliot. *Journals and Other Documents on the Life and Voyages of Christopher Columbus.* New York, 1963.

WILLIAM LEMOS

MENDOZA, ANTONIO DE (1491–1552), first Spanish viceroy of New Spain (Mexico) and second viceroy of Peru. Mendoza was born in Alcalá la Real, Spain, the second son of the second count of Tendilla, Íñigo López de Mendoza, and his second wife and third cousin, Francisca Pacheco. The count was the captain general of Granada during and following its conquest by Fernando and Isabel. He was the head of a principal family among the twenty-two families that constituted the House of Mendoza, one of the three great houses of the Castilian nobility. Antonio's brothers included Diego Hurtado de Mendoza, noted for his history of Granada and the novel *Lazarillo de Lormes*, and Bernardino de Mendoza, famous for his naval exploits in the Mediterranean.

Prior to his service in Mexico, Antonio de Mendoza served as ambassador to Hungary (1526–1528) and as a royal chamberlain in Isabel of Portugal's court. While still a teenager, he saw military service in suppressing a rebellion in Granada.

Mendoza was appointed viceroy of New Spain in 1535, six years after he first had been approached about taking that office. His rule, which lasted until 1550, was notable for strengthening the royal government through legal and institutional development. He also reformed the royal treasury, regularized the assessment of tributes on native Americans, and issued laws governing mining and the mint. He so reduced Hernando Cortés's effective power that Cortés went to Spain to seek the emperor Charles V's favor, which, however, he did not obtain. Mendoza promoted education and advocated the founding of a university. He commissioned explorations of the American southwest by Francisco Vázquez de Coronado (1540–1542) and voyages that carried Spanish exploration as far as Oregon. In 1543 he established a Spanish colony in the Philippines.

Mendoza personally led the army that crushed the Mixton rebellion in 1541, a rising of native Americans in Jalisco that might have destroyed the Spanish colony had not other Indians remained loyal to the Spanish. Mendoza also steered New Spain through the crisis of the New Laws of 1542. Faced with the potential for a Spanish revolt against royal control because the New Laws decreed an end to encomiendas, Mendoza suspended execution of the laws and worked to effect a compromise that allowed a continuation of the encomienda but under tighter royal control and for a limited number of generations. His success in thus avoiding a rebellion may be contrasted with Viceroy Blasco Núñez Vela's enforcement of the New

Laws in Peru and the resulting rebellion that cost him his life.

Once order had been restored in Peru, Mendoza was sent to be its second viceroy (1551–1552). When he arrived, Peru was in political turmoil because the audiencia of Lima had issued a decree abolishing personal service by Indians, a practice outlawed in 1542 but still customary in Peru. Mendoza attempted to moderate but not abolish this custom. Ill before he made the journey to Peru, Mendoza died on July 21, 1552, after only ten months and nine days in office.

BIBLIOGRAPHY

Aiton, Arthur S. *Antonio de Mendoza, First Viceroy of New Spain.* Durham, N.C., 1927.

Rubio Mañé, Ignacio. *Introducción al estudio de los virreyes de Nueva España, 1535–1746.* 4 vols. Mexico City, 1955.

PAUL E. HOFFMAN

MENDOZA, PEDRO GONZÁLEZ DE (1428–1495),

cardinal, archbishop of Toledo, and confidant of Fernando and Isabel. Mendoza's parents, the marquises of Santillana, intended him for a church career and arranged for his appointment as archdeacon of Guadalajara. In 1445, the young cleric went to the University of Salamanca, where he lived on his comfortable income as archdeacon, studied canon law, and translated the *Aeneid* and some books of Ovid's *Metamorphoses* at the request of his father, who was one of Spain's most renowned poets. Mendoza was appointed bishop of Calahorra (1454) and began to travel with the royal court, first representing the political interests of his militarily powerful brothers in the succession wars during the reign of King Enrique IV, then persuading Cardinal Rodrigo Borja (the future Pope Alexander VI) to support the claims of Princess Isabel. This political success launched his career up the ladder of lucrative church appointments: bishop of Sigüenza, archbishop of Seville, cardinal of Santa Croce (1472), and archbishop of Toledo (1485–1495). He also received royal and papal legitimation of his two sons and noble titles for them.

As primate of Spain and a permanent resident of the royal court, Cardinal Mendoza exercised so much influence over Fernando and Isabel that he was popularly called "the third king of Spain." Many writers speculate that, in order to have gained the confidence of the monarchs, Christopher Columbus must have been supported by Cardinal Mendoza.

BIBLIOGRAPHY

Azcona, Tarsicio de. *La elección y reforma del episcopado español en tiempo de los Reyes Católicos.* Madrid, 1960.

Azcona, Tarsicio de. *Isabel la Católica: Estudio crítico de su vida y su reinado.* Madrid, 1964.

Medina y Mendoza, Francisco de. *Vida del Cardenal D. Pedro González de Mendoza.* Memorial Histórico Español, vol. 6. Madrid, 1853.

Villalba Ruiz de Toledo, F. Javier. *El Cardenal Mendoza ante la guerra civil castellana.* Madrid, 1983.

HELEN NADER

MENÉNDEZ DE AVILÉS, PEDRO (1519–1574),

adelantado of Florida. A notable Spanish, sixteenth-century naval leader, explorer, and colonizer, Pedro de Menéndez was born in Avilés. He went to sea as a youth and led his own ship against French corsairs in the Bay of Biscay. Young Menéndez's exploits brought him a royal appointment to command the Indies fleets. He also became a ship owner in the transatlantic trade; two large galleasses were built to his order, of which one, *San Pelayo*, was of almost a thousand-tons burden.

In 1565, King Philip II contracted with Menéndez to pacify and colonize Florida, which extended from Newfoundland to the Florida Keys and west to St. Joseph's Bay in the Gulf of Mexico. Under the contract, Menéndez was named adelantado (governor and captain general), but agreed to bear much of the cost of the Florida enterprise. In return, he would enjoy certain monopolies and exemptions, and was promised a large Florida land grant, with the title of marquis, should his venture succeed.

In outfitting his Florida expedition, Menéndez used *San Pelayo* and utilized a network of relatives and friends from a closely knit Asturian family group. These associates supplemented his funds and furnished him with manpower for the Florida enterprise. In turn, they hoped to share Menéndez's royal favor and expected to receive lands in Florida. Menéndez paid his own soldiers' passage to America and promised them town lots and plantation allotments. The royal troops were to be paid from the king's treasury.

In the meantime, Jean Ribault had explored Florida for France, leaving a short-lived colony at Port-Royal, near present-day Beaufort, South Carolina. In 1564, another French captain, René Goulaine de Laudonnière, built Fort Caroline on the St. Johns River. In 1565, Ribault returned to Port-Royal with reinforcements.

On September 8, 1565, Menéndez landed in Florida and founded San Agustín (St. Augustine), the oldest continuously occupied city in the United States. Menéndez dealt rapidly with the French forces, capturing Fort Caroline and killing Jean Ribault with many of his followers. He then established reliable sources of supply in Cuba and Yucatán for his Florida colony and quelled soldiers' mutinies in the Florida garrisons. After that, Menéndez proceeded with his explorations of the east coast of North America. He signed treaties with many of the native American groups, but found himself opposed by Indians who had been allied with the French. Menéndez built forts and missions in the Florida peninsula and north to Chesapeake Bay and founded the city of Santa Elena on present-day Parris Island. He dispatched expeditions to Newfoundland and overland from Santa Elena to the Appalachian Mountains. In none of his explorations did Menéndez find the passage he sought through the continent to the Pacific and the riches of Asia.

In 1567, Menéndez was appointed captain general of Spain's first royal armada for the Indies and designed its new vessels, fast galleys called *galizabras*. While commanding the armada, Menéndez was also named governor of Cuba; his lieutenants governed it in his absence, together with Florida. He also proposed to the king his own solution for determining longitude.

As the axis of Spanish Florida began to shift northward by 1569, the south Florida forts and missions were abandoned, and more than two hundred settlers, among them Menéndez and his wife and household, came to Santa Elena to develop farms and raise livestock. Although the Spanish Crown established a subsidy to sustain the Florida garrisons and granted Menéndez another royal contract to extend his jurisdiction to Pánuco in Mexico, relations with the native Americans of Florida deteriorated into mutual hostility and war.

The settlers at Santa Elena were confined to the poor coastal soils; lacking peace with the Indians, they could not penetrate to the fertile Georgia and Carolina uplands. The Jesuit missionaries on Chesapeake Bay were killed by the Indians, and the order terminated its Florida efforts. Menéndez's enterprise was showing unmistakable signs of its eventual failure.

In February 1574, after the Sea-Beggars (Dutch rebels against Spanish rule) had captured the fortress of Middelburg, on an island on the coast of the Spanish Netherlands, Philip II ordered Menéndez to clear the English Channel of enemy vessels and reinforce the Spanish garrisons in the Netherlands. As he prepared to sail, Menéndez fell ill, evidently of typhus. He died September 17, 1574, and the fleet he had gathered at Santander never sailed.

BIBLIOGRAPHY

Lyon, Eugene. *The Enterprise of Florida: Pedro Menéndez de Avilés and the Spanish Conquest of 1565–1568.* Gainesville, Fla., 1976.

Lyon, Eugene. *Santa Elena: A Brief History of the Colony, 1566–1587.* Columbia, S.C., 1982.

Manucy, Albert C. *Florida's Menéndez: Captain-General of the Ocean Sea.* St. Augustine, Fla., 1965.

Ruidíaz y Caravía, Eugenio. *La Florida: Su conquista y colonización por Pedro Menéndez de Avilés.* 2 vols. Madrid, 1893–1894.

EUGENE LYON

MERCATOR, GERARDUS (1512–1594), Flemish cartographer, cosmographer, and instrument maker. Gerardus Mercator was born Gerhard Kremer on March 5, 1512, in the small town of Rupelmonde, Spanish Netherlands (present-day Belgium), to which his parents had recently moved from the German village of Gangelt. The family was poor. Gerhard learned what Latin he could in local schools and after his father's death in 1526–1527 his uncle sent him to 's Hertogenbosch to study at a school, one of the largest and best in Europe, run by the Brethren of the Common Life. After three and a half years with the brothers, Gerhard went to Louvain, where he enrolled at the university in 1530 as one of the poor students at Castle College. By this time he had Latinized his name to Mercator. He studied philosophy and took his master's degree in 1532.

Louvain was, at this time, a great center of learning, and Mercator made the acquaintance, among others, of the greatest astronomer and mathematician of the Low Countries, Gemma Frisius, and of the Louvain goldsmith and engraver Gaspar van der Heyden (à Myrica). Through association with these men and private study, he acquired a thorough knowledge of geography, astronomy, cartography, and surveying, including triangulation. He also learned the arts of making astronomical and surveying instruments of brass, of engraving on brass and copper, and of italic handwriting. Mercator commenced his cartographic career in Louvain but moved to Duisburg, Germany, in 1552, probably because of the repressive intolerance of the Spanish Netherlands in religious matters, and spent the rest of his life there. Besides compiling and publishing maps, Mercator also wrote a highly influential manual of italic handwriting (the first to be published outside of Italy; 1540), and attempted a "harmonization," or reconciliation, of the Four Gospels (1592). He was much involved with theological issues throughout his life and even his cartographic work (witness the introduction to his *Atlas*) was firmly rooted in religious conviction. Mercator died on December 2, 1594.

During an active career of almost sixty years, Mercator produced a long series of important and influential cartographic works: a map of the Holy Land (1537), the double-cordiform world map of 1538, a map of Flanders (1540), a pair of globes, terrestrial and celestial (1541 and 1551), maps of Europe (1554) and the British Isles (1564), the great world map (1569), a scholarly edition of Ptolemy's *Geography*, with maps (1578), and his atlas (first part, 1585; first complete edition, 1595).

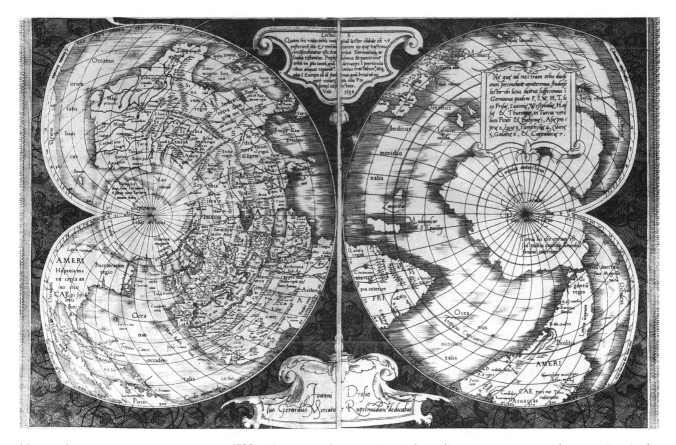

MERCATOR'S DOUBLE-CORDIFORM WORLD MAP OF 1538. This copperplate engraving is the earliest extant map to use the name *America* for both northern and southern continents. The famous Mercator projection came later, with the publication of a world map in 1569.

NEW YORK PUBLIC LIBRARY, RARE BOOK DIVISION

Mercator's research on geomagnetism anticipated Humphrey Gilbert's work by fifty years. He developed the idea that there was a magnetic pole located on the earth and not in the heavens, and suggested that its location could be determined by noting the angle of magnetic declination at two points on the earth and extending those rhumbs until they intersected.

No cartographer has been as important for the advancement of navigation as Mercator. His terrestrial globe of 1541 already showed three innovations that were developed with the navigator in mind, for it was intended that the globe actually be used at sea. First, the lines radiating from the compass roses printed on the globe are not great circles but actual loxodromes, lines of constant compass direction, and hence spiral in toward the poles. Secondly, because of the reliance that mariners placed on the compass, Mercator showed the North Magnetic Pole (in the form of *magnetum insula*), locating it in the ocean above Scandinavia. Finally, Mercator's globe was made with a hollow wooden ball, not the more usual plaster over papier-mâché, and so would stand up better to travel

and would better accept the points of the compass used to make measurements on it. The companion celestial globe, too, was viewed very much as a working tool and could be used for determining the locations of stars, the latitude of a place, zodiacal signs and degrees, the time of culmination of a star, and the duration of twilight.

Using a globe in the cabin of a pitching ship would have been an awkward operation, however, and its scale is severely limited. Flat maps, on the other hand, drawn on any of the projections then known, could not preserve the true angular relationships between places, so that navigators attempting to steer a course measured on the typical "plane chart" of the time were forced to make constant correction to be assured of a reasonably accurate landfall. Mercator set out to make a world map in sheets that would preserve the directional relationships between places and the result is the wall map of the world (1569) on the projection that bears his name. Although later mathematicians have shown how the projection can be derived using trigonometry or calculus, Mercator worked it out by trial and error, by plotting on flat paper the spiral rhumb lines from his globe of 1541. The Mercator projection has the unique attribute that any compass direction can be represented by a straight line. If a mariner wished to sail, say, between Gibraltar and Hispaniola, he simply laid a straightedge between the two points and measured the angle between this line and any meridian. If he then followed this steady compass course he would reach his destination. His course would not be the straightest possible; plotted on a globe, it would describe a spiral and not the straight line of a great circle course. But a true great circle course requires constant change in compass direction and was well beyond the abilities and instruments of sixteenth-century seamen. Mercator's chart, used in connection with a magnetic compass (and an awareness of compass deviation) gave the sailor the most reliable guide he had ever possessed.

The Mercator projection is unsurpassed for its purpose and still used on virtually all nautical charts published today, but its acceptance was slow, and apparently few navigators in the sixteenth century availed themselves of it. Several large world maps of the early seventeenth century used it as did the great sea atlas of Sir Robert Dudley, the *Arcano del mare* (1647), but so conservative was the nautical community that the use of Mercator's projection on charts for practical seamen did not become common until the end of the eighteenth century.

Mercator's *Atlas*, besides contributing the title that has come to stand for "book of maps," was tremendously influential. With its accurate and austere maps, it offered stiff competition to the later editions of the *Theatrum orbis terrarum* of Abraham Ortelius, whose florid and decorative engravings were beginning to appear dated. And whereas Ortelius had reengraved at uniform size the best available maps and published them under the names of their original authors. Mercator systematically conflated and edited all existing information to create a new work of synthesis, bearing only his name. In 1604 the copper plates of Mercator's atlas were sold to Jodocus Hondius of Amsterdam, a consummate businessman who, with his son, saw the Mercator atlas through twenty-nine editions between 1609 and 1641 and did much to launch the golden age of Dutch atlas production and to make Mercator's name a household word.

BIBLIOGRAPHY

Averdunk, Heinrich, and J. Müller-Reinhard. *Gerhard Mercator und die Geographen unter seinen Nachkommen.* Petermanns geographische Mitteilungen, supplement 182. Gotha, 1914. Reprinted Amsterdam, 1969.

Bagrow, Leo, and Robert W. Karrow, Jr. *Mapmakers of the Sixteenth Century and Their Maps: The Catalog of Cartographers of Abraham Ortelius, 1570.* Chicago, forthcoming.

Osley, A. S. *Mercator: A Monograph on the Lettering of Maps, etc., in the 16th Century Netherlands. With a Facsimile and Translation of His Treatise on the Italic Hand and a Translation of Ghim's Vita Mercatoris.* New York, 1969.

Smet, Antoine de. "Gerard Mercator." *National biografisch woordenboek* 10 (1983): 431–455.

ROBERT W. KARROW, JR.

METAL. Pre-Columbian native Americans knew how to work gold, silver, and copper. Some understood crude smelting, annealing, and soldering and used the processes to create works of art, but most of their tools were made of stone, bone, wood, and horn. When Columbus brought the first iron and steel tools to the New World, native American technology changed forever.

Copper was already commonly used by many groups in the New World. The Arctic Eskimos had copper scrapers, and Northwest Coast tribes made cold-worked copper plaques that served to indicate rank. Native Americans throughout eastern North America traded awls and pins made from northern Great Lakes raw copper. The Aztecs cast a copper-gold alloy, using the lost-wax method, and the Incas knew how to make bronze, and even how to control the tin content. Copper, however, was of little interest to the European explorers.

When Columbus arrived in the Caribbean, he found native Americans wearing ornaments of gold painstakingly extracted from placer mines. These small amounts of gold spurred expansion to the mainland, where the conquistadores found the gold and silver treasures of the Aztecs of Mexico and the Incas of Peru. Much of this treasure had been made for aesthetic purposes and for prestige, but its artistic value was lost when the silver and gold were melted down for shipment to Spain.

American Resources. Searching for the sources of the Aztec and Incan treasures, the Spaniards discovered silver west of Mexico City as early as 1531; they made large silver strikes in Zacatecas in 1546 and in Peru at Potosí in 1545. They also found some gold in Chile and New Granada. All mines were by law the property of the Crown, but colonists could exploit them upon payment of a large royalty. Although shipping costs were high and fraud through juggling books or smuggling was common, the mines brought such wealth into Europe that the resultant inflation lasted through the seventeenth century.

The conquistadores, steeped in Christian legends, believed there existed a third great treasure to match those in Mexico and Peru, and stories of Cíbola and El Dorado spurred exploration into the North American plains. This search failed, but a third source of mineral wealth did in fact exist; it was not discovered until 1848 in California, when it launched a gold rush the following year.

Until the middle of the sixteenth century, the Spanish

miners used smelting to extract silver from rich ores. Smelters used water- or hand-powered bellows and charcoal as fuel. In Mexico, the production of charcoal denuded the surrounding countryside of timber.

In 1556, German immigrants to New Spain introduced the patio amalgamation process for the extraction of silver from low-grade ores, and by the 1570s Potosí had adopted the technique. In the patio process, mules or native American labor prepared a paste from crushed ore, water, mercury, and other materials in a large open courtyard called a patio. The silver combined with the mercury as an amalgam, and the rest was washed away. Heating the amalgam drove off the mercury and left the silver behind. The mercury, reclaimed for future use, was so important to this mining process that it became a government monopoly.

The mine at Potosí was the richest of all, yielding about half the world's silver production between 1546 and 1601. But the price for this wealth could be counted in the deaths of native American miners. Although the viceroys of New Spain and Peru issued mining codes to protect them, conditions for miners grew steadily worse through the years.

European Uses of Metal in the New World. In return for the wealth of the New World, Spain introduced metal coins, arms and armor, and metal tools and equipment.

Coinage. Native Americans had no formal system of money, using instead barter and exchange systems based on such items as cacao beans and cotton textiles. Trade relationships of the Spanish colonists in the New World were crude as well. Columbus brought with him only a few coins, and the million-maravedi shipment of coins to La Española in 1505 did not stabilize the monetary system. Silver bars were debased by copper and lead, and scales and weights were unreliable. These problems were not solved until the establishment of the first New World mint in 1535.

Arms and armor. Spanish exploration of the New World coincided with the apex of the armorer's art in Europe. Sixteenth-century armor was designed for three functions: war, tournaments, and ceremony. Most Spanish soldiers in the New World wore armor designed for war, especially helmets. These ranged from a simple steel cap to more elegant curved and pointed helmets. Other armor varied from heavy Gothic suits to simple chain-mail shirts. It is an indication of their importance that weapons and coats of mail were exempt from the sales tax.

The success of cavalry depended on proper equipment. Metal parts for riding gear, such as spurs, stirrups, horseshoes, and horse armor, came from Spain. The conquistadores in Peru were so desperate for iron for horseshoes that they substituted silver and gold.

The Spanish military brought with it artillery and primitive firearms called harquebuses. These arms were important for their psychological effect, but the harquebus was unwieldy and difficult to load and fire, and the cavalry considered the weapon ungentlemanly. Although the sixteenth century saw improvements in firearms, they had limited use in the guerrilla warfare practiced by so many native Americans.

The crossbow was more common than the harquebus, but it also was of limited use, often misfiring or breaking down. Other, more useful, weapons in the Spanish arsenal were halberds, swords, rapiers, daggers, and lances. The smiths of Toledo were famous for their high standards of craftsmanship in producing swords, and a lance in the hands of a mounted man was a formidable weapon against warriors on foot.

Native Americans had little protection against Spanish weapons, although the padded armor of the Aztecs, called the *escaupil,* was adequate to repel Indian arms. Inca soldiers wore similar quilted armor, and many Spanish soldiers adopted it.

Native Americans took Spanish arms and armor as spoils of war and turned them against the Spaniards. They did not at first understand the complexities of the harquebus, but the Indians of southern Chile and the North American plains eventually adopted horses and firearms, which also changed the way they hunted. The native Americans had already developed bronze arms such as maces, heavy clubs, and hand axes, but these were simply copies of earlier stone forms and were no match for Spanish steel. Nevertheless, the Spaniards' superiority in arms and armor, and their use of cavalry, are not sufficient to explain their conquest of the New World. In the Caribbean islands the impact of European diseases and the use of native American allies also played a large role in the military strategies of the conquistadores.

Metal tools and equipment. The introduction into the New World of metal objects was of greater cultural importance than was the use of arms and armor by the conquistadores. Export of these items was tightly controlled by Spain, although the goods brought to the New World may have originated with Spanish trading partners. Knives, for instance, came from Flanders, Holland, Bohemia, and Germany, harquebuses from Holland, and clocks from Germany. Duties exacted at each point of shipment increased the cost of the import to the New World consumer as much as 75 percent; prices were the highest at the farthest outposts of the empire.

Because the monopoly on trade discouraged the independent development of many industries in the New World, all sorts of metal goods made the transatlantic passage. Sewing equipment included thimbles, scissors, pins, and wool shears. The medical kit contained copper cupping instruments, syringes, razors, lancets, and barber's scissors. A well-stocked kitchen contained tin cups, bowls, cruets, graters, and funnels, iron spoons and pans, pewter plates and bowls, bronze ollas and copper kettles, butcher knives, and spits.

Building tools and equipment included axes of various kinds, adzes, sledgehammers, crowbars, saws, chisels, augurs, planes, hinges for doors and windows, door knockers and latches, and nails of various sizes, including spikes, roofing nails, and tacks. Wagons had special metal needs such as tire nails, harping irons, cleats, washers, bolts, and linchpins. The construction of ships also demanded metal, including fastening nails, a cauldron for tar, hatchets, and iron water barrel hoops.

Religious observances, too, required special paraphernalia. Spain sent tin flasks for holy oils, copper vessels for holy water, tin and brass lanterns, silver chalices, small bells and large church bells with iron support frameworks, iron utensils for making communion wafers, and clarions, bassoons, and trumpets. And finally, the Spaniards brought with them such household and personal items as metal timepieces and jewelry, iron shoehorns, steel boxes, locks and keys, and brass picture frames and candlesticks.

Native American Adoption of Spanish Metal. Utilitarian metal items quickly replaced their native American functional equivalents in stone, bone, wood, or ceramic. New World agriculture was based on the use of the hoe and digging stick to cultivate crops, and metal garden hoes, spades, and plows were sometimes a welcome addition to native American farmers. Hunting and fishing groups added metal fishhooks and projectile points to their technology. Metal pots quickly replaced pottery and basketry vessels for cooking.

If a metal tool was more efficient than its native American analogue, it was adopted quickly. But if there was no parallel native American tool, the Spanish metal substitute might be either ignored or adapted for another use. Thus a piece of metal equipment sometimes lost its original meaning and became a personal ornament or item of prestige among native Americans.

[See also *Agriculture; Arms, Armor, and Armament.*]

BIBLIOGRAPHY

Borah, Woodrow. *Early Colonial Trade and Navigation between Mexico and Peru.* Ibero-Americana, no. 38. Berkeley, Calif., 1954.

Cespedes, Guillermo. *Latin America: The Early Years.* New York, 1974.

Haring, C. H. *The Spanish Empire in America.* New York, 1947.

Lewis, Oscar. "Plow and Hoe Culture: A Study in Contrasts." In Oscar Lewis, *Anthropological Essays.* New York, 1970.

Means, Philip Ainsworth. *Fall of the Inca Empire and the Spanish Rule in Peru, 1530–1780.* New York, 1932.

Scholes, France V. "The Supply Service of the New Mexican Missions in the Seventeenth Century." *New Mexico Historical Review* 5 (1930): 93–115; 5 (1930): 185–210; 5 (1930): 386–404.

Spencer, Robert F., and Jesse D. Jennings, et al. *The Native Americans.* New York, 1965.

Steward, Julian K. *Handbook of South American Indians.* Vol. 5. Bulletin 153, Bureau of American Ethnology. Washington, D.C., 1949.

Tarassuk, Leonid, and Claude Blair, eds. *The Complete Encyclopedia of Arms and Weapons.* New York, 1986.

Torre Revello, José. "Merchandise Brought to America by the Spaniards (1534–1586)." *Hispanic American Historical Review* 23 (1943): 773–780.

West, Robert C., and John P. Augelli. *Middle America: Its Lands and Peoples.* Englewood Cliffs, N.J., 1966.

D. K. ABBASS

MINERAL RESOURCES. The Americas are richly endowed with minerals of all kinds, but many were not discovered in the time of Columbus or in the century following his landfall. And even among some that were known, such as zinc, the technologies of the era either made little or no use of them or, as in the case of other base metals, the primitive methods of land transport and the small size of transoceanic vessels did not encourage their export. Virtually all the demand, therefore, was for precious metals and gemstones.

The Europe of the late fifteenth century had begun a long period of demographic and economic growth, which in turn involved a need for gold and silver as a necessary medium of exchange in a society where credit mechanisms were rudimentary and paper money did not yet exist. Because gold and silver were so vital, people went to even more ruthless lengths to obtain them in the years following the Columbian discoveries than they did in Brazil two centuries later or in the California gold rush of 1849. In fact the "gold lust" of the Spaniards after Columbus's first voyages of discovery became the engine of European emigration, as well as the basis for the Black Legend of Spanish cruelty.

Gold. In Columbus's lifetime or very soon after, Spaniards found gold-bearing sands and gravels in the riverbeds of La Española, Cuba, and Puerto Rico, and along the Caribbean shores of Central America. Within a generation after his death, they found more gold in southern and central Mexico and in the Andes, particularly of Colombia, but also in other locations between there and Chile.

Gold worth an estimated eight million pesos was produced in the Antilles between 1494 and around 1530, in what historians have termed the "island cycle" because the alluvial gold was exhausted in about thirty-five years. Mining methods then were almost identical to those used in the California gold rush of 1849: gravel was washed in pans or in a wooden sluice of running water nearby. Nearly all this work was carried out by Arawak labor gangs pressed into service by the early conquistadores. Their maltreatment occasioned a famous protest by Antonio de Montesinos on the Sunday before Christmas, 1509, in a thatched chapel on Santo Domingo. His sermon led to the Crown's promulgating a round of laws intended to protect the Indians and ensure their good treatment.

Prior to about 1515 most of the gold came from La Española; thereafter, most was found in Puerto Rico and to a lesser extent in Cuba (which produced only about half as much). Alluvial gold continued to be important for some time afterward, but the scene of production passed to Panama until about midcentury when gold from this source was nearly exhausted. Meanwhile, veins of gold were discovered in the highlands of Honduras and Nicaragua and, ultimately, in western Mexico, in Michoacán and Nueva Galicia. In South America, gold was mined at sites in the province of Quito, and in Colombia, in the region called Antioquia, in various regions of Upper and Lower Peru, and in Chile.

General histories have made much of the hoards of gold extorted from the Aztec Motecuhzoma II and the Inca Atahualpa, but though these represented a large and easy acquisition, they scarcely compared with the total amount

GOLD DISK WITH FIGURES. From Chimu, Peru, fourteenth to fifteenth century. The Spanish discovery of such objects fueled the conquest of the Andes.

THE METROPOLITAN MUSEUM OF ART, THE MICHAEL C. ROCKEFELLER MEMORIAL COLLECTION, BEQUEST OF NELSON A. ROCKEFELLER, 1979. (1979.206.766)

mined before midcentury by the Spaniards themselves. For instance, compare Atahualpa's ransom of 971,000 pesos worth of fine gold (over seven times that of Motecuhzoma's treasure) with the best estimates for gold that arrived—legally—and was registered at the Casa de la Contratación in Seville during the nineteen years between 1541 and 1560: over sixteen million pesos worth. And were the smuggled amounts known, that figure would likely double. (This article does not deal with the discovery and production of gold in Brazil because hardly any was found until the 1690s and thereafter, long after the time of the discoveries.)

Silver. Although gold has received most of the popular attention, it was silver that produced by far the greatest Spanish New World treasure. Moreover, because of its bulk and the more complicated industrial effort needed to extract it from the rather low-quality ore that prevailed in the Americas, it was considerably more difficult for its miners to escape payment of Crown duties. Little or none was found in the Antilles during the first decades of the expansion, however, and it was not until the conquest of Mexico by Hernando Cortés that an appreciable quantity came into Spanish hands. Even then, the amount of silver in possession of the indigenous peoples was far less than that of gold: it was less esteemed and less was found in superficial deposits. Ultimately, however, the amounts of silver extracted from both Americas dwarfed the quantities of gold. Shortly after the conquest of Mexico, Spaniards took over mining operations already being worked by Indians near Taxco, Zumpango, and Sultepec and a few years later, in Nueva Galicia at Tamazula and Compostela. Then, in the late 1540s, nearly a decade after the conquest of Peru, Gonzalo Pizarro moved into the Inca mines at Porco in Upper Peru. Production both there and in Mexico was limited before 1556, however, because the Europeans were using Indian methods to extract ore, and the yield was low.

It was only in 1556 that improved technology permitted an increase in production, and the quantities of silver obtained soon dwarfed those produced before midcentury. This was because of the invention by a colonial miner, Bartolomé de Medina, of the patio process, which led to an enormous increase in efficiency. It involved a complicated and sophisticated method of applying mercury to the crushed ore to glean silver from sulphurous compounds and the base metals—mostly tin and copper—with which it was alloyed. (American silver ore, though there were great quantities of it, was much inferior to that from European mines, as in Styria.) Meanwhile, literally dozens of huge new deposits were being discovered, most notably at Potosí in Upper Peru (1545), and in Mexico at Zacatecas (1546) and at Guanajuato and Pachuca (1550s). Soon surface deposits were exhausted and the miners began to dig shafts; until the eighteenth century, ores had to be hauled in baskets up wooden ladders on the shoulders of laborers.

The laborers, of course, were almost entirely Indians, and they were obliged to serve under the encomienda system of the allocation of indigenes to conquistadores, supposedly in return for their (religious) education. In Peru, Spaniards did not need to innovate a forced labor system as in Mexico and the Caribbean; they simply adapted the corvée-like mita system from the peasants' former Inca overlords and obliged the same lower classes to serve for stated intervals with them instead. The mine's exploitants were Spaniards, or after a generation or so, criollos—that is, their American-born heirs and descendants. Spanish (Roman) law claimed all products of the subsoil for the Crown, but it in turn awarded exploitation rights to the proprietors who had discovered or inherited the diggings. It bestowed on them a highly privileged status in order to ensure uninterrupted production. First and foremost, they could not be foreclosed by their creditors. In return, they paid a percentage of their yield, traditionally one-fifth, to the Crown and were obliged to bring their silver to government offices, which combined the functions of assaying, remelting, and taxing; there the silver was cast into uniform ingots, which bore identifying numbers. As part of the procedure, officials claimed the government's share for the royal treasury and then returned the remainder to the producers as their legitimate property.

In the course of the sixteenth century ownership of mines became highly diffuse, and workings were seldom in the hands of one individual or even one family. This was due partly to original partnership divisions but also to financial arrangements. The refining processes needed to produce pure silver from its ore were so expensive and complex that few of the mine proprietors possessed all the necessary equipment, mercury, chemicals, and labor. Hence the industry was characterized by intertwined clusters of capital devoted to various stages of production.

But that the new technology was effective—and the prospecting for new mining sites significant—there can be little question. It will afford some idea of how much yields increased during the second half of the sixteenth century if one considers that in no five-year period after 1560 did (legal) silver export from Mexico fail to exceed the total export of the entire period prior to 1550. Moreover, during the same century, Peruvian production, mainly from Potosí, dwarfed Mexican production by about four to one.

Other Minerals. Other metals, even those that were by-products of silver production, were seldom of more than local importance. Although tin, lead, zinc, and copper existed in abundance in the Americas, they are never found in export figures, for they were cheaply available on the European market. Had cannon foundries existed in the Indies (these could have been practicable in Mexico), there might have been greater industrial use of tin and copper. But as it was, Spanish colonial policy restricted the growth of such manufactures to avoid their competing with metropolitan industry (but also, perhaps, out of fear of their being used in rebellions).

Mercury, however, was the one exception, for it was used in the patio process and was largely responsible for the increased silver production after Medina's invention. Much was imported from Almadén in Castile, but appreciable quantities were discovered at Huancavelica in Peru around 1570, making the Peruvian mines nearly independent of Europe. Mexico, however, continued to require Spanish mercury throughout the century; if ships bearing mercury did not arrive as expected, production lagged visibly.

Gemstones. Less discussed in the literature than the extraction of metals is that of precious stones, which were found mostly in Colombia, in the Muzo, Coscuez, and Salmondoco mines. These appear to have been known by the indigenes prior to the conquest by Gonzalo Jiménez de Quesada. (Semiprecious stones existed in almost all American regions in abundance, but they were never items of great commercial importance.) There are no production figures available on American emeralds, rubies, or opals in the sixteenth century, and the royal government did not attempt consistently to control their production and hence tax them successfully. (Only diamonds have attracted the attention of Latin American economic historians, but their description lies beyond the compass of this article. They were not discovered in the Americas until 1720.) What is most interesting is that both the emeralds and the rubies from Colombia were of higher quality—less flawed and of better color and greater size—than those found in Asia where these gems fetched considerably higher prices than they did in Europe. Europeans appear instead to have prized diamonds, which in the sixteenth and seventeenth centuries came chiefly from mines in south India, in Golconda.

Evidence from shipwrecks suggests that American colonial jewelers were imaginative in incorporating these stones into high-quality pieces of silver- and goldsmithery, which were then brought into Europe by Spaniards returning from colonial service. There is also reason to believe that much of the gemstone production of Colombia was bought up by professional traders, who sent it off to Asia, where diamonds were common enough, but where the larger and better colored rubies and emeralds found in South America were desired by rulers and their nobility. But because jewels could so easily be concealed, as in seams of clothing, only passing references can be gleaned from memoirs as to what their distribution might have been like; it would seem that a great proportion traveled from Seville to Lisbon, where they made their way via professional traders to Goa and hence into the courts of Asian princes.

Columbus had been searching for Asia, not for the New World he encountered. Had not the presence of precious metals been immediately detected, there would have been little incentive for European colonization of the new lands in the late fifteenth and early sixteenth centuries. As it was, the ensuing gold rush virtually guaranteed European expansion into the Western Hemisphere.

[See also *Metal*.]

BIBLIOGRAPHY

Diffie, Bailey W. *Latin American Civilization: Colonial Period.* Harrisburg, Pa., 1945.

Hamilton, Earl J. "Imports of American Gold and Silver into Spain, 1503–1660." *Quarterly Journal of Economics* 43 (1931).

Haring, Clarence H. "American Gold and Silver Production in the First Half of the Sixteenth Century." *Quarterly Journal of Economics* 29 (1915).

Haring, Clarence H. *Trade and Navigation between Spain and the Indies in the Time of the Hapsburgs.* Cambridge, Mass., 1918.

Slicher van Bath, Bernard H. "Het Latijns-Americaanse goud en zilver in de koloniale tijd." *Economisch en sociaal-historisch jaarboek* 47 (1984).

Wagner, Henry R. "Early Silver Mining in New Spain." *Revista de Historia de America* 14 (1942).

GEORGE D. WINIUS

MISSIONARY MOVEMENT.

MISSIONARY MOVEMENT. From the time Columbus first made contact with the natives of the New World, one of the prime motivations for exploration and settlement was the desire on the part of the Spaniards to spread Christianity. The discovery and conquest of the Americas came immediately on the heels of the Reconquista, which had prepared the Spaniards for the new enterprise and had linked Christianization with territorial expansion. Although the methods were not always the same, the motive was similar. An important legacy of the Spaniards in the Americas is the prevalence of the Roman Catholic faith and the art and architecture it inspired.

Although no priest seems to have accompanied Columbus on his first voyage, there was no absence of religion on board. Columbus was a devout Christian, and all commentaries on the voyage speak of the important place religious devotions had in the daily life of the expedition. On the return voyage, for example, the crew, when caught in a storm, pleaded for divine intercession and at first landfall made a religious pilgrimage in thanksgiving. These, of course, were the norms of the time. The important role of missionary activity to Columbus himself is evidenced by the signature he routinely used after the voyage, *Xpo Ferens,* "He who carries Christ."

On the second voyage, Columbus brought Bernardo Buil and other friars with him, not just to minister to the Spanish settlers but also to Christianize the Indians and ensure their good treatment. In fact, the stipulated purpose of the second voyage, other than to relieve the Spaniards left on La Española, was to convert native Americans to Christianity. Second was the establishment of a trading colony. Thus the tone of the voyages of exploration and conquest was set very early. A quarter of a century later, Bernal Díaz del Castillo, a foot soldier in the conquest of Mexico, summarized his motivation as a desire to serve God and his king as well as to get rich.

The role of the missionary on an expedition was to provide spiritual support for the conquerors and to spread the Gospel among the natives. The expeditions were more corporate operations than organized military bands. Each participant provided something for the common good. Men came with their own provisions, equipment, and animals. If the expedition was successful, each received part of the booty in proportion to his investment. Similarly, the priest contributed his service as a spiritual intermediary and could receive a share usually equivalent to that of an officer. Whether he did or not depended on his status. The Catholic priesthood consists of two quite different groups. The parish priest is most often a member of the secular clergy. He lives in the world and is largely indistinguishable from other members of society, save for his celibacy and dress. Other priests are regulars, members of formally organized religious orders, such as the mendicants (Franciscans and Dominicans, among others). They follow special rules of life, often taking vows of poverty, for instance, above and beyond the vows of celibacy and obedience. Both secular and regular clergy participated in the exploration and conquest of the New World. But the regulars could not receive a portion of the booty, at least for themselves, whereas the seculars could.

In purely missionary contexts, the regulars had a slight advantage. The internal organization of the regular clergy allowed for small groups of friars to operate with limited immediate supervision, for they were somewhat self-governing bodies. The secular priest depended upon his religious superiors for authority and supervision. Thus regulars were often missionaries, and the secular clergy took over the religious administration of communities after they had been Christianized.

The missionaries played an important role in the legitimization of the conquest. Early political thinkers concluded that Spain's claim to the New World could be legally justified only in the missionary context. Consequently missionary activity had to precede military subjugation. If native peoples openly embraced Christianity and

Spanish sovereignty, no war could be made against them. As a result of the preaching of individuals such as Bartolomé de las Casas, the Spanish monarchs ordered that the natives had to reject Christianity and sovereignty before being subjected to war. To comply with this order a document known as the Requerimiento (Requirement) was read aloud to natives before the onset of battle. It outlined European history and the basics of Christian theology: the natives then were "informed" and, of their free will, could accept Christianity and Spanish rule or reject it.

The conquests of two major regions of the Americas, Mexico and Peru, provide good examples of the activity of seculars and regulars, and their relationships to missionary activity and the conquering armies. In Mexico two principal clerics accompanied Hernando Cortés —Bartolomé de Olmedo and Juan Díaz. Olmedo, a Mercedarian friar, was Cortés's private chaplain and served the spiritual needs of the army. Díaz, a secular priest, was more a member of the expedition in his own right and also served as chaplain for the troops. Both priests played major roles in the missionary activity of the expedition. Díaz baptized the nobles of Tlaxcala, Cortés's first important Indian allies. Olmedo usually celebrated mass when Cortés wanted to provide an especially good show for the natives. Olmedo died shortly after the conquest of Mexico; Díaz continued as a parish priest until his death.

In the conquest of Peru, similarly, a regular and a secular priest accompanied the expedition. The regular, Vicente de Valverde, was present when Francisco Pizarro captured the Inca ruler Atahualpa, but as a Dominican not permitted private wealth, he did not receive a share of the booty. Nevertheless, he played an important role in the conquest. As one of the most highly educated of the company, he was a personal adviser to Pizarro and spiritual leader of the band. He ultimately became bishop of Cuzco, which included all of the newly conquered territory. Juan de Sosa, on the other hand, was a secular priest who, though he was not present when Atahualpa was captured, collected a share of the booty. Like Díaz, he was more of a private member of the expedition who also happened to be a priest. He too came to serve as a chaplain for the troops.

Once the active phase of a conquest had ended, the role of the church was to continue the "spiritual conquest" of the land. As noted, this occupation usually fell to the regulars. Among the religious orders the most active, certainly in the early phases of the Spanish settlement of the Americas, were the Franciscans, who supplied twelve priests for the first organized missionary expedition to Mexico. This group arrived in 1524, led by Martín de Valencia. They were followed in 1526 by twelve Dominicans, led by Tomás Ortiz, and in 1533 by seven Augustinians under the guidance of Francisco de la Cruz. By 1559 the missionary corps had swelled to 802 religious in some 160 monasteries.

In Peru a similar pattern emerged. The Franciscans were among the first missionaries to arrive, along with Dominicans and Mercedarians. All three orders seem to have been established in Peru shortly following the conquest. The Franciscan mission was initially led by Marcos de Niza, who led a small expedition down from Mexico, although upon reaching what is now southern Panama, they seem to have returned home. In 1534 and 1535 the order established monasteries first in Quito and later in Los Reyes (present-day Lima). In 1540 twelve Dominicans arrived under the leadership of Francisco Toscano. The first Mercedarians appeared in Lima in 1535, and by 1540 they had established four monasteries, in Lima, San Miguel de Piura, Cuzco, and Guamanga.

Although the Augustinians were active in Mexico, they did not participate in the early missions in Peru. As late as 1551 the order had become established in South America, but in the sixteenth century they ranked noticeably behind the other three. In contrast, the Mercedarians participated in the spiritual conquest of Peru but did not arrive in Mexico until much later in the century. In 1593 they established a college and house of novices under the direction of the Guatemalan province. It was not until 1619 that an independent Mexican province was created.

The friars and priests encountered several obstacles to their evangelizing. The two major problems were those of communication and of the sheer size of the native population. Friars either had to teach the natives Spanish

INTRODUCING CHRISTIANITY TO NEW SPAIN. A European view, from the *Crónica de Michoacán*, an eighteenth-century copy of an earlier postconquest document. The text reads: "It is demonstrated here that once it was known that the Great Caltconzin surrendered to Cortés and the king . . . from Tzireo to Iguatzio . . . they started to surrender and ask for baptism . . . and it is shown here . . . punishments given to the ones who did not follow Christian morals . . . in their tribes."

ARCHIVO GENERAL DE LA NACIÓN, MEXICO CITY

or learn the Indian tongues themselves. Clearly the more reasonable option was that they learn the native languages, which they did. In many ways the early missionaries functioned as linguists. They listened to the languages, learned them aurally, and then wrote them down, assigning Spanish letters to the native sounds. Unfortunately there was not always a close fit between the sounds represented in Spanish and those in the Indian languages. Most notably, Spanish has no letters for the sounds "k" or "w" in most contexts but must use constructions such as "que" or "hua." The friars did not even distinguish some sounds, such as vowel length or the glottal stop, the closing off of the vocal path by the glottis and the release of air when it reopens. The glottal stop is important in the Aztec language, Nahuatl, but the Spanish friars often missed it. The early linguistic efforts usually fell to the regulars, especially the Franciscans, but eventually the secular clergy followed suit, and soon one sure method of securing a clerical position became learning a native language. The major languages, Nahuatl in Mexico and Quechua in Peru, were taught in the universities that were later founded in the colonies.

The importance of native languages in the spiritual conquest is demonstrated by the fact that the first book printed in the New World was a catechism written in Nahuatl and published in 1539 in Mexico. Throughout the sixteenth century, works in native languages continued to be an important portion of the total number of publications. Of nearly two hundred published in Mexico in the sixteenth century, thirty-five were in Nahuatl; other languages included Tarascan, Maya, Otomi, and Timucuan (from Florida). In colonial Peru similar works appeared in Quechua, Aymara, Guarani, and many other native languages.

Another means of bridging the language gap was the sixteenth-century equivalent of comic strips. This novel idea came from Jacobo de Testera, an Italian Franciscan in Mexico. He used little stick figures to portray the important features of Christian doctrine. These little catechisms have come to be known as "Testerian catechisms" in his honor. They were used with some frequency in Mexico and to a more limited extent in Peru.

Theatrical presentations soon became a popular means for spreading Christian doctrine. In all likelihood the friars used pantomime early on to explain the gospel stories. Once they had mastered the native languages, they presented European passion plays, translated into Indian languages. These plays were wildly popular—so well received that in many communities native Americans still put them on in one form or another after nearly five hundred years.

As the priests confronted the natives, several theological problems arose. Some thought that perhaps the Indians were not human, a notion that was quickly dispelled; in 1536 a papal bull confirmed Indian humanity. But then the friars wondered about the best way to proceed with the missionary effort. Should they imitate the ancient church and have the neophytes undergo a long complicated theological indoctrination before offering them the benefits of the sacraments? Or should they baptize them straight away and work later on perfecting their understanding of dogma? Although the friars were aware of the threat from pre-Columbian religions, they considered the natives more receptive to the gospel than other groups with whom they had had experience—particularly the Muslims. Native Americans were merely "heathens," that is, they had never heard the gospel of Christ (although some Christians did argue that Saint Thomas, or others, had brought Christianity to the New World in the ancient past). In contrast, the Muslims were thought of as "infidels," people who had heard the gospel but rejected it. Among the early friars there was even a romantic notion that the Indians were particularly receptive to the gospel, that in fact once they had all been baptized the Second Coming would occur. With this prospect in mind, the friars in most areas baptized first and preached second. One Franciscan lay brother, Peter of Ghent, is said to have baptized 100,000 natives in one day!

Once the initial contact was made and the friars settled into the native villages, the missionary activity became routine. On a regular basis, often daily, the priests convened the Indians for indoctrination. Men, women, and children were trained separately, according to their needs and abilities. As soon as they could, the friars established schools for the children, recognizing that they could be a potent tool for converting the elders. In Mexico, they pursued a special approach for the sons of the Indian nobility. These boys were shipped off to a school located in Santiago Tlatelolco in a neighborhood of Mexico City, where they were trained to occupy their rightful place in the native social and political order but also taught Spanish, Latin, and church doctrine. Some scholars have looked upon this as an early, intentional effort to develop a native priesthood, although this contention cannot be proved. The important role of children in the missionary effort is reflected in a legend of three children from Tlaxcala who were martyred by their parents for having openly embraced and preached Christianity.

Although the papal bull clearly established that the Indians were human, they were not offered all the sacraments of the church. In general the Indians received baptism, were often confirmed, attended mass regularly, and took the Eucharist several times a year. Sixteenth-century norms required at least an annual confession. But the administering of unction, usually reserved for the critically ill, was relatively uncommon among the natives.

Logistically it was difficult for the priests to administer the sacrament, given the thousands of natives each man tended. Matrimony was required. The native nobles often had multiple wives, something the friars abhorred. The priests forced them to recognize their first wife as the true wife and abandon the rest. Often a noble suffered circumstantial amnesia and could not remember who had come first, allowing him to choose his favorite. The sacrament of ordination, entrance to the priesthood, was denied the natives on the ground that they were newcomers to the faith. It was not until the eighteenth century that significant numbers of native Americans entered the priesthood.

The first century following Columbus's voyage saw Christianity spread throughout the Western Hemisphere. By 1592 missionaries had penetrated far into the American Southwest, the southern reaches of modern Chile, the jungles of South America, and the plains of Argentina. Their effort rivaled the military conquest of the Americas, and more important, it left a lasting mark that remains to the present day.

[See also *Religion*.]

BIBLIOGRAPHY

Phelan, John Leddy. *The Millennial Kingdom of the Franciscans in the New World*. Berkeley, 1970.

Ricard, Robert. *The Spiritual Conquest of Mexico*. Translated by Lesley Bird Simpson. Berkeley, 1966.

Tibesar, Antonine. *Franciscan Beginnings in Colonial Peru*. Washington, D.C., 1953.

JOHN F. SCHWALLER

MONTEJO, FRANCISCO DE (c. 1479–1553), Spanish conqueror of Yucatán. Born in Salamanca, Montejo went to the Americas in 1514 with Pedro Arias de Ávila (Pedrárias). From Castilla del Oro (Panama) he left for Cuba at an unknown date prior to 1518. There he acquired a ranch and other properties. In 1518, he was a captain in the Juan de Grijalba expedition, and in 1519 he joined Hernando Cortés's expedition, also as a captain. When the expedition founded the town of Veracruz, Montejo was elected one of its judges, or alcaldes.

Montejo twice served Cortés as an emissary to Charles V (1521, 1526), on the first occasion helping to secure Cortés's appointment as captain general of New Spain over the opposition of Diego Velázquez, governor of Cuba. He obtained a royal contract for the conquest of Yucatán on December 8, 1526, and sailed from Spain in the summer of 1527 with four ships and five hundred men. He landed first at Cozumel Island but abandoned it for the mainland. He marched inland against light Indian resistance until he was defeated at Aké (in north-central Yucatán). Leaving a small force in Yucatán, Montejo went

to New Spain for reinforcements. Appointed governor of Tabasco, he went there in 1529 and withdrew the men he had left in Yucatán. He resumed the conquest of Yucatán in 1530 with the founding of Campeche. By 1533, a series of campaigns seemed to establish Spanish control over western and northern Yucatán. Montejo subsequently gave the enterprise to his natural son Francisco de Montejo, who carried out the reconquest of Yucatán between 1537 and 1545, following a Maya uprising from 1533 to 1545 that had driven the Spaniards from most of the peninsula.

In 1533 the elder Montejo turned his attention to Honduras, part of which he had claimed as early as 1529. He was appointed royal governor of Honduras-Higueras in 1535, at a time when the Indians were in rebellion and Spaniards were leaving. Because he lacked financial resources, Montejo did not immediately take up his office. Instead, Pedro de Alvarado, governor of Guatemala, administered Honduras. Their rival claims to the province led to disputes in 1537 and again in 1539. In the interim, Montejo suppressed a major Indian revolt (1537–1539) and instituted modest administrative and economic reforms.

Alvarado's return to Guatemala in 1539 led to Montejo's removal as governor of Honduras and an agreement between them exchanging Chiapas, which was part of Alvarado's grant, for Montejo's claims to Honduras. Following Alvarado's death in 1541, the colonists of Honduras called Montejo to be governor (1542). However, other men were appointed governor by the audiencia of Santo Domingo and the viceroy of Mexico, and Montejo was again removed from office. The audiencia of Santo Domingo appointed him governor in 1543, but he had to give up that office when the newly created audiencia of Los Confines began its rule in the spring of 1544. Following his residencias (an inquiry at the end of his term of office) in Honduras and Chiapas, he returned to Yucatán to assume its governorship. In 1549 he was removed from that position as well. He returned to Spain where he died in 1553, having obtained few of the rewards he had sought because he had never had enough money to field large forces and because he did not cultivate patrons whose favor might have protected his claims from rivals.

BIBLIOGRAPHY

Chamberlain, Robert S. *The Conquest and Colonization of Yucatán, 1527–1550*. Washington, D.C., 1948.

Chamberlain, Robert S. *The Conquest and Colonization of Honduras, 1502–1550*. Washington, D.C., 1953.

PAUL E. HOFFMAN

MONTEZUMA. See *Motecuhzoma II*.

MONUMENTS AND MEMORIALS.

Monuments to Christopher Columbus exist throughout the United States, Mexico, Central and South American countries, and various locations in the Caribbean; Spain and Italy also boast several monuments to Columbus. Since the practice of erecting commemorative statuary to a nondivine, nonsacred, or nonaristocratic person is a modern one, originating in Europe, public monuments to Columbus did not exist much before the nineteenth century. Stylistic diversity within this large but chronologically limited group, therefore, can be attributed in part to historical developments in art; flexibility in the portrayal of Columbus—conceptually as well as physically—also accounts for the wide range of types of monuments.

The United States

The earliest notice of a Columbus monument appears in a journal of 1782 written by an officer in Comte de Rochambeau's army during the American War of Independence: "You see several notable buildings [in Philadelphia] ," wrote Jean-Baptiste-Antoine de Verger, "including the mansion where the Congress meets [Independence Hall] . . . ascending the staircase, you see the statues of Christopher Columbus and of Penn." No trace of this statue has been found, nor are there any remains of a monument created by New York's Tammany Society, also known as the Columbian Order, on the occasion of the tricentennial of Columbus's first voyage. Designed as an obelisk and of a material resembling black marble, the 1792 Columbus monument bore scenes of Columbus's life on each of its four faces. Ephemeral as these two works were, they nevertheless adumbrated the strong American interest in Columbian monuments, an interest that produced the largest number of Columbus statues in any nation. Moreover, the tradition that began in 1792 has continued unbroken to the late twentieth century.

Not all the eighteenth-century Columbian monuments were transitory. The French consul in Baltimore erected a stone obelisk on the grounds of his estate in 1792; it was moved to the Samuel Ready Institute in the 1960s. The erection of the first figural sculpture of Columbus in the United States took place in Boston, where in 1849 a Greek or Italian businessman (the sources differ) presented a marble statue of Columbus to the city. (The first figural sculpture of Columbus in the Western Hemisphere was modeled in London in 1831 and erected at Government House, Nassau, Bahamas, in 1832; it is of metal, painted white.) Although without aesthetic distinction, the Boston statue presaged many later American monuments in theme and design, being a single figure of a young man clad in fifteenth-century dress and accompanied by nautical motifs. The monument raised in Philadelphia in 1876 is similar in physical features and enlarges on the idea of Columbus as a sailor and navigator, his right hand resting

PHILADELPHIA, 1876. Statue of Christopher Columbus.

PHOTOGRAPH: E. B. HESTON

on a globe and his left holding a map; an anchor lies at his feet. Both the Boston and Philadelphia statues were produced in Italy and may have had a similar source. The Philadelphia monument, the gift of Italian Americans in celebration of the centennial of the Declaration of Independence and the world's fair, was the first statue of Columbus in the United States to be funded entirely by public subscription.

In addition to municipal funding or public subscription,

benefactors sometimes gave monuments to the community. St. Louis and Sacramento are among the cities that received Columbus statuary from private sources, the former as a gift of Henry D. Shaw in 1886 and the latter as a gift of D. O. Mills, a former resident, in 1882. The St. Louis statue, a bronze cast in Germany, was sited in Tower Grove Park, another of Shaw's bequests to the city. Mills presented Larkin Goldsmith Mead's three-figure ensemble to the state capitol in Sacramento and, though objections have been raised periodically because the legislature neither asked for the work nor was consulted about its acceptance, it has remained a featured part of the capitol interior for more than a century. Meade carved the marble in Italy and chose the unusual theme of Columbus explaining his theories to Queen Isabel; a page looking on seems added to balance the composition. The subject and its realization remain unique among Columbian monuments.

The federal government commissioned depictions of more or less the same theme—the 1492 landing—for nearly all the representations of Columbus in the U.S. Capitol. The bronze doors installed in 1863 and moved in 1871 (and again in 1961) to the east entrance to the

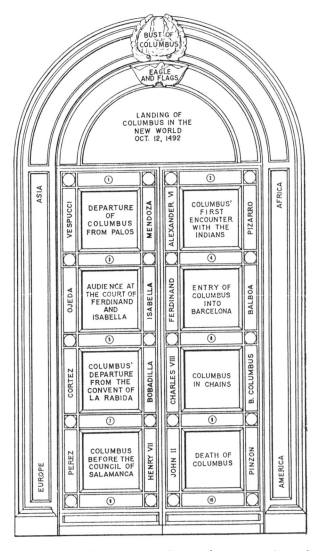

STATE CAPITOL, SACRAMENTO, CALIFORNIA, 1868. *Columbus's Last Appeal to Isabella*, Larkin Goldsmith Mead.

CALIFORNIA STATE CAPITOL MUSEUM

U.S. CAPITOL, 1863. The bronze doors at the eastern entrance to the Rotunda depicting events in the life of Columbus were designed and modeled by Randolph Rogers in Rome in 1858. They were cast in Munich in 1861. In November 1863 the doors were installed between Statuary Hall and the House extension. Because of their massiveness and great beauty, it was felt they were worthy of a more central location, and in 1871 they were moved to the Rotunda entrance. In 1961 the doors were moved again, thirty-two feet east, when the East Front of the Capitol was extended. The doors, also called the Rogers Doors, have two valves with four panels in each valve, surmounted by a semicircular tympanum. The tympanum depicts Columbus's first landfall in the New World. The eight panels depict various scenes from Columbus's life, as shown in the schematic representation. In niches on the sides of the doors and between the panels are sixteen small statues of contemporaries of Columbus: political figures, colleagues, and other explorers. Between the panels (numbers 1 to 10) are representations of historians who have written of Columbus. On the extreme edges of the doors are personifications of the continents of Asia, Europe, Africa, and America.

ARCHITECT OF THE CAPITOL

U.S. CAPITOL, 1844. *Discovery of America*, Luigi Persico.

ARCHITECT OF THE CAPITOL

Rotunda and the marble group (1836–1844) formerly at the east-facade stairway illustrate variations on this theme. The marble group, a sixteen-foot-high tableau by Luigi Persico that has been in storage since 1958, juxtaposed an armored Columbus holding a globe aloft with an awkwardly contorted seminude Indian female poised as though to flee. The doors, on the other hand, eschew the emblematical quality of Persico's statuary in favor of a carefully pictorial narrative of the main events in Columbus's life, in which the first landing in the New World is clearly the most important event. Modeled in Rome by Randolph Rogers and cast in Munich by F. von Müller, the doors have as their inspiration the North Doors of the Baptistry of Florence cathedral, which depict the life of Christ in a work by Lorenzo Ghiberti. The Capitol doors culminate in a lunette in which is placed the thematically crowning representation, Columbus's 1492 landing. As in Persico's rendition, the native Americans witnessing Columbus's debarkation are presented as awestruck, frightened primitives, a stereotype inspired and reinforced by the large mural, *The Landing of Columbus at the Island of Guanahani, West Indies* (also known as *The Landing of Columbus on San Salvador*), by John Vanderlyn, installed in the Rotunda in 1847.

The 1892 celebrations of the quadricentennial of Columbus's landing provided at least part of the impetus for the spurt of commissions for Columbian monuments at the end of the century. In New York, the monument at Columbus Circle was dedicated on October 12, 1892, a Columbus fountain for Central Park was planned but eventually abandoned, and a replica of Jeronimo Sunol's monument in Madrid was donated to the city. In Chicago, site of the 1893 World's Columbian Exposition, a fountain ornamented by a huge statue of Columbus was given to the city and statues by Mary Lawrence, Daniel Chester French, Howard Kretchmer, and Frédéric Auguste Bartholdi were exhibited at the fair. The last two became public monuments, Kretchmer's statue moved to the lakefront and Bartholdi's (cast in silver by the Gorham Company) replicated in bronze for Providence, Rhode Island. Other quadricentennial monuments to Columbus were raised in Columbus, Ohio; Boston; Baltimore; Willimantic and New Haven, Connecticut; and Scranton, Pennsylvania.

Twentieth-century Columbian monuments are also geographically widespread, with statues or busts in Pueblo, Colorado (1905); Walla Walla, Washington (1910); Detroit

CHICAGO, 1893. Small-scale bronze cast of *Columbus Sighting Land*, Frédéric-Auguste Bartholdi. The full-size original, not extant, was cast in silver for the World's Columbian Exposition.

GRAHAM GALLERY, NEW YORK

(1912); Washington, D.C. (1912); St. Paul, Minnesota (1931); Pittsburgh (1958); Memphis (1992); and Norristown, Pennsylvania (1992).

With few exceptions the sponsoring organizations of Columbian monuments have been Italian American, often under the aegis of one of the more than one hundred and fifty Italian newspapers once published in the United States. The editor of *Il Progresso d'Italia*, Carlo Barsotti, conceived of the Columbus Circle monument in New York and brought his idea to fruition; *La Tribuna Italiana* and *L'Eco d'Italia* helped raise funds for the monuments in Detroit and Philadelphia, respectively. Whatever the agency of their collective action, Italian Americans tended to choose only Italian sculptors working in Italy to carry out their commissions and this common source meant that many American monuments share stylistic traits, not only in representing a certain type of Columbus—young, with shoulder-length hair, and wearing a short Spanish tabard—but in depicting him with the attributes of a navigator, such as a globe, map, or anchor.

The most imposing of the American monuments is that

CHICAGO, 1893. Statue of Columbus at Drake Fountain, Richard Park. This work, although inspired by the celebrations of 1893, was not exhibited at the World's Columbian Exposition.

COLUMBUS, OHIO, 1892. Statue of Christopher Columbus, after Mary Lawrence. THE OHIO HISTORICAL SOCIETY

by Gaetano Russo in New York City. The statue was carved in Rome and the whole ensemble was brought to New York on an Italian warship courtesy of the Italian government. Located at the southwest entrance to Central Park, the monument rises about 24 meters (77 feet) and thus holds its own with the surrounding tall buildings. A grim-looking Columbus stands atop a rostral column (a column decorated with the prows of boats, the vessels here being bronze). He appears to be caught in mid-action, with his hand on a ship's rudder. The pedestal on which the assemblage sits is terraced with steps and culminates in a rectangular base marked with red granite corner posts. On the front of the base, above a bronze relief of the departure from Spain, a marble genius holds a globe; at the rear, a marble eagle grasps the shields of Italy and the United States.

NEW YORK CITY, 1892. Monument to Columbus at Columbus Circle, Gaetano Russo.   *BULLETIN OF PAN AMERICAN UNION*

CHICAGO, C. 1932. Statue of Christopher Columbus, Carlo Brioschi.   PHOTOGRAPH: E. B. HESTON

WASHINGTON, D.C., 1912. Two views of the statue of Christopher Columbus at Union Station, Laredo Taft.

NATIONAL PARK SERVICE

In contrast, the so-called national monument in Washington, D.C. (1912), sponsored by the U.S. Congress and the National Council of the Knights of Columbus, and the work of the sculptor Laredo Taft and the architect Daniel Burnham, offers a different conception: a fountain with a central shaft in front of which a cloaked and contemplative Columbus stands. To either side of Columbus, on the shaft, are personifications of the New World—a crouched Indian reaching for an arrow in the quiver on his back—and of the Old World—a meditative and mature European. Atop the shaft a globe rests on four large eagles with spread wings.

Most twentieth-century monuments tend to reflect the conceptions of earlier works. Statues of Columbus in Richmond, Virginia (1927), and in Newark (1927), Hoboken (1931), and Atlantic City, New Jersey (1958), testify to the strength of the navigator motif found in the Italian-produced works in Boston, Philadelphia, and New York; these later works were all carved by Italian sculptors. An Italian sculptor born abroad but whose career was conducted entirely in the United States, Carlo Brioschi, portrayed a slightly different and more theatrical Columbus for monuments now in Chicago (1933) and St. Paul (1931), each of which concentrates on a figure of mystical mien and dreamlike gestures.

Central and South America, the West Indies, and Mexico

The most appropriate location for monuments to Columbus would be the West Indies, locus of most of his activity in the Western Hemisphere. In 1891, the Chicago *Herald* raised a rough construction of local stone or coral on Watlings Island (Guanahani or San Salvador), the spot

SANTO DOMINGO, DOMINICAN REPUBLIC. Statue of Christopher Columbus. *BULLETIN OF PAN AMERICAN UNION*

WATLINGS ISLAND, 1891. Monument to Christopher Columbus sponsored by the *Chicago Herald*.

BULLETIN OF PAN AMERICAN UNION

presumed by some scholars to be the place of Columbus's first landfall. More traditional monuments were erected at other sites of Columbus's later voyages to Cuba and La Española (Hispaniola). Those in Haiti were destroyed in 1986 after the overthrow of the Duvalier regime. In Santo Domingo, the capital of the Dominican Republic, however, a monument partially funded by public subscription and erected in 1886 still dominates the city. The monument is unusual in including a nude female native American on the pedestal, her finger tracing the inscription; it is otherwise typical of the land-discovering genre of Columbian statuary found most often in North American renditions, although the bronze statue surmounting the high marble base was said to have been cast in France.

Cuba has been the home of several Columbian monuments of varying kinds, from busts to tombs. When the Cuban revolution of 1868 toppled Bourbon rule, a statue of Columbus by a French sculptor replaced a statue of Isabel II, queen of Spain until that year, that stood in the center of a park in Havana. In 1878, when Spanish rule was reinstated, the statue of Isabel returned, and the statue of Columbus was moved to the grounds of the captain general's palace. A chapel called El Templete, built to commemorate the site where the first mass was celebrated in Cuba, shelters a bust of Columbus that stands on a column. Elsewhere in Cuba, the towns of Cifuentes,

HAVANA, CUBA. *Christopher Columbus in Chains*, by Vallmitjana.
BULLETIN OF PAN AMERICAN UNION

who befriended Columbus in Spain and two missionaries to the New World. Columbus himself is portrayed as a conqueror, or even as a conjurer, for he plucks a veil from the globe he holds.

Most monuments in Central and South America, like those in the United States, appear to have been prompted by the quadricentennial observances. Honduras erected a bronze statue in Trujillo for the occasion, and Guatemala raised a unique monument in Guatemala City that placed a standing Columbus at the summit of two bronze globes, one atop the other. Earlier, in 1866, Empress Eugénie of

Bayamo, Cárdenas, and Colón all possessed public statues of the Admiral by the turn of the century.

The Caribbean monuments to Columbus include two tombs, one in the Cathedral of Santo Domingo where Columbus's body was moved at the request of his son Diego in the sixteenth century. In 1796, however, his remains were transferred to Havana where another tomb was constructed (there is a similar tomb in Spain, where, after the Spanish-American War, Columbus's bones were transferred).

Columbus monuments in Mexico, Central America, and South America reflect the historical perspectives of the encounter between Europeans and Indians as seen by the Europeans during the nineteenth century. Thus, almost all the monuments, the gift or inspiration of Europeans or Europeans of mixed descent, include some reference to religion and almost all refer to—or in some fashion resemble—the statues of conquistadores liberally sprinkled throughout the region. Therefore, some of the Columbus monuments offer rallying points for protest demonstrations on the part of Indians. In Mexico, for instance, the huge 1877 monument by Charles-Henri-Joseph Cordier, a French sculptor who resided in Mexico, has been the target of mestizo outrage because it symbolizes a Spanish invasion that debased and then ignored a thriving and mature culture. The monument's elaborate tableau pays homage not only to the Admiral but, in life-size figures of bronze on a marble base, to two priests

SAN JUAN, PUERTO RICO. Statue of Christopher Columbus.
COURTESY OF THE MUNICIPIO DE SAN JUAN

MEXICO CITY, 1877. Monument to Christopher Columbus by the French sculptor Charles-Henri-Joseph Cordier.

BULLETIN OF PAN AMERICAN UNION

France commissioned from Vincenzo Vela, a Swiss-Italian sculptor, a statue of Columbus to be erected at Colón (later Aspinwall) on the Isthmus of Panama. In Vela's conception, Columbus is shown wearing vaguely religious garb and standing beside a crouching Indian maiden, his right hand touching her gently as though to protect her.

The elaborate monument in Lima, Peru, by Salvatore Revelli seems to have been influenced by Vela's monumental grouping and is related to Genoa's monument to Columbus, not surprisingly since the artist Revelli was also a contributor to that multiauthored work. However, one source gives the date of the Lima monument's dedication as 1850, too early for Revelli to have known Vela's work; another identifies Revelli's ensemble as having been displayed at the 1867 Paris Exposition Universelle; in this case Revelli's sculpture apparently has been mistaken for that of Vela. In any event, Revelli's interpretation of Columbus's relation to the half-clothed Indian woman—a personification of America—merges a patriarchal attitude with a religious overtone. The Indian woman is coiled against Columbus's side, an arrow at her feet, and he in turn presses a cross into her left hand. His right arm draws his cloak around her as though to shield her from prying eyes and his face tilts heavenward. Columbus appears to be presenting his charge to God. The base of the monument concentrates on nautical elements in relief, the work of another Italian, Guiseppe Palombini.

Elsewhere in South America, the Columbus monuments portray a single figure. The government of Chile raised a monument in Valparaíso, a heroic-sized bronze statue of Columbus clasping a crucifix. In Buenos Aires, the Italian residents of Argentina contributed a statue of Columbus to the 1910 festivities accompanying the country's centennial. Perhaps because the celebrations commemorated the country's independence from Spain, this monument least resembles the conquistador influence. Over 6½ meters (22 feet) high, the statue instead presents Columbus, a map his only attribute, in a pose suggestive of thoughtful deliberation rather than of discovery or proselytizing. The monument to Columbus in Bogotá, Colombia, has been moved from its original site on what was the Avenida de Colón to the Avenida Eldorado. The figure, with its outstretched arm, tops a tripartite base of stone and towers over the flat terrain. Maracaibo, Venezuela, in contrast, erected a smaller but unique monument that

GUATEMALA CITY, 1893. Monument to Christopher Columbus.

BULLETIN OF PAN AMERICAN UNION

BOGOTÁ, COLOMBIA. Monument to Christopher Columbus.

LIMA, PERU. Monument to Columbus by Salvatore Revelli.

joins a bust of the Admiral to the top of a large globe that outlines on its side the contours of South America.

Europe

Among European countries, Italy and Spain compete in claiming Columbus as a national hero. The award for the greatest number of memorials dedicated to Columbus must go to Spain. Commemorative monuments may be found in Barcelona, Palos, Madrid, Huelva (a city near the monastery of La Rábida), Granada, Salamanca, and Seville. Of these, the most artistically meritorious are those at Barcelona and Madrid (the one at Granada is actually dedicated to Fernando and Isabel). Funded in part by public subscription, Barcelona's memorial was designed by a Catalonian architect, who then supervised the artists employed on the gigantic project, which took six years to complete. On the day of dedication, June 1, 1888, the ships of several nations gathered in the harbor to salute the ceremonies. The queen regent of Spain, Queen Cristina, participated in the monument's unveiling. Nearly 74 meters (240 feet) high, the monument, which stands at the harbor, is the largest of the memorials to the Admiral and won many encomiums in the nineteenth century. Columbus surmounts a Corinthian column, the base of which holds four personifications of fame, their backs arched and arms upflung. Below the column is an octagonal pedestal peopled with bronze figures representing persons known to the Admiral, as well as personifications of Castile, Aragón, León, and Catalonia. The eight lions at the foot of the monument are made of iron.

The monument in Madrid, which originated as a novel form of commemorating the 1879 marriage of King Alfonso XII to María Cristina, was unveiled in 1884 to great acclaim. Much of the praise went to the marble statue of Columbus by Jeronimo Sunol that topped the ensemble (a replica of which is located in Central Park, New York City), an original conception representing the Admiral with the standard of Castile in his right hand, his left hand outstretched and his head upraised. He appears, therefore, to be offering thanks to God, a supposition reinforced by the almost epiphanic expression animating Columbus's face. The other two parts of the monument are a square base, ornamented with both reliefs and detached figures, and an octagonal pillar. The descriptive detail of the base is late Gothic, a period style that accords well with the figural accompaniments, the Spanish coats of arms, and other embellishments. Placed in a garden setting on one of the main thoroughfares of Madrid, the site has now become more urbanized and a second, modern addition to the park, inscribed with Columbian texts and a fountain, complete the newer arrangements.

The premier Italian monument, erected in Genoa in 1862, is an altogether less soaring edifice. Though its parts are elaborate, it also is less extravagantly placed within the urban milieu. Begun in 1846, the commission took several years to complete because of a series of events, including the 1848 revolution, the death of the sculptor chosen to execute the statue of Columbus itself, and the construction of Genoa's main railroad station on the site where the cornerstone of the monument was first laid. Moved to the Piazza Acquaverde in front of the station, and now on a traffic island there, the monument eventually received the contributions of nine sculptors, some of whom, like Aristedemo Costoli, Santo Varni, and Revelli went on to create other Columbian sculpture.

Franco Sborgi has argued that the Genoese monument is of national importance because of the number of artists who contributed to it, since they constituted a pantheon of Italian sculptors. But it can also be argued that so many workers produced an unevenness of style, for the monument can be said to have its high and low points aesthetically. The figures of Columbus and the native American woman beside him represent the sculpture's best parts; in comparison, the reliefs on the base depicting the debate at Salamanca, Columbus arriving in the New World, Columbus presenting the fruits of the New World to the Spanish monarchs, and Columbus in chains appear less well-designed and are poorly executed. Nonetheless, the Genoese monument remains the foremost sculptural commemoration of Columbus, primarily because, as we have seen, all Italian American monuments in the United States and many of the monuments in Central America and South America echo its main features. In addition, its location in the birthplace of Columbus draws attention to the city's Columbian art.

[For further discussion of representations of Columbus in the visual arts, see Iconography.]

BIBLIOGRAPHY

Bump, Charles Weathers. "Public Monuments to Columbus." Reprinted in Selected Papers on Columbus and His Time. Council on National Literature, 1989.

"Columbus in Statuary." Bulletin of the Pan-American Union 34, no. 6 (1912): 775–789.

Curtis, William Eleroy. "The Columbus Monuments." The Chautauquan 16, no. 2 (1892): 138–146.

Fryd, Vivien Green. "Two Sculptures for the Capitol: Horatio Greenough's Rescue and Luigi Persico's Discovery of America." The American Art Journal 19, no. 2 (1987): 17–39.

Ponce de Leon, Nestor. The Columbus Gallery. New York, 1893.

Sborgi, Franco. "Colombo, Otto Scultori e un Piedistallo." Studi di Storia delle arti (Genoa) 5 (1983–1985): 329–458.

BARBARA GROSECLOSE

MOTECUHZOMA II (1467–1520), Aztec ruler. Motecuhzoma (Nahuatl, Angry Lord; also spelled Moteuczoma, Moteczoma, and, in a common but corrupted English form, Montezuma) was the ninth official ruler of Mexico Tenochtitlan (Spanish adaptation of Classical Nahuatl is Tenochtitlán), the preeminent member (with Tetzcoco [Spanish, Texcoco] and Tlacopan [Spanish, Tlacopán]) of the Triple Alliance that dominated a tribute empire covering much of western Mesoamerica at the time of the Conquest. He was the son of Axayacatl, the sixth Tenochca ruler (r. 1469–1481), and a princess of Itztapallapan, a community south of Mexico Tenochtitlan ruled by a dynasty derived from that center. As the great-grandson and namesake of Motecuhzoma I (r. 1440–1469), he also bore the appellation Xocoyotl (or, in the honorific form, Xocoyotzin, "the younger"). Born probably in 1467, in his youth he distinguished himself as a warrior, attaining the highest military rank, that of tlacatecatl. He succeeded his uncle, Ahuitzotl (r. 1486–1502).

According to various post-Conquest accounts, before his accession Motecuhzoma had been especially noted for his humility and religiosity. However, soon after his coronation he allegedly demonstrated his pride and arrogance by replacing all commoners on the palace staff with nobles. Inheriting a flourishing empire, he surrounded himself with particularly elaborate court ceremony, requiring all his subjects, even those of high rank, to render him slavish obeisance.

He continued to expand the empire, concentrating particularly on western Oaxaca, and he was credited with the conquest of over forty major communities in this and adjoining regions. He had less success in contending with the chief Central Mexican rival of the Triple Alliance, the powerful province of Tlaxcallan and its major allies, Huexotzinco and Cholollan. A bitter dispute between Tlaxcallan and Huexotzinco that arose about 1507/1508 appeared to provide an excellent opportunity finally to crush both of these traditional enemies, especially after Huexotzinco virtually submitted to Mexico Tenochtitlan following its defeat by Tlaxcallan. However, the Tlaxcalteca successfully defended themselves against all Triple Alliance attacks, and Huexotzinco reestablished its traditional ties with its erstwhile ally just before the arrival of Hernando Cortés. The preservation of the independence of the Tlaxcalteca was to have momentous consequences, as they played a crucial role in the overthrow of Mexico Tenochtitlan as steadfast Spanish allies.

Many omens of impending doom reportedly plagued Motecuhzoma II's last years. Just before the Conquest, he ordered his likeness, adjoining those of his royal ances-

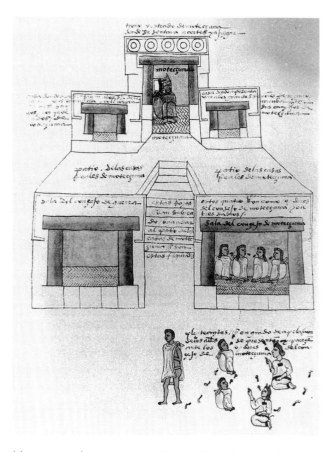

MOTECUHZOMA'S PALACE. Motecuhzoma sits at the pinnacle, chiefs just below him, and war and judiciary councils below them. From the Codex Mendoza, 1541. Original in the Bodleian Library, Oxford.   LIBRARY OF CONGRESS

tors, to be carved in the living rock at the base of the hill of Chapultepec, west of the capital. The expected return of Topiltzin Quetzalcoatl, the semilegendary Toltec ruler, to reclaim his throne appears to have significantly influenced him in his initial dealings with Cortés. Taken captive after receiving the Spanish force peaceably in the fall of 1519, Motecuhzoma II was held hostage in his father's palace until June 1520. According to the Spanish accounts, he died from wounds received while attempting to placate his own people who, under a new ruler, his brother, Cuitlahuac, had risen in revolt. Because of his seeming vacillation and his passive acceptance of his long imprisonment by Cortés, Motecuhzoma II remains a controversial and ambiguous figure. His cousin Cuauhtemoc, however, who after Cuitlahuac's death from smallpox became the final ruler of Mexico Tenochtitlan and conducted the desperate defense of the city in 1521, has become a Mexican national hero.

BIBLIOGRAPHY

Barlow, Robert H. "El derrumbe de Huexotzinco." *Cuadernos Americanos* 39, no. 2 (1948): 147–160.

Barlow, Robert H. "Las conquistas de Moteczuma Xocoyotzin." *Memorias de la Academia Mexicana de la Historia* 8, no. 2 (1949): 159–172.

García Granados, Rafael. "Moctezuma II." In vol. 1 of *Diccionario biográfico de historia antigua de Méjico.* Mexico City, 1952.

Nicholson, H. B. "The Chapultepec Cliff Sculpture of Motecuhzoma Xocoyotzin." *El México Antiguo* 9 (1959): 379–444.

Ramírez, José Fernando. "Moteczuma." Edited by Rafael García Granados. *Memorias de la Academia Mexicana de la Historia* 5–6 (1946–1947).

Romerovargas Yturbide, Ignacio. *Motecuhzoma Xocoyotzin o Moctezuma el Magnífico y la invasión de Anahuac.* 3 vols. Mexico City, 1963.

H. B. NICHOLSON

MUHAMMAD XI. See *Boabdil*.

MUSEUMS AND ARCHIVES. [This entry includes two articles: *Collections of Columbus Memorabilia* and *Overview of Documentary Sources.* The first discusses the types of artifacts that illuminate modern scholarly understanding of Columbus and his times and surveys institutions that collect, preserve, and study such materials. The second focuses on the documentary sources at the foundation of Columbus scholarship. For further discussion of these sources, see *Book of Privileges; Library of Columbus; Writings,* articles on *Book of Prophecies* and *Marginalia.* Alternative sources of Columbus research are discussed in *Archaeology.*]

Collections of Columbus Memorabilia

The basic sources for the study of Columbus's life are items associated with him, his family, and his associates. These consist of objects he owned or used, correspondence and other papers he originated or received, and contemporary public records and writings relating to Columbus in his time. These materials are sometimes to be found in private collections maintained by heirs or descendants, and frequently in public repositories such as archives, libraries, and museums. Among the best known collections in the United States of artifacts and other materials related to the Age of Discovery are the numerous museums and art galleries of the Smithsonian Institution in Washington, D.C., the Metropolitan Museum of Art and the American Museum of Natural History in New York City, and the Museum of Art in Philadelphia. The largest public libraries are the Library of Congress in Washington, D.C., the New York Public Library, and Boston Public Library. In addition to the U.S. National Archives in Washington, similar resources exist as separate entities although on a much more limited scale in the state capitals and are to be found as well as part of major libraries and historical societies.

Three-dimensional objects illustrating the character or life of an adventurer like Columbus would have included personal memorabilia, the tools of his occupation, and items related to his preoccupations. These may range from his sea chest, maps, navigational instruments, the books and charts he owned and used, and arms and armor, for example, to parts of his ships and their equipment, such as anchors. Artifacts of this character, if they survived, generally are carefully maintained and featured on display for the general public in national history or naval museums.

Equally important are records documenting Columbus's achievements, such as personal journals and diaries, letters sent and received, and official documents relating to or attesting to his attainments. These may be retained by descendants or collectors or maintained in national or local archives and sometimes in libraries. Finally, there are contemporary manuscript or printed accounts of Columbus and his accomplishments in private collections and public libraries.

Regrettably, extremely few surviving artifacts can be positively documented to have been associated with Christopher Columbus and his son Diego Colón or related to their voyages. The greatest number of these materials are in Spain. They consist chiefly of books that Columbus owned and annotated, several manuscripts that he authored, and a limited amount of his correspondence. The majority of official correspondence and state papers relating to his voyages are the property of the Spanish government and maintained in the Archivo General de Indias in Seville. A few documents relating to Christopher Columbus and Diego Colón, as well as a large collection of documents and records relating to later members of the family, are retained by the family of the present duke of Veragua and the duchess of Berwick and Alba in Madrid, head of another branch of the Columbus family. It is reported that she owns a number of original documents, a few relating to Christopher Columbus and others to his son, Diego Colón, which have been the subject of a volume entitled *Autográfos de Colón*. Following are brief accounts of the chief repositories of Columbian memorabilia.

Archivo General de Indias, Seville. The largest number of personal papers of Christopher Columbus and his son Diego relating to the voyages and the establishment of settlements in the New World are assembled in this special archive of the Spanish government. Consisting of Christopher Columbus's and Diego Colón's correspondence with the Catholic sovereigns, commissions, edicts, and the like, the archives comprise a total of approximately one hundred documents ranging from 1488 to the 1540s. A great number of these had remained the property of Columbus's descendants and passed from one generation to another of the dukes of Veragua until the nineteenth century. They were then purchased by the Spanish government from the incumbent duke of Veragua.

Duke of Veragua, Madrid. Remaining in the possession of the family of the present duke are claimed to be more than five thousand papers of the Columbus family, mostly dating after the death of Diego Colón. Notable among them are three documents signed by the Catholic sovereigns: the original grant of title dated April 30, 1492, naming Columbus admiral, viceroy, and governor of all the lands and islands he was about to discover; the deed dated May 28, 1493, naming Columbus captain general of the armada sailing for the Indies; and the original document dated June 20, 1493, granting Columbus a coat-of-arms, which is illustrated therein.

Biblioteca Colombina, Cathedral of Seville. This library of some twelve thousand to twenty thousand items was founded in 1551, based upon the bequest of Fernando Colón of approximately seven thousand manuscripts in addition to the printed books he had collected in his lifetime. The library contains a collection of printed books that Christopher Columbus owned prior to his first voyage and which he carried on his voyages as well as several others he acquired later. That he read and consulted them is attested by the presence of numerous postils in his handwriting. These books are displayed within a locked, free-standing case.

Featured in Fernando Colón's collection is a manuscript

of the navigator's Book of Prophecies, which Columbus had prepared for Queen Isabel in 1501–1502 with the assistance of the monk Gaspar Gorricio. The manuscript consists of a letter addressed by Columbus to King Fernando and Queen Isabel introducing the collection of excerpts from the Bible in addition to a number of ancient and medieval works predicting or implying the discovery of the New World and proving that his plans for discovery were not antagonistic to scripture.

The cathedral of Seville also owns a cross traditionally claimed to have been made of the gold brought from America by Columbus.

Real Academia de la Historia, Madrid. The library of this learned organization, comparable to the Royal Society of London or the American Philosophical Society, owns an original letter from Columbus to the Catholic sovereigns and a fifteenth-century (c. 1475) manuscript copy of Ptolemy's *Geography* bearing Columbus's rubric on the flyleaf.

Biblioteca Nacional, Madrid. The Department of Manuscripts of Spain's national library contains a holograph letter dated January 4, 1493, from Columbus to Rodrigo de Escobedo designating him chief of the first community established in the New World; another dated 1496–1497 from Columbus to the Catholic sovereigns relating to the discovery of La Española (Hispaniola); and a painting on wood claimed to be the earliest portrait of Columbus. It was not painted from life, however, and is believed to be Italian from about 1552.

Museo Naval, Madrid. Featured in this repository of artifacts relating to Spain's naval and maritime history is the first chart of the West Indies, drawn by Juan de la Cosa in 1500 and executed on two oxhides. The Museo Naval also owns a later copy of the Toscanelli map of 1474 and a portrait of Columbus.

Museo del Ejercito, Madrid. In the extensive collections of this museum of Spanish military history is a wide range of late-fifteenth-century arms and armor such as Columbus and his men would have worn and cannon and other weapons of the type they brought with them to the New World. None of the items is known to have been associated with Columbus's voyages, however.

Palazzo Municipale, Genoa. The chief treasure relating to Columbus in Italy is his manuscript of the Book of Prophecies entitled *Cartas, privilegias, cedulas y otras escrituras de Don Christoval Colon, Almirante Mayor del Mar Oceano, Visorey y Gobernador de las Islas y Tierra Firma* (Letters, privileges, contracts and other documents of Don Christopher Columbus, Great Admiral of the Ocean Sea, Viceroy and Governor of the Islands and the Mainland). Contained in a small folio volume of parchment bound in Spanish leather, having two silver ornaments, and enclosed in a leather bag, it was originally protected by a silver lock, now lacking. The reverse of the title page bears the Columbus arms as augmented by Columbus. The volume consists of forty-two leaves with attestations of notaries and alcaldes of Seville in whose presence the copies were made.

Following a copy of the bull of Alexander VI establishing the Line of Demarcation are nine pages of arguments by Columbus describing his contract with the Catholic sovereigns and defending his rights. Ten more pages contain a letter from Columbus to the governess of Prince Don Juan (Juan de Austria); a memorandum relating to the various copies he made of his contracts with the sovereigns and their disposition; two autograph letters from Columbus to Nicolò Oderigo, the Genoese ambassador to Spain; a copy of the reply from the director of the Banco di San Giorgio of Genoa to a letter from Columbus; an original letter from King Philip II to Ottaviano Oderigo, doge of Genoa, congratulating him upon the acquisition of this collection of documents; and a memorandum relating to Lorenzo Oderigo, who gave the collection to the Republic of Genoa. At the end of the volume is a sketch, *The Triumph of Columbus*, believed to have been drawn by Columbus. These manuscripts had been sent by Columbus to his friend Nicolò Oderigo to be deposited in the Banco di San Giorgio. Apparently Oderigo kept them for himself and it was not until 1669 that a descendant, Lorenzo Oderigo, presented them to the municipality.

During Napoleon's occupation of Italy, one copy of the manuscripts was taken to Paris, where it remains in the French ministry of foreign affairs. The other copy was acquired by Count Michelangelo Cambiasi, who surrendered it to the municipality of Genoa in 1887.

Archivio Notarile di Stato, Genoa. This repository contains a number of notarial acts of the fifteenth century relating to members of Columbus's family.

Casa Museo Colón, Las Palmas, Canary Islands. In the ancient barrio of Vegueta in Las Palmas is a house that tradition has always identified with the name of Nauta Genoves and associated with Columbus. Acquired in 1951 by the Cabildo of the Grand Canaries, it has been converted into a museum, with a Columbus Hall containing some early sixteenth-century cannons, models of Spanish caravels, a replica of a mariner's astrolabe based on the drawing in the Ribeiro map, and a copy of a portrait of Columbus. Collections of archaeological artifacts of the "Cultura Esmeraldeña" from the island of Tolita, of pre-Hispanic cultures of Mexico such as the Olmecs, and of the city of Teotihuacán are exhibited. Graphic wall displays illustrate the history of the peopling of the Americas, forms of economy in indigenous America, and the principal cities and cultures of the Americas. The museum contains no original artifacts associated with Columbus or his voyages.

Chicago Historical Society. Numerous objects that remained unclaimed or unwanted after the close of the World's Columbian Exposition of 1893 were eventually deposited with the Society, some transferred from the Field Museum of Natural History. Of particular interest are three anchors, one found at Cap-Haitien alleged to have been from *Santa María,* another claimed to have been lost off the coast of Trinidad by one of Columbus's ships on the third voyage, and an anchor found in the Ozama River, Dominican Republic, believed to have belonged to one of the ships of Columbus or his son. Although one or more of these may be authenic as claimed, their records have been misfiled and it is no longer possible to determine with certainty which is which.

Other artifacts claimed to be associated with Columbus are bricks said to have been taken from Columbus's house in Santo Domingo, an iron cross and doors from the convent of Santa Maria de La Rábida, secured at the time the building was burned; late fifteenth-century doors, three wooden shutters, and a threshold from the home in Porto Santo, Madeira, of Bartolomé Perestrelo, Columbus's father-in-law, all bearing seals of authentication by the Spanish government; and a hawkbell said to have been brought to the Americas by the first Spaniards seeking gold. Few if any of these items are satisfactorily documented.

Library of Congress, Washington, D.C. The Library's collections contain one of the four copies made under the direction of Christopher Columbus in 1501–1502 of the Book of Privileges, a collection of various grants, commissions, charters, and privileges made to Columbus by the Catholic sovereigns, in addition to copies on paper of the bulls of Pope Alexander VI of May and October 1493. This copy, consisting of forty-five folio pages on vellum, was purchased for the Library in 1901.

The Library also owns a collection of approximately three hundred mounted photographs of Columbus documents formerly owned by the duke of Veragua, the originals of which, for the most part, are now in the Archivo General de Indias, in addition to a collection of photographs of pages of the Book of Privileges in the Municipal Palace in Genoa.

Columbus Chapel, Boal Mansion Museum, Boalsburg, Pennsylvania. Founded in 1951 and installed in the Boal family estate is a collection of materials relating to later descendants of Christopher Columbus and collateral branches of the family. Featured is the interior of a sixteenth-century chapel from a Spanish castle said to have been once owned by Diego Colón, which later became the home of Columbus's descendants. It was brought from Spain in 1909 and re-erected on the Boal family estate. In the interior are a grand escutcheon of the Columbus arms, numerous religious paintings, and other items, such as a reliquary with fragments said to be from the left arm of the True Cross. A portable "admiral's desk" is claimed to have been associated with Christopher or Diego. The museum also holds a collection of more than 165,000 pages of documents spanning four and a half centuries, from 1451 to 1902. More than half of the papers relate to three Columbus descendants of the late eighteenth and early nineteenth centuries—Joseph Joaquim Colón, his son Diego Mariano, and his grandson, Diego Santiago. Many of the records concern the endless conflict between this line of the Columbus family, which ended when Diego Santiago died without an heir, and the branch holding the dukedom of Veragua. None of the documents is positively identified to have been associated with Christopher Columbus or his sons.

Upon her death, Diego Santiago's wife left the family fortune to her French nephews and nieces, one of whom became the wife of an Irish American named Theodore Boal. It was as a consequence of this marriage that the chapel interior and collection of papers were brought to the United States.

The Columbus Memorial Lighthouse, Dominican Republic. Still under construction in 1991 is a landmark known as "El Faro a Colón," a lighthouse erected as a memorial to Christopher Columbus. The installation will contain six museums dedicated to aspects of the explorer's career. Included are a library of rare and hard-to-find books; an archive concerned with the history of the planning and construction of the lighthouse project, containing architectural plans and models; and a unit devoted to the history of cartography, featuring a collection of maps of the Americas. One of the museums will be dedicated to underwater archaeology, with artifacts recovered from sites in the region; another will be devoted to ceramics produced over the past five centuries. Central in theme to the installation is a museum commemorating Columbus himself, featuring displays of collections of coins, stamps, portraits, and works in gold and silver.

BIBLIOGRAPHY

[Bedini, Silvio A., and José Ibañez-Cerda]. *Colón y su tiempo.* Madrid, 1976.

Casa Museo Colón: *Guia Didactica.* Grand Canaries, n.d.

Davenport, Frances G. "Documents. Texts of Columbus's Privileges." *American Historical Review* 14 (1909): 764–777.

Garner, Richard L., and Donald C. Henderson. *Columbus and Related Family Papers, 1451–1902. An Inventory of the Boal Collection.* University Park, Pa., 1975.

Pérez Montás, Eugenio, and Manuel Valverde Podesta. "The Columbus Memorial Lighthouse." *La Española* (Dominican Republic Commissión del Quinto Centenario) 92, no. 3 (October 1988): 66.

Putnam, Herbert. "The Columbus Codex." *The Critic,* March 1903, pp. 244–251.

Watts, Pauline Moffitt. "Columbus's Crusade." *Humanities* 6, no. 6 (1985): 15–17.

SILVIO A. BEDINI

Overview of Documentary Sources

Considering the significance of his voyages of discovery from 1492 through 1503, original documents that deal with Christopher Columbus are scarce. Ninety-three such documents are located in nine archives in Spain, one in Italy, and one in Mexico. None of the diaries of the four voyages is a holograph; the diaries consist of abstracts prepared by Bartolomé de las Casas. Careful textual analysis can reveal original portions of the diaries. The total array of information on Columbus is a composite of scattered holograph documents, printed copies and translations of documents that are now lost, and corroborative documents by contemporaries.

The most important collection of material on Columbus was the library built up by his youngest son Fernando. Known today as the Biblioteca Colombina, this library once held all Columbus's personal papers and thousands of books that were still rarities in sixteenth-century Europe. The collection, housed in the cathedral of Seville, has dwindled to some two thousand items from an estimated twelve to twenty thousand in the original bequest. Several books contain marginal notes by Columbus.

Another important collection is that of Martín Fernández de Navarrete (1765–1844), who was commissioned by the king of Spain in 1789 to copy extensively the documents of voyages and discoveries in all Spanish archives. The materials in the Navarrete Collection are held in the Museo Naval, Madrid, which is a major resource for maritime history since the time of Columbus, although caution is advised in using printed versions of the collection because of occasional errors in paleographic transcription.

In anticipation of the four hundredth anniversary of the discovery of America in 1892, the Italian government commissioned the gathering of all known information on Columbus and his voyages from libraries and archives throughout Europe. The result was the compilation of the *Raccolta di documenti e studi pubblicati dalla R. Commissione Colombiana per quarto centenario dalla scoperta dell'America* (six parts, 14 vols. and supplement). The *Raccolta* remains the single best source of documents for Columbian research.

Documents on the early life of Columbus are preserved in the archives of the city of Genoa and also in its notarial archives. Some of these documents have been published by the city in Italian, German, and English editions. The earliest manuscript biography of the Admiral, by Hernán Pérez de Oliva (1531), is in the Yale University Library.

Correspondence between Columbus and Paolo dal Pozzo Toscanelli can be found in the Biblioteca Colombina in Seville.

The diaries of the four voyages are the focus of most Columbian research. The journal of the first voyage is based on an abstract by Las Casas, *El libro de la primera navegación,* which is in the Biblioteca Nacional, Madrid. Columbus's synoptic report to the Spanish Crown has survived only as a printed document, the earliest copy being in the New York Public Library. No original or abstract exists for the second voyage, thus forcing historians and commentators to reconstruct the voyage mainly from letters by Michele da Cuneo, a Latin summation by Nicolo Syllacio, and the observations of Fernando Colón. The journal of the third voyage depends on an abstract by Las Casas; the original manuscript is in the library of the Real Academia de la Historia in Madrid. Columbus's summary report to the Crown was copied by Las Casas and is in the Biblioteca Nacional, Madrid. The fourth or "high" voyage was abstracted by Las Casas in his *Historia de las Indias* and is also recounted by Fernando Colón in *Historie del S. D. Fernando Colombo.* The Royal Instructions for the voyage were copied by Columbus in his Libro de Privilegios (Book of privileges), which is in the library of the Real Academia de la Historia. The Archivo de Simancas preserves a copy of the muster and payroll for the fourth voyage.

The Archivo General de Indias, Seville, retains the Pleitos Colombinos (in the section of the Patronato), which are a rich source of corroborative material regarding the voyages and the claims of discovery. The texts of these lawsuits brought by and against Columbus and his heirs have been published at various times, but their accuracy is frequently held in question by scholars. Holograph documents of major importance can also be found in the archives as part of the collection of the Casa de la Contratación; pertinent documents are also in the section Indiferente General.

The Archivo General de Protocols, Seville, has two original Columbus documents and many others pertaining to relatives and crew members; it is an important depository of primary sources.

The Archivo de la Casa de Alba, Madrid, contains many significant documents, especially correspondence, on Columbus and his heirs. As is true with many other subjects, the archives of private families in Spain are rich and indispensable sources of history.

One of the best known and later works of Columbus, the Libro de las Profecías (Book of prophecies), is housed in the Biblioteca Colombina in Seville and a copy is at the Archivo Histórico Nacional, Madrid. As noted above, the Biblioteca Nacional has several essential documents in its section of reserved manuscripts.

Detailed citation of Columbian documents is an unusually complex matter because what is known about Columbus is taken from a composite of extant originals, early copies of original documents that have been lost, and printed abstracts of information once contained in the Columbus library as preserved and enriched by Fernando Colón. One is best advised to consult either the major compilation of documentary material in the *Raccolta* or the more reliable translations cited below.

After the surge of interest in Columbiana receded in the early twentieth century, attention was focused on archival lacunae and errors in publication. Alicia Bache Gould worked through much archival minutiae to develop her *Nueva lista documentada de los tripulantes de Colón* (Newly documented list of Columbus's crew). Her work has shown the need for even more careful synthesis of widely scattered data.

Most English-speaking scholars recognize the preeminent work of Samuel Eliot Morison, whose *Admiral of the Ocean Sea* remains the classic biography of Columbus. Morison's careful attention to documentary detail is seen in the first, two-volume edition (1942), and his publication of several key documents in *Journals and Other Documents* provides the English reader with a ready and reliable source of documentary information, since the paleography of sixteenth-century originals is uniformly difficult.

BIBLIOGRAPHY

Dunn, Oliver C., and James E. Kelly, Jr. *The* Diario *of Christopher Columbus's First Voyage to America, 1492–1493.* Norman, Okla., 1989.

Morison, Samuel Eliot. *Admiral of the Ocean Sea: A Life of Christopher Columbus.* 2 vols. Boston, 1942.

Morison, Samuel Eliot. *Journals and Other Documents on the Life and Voyages of Christopher Columbus.* New York, 1963.

Taviani, Paolo Emilio. *Christopher Columbus: The Grand Design.* London, 1985.

Varela, Consuelo. *Cristóbal Colón: Textos y documentos completos.* Madrid, 1984.

CHARLES W. POLZER

MUSLIMS IN SPAIN. The first Spaniards in the Americas were unlike other European Christians in one crucial respect: for more than seven hundred years their ancestors had lived near, with, or even as Muslims. Yet for the next century subsequent generations would gradually eliminate the physical presence of Muslims and any cultivation of their significance. Between the early seventeenth century and the end of World War II, this exclusion of the Muslim past from Spanish national identity came to dominate historical scholarship. As a result, the respective histories of Christians, Jews, and Muslims in Spain fell to three almost mutually exclusive sets of academic specialists.

However, Américo Castro's *España en su historia* (1948; English ed., *The Structure of Spanish History*, 1954) generated a debate that restructured the study of Spanish history for generations to come. In that work Castro insisted that modern Spanish identity was inconceivable without the centuries of interaction among Christians, Muslims, and Jews. Conversely, Claudio Sánchez-Albornoz, in *España: Un enigma histórico* (1956), described modern Spanish culture as essentially continuous with its pre-Islamic, that is, Roman or Visigothic, past. While late twentieth-century scholarship has mediated these extremes, it has leaned toward Castro, stressing the significance of intercommunal interaction while accounting for its changing patterns and structures with greater subtlety and precision. These changes occurred in three major phases.

During the first phase, from the eighth to the eleventh century, Muslims controlled most of the Iberian peninsula, assimilating much of the indigenous population to Islam and incorporating unconverted Jews and Christians as quasi-autonomous subject communities, while leaving Christians in control of a number of kingdoms in the far north. During this period, religious differences did not determine social relations.

Arab Muslims arrived in Egypt in the 630s and 640s, as others were expanding into Syria and Iran. By the beginning of the eighth century, this expansion had reached present-day Morocco, and most of North Africa's indigenous Berber peoples had become Muslim. In 711, a Berber-Arab army of about seven thousand, led by Tariq ibn Ziyad, landed near modern-day Gibraltar (Jebel Tariq), assisted by the flotilla of Count Julian, the Byzantine exarch of Ceuta. A few months later, a decisive defeat of the Visigothic king Roderick opened the way to rapid conquest. Within a year, Muslims controlled virtually everything south of the Duero and Ebro rivers. Although raiding across the Pyrenees continued after Charles Martel's victory at Poitiers (732), the Muslims, or Moros (Moors) as the Christians called them, made no effort to eliminate remaining Christian kingdoms south of the Pyrenees, to which a number of defeated Visigothic nobles had fled. Thus the anti-Muslim resistance that soon began in these kingdoms was led largely by Christians whose territory had never been conquered. For that reason, many scholars have accepted the concept of Reconquista as a subjective reality but not as an objective fact.

As early as 716, the Muslims were calling their territory "al-Andalus," a term that may have come from "Vandalicia," the Visigothic name for the peninsula's southernmost province. At first Berbers outnumbered Arabs; soon both groups constituted a minority of the Muslim population, which was increasingly made up of indigenous, Hispano-Roman converts (*musalima* or *muwalladun*). However, the spread of Arabic language and culture facilitated interaction and intermarriage among the various Muslim groups, unconverted Christians (Mozarabs), and Jews. The growth of bilingualism in Romance and Arabic promoted further cross-fertilization. An important symbol of this cultural fusion is the literary genre of the *muwashshah*, long Hebrew or Arabic poems that end with short passages in Romance, known as *kharjas*, the oldest poetic texts in any European vernacular.

Al-Andalus was administered by representatives of the Muslim caliph in the East until a refugee prince, Abd ar-Rahman I, established the Umayyad dynasty, which ruled until 1012. By the reign of the dynasty's most famous member, Abd ar-Rahman III an-Nasir (r. 912–961), al-Andalus was open to wider Muslim culture, to increased contact with Byzantium and Greek learning, and especially to the technological diffusion that the expansion of Islam had encouraged. Political, cultural, and economic interaction across religious frontiers was common, especially by Christians wanting to take advantage of the general superiority of Muslim culture in areas such as medicine. The last member of the Umayyad dynasty symbolized this intermixing in his nickname Sanchuelo, which derived from his maternal grandfather, the Christian king of Pamplona.

The second phase of changes occurred from the eleventh to the fifteenth century. Al-Andalus shrank substantially, yet Christians tended to treat subject Jews and Muslims (now known as Mudejares) along the lines Muslims had treated subject Jews and Christians, and bilingualism continued to promote important cross-cultural exchange.

When Umayyad rule ended, al-Andalus divided into a number of separate states, often known as Party Kingdoms. Simultaneously, the strength and quality of Christian leadership improved. In 1085, Alfonso VI of Castile occupied Toledo. The chief architect of the Reconquista, Alfonso VIII (r. 1158–1214), defeated a large Muslim army at Las Navas de Tolosa (1212) and thereby opened the way to rapid Christian advances. By 1248, Córdoba, Valencia, and Seville were also in Christian hands. The one major remaining Muslim kingdom, Granada, was ruled by the founder of the Nasrid dynasty, Muhammad I al-Ghalib (r. 1238–1273), who exchanged a tributary relationship with Castile for an independence that would last 250 years.

Despite these major changes in the balance of power, cultural boundaries remained porous and Muslims remained tolerated as a subject population, partly for practical reasons. Like Jews, Muslims performed occupa-

tional and economic functions that Christians did not, and without Muslim numbers the Christians could not populate and maintain the prosperity of their conquered territories. Some Muslims became Christians (conversos); others retained their identity, even as knowledge of Arabic declined, helped by the inspiration of Muslim Granada, where, in the last part of the fourteenth century, the Alhambra was completed, symbolizing efforts to preserve the best of Muslim culture from the threat of extinction.

Ironically, this state of affairs produced some of the most productive intercommunal exchange and some of the Muslims' greatest cultural achievements. Alfonso X, known as the King of the Three Religions, fostered collaborative learning. Raymond Lull (d. 1315), well-known Majorcan scholar and writer, knew Arabic better than Latin and was influenced by Sufism and the teachings of the Jewish philosopher Maimonides, who was in turn also influenced by Muslim thinkers. The Mudejares were responsible for a cultural synthesis, especially in architecture, that affected even areas like Aragón and Castile, which did not have direct contact with Muslims. Some craftsmen working in the Mudejar style were actually Christians.

The third phase of structural changes occurred from the fifteenth to the seventeenth century. During this period, religious affiliation began to define social relations. As religion emerged as the unifying factor among rival Christian leaders, intolerance of Muslims increased. Even when baptized and relocated, Muslims proved unassimilable. Increasingly the symbol of everything Christians were not, they were ultimately expelled.

The union of Aragón and Castile in 1469 led to the rapid conquest of remaining Muslim centers. Although the Granada capitulation treaty (1492) contained promises of continued religious tolerance for Muslims, now dubbed Moriscos (a pejorative form of Moros), pressure for their conversion grew. At first Christian leaders tried aggressive persuasion; however, when such measures as the public burning of Islamic books led to Morisco revolts, Christian leaders resorted to more forceful means. A 1501 decree gave Moriscos a choice between baptism and expulsion. At midcentury, even more extreme orders banned the use of Arabic, the wearing of Arab dress, and the covert practice of Islam, which was widespread. In the ensuing half-century, the presence of the Morisco nemesis helped harden Spanish Christian notions of religious and racial purity. In 1609, Philip III gave the final expulsion order, despite the major economic loss it entailed. During the next five years, an estimated 300,000 to 500,000 Moriscos left, some for France, some for Egypt or Constantinople, most for North Africa, where their incomplete assimilation has resulted in the partial survival of Andalusian culture.

Some, as corsairs, continued to affect Mediterranean affairs for years to come.

The Moriscos were not absorbed for many reasons. Granada's intransigence in its last decades had left Muslims suspect. As Spain committed more and more fighting men to the New World and at the same time attempted to become an imperial power, the Moriscos' identification with foreign Muslim enemies, such as the Ottomans, became increasingly threatening. In fact, the Moriscos did look to other Muslims for inspiration and support, both in their covert practice of Islam and their mounting of rebellions. For example, in their 1569 revolt, Granada Moriscos sought and received the help of the Ottoman governor of Algiers. Although knowledge of Arabic had declined sharply, the Moriscos cultivated their identity through Aljamiado literature, which they wrote in Romance using Arabic script. With Muslims viewed as racially alien as well as religiously disloyal, the intermarriage that had characterized earlier times became impossible. A higher birth-rate among Moriscos, partly the result of the increase of celibacy among Christians, may also have been threatening.

Nine hundred years of interaction had left Spain's "three histories" inextricably intertwined. Even in defeat, Muslim culture continued to exert its influence, as in Charles V's Renaissance palace in the Alhambra and the cathedral in the middle of the Great Mosque at Córdoba. Muslim culture, as absorbed by Spanish Christians, also indirectly influenced the New World in the form of family honor codes, home design, and the plateresque style of architecture. Romance and Spanish have been filled with Arabic loanwords, be they chemical, culinary, agricultural, technological, social, or scientific. Muslims introduced new crops, such as sugar cane, rice, cotton, and a number of fruits. Their wind-tower technology still heats and cools some Spanish homes, and their irrigation technologies still water some Spanish fields.

The significance of Islam for the Spaniards extended beyond Spain. When Spanish explorers happened upon the Americas, they were seeking a route to the Indian Ocean, where Muslim power was still increasing, so as to gain direct access to one of the world's most lucrative economic systems. By 1500, Muslims had rounded the Malay Peninsula and the northern coasts of Sumatra and Java and were pressing into the Moluccas and what became the Philippines. By the time Ferdinand Magellan

EXPULSION OF THE MUSLIMS FROM SPAIN. Drawing by Vincente Carducho.   MUSEO DEL PRADO

THE ALHAMBRA. Court of the Lions.   Spanish National Tourist Office

sailed across the Pacific from Mexico and arrived in the Philippines in 1521, conversions to Islam were increasing as far north as Manila. Muslim expansion into Southeast Asia was the result of the long-term, hemispheric political and economic changes that had brought them to al-Andalus in the first place. Likewise, the Spanish triumph in the Philippines, which reduced Muslims to a minority, was part of global political and economic changes that had begun with the Reconquista and were soon to displace the Ottomans in Europe and the Mediterranean. This connection between the geographical extremities of Islamic power is symbolized by the Spanish name for Muslims in the Philippines, Moros (Moors), the same name they had been given at home so long ago.

[See also *Granada; Ottoman Empire; Reconquista; Spain.*]

BIBLIOGRAPHY

Burns, Robert Ignatius. *Muslims, Christians, and Jews in the Crusader Kingdom of Valencia: Societies in Symbiosis.* Cambridge, 1985.

Cardaillac, Louis. *Morisques et Chrétiens: Un affrontement polémique (1492–1640).* Paris, 1977.

Castro, Américo. *The Spaniards: An Introduction to Their History.* Translated by Willard F. King and Selma Margaretten. Berkeley, Los Angeles, and London, 1971.

Chejne, Anwar G. *Islam and the West: The Moriscos, A Social and Cultural History.* Albany, 1983.

Glick, Thomas F. *Islamic and Christian Spain in the Early Middle Ages.* Princeton, 1979.

Gómez, Emilio Garcia. "Moorish Spain: The Golden Age of Cordoba and Granada." In *Islam and the Arab World,* edited by Bernard Lewis. New York, 1976.

Hess, Andrew C. *The Forgotten Frontier: A History of the Sixteenth-Century Ibero-African Frontier.* Chicago, 1978.

Jackson, Gabriel. *The Making of Medieval Spain.* New York, 1972.

McKendrick, Melveena. *The Horizon Concise History of Spain.* New York, 1972.

Watt, W. Montgomery, and Pierre Cachia. *A History of Islamic Spain.* Edinburgh, 1965.

Marilyn Robinson Waldman

MYTH OF COLUMBUS. The myth of Columbus portrays his life and accomplishments in simplistic terms, echoing the portrayals of heroes in classical mythology. The complexity of Columbus's character and the full historical context of his life and voyages are ignored in order to illustrate moral lessons about good and evil. Such portrayals are common in textbooks, but they have also appeared in books designed for adult audiences.

The myth of Columbus stems in part from incomplete historical evidence. Even if his life were fully documented, it is likely that some distortions would have occurred over time, simply because he was a transcendent historical character. As it is, parts of his life are well-documented despite the passage of five hundred years, and other parts remain obscure. Columbus himself wrote little about his background and consciously exaggerated his accomplishments as an adult, bitterly blaming others for the misfortunes and reverses he suffered. Both his bitterness and his exalted sense of his own worth have come down to us in the biography attributed to his second son, Fernando, and in the historical works of Bartolomé de las Casas, who had access to Columbus's family papers in the first half of the sixteenth century. The uneven availability of sound evidence plus distortions promulgated by Fernando and Las Casas have both contributed to the myth.

Of the dozens of misconceptions and distortions that characterize the mythic view of Columbus, only a few will be discussed here. One persistent misconception deals with his supposedly mysterious origins. Fernando's biography and many other sources contemporary with Columbus indicated that he was Genoese, and the few times Columbus mentioned his birthplace, he named Genoa. No one seemed to doubt it before the end of the seventeenth century. Nonetheless, from then on a series of writers claimed that Columbus was English, Spanish, Portuguese, Greek, or some other nationality. In the nineteenth century the notion surfaced that he and his family were of Jewish ancestry, wherever they originated. Columbus's own reticence and the scant documentation discovered for his early life encouraged these speculations.

In the late nineteenth century, however, Italian scholars uncovered a wealth of notarial documents and other papers that proved beyond a shadow of a doubt that Columbus's family was Genoese, originating in the mountains that formed part of the city's hinterland. Columbus was born in or near the city of Genoa, probably in mid-1451. His ancestors were Christian landowners, woolworkers, minor merchants, shopkeepers, and sometime participants in Genoa's volatile partisan politics. Although Fernando's biography went to great lengths to suggest that the family was quite distinguished socially and intellectually, nothing in the documentation supports that suggestion. In fact, the family's humble position in Genoese society may explain Columbus's reticence about it. He was highly ambitious for status, wealth, and fame; revealing his true origins would not have helped him achieve his ambitions.

Because the family owned land, and because Columbus's father held a few minor official posts in Genoa, it is highly likely that the family was Christian and always had been: Jews could neither own land nor hold official posts. Columbus's own writings emphasize his strong Christian beliefs and his sense of being chosen by God to advance the spread of Christianity. He urged Fernando and Isabel, the royal sponsors of his 1492 voyage, to bar Jews and Muslims from the lands he had claimed for Castile, and he suggested that they use the profits from those lands to finance the Christian recapture of Jerusalem from the Muslims of the Ottoman Empire. Despite the findings of scholars, the myth that Columbus's origins are shrouded in mystery and that he may have been of Jewish ancestry continues to appear.

Another myth—or set of myths—deals with the formulation of Columbus's great notion that one could reach Asia in the far east of the known world by sailing west. Fernando's biography emphasizes the scholarly sources for that idea: the academic geographers whose works were newly available in the late fifteenth century after Johannes Gutenberg's invention of movable type. He also mentioned his father's experience at sea and the tales told by other mariners and merchants, but his obvious aim was to portray his father as a scholar and an intellectual, not just a mariner. From Fernando's efforts comes the myth of Columbus the scientist and intellectual. By contrast, modern scholars generally agree that Columbus's experiences of Atlantic winds and currents planted the seeds for

his great notion, inspiring him to collect tales of possible lands to the west. Columbus went to sea as a teenager, eventually traveling over most of the Mediterranean and into the Atlantic on commercial voyages for various Genoese merchants. He found himself in Lisbon in 1476 and remained in Portugal and its Atlantic islands for nearly a decade, when he was not at sea. During that period, he probably continued as a seagoing merchant, battening on the contacts he retained with his Genoese homeland and with the Italian communities established in Portugal. Undoubtedly he traveled to the Atlantic islands belonging to both Portugal and Castile, West Africa, and the British Isles, and perhaps Iceland as well. In Portugal he married into an Italian-Portuguese family of some distinction; his wife's family had important mercantile, maritime, and political connections. During his Portuguese sojourn he formed the idea of sailing west to establish a shorter route to the markets of Asia, but his formulation may have had little to do with research. Scholars now think that he sought out academic sources only later, to improve the chances that his idea would find official acceptance and financial support.

At the opposite end of the spectrum from the myth of Columbus the intellectual and scientist is the anti-heroic myth that Columbus had some secret knowledge of what lay west of Europe in the Ocean Sea. Fernando's biography mentions various mariners who claimed to have seen land far to the west of Europe. From one of them, the argument goes, Columbus acquired certain knowledge that land could easily be reached by sailing westward from Europe. The success of his voyage was therefore a certainty, rather than an audacious gamble. Some modern authors have claimed that Viking voyages four centuries before Columbus produced maps of parts of North America. A few claim that Columbus had seen such a map, which provided him with proof that his notion would succeed, or even inspired the notion in the first place. In other words, they credit the Vikings not only with their own voyages in the eleventh century, but with inspiring Columbus's voyages in the fifteenth. Most scholars dismiss all supposed Viking maps as forgeries and argue that, first, even if they were authentic, the chances are very slim that Columbus could have known about them, and, second, if he had known about them, he would have sailed northwest rather than southwest to find the lands depicted. Even without maps, however, proponents of the myth of secret knowledge continue to argue that Columbus learned about the location of western lands from others, rather than formulating his notions independently.

Another set of heroic myths about Columbus deals with his search for support. The king of Portugal declined to sponsor him, presumably because the Portuguese were already pursuing an eastern sea-route to Asia toward the south around the African continent. Nonetheless, the king sent out a secret expedition to test Columbus's theory. In the heroic view of Columbus, his rejection and betrayal by the king of Portugal is usually presented as the first of a long series of trials in which he was unjustly denied and shamefully treated by nearly everyone he approached for support. Although there is some truth to such views, they still perpetuate a heroic myth about Columbus that distorts the historical record.

Seeking other royal sponsorship, Columbus moved to Spain in 1485, eventually persuading Queen Isabel of Castile and her consort, King Fernando of Aragón, to support his scheme. His long wait for royal backing and his repeated rejections by royal commissions are used in the heroic myth to show his perseverance in the face of ignorance and prejudice. In this view, Spain and its monarchs deserve almost no credit for the success of the 1492 voyage. Columbus did have to wait seven years before persuading the monarchs to support him. What the heroic myth ignores is that his geographical calculations of the size of the earth were quite wrong according to the best academic geographers of his day. It is hardly surprising that he failed to persuade them. Moreover, through the years that the Spanish monarchs kept Columbus in a state of frustrated anticipation, they provided him with several grants for his expenses, even when the royal treasury was dangerously strained by the war against Muslim Granada. When they finally agreed to sponsor his voyage, they did so despite the judgment of their expert advisers that his scheme was impractical.

Columbus embarked in 1492 in search of the famous markets of Asia and any other lands he might encounter along the way. Columbus's subsequent relations with the Spanish monarchs are distorted by a broad set of myths about his character and behavior that can fit either the heroic or the anti-heroic version of his life. Landing on an island in the Caribbean after a calm voyage of thirty-three days from the Canary Islands, he was sure he had arrived in Asia. He dubbed the local inhabitants "Indians," and the islands the "West Indies," assuming that he was somewhere in South Asia, west of the East Indies that Marco Polo had visited. Concerned with producing a profit to justify the support he had received, Columbus searched during the next several months for the rich ports of the Great Khan. Not finding them, he shifted his emphasis to a search for local trade goods and other commodities such as slaves that might be used to produce commercial profits in the immediate future. He also detained several natives against their will to take back to Spain, Christianize, and train as interpreters. The heroic myth of Columbus ignores the implications of these

actions and portrays him in one-dimensional terms as a daring explorer with only high-minded objectives.

Columbus was greeted as a hero upon returning to Spain and received substantial administrative responsibilities from the queen of Castile, in whose name he had claimed the islands. Within a few years, however, he proved incapable of carrying out those responsibilities, and the queen conferred them on others. Although the myth of Columbus blames Spanish ingratitude for his change of fortune, scholars have ample evidence to show that he brought his troubles on himself. Among other actions that turned the Crown against him, Columbus was eager to capture local inhabitants in the West Indies to sell as slaves. That was one of the easiest ways to turn a profit until the land could be developed. Despite strong sentiments by the Crown that slave-taking could only be justified in the context of a just war, Columbus continued to take slaves in other circumstances. Coupled with his obvious inability to govern the Spanish colonies established in the islands, his actions led to his ignominious arrest and to the Crown's withdrawal of his administrative duties. Personally, however, Columbus continued to enjoy honorable and friendly treatment from the monarchs, and he and his family grew rich from the offices and commercial privileges they held in the Indies. In the heroic myth of Columbus, his troubles with the Crown are blamed on the perfidy and greed of others, never on his own actions and flaws in character. Indeed, Columbus himself promulgated this interpretation in his letters to the Crown and in his subsequent legal battles to regain his titles and monopolies.

In all, Columbus made four voyages across the Atlantic, returning from the last in 1504, shortly before Queen Isabel died. By then the Crown had begun the process of colonizing the islands and bringing settlers under bureaucratic control, even as it continued to sponsor further exploration. Many individuals had been given royal approval for their expeditions, breaking the exclusive monopoly that had once been given to Columbus. Angry and disappointed, Columbus spent his last two years trying to regain all of the titles, offices, and privileges that had been withdrawn. He died in 1506, wealthy and still possessing many honorific and financial rewards, but embittered nonetheless.

The anti-heroic myth of Columbus sees only the negative sides to his character and his actions in the Western Hemisphere. In this portrait, Columbus emerges as an insensitive and brutal slaver, interested only in gold, who began the destruction of indigenous societies in the Caribbean by waging a genocidal war against the native peoples. To writers appalled by the destruction of native societies that followed in the wake of European expansion, Columbus stands as the first evil example of the European conqueror.

Not surprisingly, the interpretation favored by scholars relies on all the documentary evidence available and produces a view that avoids simplistic conclusions of every stripe. Columbus was not only a skilled mariner, master salesman, and daring explorer, but also an inept and arrogant administrator, and a merchant whose conscience was not troubled by taking and selling slaves. Columbus worked tirelessly to enhance the wealth and status of his family, but he was also a religious visionary who dreamed of recapturing Jerusalem for the glory of Christianity. In many ways he was a figure larger than life, whose reality lies somewhere between the heroic and the anti-heroic myths that have formed around him. Nonetheless, because of the far-reaching consequences of his voyages and the general human trait to seek simple explanations for complex reality, the mythic views of Columbus seem likely to continue.

[For detailed discussion of Columbus's life and works, see the various articles under *Columbus, Christopher*.]

BIBLIOGRAPHY

Books that Promote Simplistic Heroic Myths about Columbus

Columbus, Ferdinand. *The Life of the Admiral Christopher Columbus*. Translated by Benjamin Keen. New Brunswick, 1959.

Irving, Washington. *The Life and Voyages of Christopher Columbus*. 1828. Edited by John Harmon McElroy. Reprint, Boston, 1981.

Las Casas, Bartolomé de. *Historia de las Indias*. 3 vols. Edited by Agustín Millares Carló. Mexico City, 1951.

Books that Promote a Balanced Interpretation of Columbus

Ballesteros Beretta, Antonio. *Cristóbal Colón y el descubrimiento de América*. 2 vols. Barcelona, 1945.

Heers, Jacques. *Christophe Colomb*. Paris, 1981.

Taviani, Paolo Emilio. *Christopher Columbus: The Grand Design*. Translated by William Weaver. London, 1985.

Winsor, Justin. *Christopher Columbus and How He Received and Imparted the Spirit of Discovery*. Boston, 1892.

CARLA RAHN PHILLIPS

N

NAMING OF AMERICA. See *America, Naming of.*

NAPLES. The Kingdom of Naples grew from the early twelfth-century Norman conquests of Byzantine, Lombard, and Muslim lands in southern Italy and Sicily to become one of the great powers of Renaissance Italy. Limited to the lower third of the Italian mainland by the revolt of Sicily in the Sicilian Vespers of 1282, the Kingdom of Naples itself became the object of Angevin-Aragonese dynastic rivals in the late Middle Ages and continued to be fought over by their French and Spanish heirs after the 1494 invasion of Italy. With the Spanish victory and viceroyalty established by 1503 in neat parallel with the Spanish conquests in the New World, the Kingdom of Naples remained under Spanish rule through the sixteenth and seventeenth centuries.

The fluctuating fortunes of Neapolitan political history had already become a commonplace by the time of the Spanish conquest. In *The Prince,* Niccolò Machiavelli used Naples and Milan as examples of newly acquired principalities to be tamed; and in *The Discourses,* he argued that the Kingdom of Naples, typical of a state without equality, was incapable of establishing a republic. In his *History of Italy,* Francesco Guicciardini combined his themes of internecine quarrels and princely caprice in the Italian states with the standard portrait of an ineffectual and division-riven Kingdom of Naples. He coined an inverted aphorism to characterize the 1494 fall of Naples: "The French king—beyond the example even of Julius Caesar—first conquered, then saw." Even after three-quarters of a century of Spanish rule, the Venetian ambassador in 1580 still portrayed the Kingdom of Naples with its "frequent and turbulent revolutions" as the prime exemplar of "the various and marvelous mutations of states and governments which are diversely represented in history." Despite being "put in perpetual bondage so many times by its enemies," Naples was uniquely capable of transforming itself from conquered to conqueror, "always boasting liberty and dominion equal to the greatness of these same enemies."

Unstable political formations reflected the internal organization of a kingdom fractured by a factious feudal nobility whose agricultural interests allied them with foreign merchants and inhibited communal towns from developing native commerce and industry. The feuding local nobility maintained its regional power based largely upon the profits of raw agricultural exports shipped by Tuscan, Venetian, Catalan, and Genoese merchants to northern Italian cities. In the fifteenth century, the Adriatic ports of Manfredonia, Barletta, and Bari provided the chief products, olive oil, wheat, and wool, while the city of Naples continued to be an important port for silk exports, textile and metal imports, and products exchanged in western Mediterranean trade. Caught between foreign mercantile expansion and native baronial domination of the provincial communes, the kingdom remained compartmentalized into regional, unarticulated markets and dependent upon foreign investment and foreign demand, ripe for foreign intervention and conquest.

Population growth exacerbated the problem of the lack of economic integration. In the sixteenth century, the kingdom's population doubled from about 1.3 million inhabitants to 2.5 million. And no division better exemplifies the extremes found in the kingdom than the dichotomy between capital city and countryside. The capital city of Naples, with over 100,000 inhabitants in 1500, grew to be the largest city in western Europe, with 250,000 inhabitants at the end of the sixteenth century. At the same time, no city in the kingdom's twelve provinces numbered more than 20,000 during this period. From the late Middle Ages, then, the city of Naples was the unique cosmopolis of a rural kingdom, and the resident Angevin and Aragonese courts provided a brilliant cultural life for its teeming population.

The Angevin dynasty of Naples (1268–1435) came to the kingdom through papal invitation after the defeat of Frederick II, his son Manfred, and the Hohenstaufens. Before the 1348 plague, Angevin Naples basked in the Guelph sun of banking, financial, and commercial interests. King Robert (1309–1343) was a patron of Petrarch and of the young Boccaccio, who lived, worked, and studied in Naples from the age of fourteen to twenty-seven between 1327 and 1341. Since this cadet French dynasty owed its investiture to the pope, it attempted to solidify its claims in the kingdom by granting new titles and ever-greater privileges to the increasingly independent native nobility. Baronial antagonism erupted in civil wars that racked the kingdom during the reign of the last of the Neapolitan Angevins, the childless Queen Giovanna II (1414–1435). From her death in 1435, her Angevin heir, René of Anjou, fought over the Kingdom of Naples with Alfonso V, king of Aragón and Sicily since 1416, who was attempting to create an empire in the western Mediterranean, often at the expense of the Genoese.

Alfonso (1443–1458) successfully conquered Naples in 1443 and established himself as one of the most able rulers and generous patrons of fifteenth-century Italy. He forged diplomatic ties with Milan, repaired quarrels with the papacy, but adamantly maintained aggressive action against the rival Genoese, who were driven further into the pro-Angevin French camp. Alfonso's literary and humanist patronage, which gained him the title of "the Magnanimous," fostered a court of talented humanists including such long-term residents as Panormita, Lorenzo Valla, Bartolomeo Facio, Giannozzo Manetti, and Giovanni Pontano.

Alfonso's illegitimate son and successor in Naples, Ferrante (1458–1494), continued such patronage, but shifted his cultural largesse to vernacular works, music, and law in accordance with personal interest and contemporary exigencies. Ferrante employed all the propaganda skills of the humanist movement in order to combat the interminable opposition from René and Jean of Anjou (the Angevin claimants to Naples), from Genoese and papal resistance to Catalan-Aragonese pretensions in the Tyrrhenian Sea, from two revolts by local baronial factions aligned to the Angevin French forces, and from the Ottoman Turkish threat after the occupation of Otranto in 1480–1481. Influenced by the late fifteenth-century crisis in Naples, Neapolitan humanist literature was characterized by realistic examination of the role of fortune and *virtù* (ingenuity or ability) and the uncertainty of military

action and dedicated itself to princely values intent upon overcoming internal and external political threats. (Christopher Columbus, according to his son Fernando's *Life*, is reputed to have been in command of a corsair ship in the service of René of Anjou during this period, possibly in 1472–1473.)

The French invasions of Italy in 1494 marked the end of an independent Neapolitan dynasty. First conquered by Charles VIII of France and then fought over by French and Spanish troops in the last decade of the fifteenth century, Naples became the proving ground for numerous military innovations championed by the victorious Spanish general, Gonzalo Fernández de Córdoba, the Great Captain. Among the poignant stories of the French invasions, none strikes more deeply than the faithful service of the great Neapolitan poet Jacopo Sannazaro to the last Aragonese king, Federico (1496–1502), in French exile.

Naples emerged from the wars as a cornerstone in the Spanish imperial system in Italy. The Spanish conquest of Naples subordinated the independent nobles' pretensions to the Crown, erected a bulwark against Turkish and French invasions, and established a bureaucratic government that further elaborated the long tradition of Neapolitan law. The Viceroy Pedro de Toledo (1532–1553) is credited with giving Naples its definitive Spanish character as well as solidifying an alliance with Tuscany through the marriage of his daughter Eleonora to Cosimo I, duke of Florence. Finally, in an irony of history typical of the inversions of fortune in Naples, the Aragonese dynasty's most hated Italian enemies, the Genoese, eventually became bankers to the Spanish Crown in the sixteenth century and, thus, indirectly conquered the Kingdom of Naples through trade and finance.

BIBLIOGRAPHY

Abulafia, David. *The Two Italies: Economic Relations between the Norman Kingdom of Sicily and the Northern Communes.* Cambridge, 1977.

Bentley, Jerry H. *Politics and Culture in Renaissance Naples.* Princeton, 1987.

Calabria, Antonio, and John A. Marino, eds. and trans. *Good Government in Spanish Naples.* New York and Bern, 1990.

Croce, Benedetto. *History of the Kingdom of Naples.* Translated by Frances Frenaye. Chicago, 1970.

Ryder, Alan. *The Kingdom of Naples under Alfonso the Magnanimous: The Making of a Modern State.* Oxford, 1976.

JOHN A. MARINO

NARVÁEZ, PÁNFILO DE (1470?–1528), Spanish conquistador. Born either in Valladolid or Cuellar, Narváez came to the New World looking for adventure. By 1509 he commanded a company of archers in the conquest of

Jamaica. Tall, bearded, affable, and hearty, with a deep, booming voice, Narváez was invited to join his old friend Diego Velázquez de León in the conquest of Cuba in 1513. His company of battle-hardened veterans cut a bloody swath through the island, so sickening the chaplain, Bartolomé de las Casas, that he abandoned the army with a holy curse on his lips, later writing that Narváez himself had killed two thousand Indians in the gruesome slaughter. For his efforts Narváez received rich grants of land and Indians to serve his whims. His wealth grew even more when he married a rich widow, María de Valenzuela.

In 1520 Velázquez sent him to the mainland to arrest the insubordinate Hernando Cortés. On May 27, after weeks of fruitless negotiation, the outnumbered army of Cortés infiltrated the Narváez encampment at Cempoala (near present-day Vera Cruz) in a brilliant and daring night attack. Narváez himself was badly wounded and lost an eye, and his entire army was captured. Most of his men joined Cortés for a renewed march on the Aztec capital, Tenochtitlán, but Narváez was imprisoned and later returned to Spain.

His phenomenal success in Cuba, where the royal share of profit from the gold mines added immense sums to the Spanish treasury, gave Narváez easy access to the king. In 1527 he returned once more to the New World, this time with an army, a fleet, and a royal grant allowing him to explore, settle, and govern Florida. But, unnerved by the harrowing Atlantic voyage, a fourth of his army deserted when the fleet made its first stop at Santo Domingo. Other losses followed, but Narváez finally managed to land his forces near Tampa Bay on April 14, 1528, where he took possession in the name of the Spanish king.

Foolishly sending his fleet away, Narváez marched his men north and west to the supposedly rich town of Apalache. Here they found a hostile reception in a miserable little village. After several more weeks of fruitless marching through dense forests and disease-ridden swamps, Narváez ordered his men to build boats for an attempt to reach Mexico. Short of food, the men slaughtered and ate their horses, turning the hides into water containers and fashioning tools from the spurs, bits, and stirrups. One way and another, Narváez and his men constructed five bargelike vessels. With about fifty men in each boat they set off along the coast on September 22, 1528. The water bottles rotted almost immediately and food quickly ran out. In about a month they passed the mouth of the Mississippi, but two of the boats were lost. Desperate and hungry, Narváez told his men to fend for themselves as best they could, sailed off, and was lost in the waters of the Gulf of Mexico. The others landed, and four survivors, including Alvar Núñez Cabeza de Vaca, eventually made their way across the continent and back to Mexico.

BIBLIOGRAPHY

Davenport, Harbert, ed. "The Expedition of Pánfilo de Narváez, by Gonzalo Fernández de Oviedo." *Southwestern Historical Quarterly* 27 (1923).

Goodwyn, Frank. "Pánfilo de Narváez, a Character Study of the First Spanish Leader to Land an Expedition to Texas," *Hispanic American Historical Review* 29 (1949).

Hallenbeck, Cleve. *Alvar Núñez Cabeza de Vaca: The Journey and Route of the First European to Cross the Continent of North America.* Glendale, Calif., 1940.

Vigil, Ralph H. "A Reappraisal of the Expedition of Pánfilo de Narváez to Mexico in 1520." *Revista de Historia de America,* nos. 77–78 (1974).

HARRY KELSEY

NAUTICAL CHARTS. Despite the inclusion of nautical information in a few world maps and in some maps of islands, the only charts effectively used by sailors in the decades before Columbus's first voyage to the Western Hemisphere are of two types: those now known as portolan charts and the earliest plane charts produced by Portuguese hydrographers. The name portolan chart is derived from the name for written sailing directions *(portolani)*. Used in the Mediterranean from the late thirteenth century, these charts are distinguished from other medieval and Renaissance maps by the remarkable accuracy with which the regions are shown. These manuscripts, drawn in ink on vellum, divide into two groups: small atlases, each with openings devoted to a particular maritime basin, and large, single charts of the Mediterranean and the Black seas.

The portolan charts were true navigational instruments and, regardless of when they were drawn, exhibit similar characteristics. Their most prominent feature is the network of rhumb lines *(marteloio)* on which they are constructed. This complex system of straight lines spreads out from the center of a circle or from several implicit circles, placed side by side. The lines represent the thirty-two directions of the wind rose, each wind distinguished by color. Black represents the eight main winds; green, the half winds; and red, the quarter winds.

A second prominent characteristic is the scale, present in all these charts. Normally, the scale's large divisions are subdivided into five parts; the value of these parts, known to the users, was indicated only in the late examples. A third characteristic is the profusion of place-names, written perpendicular to the coastlines in the interior of the land masses. These place-names—written in black or red, according to their importance—identify the ports, havens, capes, reefs, bays, and promontories that the sailor needed to know. The principal, though not exclusive, concern of these charts is the outline of the coast. Inlets,

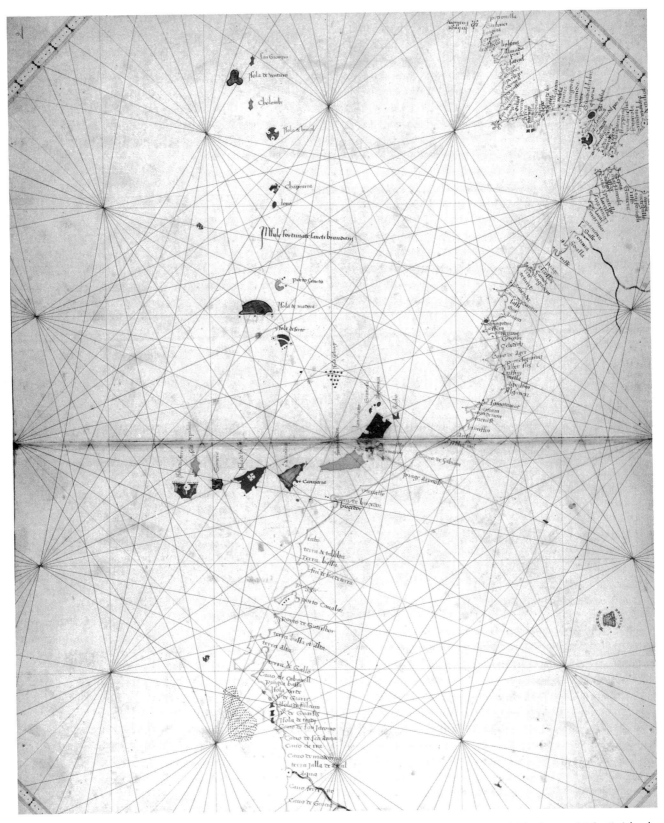

NAUTICAL CHART BY GRAZIOSO BENINCASA, 1467. Showing the Iberian and West African coasts, the Strait of Gibraltar, and Atlantic islands.

promontories, and estuaries are emphasized. Reefs are indicated by small crosses, sandbanks and shallows by dots, and islands and deltas by color.

Surviving examples indicate that these charts were owned mainly by princes and scholars, who influenced their geopolitical, theoretical, and religious content. However, these charts were originally intended for and developed by seamen. They reflect a specific navigational technique, dead reckoning, which was still in use at the time of Columbus. Essentially, this technique depends on the mariner's knowledge of the course set and the distance run, to which, respectively, the *marteloio* and the scale correspond. To effect a cross-sea route, the user would open a pair of dividers on the chart with one point on the port of departure and the other on the destination. He then looked for the closest parallel rhumb line, which showed the direction to follow. Since the chart had neither top nor bottom, the mariner could turn the chart in any direction he intended to sail and from which he would try not to deviate. If he lost his course, the mathematical tables, known as the *toleta de marteloio*, used since at least 1436, allowed the navigator to make the best use of the chart's network system in order to recover the course. Columbus's log book for the first voyage shows him trying to follow a constant course, guided by a magnetic compass, carefully measuring with a sandglass the distance run between each change of course, and scrupulously pricking off this distance on his charts, an operation that he calls *echar punto* or *cartear*.

At the end of the thirteenth century, merchants and explorers started to sail beyond the Mediterranean and to confront the unique problems of ocean navigation. Nautical charts began to take account of the nautical mile of a different value in the Atlantic and of the importance of the tides, which controlled the entry to and exit from harbors. The cartographic region was enlarged, and in the fifteenth century, charts were extended to the "Mediterranean Atlantic" between Madeira, the Azores, and the Canaries. Other Atlantic islands, both real (Cape Verde Islands) and imaginary (Antilia), were added, and, lastly, the West African coast beyond Cape Bojador, the southern limit of medieval navigation, was incorporated into the charts.

The addition of new lands, made at different times and using names that rarely agreed with other sources, has provoked endless controversies about the priority of one nation's discovery over another's and the anticipation by the charts of knowledge of a certain region before its documented discovery. For example, it has been claimed, though unconvincingly, that the island of Antilia, first identified on the 1424 Zuane Pizzigano chart, is a depiction of the most easterly part of the American continent. Such discussions obscure the more important aspects of the charts: the capacity of the rhumb-line system to be enlarged indefinitely allowed it to record, with remarkable confidence, the outline and respective position of newly attained lands. The empirical knowledge gained by seamen became known internationally, which is reflected in the charts' mixture of Latinate languages. Information concerning new discoveries consequently circulated rapidly, despite the official secrecy imposed by governments and merchant associations.

The Columbus brothers, particularly while in Lisbon, were apparently familiar with the most recent Portuguese discoveries and their incorporation into sea charts. Fernando Colón reports that Christopher Columbus had observed with interest charts belonging to his father-in-law, Bartolomeo Perestrelo, himself a navigator and erstwhile governor of Porto Santo. Most telling are the marginal annotations in books from Columbus's library, which reveal that Bartolomé Colón witnessed the return of Bartolomeu Dias to Lisbon and that he was aware of the *Carta navigationis* in which Dias recorded his voyage. Columbus himself noted the charts' inaccurate rendering of the length of the north-south journey from England to Guinea in comparison to positions established by a quadrant measuring solar altitude.

Having observed such discrepancies, Columbus showed his concern in correcting charts, for, like many sea officers in the fifteenth century, the Columbus brothers were chart makers. That they practiced this craft as a trade is, however, not certain, even during their stay in Seville. Nevertheless, both are said to have been talented draftsmen, and several documents, notably the logbooks and the accounts of the lawsuits against the Crown (the *Pleitos Colombinos*), reveal Columbus plotting the smallest of islands in a chart. His successors in the exploration of the American continent used the "charts that the Admiral had made, because he alone can make charts of all he discovered." At the end of the formal introduction to his journal of the first voyage, Columbus announces his intention "to make a new sea chart where he will place all the seas and the lands of the Ocean Sea in the places where they belong and under their winds."

Though none of the charts ascribed to the Columbus brothers carries their signatures, two of them merit special attention. The first, drawn on a relatively large scale and showing La Española (Hispaniola), is the sketch preserved in the collection of the dukes of Alba. This is a rare, if not unique, example of preparatory rough sketches for hydrographic use. By assembling several of them, the chart allows a far larger region to be drawn. The writing on this sketch is probably that of Columbus, and precise details given on the northwest coast of the island and the site of "Natividad" (La Navidad) suggest that it was drawn, at the latest, in the course of the second voyage, in December 1493.

The second is the anonymous chart preserved in the Bibliothèque Nationale, Paris. The attribution of this chart to Columbus is fraught with difficulties. However, this document is noteworthy as much for the maritime and commercial experience it illustrates as for its representation of the world. The same parchment, in effect, juxtaposes a portolan chart of the Atlantic with a tripartite *mappamundi*. The Atlantic portolan chart extends from Iceland to the mouth of the Congo River in Africa, with detailed commentaries near points on the coast that Columbus frequented after 1476. The *mappamundi*, on the other hand, is surrounded by celestial spheres (thereby displaying a geocentric universe) and shows Africa all the way to the Cape of Good Hope. Two maps in one, they share legends in Latin, the majority of them borrowed from Pierre d'Ailly's *Imago mundi*, a work central to the theoretical education of Columbus. This unusual linking of two types of maps recalls Columbus's own reference to his maps, "all of which also carry a sphere."

Except for the rough sketch drawn by the Admiral himself, the first nautical charts that incorporated hydrographic material from the voyages of Columbus are later than 1500. They are large manuscript planispheres that include first-hand documentation. One is Turkish and may owe its outline to a chart drawn in 1498. It was obtained from a companion of Columbus, who became a slave in the Ottoman fleet. Another, the oldest, is Spanish and was signed by Juan de la Cosa in 1500. Cosa was the cartographer of the second voyage, and he himself explored the Venezuelan coast in 1499. The other charts are Italian (Cantino, 1502; Caverio [Canerio], c. 1505), but they are copies of the *padrão real*, the official Portuguese chart. In light of the scale of these documents and their silence concerning specific areas, they give little information regarding Columbus's first landfall or the shape of the coast surveyed during the fourth voyage. Finally, contrary to the *mappaemundi*, they give only a slight hint of Columbus's conviction that he had reached Asia.

On the other hand, each of these documents is instructive regarding the difficulties encountered by the cartographers of this period, especially in the compilation of a new map of the entire world from discrete and disjointed individual surveys. Cartographers devised new solutions, which themselves generated other difficulties. The elements they had to contend with were magnetic variation, scale, and latitude. For example, Juan de la Cosa's map places the northern Bahamas at an excessively high latitude, and Jamaica, La Española, and Puerto Rico, which should be on the same parallel, are rotated fourteen degrees from the horizontal. There may be two explanations for this: the magnetic variation in the West Indies at this time and the use of two different scales—one for the

Old World, another for the New World—which made the islands too large to fit in their correct positions. In spite of these problems, Cosa's map accurately depicts the course of Columbus's second voyage. This may be seen by placing a straightedge on the map, connecting Ferro (Hierro) in the Canary Islands to Dominica in the West Indies; the straightedge will be parallel to the west-by-south rhumb line, as indicated by Columbus himself. The Cantino map, famous for being the first to show the Line of Demarcation, is equally important in the history of nautical charts for its accurate delineation of Africa. This accuracy results from the fact that from about 1485 Portuguese hydrographers had been sent to the African coast in order to measure solar altitude, or latitude, with a quadrant and thereby more precisely establish the positions of specific places.

The Caverio chart (c. 1505) was one of the first charts to show a latitude scale. The use of latitude measurements reflects an enormous step forward in the history of surveying space, but it conflicted with essential aspects of the portolan charts. For example, dead reckoning functions with magnetic north; the quadrant uses geographic north. In addition, when using the same length for one degree in any parallel of the chart, the dead-reckoning method does not take into account the convergence of meridians. Thus, this new type of nautical chart, which was to be called a plane chart, was difficult for navigators. Sailors tried to get around the problem by using two or more scales of latitude for different areas on the same chart.

In 1516, the Caverio chart was used by Martin Waldseemüller as a model for the first printed planisphere shaped as a nautical chart, the *Carta marina navigatoria Portugallen navigationes*, and meridians showing longitude appear on charts very soon after Magellan's circumnavigation. But neither printed charts nor longitude would be of any practical use for navigation or chart making for a long time.

[See also *Cartography; Dead Reckoning; Latitude; Longitude; Mappamundi; Sailing Directions.*]

BIBLIOGRAPHY

Campbell, Tony. "Portolan Charts from the Late Thirteenth Century to 1500." In vol. 1 of *The History of Cartography*, edited by J. B. Harley and David Woodward. Chicago and London, 1987.

Harrisse, Henry. *The Discovery of North America*. Paris, 1892. Reprint, Amsterdam, 1961.

Kelley, James E., Jr. "The Map of the Bahamas Implied by Chave's Derrotero. What Is Its Relevance to the First Landfall Question?" *Imago Mundi* 42 (1990): 26–45.

Martínez, Ricardo Cezero. "Aportación al estudio de la carta de Juan de la Cosa." In *Géographie du monde au moyen âge et à la Renaissance*, edited by Monique Pelletier. Paris, 1989.

Mollat du Jourdin, Michel, and Monique de la Roncière, with Marie-Madeleine Azard, Isabelle Raynaud-Nguyen, and Marie-Antoinette Vannerau. *Sea Charts of the Early Explorers.* Translated by L. le R. Dethan. New York, 1984.

Raynaud-Nguyen, Isabelle. "Les portulans: Textes et iconographie." *Iconographie médievale.* Paris, 1990.

Skelton, R. A. "The Cartography of Columbus' First Voyage." In *Journal of Christopher Columbus.* Translated by Cecil Jane. London, 1960.

ISABELLE RAYNAUD-NGUYEN
Translated from French by Mary Pedley

NAVIDAD, LA. See *Settlements,* article on *La Navidad.*

NAVIGATION. [This entry includes two articles that survey European technologies of navigation at the time of European overseas exploration and expansion:

Art, Practice, and Theory
Instruments of Navigation

For related general discussions of navigating at sea, see *Cartography; Shipbuilding; Tides and Currents; Weather and Wind.*]

Art, Practice, and Theory

Western nautical science based on measurement, rather than on traditional skills, originated in the Mediterranean, where by the end of the thirteenth century the navigator was in possession of the mariner's compass, systematically compiled sailing directions based on compass direction and estimated distance, and the portolan chart. Distance was estimated with the help of the timeglass, or running-glass, and a trigonometrical table or diagram, essentially solutions for a series of right-angle triangles, that told him how far he had been pushed off his intended course by headwinds and how to regain it. Mediterranean navigation, which developed rapidly during the thirteenth century in response to expansion of trade by Italian city-states with Egypt and the Levant and, to a lesser extent, the voyages of the Crusades, was essentially based on dead reckoning, the determination of position from the course and distance made good since the last known position. There was no means of fixing position offshore, but the Mediterranean seaman would seldom have been out of sight of land for more than a few days at a time, and although there are known currents the sea is virtually tideless and thus without tidal streams. Further, since both sailing directions and the chart were based on magnetic compass bearings, magnetic declination, or variation, was of no account, and, in a sea that stretches east and west over a narrow belt of latitude, neither was the convergence of the meridians toward the poles. In this special environment dead reckoning was developed to a fine art.

It was the Portuguese, during the fifteenth century, who developed and adapted Mediterranean methods of navigation to the more stringent demands of the open ocean and thus made the great European voyages of discovery possible. It was in Portugal, probably during the period 1478 to 1485, that Columbus acquired his knowledge of navigation.

On the Atlantic coasts of Europe a knowledge of the tides had been central to navigation, both to predict the depth of water within ports and harbors and to determine the direction and strength of the tidal stream that could so affect a passage. The assumption, acceptable within a narrow latitude belt, that meridians lay parallel to one another, became meaningless once latitude navigation had been introduced, for it became clear that an east-west course could carry a ship north or south of its intended latitude. Magnetic variation, too, became a problem on long voyages; positions defined by magnetic bearings on the chart often became irreconcilable with those obtained by astronomical observation.

The tides are of course caused by the attraction of the moon and, to a lesser extent, the far more distant sun on the waters of the earth. As long ago as the seventh century, Bede the Venerable had propounded his own theory of the tides and concluded, among other things, that although high water does not necessarily arrive simultaneously at all places on a meridian, it does occur at any one place when the moon is at the same position in the sky. The daily retardation of both the moon and the tides, which results from the fact that while the earth rotates on its axis once in twenty-four hours, the moon revolves counterclockwise around the earth (taking the high waters with it) in about thirty days, was accepted by Bede as forty-eight minutes. Seamen, however, were accustomed to telling the time at sea in terms of a compass bearing of the sun, so that each of the thirty-two points represented forty-five minutes, which was found to be a more convenient figure for the daily retardation of the tide. If they knew the time of high water at new moon they could thus use the compass rose to find the time of high water on any other day when the age of the moon, the time elapsed since new moon, was known. The "establishment of the port" at any place is the interval between the time the moon crosses the meridian and the time of high water. In early tide tables these values were expressed for different places in terms of compass directions, so that a phrase like "Flood tide, moon north-east, south-west" would mean that at new moon high water would occur three hours after the moon had crossed the midnight line and meridian. The lowest ebb would be six hours later and the following day the figures would be forty-five minutes later. To find the age of the moon the seaman needed to know the golden number (or prime), which he could deduce from the date, and that gave him the epact, from which he could calculate the moon's age by rote.

The earliest tidal diagram to survive is on the splendid Catalan atlas, dated 1375, attributed to Abraham Crescas and presented to the French court by the king of Aragón. It shows, in the form of a circular diagram and in terms of the eight named Mediterranean winds (directions were thus identified), the bearing of the moon at high and low water on the first day of new moon for a number of ports on the Atlantic seaboard. In the mid-sixteenth century, the Breton cartographer Guillaume Brouscon produced a handier form of tidal chartlet on which ports were linked with the appropriate bearings on the compass rose to show the establishment. Duarte Pacheco Pereira, the distinguished Portuguese pilot and contemporary of Columbus, devotes a chapter of his *Esmeraldo de situ orbis* (1505) to computing "the ebb and flow of the sea in the greater part of Spain and likewise in other regions where there are tides."

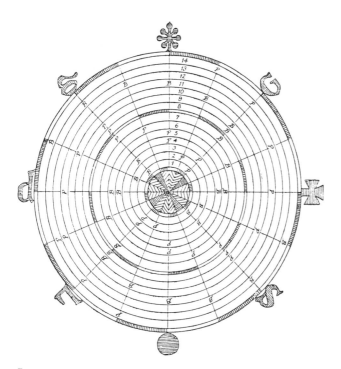

ESTABLISHMENT OF PORT. The earliest depiction of the establishment of port, from the Catalan Atlas of 1375. Bearings of the moon at high water (the *P*s) and low water (*B*s) are shown in terms of the winds for fourteen ports, identified by number. Number thirteen, for instance, is Sandwich; fourteen is the mouth of the Seine.

FROM E. G. R. TAYLOR, *THE HAVEN-FINDING ART*, LONDON, 1956

Navigators of the waters of the European continental shelf were clearly concerned with tides, the depth of water, and the nature of the sea bottom, samples of which could be brought up by a sounding lead armed with tallow. Pilot books, based on the accumulated experience of shipmasters and pilots, are of course as old as seafaring itself, and they reflect the navigational practice of their time and place. Thus the emphasis in the earliest surviving English "rutter" (from the French, *routier*), possibly dating from the fourteenth century, was all on tides and depths: "Upon Lizard there is great stones, as it were beans, and it is ragged stone. Upon Portland there is fair white sand and 24 fathoms," reads one passage; another, "A south moon maketh high water within Wight, and all the havens be full at west-south-west moon between Start and the Lizard." By contrast, Mediterranean pilot books emphasized direction and distances between coastal points. The earliest to survive, the *Compasso da navigare*, dating from between 1250 and 1260, is written in Italian and gives instructions, in terms of compass points and distance measured in Mediterranean miles (one Mediterranean mile equals five-sixths of the Roman mile), for navigating around the Mediterranean coasts eastward from Cape St. Vincent along the European shore and then along the African shore to Safi in Morocco; a bearing is then given between Safi and Cape St. Vincent. This last feature counters the idea that the early navigator was expected to cling to the coast, but such pilot books were nevertheless coastal in character as compared with later Iberian pilot books, which gave, for instance, lists of latitudes, tidal information, and sailing routes that took into account the ocean wind and current circulation. The *Compasso* distinguishes sixty-four directions, or rhumbs, arrived at by successively halving and rehalving the four quarters of the horizon, from which we can deduce that by then the magnetized needle must have been attached to the compass card. Directions in the Mediterranean were defined in terms of winds, which were named after their place of origin or character. There were eight named divisions, the four cardinal points, Tramontana (north), Mezzodi (south), Levante (east), and Ponente (west), and the four winds Greco, Scirocco, Garbino, and Maestro. Intermediate directions were named by combining the rhumbs, as, for example, "Tramonta a quarter wind Greco." The compass and wind roses on portolan charts, however, continued to show for the most part a sixteen-fold division. The division used in northern Europe, based on the four cardinal points, north, south, east, and west, proved less complicated and was adopted by the Portuguese and later the Spanish during the Age of Discovery.

The first written evidence for the existence of the mariner's compass dates from 1187, when Alexander Neckham, an English monk who lectured in the University of Paris, described how seamen, when the sun and stars were covered by clouds, used an iron needle magnetized by a piece of lodestone and floating in a bowl of water to indicate the direction of north. It is clear from the context, however, that when Neckham wrote the device had been in use for some time, and there is evidence from the changing pattern of trade in the last thirty years of the century that Genoese ships were already regularly sailing out of sight of land using the stone and needle technique. By the end of the thirteenth century, with the card attached to the needle, the compass had become a seagoing instrument indicating all directions all the time. There is no evidence that the magnetic compass was introduced to the Mediterranean by the Arabs or from China, as is sometimes held.

Whether sea charts in any recognizable form were used in antiquity is a matter of dispute; in any case, all knowledge of them seems to have been forgotten by the Middle Ages. The earliest extant reference to the chart is in the Latin account of a voyage made by King Louis IX of France from his new port of Aigues-Mortes to Tunis in 1250. The fleet was forced by heavy weather to seek shelter in Cagliari Bay, and to reassure the king he was shown the position on a sea chart (although the Latin chronicler calls it a *mappamundi*). The earliest surviving sea chart is the Carte Pisane, dated about 1290 and now in the Bibliothèque Nationale in Paris. It is clearly not the first portolan chart (a name taken from the port books or sailing directions from which, it may be assumed, the displayed information was derived, but it remains one of the most important documents in the history of navigation and deserves particular attention. Almost certainly of Genoese origin, it is drawn on an outstretched sheepskin, the neck (unusually) to the right. The coastline presents an astonishingly faithful representation of the shape of the Mediterranean. The chart carries no graticule, but a scale of miles is displayed in two places, each at a right angle to the other, presumably to take into account shrinkage. The portolan chart was indeed the first map of any kind to carry a scale, and for that reason alone is held to mark a turning point in the history of cartography. If one compares the Carte Pisane, for example, with a contemporary land map such as the Hereford world map, it is obvious that whereas the former is scientifically based, the latter is based on theology. The origins of the chart remain obscure and the problem of sources apparently intractable. But, as E. G. R. Taylor has pointed out, the nautical chart did not develop gradually but appeared suddenly, complete and excellent in all its essential features, which remained unaltered for over 250 years.

At the beginning of the thirteenth century the Hindu (Arabic) system of numerals was introduced to the West, largely through the influence of Leonardo of Pisa (Fibo-nacci). Arithmetic was thus brought within reach of the ordinary man, including the navigator. One of the most intriguing features of the Carte Pisane is the construction diagram by means of which the network of rhumbs showing direction was laid down, for it is based on Euclid's method of making a perpendicular and shows the clear intervention of a mathematician. The coastline will have been drawn from information collected by trading ships, from local pilot books, and no doubt from the sketches of the pilots themselves, and then transferred to the chart by the method of scale squares still used by draftsmen today. The portolan chart is not based on any projection, but tests on a number of charts in the British Library suggest that the network of rhumbs was laid down before the coastline. It is tempting to relate the Carte Pisane historically with the *Compasso da navigare*, but all we can be sure of is that some central authority must have been responsible for collating the work necessary for each, and that neither document would have been possible without the magnetic compass.

To navigate with the chart the pilot or master would join, say, his point of departure with his destination using a straight-edged rule and then with dividers (compasses) find the rhumb most closely parallel. Traced back to its parent rose, this rhumb would give him the course. A color code was used for the rhumbs: black or brown for the eight winds, green for the eight half winds, and red for the sixteen quarter winds. Distance run at sea was estimated by the master or pilot from their experience of the ship in different conditions, using the timeglass as a measure of time. (The common log was not introduced until the sixteenth century.) The experienced seaman would be able to estimate the speed of the ship fairly accurately, based on his seaman's eye and notes on previous passages in differing wind and sea conditions. Leeway, the angle between the ship's fore-and-aft line and the wake, would be added or subtracted from the course steered to derive the course made good; a line with a wooden block on the end was sometimes towed astern to indicate the leeway angle. Because a sailing vessel's course is governed by the wind direction and it is seldom possible to maintain the same course throughout the voyage, it was important to keep an accurate record of the courses made good and the distances run. Estimates were normally made every hour, and at the end of each watch, or perhaps once a day, the pilot would calculate from the record the ship's progress toward its destination. The Mediterranean seaman had access to a set of what were in effect trigonometrical tables, the *toleta de marteloio*, first referred to by the Catalan mathematician Ramon Lull late in the thirteenth century. The tables, similar in concept to the modern traverse table, told the pilot how far the ship had diverged from the intended track for each of the quarter winds in a quadrant, and how far he had progressed along the intended track. A second part of the table gave him the distance along each of the quarter winds he would have to sail to regain the intended track. By the middle of the thirteenth century mathematical navigation was sufficiently advanced for the tables to be used outside the Mediterranean, but there is no hard evidence that they were. When altitude navigation was introduced by the Portuguese, the rules for "raising a degree," by means of which distance run was deduced from the course made good and the change in the sun's altitude, took the place of the *toleta*.

Although pilots had steered by the sun and stars from time immemorial, there is no evidence that astronomical navigation, in the sense of fixing position through observation of the sun and stars, was used in the Mediterranean before the seventeenth century, nor, within the confined limits of latitude of that sea, can there have been much call for it. The accuracy of dead reckoning in the Mediterranean from early on can be gauged by comparing the coastal outline of the Carte Pisane, slewed round a point to correct for the easterly variation, with a modern map of the area.

In 1317 King Dinis of Portugal appointed as hereditary admiral of his fleet the Genoese Manuel Pessagno, who brought with him a number of seamen skilled in the use of Mediterranean methods. There can be no doubt that by the time of the discoveries Portuguese pilots and masters would have been thoroughly familiar with Mediterranean dead-reckoning techniques. However, once they had passed Cape Bojador in 1435, beyond which was supposed to lie the sea of darkness, the Portuguese explorers found dead reckoning less and less adequate as they proceeded southward along the Atlantic coast of Africa. In uncharted waters, an indication of position only in relation to last known position presented problems, and the errors were of course cumulative. However, the crucial issue became the return from the Guinea coast to Portugal, since the most expeditious route, it was soon established, involved taking a long leg westward into the Atlantic to cross the northeast trades and pick up the variables more or less in the latitude of the Azores, a voyage that could take over two months out of sight of land. The route back, termed the *volta del mar*, varied according to the season, the intended landfall, and the point of departure.

That there were people in Portugal capable of adapting astronomy to the needs of navigation is shown by early tables, such as the 1339 Almanac of Coimbra. It seems more likely, however, that the initiative in this innovation came from pilots, who would undoubtedly have noticed the difference in altitude of the North Star at Lisbon and in Guinea. Latitude is of course defined by the elevation of the polestar, but the procedures introduced by Portuguese pilots in the 1450s to check distance sailed in a north-south direction between two observations of the North Star had nothing to do with establishing latitude, which indeed was not then marked on charts. The difference in angle between the two observations was to be multiplied by 16⅔ to give the linear distance in leagues (a figure later changed to 17½, still an underestimate). Observations were made with the seaman's quadrant, a simplified version of the astronomer's instrument, and in the early days of altura navigation, as it was called, it became the practice to mark on the scale the names of the various capes, islands, and landmarks whose star altitudes had been observed. At the same time, astronomers at home were compiling lists of latitudes, which by 1473 had reached the equator. It should be emphasized, however, that until latitude navigation was introduced after 1485 (when João II's mathematical commission worked out the procedures), altura navigation did not involve concepts of latitude.

The North Star does not of course lie on the axis of the earth's rotation, the pole of the sky, but describes a small circle in its counterclockwise path about it. This means that a correction has to be made to the altitudes observed to allow for the star's position in relation to the true pole, a correction that can be ascertained by the position of the Guard Stars in the Little Dipper (Ursa Minor). A mnemonic, in the form of an imaginary figure in the sky with the pole at his stomach, his head above, feet below, and outstretched arms left and right, had been used by the medieval seaman to help him remember the midnight positions of the Guards throughout the year; the mnemonic would be used to tell the time by Polaris. A similar mnemonic was now adapted to give the navigator the correction to the altitude of the North Star, originally when it was at the height of the true pole (as it would be twice every twenty-four hours) and later at any one of eight positions on its circle of declination. An observation would be made on departure, typically at Lisbon, and a further observation two or three days later when the Guards were in the same position relative to the star. Later versions of the Regiment (rule) of the North Star, as the instructions were called, gave the corrections in degrees and fractions of a degree, principally for measuring departure altitudes from points other than Lisbon.

As the equator was approached and finally crossed, in 1471, observations of the North Star became impossible, and although procedures were worked out for observing one of the circumpolar stars in the Southern Cross, the obvious body for these observations was now the sun. The sun, however, in its apparent path around the earth follows the ecliptic, not the equinoctial, and a daily correction must therefore be made to its noonday altitude to allow for its declination, the angular distance north or

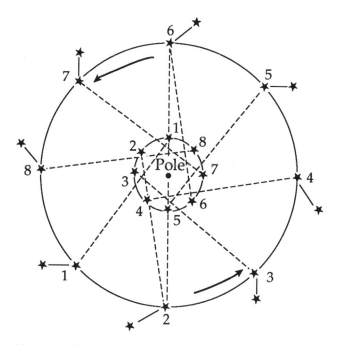

USE OF THE GUARD STARS. The relative positions of the two Guard Stars for different altitudes of the North Star.

JOURNAL OF THE INSTITUTE OF NAVIGATION, LONDON

south of the equator, or equinoctial. The practice had already developed of observing the sun to check linear distance traveled in a north-south direction, provided the observations were not more than a day or two apart—in other words, provided that the declination had not changed so as to significantly affect the result. Tables of the sun's declination had of course long been used by Iberian astronomer-astrologers, and in 1484 King João II of Portugal appointed a mathematical commission to look into the feasibility of using observations of the sun to determine latitude at sea. This was one of the most significant developments in the history of navigation and marks the foundation of positional astronomy. A leading member of the commission was José Vizinho, a Jewish scholar and former pupil of Abraham Zacuto. Vizinho, who had been a member of the commission that rejected Columbus's offer to the king of Portugal, was author, or perhaps editor, of the *Regimento do astrolabio e do quadrante*, the oldest surviving Portuguese navigation manual of which it seems likely hand-copies had been available to masters and pilots. Such copies would date from the 1480s, though the earliest known printed version is from 1509. The manual must have epitomized the conclusions of the mathematical commission and summarized the new navigational techniques. In 1485 Vizinho was sent on a voyage to Guinea (Columbus claims to have been on the same voyage) to test the practicability of the

procedures proposed for observing the sun and to check the values of declination from Zacuto's tables.

The surviving copy of the manual dating from 1509, known as the Manual of Munich, is in two parts, the second of which is a Portuguese translation of Johannes de Sacrobosco's treatise *De sphaera* (On the sphere), a thirteenth-century textbook on cosmography based on the *Almagest*. The first part contains instructions for determining latitude by the sun's meridian altitude, with seventeen examples differing according to whether the observer is north or south of the equator and whether the declination is north or south; rules for observing the North Star; rules for raising the pole (replacing the *toleta de marteloio*); a list of latitudes north of the equator; and a calendar for the year starting on March 1, with the sun's position within the signs of the zodiac and its daily declination. The next printed copy to survive, dating from circa 1519 and known as the manual of Evora, contains in addition rules for telling time by the North Star and instructions for finding the time of high water.

The rule for raising a degree became necessary when instead of sailing direct for a destination, the pilot would attempt to sail to a point one hundred leagues east or west of it and then sail along the altura (or latitude) to it. The rule, instead of dealing in terms of relative direction, as had the *toleta de marteloio*, told the pilot how far the ship must sail on each of the eight rhumbs to raise one degree and how far east or west it will have sailed in the process. The procedure at sea now became to observe the latitude daily, from sun or star, to record carefully the courses made good and estimated distances run, and to determine from the observed latitude and the mean course and distance sailed the distance made good east or west. It is possible that the introduction of latitude navigation, that is to say measurement of angular distance north or south of the equator, owed something to the publication about this time of Ptolemaic maps with a latitude scale. In any event, it quickly became apparent that, to get the full benefit of the new methods, latitude would have to be marked on the charts. This required a resurvey of the African coast based on dead reckoning and observed latitudes instead of on magnetic bearing and distance. In the 150 years following the doubling, or rounding, of Cape Bojador (1434), some three hundred miles of coastline had been surveyed each year, the results closely guarded in the Casa de India e Guinea in Lisbon, where the chief cosmographer to the king was responsible for keeping the master charts up to date and compiling sailing directions, almanacs, and manuals, as well as for training and certifying pilots.

The marine chart, to the seaman at least, was essentially a compass chart, on which the direction of the rhumbs corresponded with the rhumbs on his compass card. The compass was assumed to point true north, and, in spite of the convergence of the meridians, north-south lines on the chart were assumed to be parallel. Further, courses between points were assumed to be straight lines, not great circles. All this raised problems once a latitude scale was marked on the chart (the first was in 1502), for it became impossible to relate celestially observed latitudes with a chart based on bearing and distance. A solution attempted by the Portuguese cartographer Pedro Reinel on his 1504 chart of the North Atlantic was to provide an oblique meridian in the vicinity of Labrador to enable the seaman to reconcile his latitude with the direction of the coastline. But the seaman would have none of it; he expected the bearings on his chart to coincide with those on his compass. Columbus is credited with the first written mention of magnetic variation, but the language he uses ("northeasting" and "northwesting") is that of the Portuguese pilots, who could scarcely have failed to notice the phenomenon when they ran down the latitude to their destination. But it was little understood, was attributed to various causes, and its importance was underrated. It was not until 1538 that João de Castro would conclude that variation was not linked to longitude.

The sphericity of the earth had never been in doubt, and Sacrobosco's text printed in the navigation manuals gave a thorough description of it. But the plain chart still took no account of the fact that on a sphere north-south lines converge at the poles. In practice, however, pilots had to compensate for convergence; on the crossing from Brazil to the Cape of Good Hope, for example, it was the custom to increase the estimated distance sailed each day to compensate for chart error. Pedro Nunes, the Jewish mathematician and scholar who was cosmographer to the king of Portugal, in a tract in defense of the sea chart published in 1537, examined the problem of convergence and showed that on the sphere the direct line from one place to another is not a line of constant bearing, as it is on a plane surface. Rhumb lines, he showed, spiral toward the poles, but it was another fifty years before Gerardus Mercator published his world atlas on a projection that allowed the seaman to go on treating his rhumbs as straight lines.

There were numerous attempts in the early part of the sixteenth century to improve the instrumental accuracy of both the mariner's astrolabe, which was used largely for observations of the sun, and the seaman's quadrant; Nunes, in particular, applied his invention of the nonius (a contrivance for graduating mathematical instruments) to increase precision in reading the scale. It is difficult to assess the accuracy of either instrument at sea. The large astrolabe, such as the one Vasco da Gama used ashore at St. Helen's Bay in 1497, seems to have become at some point standard equipment for onshore observations, and

on that particular occasion it certainly proved its value. Of the instruments used at sea, smaller and generally of brass or bronze, all one can say with any certainty is that they proved accurate enough to enable the pilot to approach a destination on an east-west bearing so that he would eventually be able to identify landmarks. In 1499 Vasco da Gama brought back from the Indian Ocean the Arabic *kamal,* or *tavoletas de India,* as the Portuguese called it, a tablet of wood through which a knotted line was threaded and the tablet held, by means of the line, at a distance from the eye such that it just spans the space between the body observed and the horizon, thus giving the altitude. Pedro Álvares Cabral's pilot was charged with the mission of assessing the astrolabe, quadrant, and *kamal* on the first long voyage after Da Gama's return. His report on the *kamal* was unfavorable. However, another instrument based on the same principle, the forestaff, began to appear at sea in the early years of the sixteenth century. It was similar to but not identical with the Jacob's staff used by medieval surveyors and consisted of a wooden staff about a meter long with a movable crosspiece or transversal to measure the required angle of altitude. It seems to have been more popular with Spanish than with Portuguese seamen (except as used for measuring angular distances between the constellations), possibly because

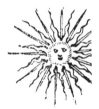

ORI ZONTE

OBSERVING THE SUN. With the mariner's astrolabe. Earliest known illustration, from Pedro de Medina's *Regimento de navigacion.*

NATIONAL MARITIME MUSEUM, GREENWICH

Nunes had condemned its use, perhaps because of the ocular parallax error.

The early years of the sixteenth century witnessed the climax of Portuguese navigational achievements, and the works of Pedro Nunes, João de Castro (the chief pilot of the Portuguese Indies fleet), and Duarte Pacheco Pereira, whose *Esmeraldo de situ orbis* (1505) remains the classic guide to navigation at the time, are fitting monuments. Portuguese understanding of the wind and current systems of the ocean had enabled them to sail with confidence into the Atlantic and round the Cape to India and the Far East, and their observations of the sun and stars laid the foundation of astronomical navigation at sea. Systematic surveys of the African coast using observed latitudes increased the reliability and usefulness of the sea chart. Less than ten years after Columbus had discovered America, the Catholic monarchs, Fernando and Isabel, aware that the fate of the Indies would ultimately depend on the skill of the pilots in the Indies fleet, in 1502 established in Seville the Casa de la Contratación, the principal functions of which were the training and certification of pilots, the maintenance of the Padron Real (a master chart of all the known seas), and the inspection and certification of navigational instruments. The key figure in this enterprise was the pilot major, and over the next fifty years the position was held by a succession of distinguished navigators, including Juan de la Cosa, Amerigo Vespucci, and Sebastian Cabot. In 1519 the post of chief hydrographer was created, and four years later that of cosmographer, who was responsible for the manufacture of charts and navigating instruments. The first hydrographer was the eminent Portuguese cartographer Diogo Ribeiro, who in 1525 introduced a marked improvement in survey techniques in which positions were charted by observed latitudes and magnetic bearings corrected for variation.

The invention of printing led to a greater dissemination of navigational knowledge, both in the wider circulation of navigation manuals and in the ability to reproduce exact copies of charts in large numbers. The *Compasso da navigare*, the thirteenth-century pilot book, was first printed in Venice in 1490, and a rutter of the European coasts attributed to Cadamosto was printed in the same year. Columbus's letter to his sovereigns on his return from the first voyage was printed in Spanish that April, and four further editions were published within a year. The almost total lack of navigational works printed in Portugal during most of the sixteenth century explains why Portuguese nautical science, once so jealously guarded, was now, during the period of Spanish colonial expansion, disseminated largely by Portuguese cartographers, pilots, and shipmasters employed abroad. The first navigation manual to be printed in Spanish, Fernández de Enciso's *Suma de geographia* (1518), which included sailing directions for American waters and which preserved the four-year solar declination tables prepared by Abraham Zacuto for Vasco da Gama's Indian voyage, was loosely based on a hand-copy of a work by the Portuguese Andres Pires. The second was an important work, *Tractado del esphera* (1535), by the Portuguese navigator Francisco Faleiro. With his brother Ruy, Faleiro had been closely involved with the navigational preparations for Magellan's circumnavigation. Pedro de Medina's *Arte de navegar* (1545) and Martin Cortés's *Breve compendio de la esfera e del arte de navegar* (1551) were both works of seminal importance to the development of navigation whose origins can be traced to the Portuguese manuals of Munich and Evora.

The problem of finding longitude would remain for another two hundred years, until the invention of the marine chronometer allowed time at sea to be treated as a measure of the earth's rotation. But there were attempts to solve the problem. Columbus twice, in 1494 and in 1504, observed lunar eclipses to this end using Zacuto's astronomical tables, but his objective was cosmographical rather than navigational. Vespucci claimed to have determined the longitude off the coast of Venezuela in 1499, but the claim is not generally credited. Magellan took with him instructions drawn up by Ruy Faleiro for determining longitude by lunar distances, and observations were made along the eastern seaboard of South America, but the results are not easily interpreted.

[See also *Altura Sailing; Dead Reckoning; Latitude; Longitude; Lunar Phenomena; Nautical Charts; Piloting; Solar Phenomena.*]

BIBLIOGRAPHY

Albuquerque, Luís de. *Astronomical Navigation.* Lisbon, 1988.

Albuquerque, Luís de. *Instruments of Navigation.* Lisbon, 1988.

Cortesão, Armando. *History of Portuguese Cartography.* 2 vols. Coimbra, 1969.

Da Costa, A. Fontoura. *A Marinharia dos descobrimentos.* Lisbon, 1933.

Hourani, G. F. *Arab Seafaring in the Indian Ocean in Ancient and Early Medieval Times.* Princeton, 1951.

Mota, Teixeira de. "Atlantic Winds and Ocean Currents in Portuguese Nautical Documents of the Sixteenth Century." *Proceedings of the Royal Society of Edinburgh,* section B, 23 (1972).

Pacheco Pereira, Duarte. *Esmeraldo de situ orbis.* Translated and edited by G. H. T. Kimble. London, 1937.

Randles, W. G. L. *Portuguese and Spanish Attempts to Measure Longitude in the 16th Century.* Coimbra, 1985.

Taylor, E. G. R. "The Navigating Manual of Columbus." *Journal of the Institute of Navigation* 5, no. 1 (1952): 42–54.

Taylor, E. G. R. *The Haven Finding Art: A History of Navigation from Odysseus to Captain Cook.* London, 1956.

Waters, David W. *The Rutters of the Sea.* New Haven and London, 1967.

Waters, David W. *Reflections upon Some Navigational and Hydrographic Problems of the XVth Century Related to the Voyage of Bartolomeu Dias, 1487–88.* Lisbon, 1988.

M. W. RICHEY

Instruments of Navigation

Navigation is an art and a craft as well as a science. People have regularly found their way across vast areas of sea without the benefit of any technological devices, using no other aids than their memory of traditional, codified star lore and local marine conditions, together with their own cumulative experience, as the Polynesians still did in very recent times. Even after the introduction of navigational instruments, seamanship still relied on the observation of winds and currents and other natural phenomena; as late as 1697, Martin Martin noted how the inhabitants of St. Kilda preferred to observe the direction of the flight of birds than to use a compass.

Very little is known about the practice of navigation in northern Europe and the Mediterranean region in early times. It may be inferred from Lucan's *Bellum civile* (A.D. 62 or 63) that observation of the stars in relation to the top of the mast and to the marine horizon was a navigational technique practiced in the Mediterranean. In addition to the polestar (at that time several degrees away from the celestial pole), Sirius, a bright star, may also have been important and may have been the original Stella Maris. Norse sagas refer to a *husanotra,* apparently a device used in navigation, but its nature and exact function remain unclear, as is the possible influence of the Northmen's open sea navigation in the North Atlantic upon that in more southerly latitudes. Most intentional sea voyages were coastal, only occasionally and briefly venturing out of sight of land. In northern Europe especially, the continental shelf and tidal waves encouraged the use of lead and line, probably the most ancient of navigational instruments. By the end of the thirteenth century, sailors on the Mediterranean could have used a chart, a magnetic compass, and sailing directions (written instructions for navigation in a particular area), and possibly a timeglass (sandglass). The Mediterranean is virtually tideless and there are many islands to provide stages or shelter during a voyage. To a large extent, sailing was concentrated during the summer months when the visibility was good and the sea tended to be calm. Sailing was by dead reckoning, that is, by attempting to determine the ship's position by calculation of the distance and direction traveled from the starting point. Directions were given in the sailing directions, according to the traditional wind directions, as winds, half-winds, or quarter-winds, and the

distance sailed was measured by estimating the ship's speed and relating it to the time elapsed from departure.

But the determination of position at sea is pointless if there is no geographical framework to which it can be related. In the case of a sea such as the Mediterranean, almost entirely surrounded by land, the need was for accurate mapping of the coasts and the ports. Charts (it is customary to refer to land maps as "maps," and to sea maps as "charts") showing a network of lines radiating from a compass rose and parallel lines enabled a navigator to set a course from a port on one coast of the Mediterranean to a port on the opposite coast, using his magnetic compass to help him steer the ship along, or close to, one of these "rhumb" lines. The introduction to the Mediterranean seafaring community, during the latter part of the twelfth and during the thirteenth centuries, of the magnetic compass and the chart is, perhaps, the first important impact of a wider science and technology on the practical, traditional, world of the seaman, but the details of its impact remain obscure. When, in 1377, Ibn Khaldun (b. Tunis 1332; d. Cairo 1406) prepared the *Muqaddima,* the prolegomena to his universal history, he described the Mediterranean chart and its use, but added that nothing similar existed for the "Surrounding Sea" (the Atlantic Ocean) and therefore ships did not enter that sea because, if they lost sight of shore, they would be unlikely to find their way back.

As the Portuguese found when they began to explore as far as Guinea along the west coast of Africa in the fifteenth century, the winds and currents in the ocean were such as to encourage them to sail back to Portugal in a large arc toward the west, rather than to return by their outward, coastal, route; this was known as the Guinea track and later as the Elmina track. From about 1460, when sailing in the Atlantic Ocean out of sight of land, they adopted an elementary form of astronomical navigation. As they sailed northward, the sailors observed the polestar, measuring its altitude with the aid of a quadrant; when its altitude matched that observed at Lisbon, they then had merely to sail due east in order to reach Lisbon. This simple idea was beset with problems: possible invisibility of the polestar because the sky was overcast, errors in keeping to the required course because of wind or rough seas, and the fact that the polestar was not then as close to the true celestial pole as it is today. This last problem was resolved by ingenious mnemonic diagrams *(rodas)* giving the altitudes of the polestar at successive positions in its apparent rotation about the true pole. To enable a similar procedure to be used in daylight, tables of the midday position of the sun (solar declination), called *regimentos,* were produced. The astronomical techniques required for oceanic navigation, such as "running down the latitude" described above, were gradually refined and generalized.

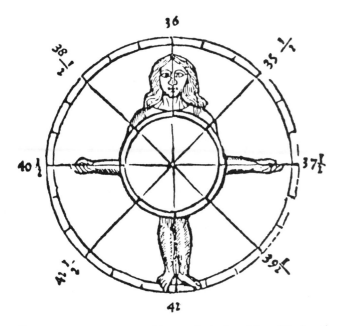

Roda das alturas do norte. Mnemonic device giving altitudes of the polestar at Lisbon. The head of the man represents north, and eight altitudes of the polestar on its circle of declination are given. From Valentim Fernandez's *Reportório dos tempos*, Lisbon, 1518.

When in 1497–1498 Vasco da Gama sailed around the Cape of Good Hope and by way of the east coast of Africa discovered, for Europeans, a sea-route to India, he took with him a number of quadrants and astrolabes, but we do not know whether the latter were traditional planispheric astrolabes or mariner's astrolabes. When he wished accurately to determine his latitude in the Bay of St. Helena, he set up his large astrolabe on land; this underlines the difficulty of using angular sighting instruments on the moving deck of a ship, a difficulty only partly overcome by averaging successive observations. At Malindi (present-day Kenya), Da Gama took on board a local, possibly Indian, navigator to guide him across the Indian Ocean; this navigator, no doubt fully cognizant of the traditional rutters in verse that were learned by heart, scorned Da Gama's instruments, saying that the only instrument used by his fellow navigators was a wooden tablet with a knotted string attached, now generally known as the *kamal*, an alternative approach to oceanic navigation despite the long tradition in Islamic lands of metal, angle-measuring instruments such as the astrolabe and the quadrant. In fact, any astronomer, Hellenistic or later, Islamic or European, from the time of Ptolemy of Alexandria (about A.D. 150) could have indicated to a mariner some form of altitude navigation, but the application of this knowledge required not only developments in cartography and its associated concepts, but also a

communication between astronomer and seaman that was rare in the early history of navigation. Other navigational problems that beset late medieval navigators venturing upon oceanic voyages were the varying magnetic declination (a magnetic needle, as in a marine compass, does not usually point to true geographical north because magnetic north lies to the east or west of true north and moves about over time) and the impossibility then of knowing longitude, the other coordinate apart from latitude required to determine a ship's position at sea. Magnetic variation was proposed by Edward Wright (1558–1615) in his preface to William Gilbert's *De magnete* (1600) as a means of determining longitude, and Galileo favored lunar distances, but it was the development of the marine chronometer that provided the practical solution. It was not until John Harrison constructed his chronometers in the mid-eighteenth century that this solution was achieved. However, the transportation of clocks for finding longitude (albeit on land) by comparing local time with standard time had been proposed as early as 1530 by Gemma Frisius in his *De principiis astronomicae et cosmographiae*, published at Louvain and Antwerp.

Accurate angular measurement, whether in the vertical plane (for solar and stellar observation) or in the horizontal (for azimuths), requires instruments. The few astronomical instruments and compasses available in the medieval period were not suited for use at sea on the deck of a moving vessel. From the end of the fifteenth century, adaptations of these instruments were devised for mariners. The *pilóto-mayor* (chief navigator) of the Casa de la Contratación (House of Commerce), founded in Seville in 1503, was charged, among other matters, with examining

THREE FIFTEENTH-CENTURY EQUINOCTIAL SUNDIALS. The middle example includes a compass needle. The instrument is oriented by use of its hour-ring and a compass.

MUSEUM OF THE HISTORY OF SCIENCE, OXFORD

and certifying instruments made by the navigators of the Casa. In 1523, it was found necessary to create the post of *cosmógrafo, maestro de hacer cartas, astrolabios y otros ingenios de navegación* (cosmographer, master of the manufacture of charts, astrolabes and other navigational devices). Practical navigators, therefore, were responsible for the supervision of the production and use of instruments, because in Spain, as in Portugal, the nature of the incentive to create an astronomical navigation and the absence of a nascent instrument-making industry resulted in the manufacture of nautical instruments remaining for some time in the hands of the practical navigators. In northern Europe, however, by the time the translation of Spanish nautical books brought astronomical navigation first to the Dutch and then to the English, specialist instrument-making workshops, which had proliferated for the manufacture of astrolabes, sundials, magnetic compasses, dividers, and other instruments for rich amateurs of science, land-travelers, surveyors, and mathematicians existed to fulfill the demand for navigational instruments and flourished from the latter part of the sixteenth century onward.

The voyages of Christopher Columbus occurred between the beginnings of the use of any reliable instrument in oceanic navigation and the serious attempts to improve upon this primitive situation, as when João de Castro tried an instrument *(estormento de sombras)* newly designed by Pedro Nunes in the course of his journey to Goa in 1538 (Armando Cortesão and Luís de Albuquerque, eds., *Obras completas de D. João de Castro*, vol. 1, Coimbra, 1968, pp. 115ff.). Columbus certainly used a quadrant, marine compasses, charts, timeglasses, log and line, lead and line, and probably portable sundials, and he had with him an "astrolabio" on the first voyage, but of what type remains unknown. All of these, with the exception of the quadrant and the astrolabe, formed part of a navigator's equipment from the beginning of the twelfth century onward. However, the mariners for whom *Le grand routier et pilotage* of Pierre Garcie (dated in May 1438; the earliest known printed edition dates only from 1521) was written had no chart, though it was assumed that they had lead and line and a compass. The quadrant, no doubt, was part of Columbus's Portuguese background, for despite his Genoese origins and his later association with the Spanish court, Columbus was a Portuguese navigator in training, experience, and exploratory aims. Evidence of this is found in the detailed analyses of his language by Consuelo Varela and by R. J. Penny.

[See also *Armillary Sphere; Astrolabe; Compass; Cross-Staff; Kamal; Lead and Line; Quadrant; Timeglass.*]

BIBLIOGRAPHY

Albuquerque, Luís de. "Astronomical Navigation" and "Instruments for Measuring Altitude and the Art of Navigation." In vol. 2 of *History of Portuguese Cartography*, edited by Armando Cortesão. Agrupamento de estudos de cartografia antiga, vol. 8. Coimbra, 1971.

Fontoura da Costa, A. *A marinharia dos descobrimentos*. 2d ed. Lisbon, 1939.

Godinho, Vitorino Magalhães. "Navegação oceánica e origens da náutica astronómica." Reprinted in vol. 1 of *Ensaios*, pp. 179–227. Lisbon, 1968.

Ife, B. W., ed. and trans. *Christopher Columbus. Journal of the First Voyage (Diario del primer viaje) 1492. Together with an Essay on Columbus's Language by R. J. Penny*. Warminster, 1990.

Maddison, Francis. *Medieval Scientific Instruments and the Development of Navigational Instruments in the XVth and XVIth Centuries*. Agrupamento de estudos de cartografia antiga, vol. 30. Coimbra, 1969.

Marcus, G. J. *The Conquest of the North Atlantic*. Woodbridge, Suffolk, 1980.

Poulle, Emmanuel. *Les conditions de la navigation astronomique au XVe siècle*. Agrupamento de estudos de cartografia antiga, vol. 27. Coimbra, 1969.

Taylor, E. G. R. *The Haven-Finding Art: A History of Navigation from Odysseus to Captain Cook*. Rev. ed. London, 1971.

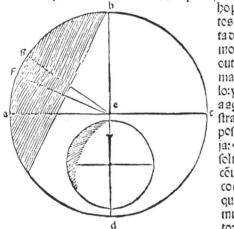

faber o que correram as fombras polla diftancia que ha a hum põ to firo: faremos noffa obferuação per efta arte. Tomaremos a altura do fol pello eftrelabio: e na lamina das fombras. a. b. c. d. que no centro. e. tem o eftilo perpendicular: notaremos o lugar da cir cúferencia que a fombra nos amoftra: o qual feja nefte entempo. ho põto. f. per quã tos graos fe apar ta do ponto. d. co mo faziamos no outro modo de to mar a altura do po lo: ymaginando q a agulha nos amo ftra ho meridiano pofto que affi nã fe ja: e fituaremos o fol no globo como cõuẽ: e dahi apou co efpaço de tẽpo é que a fombra faça mudança fenfiuel: tomaremos a to mar o fol pello eftrelabio: e notar outra vez o lugar da fombra q fe ja nõ ponto. g. e fituaremos feguda vez ho fol em feu lugar no glo bo: ou começãdo do meridiano jmaginario como ao princípio: ou

ESTORMENTO DE SOMBRAS. As illustrated and discussed in Pedro Nunes's *Tratado da sphera* (Lisbon, 1537). A horizontal plate, *a, b, c, d*, has an inset compass. In the center, at *e*, is a vertical style that casts a shadow of the sun on a scale of degrees around the circumference of the plate (the lines *ef* and *eg* show possible positions of the shadow). The compass has a south-pointing needle.

Turner, Anthony. *Early Scientific Instruments: 1400–1800.* London, 1987.

Varela, Consuelo, ed. *Cristóbal Colón: Textos y documentos completos. Relaciones de viajes, cartas y memoriales.* Madrid, 1982.

FRANCIS MADDISON

NEW SEVILLE. See *Settlements*, article on *Sevilla la Nueva.*

NIÑA. Columbus's favorite ship, *Niña*, was a caravel and smallest of the three ships of his first voyage of discovery. After *Santa María*, his flagship, was wrecked on a reef just off the northern coast of La Española on Christmas morning, 1492, he transferred to *Niña* and made her his flagship for the return voyage to Spain. Despite encountering two fierce storms en route, she safely carried him home with the triumphant, world-changing news of his historic discoveries. In an entry in his log on February 12, 1493, Columbus states, "If she had not been very staunch and well found, I fear we would have been lost."

On departure from Palos, Spain, on August 3, 1492, at the start of the first voyage, *Niña* sailed with the traditional lateen rig of most caravels. With their triangular sails gracefully set on long slanting yards, these sharp-ended, light-displacement caravels were fast, maneuverable, and capable of sailing close to the wind, making them relatively independent of the variable directions of coastal winds. Having earlier participated in Portuguese voyages of discovery along the Atlantic coast of Africa, Columbus knew of the prevailing east to west trade winds at the latitude of the Canary Islands, from which he planned to take his departure on a westerly course to the Indies. With the wind coming from astern, the triangular lateen sails were less effective and far more difficult to handle than square sails. Accordingly, on arrival at the Canary Islands, he converted *Niña* to a "carabela redonda," a class of ship with rigging similar to the *Pinta*'s, with square sails on mainmast and foremast but retaining the small lateen mizzen to help in retaining much of her ability to sail to windward.

A bowsprit, an unnecessary appendage with the lateen rig but an important adjunct to the square rig, was also installed to accommodate a headstay for the new foremast and the bowlines of both the foresail and mainsail. Bowlines were attached by means of a bridle at about the midpoint of the two vertical edges of the square sails and led as far forward as possible. The purpose of the bowlines, in conjunction with the tack lines, was to haul forward the leading edges of the two sails to both flatten and steady them to improve the ship's ability to sail as close as possible into the wind.

Niña's registered name was *Santa Clara* after the patron saint of Moguer where she had been constructed. Such religious names were typical of Spanish ships of the period. Also typical was her nickname *Niña*, the feminization of the name of her popular master and owner, Juan Niño of Moguer. As with all ships built prior to the seventeenth century, no original plans or even sketches of the *Niña* exist. More is known about *Niña* than about any other ship of the period, however. This is principally because of the *Libro de armadas*, a four-hundred-page bundle of handwritten documents discovered in the Archive of the Indies in Seville by Eugene Lyon in 1986. It records the complete bill of lading of *Niña* for her 1498 resupply voyage to the colony at Santo Domingo, capital of La Española. Lyon calculated this 1498 lading to be just over fifty-two tons. It also has been documented that on a commercial voyage to Rome in 1497, she carried a cargo of fifty-one tons. Michele da Cuneo, a Genoese nobleman who accompanied Columbus aboard *Niña* in the exploration of Cuba and Jamaica during the second voyage, recorded in his excellent historical account that *Niña* was "about 60 tons," a figure that probably reflects her maximum capacity. For the 1498 voyage, *Niña* had a small fourth mast, a lateen-rigged countermizzen, stepped on her stern aft of the mizzenmast.

The Portuguese *Livro nautico* is considered to be the best source of information on the dimensional proportions and general characteristics of a typical caravel of the Columbus period. Capt. José María Martinez–Hidalgo, Spain's foremost authority on Columbus's ships and former director of the Maritime Museum in Barcelona, bases his design of *Niña* on this source and uses ratios of 1 for beam, 2.4 for length of keel, and 3.33 for length of hull. Master shipwrights of the period would know from personal and inherited experience that to carry a cargo of no more than sixty tons, a ship of the caravel type should have roughly the following dimensions: beam, twenty-one feet; length of keel, fifty feet (21×2.4); length of hull, seventy feet (21×3.33); and draft of slightly less than six feet.

Contrary to a few reports that have been ridiculed by most maritime historians, *Niña* had a full-length main deck, which extended from bow to stern. Her sheer line forward was unbroken by any raised forecastle deck such as had been constructed on *Pinta*. Since *Niña* was still lateen-rigged when she left Palos, such an elevated structure at the bow would have obstructed the free movement of the lower end of her long slanting main yard from one side of the ship to the other. From *Niña*'s remarkable success at repeatedly surviving severe storms on each of her three voyages to the New World, it seems

MODEL OF *NIÑA*. By José María Martinez-Hidalgo.

MUSEU MARÍTIM DE BARCELONA

BIBLIOGRAPHY

Fonseca, Quirino da. *A Carvela Portuguesa.* 2 vols. Lisbon, 1973.
Martinez-Hidalgo, José Mariá. *Columbus' Ships.* Barre, Mass., 1966.

WILLIAM LEMOS

NIÑO, JUAN (fl. late 1400s), owner and master of *Niña*. Niño was a leading member of one of the most respected seafaring families of Moguer, all of whom were strong supporters of Columbus. Their social and economic status in Moguer was comparable to that of the Pinzón family in Palos. As with the Pinzóns, the willingness of the Niños to join Columbus in his effort to find the Indies by sailing west across the Mar Tenebroso (Dark Sea) strongly influenced local seamen to overcome their reluctance to sign on for such a dubious venture.

Eldest of three brothers who participated in the first voyage, Juan Niño owned *Niña* and sailed aboard her as master. The official name of his caravel was *Santa Clara*, but, as was customary, the ship was always referred to by her nickname, *Niña*. This use of the feminine form of the owner's family name was a typical reflection of the affection and respect in which Juan Niño was held by all with whom he sailed. He is reported to have been Columbus's favorite shipmate. It is easy to understand how such a relationship might have developed aboard *Niña* during her encounter with two fierce storms while homeward bound on the first voyage. Her survival was evidence of superb seamanship, to which the veteran Juan Niño undoubtedly contributed in full measure. As a demonstration of his respect, Columbus reportedly took Niño with him on the triumphant journey from Seville across Spain to the royal court in Barcelona at the conclusion of the first voyage.

Another incident that may have contributed to their mutual respect occurred in mid-October 1492. The crewmen of all three ships, having been at sea for two months since departing Palos, had given up hope of finding land to the west and had become fearful for their lives. Because of the incessant easterly winds prevailing in the ocean, the crewmen believed that if they went any farther to the west they could never make it back to Spain against the head winds they assumed would be opposing them. Niño is reported to have joined with the masters of the other two ships to report these fears to the Admiral. It is not recorded whether the three masters themselves shared that fear, but it was appropriate for them to make known to the fleet commander the concerns of the crews. The Admiral, attempting to assuage their anxiety, replied that God had given them these favorable winds and would give them other favorable winds to return. He then suggested

that she did not suffer from the absence of a raised forecastle. Like *Pinta*, however, she had a raised half deck aft of the mainmast.

Access to the hold was provided by two center-line hatches in the main deck. The main cargo hatch in the waist, just forward of the mainmast, was of a size such that a wine tun (barrel) of 1 meter by 1.5 meters could be lowered through it. A second smaller hatch was located aft under the half deck. Both hatches were fitted with covers to prevent heavy seas sweeping over the deck from pouring into the hold. Her hold was open from stem to stern with no watertight bulkheads to control flooding.

The excavation by the Institute of Nautical Archaeology during the 1980s of the remains of two discovery-era caravels wrecked by severe storms in the Caribbean, one on Molasses Reef in the Turks and Caicos islands and the other at Highborn Cay in the Bahamas, has provided important construction details not previously available. This new information, combined with documented rules of thumb used by shipwrights of the Age of Discovery, has made it possible to construct a more authentic replica of caravels of the period than could be done in the past.

that they might set a limit of three or four days and hold to the course they were following; if they did not sight land within that time, they could turn back if they wished. With this agreement they continued their voyage, and within that time they found land.

Niña was one of the twenty ships composing the armada of the second voyage, and Niño sailed again as her master, departing the Bay of Cádiz on September 25, 1493, only six months after returning from the first voyage. After their arrival, Columbus decided that, for his planned exploration of Cuba in the spring of 1494, he needed a fast, maneuverable caravel of shallow draft as his flagship rather than the large and cumbersome *Mariagalante* in which he had sailed from Spain. He chose his old favorite, *Niña*, and purchased her from Niño, who then decided to return to Spain in one of the ships being sent back for additional provisions. Regrettably, from that time onward, the historical record of this respected seafarer is blank.

BIBLIOGRAPHY

Gould, Alicia B. *Nueva lista documentada de los tripulantes de Colón en 1492.* Madrid, 1984.
Irving, Washington. *The Life and Voyages of Christopher Columbus and His Companions.* 3 vols. New York, 1849.

WILLIAM LEMOS

NIÑO, PERALONSO (fl. late 1400s), chief pilot of *Santa María.* Member of a respected seafaring family from Moguer, Niño was well known in the seaport region of Huelva, Moguer, and Palos and very helpful to Columbus in overcoming the initial refusal by seafaring men in the three villages to be led by this unknown foreigner who proposed to reach Cipangu (Japan) and Cathay (China) by sailing west across the Mar Tenebroso (Dark Sea). Although most of the official records of the second voyage have been lost, it is believed that Niño also accompanied the Admiral on the outward-bound portion of that voyage, returning to Spain with the fleet of Antonio de Torres on March 7, 1494. He next participated in a 1496 voyage of two caravels and a nao, which he commanded, laden with provisions for the colony at La Isabela, then capital of La Española.

Niño arrived there early in July and delivered a message from the Spanish sovereigns ordering that the capital be transferred from La Isabela on the north coast to a new colony to be established on the south coast, which became present-day Santo Domingo. He also delivered a letter from the Admiral stating that the slave trade could continue provided that the Indians were genuine prisoners of war. Accordingly, three hundred Indians, all designated as "prisoners," were rounded up and sent to market

in Spain aboard Niño's ships. The proceeds of their sale were used by Bishop Juan Rodríguez de Fonseca, agent of the Crown, to help finance Columbus's third voyage.

In mid-1499, Bishop Fonseca authorized a number of adventurers to undertake privately funded expeditions to the New World. Peralonso Niño was quick to respond to this opportunity and, like Alonso de Ojeda before him, sought financial support from wealthy merchants in Seville. The only merchant who was willing to provide the necessary funds was Luis Guerra, but his offer was conditional: his brother, Cristóbal Guerra, must be in command of the expedition. Niño's financial condition was such that his only recourse was to accept a subordinate position on his own expedition.

Early in June 1499, Niño sailed from the port of Palos in a small caravel of only fifty tons burden, manned by a crew of thirty-three men. His landfall on the unnamed southern continent was only a short distance from that of Columbus, whose route he had followed. Proceeding to the northwest through the Gulf of Paria and entering the Caribbean, he headed directly for the island of Margarita, just off the northeast coast of present-day Venezuela, which Columbus had reported as being rich in pearls. Finding the natives hospitable and the pearls beautiful, large, and plentiful, the crew remained there for several weeks.

Accounts of the voyage by early historians indicate that, after amassing a substantial quantity of pearls, Guerra and Niño proceeded along the coast to the west for an unspecified but probably short distance. At their first attempt to go ashore, they were confronted by hostile Indians who had previously been stirred up by the belligerent Ojeda. Guerra, who had wisely permitted the more experienced Niño to exercise de facto command of the expedition, insisted at this point on a hasty retreat and departure with their precious cargo from this hostile coast. After an uneventful voyage home, they reached Spain early in February 1500.

On February 13, 1502, Peralonso Niño sailed once again from Cádiz as chief pilot of the flagship of a magnificent fleet of thirty ships carrying twenty-five hundred mariners, colonists, and men-at-arms to Santo Domingo, the new capital of La Española. Aboard the flagship was Nicolás de Ovando, newly appointed governor of the Indies. The outward-bound passage was uneventful, but the attempted return voyage was a disaster. Ignoring a timely warning by Columbus of an approaching hurricane, Ovando ordered the fleet to sail. The ill-fated ships had just entered the Mona Passage between La Española and Puerto Rico when the hurricane struck. Several ships capsized at sea, and most of those that survived the initial burst of fury were driven ashore and pounded to bits. Only five of the thirty ships survived. Over five hundred men were lost, among them the fleet commander, Antonio de Torres, and his chief pilot, Peralonso Niño.

BIBLIOGRAPHY

Gould, Alicia B. *Nueva lista documentada de los tripulantes de Colón en 1492.* Madrid, 1984.

Irving, Washington. *The Life and Voyages of Christopher Columbus and His Companions.* 3 vols. New York, 1849.

WILLIAM LEMOS

NORTHWEST PASSAGE.

As merchants and explorers came gradually to realize that America formed a separate continent between Europe and the East, they took up the search for the Northwest Passage to Asia. England, because it was excluded from sharing in the riches of eastern commerce by the prior discoveries and monopolistic claims of Spain and Portugal, based on the terms of the Treaty of Tordesillas (1494), was particularly interested in a northern route. "There is left one way to discover, which is unto the North," the merchant adventurer Robert Thorne the Younger wrote in an address to King Henry VIII in 1531.

The first voyage in search of the Northwest Passage apparently was that of Sebastian Cabot for Henry VIII in 1508–1509, but contemporary records are sparse. J. A. Williamson suggests that Cabot may have sailed through Hudson Strait into Hudson Bay, which he believed to be open ocean on the route to the East. The evidence rests partly on Cabot's later claims to have discovered the Northwest Passage and also on maps that appear to show the discovery, the earliest being a woodcut globe made in about 1530 in Nürnberg. It is depicted in a portrait of ambassadors at Hampton Court in England, painted by Hans Holbein in 1533. The Northwest Passage appears on the globe as a long strait between America and Asia, with its eastern entrance located about 50° to 55°N.

The globe appears to have been the prototype for a series of maps and globes showing a northwest "Fretum arcticum sive fretum trium fratrum" (Arctic strait or strait of the three brothers). The three have been identified as the Côrte-Real brothers, Portuguese explorers of Labrador in 1500–1501.

The most influential works were those of Gemma Frisius, the Flemish geographer, and his celebrated pupil Gerardus Mercator. Their terrestrial globes (Gemma's, 1536; Mercator's, 1541) became well known in England. Gemma Frisius's globe depicting the "Fretum trium fratum" came to be accepted as an authoritative record of Cabot's discovery of the Northwest Passage. Cabot's own world map, revised and published in London in 1549, was on display in Queen Elizabeth's gallery in Whitehall in the

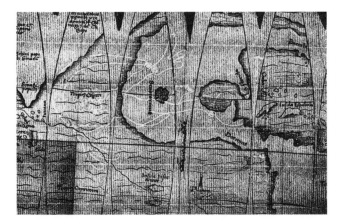

GLOBE GORES FOR THE "AMBASSADORS' GLOBE." Nürnberg, circa 1530. Detail, showing a northwest passage (as a long strait running east to west along upper right side of image).

1560s and was consulted by promoters of northern exploration. Upon returning to England in 1547 after forty years in Spanish service, Cabot was hailed as the leading expert on Arctic exploration.

In the 1560s plans for the discovery and exploration of the Northwest Passage were taken up with Sir Humphrey Gilbert, the leading promoter. His manuscript *Discourse of a Discoverie for a Newe Passage to Cataia* (1566) set out proof of the existence of a northwest, as opposed to a northeast, passage. Published in 1576, the *Discourse* was illustrated by a reduced version of a large world map of 1564 prepared by Ortelius (Abraham Oertel), which shows an easy route into the Pacific. The publication was intended to encourage the newly founded Company of Cathay, which dispatched Martin Frobisher's three expeditions (1576, 1577, 1578), the first to be sent to the northwest in the reign of Elizabeth I.

In 1576 the discovery of the so-called Frobisher Strait seemed to open a passage to the Pacific. The strait was in fact an inlet, now known as Frobisher Bay, on the coast of Baffin Island. The queen named the newly discovered land "Meta Incognita" (Unknown Goal). The second voyage (1577) was a more elaborate operation, in which the queen invested a thousand pounds. One of its aims was to extract ore, samples of which had been brought back from the first voyage. The enterprise had become a treasure hunt. The third voyage in 1578 carried 120 colonists in eleven ships to establish a mining settlement, but that plan was aborted by a shipwreck. Seeking to regain the Frobisher Strait, he made a new discovery by sailing two hundred leagues into Hudson Strait, which he called "The Mistaken Straightes." It seemed to be "the passage which we seek to find to the rich countrey of Cathaya."

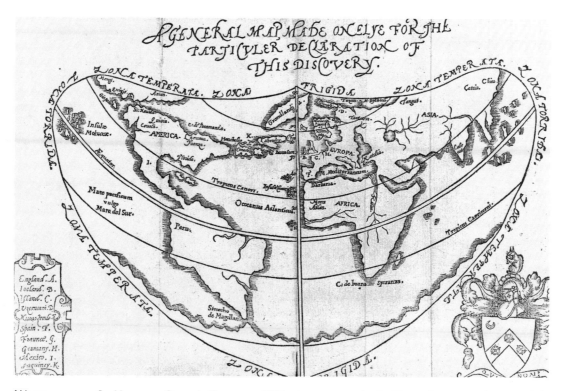

WORLD MAP FROM SIR HUMPHREY GILBERT'S *DISCOURSE*, 1576. A passage to the Pacific can be seen in the upper left corner of the map.

Frobisher returned with more supplies of ore, but the previous samples had proved to be worthless. The Company of Cathay and its financial promoter, Michael Lok, were bankrupt. Interest in the voyages, however, prompted a spate of publications in England and abroad. Dionyse Settle's account of the second voyage (1577) was issued in three foreign editions. George Best's *True Discourse*, an account of the three voyages published in London in 1587, has been described as a manual of "Arctic seamanship."

Of special interest were the reports of Eskimos (Inuits). One had been brought home from the first voyage in 1576, and three from the second in 1577. Their Asiatic appearance encouraged the belief in the Northwest Passage. Michael Lok described the Eskimo as Frobisher's "strange man of Cathay." Drawings of individuals and scenes from the second voyage made the Eskimos famous throughout Europe, and they gained ethnographical significance as the stereotype of exotic peoples. William C. Sturtevant and David B. Quinn comment that these Eskimos are rare examples of named individuals whose portraits have come to typify whole populations.

Frobisher's discoveries suggested two possible routes, which are depicted on the maps in Best's *Discourse*. The world map illustrating the first voyage shows "Frobusshers Straightes" as a wide channel between America and one of Mercator's mythical polar islands. On the map of the North Atlantic, perhaps by James Beare, illustrating the third voyage, "The Mistaken Straightes" lie immediately north of the continent, and "Frobisshers Streights" are marked farther to the north between the islands of Meta Incognita. The landmass of Greenland is depicted still farther north.

This map helps explain a major cartographic error by which Frobisher Strait and Meta Incognita came to be displaced from North America to Greenland. The maps Frobisher took with him, "Carta de navegar de Nicolo et Antonio Zeni . . . MCCCLXXX" published in 1558 and Mercator's world chart of 1569, mark to the south of the latitude of Iceland the nonexistent island of Frisland (a duplicate of Iceland) and locate the southern tip of Greenland at 65°40' instead of 59°45' N. Thus Frobisher identified his first landfall as being on Frisland, whereas it was near Cape Farewell on the southern tip of Greenland. Best's map shows "West-Ingland olim West Friseland" in mid-Atlantic and fits Greenland into the north of America.

For the next three hundred years Frobisher Strait and Meta Incognita were depicted in southern Greenland. Their true location remained unknown until the American explorer Capt. C. F. Hall, on an expedition in 1861–1862,

ESKIMO SCENE. From Dionyse Settle's account (Nürnberg, 1580) of Frobisher's second voyage. The father, mother, and child shown on the shore are the three Eskimos brought to London in 1577.

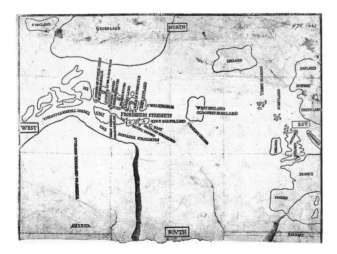

MAP OF FROBISHER'S DISCOVERIES. From George Best's *True Discourse of the Late Voyages of Discoverie*, 1578.

GERARDUS MERCATOR'S WORLD MAP OF 1569. Inset, showing polar regions.

identified with the help of the Eskimos the site of Meta Incognita from relics on Kodlunarn Island, which means "white man's island."

The three voyages of John Davis in 1585, 1586, and 1587 had their origin in plans of the geographer John Dee to exploit Sir Humphrey Gilbert's rights to American lands north of 50° N. Dee abandoned the project, but his associate Adrian Gilbert of Sandridge, Devon, Sir Humphrey's brother, obtained the patent for discovery. Davis, also of Sandridge, sailed as navigator, and William Sanderson, the London merchant, provided the financing.

On the first voyage, in 1585, Davis sailed up the strait named after him to 66°40' N, which he found clear of ice. He reported to Sir Francis Walsingham, secretary of state, that "the northwest passage is a matter nothyne doubtful . . . the sea nauigable, voyd of yse, the ayre tollerable, and the waters very depe." On the second voyage the next year, he returned to the strait without gaining much new information. On the third, in 1587, he reached his farthest point north, naming it Hope Sanderson at 72°49' N. Crossing the strait, he came upon "a very great gulfe," which was Hudson Strait. Without realizing it he had rediscovered Frobisher's "Mistaken Straightes" of 1578. On his return, he reported to Sanderson that at 73° he had found the sea all open: "The passage is most certaine, the execution most easie." Davis had in fact discovered the entrance to Lancaster Sound, where the Northwest Passage begins.

Davis gave a report of his voyages in *The Worldes Hydrographical Description* (London, 1595). For a record of his discoveries he referred the reader to the terrestrial globe of Emery Molyneux, which was published in 1592 at Sanderson's expense. The globe shows the northern outlet of Davis Strait as the only route available for a northwest passage. Frobisher's discoveries are marked in southern Greenland. The globe thus makes clear why Davis never realized that he was sailing in the same region as Frobisher and had rediscovered the same strait and bays.

In the early years of the seventeenth century the search

TERRESTRIAL GLOBE OF EMERY MOLYNEUX, 1592. Detail, showing a northwest passage and the discoveries of John Davis.

for the Northwest Passage centered on Hudson Strait. In 1602 George Weymouth sailed to the northwest for the English East India Company (founded in 1600), carrying letters from Elizabeth to the emperor of China. He explored Frobisher Strait, proving it to be a bay, and noted the current from Hudson Strait.

In 1610 Henry Hudson set out to explore the inlets of Davis Strait. He passed through Hudson Strait into Hudson Bay; he saw the bay as a spacious sea and thought he had found the passage. The expedition wintered in James Bay. The men mutinied, and Hudson was set adrift and never seen again. The survivors on their return reported that they had found the passage.

Thomas Button and Robert Bylot, who had been on Hudson's voyage, returned to Hudson Bay in 1612 to look for him. After navigating the west coast of the bay, they realized they had not found a passage. Bylot sailed again in 1615 with William Baffin as chief pilot and explored Baffinland. In 1616 Baffin and Bylot searched Davis Strait and reported it to be a great bay. This phase of exploration ended with the separate expeditions of Capt. Luke Foxe of Hull and Thomas James of Bristol to Hudson Bay, where they encountered each other in 1631.

The English voyages in search of the Northwest Passage

had been pursued with great determination under the harshest of conditions. Thomas Blundeville, the mathematician, commented on Arctic voyages in 1613, "I can greatly commend those valiant mindes that doe attempt such desperate voyages, and the rather when they doe it for knowledge sake, and profit their Countrey, and not altogether for private gaine and lucre."

Admiral Sir William Monson made a more practical assessment in his "Discourse Concerning the North-west Passage," revised for publication before his death in 1643: "If the passage be found, I confess there is something gained in the distance, but nothing in the navigation. . . . Little good is like to ensue of it, because of the hazard of cold, of ice, and of unknown seas." Recommending the route via the Cape of Good Hope, he wrote, "Let me now appeal to the opinion of any mariner whether it were not better for a man to sail six thousand leagues in a certain and known navigation. . .than three thousand in an uncertain sea as we shall find to the northward."

The Northwest Passage nevertheless remained a dominant feature of the world map, and the straits captured the imagination even of the poets. John Donne, referring to the western end of the passage, the Strait of Anian, wrote, probably in 1623:

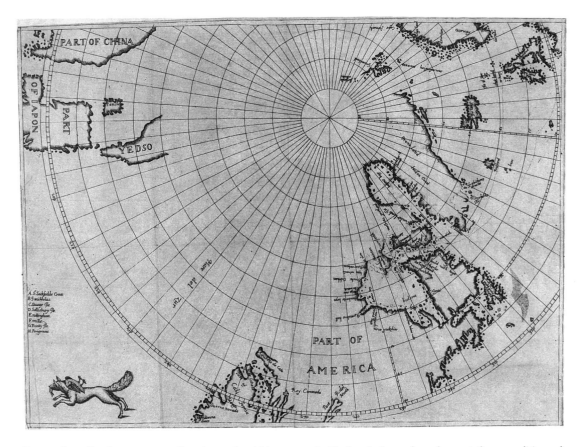

CAPTAIN LUKE FOXE'S POLAR MAP. Showing path of his voyage to Hudson's Bay, where he met the expedition of Thomas James in 1631.   BY PERMISSION OF THE TRUSTEES OF THE BRITISH LIBRARY

Is the Pacific Sea my home? Or are
The eastern riches? Is Jerusalem?
Anyan, and Magellan, and Gibraltar,
All straits, and none but straits, are ways to them,
Whether where Japhet dwelt, or Cham, or Shem.
    ("Hymn to God my God, in my Sicknesse," 1635)

[See also *Canada*.]

BIBLIOGRAPHY

Cumming, W. P., R. A. Skelton, and D. B. Quinn. *The Discovery of North America.* London, 1971.

Monson, William. "Sir William Monson's Naval Tracts." In *A Collection of Voyages and Travels,* edited by A. Churchill and J. Churchill, vol. 3. London, 1732.

Quinn, D. B., ed. *New American World: A Documentary History of North America to 1612.* New York, 1975.

Skelton, R. A. *Explorers' Maps.* London, 1958.

Sturtevant, William C., and David B. Quinn. "This New Prey: Eskimos in Europe in 1567, 1576, and 1577." In *Indians and Europe,* edited by Christian F. Feest. Aachen, 1987.

Wallis, Helen. "England's Search for the Northern Passages in the Sixteenth and Early Seventeenth Centuries." In *Unveiling the Arctic,* edited by Louis Rey. Calgary, 1984. Also in *Arctic* 37 (1984): 453–472.

Williamson, J. A. *The Cabot Voyages and British Discovery under Henry VII.* Cambridge, 1962.

HELEN WALLIS

NUEVA CÁDIZ. See *Settlements,* article on *Nueva Cádiz.*

NÚÑEZ CABEZA DE VACA, ALVAR. See *Cabeza de Vaca, Alvar Núñez.*

NÚÑEZ DE BALBOA, VASCO. See *Balboa, Vasco Núñez de.*

O

OJEDA, ALONSO DE (1466–c. 1515), ship's captain and squadron commander. Ojeda was one of the many gentlemen adventurers who eagerly accompanied Columbus on the second voyage, anticipating excitement and riches. He soon distinguished himself both afloat and ashore by his boldness and energy. He was a native of Cuenca and had been brought up as a page in the service of the Duke of Medinacelli, one of the most powerful nobles in Spain and an important ally of Fernando and Isabel in their efforts to expel the Moors from Spain. Ojeda, ever ambitious, made good and frequent use of his close connections with the nobility.

After the seventeen ships of the second voyage reached the north coast of La Española and a new settlement named La Isabela had been established, Columbus placed Ojeda in command of an expedition into the interior to find the long-sought mines of Cibao, reported by the Indians to be rich in gold. Immediately after participating in the first Mass to be celebrated in the New World on January 6, 1494, the Feast of the Epiphany, Ojeda set off. Two weeks later he returned with enough samples of gold to cause Columbus to write to the sovereigns that he hoped soon to "be able to give them as much gold as the iron mines of Biscay." Unfortunately, while leading a second expedition into the interior, the impulsive Ojeda overzealously punished a cacique (native chief) and two other Indians for a minor infraction. "This," wrote Bartolomé de las Casas, author of *Historia de las Indias*, "was the first injustice, with vain and erroneous pretension of doing justice, that was committed in these Indies against the Indians, and the beginning of the shedding of blood, which has since flowed so copiously in this island." Despite this rash act, Ojeda retained the trust of Columbus and later was instrumental in putting down a strong uprising by the Indians.

Ojeda did not accompany Columbus on his third voyage, being ambitious to gain a command of his own. As a welcome visitor to the royal court, he was able to read letters from Columbus recounting his discovery of the island of Trinidad and the mainland coast of present-day Venezuela, glowingly described as abounding in drugs and spices, gold and silver, and pearls. Excited by these tidings, Ojeda sought authorization to undertake a voyage of discovery to this new region. Bishop Juan Rodríguez de Fonseca, principal agent of the Crown in managing the affairs of the Indies and no friend of Columbus, promptly granted Ojeda a commission to trespass on the Admiral's domain. With the avid assistance of wealthy merchants in Seville, Ojeda soon equipped a squadron of four ships at Puerto de Santa María near Cádiz. He chose Juan de la Cosa, famed for his 1500 chart of the New World, as his chief pilot. Also joining him on the voyage was Amerigo Vespucci whose widely published account of this voyage, falsely dated two years early without mention of Ojeda, resulted in the New World being named America.

Departing Puerto de Santa María on May 20, 1499, Ojeda, although trying to adhere to Columbus's course, made landfall about six hundred miles southeast of the point where Columbus had first sighted South America. From this point Ojeda sailed along the coast to the northwest, stopped briefly at Trinidad, and making use of a chart of the area drawn by Columbus, passed through the Gulf of Paria into the Caribbean and proceeded along the coast to the west. Like Columbus, he neglected to avail himself of a treasure trove of large and beautiful pearls available in quantity along the shores of the island of Margarita just off the north coast of Venezuela. Instead, he chose to continue along the coast, discovering en route the islands now known as Bonaire, Curaçao, and Aruba. He finally reached as far west as the northern tip of present-day Colombia, not realizing how close he was to the Isthmus of Panama and the Pacific Ocean. Having failed to find any of the Oriental splendors he had sought, he turned to the north and took course for La Española, ignoring specific instructions to stay away from that island. Repulsed there, he stopped at several islands in the Bahamas, carrying off numerous natives to be sold as slaves when he reached Cádiz in June 1500.

Even though Ojeda had failed to find any of the riches he sought for himself and the merchants of Seville, his exploration of virtually the entire northern coast of the southern continent secured for him an authorization for a second voyage to establish a colony on that coast. He soon found associates willing to join him in fitting out another squadron of four ships and sailed from Cádiz in January 1502. This venture also came to naught when the Indians, repeatedly provoked by Ojeda, became hostile. In May, Ojeda's discontented partners rebelled, took him prisoner, and sent him to La Española, where he arrived in September 1502.

In 1508, King Fernando, sole ruler of Spain following the death of Isabel on November 26, 1504, sought an able commander to establish colonies on the coast of gold-rich Veragua (Panama). Juan de la Cosa, the chart maker, interceded in favor of Ojeda and won for him the post of governor of New Andalusia, an undefined area including what is now the Caribbean coast of Colombia. At his own expense, Juan de la Cosa fitted out three ships in which he set sail for La Española with about two hundred men. This final venture of Ojeda, like so many of his past ventures, also was doomed to failure by his belligerence toward the Indians. His recklessness resulted in the death of his staunch supporter Juan de la Cosa by a poison-tipped arrow. Ojeda managed to escape to La Española where he later died in poverty.

BIBLIOGRAPHY

Gould, Alicia B. *Nueva lista documentada de los tripulantes de Colón en 1492.* Madrid, 1984.
Irving, Washington. *The Life and Voyages of Christopher Columbus and His Companions.* 3 vols. New York, 1849.

WILLIAM LEMOS

ORELLANA, FRANCISCO DE (c. 1511–1546), Spanish explorer and soldier; first European to descend the Amazon River. Born in Trujillo, Spain, Orellana may have been related to the Pizarros. In about 1527 he went to the Indies, probably to Nicaragua. From there he went to Peru, probably after 1533. In 1535 he helped to conquer Portoviejo and became a resident of the Spanish town of that name. He took a dozen horsemen to Lima during the first Inca rebellion in 1536 and sided with the Pizarros in

the battle of Las Salinas on April 26, 1538. Later that year he founded Guayaquil, Ecuador, and served as its first captain general and governor.

When Gonzalo Pizarro set out from Quito in 1540 in search of the mythic El Dorado and the land of cinnamon in the Coca River basin on the eastern slopes of the Ecuadorian Andes, Orellana joined the expedition as the leader of twenty horsemen and was given the position of second-in-command. In February 1542, he was sent to search for food with fifty men and a small boat that the Spanish had built on the banks of the Coca River. Unable to return upstream against the current, Orellana continued down the Coca and Napo rivers into the Amazon River. During a stop at Aparia, the land was claimed for Spain and a second ship was built. He later claimed to have encountered and fought with the "Amazons" of mythic fame. His boats entered the Atlantic Ocean on August 26 and sailed northwest to Nueva Cádiz, Cubagua, where they arrived on September 9 and 11, 1542. His party was the first group of Europeans to navigate the length of the Amazon River.

Returning to Spain, Orellana obtained the governorship of the south side of the Amazon Basin west of the Tordesillas Line of Demarcation. He departed Sanlúcar de Barrameda on May 11, 1545, with four ships and four hundred Spaniards. By the time he reached the mouth of the Amazon River in December, he had only two ships and less than half of the men.

The expedition worked its way one hundred leagues upstream before pausing for the first three months of 1546 to build a brigantine to replace one of the ships. Over fifty men died of hunger during this delay. Ascending another twenty leagues, the party lost the last of the original ships. Orellana broke off his efforts not long after this shipwreck and died before he could return down the Amazon. His widow and the remaining members of the expedition abandoned the enterprise and sailed to Margarita, arriving in December 1546.

BIBLIOGRAPHY

Benites Vinueza, Leopoldo. *Los descubridores del Amazonas: "La expedición de Orellana."* Madrid, 1976.
Medina, José Toribio. *The Discovery of the Amazon.* Translated by Bertram T. Lee. Edited by H. C. Heaton. New York, 1934.

PAUL E. HOFFMAN

ORTELIUS, ABRAHAM (1527–1598), Flemish cartographer and publisher. Abraham Oertel, known by the Latinized name Ortelius, was born into the family of an Antwerp antique merchant. His education evidently did not extend much beyond the curriculum of the typical

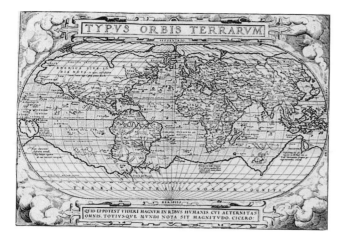

ORTELIUS'S MAP OF THE WORLD. From *Theatrum Orbis Terrarum.*
ELSEVIER PUBLISHING PROJECTS, AMSTERDAM

Latin school, where he also received some instruction in Greek and mathematics. His father died when he was twelve and his mother took over the family business. Together with his sisters, Anne and Elizabeth, Abraham took up the coloring of maps and was admitted to the painters' guild as an "illuminator of maps" in 1547. In time he took over the operation of the family shop and dealt in antiques, coins, maps, and books, with the book and map trade gradually becoming his primary occupation.

Having prospered, he began to form an extensive collection of medals, coins, and antiques (which he exhibited in his home as a kind of private museum), as well as a library of many volumes. He traveled widely on business, studied the history and geography of the places he visited, made contacts with scholars and editors, and carried on an extensive correspondence, some of which has been preserved and forms the primary source of information about his life and work.

Ortelius's career as a cartographer began in 1564 when he published a large and ambitious wall map of the world, followed in the next few years by several other separate maps. But his chief monument, and his greatest contribution to the Age of Discovery, was his atlas, the *Theatrum orbis terrarum* (Theater of the world), published in Antwerp in 1570. Earlier collections of maps had been published (most notably, those accompanying Ptolemy's *Geography*), but Ortelius's contribution was to collect the newest and best maps available for all parts of the world, have them engraved to a uniform size, and publish them together in book form. The result is usually thought of as constituting the first modern atlas. The atlas seems to have had its origins in the need to supply merchant-traders in the Low Countries with geographical information so that they could calculate freight costs and plan efficient trade routes while avoiding wars and civil disturbances. The appeal of the *Theatrum,* however, went well beyond the commercial world, and scholars all over Europe were virtually unanimous in their praise. Gerardus Mercator summed up the value of the *Theatrum* when he thanked Ortelius for having "selected the best descriptions of each region and collected them into one manual, which can be bought at small cost, kept in a small space and even carried about wherever we please."

Demand for the *Theatrum* was remarkable. Altogether some twenty-four editions appeared during Ortelius's lifetime, and another ten after his death in 1598. The original Latin text of the geographical descriptions that accompanied the maps was translated into the major vernacular languages of Europe, and by 1608, editions had been published in Dutch, German, French, Spanish, English, and Italian. The number of map sheets grew from 53 in 1570 to 167 in the last edition, in 1612. Answering the need for even lower costs and greater portability were the pocket-sized versions of the *Theatrum,* of which thirty editions were published. One of the unique contributions of the *Theatrum* was Ortelius's scrupulousness in crediting individual cartographers and his inclusion of a catalog of all the maps known to him, a document of primary importance for the history of sixteenth-century cartography.

It is difficult to overemphasize the importance of Ortelius's atlas for the spread of information about the world, including the relatively new discoveries in America. The first edition included only a single map of North and South America, but by 1590, eight new maps had been added, showing the results of Spanish and French explorations up to about mid-century. Maps of central Mexico, Sinaloa, and the West Indies appeared in editions after 1579, and five years later these were joined by maps of northwestern South America, the southeastern United States, and the San Luis Potosí region of Mexico. A new map of the Americas appeared in 1587 and one of the Pacific Ocean in 1590. These were far from being the earliest depictions of the New World on printed maps, but they were certainly the most widely available. The unique value of Ortelius's atlas as a compendium of geographical knowledge is attested by the fact that at the court of Philip II, with the resources of the great cosmographers and the Casa de la Contratación at its disposal, the *Theatrum* was consulted regularly as a tool of statecraft.

BIBLIOGRAPHY

Bagrow, Leo, and Robert W. Karrow, Jr. *Mapmakers of the Sixteenth Century and Their Maps: The Catalog of Cartographers of Abraham Ortelius, 1570.* Chicago, forthcoming.

Hessels, Jan H. *Abrahami Ortelii (geographi antverpiensis) et virorum eruditorum ad eundem et ad Jacobum Colium Orte-*

lianum . . . epistulae. Cambridge, 1887. Reprint, Osnabrück, 1969.

Koeman, Cornelis. The History of Abraham Ortelius and His Theatrum orbis terrarum. New York, 1964.

ROBERT W. KARROW, JR.

OTTOMAN EMPIRE. The name of this empire came from Osman, a Turkish nomad chief (d. 1324) who founded it at the turn of the fourteenth century near the northwest edge of the Anatolian plateau. Although Europeans spoke of it as an empire, the Ottomans themselves wrote of it as the Al-i Osman, or "House of Osman." By Columbus's time, the Ottomans had conquered the Balkans, including Constantinople (1453) as well as most of Anatolia; the Byzantine state of Trebizond fell in 1461 and the major Anatolian Muslim rival of the Ottomans, the emirate of Karaman, was conquered in 1468.

Sultan Mehmed II the Conqueror (r. 1444–1446, 1451–1481) had been responsible for these last additions to Ottoman soil, and in his lifetime the empire increased in size by about 50 percent. In fact, one of his armies briefly occupied the Italian port of Otranto in the last months of his reign. The sultanate of his son, Bayezid II (r. 1481–1512), did not add to the empire so much as consolidate it: strategic points in the Aegean and the Danube delta came under Ottoman rule, but in the main Bayezid II had to fend off, in the early years of his reign, the attempts of his brother Jem to supplant him and, in his later years, the rise of Isma'il I to power in Iran and the Safavid attempts to arouse the nomads of Anatolia against Ottoman rule. One notable addition to the population of the empire was a number of Jews, refugees from Spain who left their homes in 1492. By the end of the century they had established themselves in Thessaloníki (Salonika) and Istanbul, where they had set up a printing press.

Bayezid's successors set a faster tempo for conquest. Selim I (r. 1512–1520), known as Selim the Grim, defeated the Safavids at the Battle of Chaldiran (1514) and briefly occupied their capital, Tabriz. After this time Ottoman rule over Anatolia remained secure. In 1516 Selim marched east and south against the Mamluks of Syria and Egypt. At Marj Dabiq, near Aleppo, Selim's army defeated the Mamluks, and at the beginning of 1517 he entered Cairo. With the conquest of the Mamluk domains the Ottomans came to rule over Arabic-speaking lands and became the protectors of Mecca and Medina, the holy cities in Arabia. Further, the Ottomans now had a third sea frontier to defend, for to the Black Sea and the eastern Mediterranean was now added the Red Sea and its outlet onto the Indian Ocean, for which the Ottomans contested with the Portuguese during the sixteenth century.

Selim's son and successor was Süleyman the Magnifi-cent (r. 1520–1566), whom the Turks called Kanuni, or the lawgiver. Süleyman caught the imagination of European authors, artists, and travelers, not least for his conquests of Rhodes, Iraq, Yemen, and parts of Hungary and his subordination of much of the North African coast and lands north of the Black Sea and the Danube. Most celebrated was his siege of Vienna in 1529. In all, Süleyman spent ten of his forty-six years of rule on campaigns.

At the death of Süleyman in 1566, the area under direct Ottoman control included about 1,190,000 square kilometers (460,000 square miles) in Asia, 570,000 (220,000) in Europe, and 490,000 (190,000) in Africa, for a total of around 2,255,000 square kilometers (870,000 square miles). An additional 905,000 square kilometers (350,000 square miles) lay under tributary rulers in central Europe and south Russia. Ottoman writ held sway along the coast of North Africa, in Egypt and the Nile basin, the coasts of Arabia, the Fertile Crescent (Syria, Iraq), Anatolia as far east as Lake Van and as far north as Kars, the Balkans, and most of Hungary; nor was it ignored in the tributary states of Walachia, Transylvania, Moldavia, and the Khanate of Crimea.

The Ottomans had originally ruled over a population that was largely Christian, especially in the Balkans, but by the sixteenth century Islam was predominant in most of Anatolia, and the conquests of Selim I and Süleyman had added large Muslim populations. In North Africa and the Levant, most people spoke Arabic; in Anatolia, while Turkish was the lingua franca, Christians spoke Greek or Armenian; and in the Balkans, Turkish at this time was more a language of administration, with the overwhelmingly Christian population speaking their traditional languages: Greek, the Slavic languages, Hungarian, and Rumanian.

The Ottomans were Muslims and ruled with a view to the protection and expansion of Muslim dominion. Nonetheless, they allowed non-Muslims to practice their religions in return for additional taxes and restrictions. The organized Christian and Jewish communities enjoyed a certain amount of autonomy and were responsible to the sultan through the community's head. Mehmed the Conqueror and his successors appointed the patriarchs of the Greek Orthodox and Armenian churches, and at some point the Jews had a grand rabbi. The sultans placed garrisons in some of the cities of the empire for the protection of the Christians and Jews.

The Ottoman Empire was the first of the "gunpowder empires" in the Near East: the Ottoman armies won at Chaldiran and Marj Dabiq thanks to their use of gunpowder weapons. What impressed European observers the most, however, was the organization of Ottoman governance, for the Ottoman enterprise rested upon the services of officials many of whom, at all levels of government, were legally slaves. The Habsburg ambassador Oghier Ghiselin de Busbecq suggested that the Ottoman government was a true meritocracy, not bound by a traditional nobility. In some years the central government sent out men to conscript Christian youths, a process known as the *devshirme*. These youths were converted to Islam and schooled for a number of years, with some graduates joining the bureaucracy, where in principle a talented man could rise to head the imperial administration as grand *vezir*, and with others, joining the Janissary Corps, the crack infantry of the sultans.

Although the empire included a number of large and historic cities (Istanbul, Damascus, Jerusalem, and Cairo), it was fundamentally an agrarian society, and during the age of Columbus there was little long-distance trade in agricultural commodities. The spice and silk trades flourished, however, and it was not until the later sixteenth century that the shift of trade routes around the horn of Africa and the influx of American silver had an impact upon the Ottoman economy. There were Ottomans who took an interest in what was occurring in other markets. For their part, Europeans, especially in the Habsburg domains and Italy, had an interest in this formidable enemy and possible trading partner. Although they did not know much of the Ottomans' early history, diplomats and merchants gathered together accounts of court life and attempted to influence Ottoman decisions through quiet diplomacy with some of the higher bureaucrats and grand *vezirs*. These accounts have not lost their interest or charm with the slow opening of the vast Ottoman archives to modern researchers.

BIBLIOGRAPHY

Inalcik, Halil. *The Ottoman Empire: The Classical Age.* London, 1973. Reprint, 1990.

Tietze, Andreas, ed. *Turkologischer Anzeiger.* An annual of current literature in all languages. Vienna, 1976–.

RUDI PAUL LINDNER

OVANDO, NICOLÁS DE (c. 1451–1511), governor of the Indies (1501–1509). Born in Brozas, Extremadura, died in Seville, May 29, 1511, Ovando was the son of Capt. Diego de Ovando, who, in the civil wars preceding the marriage of Isabel of Castile and Fernando of Aragón, opted for the winning side. In 1473 his younger son Nicolás was given the commandery of Lares in the Order of Alcántara. As a member of the military order, called frey rather than fray, he took monastic vows in addition to one that obliged him to fight the infidel.

Because of Nicolás de Ovando's performance in the civil wars and his proven loyalty to the Crown, Queen Isabel in

OVANDO ORDERS THE FIRST CONSTRUCTION OF SHIPS IN THE NEW WORLD. Engraving from Théodor de Bry's *Americae*. Frankfurt, 1594.

1501 appointed him to the post of first royal governor of the Indies, in succession to Christopher Columbus. Under the Admiral, the infant colony in Santo Domingo had fallen into disarray, and the interim attempt to cope with the difficulties by Francisco de Bobadilla had failed. Ovando arrived on April 15, 1502, with a fleet of thirty ships and about twenty-five hundred settlers. Among them were soldiers, artisans, and professionals, some of whom brought their families, and priests.

During the decade of Ovando's administration he followed his instructions from the Crown, which can be grouped under four headings: to implement the transfer of powers of government from Columbus to the Crown; to establish royal jurisdiction over planters, miners, and future towns; to encourage economic development; and to put the church on a firm foundation.

Ovando brought with him royal laws comparable, by and large, to those practiced by the military orders during the years of the reconquest. His "mission of civilization" was to convert the Indians to the Catholic faith and teach them to live as Spaniards. He thus represented the continuity of an ancient tradition.

La Española, however, was not Spain, nor were the Indians Moors. The Spanish colonists, moreover, were split in their loyalties, many supporting the Columbuses. The physical setting, the challenges to authority, and the demands on the governor to do justice by both the Indians and the settlers under Crown law demanded adjustments in almost every detail.

Ovando's powers to deal with Columbus were legally

justifiable, but his actions were shadowed by his lengthy abandonment of the marooned discoverer in Jamaica. His confrontation with the natives, whom he feared as possible agents of rebellion, led to the infamous hanging of the cacique Anacaona. The settlement of the countryside by the system of repartimiento (Indian forced labor) cost many Indian lives and was destructive of the indigenous culture. But in the more customary enterprises of stabilizing a mixed rural and mining economy, founding towns, stimulating construction of stone houses, and planning a cathedral and a hospital, which represented the "civilizing" mission of Castile, he carried out the will of the Crown. Recalled in 1509, Ovando, who had by then been elected and confirmed as *comendador mayor* of Alcántara (that is, as head of this military order of knights), left La Española. This colony had become a little Spain, with the Americas a challenge yet to be met.

BIBLIOGRAPHY

Lamb, Ursula. "Cristóbal de Tapia v. Nicolás de Ovando: A Residencia Fragment." *Hispanic American Historical Review* 33 (1953).

Lamb, Ursula. *Frey Nicolás de Ovando, Gobernador de las Indias (1501–1509).* 2d ed. Santo Domingo, Dom. Rep., 1977.

Demorizi, Emilio Rodríguez. *El Pleito Ovando-Tapia: Comienzo de la vida urbana en America.* Santo Domingo, Dom. Rep., 1978.

URSULA LAMB

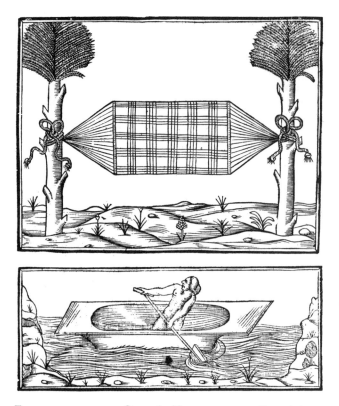

TWO WOODCUTS FROM OVIEDO'S *HISTORIA GENERAL*. *Top*: A hammock, a native American invention that soon found use in European sailing vessels. *Bottom*: Indian in a canoe. These are from the second edition of the *Historia general*, published in Salamanca in 1547 under the title *Cronica de las Indias*.

NEW YORK PUBLIC LIBRARY, RARE BOOK DIVISION

OVIEDO, GONZALO FERNÁNDEZ DE (1478–1557), royal official.

Known widely among historians and bibliographers simply as Oviedo, Gonzalo Fernández de Oviedo y Valdés spent almost fifty years in the New World and wrote two important works on the Indies and Tierra Firme (present-day Colombia and Panama). The first, *De la natural historia de las Indias*, published at Toledo in 1526, treated of the flora, fauna, and geography of the Caribbean, principally La Española, and of Tierra Firme. In one chapter he described the customs and folklore of the native inhabitants, displaying little regard for their humanity or capacity. The second work, *Historia general y natural de las Indias, islas y Tierra Firme del mar Océano*, was a larger and more significant manuscript, which, though it too included natural history and comment on Indian societies, chiefly chronicled Spain's political adventures in the same regions. The first part was published at Seville in 1535; the second at Valladolid in 1557, the year of Oviedo's death. Additional parts, suppressed probably by his ideological rival, Bartolomé de las Casas, did not appear in print until the nineteenth century.

Born at Madrid of Asturian parents, Oviedo briefly entered the service of the Infante Juan, only son of Fernando and Isabel, and came to know Columbus and the Pinzón family. During two years of military service in Italy he acquired a Renaissance taste for literature and the arts. On returning to Spain at age twenty-four, he married the Toledo beauty Margarita de Vergara, who died ten months later in childbirth. He would marry twice more.

In 1514 he made the first of his twelve Atlantic crossings, sailing (along with Bernal Díaz del Castillo and Hernando de Soto) on the expedition of Pedro Arias de Ávila (Pedrárias Dávila) to assume newly appointed duties as *veedor*, or inspector of gold smelting, on Tierra Firme. With Pedrárias, who established a tyrannical governorship at Darién, Oviedo had a continually hostile relationship. In 1532 he received the newly minted position of chronicler of the Indies, and the inspectorship of gold foundries passed to a son. In the following year he assumed the additional post of *alcalde*, or governor, of the fortress at Santo Domingo.

In his travels Oviedo became the first New World field naturalist, describing and illustrating in his own hand numerous animals, fish, and plants. To him also linguists owe their first knowledge of Indian words from which were derived such terms as *canoe, hurricane, maize,* and *hammock.* His nature writings enjoyed a wide vogue in Spain and throughout Europe.

Oviedo's attitude toward the native peoples had a strong impact in Spain, where Las Casas singled him out as "a deadly enemy of the Indians" for the way in which he denigrated their customs and capacities. In Oviedo's vision the Indians were lazy, corrupt, vicious, idolatrous, bestial, and deserving of enslavement, the last of which he himself practiced. In his famous disputation with Las Casas in 1550, Juan Ginés de Sepúlveda relied heavily on the *Historia general* in his attempt to demonstrate that the Indians were lacking in intellectual and religious capacity and thus could be justly warred upon. On the other side, Las Casas in his formal argument, the *Apologética historia,* answered the royal historian's positions point by point.

As a footnote, Oviedo deserves to be remembered as the first Spaniard to read aloud in the New World the formidable theological proclamation called the *Reque-rimiento,* which, if not heeded by its native audience, justified war and enslavement. On June 14, 1514, Oviedo dutifully declaimed before a deserted village inland from Darién, to the laughter of a military guard. He died on July 27, 1557, at Santo Domingo.

BIBLIOGRAPHY

Hanke, Lewis. *All Mankind Is One: A Study of the Disputation between Bartolomé de las Casas and Juan Ginés de Sepúlveda in 1550 on the Intellectual and Religious Capacity of the American Indians.* De Kalb, Ill., 1974.

Pérez de Tudela Bueso, Juan, et al. *Homenaje a Gonzalo Fernández de Oviedo en el IV centenario de su muerte.* Madrid, 1957.

Pérez de Tudela Bueso, Juan. "Vida y Escritos de Gonzalo Fernández de Oviedo." In Gonzalo Fernández de Oviedo, *Historia general y natural de las Indias,* vol. 1. Madrid, 1959.

Restrepo Uribe, Fernando. "Gonzalo Fernández de Oviedo, primer cronista de Indias." *Boletín de Historia y Antigüedades* 74, no. 757 (April–June 1987): 245–257.

MICHAEL GANNON

P

PACHECO PEREIRA, DUARTE (c. 1460–c. 1533), Portuguese explorer, navigator, conquistador, cosmographer, and author of *Esmeraldo de situ orbis.* Duarte Pacheco Pereira, called the Great Pacheco and the Portuguese Achilles by the poet Luis Vaz de Camões, was born in Lisbon, the son of the seafarer and solider João Pacheco and Isabel Pereira. Little is known of his early life. Recent studies have challenged the view that young Pacheco Pereira was present in North Africa at the Portuguese conquest of Arzila and the occupation of Tangier in 1471. However, during the reign of João II (1481–1495), he made several voyages to the Guinea coast of Africa and explored the region around the Senegal River and the kingdom of Benin, whose capital he visited four times. In 1488 when Bartolomeu Dias was returning from his expedition around the Cape of Good Hope, he picked up Pacheco Pereira, who was seriously ill, from the island of Principe in the Gulf of Guinea and brought him back to Portugal. About that time, Pacheco Pereira, already a knight in the household of King João, became a member of the king's guard. He resided in Lisbon and because of his navigational experience was a technical adviser to the Portuguese delegation that was given the task of negotiating the Treaty of Tordesillas (1494) and signed the document as a witness.

In Book I, chapter 2 of Pacheco Pereira's *Esmeraldo de situ orbis,* there is an ambiguous statement regarding an expedition in 1498 "in which your Highness ordered us to explore the Western region, . . . a very large landmass with many large islands adjacent." It is not clear whether the author uses the word *us* to refer to himself or to the Portuguese in general. Some scholars assert that he, rather than Pedro Álvares Cabral, discovered Brazil. Others argue that his 1498 voyage was to the north and that it touched Florida, and therefore that the Portuguese dis-

covered the North American mainland. Still others conjecture that the 1498 explorers sighted the Yucatán. Though it seems that there was indeed a 1498 voyage to the west, it most probably did not touch Brazil or King Manuel I would have proudly announced the news to Europe, as he did in 1501 after Cabral's landfall the previous year. Furthermore, there is no evidence that Pacheco Pereira was a member of Cabral's armada, as some writers have alleged.

In 1503 Pacheco Pereira was captain of one of the three ships in Afonso de Albuquerque's expedition to India. While there, he organized the defense of Cochin against the attacks of the ruler of Calicut. His military exploits earned him great praise from the most important Portuguese chroniclers of the sixteenth century.

He returned to Lisbon in mid-1505 as captain of one of the ships in the armada of Lopo Soares and was warmly received by King Manuel. It was about this time that he began writing *Esmeraldo de situ orbis,* which he described as "a book of cosmography and navigation." He seems to have completed all or most of it by 1508. Toward the end of 1508, King Manuel ordered him to track down the French corsair Mondragon; in a battle off Cape Finisterre on January 18, 1509, he sank one ship and captured three others as well as Mondragon himself. In 1511 he commanded a fleet sent to the aid of Tangier, which was besieged by the king of Fès. By 1512 he had married Antónia de Albuquerque, daughter of Jorge Garcês, secretary of King Manuel, and maternal granddaughter of Duarte Galvão, who had held a similar post under King João II.

In 1519 Pacheco Pereira was named governor of São Jorge da Mina for three years. In 1522 he was arrested and brought back to Portugal at the orders of King Manuel's successor, João III (r. 1521–1557). After a period of imprisonment, he was released by João and granted a pension. The exact date of his death is unknown, although there is evidence that he died in late 1532 or early in 1533.

Duarte Pacheco Pereira's *Esmeraldo de situ orbis*, first published in 1892, almost four centuries after being penned (the original manuscript is missing and only two eighteenth-century copies exist), combines a partial chronicle of Portuguese overseas discovery with a cosmography of the world. It also attempts—not always successfully—to synthesize the wisdom of the ancients with Portuguese experience. For example, the author believed that six-sevenths of the world was land enclosing a sea. At the same time, his projections regarding latitude were some of the most accurate of his day. The two extant manuscripts also give detailed sailing instructions for coasting the western part of Africa, with descriptions of that region.

BIBLIOGRAPHY

Bensaude, Joaquim. *L'astronomie nautique au Portugal à l'époque des grandes découvertes*. Bern, 1912.

Carvalho, Joaquim Barradas de. *À la recherche de la spécificité de la renaissance portugaise: L' "Esmeraldo de situ orbis" de Duarte Pacheco Pereira et la littérature portugaise de voyages à l'époque des grandes découvertes*. 2 vols. Paris, 1983.

Dias, Carlos Malheiro. *História da colonização portuguesa do Brasil*. 3 vols. Porto, 1921–1926.

Morison, Samuel Eliot. *Portuguese Voyages to America in the Fifteenth Century*. Cambridge, Mass., 1940.

Pacheco Pereira, Duarte. *Esmeraldo de situ orbis*. Translated and edited by G. H. T. Kimble. London, 1937.

Pacheco Pereira, Duarte. *Esmeraldo de situ orbis*, 3d ed. Lisbon, 1954.

FRANCIS A. DUTRA

PACIFICATION, CONQUEST, AND GENOCIDE.

The people who met Christopher Columbus at the end of his first voyage, the Taínos (from their word for "noble," or "good"), were described by Columbus as the best and most gentle people on earth. In 1492 there may have been as many as two million (estimates range from one hundred thousand to eight million) Taínos living on La Española (Hispaniola). The chroniclers described Jamaica and Puerto Rico as equally populous and the Bahamas and Cuba as supporting somewhat less dense populations. Within fifty years the Taíno peoples who occupied these islands were replaced by native peoples from other islands and the mainland and by Africans.

The destruction of the native West Indian societies occurred in two stages. The first came between 1492 and 1500 under the administration of Christopher Columbus, who undertook what he called the "pacification" of the Taínos. The second stage commenced with the arrival of

Governor Nicolás de Ovando in 1502. Ovando destroyed what remained of the Taíno political structure on La Española and encouraged the brutal conquest of neighboring islands. These stages were separated by a brief respite during the two-year administration of Francisco de Bobadilla.

It must be noted that historical accounts of this period draw heavily on the writings of Bartolomé de las Casas. Las Casas, who arrived in La Española in 1502, was the first priest ordained in the New World, in 1510; he was appointed "protector of the Indians" by Cardinal Francisco Jiménez de Cisneros, archbishop of Toledo. Because of their moral and political overtones, his writings have been used to support modern political objectives. On the one hand, his denunciation of his countrymen's treatment of native peoples was so severe that it was used to fuel the anti-Hispanic sentiments embodied in the Black Legend of the seventeenth and eighteenth centuries, which drew upon the most horrifying details in the Las Casas polemic, and was intended not to reform Spanish policy but to denigrate Spanish character. On the other hand, Las Casas's use of exaggeration to amplify his argument has led others to reject his history as inaccurate. The following discussion seeks a middle ground.

Pacification. Christopher Columbus's efforts to establish a colony on La Española were directed toward one end: he sought to extract the wealth of the Indies and to export it to Spain to enrich himself and the Crown. During the seven years that he was governor of La Española, he enumerated three sources of wealth: gold, brazilwood (a source of a red dye), and slaves. Complicated interactions between Columbus, his countrymen, and the native Taínos affected which of these sources was emphasized at any particular time. Columbus was clearly most interested in gold. He demanded that every Taíno over fourteen years of age pay one Flemish hawkbell (85 grams or 3 ounces) of gold or an arroba (11 kilograms or 25 pounds) of cotton every three months. These payments were to be collected by the Taíno caciques.

At first, relations with the Taínos were amiable. Columbus established a lifelong bond with the Taíno cacique Guacanagarí. Guacanagarí helped to salvage the contents of *Santa María*, which sank on December 24, 1492; it was in his village that the first Spanish fort, called La Navidad, was built; he also accompanied Columbus during the forced occupation of the interior in March 1495. Given Columbus's relationship with Guacanagarí, it is inferred that those who willingly submitted to his demands were treated as friends, while those who opposed him were treated as enemies.

Although native rights were not acknowledged, the issue was one of power and not race. The treatment of the Taínos was undeniably cruel, but it paralleled the treatment of Spaniards. Spaniard and Indian alike had their ears and noses cut off for stealing, and Spaniards who committed treason were hung. When Ovando burned the chiefs of Jaraguá in 1502, the Taino *cacica* (female chief) Anacaona was hanged because a person of her rank had earned that form of execution over a form—burning—suited for persons of lower rank.

Columbus began his colony with both a friend and an enemy. His friend, Guacanagarí, was not blamed for the destruction of La Navidad. Blame and retribution centered on Caonabó, who was arguably the most powerful cacique on the island. The area over which he ruled was one of the five principal *cacicazgos* on the island; it was located in the Cibao, the primary gold-producing region on La Española. Guacanagarí was a lesser cacique whose influence may not have extended much beyond his village.

One of Caonabó's names, Guacaonabo (Taíno caciques had many names that reflected their power and political alliances), was translated as "gold house." The name was interpreted as meaning that he controlled the gold deposits. Although his *cacicazgo* did include major gold deposits, the Taínos did not display the same enthusiasm for gold as did the Spanish. The capture of Caonabó became Columbus's first objective and was accomplished by subterfuge in 1494.

By 1494 the Taínos were already tired of the burdens that were placed on them. As Las Casas described the situation, even the most miserable of convicts from Spain demanded royal treatment from the natives and simply took what they desired. The situation was made worse by a famine that began in 1494. Many of the Taínos moved away from the Spaniards or went into hiding, held the Spaniards in mortal horror, refused obedience, and began to avenge themselves against individual Spaniards.

The only solution for the Taínos was to defeat the Spaniards. An army of at least fifteen thousand (but perhaps as many as one hundred thousand) was assembled in the central part of the island with Guarionex as the reluctant commander-in-chief. The Taíno forces were joined by certain Spaniards in open rebellion against Columbus. The Admiral and his brother Bartolomé Colón marched into the interior with an army of two hundred footsoldiers, twenty horsemen, twenty dogs, and Guacanagarí and his men. Vastly outnumbered, and faced with certain defeat, Bartolomé staged a midnight raid on the villages in which the Taínos were assembling. This breach of Taíno battle etiquette proved effective. Fourteen chiefs were captured, including Guarionex. Las Casas wrote that the next morning about six thousand men arrived without weapons and begged for the release of their leaders. The leaders who had instigated the uprising were burned, but Guarionex and others were released. In this way the interior of the island was "pacified."

In an effort to maintain peaceful relations, Columbus promised Guarionex and the other chiefs that, in return for tribute payments, he would keep the Spaniards from roaming free. In effect, the Taínos would have only one master, Christopher Columbus. This solution proved unsuccessful. The tribute demanded was beyond their means, even after the demands were halved. Moreover, the inability of the Taíno chiefs to meet tribute payments may have been caused by the loss of up to one-third of the native population in the central area. The gold fields were not producing a good return, and there was growing discontent among Spaniard and Taíno alike. With the conquest of the interior completed, efforts were made to bring the rest of the island into the tribute system. The *cacicazgo* of Jaraguá, in the west, was approached and began to pay tribute in the form of cotton and food, and *cacicazgos* on the east coast continued to supply Spanish ships with cassava bread.

Treatment of the Indians was strongly influenced by relations among the Spaniards. The Spaniards continued to fight among themselves, and despite promises to the Taíno chiefs, the colony was out of control. When a group of three hundred disenchanted colonists left La Española in 1498, the three hundred who remained were equally divided between Columbus, who controlled the center of the island, and Francisco Roldán whose rebels held the west. Roldán took up residence in Jaraguá, thus ending tribute payments to Columbus, and both groups plundered the *cacicazgos* on the north coast.

The peace that was negotiated between Roldán and Columbus included the allocation of native peoples to individual Spaniards. This practice of allocating Indians and their land in *repartimientos*, and later encomiendas, was to characterize the Spaniards' treatment of native peoples in their other colonies. In theory, encomenderos were responsible for the spiritual and corporal well being of their natives. In practice, the natives were often treated as slaves.

Columbus also drew royal disfavor over the issue of slavery. As early as 1493, Columbus proposed the export of natives to Spain, citing the activities of the Portuguese in Africa as an example. Columbus sent 550 slaves to Spain in 1495. In 1499 he proposed the export of slaves and dyewood as the means for resurrecting La Española's failed economy. The Crown resisted all efforts to send native West Indians to Spain as slaves. When Columbus awarded one Taíno to each of the colonists who left La Española in 1498, Queen Isabel set the natives free and returned them to La Española.

When Francisco de Bobadilla arrived at Santo Domingo in July 1500, his first sight was of two gallows, a Spaniard hanging from each. Five Spaniards had been executed in the past week and five others awaited execution. Bobadilla had been sent by the Crown to investigate turmoil in the colony and to become the new governor after he had completed his investigations. Instead, he immediately seized control of the government, arrested Christopher Columbus and Bartolomé and Diego Colón and sent them back to Spain in chains. After the removal of Columbus there was a brief respite. Bobadilla returned control of the colony to the Crown. The award of larger shares of gold placers encouraged the three hundred Spaniards who remained, and gold for the first time produced good returns.

Conditions also improved somewhat for the Taínos. A royal *cédula* (decree) declared that the Indians were free vassals of the Crown of Castile. The Spanish contingent was small, and there were no new repartimientos, uprisings, or reprisals. However, no Indians were released from previous repartimientos, and they continued to suffer under the burden of being the major suppliers of food as well as the source of labor for the gold mines. This brief peace was soon shattered.

Conquest. In April 1502, Nicolás de Ovando replaced Bobadilla as governor. Ovando arrived with about twenty-five hundred persons, and the new arrivals had an immediate and devastating impact. Las Casas reported that sickness broke out and that one thousand of the new arrivals died and more became ill. The Spaniards who headed directly for the gold fields introduced diseases into an already unhealthy environment where the death toll among the Taínos reached 25 to 30 percent of each *demora* (work gang).

The *demora* was supposed to provide a measure of protection to the Indians. Indians would work in the mines for only six to eight months, after which they would return to their fields. In theory, the natives retained their freedom in exchange for a period of labor. In practice, the system failed to instill a sense of responsibility toward the Indians. While slaveowners had to see to the needs of their slaves, if only because they represented a financial investment, the *demora* was a revolving door of free labor. Indians in a *demora* were treated as expendable because new Indians were always arriving and because the period of labor was limited. Their labor was lost when their period of service ended.

Ovando also brought a change of emphasis. The principal effort of his first two years was to gain control of the entire island. He accomplished this by breaking apart the native political structure. In the fall of 1503, Ovando marched his forces into the *cacicazgo* of Jaraguá. The leaders of Jaraguá had peacefully submitted to tribute demands of Bartolomé Colón in 1496 and had cooperated with Roldán when he took control of this area. Ovando had eighty-four caciques burned and hanged, including the paramount *cacica*, Anacaona. Attention was next directed to the conquest of the southeastern peninsula in 1504, during which the *cacicazgo* of Higüayo was overrun and the last major Taíno cacique was deposed. All the natives were then assigned in repartimientos to the Crown or to individual Spaniards.

Throughout this period the Crown maintained that the Indians were vassals entitled to proper care and wages. These rights were largely ignored by Spaniards in La Española and were eventually abrogated. In 1503, Queen Isabel declared that the rebellious people "called Cannibals" could be captured and sold as slaves. In May 1509, in response to the dramatic decline in the Taíno population, King Fernando ordered Ovando to import all the Indians he could from neighboring islands.

The Bahamas became the immediate focus of slaving expeditions, and were depopulated by 1520. Pietro Martire d'Anghiera reported that forty thousand Lucayans were removed from the Bahamas. The Lucayans commanded a high price, 150 pesos per person, compared to the normal rate of five pesos, because they were in demand as divers on the pearl coast. The conquest soon spread to the neighboring islands. Cuba, Puerto Rico, and Jamaica were all brutally conquered. Las Casas claimed that the conquest of Cuba was so brutal it caused him to renounce his encomienda and to become an activist for native rights.

Genocide. Defined as the systematic extermination of a national or racial group, the term *genocide* is used here to characterize the extinction of the Taínos within two generations of the arrival of Columbus. Warfare, forced labor, disease, and miscegenation were the main agents of extermination. Las Casas claimed that three to four million Taínos were living in La Española in 1492, and he mourned the loss of five hundred thousand Lucayan souls. Historical demographers have increased the former number to eight million by using certain projection techniques, while at the same time discounting the latter. However, archaeologists who work with the material evidence have put the Taíno population at somewhere between four hundred thousand and two million. For the Bahamas, a population of about forty thousand is reasonable. The loss of several million native peoples in the West Indies is the most devastating result of contact with Europeans.

It is in the polemical writings of Las Casas that the mistreatment of the Indians is most completely expressed. Las Casas continuously chastises his countrymen for their disregard of native rights. He describes conditions in these words: "they thought nothing of knifing Indians by the tens and twenties and cutting slices off them to test the sharpness of their blades" and "they [the Taínos] saw themselves each day perishing by the cruel and inhuman treatment of the Spaniards, crushed to the earth by horses, cut in pieces by swords, eaten and torn by dogs, many buried alive and suffering all kinds of exquisite tortures."

But were such random acts of violence the exception or the rule? The worst offenses occurred during the Conquest. As colonists settled onto encomiendas, their profits depended on the well-being of their subjects. There was no economic benefit to killing Taínos for sport.

During the Conquest, Spanish battle strategy seems to reflect the lessons of their war with the Moors. On a large scale, horses, dogs, and European weapons were used to devastating effect. But to the surprise of the Taínos, the Spanish would then initiate amiable relations provided the defeated submitted to their demands. This behavior reflects certain expectations of conquest and submission. Other European tactics were also employed. Caciques were taken hostage to ensure the cooperation of their subjects, individuals were made an example of to frighten others into submission, and punishments such as hanging, burning, and facial disfigurement were exacted.

The purpose of conquest warfare was not to destroy the native population, but to secure the cooperation of the people in the extraction of wealth. Although casualties in war were certainly high, these would have been greatly exceeded by deaths in the gold fields. The *demora* system, with its 25 to 30 percent mortality, has been described above. Death resulted from inadequate nutrition (workers were fed only cassava bread) and to unhealthful conditions that promoted the spread of diseases.

The greatest loss of human life came from diseases. Native Americans presented "virgin soil" conditions to infectious European parasites, conditions under which mortality can reach 30 to 100 percent. More than a dozen potentially fatal diseases were carried into the Americas by unhealthy Europeans. It is clear that Taínos were dying from European diseases as early as 1493. However, the continued operation of *cacicazgos* in La Española indicate that diseases had only local effects prior to the smallpox epidemic of 1517, by which time most of the Taínos were already dead.

In their *Essays in Population History,* the historical demographers Sherburne Cook and Woodrow Borah projected annual rates of decline from 1496 to 1504 that exceeded 30 percent per year and totaled more than three million people of an original population of seven to eight million. Yet while this massive islandwide depopulation was supposedly going on, the *cacicazgo* of Jaraguá continued to function and to pay tribute. It is impossible that this *cacicazgo* could have survived intact while undergoing such massive depopulation.

Finally, the native societies lost their identity through the intermarriage of Spaniard and Indian and by bastardization. There were few Spanish women on La Española. An accounting in 1514 listed 392 *vecinos* (inhabitants) of whom 92 had Spanish wives and 54 had native wives. The outbreak of syphilis in La Española and Europe is evidence that a number of the Spaniards and Taínos engaged in intercourse. The result was the creation of a mestizo population, today the largest segment of Hispanic Americans.

Archaeologists have examined this exchange of cultural and genetic information as a process called transculturation. The adoption of native pottery by the Spaniards is one of the most obvious types of transculturation. The replacement of native peoples by those with a European ancestry is another. Taíno culture disappeared by 1505, Taíno art by 1530, and the Taíno population by 1545.

[See also *Black Legend; Disease and Demography; Encomienda; Indian America,* especially the article on *Taínos; Slavery; Syphilis.*]

BIBLIOGRAPHY

Cook, Sherburne F., and Woodrow Borah. "The Aboriginal Population of Hispaniola." In vol. 1 of *Essays in Population History.* Berkeley, Calif., 1971.

Crosby, Alfred W. *The Columbian Exchange: Biological and Cultural Consequences of 1492.* Westport, Conn., 1972.

Keegan, William F., ed. *Hispanic/Native American Interactions in the Caribbean: A Sourcebook.* New York, 1991.

Las Casas, Bartolomé de. *Historia de las Indias.* 3 vols. Mexico City, 1951.

Sale, Kirkpatrick. *The Conquest of Paradise.* New York, 1990.

Sauer, Carl Ortwin. *The Early Spanish Main.* Berkeley, Calif., 1966.

Wilson, Samuel M. *Hispaniola: Caribbean Chiefdoms in the Age of Columbus.* Tuscaloosa, Ala., 1990.

WILLIAM F. KEEGAN

PAINTING. For discussion of Columbus as a figure in painting, see *Iconography,* articles on *Early European Portraits* and *American Painting.*

PALOS DE LA FRONTERA. In 1492, when Columbus launched his momentous voyage from Palos, the town was barely a century old. King Juan I of Castile had legally separated the squatter settlement of Palos from the town of Moguer in 1380, established it as a town, and sold it to a nobleman from Seville, Alvar Pérez de Guzmán, for 160,000 maravedis.

Pérez de Guzmán proceeded to develop the economic infrastructure of his new town in order to attract families. He received from the king an exemption from all royal taxes for the first fifty families that would settle in Palos. With almost no level land for plowing and growing wheat, Pérez de Guzmán planted olive trees on the hillsides and built a warehouse on the beach where local seamen could store their merchandise and auction their fish. He drew up municipal ordinances and founded a town government. After his death in 1394, his heirs authorized the building of a Franciscan monastery, Santa María de La Rábida, within the municipal boundaries.

The town council, which was elected annually by the local citizens upon approval by the lord, expanded the town's economy. By the mid-fifteenth century, Palos had a municipal shipyard, extensive salt pans, and a town marketplace. The town's financial obligation to its lord was to pay a 5 percent sales tax on the fish auctioned to wholesalers and to harvest the lord's olive crop during November.

Prosperity attracted new settlers, even though these latecomers did not receive the royal tax exemptions. Most Palos citizens made their living from the sea as fishermen, import-export merchants, shipbuilders, and pirates. Fish, olive oil, and salt were the town's major exports, and wheat its major import. By 1478, the town's population had grown to six hundred households.

Palos became an extremely prosperous town and its lordship a valuable possession. In 1479, a descendant of Alvar Pérez de Guzmán sold one-twelfth of the town's lordship to the duke of Medina Sidonia for the price of 2,200,000 maravedis. On June 24, 1492, another descendant sold his half of the lordship to Queen Isabel for 16,400,000 maravedis, which the royal treasury paid in annual installments during the next six years.

The town of Palos had already entered the royal service a month earlier. In a town meeting in the parish church of San Jorge on May 23, 1492, the town crier read an order from Queen Isabel commanding Palos to contribute two caravels for royal service for twelve months. The town clerk, Francisco Fernández, recorded that in addition to the usual two town judges and three town councilmen, two noncitizens were present: a Franciscan from La Rábida, Juan Pérez, and a foreign businessman, Christopher Columbus. The town council released municipal funds to lease two Palos caravels, *Niña* and *Pinta*, and local business leaders from the Pinzón family agreed to captain the ships.

BIBLIOGRAPHY

Ladero Quesada, Miguel Angel. "Palos en vísperas del descubrimiento." *Revista de Indias* 38 (1978): 471–506.
Manzano Manzano, Juan. *Cristóbal Colón, siete años decisivos de su vida (1485–1492)*. Madrid, 1963.

HELEN NADER

PANÉ, RAMÓN (d. around 1498), author of early ethnological study of the Taínos. Ramón Pané arrived in La Española on Columbus's second voyage. Following orders from the Admiral, he went to live among the indigenous people of the island in order to study their "beliefs and idolatries." Pané learned their language, listened to their sacred songs and mythical tales, and submitted his findings in a report that he gave to Columbus around 1498. Known as *Relación acerca de las antigüedades de los indios* (Report on the antiquities of the Indians), this document is the first book written on American soil in a European language and marks the beginning of the ethnological study of American peoples.

The importance of this report went almost unnoticed, and its data were scarcely used because of problems understanding the text. In Spain, the manuscript was passed from Pietro Martire d'Anghiera (Peter Martyr) to Bartolomé de las Casas and Fernando Colón. The first two took note of its content, and Fernando included it in its entirety in his biography of his father, *History of the Admiral Cristopher Columbus by His Son*. Fernando Colón's work, which was left unpublished at his death in 1539, was brought to Venice, and in 1571 an Italian translation was printed by Alfonso de Ulloa. Fernando's original manuscript and Pané's original report are lost. All that have survived are d'Anghiera's notes in Latin, the summary in Spanish by Las Casas, and Ulloa's translation.

Many of the difficulties with the text could have been avoided if the original Italian translation had been better written. But Ulloa left an incomplete and hastily prepared manuscript. The translation is hence an uncertain rendering, with extensive use of indigenous terminology and several lacunae.

Following careful editing and research, the text now reveals a fascinating mythical world. It tells of the creation of the sun, the moon, the sea, and the fish; of the appearance of humans on the earth and their exploits until they arrived at the Caribbean islands; of the acquisition of fire and the cultivation and use of yucca and manioc; and of the transition from a nomadic to a sedentary life and the subsequent codification of habits and customs. It also lists the functions and attributes of the gods who inhabit the pantheon: the Supreme Being, lord of agriculture and sea activities; the Mother of God, mistress over the springs and tides and a compassionate protector of women in labor; and the Twins, the givers of the sun and the rain, among others. Finally, it narrates the moment when one of these gods announces the fateful forecast that strangers who wore clothes would come and devastate the land and people.

The reports transcribed by Pané have kept something of the original tone of the sacred hymns and epic legends, thus constituting an early record of the oral poetry and the narrative prose of the Antilles. They also serve to explain the arcane meaning of numerous handicrafts created by the Taíno potters and engravers and thus add an unexpectedly rich chapter to the history of the pre-Hispanic arts of the region, which was hitherto missing. Pané's account is no longer the forgotten evidence of an obscure friar; it has become one of the fundamental works of Hispanoamerican culture.

BIBLIOGRAPHY

Pané, Ramón. *Relación acera de las antigüedades de los Indios.* 8th ed. Mexico City, 1989.

JOSÉ JUAN ARROM
Translated from Spanish by Paola Carù

PAPACY. In the fifteenth and sixteenth centuries, the papacy was preoccupied with four principal concerns: the institutional unity of the Roman Catholic Church, peace among Christian princes and a crusade against Islam, church reform, and the defense and propagation of the faith.

Determined to prevent another Western Schism such as that of 1378 to 1417, during which the Roman, Avignonese, and Pisan popes each laid claim to the papacy, the popes from Martin V (r. 1417–1431) onward worked to preserve church unity by affirming the supreme authority of the Roman pontiff. Conciliarism, which asserted the ultimate authority of councils over the church and called for their frequent and regular convocation as set out by the Council of Constance (1414–1418), was stymied at the Council of Pavia-Siena (1423), sabotaged and discredited at Basel (1431–1449), refuted at Ferrara-Florence-Rome (1438–1445), deflated at Pisa-Milan-Asti-Lyon (1511–1512), and eviscerated at Lateran V (1512–1517). The attempt of the College of Cardinals to give the church an oligarchic constitution was countered by successive pontiffs' packing the college with their relatives and clients, and it ultimately failed when Sixtus V in 1587 legislated the transformation of the baronial cardinals into docile bureaucrats. The efforts of national states to set up autonomous local churches (e.g., the English Statutes of Provisors and Praemunire, 1351–1393; the French Pragmatic Sanction of Bourges, 1438; and the German Acceptance of Mainz, 1439) were in some cases checked and replaced by concordats regulating the relations between the papacy and the local church (e.g., for the Holy Roman Empire by the Concordat of Vienna, 1448; for France by that of Bologna, 1516; and for Spain by a series of papal bulls, culminating in *Eximinae devotionis affectus* of 1523). In other cases independent Protestant churches were established (e.g., Sweden in 1524 and England in 1534).

To guarantee the independence of the papacy from secular control, the popes labored to regain full sovereignty over their traditional Papal States in central Italy by subduing rebellious local lords and republican movements and by securing their territory's integrity and independence through a series of foreign alliances. Rome, the capital of the Papal States, was gradually transformed into the center of ecclesiastical and civil government with papal palaces and chapels, curial offices, cardinals' residences, and educational and cultural institutions. Christian pilgrims thronged its churches and processional thoroughfares, and visited the recently discovered (1578) catacombs. Some of the greatest artists and architects of this period such as Botticelli, Michelangelo, Raphael, Bramante, and Caravaggio contributed to making Rome a treasury of sacred art.

As head of Latin Christendom the papacy worked to end conflicts among Christians and to rally them to a defense of the Christian religion against Islam. Despite a series of papally supported campaigns to check the advance of the Turks in the Balkans and assist the embattled Byzantine Empire, Muslim forces defeated a huge Christian army at Kossovo in Serbia (1448), took Constantinople (1453), and within ten years conquered almost all the lands south of the Save and Danube rivers. The armies of Süleyman later took Belgrade in 1522, Rhodes in 1523, and most of Hungary in 1526, and unsuccessfully laid siege to Vienna in 1529.

Pope Paul III sent aid to the frontline Habsburg lands but found that his efforts to reconcile the Valois and Habsburgs, so that Emperor Charles V could confront the Turks, were hampered by King Francis I's alliance with Süleyman. As a member of the Holy League allied with Venice, Genoa, and Spain, the papacy provided money and ships for the failed efforts of 1537–1540, for the successful defense of Malta in 1565, and for the great but temporary Christian victory of Lepanto in 1571. That same year, however, Cyprus was conquered by the Turks. With offers of indulgences and patronage rights, the papacy successfully encouraged the Iberian monarchs to complete the Reconquista of Spain (Granada fell in 1492) and to take the fight against Islam to North Africa and the Arabian Sea.

As heads of the Roman Catholic Church the popes were called upon to reform the officials, procedures, and fees of the Roman Curia and to eliminate institutional abuses and moral misconduct throughout Christendom. Because many of these reforms involved a diminution in papal prerogatives and revenues at the very time the popes were struggling to strengthen their authority and to finance a restoration of Rome and the Papal States and a crusade against the Turks, the pontiffs were slow to act. They did, however, actively support the reform efforts of others: the movements to restore a pristine observance of rules by the older monastic and mendicant orders, the foundation of new religious orders (e.g., Theatines, Ursulines, Barnabites, Jesuits, and Oratorians), and local reforms by bishops, civil authorities, and special legates.

Beginning with the pontificate of Paul III (r. 1534–1549), the papacy assumed a role of leadership, enacting measures to reform the Curia, celebrating the Council of Trent (1545–1563), which issued numerous decrees reforming clerical education, preaching, appointment to church office, and religious practices, and finally seeing to the enforcement of these decrees. By the end of the sixteenth century the papacy was the driving force behind Catholic reform.

The defense and propagation of the Roman Catholic Church was the papacy's primary responsibility. Its efforts to restore communion with the Eastern Christian churches on the basis of an agreement on essential beliefs and practices resulted in the often only temporary unions negotiated at the Council of Ferrara-Florence-Rome (1438–1445) with the Greeks and Armenians (1439), Copts (1442), Syrians (1444), and Maronites on Cyprus (1445), and in the permanent union at the Fifth Lateran Council (1512–1517) with the Maronites of Lebanon. Protracted and confusing negotiations, however, ultimately failed to bring the Ethiopian church into permanent communion with Rome. In 1553 a group of the Chaldean Christians of Mesopotamia formally united with Rome, and in 1599 those of the Malabar coast of India also recognized papal authority at the Synod of Diamper. The largest group to enter permanently into union with Rome was the Ukrainians in 1595.

The efforts to suppress heresy within the Latin church were seldom successful. Despite persecution, the followers of Peter Waldo (d. 1217), known as Waldensians, survived in Savoy to be later absorbed for the most part by Protestantism. So too were the Lollard followers of John Wycliffe (d. 1384) in England and the Hussite disciples of Jan Huss (d. 1415) in Bohemia. Not appreciating at first the seriousness of the challenge coming from such Protestant theologians as Martin Luther (1483–1546) and Ulrich Zwingli (1484–1531), the papacy attempted to manage the problem by diplomacy and then resorted to public condemnations. Its effort to rally Catholic theologians, prelates, and lay leaders to a defense of the Catholic Church succeeded for the most part only in regions of southern Germany and the Rhineland. The English monarchs, with the exception of Mary I (r. 1553–1558), took that country at first into schism and then into Protestantism. Recourse to military means kept the followers of John Calvin (1509–1564) in check in France and present-day Belgium, but not in the Netherlands or Scotland.

But the most effective ways by which the papacy met the challenge of Protestantism were to clarify and explain Catholic doctrine at the Council of Trent (1545–1563), to support the preaching of the Capuchins (founded 1528) and the educational work of the Jesuits (f. 1540), and to suppress heresy through such instruments as indices of prohibited books and the Spanish (f. 1478) and Roman

(f. 1542) inquisitions. The vast bulk of the cases tried by these tribunals, however, involved questions of moral conduct, and the Spanish institution at first dealt primarily with feigned conversions from Judaism.

The task of propagating Catholicism in the newly discovered lands was entrusted by the papacy to the rulers of Portugal and Spain. Because the conversion of natives was considered more easily accomplished if political control were in the hands of a Christian, the popes invoked a theocratic theory generally accepted by canonists of the high and later medieval period, and as the acknowledged vicars of Christ to whom, it was believed, belongs the earth and all that is in it, they granted particular Christian princes dominion over certain territories. The grant of islands as papal fiefs may have been based on the Donation of Constantine.

To encourage the crusading efforts of the Iberian kings, the popes over the centuries issued bulls granting them special ecclesiastical patronage rights in the conquered lands. Thus in 1095 Urban II by the bull *Tuae dilectissime* granted to Pedro I of Aragón and his successors patronage rights over all the churches (except bishoprics) established on lands taken from the Moors. Eugenius IV in 1436 by the bull *Laudibus et honore* granted these same rights to Juan II of Castile and his successors. Not until *Orthodoxae fidei* (1486) of Innocent VIII were these patronage rights extended to include bishoprics, major canonries, and dignities in cathedral and principal churches, and other well-endowed benefices in Granada, the Canary Islands, and Puerto Real, a town recently founded near Cádiz by Fernando and Isabel. By the bull *Eximiae devotionis sinceritas* (1493), Alexander VI granted to the Spanish monarchs and their successors the right of presentation to all ecclesiastical benefices in the newly discovered lands of America. That this grant also included bishoprics was clarified only in 1508 by Julius II's bull *Universalis ecclesiae regimini* addressed to Fernando of Aragón and his daughter Juana of Castile. Sovereignty over the American territory had been granted to Fernando and Isabel and their successors by Alexander VI's bulls *Inter caetera divinae* of May 3–4, 1493, and *Dudum siquidem* of September 26, 1493.

The Portuguese had received similar grants of sovereignty earlier. Although Clement IV by *Sicut exhibitae* (1344) had granted to a member of the royal house of Castile, Luis de Cerda, permission to conquer and hold as a papal fief the Canary Islands (a military feat de Cerda never accomplished), Eugenius IV by *Romanus pontifex* (1436) granted to King Duarte of Portugal the right to conquer and hold independently these islands. Exclusive Portuguese sovereignty over Saracen lands in West Africa and those of infidels and pagans farther to the south and elsewhere to be conquered and Christianized was granted by *Romanus pontifex* (1455) of Nicholas V to Afonso V of Portugal. A year later at the request of King Afonso and his uncle Henry the Navigator, who was Administrator of the Order of Christ, Calixtus III by *Inter caetera quae* confirmed the grants of his predecessors and turned over to the Order of Christ ordinary spiritual jurisdiction over the conquered region from Capes Bojador and Não (also known as Nam, Nun, and Noun) in West Africa south to India and beyond. Leo X by *Dum fidei constantiam* (1514) confirmed the order's jurisdiction and accorded to the Portuguese kings the right to propose candidates for church offices in these overseas lands. When Julius III incorporated the grand mastership of the Order of Christ into the Crown of Portugal by the bull *Praeclara charissimi* (1551), the order's jurisdictional rights also passed to the Portuguese kings.

Although having recourse to the papacy had helped sort out some of their rival claims, the Spanish and Portuguese monarchs also came to their own negotiated agreement in the Treaty of Alcáçovas (1479). In addition to settling the disputed Castilian succession, Portugal recognized Castilian sovereignty over the Canary Islands, and Fernando and Isabel acknowledged Portuguese control over the Azores, the Madeiras, the Cape Verde Islands, and the West African mainland. By his bull *Aeternae Regis clementia* (1481), Sixtus IV confirmed the concessions made by Nicholas V and Calixtus III to the Portuguese and agreed to punish with spiritual penalties anyone who violated the terms of the Treaty of Alcáçovas. Thus the later division of the new lands between Castile and Portugal by Alexander VI's *Inter caetera divinae* (1493) had both papal and secular precedents. Similarly when the Spanish and Portuguese monarchs independently agreed after ten months of negotiations to settle their differences by moving the Line of Demarcation to 370 leagues west of the Azores and Cape Verde Islands in the Treaty of Tordesillas of June 7, 1494, the papacy once again confirmed this accord by the bull *Ea quae* (1506) of Julius II. In all these agreements the Iberian monarchs agreed to work as vicars of the pope for the propagation of the Christian religion in their lands.

The delegation to the Iberian monarchs of responsibility for the church in the new lands was not complete, however. The papacy formally instituted new dioceses and gave final approval to the appointment of their bishops. Popes also acted to encourage the creation of an indigenous clergy. They supported Portuguese efforts in this regard. In 1518 Leo X, acting on the advice of King Manuel I, appointed the son of the Christian king of the Congo, Ndoadidiki Ne-Kinu a Mumemba (c. 1495–c. 1531), also known by his Christian name of Henrique, as titular bishop of Utica, vicar apostolic of the Congo, and coadjutor to the bishop of Funchal. That same year, moreover, the pope issued the brief *Exponi nobis* ordering ordinaries to train and ordain to the priesthood native Christians. The Lisbon monastery of San Eloi had already trained native clergy for Africa and Asia for many years. In 1541 the Seminary of the Holy Faith opened in Goa to train similar indigenous clergy, and in 1571 another seminary opened on São Tomé Island to train African clergy. A seminary to train native clergy for Japan did not produce its first priests until 1601.

When Spanish efforts to create an indigenous clergy faltered, papal intervention was required. In Mexico the College of Santiago de Tlatelolco was founded in 1536 to train local clergy but soon desisted owing to fierce criticism by those who held that the Indians, if not incapable of Christianity, were too new to the Christian religion, dull, incontinent, inconstant, and proud to be ordained. At the urging of the Dominicans Bishop Julián Garcés and Fray Bernardino de Minaya, Paul III issued the bull *Sublimis Deus* (1537), which affirmed that Indians were capable of becoming Christians and that even as non-Christians they should retain their liberty and possessions. The First Mexican Provincial Council (1555) and the Second Provincial Council of Lima (1567–1568) prohibited the ordination of natives, but both decrees had to be modified in subsequent councils because of a 1576 decree of Gregory XIII allowing the ordination of mestizos. Thus, at significant points the popes intervened to ensure that missionary churches under Iberian royal patronage were in substantial conformity with the practices of the Catholic Church elsewhere.

[See also *Inquisition; Line of Demarcation; Missionary Movement; Reconquista; Religion; Rome; Spirituality of Columbus; Treaty of Alcáçovas; Treaty of Tordesillas*.]

BIBLIOGRAPHY

Bontinck, François. "Ndoadidiki Ne-Kinu a Mumemba, premier évêque Kongo (c. 1495–c. 1531)." *Revue africaine de théologie* 3 (1979): 149–169.

Boxer, Charles R. *The Church Militant and Iberian Expansion, 1440–1770.* The Johns Hopkins Symposia in Comparative History, no. 10. Baltimore, 1978.

Castañeda Delgado, Paulino. *La teocracia papal y la conquista de América.* Vitoria, 1968.

Hanke, Lewis. *All Mankind Is One: A Study of the Disputation between Bartolomé de Las Casas and Juan Gines de Sepúlveda in 1550 on the Intellectual and Religious Capacity of the American Indians.* De Kalb, Ill., 1974.

Muldoon, James. *Popes, Lawyers, and Infidels.* Philadelphia, 1979.

Pastor, Ludwig von. *History of the Popes from the Close of the Middle Ages.* Vols. 1–22. Translated by Frederick Ignatius Antrobus and Ralph Francis Kerr. St. Louis, 1923–1932.

Prodi, Paolo. *Il sovrano pontifice: Un corpo e due anime: Le monarchia papale nella prima età moderna.* Annali dell' Istituto storico italo-germanico, Monografia 3. Bologna, 1983.

Ricard, Robert. *The Spiritual Conquest of Mexico: An Essay on the Apostolate and the Evangelizing Methods of the Mendicant Orders in New Spain, 1523–1572.* Translated by Lesley Byrd Simpson. Berkeley, 1966.

Setton, Kenneth M. *The Papacy and the Levant (1204–1571).* 4 vols. Memoirs of the American Philosophical Society, vols. 114, 127, 161, 162. Philadelphia, 1976–1984.

Shiels, W. Eugene. *King and Church: The Rise and Fall of the Patronato Real.* Chicago, 1961.

Thomson, John A. F. *Popes and Princes, 1417–1517: Politics and Polity in the Late Medieval Church.* London, 1980.

NELSON H. MINNICH

PEDRÁRIAS. See *Ávila, Pedro Arias de.*

PERESTRELO Y MONIZ, FELIPA (c. 1454–c. 1484), wife of Christopher Columbus. Felipa Perestrelo y Moniz was born to one of the most illustrious noble families of Portugal. She was the daughter of Bartolomeu Perestrelo, the son of Filippo Pallastrelli of Piacenza, and Isabella Moniz, Bartolomeu's second or third wife.

On August 26, 1479, Christopher Columbus left Genoa for the last time and returned to Lisbon, where he had met and would marry Felipa Perestrelo y Moniz. The date of the wedding is unknown, but it is assumed to have occurred either between Epiphany and Lent, 1479, or between September 20 and October 21, 1479. These dates are probable, for Gonzalo Fernández de Oviedo states that Columbus "made himself a naturalized subject of that land by his marriage," and on August 25, 1479, Columbus stated that he was still "civis Januae" (citizen of Genoa). Hence, either he was not yet married or he had been married only a few months and had not yet acquired his new citizenship.

According to Columbus's son Fernando Colón, Columbus met his wife in the chapel of the Convento dos Santos, where they were later married. Columbus told his son that the marriage was based on love, but this claim does not exclude the possibility that there were other, mundane considerations for Columbus's choice of a bride.

One was her noble lineage. Both her father and mother were descendants of noble families. Throughout Columbus's life there is evidence that he aspired to the state of nobility denied him by birth. Nobility, more than money, was the reward he stipulated for his voyage of discovery. His wife's family was just what he wished his own father's had been—and, indeed, as he persuaded himself that it had been, boasting of it to his son Fernando, who perpetuated the illusion in his biography of his father.

A second possible reason for considering the marriage was the fact that, according to Fernando Colón and Bartolomé de las Casas, Felipa's father, Bartolomeu Perestrelo, had been "a great seafaring man." Although historians may regard this characterization as an exaggeration, there is some justification for the claim. Felipa's father, who had been dead for twenty years when she married Columbus, may have been neither great seafarer nor explorer, but he had been governor of Porto Santo. The fact that Prince Henry the Navigator had assigned him an island of such importance to Atlantic exploration suggests that Bartolomeu Perestrelo not only had been descended from nobility but had known the sea. It is interesting to note that the husband of his wife's stepsister, Pedro Correa da Cunha, was the present governor of Porto Santo. He would now be Columbus's brother-in-law, and in light of the significance of the island, the potential importance of the relationship was undoubtedly evident to Columbus.

It is not possible to claim with certainty that Columbus's marriage influenced his great plan. But it is evident that the marriage was important to the genesis of the great discovery.

Christopher Columbus and Felipa Perestrelo y Moniz had one child, Diego Colón, who was born on Porto Santo around 1480. Little more is known of the Admiral's wife, who died before Columbus left Portugal in 1485.

BIBLIOGRAPHY

Ballesteros Beretta, Antonio. *Cristóbal Colón y el descubrimiento de América.* Vol. 1. Barcelona and Buenos Aires, 1945.

Taviani, Paolo Emilio. *Christopher Columbus: The Grand Design.* London, 1985.

Treen, Maria de Freitas. *The Admiral and His Lady: Columbus and Filipa of Portugal.* New York, 1989.

PAOLO EMILIO TAVIANI

PETER MARTYR. See *Anghiera, Pietro Martire d'.*

PHILIP II (1527–1598), king of Spain. When his father, Charles V, abdicated in 1555–1556, Philip inherited Spain and its possessions in America, Italy, and the Low Countries. From the first, this vast empire was threatened by hostile powers, the most important of which were France and the Ottoman Empire. The French were distracted by civil wars after their defeat by Philip's armies at Saint-Quentin (1557), but the Turks continued to present a threat even after the Spanish-Italian naval victory at Lepanto (Náypaktos) in 1571.

In 1566, Philip's efforts to reform both church and state in the Netherlands led to revolt. His army, though superior to others of the day, was able to secure only the ten southern provinces by 1579. The north soon proclaimed its independence as the United Provinces of the Netherlands, but the king's exalted conception of royal

PHILIP II. At age fifty-nine.

authority and his devotion to the Catholic cause made it impossible for him to abandon the struggle. Meanwhile, English support for the rebels caused Philip to launch the disastrous Armada of 1588 and a second invasion attempt in 1597; fear of an alliance between the French Huguenots and their Dutch coreligionists led to a series of campaigns in France after 1589. Within Spain, Philip was forced to suppress rebellions by the Moriscos (1568–1570) and the Aragonese (1591). In spite of these problems, Philip invaded Portugal in 1580 and asserted his claim to the Portuguese throne after King Henry died without heirs. He was now the ruler of a second vast empire, though he was careful to preserve Portuguese institutions and governed with the aid of Portuguese ministers.

Philip's vigorous defense of his prerogatives and the ongoing war with the Turks were enormously expensive. His policies would have been impossible without the treasures of the New World, which during most of his reign contributed between 20 and 25 percent of Spain's total revenues. Protection of the American colonies and of their lifeline, the annual treasure fleet, was therefore one of the king's primary strategic goals. This elaborate system of convoys was established at the beginning of his reign

and strengthened continually thereafter. A French colony in Florida was destroyed in 1565, and Caribbean strongholds were fortified after the English raids of 1585–1586. After the defeat of the Armada in 1588 led Philip to rebuild and strengthen his Atlantic fleet, the American colonies remained almost inviolate for the remainder of his reign.

Internally, revolts by the descendants of the conquistadores in 1552–1554 and in 1565 convinced Philip that the colonies were threatened by anarchy. A committee under the presidency of Juan de Ovando reformed the Council of the Indies (1570–1572) and promulgated the Ordinances of 1573, which confirmed the rights of the Indians and attempted to set them on the road to self-government by locating them in fixed settlements. Disorder among the colonists and Indian raids on the frontiers were suppressed by two unusually competent viceroys, Martin Enríquez in Mexico and Francisco de Toledo in Peru. A *recopilación* of all laws pertaining to the Indies was begun, and in 1571 the Inquisition was extended to America. Philip may therefore be credited with establishing the basic system of Spanish colonial administration. He seems to have been in general agreement with the views of Bartolomé de las Casas, though unlike the Dominican, he questioned the morality of African slavery. The king's reformist impulses were constrained only by the desperate need for American bullion.

In the end, even the riches of the Indies proved insufficient to support Philip's policies, and Spain entered upon a long period of economic decline the ravages of which were evident well before his death. The reign of Philip II was nevertheless regarded as a golden age, and the king himself enjoyed a large measure of personal popularity. Hardworking, conscientious, and dignified, he was respected by his subjects for his piety and devotion to justice. His personal life, however, was tragic. His first wife, Maria of Portugal, died after two years of marriage, leaving him a son, Carlos, who died at twenty-three after being placed under arrest for his violent and unstable behavior. Philip was widely, and falsely, accused of murdering him. An unhappy marriage to Mary I of England was barren, and a third wife, Elizabeth of Valois, died young, leaving him two daughters to whom he was devoted. He had four sons by his fourth wife, Anne of Austria, but three of them died in childhood, leaving the survivor, the indolent Philip III, to inherit an exhausted empire that nevertheless spanned the entire world.

BIBLIOGRAPHY

Elliott, J. H. *Imperial Spain.* New York, 1963.
Lynch, John. *Spain under the Habsburgs.* 2 vols. 2d. ed. New York, 1981.
Parker, Geoffrey. *Philip II.* Boston, 1978.
Pierson, Peter. *Philip II of Spain.* London, 1975.

WILLIAM S. MALTBY

PICCOLOMINI, ENEA SILVIO. See *Pius II.*

PILOTING. The art of piloting, or pilotage, is conveniently distinguished from open-ocean navigation by the fact that it is a skill based on experience and judgment, whereas ocean navigation relies on measurement and mathematics. The distinction, however, cannot be too rigidly drawn. Although astronomical navigation, which is the salient feature of ocean navigation, was developed by the Atlantic-coast Portuguese and Spaniards during the Age of Discovery, mathematical navigation was born in the Mediterranean, where the deep basins and steep coastal formations and the absence of tidal streams favored techniques based on accurate measurements. The mariner's compass, the nautical chart, and the pilot books based on precise bearings and distances were all Mediterranean developments.

On the Atlantic seaboard conditions were quite different. The rise and fall of the tide governed not only the depths in harbors and anchorages but also the ebb and flow of the often fierce tidal streams that dominated coastal passage making. During the Columbian period, the skill of the pilot lay in his ability to conduct his ship from cape to cape in coastal waters; he drew on his knowledge of off-lying dangers, local sets (directions in which local currents flow), landmarks and seamarks, bottom depths, bottom composition, and tides. By the beginning of the fourteenth century Genoese ships were trading directly with ports in the English Channel, across the Bay of Biscay from Cape Finisterre to within soundings, or within the one-hundred-fathom line, in the approaches to the Channel, using the nautical chart, the magnetic compass, and the sounding lead. No doubt Mediterranean methods were then adapted to the tidal waters and shallow depths on the continental shelf of northwest Europe. The Portuguese, too, were by this time trading with Galway and Flanders and would have been familiar with the Breton and English methods of pilotage, which were largely dependent on the log and line and traditional knowledge gained from centuries of experience.

In Columbus's day the speed of a ship through the water was a matter of estimate, not direct measurement, and one of the skills of the pilot was determining the course and distance made good each day on the basis of his estimate of speed over a given period of time or on each leg of a traverse. In the Mediterranean, the tideless conditions favored the use of compass, bearing-and-distance chart, timeglass (to measure intervals of time), and the *toleta de marteloio*. With these methods he could determine the course made good since the last known position—the process known as dead reckoning. On the Atlantic seaboard, currents of unknown velocity and the ebb and flow of the tides upset this straightforward pattern, and the pilot had to rely more on his own resources and the traditional knowledge acquired, likely as not, through a long period of apprenticeship. As late as 1632, Adriaan Metius, a Dutch mathematician who wrote on astronomy and navigation, held that the determination of the number of miles run in twenty-four hours by a ship in ballast or laden with cargo could neither be described, explained, nor taught; only by long experience could the art of estimating the speed of voyages along familiar routes be mastered. Once the system of altura navigation had been introduced, there was some independent check of the distance traveled in a north-south direction, but the interpretation still depended on the pilot's judgment. The pilot took account of the conditions of lading, the strength of the wind, and the points of sailing taken on a course (running, making to windward, or reaching). He knew his ship, and though he might on occasion time the passage of a chip thrown overboard between two bolt-heads, using the repetition of some jingle to measure the interval of time, by and large he would trust his own judgment in estimating speed.

The timeglass, turned every half hour or hour, was used both to regulate the watch keeping and to help keep the reckoning. By night, the pilot would keep time by observing the constellation Little Dipper (Ursa Minor) and the star Kochab, the brighter of the two Guard Stars, using mnemonic rules based on the midnight position of the Guard Stars throughout the year. By day he would use a compass bearing of the sun, treating the compass rose as a clock face, each of the thirty-two points representing forty-five minutes, an inherently inaccurate system that nevertheless sufficed. Before the solution of the longitude problem, time of day, as opposed to measurement of the passage of time, was required principally for the prediction of tides. The "establishment of the port" at any place is the interval between the time the moon crosses the meridian and the actual time of high water, generally expressed in early tide tables and diagrams as a compass direction. From the "golden number," deduced from the date, from which he could calculate the epact, the pilot was able to determine the age of the moon (information he would later get from his almanac) and so the state of the tide for any port where the establishment was known.

During the Age of Discovery, the pilot was the ship's navigator. In the latter part of the fifteenth century, when oceanic navigation, which was necessarily mathematically based, was introduced, the manner in which the pilot exercised his responsibilities necessarily changed too.

[See also *Altura Sailing; Compass; Nautical Charts; Navigation; Timeglass; Timetelling.*]

BIBLIOGRAPHY

Crone, Ernst. *How Did the Navigator Determine the Speed of His Ship and the Distance Run?* Coimbra, 1969.

Waters, David W. "Early Time and Distance Measurements at Sea." *Journal of the Institute of Navigation* 8, no. 2 (1955): 153–173.

Waters, David W. *The Rutters of the Sea.* New Haven and London, 1967.

M. W. Richey

BIBLIOGRAPHY

Bascolo, Alberto. *Il genovese Franceso Pinelli amico a Siviglia di Christoforo Colombo.* Saggi su Christoforo Colombo. Rome, 1986.

Manzano Manzano, Antonio. *Christóbal Colón: Siete años decisivos de la vida, 1485–1492.* Madrid, 1964.

Taviani, Paolo Emilio. *Christopher Columbus: The Grand Design.* London, 1985.

Paolo Emilio Taviani
Translated from Italian by Rodica Diaconescu-Blumenfeld

PINELLI, FRANCESCO

(c. 1450–1509), primary financier of Columbus's first voyage. Pinelli was born to an ancient family, which was among the wealthiest in Genoa in 1528. He lived in Valencia for a time and then moved to Seville as a civil servant to the Crown. He acted as the monarchs' guarantor for a loan of five million maravedis they had contracted with the duke of Medina Sidonia, and Pinelli himself loaned them one million maravedis for the purpose of transporting the last Saracen king of Granada to Africa.

The Spanish monarchs made no cash contributions to Columbus's first voyage. Rather, they provided two caravels (*Pinta* and *Niña*) that they had received from the inhabitants of Palos as fines for crimes they had committed. Money for the expedition was raised through loans made to the minister Luis de Santángel by Italian merchants residing in Spain. The largest of these (1,140,000 maravedis) came from Pinelli. Other loans came from Giannotto Berardi, Jacopo di Negro, Luis Doria, Gaspare Spinola, Francesco Rivarolo, and Francesco Castagno.

There are also several factors linking Pope Innocent VIII to the sponsorship of the voyage. First is the fact that the Pinellis, a Genoese family, were related to the Cibo family, to which the pope belonged. And documents, which scholars are still examining, have recently been uncovered in Genoa, Spain, and the Vatican that point to the pope's direct involvement in the project. Moreover, it is known that Martín Alonso Pinzón, before returning to Palos and joining Columbus's venture, was in Rome for the unloading of a ship's cargo. According to certain indications from the Pleitos Colombinos, he probably visited the papal court while in Rome. And finally, Monsignors Antonio and Alessandro Geraldini, who gave substantial support to Columbus between 1486 and 1492, undoubtedly had direct contact with the pope.

It is difficult, however, to draw a complete picture of the sponsorship of the voyage. It is only certain that those who invested in it knew they would make money if the voyage went well. If it did not, they would, in any case, have earned the favor of the Spanish monarchy and, apparently, the papacy.

PINTA.

The *Pinta* was a caravel, the sort of vessel most frequently used by both the Portuguese and the Spanish in voyages of discovery during the late fifteenth and early sixteenth centuries. With their relatively light displacement, shallow draft, and sharp-ended hulls, and driven by the relatively efficient sails of their traditional lateen rig, they were fast, maneuverable, and capable of sailing to windward. These qualities minimized the frustrations of shoal waters and adverse winds likely to be encountered when exploring the unknown.

Like so much about ships of the period, the derivation of the caravel is controversial. Most maritime historians, however, credit the Arabs with development of both the lateen rig and the basic hull form. The Moors called a ship of this type a carabo or caravo from which the Spanish and Portuguese derived the diminutive forms carabela and caravela.

Pinta, by all accounts, was the fastest of the three ships of Columbus's fleet on his historic first voyage of discovery. This is readily explained by her finer lines as compared to those of *Santa María* and by her slightly greater length as compared to that of *Niña*. At some time prior to *Pinta*'s departure from Palos on the first voyage, her rig had been changed from the traditional lateen rig to "carabela redonda," square-rigged on foremast and mainmast with lateen-rigged mizzen. This was a far more practical rig for prolonged downwind open-ocean sailing, yet retained an only slightly reduced capability to sail to windward. Her conversion to a square-rigged configuration made it possible to improve her seaworthiness by the addition of a small raised forecastle deck, which, with her former lateen rig, would have been an obstruction to the lower end of her long, slanting lateen yard. A bowsprit, an unnecessary appendage with the lateen rig but an important adjunct to the square rig, had also been installed for accommodating the headstay of the foremast and the bowlines of the foresail and mainsail. Bowlines were attached by means of a bridle at about the midpoint of the two vertical edges of the square sails and led as far forward as possible. The purpose of bowlines, in conjunction with tack lines, was to haul forward the leading edges of the square sails to flatten and steady them for improved performance in sailing as close as possible into the wind.

There is consensus among maritime historians that *Pinta* had a cargo-carrying capacity of about sixty-five tons. From that value and from commonly used contemporary rules of thumb for hull proportions, it has been possible to arrive at reasonable assumptions of hull dimensions and shape. For a late-fifteenth-century caravel, the accepted hull proportions were in the approximate ratio of 1 for breadth or beam, 2.4 for length of keel, and 3.33 for overall length of hull. The master shipwright builder of *Pinta* would have known from his own long experience and from knowledge inherited from his father and forefathers that if the ship was to be of sixty-five tons burden her hull dimensions, using these ratios, should be roughly twenty-two feet for breadth or beam, fifty-three feet for length of keel, and seventy-three feet for overall length of hull.

Access to the hold was provided by two center-line hatches in the main deck. The main cargo hatch in the waist, just forward of the mainmast, was of a size such that a wine tun (barrel) of 1 meter by 1.5 meters could be lowered through it. A second smaller hatch was located aft under the half deck. Both hatches were fitted with covers to prevent heavy seas sweeping over the deck from pouring into the hold, which had no watertight bulkheads to control flooding.

In order to move beyond the mere external appearance of discovery-period ships and develop hard evidence of specific construction details, it is necessary is examine the relatively recent important findings of nautical archaeologists. The Institute of Nautical Archaeology at College Station, Texas, deserves great credit for important work in this field.

In 1982 the institute formed a group headed by Donald Keith to locate, survey, and excavate the wrecks of discovery-period ships in the Caribbean. Two shipwrecks they have surveyed and excavated are deemed to be of the discovery era. One is located on Molasses Reef near the Turks and Caicos Islands and the other just off the north shore of Highborn Cay in the northern Bahamas. The size and shape of the reasonably intact mound of stone ballast at the Molasses Reef wreck site indicates that the ship was of the approximate tonnage of *Pinta*, a common size for caravels of that period. A Florida-based treasure hunting company, Caribbean Ventures, which discovered the wreck, claimed it to be *Pinta* and one of four caravels in a fleet commanded by Vicente Yáñez Pinzón used during a voyage of exploration in 1499–1500. (Pinzón had been captain of *Niña* on Columbus's first voyage.) It is known that shortly after departing La Española on the return trip to Spain, Pinzón's ships encountered a severe storm and two of the caravels were lost. Most maritime historians,

however, believe there is insufficient evidence to support the claim that it is, in fact, *Pinta*.

Under the mounds of stone ballast at both the Molasses Reef and Highborn Cay shipwreck sites the institute's team found sections of the wooden hulls, which revealed valuable construction details. Substantial portions of hand-hewn keel, keelson, floor timbers, and other structural members were recovered and provided important information on their shape, dimensions, and methods of assembly and attachment. Among recovered artifacts were authenticated fifteenth-century wrought-iron breech-loading cannons (lombards) with separate breech blocks, breech-loading as well as muzzle-loading swivel guns with various types of shot for all, and several large anchors. Numerous wrought-iron hull fastenings and other fittings were found scattered about the sites. Iron gudgeons and pintles, hinge-like fittings used to fasten the rudder to the sternpost, provided information on the thickness of the sternpost and rudder. Several sets of iron rigging components provided indications of how the ships' standing rigging had been fastened to the hulls. With this sort of detailed information from shipwrecks, our knowledge of Columbus-era ships has been enhanced to a degree that now permits replicas of the two principal types, naos and caravels, to be constructed with high assurance of authenticity.

BIBLIOGRAPHY

Keith, Donald. *The Molasses Reef Wreck.* Institute of Nautical Archaeology. College Station, Tex., 1987.

Martinez-Hidalgo, José María. *Columbus' Ships.* Barre, Mass., 1966.

WILLIAM LEMOS

PINTO, FERNÃO MENDES (c. 1510–1583), merchant adventurer and author. Pinto's *Peregrination* is one of the most remarkable traveler's tales of the sixteenth century. It purports to be an autobiographical account of twenty-one years in the life of a man who traveled to almost every known—and unknown, at the time—part of Asia. In the year 1537, Pinto says, he sailed for India where he was shipwrecked, taken captive, and sold innumerable times. He was based in Malacca where he arrived in 1539, in the employ of the captain of the fortress whom he served as an ambassador-at-large to the neighboring kingdoms of Sumatra, Malaysia, and Martaban. Around 1540, after spending time in Burma and Siam, he shifted his activities to trading voyages in the China Seas and is known to have made four voyages to Japan.

Pinto claims to have been one of the first Europeans to have reached Japan, in 1542 or 1543, aboard a Chinese pirate junk that was blown off course and landed on the

FERNÃO MENDES PINTO. Statue dedicated in Almada, Portugal, 1983.

From its inception the work was enjoyed as an amusing traveler's tale, the first in European literature to tell of pirate battles on the high seas in the distant lands of the Orient. But this was far from the author's intention. A close reading reveals that *Peregrination* is a work of corrosive satire in which the author attacks the religious and political institutions of sixteenth-century Portugal. It is also a sweeping condemnation of the ideology of the crusade against the Moors, an extension of the crusade to liberate Iberia; this ideology was the justification for the overseas empire of the Portuguese, at least in Africa and Asia, and lay behind many of its excesses. Written in a period of religious strife, it is a rare book indeed in its plea for religious tolerance as a moral injunction from God. It is an early, if not the first, example, at the beginning of the age of European colonialism, of a literary work questioning the morality of the overseas conquests of the Portuguese.

Pinto's book is unquestionably an amalgam of everything he ever saw, heard, or read about Asia. But his genius lay in his ability to interweave it all into what has been described by Maurice Collis as "the most authentic picture of 16th-century Asia that has been written or that ever will be written."

BIBLIOGRAPHY

Collis, Maurice. *The Grand Peregrination.* 2d ed. London, 1990.
Le Gentil, Georges. *Les portugais en Extrême-Orient: Fernão Mendes Pinto, un précurseur de l'exotisme au XVIème siècle.* Paris, 1947.
Pinto, Fernão Mendes. *The Travels of Mendes Pinto.* Translated and edited by Rebecca D. Catz. Chicago, 1989.
Saraiva, António José. *Fernão Mendes Pinto ou a sátira picaresca da ideologia senhorial.* Lisbon, 1958. Reprint in *História da Cultura em Portugal* 3 (1962): 343–496.

REBECCA CATZ

island of Tanegashima—some fifty years after Columbus thought he had reached the Cipangu (Japan) he sought. If Pinto is to be believed, he was one of a group of three Portuguese who were indeed the first Europeans to set foot in Japan—thereby fulfilling Columbus's dream.

Sometime during his years in Asia, Pinto amassed a fortune. It was as a wealthy merchant on his third voyage to Japan that he met Francis Xavier, in 1551, and lent him the money to build the first Christian church in Japan. In 1554 Pinto joined the Society of Jesus (Jesuits) and took part in and paid for a diplomatic and evangelical mission to Japan. Two years later he was separated from the order at his own request, and in 1558 returned to Portugal.

Disappointed in his hopes of obtaining a royal sinecure, Pinto left the court after four years of fruitless petitioning. He married and retired to an estate in Almada, across the river from Lisbon. There he raised a family and wrote *Peregrination*, which became a classic of Portuguese literature; in the seventeenth century it rivaled in popularity Cervantes's *Don Quixote*.

PINZÓN, FRANCISCO MARTÍN (died c. 1500), master of *Pinta*. Francisco Martín Pinzón was the youngest member of the highly regarded Pinzón family of Palos. He was considered to be a competent mariner but seems to have lacked the forcefulness and ambition of his famous brothers, Martín Alonso and Vicente Yáñez, who overshadow him in the historical record. Nevertheless, when Martín Alonso Pinzón, the oldest and most reknowned of the brothers agreed to participate in the first of Columbus's voyages as captain of *Pinta*, he chose his young brother to serve as master instead of Cristóbal Quintero, *Pinta*'s owner, who normally would have been given that position.

Although the captain was in overall command of the ship, the master was in charge of the crew and responsible for their performance at sea and in port. Other responsibilities included the proper stowage of the cargo and all the ship's supplies and provisions, getting the ship under way with all appropriate sails set, managing the operation of the ship at sea, and anchoring the ship in a suitable location at the destination port. Unfortunately, no historical record exists of Francisco Martín's performance as master of *Pinta*. Whenever *Pinta* is mentioned in Columbus's log of the first voyage, as it is on a number of occasions, reference is made only to the captain.

On the return voyage to Spain in January and February 1493, *Pinta* became separated from *Niña* during a severe storm in the vicinity of the Azores. Driven to the northeast by the storm, *Pinta* finally made landfall on the northwest coast of Spain and sought refuge in the harbor of Bayona, near Vigo, to effect repairs. Not knowing whether *Niña* had survived the storm but certain that he had been first to reach Spain with news of the discoveries, Martín Alonso Pinzón sent word to the sovereigns in Barcelona announcing his arrival and requesting permission to come to court in person to make his report. To his dismay, and undoubtedly to that of Francisco Martín as well, the request for an audience was rebuffed. Crestfallen, the two Pinzóns set sail for Palos, reaching there on March 15 only a few hours after the Admiral's safe arrival. The sight of *Niña* already there, riding securely at anchor, was a shock. When they disembarked, they retired quietly to their home in Palos.

According to Alicia B. Gould, noted historian who spent many years searching for documentation of members of the crews of Columbus's ships of discovery, "Francisco Martín Pinzón has no historical importance, neither in that year [1492] nor later. Not one action nor one word about him comes down to us of his performance aboard ship in 1492, even though he held a position of importance; and of his later life very little is known." A notarial record in the Archive General of Simancas regarding the death of his mother, Mayor Vicente, in 1505 indicates that Francisco Martín Pinzón had predeceased her on an unspecified date. Apparently his death was as unheralded as his life seems to have been.

BIBLIOGRAPHY

Gould, Alicia B. *Nueva lista documentada de los tripulantes de Colón en 1492*. Madrid, 1984.
Manzano, Juan Manzano. *Los Pinzones y el descubrimiento de America*. 3 vols. Madrid, 1988.

WILLIAM LEMOS

PINZÓN, MARTÍN ALONSO (d. 1493), captain of *Pinta*. Martín Alonso Pinzón has been credited by many as the one person, apart from Columbus, most responsible for the success of the first voyage. In judicial proceedings (known as the Pleitos) between the heirs of Columbus and the Spanish Crown, convened in 1513, the Crown attempted to establish that Columbus was merely the nominal head of the voyage of discovery. It was Martín Alonso Pinzón, the Crown asserted, who had instigated, organized, and carried it out. Although controversy on this subject continues, most historians agree that the preponderance of evidence supports the view that Columbus conceived the plan to reach the Indies by sailing west, was responsible for convincing the sovereigns of its merit, and provided the leadership that resulted in discoveries of such significance to the world.

Yet there is little doubt that Martín Alonso and, to a lesser extent, his brothers Vicente Yáñez and Francisco Martín, all of the maritime village of Palos, were highly influential in overcoming the initial refusal by seafaring men in Palos, Moguer, and Huelva to participate in the dubious venture. They had no wish to be led by an unknown foreigner who foolishly, in their view, proposed to reach the distant Oriental regions of Cipangu (Japan) and Cathay (China) by a western route across the Mar Tenebroso (Dark Sea). To many of them, that sea abounded in countless terrors. In many testimonials offered during the Pleitos, Martín Alonso Pinzón was lauded as the most capable and honored ship captain in all the seaports of the Palos region. When Columbus came to him for help in recruiting seamen, he quickly volunteered to be captain of *Pinta*, one of the two ships provided for the venture by the town of Palos under orders from the Spanish sovereigns. During the Pleitos, a witness reported that Martín Alonso exhorted seamen of the region with the words, "Friends, come away with us. You are living here in misery. Come with us on this voyage, and to my certain knowledge, we shall find houses roofed with gold and all of you will return prosperous and happy." Another witness reported, "It was because of this assurance of prosperity and the general trust in him that so many agreed to go with him."

Also during the proceedings, Arias Pérez Pinzón, the older of Martín Alonso's two sons, testified that in early 1492 a friend of his father's, employed as a cosmographer in the Vatican Library, had given Martín Alonso a copy of a document indicating that Japan could be reached by sailing westward across the Atlantic. His father, impressed by this story, decided to attempt such a voyage himself. Soon thereafter, Martín Alonso discovered that Columbus was at the Franciscan friary of La Rábida, preparing to leave for France after learning that the Spanish sovereigns had rejected his plan for reaching the Indies. Martín Alonso, according to his son, showed Columbus his copy of the Vatican document and persuaded him to visit the sovereigns once more. Having done this, Columbus finally was successful in gaining royal approval for his enterprise. On returning to Palos, however, he tried for two months to procure ships and recruit men before turning for help to Martín Alonso, who succeeded where Columbus had failed.

Other testimony asserted that two interventions by Martín Alonso just prior to the first landfall in the Indies were vital to the success of the first voyage. By October 6, having lost faith in Columbus's pronouncements that they would reach the Indies at a distance of no more than 750 leagues (approximately 2,115 nautical miles) west of the Canary Islands, the seamen of the *Santa María* began to grumble and urge that the ship return to Spain before it became too late. According to testimony in the Pleitos, Martín Alonso proclaimed his support of Columbus and persuaded the men to continue on. Four days later, on October 10, against the opposition of the seamen of all three ships, Martín Alonso, with cries of "Adelante! Adelante! [Onward]," reportedly again convinced the men to continue the journey for three more days.

The Las Casas transcript of Columbus's log of the first voyage confirms an intervention by Martín Alonso on October 6, but of a different nature. The entry on that day states, "This night Martín Alonso said that it would be well to steer southwest by west for the island of Cipangu as indicated by the chart that Cristóbal Colón had shown him. It did not appear to the Admiral that they ought to change course because if the new course was incorrect they might miss the island and it would be safer to continue to the west and discover the mainland before going to the islands." The transcript for October 10 makes no mention of Martín Alonso but does confirm grumbling by the crew: "The men could now bear no more and complained of the long voyage. The Admiral cheered them on as best he could, telling them of great rewards they would soon gain and adding that they complained in vain because having set out for the Indies they must continue until, with the help of God, they found them."

Two days later, at two o'clock in the morning of October 12, 1492, Rodrigo de Triana, a seaman on *Pinta*, made the first sighting of land in the Indies, later confirmed to be an island of the Bahamas, which was called Guanahani by the natives. Martín Alonso Pinzón quickly verified the sighting and ordered the already loaded lombard to be fired as the signal of landfall and shortened sail to permit the flagship to catch up. When *Santa María* arrived, the Admiral also shortened sail and, with the fleet headed straight for an uncharted lee shore, ordered all three ships to lay-to until daylight. Finding a suitable anchorage on the leeward side of the island, the Admiral, accompanied by Martín Alonso Pinzón, Vicente Yáñez Pinzón (captain of *Niña*), Rodrigo de Escobedo (secretary of the fleet), and Rodrigo Sánchez (comptroller of the fleet), went ashore with royal banners flying. After a prayer of thanksgiving, Columbus took

possession of the island for the king and queen and named it San Salvador.

The fleet departed San Salvador to the southwest on October 15, taking with them six natives as guides. They sighted and assigned names to a number of islands, finally reaching the north coast of Cuba on October 28. After exploring along this coast for three weeks without finding evidence of the anticipated splendors and riches of the Orient, Martín Alonso became impatient and decided to strike off on his own. The Las Casas transcript of the log entry for November 21 states, "This day Martín Alonso Pinzón sailed away with the *Pinta* without the permission and contrary to the wish of the Admiral but rather through greed, thinking that an Indian whom the Admiral had ordered aboard that caravel would give him much gold; and so he went away without waiting, without the excuse of bad weather, merely because he wished to do so." Testimony given in the Pleitos stated that after departing, Martín Alonso sailed east and discovered a large island that he believed to be Cipangu. He christened a river on its north coast with his name ("Río de Martín Alonso") and found evidence of gold in the mountains.

On January 6, 1493, Martín Alonso rejoined the Admiral who had also come upon the same island and named it La

MARTÍN ALONSO PINZÓN.   MUSEO NAVAL, MADRID

Española (Hispaniola). Having lost *Santa María* on a reef on Christmas night, Columbus was making preparations to return to Spain in *Niña*. The two remaining ships of the expedition headed east along the north coast of La Española, exploring as they went, and on January 16 took departure for Spain. A severe storm just west of the Azores separated them once again. *Pinta* was driven by the gale to a landfall on the northwest coast of Spain and sought refuge in the port of Bayona in Galicia.

Not knowing whether *Niña* had survived the storm but certain that he had been first to reach Spain with news of the discoveries, Martín Alonso promptly sent word to the sovereigns in Barcelona, announcing his arrival and requesting permission to come to court in person to make his report. Confident of a favorable response and eager to make the journey to Barcelona as early as possible, he remained in Bayona awaiting the expected summons. To his dismay, his request for an audience was rebuffed. Crestfallen, he set sail for Palos, reaching there on March 15 only a few hours after the Admiral's safe arrival. The shock of finding *Niña* already there, riding securely at anchor, struck a mortal blow. Older than Columbus, he was broken in health from the rigors of the voyage and mortified over the honors to be bestowed upon a man whose authority he had been unwilling to acknowledge. Martín Alonso Pinzón went directly to his country home near Palos and died in despair within the month.

BIBLIOGRAPHY

Gould, Alicia B. *Nueva lista documentada de los tripulantes de Colón en 1492.* Madrid, 1984.
Manzano, Juan Manzano. *Los Pinzones y el descubrimiento de America.* 3 vols. Madrid, 1988.

WILLIAM LEMOS

PINZÓN, VICENTE YÁÑEZ (c. 1461–c. 1513), captain of *Niña* and explorer. Vicente Yáñez Pinzón and his brothers Martín Alonso and Francisco Martín, captain and master, respectively, of *Pinta* on Columbus's first voyage, were respected members of the seafaring community of Palos and well known in the adjoining communities of Huelva and Moguer. Their commitment to Columbus and his enterprise helped overcome the initial reluctance of local seamen to sign on as crewmen in such a questionable venture. During the first voyage, Martín Alonso became disgruntled at finding no evidence of the anticipated riches of the Orient and left the formation to explore on his own without authorization from Columbus. But Vicente Yáñez loyally remained with the Admiral. On Christmas night when *Santa María* ran aground through the negligence of Juan de la Cosa, her owner and master, Vicente Yáñez again proved his loyalty by sending one of

Niña's boats to assist Columbus. He also refused to grant refuge to La Cosa, who had fled from his grounded ship, disregarding a direct order from the Admiral to set out a kedge anchor by which the ship might have been hauled off the reef.

The death of the eldest brother, Martín Alonso, soon after his return from the first voyage and the initial failure of the Spanish sovereigns to recognize the Pinzóns' vital role in the voyage instilled in the two surviving brothers a feeling of jealous hostility toward Columbus. Neither of the brothers took part in any of Columbus's subsequent voyages. When command of private expeditions became available in 1499, Vicente Yáñez was quick to respond. His perceived hostility toward Columbus worked in his favor, since Bishop Juan Rodríguez Fonseca, who was granting authorizations for expeditions, had long harbored a similar hostility.

Unlike Alonso de Ojeda and Peralonso Niño, other maritime adventurers who had obtained financial backing for their expeditions from wealthy merchants in Seville, Vicente Yáñez was obliged to fit out his four caravels on credit from mercenary ship outfitters in Palos. Among his crew were two nephews, several seamen, and a pilot who had been with Columbus when he discovered the Gulf of Paria and the continental landmass of South America. They put to sea from Palos early in December 1499, bypassing both the Canary Islands and the Cape Verde Islands and pressing on instead to the southwest for the southern mainland.

Pinzón deliberately took a more southerly course than Columbus had on his third voyage in order to make a landfall farther south on the mainland. This course took him across the equator. At that point, the North Star was no longer visible, and he was deprived of the only celestial means known to him for determining his latitude. The southern skies were completely foreign to him. But since seafarers of the period kept track of their position principally by dead-reckoning navigation—that is, by keeping a record of compass courses, estimated speeds, and leeway—Pinzón probably did not feel handicapped by the disappearance of the North Star. He continued on to the southwest until he reckoned his latitude to be eight degrees south of the equator, at which point he changed course to the west to find land. On January 28, 1500, nearly two months after leaving Palos, he finally sighted the easternmost promontory of the southern continent. As a sign of his relief, he named it Santa María de la Consolación and took formal possession for the Spanish Crown.

Finding the natives in the area decidedly inhospitable, Pinzón reportedly sailed off to the northwest, indicating that his landfall had been at what is now Cabo de São Roque at about five degrees south latitude rather than his reckoned eight degrees, a not unusual discrepancy in dead reckoning after nearly two months at sea. In a second attempted landing along the coast, he and his crew encountered more hostile Indians, resulting in the death of several Spaniards and the wounding of many more. Sailing on to the northwest, Pinzón recrossed the equator and was astounded to find that the seawater was so fresh he was able to refill his casks. Standing in toward the coast, he discovered the mouth of an immense river that was, of course, what we now know as the Amazon. Here, for the first time on this voyage, he found the Indians to be friendly. But finding no gold or other riches, he departed, emulating other early explorers by carrying off thirty-six of the natives as captives.

The North Star having reappeared above the horizon, Pinzón proceeded along the coast to the northwest with renewed confidence, passing the mouths of the Essequibo and Orinoco rivers, which had already been encountered by Ojeda, and eventually reached the Gulf of Paria, where Columbus had discovered the southern continent. Landing there and finding a magnificent stand of tall, straight trees, he ordered some to be cut down and loaded aboard as cargo. There is no record of his attempt to acquire any of the plentiful and valuable pearls along the coast just to the west of Paria. Instead, he set off for La Española, arriving there in late June 1500 and stopping only briefly to refit his ships for the long voyage home.

Departing La Española in July, Pinzón sailed north to the Bahamas, presumably profiting from the experience gained with Columbus in 1492 when they had headed north to find the favorable band of westerly winds to take them swiftly home. His four ships, apparently anchored at a location for which there is no existing record, were struck by a fierce hurricane, which sank two of his ships and severely damaged the remaining two. The survivors, Pinzón among them, returned to La Española, repaired the damages, and set off once again for Spain, anchoring at Palos at the end of September. The merchants to whom Pinzón was in debt for most of the expenses of the expedition promptly seized the two ships and their cargo. A petition to the Crown saved him from imprisonment and ruin, but the damage done by the hurricane stripped him of any financial gain from the voyage.

On September 5, 1501, Vicente Yáñez Pinzón received royal authorization to colonize and govern the lands he had discovered in the vicinity of the Amazon River, but there is no record of his ever exploiting that authorization. In 1506 and again in 1508, expeditions under the joint command of Pinzón and Juan Díaz de Solís attempted in vain to find a strait or passage to the Indian Ocean. On the 1508 expedition they sailed as far as forty degrees south latitude, but the honor of discovering the strait was to go to Ferdinand Magellan. In belated recognition of the important contributions made by the Pinzón family to the discovery of the Indies, Emperor Charles V, in 1519, granted their descendants a coat of arms emblazoned with three caravels and an island covered with Indians.

BIBLIOGRAPHY

Gould, Alicia B. *Nueva lista documentada de los tripulantes de Colón en 1492.* Madrid, 1984.
Manzano, Juan Manzano. *Los Pinzones y el descubrimiento de America.* 3 vols. Madrid, 1988.

WILLIAM LEMOS

PIUS II (1405–1464), pope, diplomat, poet laureate, bishop, and historian. Enea Silvio (Latin, Aeneas Silvius) was born at Corsignano, Piccolomini, Tuscany (later called Pienza after his papal name). The eldest of eighteen children of an impoverished aristocratic family, he was educated at Siena and Florence. As secretary to the bishop of Fermo, he attended the Council of Basel from 1431 to 1435, but fled because he was involved, as secretary to the bishop of Novara, in a plot against Pope Eugenius IV. He became secretary to Cardinal Nicolas Albergati and attended the Congress of Arras. Next he journeyed to Scotland, while suffering terribly after walking barefoot through snow to carry out a vow, to persuade James I to harass the English; the cardinal hoped that this would end the Hundred Years' War. In 1436 he returned to Basel and played a part in "deposing" Eugenius IV, who retaliated by dissolving the council. In 1440, Felix V (a layman and duke of Savoy, elected by the council the previous year but not recognized by the Vatican) made Enea Silvio papal secretary. Two years later, Emperor Frederick III appointed him poet laureate and private secretary; in 1445 he made his peace with Eugenius. He took holy orders in 1446, and promotion was rapid: he became bishop of Trieste in 1447, bishop of Siena in 1450, and a prince and cardinal in 1456.

In 1458 he was elected pope, taking the name Pius II, with the help of Rodrigo Borgia (later Pope Alexander VI). When Pius's open letter to Sultan Muhammad II suggesting that he convert to Christianity proved ineffective, he proposed a new crusade. In 1464, despite loss of German support, he set out from Venice as a crusader, but died at Ancona.

Enea Silvio produced numerous works in many spheres. Before he became a cleric, he wrote poems in Tuscan and Latin; a novel, *Historia de Eurialo et Lucretia,* in the style of Boccaccio; a Plautine play, *Chrysis;* and letters and essays on many subjects. His commentaries on the Council of Basel are exhaustive.

His geographical work, also known as *Cosmographia,* has the full title *Historia rerum ubique gestarum locorumque descriptio;* since it was never completed, its

PIUS II. Engraving, from André Thevet's *Portraits et vies des hommes illustres*. Paris, 1584.

constituent parts are often quoted under their own titles. Perhaps his most important comments from this work concern long-distance voyages. In *De mundo in universo*, Pius writes

> It has been disputed whether this island [the known world] can be circumnavigated. Strabo the Cretan [actually of Amasia in Pontus] thought the Southern Sea could certainly not be navigated because of intolerable heat, or the northern because it was frozen. Solinus quotes Juba as claiming that in the whole of the South . . . all the sea encircling Africa, from India back to Spain, is navigable, adding stopping-places and distances. Pliny of Verona [actually of Comol] . . . quotes Cornelius Nepos [in fact, Strabo] as writing that one Eudoxus, a contemporary, fleeing from King Lathyrus, sailed from the Arabian Gulf as far as Cadiz.

From this extract and its context it is clear that Pius rejected Ptolemy's notion that southern Africa is connected to southern Asia. It may have been his influence that led to the alteration of the coastline in the pre-1460 Wilczek-Brown Ptolemaic map of southern Africa.

Pius's use of the word *hodie* (today) in his description of navigation in the eastern Atlantic reflects the assertion of the ancient Roman scholar Pliny the Elder: "totus hodie navigatur occidens" (today men sail over the whole of the West). He shows no sign of having seen Fra Mauro's map of 1459. His descriptions of Asiatic peoples are likewise derived from ancient geographers. It is probably thanks to Pius's work that an Arctic island inhabited by Aronphei appears in Johan Ruysch's map in the 1508 Rome edition of Ptolemy, of which a palimpsest has been deciphered. When Columbus reached Cuba, he thought it was Cipangu (Japan), evidently concluding from Solinus as quoted by Enea Silvio that the inhabitants were Seres, "mild, very quiet and preferring to show their bodies rather than dress."

Pius II's impact on Columbus and other Renaissance explorers should not be exaggerated. As a keen interpretation of classical geographers, his work was read with attention. His interest in contemporary geography, however, was linked not so much with exploration as with his attempt to limit Turkish expansion. He was a close friend of Nicholas of Cusa, corresponded regularly with him, and at the outset of his papacy promoted him. It is hence likely that Pius II furthered Nicholas's cartographic activities; however, any connection between these activities and areas of exploration is speculative.

BIBLIOGRAPHY

Aeneas Silvius (Pius II) *Opera*. Basel, 1571. Reprint, Frankfurt am Main, 1967.

Dilke, O. A. W., and Margaret S. Dilke. "The Wilczek-Brown Codex of Ptolemy Maps." *Imago Mundi* 40 (1988): 119–124.

Gasparrini Leporace, Tullia. *Il mappamondo di Fra Mauro*. Rome, 1956.

McGuirk, Donald L. "Ruysch World Map: Census and Commentary." *Imago Mundi* 41 (1989): 133–141.

Mitchell, R. J. *The Laurels and the Tiara: Pope Pius II, 1458–1464*. London, 1962.

O. A. W. DILKE

PIZARRO, FRANCISCO (1478–1541), Spanish conqueror of the Incas and governor of Peru. Francisco Pizarro was the illegitimate son of Gonzalo Pizarro, a royal captain of infantry and member of a recently established hidalgo family in Trujillo, Extremadura, Spain, and Francisca González, a servant of nuns and the daughter of a poor farmer. Pizarro spent much of his childhood in his paternal grandfather's home as well as with his mother's humbler relatives. He may have done agricultural work or practiced a manual trade in his earlier years. The sixteenth-century chronicler Francisco López de Gómara reported that the infant Pizarro was left at a church door, was suckled by a sow, and later was reluctantly recognized by his father and put to work herding swine. However, James Lockhart presents documentary evidence that this was a malicious story invented by Gómara, whose intention was to enhance the qualities and military successes of Hernando Cortés, Pizarro's rival.

Pizarro had some military experience in Italy before he arrived in the New World in 1502 in the fleet of Nicolás de Ovando, the governor of La Española. He either accompanied his uncle, Juan Pizarro, or was sent to join him in Santo Domingo. He became a leader in La Española, joined Alonso de Ojeda's expedition to the Gulf of Urabá in 1509, and shortly thereafter was left in charge of it as lieutenant general when Ojeda was recalled. He was second in command to Vasco Núñez de Balboa when he saw the Pacific for the first time. Governor Pedrárias (Pedro Arias de Ávila) sent Pizarro to arrest Balboa, and thereby conferred on him the enterprise of the discovery and conquest of Peru.

Pizarro was a tall, hollow-cheeked, thin-bearded, grim man of few words, ambitious but never flashy. He was well respected. When Panama was founded in 1519, he was a prominent citizen, council member, one of the largest encomenderos, and later an alcalde. Pizarro was formed

FRANCISCO PIZARRO. Engraving.

by his experience in the New World. He was pragmatic and defended the customs of the Americas over Spanish legalism, valued seniority in the colonies, and despised those with less experience. He favored his old companions and resented all royal or ecclesiastical supervision. Though proud of his hidalgo lineage and willing to appeal to his rank over his subordinates, he preferred to fight as a footman, the only way to fight in the isthmian jungles. He was illiterate, had never learned noble pastimes, and knew nothing of business or law, and so preferred the plebian amusements of gambling and sporting and liked to work. He was indifferent to everyone, never offered praise, was suspicious and implacable, but able to cut through verbiage and pretense. His ambition was to rule Peru as the governor and to leave his legacy to his descendants.

When the first Peru expedition was organized (1523–1524), Pizarro was senior to almost anyone else in Panama and had the longest experience of command. He was therefore put in charge. Pizarro and Diego de Almagro bore the heaviest burden of the financial support and Fernando de Luque contributed in lesser measure. In 1526 Pizarro led a second expedition to Peru, but it retired to Gallo Island off the coast of Ecuador. In 1527 Pedro de los Ríos, the governor of Panama, gave the men on Gallo the choice of returning to Panama or remaining on Gallo. Pizarro spoke in favor of remaining and thirteen men did so. No record exists of Pizarro's exact words, but the flowery speech attributed to him is not in keeping with his character. In 1528–1530 Pizarro returned to Spain by way of Panama, and in a document called the Capitulation, the Crown granted him the governorship of Peru and authorization to conquer the country. He was also made a knight of the Order of Santiago. Among the men he recruited for this expedition were his brothers Juan, Hernando, and Gonzalo, and many Trujillans and other Extremadurans.

In 1532 his expedition occupied Tumbes in the northern part of the Inca Empire, where he founded the first Peruvian settlement, San Miguel (Piura). When he entered Cajamarca to capture the Inca Atahualpa, he found it deserted and the Inca encamped nearby. When Atahualpa returned on November 16, 1532, he was ambushed by Pizarro's troops. Atahualpa offered a ransom of a room filled with gold and silver in return for his life, but Pizarro had him executed in July 1533. Though Pizarro at first founded Jauja as the capital of Peru and Cuzco, he later abandoned it and moved the capital to Lima in 1535. He later founded Trujillo and San Juan de la Frontera (Huamanga, now Ayacucho). Charles V made Pizarro a marquis in 1537 but Pizarro never chose a territorial title. In 1536–1537 the Indians laid a seige to Cuzco, which Almagro ended, seizing the city for himself. Pizarro's army defeated

Almagro at the battle of Salinas (Cuzco) in 1537 and executed him. In retaliation the partisans of Almagro's son, Diego de Almagro, assassinated Pizarro in Lima in 1541.

Pizarro left four mestizo children by two Indian mistresses. Francisca Pizarro, his legitimized daughter by Inés Yupanqui Huaylas, a daughter of Huayna Capac, lived the longest of all his children, received Pizarro's encomienda, and married his brother Hernando. His son Gonzalo Pizarro was also legitimized. His second mistress, Añas Yupanqui, a daughter of either Atahualpa or Huayna Capac, known as Doña Angelina, bore two (never legitimized) sons, Francisco Pizarro, a companion to Garcilaso de la Vega, and Juan Pizarro, who died in childhood.

BIBLIOGRAPHY

Cieza de León, Pedro de. *Tercera parte de la crónica del Perú.* Lima, 1946.
Hemming, John. *The Conquest of the Incas.* San Diego, 1970.
Lockhart, James. *The Men of Cajamarca.* Austin, Tex., 1972.
Pérez de Tudela, Juan, ed. *Crónicas del Perú.* Vol. I. Madrid, 1963.

JEANETTE SHERBONDY

PIZARRO, GONZALO (c. 1512–1548), youngest brother of Francisco Pizarro and his successor as governor of Peru. Gonzalo Pizarro was the illegitimate son of Gonzalo Pizarro and María Alonso and like his full brother, Juan Pizarro, was brought up in his father's household. He was quite young when the Incas were defeated at Cajamarca and is mostly known for the great rebellion he led against the Crown's authorities. He was arrogant, rash, and imprudent. While Hernando's ambition was to return to Spain with his wealth, Gonzalo Pizarro's was to stay in Peru and maintain the Pizarro family power and interests.

He became a major actor in the conquest of Peru upon the death of Juan Pizarro during the seige of Cuzco, when Hernando Pizarro made him captain of cavalry. After the battle of Salinas, Francisco groomed him as his second in command. He founded La Plata (Charcas) and had encomiendas in Cuzco, Charcas, and Arequipa. He was sent to Quito to govern the region and while there, led an expedition into the Amazon. When he returned, he learned that Francisco had been assassinated and that, even though Francisco had designated Gonzalo in his will as his successor, Vaca de Castro, the royal representative, had cheated him of his governorship. Vaca de Castro banished him to Charcas. When the first viceroy, Blasco Núñez de Vela, arrived in 1544, Pizarro organized a rebellion of the Peruvian Spaniards and was appointed governor of Peru by the audiencia. He ruled for about four years. In 1548, however, the royal forces of Pedro de la Gasca defeated Pizarro at the battle of Jaquijahuana, near Cuzco, and he was executed.

BIBLIOGRAPHY

Hemming, John. *The Conquest of the Incas.* San Diego, 1970.
Lockhart, James. *The Men of Cajamarca.* Austin, Tex., 1972.

JEANETTE SHERBONDY

PIZARRO, HERNANDO (1501–1578), brother of Francisco Pizarro, second-in-command in the conquest of Peru. Hernando Pizarro, the legitimate son of Gonzalo Pizarro and Isabel de Vargas, was his older brother, Francisco Pizarro's, right-hand man in the conquest of Peru. His upbringing in his father's household in Trujillo, Extremadura, Spain, had been very different from Francisco's. He was fully literate, had had extensive military experience in Europe as captain of infantry, had a horse, was knowledgeable in financial affairs, and was more comfortable with words than Francisco and even witty. His one outstanding personal trait, however, was self-centeredness. In appearance he was a massive, heavy man.

At Cajamarca he led a group of horsemen in the ambush of Atahualpa. His share in the ransom was the largest after Francisco's. He led the expedition that took the temple of Pachacámac. As Francisco Pizarro's major emissary to Spain, he conveyed part of the king's portion of the ransom to Spain as well as his own share. The Crown immediately sent him back to Peru, where he took over as lieutenant governor of Cuzco from his younger brother, Juan. He led the defense of Cuzco during the seige in 1536–1537, but when Cuzco was seized by Diego de Almagro, he was imprisoned. Upon his release, he defeated Almagro's army at the battle of Salinas and executed Almagro. He led an expedition into Collasuyu and in 1539 returned to Spain, where the Crown imprisoned him indefinitely for the execution of Almagro. He married his niece, Francisca Pizarro, Francisco's sole heir, in 1552, thus consolidating their vast wealth.

BIBLIOGRAPHY

Hemming, John. *The Conquest of the Incas.* San Diego, 1970.
Lockhart, James. *The Men of Cajamarca.* Austin, Tex., 1972.

JEANETTE SHERBONDY

PIZARRO, JUAN (c. 1509–1536), brother of Francisco Pizarro, Spanish conqueror of Peru. Illegitimate son of Captain Gonzalo Pizarro and María Alonso, Juan Pizarro grew up in his father's household in Trujillo, Extremadura, Spain, in the style of a hidalgo. He could sign his name but was otherwise illiterate. He was popular, magnanimous, and considerate. As a brother of Francisco, he was put in positions of responsibility even though he was young, the second youngest of the four Pizarro brothers in the conquest of Peru. At Cajamarca, Francisco put him in charge of one-half of the foot soldiers. He received the fourth largest share in the gold and silver of Atahualpa's ransom. He was a member of the council of Cuzco at its founding and represented the Pizarro family interests. He led the Pizarro faction in resisting Almagro's takeover of Cuzco. Juan was appointed captain general and then corregidor of Cuzco. He was mortally wounded in the seige of Cuzco and died two weeks later. He never married, but had at least one mestizo daughter in Peru, Isabel, to whom he left a dowry.

BIBLIOGRAPHY

Hemming, John. *The Conquest of the Incas*. San Diego, 1970.
Lockhart, James. *The Men of Cajamarca*. Austin, Tex., 1972.

JEANETTE SHERBONDY

PIZZIGANO CHART. The Pizzigano chart, dated 1424 and signed by Zuane Pizzigano, is preserved in the James Ford Bell Library of the University of Minnesota, Minneapolis. It is intricately bound up with the debate concerning a possible pre-Columbian discovery of America by the Portuguese.

In 1954, the chart was introduced in extravagant terms by the Portuguese historian Armando Cortesão, to whom we are indebted for its study and publication in a work published by the University of Coimbra. In the opinion of Cortesão, the chart represents the Antilles, Caribbean islands, which are given Portuguese names. If this were so, the discovery of America would have to be attributed to the Portuguese, and at a date far earlier than the one generally accepted today. (Note that even in Portugal, the first steps toward the discoveries promoted by Henry the Navigator were just being taken in 1424.) An acceptance of this idea would be nothing less than revolutionary and would detract considerably from the glory of the discoveries of the successive navigators who touched at the American continent, beginning with Christopher Columbus in 1492.

Needless to say, the opinions advanced by Armando Cortesão did not meet with unanimous acceptance among the international community of scholars of the history of discovery and ancient cartography. Quite the contrary, his conclusions were rejected by the great majority of them, especially the numerous defenders of the glories of Columbus. Even in Portugal, Cortesão's hypotheses were regarded as somewhat unsubstantiated. Among Portuguese specialists, Jaime Cortesão, in his latest publications, has reexamined, accepted, and developed the theses presented by his brother, regarding them as support for his own views on the policy of secrecy of the Portuguese Crown concerning western voyages and discoveries, a policy that began as far back as the time of Henry the Navigator. Few Portuguese scholars, however, share his enthusiasm.

The enigmatic document at the center of the debate is an Atlantic chart representing the European and African coasts (as far south as the Canary Islands) and a great number of islands, including the "fantastic isles" hypothetically identified with the Azores. To the West, beyond these, two large islands are represented ("Antilia" and "Satanazes") as well as two smaller islands ("Saya" and "Ymana").

The question arises as to whether these last four islands, especially, should be related to some actual discovery of land or rather added to the list of the many numerous fantastic islands with which Mediterranean cartography populated the Atlantic. According to Amando Cortesão, these islands represent the Antilles, and their names are typical Portuguese words. Moreover, he claims, the representation of the larger Antilles island would have some connection with the Portuguese myth of the "Island of the Seven Cities" (the myth that seven Portuguese bishops escaped from the invasion of the Iberian Peninsula by the Arabs and went to an island in the West, with Portuguese populations following them, and there they founded seven cities). Its appearance may also have been related to rumors within the circles of cartography, which came by way of a Portuguese model that found its way to Italy, of actual discoveries made by the Portuguese in the West in an earlier period. Cortesão also argues that the chart shows an incipient representation of the archipelago of Cape Verde, in the form of an island called "Himadoro" surrounded by islets south of the Canaries, which would suggest that the discoveries along the African coast would also have to be pushed back to an earlier time.

Without doubt, some of these hypotheses are quite acceptable, but others are less so. Even if the Portuguese origin of the place names and the general character of the chart were confirmed, it would still have to be proved that the land masses represented are not fantastic, that they correspond to an actual discovery of lands, and that those lands are American.

Even apart from these issues, the implications of this chart are by no means insignificant. As Jaime Cortesão notes, it is the earliest European map on which the main focus is no longer the Mediterranean but rather the Atlantic and the lands, real or fantastic, in and around it.

[For further discussion and an illustration of the Pizzigano chart, see *Cartography*.]

BIBLIOGRAPHY

Campbell, Tony. "Census of Pre-Sixteenth-Century Portolan Charts." *Imago Mundi* 38 (1986): 67–94.
Cortesão, Armando. *The Nautical Chart of 1492 and the Early Discovery and Cartographical Representation of America.* Coimbra, 1954.

Cortesão, Armando. "Pizzigano's Chart of 1424." *Revista da Universidade de Coimbra* 24 (1970).

Harley, J. B., and David Woodward, eds. *The History of Cartography*. Vol. 1, *Cartography in Prehistoric, Ancient and Medieval Europe and the Mediterranean*. Chicago, 1987.

Marques, Alfredo Pinheiro. "Novos elementos sobre a cartografia portuguesa vinte e sete anos depois da primeira publicacão dos portugaliae monumenta cartographica" (New materials relating to Portuguese cartography twenty-seven years after the first publication of "Portugaliae Monumenta Cartographica"). In vol. 6 of *Portugaliae Monumenta Cartographica*, edited by Armando Cortesão and Avelimo Teixeira da Mota. Lisbon, 1988.

Marques, Alfredo Pinheiro. *Origem e desenvolvimento da cartografia portuguesa na época dos descobrimentos*. Lisbon, 1988.

Marques, Alfredo Pinheiro. "Um novo mapa e a sua representação do Atlantico pre-Colombiano." *Oceanos* (Lisbon) 1 (1989): 55–57.

Taylor, E. G. R. "Imaginary Islands: A Problem Solved." *Geographical Journal* 130 (1964).

Vigneras, Louis-André. *La búsqueda del paraíso y las legendarias islas del Atlántico*. Valladolid, 1976.

ALFREDO PINHEIRO MARQUES
Translated from Portuguese by Rebecca Catz

PLANTS. See *Flora*.

PLEITOS COLOMBINOS. See *Lawsuits*.

POLITICAL INSTITUTIONS. [This article surveys the political landscape of Europe in the Age of Discovery and focuses on the structures of Spanish power and authority. For discussion of other European nations and city states, see *England; Florence; France; Genoa; Naples; Portugal; Rome; Venetian Republic.* See also *Papacy.* For discussion of the political organizations of the peoples of the New World, see *Indian America*, especially the articles on the Aztecs, Incas, and Mayas. The political institutions of Africa and Asia are discussed in *Africa; China; Cipangu; Ottoman Empire*.]

As the European Middle Ages drew to a close, the two great universal powers, the papacy and the empire, were in decline. The Renaissance popes had only recently overcome the challenge of conciliarism, that is, the idea that a general council had supreme authority in the church, even over the pope. Despite the increasingly loud cry for reform of the church in head and members, the popes were fearful of convoking a reform council, lest the specter of conciliarism should reappear. The Holy Roman Empire, ruled by the Habsburgs from their base in Austria, was in the process of disintegration into a collection of petty autonomous states. The empire's southern frontier was menaced by the presence of the Ottoman Turks in the Balkan peninsula. New nation-states were beginning to take shape in England, France, Spain, and Portugal. As the Hundred Years' War came to an end, England suffered through the dynastic Wars of the Roses and then enjoyed a resurgence under the Tudor dynasty that came to power in 1485. France, freed of the burden of the Hundred Years' War, also endured a period of civil war as the dukes of Burgundy tried to create an independent kingdom on France's eastern frontier. When King Charles VIII (r. 1483–1498) embarked on an adventuresome policy by invading Italy in 1494, he not only aroused the opposition of the papacy and the north Italian states, but initiated a long rivalry between France and Spain. Portugal, under Kings João II (r. 1481–1495) and Manuel I (r. 1495–1521) continued the work of colonization and exploration in the Atlantic begun by Henry the Navigator (d. 1461). Before the close of the century the Portuguese captain Bartolomeu Dias reached the southernmost tip of Africa and Vasco da Gama completed the roundtrip from Portugal to India.

The most momentous development in fifteenth-century Spain was the union of Castile and Aragón, the two most powerful Hispanic kingdoms. The basis for the union was laid in 1469 by the marriage of Isabel of Castile (r. 1474–1504) and Fernando of Aragón (r. 1479–1516). The fundamental equality of the sovereigns and their joint action was symbolized in various ways such as their motto, *tanto monta, monta tanto* ("one is equal to the other"), and the yoke and the arrows they adopted as their arms. In 1494 Pope Alexander VI accorded them the honorific title "los reyes católicos," or "the Catholic monarchs," in recognition of their triumph over the Moors of Granada and their establishment of religious unity in their realms.

The union of their kingdoms was a purely personal one, as each retained its identity and distinctive institutions and laws. Isabel, as queen proprietress of Castile, exercised the fullness of authority in her kingdom, but in 1475 she shared that responsibility with Fernando, so much so that public documents ordinarily were issued in the names of both. Fernando in 1481 also acknowledged her as coruler in Aragón. Although they might have simply called themselves monarchs of Spain, they maintained the traditional royal intitulation that recorded the separate identity of the eighteen kingdoms and several counties under their rule. After 1492 the Kingdom of Granada was added to the list.

The idea of the state as an entity distinct from the sovereigns, the people, and the territory of the realm was well developed in the time of Fernando and Isabel. The state was an abstraction, something intangible, but nevertheless having a real existence. Described as the *estado del reino* (state of the realm) or the *cosa publica* (republic), it was often compared to the human body. As the head of the body politic, the ruler was responsible for preserving and maintaining the state. The sum of the ruler's rights and powers was expressed by the term *corona real* (royal crown). The development of a patriotism that exalted the homeland of Castile and extolled the virtues of the Castilian nation assisted the monarchs in carrying out their responsibilities.

Fernando and Isabel's primary task was to restore the authority and prestige of the monarchy that had been seriously undermined by the ineptitude of preceding rulers. Poets and theorists, hoping that the king and queen would bring about a new age of greatness for Spain, exhorted them and applauded their efforts.

The monarchy retained a secular character that distinguished it from the monarchies in France and England where so much emphasis was placed upon the priestly or sacred character of the institution. Neither Fernando nor Isabel was anointed and crowned by an archbishop as was customary elsewhere. Rather, each was acclaimed and received an oath of allegiance and pledged to uphold the laws of the land. Although it is commonplace to describe their government as a form of royal absolutism, one should understand that in relative terms. Royal authority was always limited by circumstances and even by institutions. The Catholic monarchs made those institutions work more effectively and so greatly strengthened royal power.

As yet there was no fixed capital, although Valladolid and Toledo (and Granada after its fall in 1492) were favorite residences. The monarchs were basically itinerants, traveling their realm in the company of their household and court. In order to carry out their responsibilities, they surrounded themselves with persons distinguished by talent rather than ancestry. The magnates were drawn to the monarchy by honors and stipends, but the duties of administration most often were entrusted to members of the lesser nobility or the bourgeoisie. A major change in administration was the prominent role given to legists (*letrados*) trained in Roman law, whose principal concern was to maintain and expand the authority of the Crown. The royal council, or *consejo real*, reorganized in the Cortes of Toledo in 1480, advised the monarchs on all affairs touching the Kingdom of Castile, but it also acted on its own initiative. Prelates, nobles, and others might attend the council, but the voting members were one prelate, three knights, and eight or nine legists. The council retained a traditional function as the highest judicial tribunal, but it assumed more and more responsibility for government, administration, finance, and foreign policy. The secretaries, with custody of the royal seals, were especially influential because they had direct and continual access to the sovereigns. They intervened in all major and minor affairs and served as a link between the king and queen and the council. Aragonese affairs were handled by the Consejo de Aragón, whose members ordinarily remained with the king in Castile rather than in Aragón.

Several additional councils were created for exceptional purposes. In the late thirteenth and early fourteenth centuries the towns had organized associations, or hermandades, in times of crisis to defend their rights. In 1476 Fernando and Isabel established the Santa Hermandad and placed it under the control of the Consejo de la Santa Hermandad. As its purpose was to restore law and order in the towns and in the countryside, the hermandad maintained a militia that guaranteed public security and pursued criminals. Abuses, however, provoked the townspeople who asked that the hermandad be dissolved. Only in 1498, when the king and queen were satisfied that it had done its work, did they take that step.

As the military orders of Calatrava, Santiago, and Alcantara had participated in the factional struggles of the preceding reigns, Fernando and Isabel decided to bring the extensive resources of the orders under royal control. With papal consent, they united the administration of the orders to the Crown between 1489 and 1494. They also created the Consejo de las Ordenes in 1495 to administer the orders on their behalf. Pope Adrian VI in 1523 annexed the masterships to the Spanish Crown in perpetuity. After the papacy approved the establishment of the Inquisition in Castile, the Catholic sovereigns set up the Consejo de la suprema y general Inquisición in 1483 through which they controlled the appointment of inquisitors and directed their activities. Though this was primarily a Castilian institution, its authority also extended to Aragón. Finally, the Consejo de las Indias, established at Seville in 1511, controlled all activities relating to the exploration and colonization of the New World.

Fernando and Isabel convened the Cortes of Castile in 1476 and 1480 to promulgate their reform program but neglected to summon it again until 1498. By the more efficient collection of taxes and the development of other financial resources, the Crown was not dependent upon subsidies voted by the Cortes. The Cortes was summoned in 1498 and on several occasions thereafter principally to acknowledge the heir to the throne. The Cortes could scarcely claim to represent the estates of the realm because the prelates and magnates seldom attended, and only eighteen towns, with two representatives each, were entitled to speak for the third estate. The Castilian Cortes met only nine times in Isabel's reign of thirty years, and Fernando summoned the Catalán parliament, or *corts*, only seven times. Meetings of the parliaments of Aragón and Valencia were equally infrequent. Thus by careful manipulation, the monarchy thwarted any challenge that the Cortes might represent.

Fernando and Isabel took seriously their responsibility to administer justice to all and for that purpose promulgated many laws, or *pragmáticas*, which were printed in 1503. They also authorized Alonso Díaz de Montalvo to publish in 1484 a collection of laws entitled *Ordenanzas reales de Castilla*. New editions of the laws of Catalonia and Aragón were published by Fernando's order. The monarchs also encouraged the towns to revise and publish their *fueros* (municipal charters) and ordinances, eliminating contradictory laws or others no longer in force. The printing press disseminated the books of laws more widely than ever before.

The royal council remained the supreme tribunal, but the *audiencia*, a special court of justice that was developed in the fourteenth century, was now revitalized and, called the *chancillería*, was established at Valladolid. Ordinances drawn up in 1486 regulated the activities of the president, the *oidores*, who were responsible for civil cases, and the *alcaldes*, who dealt with criminal matters. There were also noble judges who heard suits involving the nobility. For the most part, these judges were laymen rather than clergy as had often been the case in the past. In view of the great territorial extension of the Kingdom of Castile, a similar tribunal to handle litigation south of the Tagus River was created at Ciudad Real in 1494 and transferred to Granada in 1505.

Fernando and Isabel greatly increased their revenues by recovering estates alienated from the Crown and by the more efficient collection and administration of taxes. Royal income rose from 27 million maravedis in 1470 to 317 million in 1504. Although the royal council had general oversight of finances, a more elaborate administrative apparatus was developed. The *mayordomo mayor* (chief steward) and three subordinate *contadores mayores* (chief accountants) were entrusted with daily responsibility for managing the royal finances. The tax system was essentially the same as before, even to the point of continuing the immunities of the nobility and the clergy. The most important sources of revenue were the *alcabala*, or sales tax (about 70–80 percent of the total revenue), customs duties known as *diezmo* and *almojarifazgo*, the *servicio y montazgo* levied on transhumant sheep, ecclesiastical contributions such as the *tercias reales* (two-ninths of the tithe), and papal subsidies for the crusade against Granada. Of lesser value were the *servicios* voted by the Cortes. The Crown also benefited from its monopoly of salt and the coinage. The Crown still contracted with tax farmers who were authorized to collect various taxes, provided that the government received a specified amount. The tax farmer retained any surpluses as profit. The towns also contracted to pay fixed sums.

The office of *adelantado mayor* (provincial governor), which had had responsibility for territorial administration, was now in a state of decline. Many of its duties were taken over by *corregidores*, usually knights or legists dispatched permanently to most of the Castilian towns after 1480. As these officials enjoyed supreme judicial and administrative authority, the towns lost much of their traditional autonomy. By nominating the *regidores* who formed the municipal council, or *cabildo*, and the procurators whom the towns sent to the Cortes, the Crown exercised far more direct control over municipal affairs than ever before.

Some towns that had once depended directly on the Crown had been alienated by the preceding Trastámara kings and were now held in lordship by nobles or prelates. Fernando and Isabel established a few minor lordships and attempted to clarify seigneurial jurisdiction.

The king and queen reemphasized the principle that all able-bodied citizens had the responsibility to be prepared to defend the realm. In practice the royal army was formed by the municipal militias, by contingents brought by the military orders, and by the nobles in fulfillment of their duty as royal vassals. As a consequence of a concerted effort to develop a permanent army, the Crown had at its disposal in 1504 a force of about eight thousand, consisting of men-at-arms, light cavalry, artillery, and infantry.

By restoring the prestige and authority of the monarchy and repairing the governmental structures that had been so damaged during the previous three-quarters of a century, Fernando and Isabel prepared Spain to dominate Europe in the sixteenth century.

[See also *Isabel and Fernando; Spain.*]

BIBLIOGRAPHY

Azcona, Tarsicio de. *Isabel la Católica: Estudio critico de su vida y su reinado*. Madrid, 1964.

Ladero Quesada, Miguel Angel. *La Hacienda Real de Castilla en el siglo XV*. La Laguna de Tenerife, 1973.

Lunenfeld, Marvin. *The Council of the Santa Hermandad: A Study of the Pacification Forces of Ferdinand and Isabella*. Coral Gables, Fla., 1970.

Lunenfeld, Marvin. *Keepers of the City: The Corregidores of Isabella I of Castile (1474–1504)*. Cambridge, 1987.

JOSEPH F. O'CALLAGHAN

POLO, MARCO (1254?–1324), Italian traveler and writer. Most of what is known about Polo, his travels in Asia, and the origin of his famous book is drawn from the biographical portions of that ghostwritten masterpiece. He was born of a Venetian merchant family of Dalmatian ancestry, and, as a young man, accompanied his father, Niccolò, and uncle, Maffeo, on an overland journey to Mongol China, where they resided from 1275 to 1292. This trip was preceded by a visit of the elder Polos to the court of Kublai Khan in the late 1260s. The earlier journey was the outcome of a commercial venture among the western Mongols; but when Niccolò and Maffeo returned to the West, they came as ambassadors of the Grand Khan bearing the request to the pope to dispatch one hundred learned missionaries to undertake the conversion of the Mongols to Christianity. This request was only partially fulfilled when, accompanied by the seventeen-year-old Marco, they returned to China in an embassy appointed by Pope Gregory X, who, as the former papal legate in the Holy Land, had strong interests in extending Christianity in Asia.

According to his book, Polo served the Mongol government in an official capacity, which enabled him to travel in southern China and Indochina on fact-finding missions for the Grand Khan. Whether his book derived from the notes and memoranda prepared during these official trips is

MARCO POLO. As depicted on the frontispiece of the first printed edition of Marco Polo's book of travels (Nürnberg, 1477), showing the author as a young German knight.

unknown. The chance to return home was provided by the family's appointment as members of a bridal party that escorted a Mongol princess to the court of the Persian khan. The return journey was made by the sea route from China, through the straits of Singapore and Malacca, to Ceylon, along the western coast of India, and thence to Hormuz on the Persian Gulf—an itinerary that attracted considerable interest among European explorers of a later period.

Polo's book was produced while he was imprisoned in Genoa (1298–1299) following his capture during a naval battle between Venice and Genoa. In prison he met the author of several Arthurian romances, Rustichello (or Rusticiano) of Pisa, to whom he related his experiences in Asia and who composed them in the distinctive Italianized French dialect of Rustichello's own surviving romances. It was probably Rustichello who gave Polo's book its flourishes of chivalric rhetoric and much of its legendary content. The book, known in English as *The Travels*, circulated under various titles: *The Description of the World, The Million, The Book of the Customs and Conditions of the Oriental Regions*, and simply *The Book of Marvels*. Its Italian title, *Il milione*, may reflect the skepticism of readers as to the author's truthfulness, although the word became attached to Polo's surname and may have originally been part of it. *Description of the World* was probably the more appropriate title, since it conveyed Polo's intention to compose a grand ethnographical and geographical encyclopedia of the peoples and places he had encountered in his travels (and some he had not).

During the fourteenth and fifteenth centuries, the book was translated into most of the European vernacular languages and twice into Latin. Francesco Pipino's Latin translation (1320), which was commissioned by the Dominicans, and which in its printed edition (1485?) was read by Columbus, was preceded by a prolog in which the translator argued the book's usefulness for converting pagans. The *Description* survives in some 140 manuscript copies, which vary greatly because of deletions and interpolations by generations of translators and copyists. After the invention of printing, the book appeared in almost 160 separate editions from 1477 on.

Lingering suspicion as to the author's possible exaggerations did not appear to diminish its appeal to readers who were strongly attracted to exotic travel writing and similar books of "marvels" such as Sir John Mandeville's *Travels* (1356?). Its influence on geographical knowledge and cartography only gradually became apparent as in the world maps of Abraham Crescas (1376?) and Fra Mauro (1459), which it provided with names and physical locations. The European voyages of exploration and discovery during the late fifteenth and the sixteenth centuries gave

Polo's book new influence. The efforts of Pope Eugenius IV (1431–1447) and the Council of Ferrara-Florence (1438–1442) to unite the western and eastern churches and to expand the bounds of Latin Christendom promoted interest in earlier reports of Christians in India and China such as those of Polo concerning the Church of Saint Thomas at Mylapore, India, and the Nestorian communities among the Mongols. The papal secretary and humanist, Poggio Bracciolini, published in 1492 a narrative of the travels of the Venetian Niccolò de' Conti (c. 1395–1469) in Southeast Asia, which was republished in Portuguese (1502) and Spanish (1503) translations in volumes that also included Polo's book.

Giovanni Battista Ramusio (1485–1557), Polo's first biographer, was the source of the report that Prince Pedro, Henry the Navigator's brother, acquired a copy of the *Description* from the Venetians. Columbus's interest in the book is shown by the annotations in his personal copy and by his lament to the Spanish sovereigns in the prologue to his logbook concerning the lost opportunity to convert the subjects of the "Great Khan of India." Polo's influence on Columbus and his successors was possibly more inspirational than scientifically nautical. His descriptions of the wealth of the Spice Islands and the Indies were appealing to the "insular romanticism" of Europeans who compiled gazetteers of the world's islands. Ramusio, the anthologist of sixteenth-century travel writing, compared Polo very favorably with Columbus, and by reprinting the *Description* in his collection of famous voyages (1559) made a place for Polo in the history of European exploration and discovery. By 1600 the growth of geographical knowledge had displaced Polo and his book from among the canon of authorities of European expansion.

BIBLIOGRAPHY

Moule, A. C., and Paul Pelliot. *Marco Polo: The Description of the World.* 2 vols. London, 1938.

Olschki, Leonardo. *Marco Polo's Asia: An Introduction to His "Description of the World" Called "Il Milione."* Translated by John A. Scott. Berkeley and Los Angeles, 1960.

Reichert, Folker. "Columbus und Marco Polo—Asien in Amerika," *Zeitschrift für historische Forschung* 15, no. 1 (1988): 1–63.

Yule, Sir Henry. *The Book of Ser Marco Polo the Venetian concerning the Kingdoms and Marvels of the East.* 3d ed. Revised by Henri Cordier. 2 vols. London, 1926.

W. R. JONES

PONCE DE LEÓN, JUAN (1474–1521), Spanish explorer and founder of San Juan, Puerto Rico. Ponce de León was born in San Servás de Campos, province of Palencia, in Old Castile in 1474, the year attested by him in an inquiry into the death of Cristóbal de Sotomayor during Puerto Rico's general Indian uprising in 1511. He was a veteran of the reconquest of Spain from the Moors and volunteered in 1493 for Columbus's second voyage of discovery to the New World.

He was the nephew of Rodrigo Ponce de León, Spain's outstanding hero of the Reconquista, first duke and marquis of Cádiz, and third count of Arcos. Ponce de León has been erroneously described as a "peon," or laborer. The contemporary meaning of *peon* was "foot soldier," and on that second voyage even noble caballeros had to walk, since there were no horses.

In La Española he founded the town of Salvaleón de Higüey, and on June 24, 1506, with a crew of one hundred, he sailed to the place he had landed in 1493, identified in nautical charts as *aguada*, or "watering place." There he built a fort and houses, which were destroyed during the 1511 Indian uprising but were soon rebuilt and named San Germán by Miguel Díaz d'Aux. In 1508 he also founded the town of Caparra, which was resettled in 1520 on the site of present-day San Juan as a capital city.

On February 23, 1511, he was commissioned by the king to conduct punitive expeditions against the Carib Indians. These forays took him as far as the Gulf of Darien and Yucatán in Mexico, in the course of which he discovered the "islands of Bimini," which he named Florida.

Ponce de León was an outstanding conquistador, settler, and partner in an agricultural enterprise with the king of Spain. When a court ordered him to vacate the governorship of Puerto Rico in favor of Columbus's heir, Diego Colón, King Fernando invited him to court to reward him for his deeds. As compensation for the lost governorship, the king, on September 27, 1514, appointed him adelantado of the lands he had discovered, known as Bimini and Florida, which extended from forty leagues north of Panuco in Mexico to Newfoundland.

A scientific-minded and cultured nobleman, Ponce de León served at one time or another as notary, Indian overseer, government comptroller and treasurer, public works overseer, surveyor, gold prospector, king's courier to Vasco Núñez de Balboa and Pedrárias Dávila (Pedro Arias de Ávila) in Darién, warden of Fortaleza Palace in San Juan, municipal assemblyman of San Juan, land and sea captain, navigator, and cosmographer. His ship's log for the trip from Puerto Rico to Florida and Yucatán in 1513 shows that he developed a graphical system for estimating accurate latitudes from his quadrant readings; this preceded the Nonio and Vernier instruments for measuring distances too small for visual reading.

Acting as a military engineer, he designed fortresses and towns. Their streets radiated from a central plaza containing a church, hospital, city hall, and jail nearby to which would be a tall post where punishment was meted out. The residential lots were sized according to the citizens' standing in the community.

Ponce de León discovered Mexico in 1516, landing at San Juan de Ulúa near Veracruz, as attested by Spanish records and Maya codexes. His sea chart guided Hernando Cortés who landed there in 1519. It was Ponce de León who dispatched an armed ship to Veracruz to reinforce Cortés for a counterattack on the Indians who had driven him from the capital city of Tenochtitlán.

Ponce de León's chart and log of his 1513 voyage to Florida and Yucatán provide one possible solution to the identity of the first island discovered in the New World, Guanahani; Guanahani was known in the neighboring island of Ciguateo (now Eleuthera) by the name of Guanimá (now Cat Island). During that same voyage he discovered the Gulf Stream while crossing it from the Bahamas toward Florida. He describes in his ship's log its tremendous force: on a very clear day the current near the coast was stronger than a stiff contrary wind.

Ponce de León settled at Charlotte Harbor in Florida in 1521, but that year the Calusa Indians attacked the settlement. An arrow pierced Ponce de León's armor and his left thigh, forcing him to sail to Havana for treatment, where he died. His remains now rest in a marble mausoleum in the San Juan cathedral. He has been remembered in history mostly for his putative search for the "Fountain of Youth" spoken of in Indian legends. But he was in reality a man of many achievements and the first European to land in and explore the continental United States.

BIBLIOGRAPHY

Tió, Aurelio. *Nuevas fuentes para la historia de Puerto Rico.* Barcelona, 1961.

AURELIO TIÓ

PORTOLANO. See *Cartography; Nautical Charts; Sailing Directions.*

PORTO SANTO. Porto Santo, one of the Madeira Islands, sometimes called the golden island or the windmill island, lies 64 kilometers (40 miles) northeast of Funchal, Madeira. The island is 11 by 6 kilometers (7 by 4 miles) with a circumference of 38 kilometers (24 miles). Its capital is Vila Baleira.

Porto Santo is low lying and flat except for the high peaks at each end. The population in the fifteenth century is estimated at six hundred inhabitants. The highest point is Pico do Facho (*facho* means "torch," and it was from this peak that signals warning of approaching pirates were sent). The climate is drier and warmer than Madeira. Wind blows every day and the original settlers built windmills to pump water and grind grain. Very little now grows in the chalky limestone soil, and the landscape has an ocher color except after a rain, when it becomes light green.

The island was discovered by mariners trading between Bristol, England, and Genoa in the 1340s. A legendary account claims that during 1344, Robert McKean in his cog *Le Welyfare* abducted his lover, Anna of Hereford; thirteen days later his ship met a storm and was wrecked off Madeira. Moors picked up the survivors and imprisoned them, from whence the story of the islands spread. The Medici Map of Genoese origin dated 1351 indicates this island with the name Porto Santo (Italian, Porto Seo).

The island's association with Christopher Columbus begins with the forebears of his wife. In 1419, João Gonçalves and Tristram Vaz were blown to Porto Santo by a storm. In their company was Bartolomeu Perestrelo, whose daughter, Felipa Moniz, would marry Columbus in 1479. In 1446, the island had been granted by royal charter to Bartolomeu Perestrelo, making him lord proprietor during the reign of Dom Duarte, king of Portugal. The island was controlled by him and his heirs until April 7, 1497, except for the period from 1458 to 1470 when it was owned by Pedro Correira da Cunha, governor of Graciosa. The Perestrelo family regained ownership in 1470, and in 1497, the island was incorporated under the Crown of the Portuguese kingdom to be governed by the laws and king of Portugal.

In the traditional account, Columbus, Felipa, and their infant son stayed with Bartolomeu Perestrelo II in Porto Santo for two years (1478–1480) while Columbus tried to set himself up as a sugar trader in Funchal. By this time, the island had been ruined for agriculture by infestations of rabbits and the harvesting of dragon trees; earlier documents show the island to have been a source of beef, wild pig, and wild rabbit.

Still standing is the church where Columbus was supposed to have worshiped, Nossa Señhora da Piedade, which dates from 1494. Down a narrow lane beside the church is a white-washed house dating from the time Columbus was in the islands. A museum in Vila Baleira dedicated to Columbus was opened in 1987.

[See also *Madeira.*]

BIBLIOGRAPHY

Azurara, Gomes Eanes de. *Crónica da Guiné.* Edited by Livraria Civilizacão. Oporto, 1973.

Cadamosto, Luis de. *Navegacão de Luis de Cadamosto.* Lisbon, 1944.

Carita, Rui. *Historia da Madeira, 1420–1566.* Funchal, 1989.

Frutuoso, Gaspar. *As Saudades da Terra.* Lisbon, 1590. Reprint, edited by Alvaro Azevedo. Funchal, 1873.

J. DONALD SILVA

PORTUGAL. Portugal emerged as an independent nation in the year 1140 by liberating the western corner of the Iberian Peninsula, which had been overrun by the Moors. Under Afonso III (r. 1248–1279), who finally drove the last of the Moors southward across the sea, Portugal achieved its present-day boundaries, which from 1263 remained permanently fixed. Under Dinis I (r. 1279–1325), Portugal entered upon an era of colonial and maritime expansion. A Genoese, Manuel Pessagno, was hired as hereditary admiral of the Portuguese navy, and some twenty Genoese seamen entered the service of the king of Portugal—forerunners of Columbus, a later compatriot whose exploits were to be far more significant for both Portugal and the world.

On the death of King Fernando I (r. 1367–1383), whose sole heiress was married to Juan I of Castile, a popular revolution overthrew the dynasty out of fear of Spain's claiming the throne. In 1385, João of Aviz, illegitimate son of Pedro I (r. 1357–1367), was proclaimed king after a resounding victory on the battlefield of Aljubarrota. That same year, João married Philippa of Lancaster, daughter of John of Gaunt, and the Portuguese court entered one of the most promising periods in its history. The couple's third son, Henry, who became known as the Navigator,

earned a large place in the history of Portugal and the world for his contributions to nautical science.

The first stage of the overseas expansion of Europe can be regarded as beginning with the capture of Ceuta (on the Moroccan coast) by the Portuguese in 1415. Ceuta was literally the opening gun in the great adventure that did not end until a large part of the known world came within the sphere of Portuguese influence. The three oldest sons of King João I were anointed for their heroism in the capture of such a glorious prize, though no one could foresee then that Ceuta was the initial step toward the conquest of Africa. But the main impulses behind the Age of Discovery undoubtedly were a mix of religious, economic, strategic, and political factors, all of which were celebrated in the literature of the period. The lyricism of the Middle Ages, the melancholy and simple melodies that distinguished the abundant poetry of Galicia and Portugal, was to give way to a severe but exultant prose—the chronicles of the historians who found more inspiration in the exploits of warriors and crusaders, explorers and adventurers, than in the love affairs of peasant girls and shepherds. History and historical evocation were the most original forms of expression during the fifteenth century.

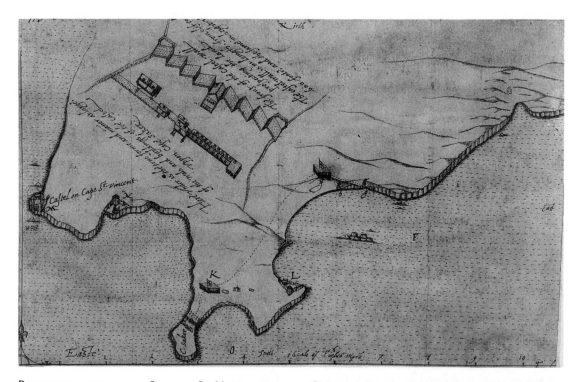

PLAN OF THE WORKS OF CAPES SAKER AND ST. VINCENT IN SOUTHERN PORTUGAL. Showing some of the installations where, according to tradition, Henry the Navigator sponsored much research and innovation in the art of navigation. The site advantageously faced Africa and the shipping routes between the Mediterranean and the Atlantic. This English drawing is from 1587.

The seizure of Ceuta in 1415 and, more important, its retention were probably inspired mainly by crusading ardor to deal a blow at the infidel and the desire of the half-English princes of Portugal to be dubbed knights on the field of battle in a spectacular manner. But there is no doubt that the occupation of Ceuta enabled the Portuguese to obtain some information about the territory of the native peoples in the Upper Niger and Senegal river regions where there was gold. Under the aegis of Prince Henry the Navigator, Portuguese ships went out along the coast of Africa, following up on the information.

The next stage in the Portuguese expansion began with the discovery, or rather the rediscovery, of the islands that lay not far from Portugal proper—the Azores and Madeiras. In all probability they were rediscovered by Portuguese vessels returning from the African coast. The Madeiras became a Portuguese outpost at a very early date after their rediscovery by João Gonçalves Zarco who sighted Porto Santo in 1418. The formal discovery of the Azores has been attributed to Gonçalo Velho Cabral who, in 1431, was instructed by Prince Henry to sail westward in search of these islands, which appeared on early maps. The colonization of both uninhabited archipelagoes followed quickly.

The next step toward conquering Africa geographically was to round Cape Bojador (present-day Boujdour, Western Sahara) and move on to Cape Verde. But for a long time terror inspired by ancient legends kept the Portuguese from sailing around the cape. In 1433 Henry sent out Gil Eanes to prove that it was possible to go beyond Bojador. Eanes failed on that trip but succeeded on a second try, demonstrating that it was possible to sail southward beyond the line that ignorance had set as the outward limit of navigability. In 1444 a voyage under the command of Nuno Tristão pushed still farther south and saw for the first time the lands where black Africans lived, far beyond the territories of the Islamized Moors. Between 1445 and 1448, caravel after caravel sailed out of Portugal bent on expanding the knowledge already acquired and pushing the known frontier farther and farther south. After a hiatus, the voyages resumed, and from 1470 to 1475, under Afonso V (r. 1438–1481), they were leased on a monopoly basis to Fernão Gomes, a wealthy Lisbon merchant. He discovered a large stretch of the Guinea coast, which was opened up to Portuguese enterprise and trade.

From 1480 on, the *mare clausum* (closed sea) policy in the Gulf of Guinea was enforced by Prince João, son and heir of Afonso V, who had placed him in charge of the African voyages. Coast guard squadrons had orders to execute on sight any intruder who was found south of the parallel of the Canaries. In 1481 the prince ascended the throne as João II (r. 1481–1495) and issued orders to Diogo de Azambuja to construct a castle at São Jorge da Mina (on what was later known as the Gold Coast), which was completed in 1482 and became the principal source of gold in the fifteenth century. It is believed that Columbus made one or two voyages to São Jorge in the company of Azambuja.

About the same time, João II ordered the first voyage of exploration undertaken by Diogo Cão (1482–1484) to sail beyond the then known limits of the African coast, south of the Gulf of Guinea, below the equator. He reached the Zaire River, sailed beyond it, and got as far as Cape Lobo on the coast of Angola, where he mistakenly believed he had reached the tip of Africa and the waters of the Indian Ocean. On this voyage he made contact with the Kingdom of the Congo where he established friendly relations that were later to bear fruit.

In the meantime, while the first voyage of Diogo Cão was underway, another explorer, João Afonso de Aveiro, was sent overland into the interior of Africa, starting from the coasts of Benin and present-day Nigeria. He announced on his return that he had heard of the presence in the area of Prester John, a legendary African potentate for whom the Europeans had been searching for years. Toward the end of 1484 or the beginning of 1485, Columbus appeared in audience before the king with a proposal for reaching the Indies by sailing west. King João submitted his proposal to a scientific council, which rejected it. It was at that time that a disappointed Columbus left Portugal for Spain. It is possible that one of the reasons for his rejection, among others, was the information brought back by Diogo Cão and João Afonso de Aveiro, information that led the king to believe that the Portuguese were already on the threshold of India.

During the years 1485–1486, Diogo Cão was sent out on a second expedition. He had passed beyond the limits of his first voyage and reached a point on the African coast called Serra Parda when he realized he had been mistaken in believing he had reached the tip of Africa on his previous voyage. There now appeared to be no end to the African coast, which continued farther south. He set up a commemorative pillar and returned to Portugal in 1486 with a plan for reaching southern Africa by cutting a wide circuit to the west, as Vasco da Gama was to do later on his momentous journey to India in 1497–1499.

The crusading impulse and the search for Guinea gold were soon reinforced by the quest for Prester John. This mythical potentate was vaguely located in the "Indies"—an elastic term often embracing Ethiopia and East Africa as well as what little was known of Asia. The passage of time, travelers' tales such as Marco Polo's, and wishful thinking combined to build up the medieval belief that Prester John was a mighty schismatical Christian priest-king. As early as the twelfth century the news had spread over Europe that

Prester John was real and had communicated with the pope. His domains were believed to lie somewhere behind those of the Islamic powers, which occupied a wide belt of territory from Morocco to the Black Sea. The opening up of the route to the Far East via the cape was undoubtedly partly motivated by the desire of the Portuguese to locate Prester John and, with his assistance, squeeze Islam from two sides. Both Prince Henry and, long after Henry's death, King João II were obsessed by the desire to establish contact with Prester John.

King João decided to investigate both by land and by sea. Two expeditions were sent out almost at the same time. The one would travel overland via Egypt and the Red Sea to take passage on an Arab dhow for Indian ports to study Indian Ocean navigation, to see the lands in which spices grow, and then to cross the sea again and seek the Christian realm of Prester John in Abyssinia. The other was to pursue the Atlantic route from the point at which Diogo Cão had turned back. João picked his men carefully. Pero da Covilhã and Afonso de Paiva, polyglot adventurers with diplomatic tact and fluent Arabic, would risk the perils of wandering disguised through Muslim lands, while the stout seaman Bartolomeu Dias would lead his caravels beyond all distances known to Europeans.

It was Dias who was destined to discover the Cape of Good Hope and prepare the way for the exploit of Vasco da Gama in reaching the Indies. In August of 1486, Dias departed from Lisbon with three ships, the purpose of which was to continue the work so promisingly begun by Diogo Cão who had reached a spot on the coast of southwestern Africa (present-day Namibia), where he set up a pillar and moved down the African coast. Dias finally rounded and pushed up the other side of Africa to halfway between the cape and Port Elizabeth before turning back. He had found Africa's southern limit and demonstrated that it was possible to navigate around it and into the Indian Ocean. Dias returned from the cape in December of 1488. It is believed that Columbus was present at court when Dias announced his discovery.

João II now began preparations for the voyage that was to be commanded by Vasco da Gama, but the king died in 1495, before they were far advanced. The fruits of the seeds sown by him and by Prince Henry the Navigator and other forgotten pilots and navigators were now reaped by King Manuel I (r. 1495–1521), starting with Da Gama's voyage in 1497–1499. On July 9, 1497, the little fleet of four vessels sailed down the Tagus. Four months later Da Gama cast anchor in St. Helena Bay, South Africa, and then quickly rounded the cape and proceeded up the east coast of Africa. After calling at various Arab-Swahili ports along the coast, Da Gama reached Malindi, where he received the help of Ahmad Ibn Madjid, the most famous Arab pilot of his age, who knew the Indian Ocean better than any other man alive. Thanks to his guidance, the Portuguese

were able to reach Calicut, the major emporium of the pepper trade on the Malabar coast, thereby ushering in a new era for India and the world—an age of maritime power and authority based on control of the seas by European nations.

On April 22, 1500, a year after Da Gama's return to Portugal, Pedro Álvares Cabral, on his way to India, sailed much farther west into the South Atlantic than Da Gama had and sighted land. A week later Cabral took possession of this unknown territory in the name of Portugal, but since his business lay elsewhere, he did not linger. He simply took on water and named the newly found land Terra da Vera Cruz. Thus, the vast country of Brazil was discovered—by chance, if we are to believe the common version, and its exploration was left largely to chance for a long time afterward.

Portuguese naval supremacy in the Indian Ocean was achieved early on with Francisco de Almeida's great victory over a combined Muslim fleet off Diu in 1509, and it was not seriously challenged until the appearance of the Dutch and English in the Indian Ocean nearly a century later. But the foundations of the Portuguese eastern empire were laid by Afonso de Albuquerque who wrested the landlocked island of Goa from the Muslim sultan of Bijapur in 1510. By capturing Malacca in 1511, Albuquerque secured the main emporium for the spice trade and the strategic key to the South China Sea and to Indonesia. With the seizure of Hormuz in the Persian Gulf in 1515, he obtained control of those waters and of one of two routes by which the spice trade was carried on with the Levant.

The three key strong points of Hormuz, Goa, and Malacca were soon supplemented by a large number of other fortified settlements and trading posts extending from Sofala to southeastern Africa to Ternate in the Moluccas. In addition, the Portuguese established a number of unfortified settlements. Elsewhere, native shipping was allowed to continue as before, provided that the owners took out Portuguese licenses. Unlicensed ships were liable to be seized or sunk, particularly if they belonged to Muslim traders. East of Malacca the situation was different. Beyond Malacca, the Portuguese were merely one more cog in the existing pattern of trade, nor was it long before they had to compete with the Spaniards who were seeking the same goal from the opposite direction. Once the Spaniards realized that Columbus had not discovered the golden lands of Cathay and Cipangu so enthusiastically described by Marco Polo, and before they found the treasures of Aztec Mexico and Inca Peru, one of their chief objectives was to get around the newfound American continent that was barring their way to East Asia. This they finally achieved with what must surely rank as the most outstanding voyage of all time—the circumnavigation of the world organized and begun by the Portuguese Ferdinand Magellan, in the service of the Crown of

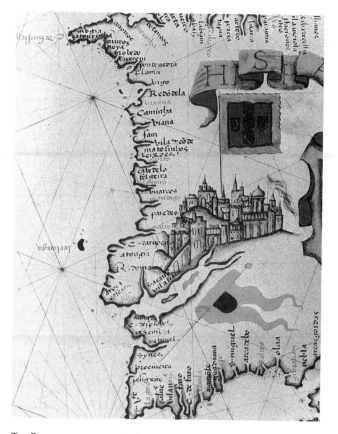

THE PORTUGUESE COAST. In the center, Lisbon and the Tagus River. From Diego Homen's atlas, 1563.

Castile, and completed by the Basque Juan Sebastián de Elcano, who sailed *Victoria* into the harbor of Sanlúcar de Barrameda on September 8, 1522, after an absence of almost three years.

The Portuguese Empire reached its peak during the sixteenth century and then went into decline. With the appearance of European rivals in the Far East and Africa, Portugal was unable to do more than maintain what it already possessed. It lost the prestige it had gained from being for so many years the sole European influence in these areas. For a long time the Portuguese expended their fortune and energy in preventing the Dutch in particular from seizing their possessions in Brazil, India, the Indonesian islands, and Africa. One of their problems was a shortage of manpower; there were never enough soldiers to man the forts. Exact figures for the Portuguese overseas population in the sixteenth and seventeenth centuries are lacking, but apparently there were never more than between six and ten thousand able-bodied men manning an empire that at its peak extended from South America to the Spice Islands. The population in Portugal at this time probably fluctuated at around a million, and a heavy annual emigration from the mother country was needed to fill the gaps in manpower caused by tropical diseases and battles with the Dutch during the first forty years of the seventeenth century.

During the early part of the reign of Sebastião (r. 1568–1578), divisions and conflicts within the Portuguese court led to neglect of the defenses of India. In 1578, Sebastião led the Portuguese to a resounding defeat on the battlefield of Morocco. His death in that battle threw the nation into a dynastic crisis, since he died without an heir. For two years, the aged Cardinal Henrique, brother of King João III (r. 1521–1557), sat on the throne of Portugal, but he died in 1580, also without an heir.

Then came forced union with Spain, after Philip II backed his claim to the Portuguese throne with well-placed money and military might. For sixty years, Spanish interests prevailed and Portugal was dragged into every conflict in which the Spaniards were involved. Spain's enemies determined those whom Portugal engaged in combat. The effects were disastrous for the immense Portuguese Empire, which was now open to depredations actually directed against Philip II and Spain. This period (known as the "Spanish captivity" to the Portuguese) also left the Portuguese vulnerable to the ambitions of the Dutch, whose incursions in the waters of the Far East ruined the Portuguese Empire there. Only Macao on the Chinese coast remained in Portuguese hands.

The opening years of the seventeenth century saw a bitter clash of rivalries and ambitions among all the European states, which now joined in the scramble for overseas possessions. In addition to the Dutch and English, the French East India Company was established in 1604, and even Denmark founded a similar enterprise in 1616, constructing a fortress and commercial depots on the Malabar coast of India.

On December 1, 1640, Portuguese insurgents assassinated the Spanish viceregal adviser, Miguel de Vasconcelos, and escorted Philip IV's representative in Portugal, Margaret of Savoy, to the frontier. John of Braganza, a descendant of King Manuel I, was proclaimed king of Portugal. The revival of independent Portugal was now complete, and another cycle in the national history was about to begin.

[See also *Africa; Colonization,* article on *Portuguese Colonization; Lisbon;* and biographies of figures mentioned herein.]

BIBLIOGRAPHY

Boxer, Charles Ralph. *Four Centuries of Portuguese Expansion, 1415–1825.* Berkeley and Los Angeles, 1969.

Lach, Donald F. *The Century of Discovery.* Vol. 1 of *Asia in the Making of Europe.* Chicago and London, 1965.

Pattee, Richard. *Portugal and the Portuguese World.* Milwaukee, 1957.

Sanceau, Elaine. *Good Hope: The Voyage of Vasco da Gama.* Lisbon, 1967.

Sanceau, Elaine. *The Reign of the Fortunate King, 1495–1521.* Hamden, Conn., 1969.

REBECCA CATZ

POSTILS. For discussion of Columbus's marginal notations in the books he owned, see *Library of Columbus; Writings,* article on *Marginalia.*

PRESTER JOHN. Prester (the Priest) John was the legendary monarch of an imaginary Christian kingdom variously located in India, central Asia, and Africa. The first mentions of Prester John in western European letters appear in the twelfth century. In his *Chronicon,* the historian Otto of Freising relates that in 1145 he interviewed a Syrian bishop in Rome who described a kingdom far to the east ruled by a Nestorian Christian named Prester John. Nestorian Christians were usually Persians, so it is not incongruent that the bishop told Otto that Prester John was a descendant of the Magi. He had been on his way with armies to aid the crusaders in the Holy Land but was unable to cross the Tigris River. He was said to have lingered for several years in hopes that it would freeze over during the winter and allow his forces to pass.

Somewhat later in the same century, around 1165, a letter purportedly written by Prester John himself to the Byzantine emperor, Manuel I, began to circulate in western Europe. In this letter, Prester John describes his fantastic kingdom in some detail. Located but three days' journey from the Terrestrial Paradise, he says, it is replete with precious and magical stones and with plants and animals that have special powers. Its inhabitants live in perpetual peace and harmony and may drink from the waters of a "transparent spring" located at the foot of Mount Olympus, waters that endow them with eternal youth and health. The history of this letter is complex. It was probably originally written in Latin in western Europe, though some versions claim to be translations from Arabic or Greek. Many manuscripts survive; they frequently contain additions and variations reflective of shifting popular conceptions regarding the "marvels of the East."

These twelfth-century sources engendered an ongoing series of attempts to communicate with or actually visit Prester John. In 1177, Pope Alexander III wrote a letter to Prester John proposing to instruct him in Roman Christianity and to help him secure a church of his own in Jerusalem. In the thirteenth century, a new phase of European contacts with inner Asia and the Far East was inaugurated by the westward surges of the Mongols under Genghis (Chingis) Khan. European travelers, from Gio-

PRESTER JOHN. From Francisco Alvares's *Truthful Information of the Lands of Prester John,* 1540.

vanni da Pian del Carpini in the middle of the century to Odoric of Pordenone in the early decades of the fourteenth century, sought to locate the legendary kingdom somewhere within the previously unknown regions opened to them.

In his *History of the Mongols,* Carpini calls Prester John the king of Greater India and describes in some detail a bizarre battle between his forces and a "black people" called Ethiopians. Willem van Ruysbroeck, writing an account of a journey to the court of Mangku Khan in the 1250s, says that Prester John is a Nestorian Christian, the ruler of a people called the Naimans whose home appears to be somewhere in the steppes of inner Asia. In his famous *Travels (Il Milione),* written in the final years of the thirteenth century, Marco Polo devotes several passages to Prester John. He relates that the dominions of Prester John and his descendants lay in a region called Tenduc and that he ruled a people named the Kerait (Kairites). He apparently considered Prester John to be a hereditary title rather than the name of a particular individual. In one passage he describes how the first Prester John was slain in battle by Genghis Khan; in another he mentions that the present ruler of Tenduc is of the lineage of Prester John and bears that title, though his given name is George. The letters of Giovanni da Montecorvino, written from Peking (Beijing) in the first decade of the fourteenth century, and the narrative of Odoric of Pordenone, written somewhat later, both parallel the account of Marco Polo.

Sometime around the middle of the fourteenth century, an obscure Florentine Franciscan by the name of Giovanni dei Marignolli wrote an account of a papal legation to the Far East in which he describes the kingdom of Prester John as being located in Ethiopia. The tradition of locating Prester John's kingdom in East Africa rather than on the eastern fringes of Asia seems to have prevailed among the Portuguese explorers of the fifteenth century. Portuguese navigators working their way down the west coast of Africa sought to establish contact with this legendary ruler and to establish a workable access to his kingdom. In 1499, when Vasco da Gama returned to Portugal from his famous voyage around the southern tip of Africa, he reported hearing of a king who ruled the interior somewhere near Mozambique.

Christopher Columbus's readings—of Marco Polo's *Travels,* for example—would have acquainted him with the legendary kingdom of Prester John. But he does not seem to have been as preoccupied with locating it as he was with reaching Cipangu (Japan) and the court of the Grand Khan. At least one of Columbus's prominent successors in the exploration of the Caribbean, Juan Ponce de León, seems to have believed that at one point he might be proximate to the Fountain of Youth supposedly located in Prester John's kingdom. According to the sixteenth-century *Historia general y natural de las Indias* by Gonzalo Fernández de Oviedo, in 1512 Ponce de León and his men heard tales of the existence of the Fountain of Youth in the Bimini Islands north of Cuba. Their efforts to locate it, which apparently were not casual, provide evidence of the enduring power of the imagined presence of this isolated Christian monarch and the unparalleled riches of his kingdom.

[See also *Geography, Imaginary; Grand Khan; Terrestrial Paradise.*]

BIBLIOGRAPHY

Boas, George. *Essays on Primitivism and Related Ideas in the Middle Ages.* New York, 1978.

Gumilev, L. N. *Searches for an Imaginary Kingdom: The Legend of the Kingdom of Prester John.* Cambridge, 1987.

Lach, Donald F. *Asia in the Making of Europe.* Vol. 1. Chicago, 1965.

Polo, Marco. *The Travels.* New York, 1958.

Quinn, David B., ed. *America from Concept to Discovery: Early Exploration of North America.* Vol. 1 of *New American World: A Documentary History of North America to 1612.* New York, 1979.

Yule, Henry. *Cathay and the Way Thither: Being a Collection of Medieval Notices of China.* Taipei, 1966.

PAULINE MOFFITT WATTS

PRINTING. Although printing with movable characters was invented in China in the early eleventh century A.D., it is generally accepted that the technique was reinvented in the West by Johann Gensfleisch zur Laden (c. 1394/1399–1468), better known as Johann Gutenberg, and was first used at Mainz in the 1450s, at a time when technical and commercial conditions in Germany were ripe for such a development. It is, however, probable that others in Europe were working toward the same invention at about the same time.

Mainz was a metalworking center, and Gutenberg was familiar with the goldsmith's craft. When in 1428 local patrician families like his own were deprived of their civic privileges in the Guild Rebellion, he settled in Strasbourg, where, as early as the mid-1430s, he and his partners began the slow elaboration of certain processes connected with printing. As he was secretive about his inventions, contemporary documents are not explicit about them. In 1448 he was back in Mainz. The development and application of his inventions required considerable investment, so in 1449 or 1450 he turned to a lawyer, Johann Fust, for a substantial loan. A subsequent sum was also loaned by Fust in exchange for a partnership in Gutenberg's project. In 1455, by which time Gutenberg had perfected the process of printing with movable metal types, Fust appears to have foreclosed on him, for reasons which remain unclear. Some, at least, of Gutenberg's stock and equipment passed to Fust, who thenceforth ran a printing office with Gutenberg's former associate, a calligrapher named Peter Schöffer. Together they produced, or at least completed, the famous Mainz Psalter of 1457, the first known book printed in the West to carry a date and also the name of its printers.

The magnificent forty-two-line folio Bible printed at Mainz in the period 1453–1455 is usually attributed to Gutenberg and named after him; it was either nearing completion or already finished at the time of his apparent dispute with Fust. Although Gutenberg continued to have access to printing equipment after 1455, it is not certain what he produced, because he never put his name to any printed item.

Gutenberg's invention required him to adapt various techniques, instruments, and material already employed by skilled metalworkers, printers of woodcuts, and scribes. He also developed completely new ones. Probably his most outstanding achievement was to invent an adjustable mold in which thousands of pieces of type, all of the same height but of varying widths (the letters *i* and *m*, for example, require bodies of different widths), could be cast rapidly yet with great precision. Gutenberg so perfected the processes involved in printing that they were not fundamentally altered until the nineteenth century.

Presses, often operated by peripatetic German craftsmen, spread from the Rhine Valley to much of the rest of Europe within some twenty years of the invention of printing. Printed books first appeared in Italy in 1465, Bohemia in 1468, France and Switzerland in 1470, Spain perhaps in 1472, Hungary and Poland in 1473, the Low Countries in 1473 or 1474, and England in 1475 or 1476. From the outset, printing was a business, and most printers were motivated by profit rather than any more high-minded ambitions. Commercial cities like Venice, Lyons, Basel, and Seville, situated on major trade routes

THE GUTENBERG PRESS. A reconstruction at Mainz.

ELSEVIER PUBLISHING PROJECTS, AMSTERDAM

along which printed books could be distributed like other merchandise, were generally more important printing centers than university cities such as Oxford or Heidelberg. When, for instance, the great humanist printer Aldo Manuzio (Aldus Manutius) began printing in 1494 or 1495, he chose to work in Venice, a commercial center that dominated European printing in the fifteenth and early sixteenth centuries, rather than Florence. Modern reassessments of Manuzio's career emphasize the importance of economic considerations for even the most scholarly of printers.

About 77 percent of all books printed in the fifteenth century were in the international language, Latin, allowing printers to export their products to other countries. Indeed, the rise and influence of humanism throughout Europe was closely linked to that of printing. The new craft's early opponents have too frequently been thought to reflect a universal contemporary judgment that printed books were an inferior substitute for the manuscripts that the first printed editions imitated. Italian humanists were enthusiastic patrons of the presses, however. Pico della Mirandola, for example, chose printed rather than manuscript versions of several works, presumably because he believed the former to be more accurate. In the sixteenth century, humanist scholars and certain notable printers cooperated closely. Erasmus, for instance, was associated with Josse Bade in Paris, Johann Froben in Basel, and Manuzio in Venice; he even spent considerable time revising his *Adagia* in the latter's office.

Initially, apart from the printing of indulgences, administrative forms and notices, and the ephemeral broadsheets (which have disappeared in incalculable numbers), the early presses tended to print time-honored works of the ancients and of the Middle Ages, reproducing in particular those texts that had already been most in demand before the advent of printing. Only later did contemporary authors begin to write specifically to be printed and publishers need to search for new works to satisfy demand.

By far the largest proportion of books printed at the time of Columbus were religious (over 40 percent), and it is no coincidence that the first printed book was the Bible. The scriptures became widely available in Latin and in some of the vernacular languages, leading, in the sixteenth century, to intense debate among both Catholics and Protestant Reformers about the desirability of general access to Holy Writ. While numerous works of scholastic theology for the universities and simple manuals for confessors were issued, liturgical editions and books of hours became a staple for the new presses. Likewise, devotional works proved best-sellers. The most popular were the fifteenth-century *Imitation of Christ,* attributed to Thomas à Kempis, of which some one hundred Latin and vernacular editions appeared before 1501, and the thirteenth-century *Golden Legend* by Jacobus de Voragine, of which at least 130 Latin and vernacular editions were printed before 1501. Indeed, a major effect of the advent of printing was to multiply the number of books of popular piety generally available.

The range of works printed in the fifteenth century was extremely varied, however; commercial considerations underlay the process of selection from among the thousands of works available in manuscript. Classical, medieval, and contemporary literature account for some 30 percent of the presses' known output, law for just over 10 percent, and books on scientific subjects for approximately 10 percent, while one of the most profitable categories for publishers would have been schoolbooks. It is certain that huge numbers of Latin grammars, particularly that of Donatus, were printed, but whole editions, now lost, must have been thumbed to pieces by students.

Classical works became widely available, often in scholarly editions printed in Italy, but, despite the humanists' recent rediscovery of works by the ancients, it was the classical texts popular throughout the Middle Ages that were most frequently issued. In the course of the second half of the fifteenth century many printed editions appeared of Aesop, Aristotle, Boethius, the pseudo-Cato, Cicero, Juvenal, Livy, Lucian, Ovid, Persius, Plautus, Sallust, Seneca, Terence, Vegetius, and Virgil. Works by these authors were read throughout Europe, as were vernacular translations of Latin works, printed translations from other vernacular languages, and works originally written in the vernacular in which they were printed. Boccaccio, Dante, Petrarch, and amatory romances were universally popular. The medieval chronicles and other works considered by contemporaries to be historical were frequently issued. Aristotle, Euclid, Pliny, and Ptolemy were among the scientific authors most often printed.

The eventual effects of the wide dissemination of ideas and information permitted by printing constituted a communications revolution. This has tempted some historians to view the advent of the presses as a major turning point in Western history and to attribute almost every intellectual or ideological development which took place after Gutenberg to his invention. Not only does the output of the presses in Columbus's lifetime provide much evidence of continuity with the manuscript age, however, but early printing generally did not hasten the acceptance of new ideas or knowledge. It should also be remembered that printing was a neutral medium exploited by both innovators and conservatives. However revolutionary its eventual consequences, it neither did away with the scribes—who often copied printed books—nor did it convert a largely oral culture to a written one overnight.

A major effect of the advent of printing was the rise of a new industry with its related crafts and a large wholesale import-export trade of books. France, Italy, Germany, and the Low Countries were net exporters of printed books while countries on the periphery of Europe, like Spain, Portugal, England, and Poland, were importers. The production and availability of books were dramatically increased by printing: by 1500 there were some 250 printing centers, which had issued at least 27,000 surviving editions. In two generations, more than 10 million books had been produced mechanically at a time when the population of Europe numbered fewer than 100 million inhabitants. But, rather than immediately creating a new demand, the presses supplied the burgeoning market that already existed for manuscript books, a result of increasing levels of literacy during the first half of the fifteenth century.

Although printing enormously increased the availability of books, which were generally cheaper than manuscripts, it does not seem immediately to have had a radical effect on levels of literacy or on the ownership of books. The same sorts of readers who once acquired manuscripts simply acquired a greater amount of written material. Indeed, the collapse of many printers in Italy in the 1470s and again by 1500 suggests that the market was limited and printing rapidly glutted it.

As a result of the new availability of books, scholars could now readily consult a range of works that previously would have taken them a lifetime to copy or acquire. Large collections were made, the most notable of which— although untypically extensive—was that of Columbus's illegitimate son, Fernando Colón, who had amassed more than 15,000 volumes in his Seville library by the time of his death in 1539. Liberated from the need constantly to travel to study manuscripts or to spend time copying them or having them copied for their own use, scholars enjoyed increased opportunities both for wider research and for comparing conflicting ideas, a significant development in intellectual history.

While errors always crept into manuscript text and diagrams as they were copied and recopied, some works becoming hopelessly garbled in the process, the possibility of printing numerous identical copies of a work encouraged scholarly editors to correct such errors and to publish the most accurate version they could. This had the effect of fixing texts, various forms of which had previously coexisted. Books could also be regularly revised in the light of new discoveries, as happened with successive editions of Ptolemy's *Geography*. This work had lost its maps during the Middle Ages and was provided with substitutes only after its first printed edition; the maps were subsequently updated as new information became available.

PRINTING. Woodcut by Jost Amman.

Yet all editors and printers were not scholars, and printing also allowed defective texts to be widely disseminated, and outmoded orthodoxies and traditional prejudices to be reinforced. For example, Diego de Valera's popular *Historia de España abreviada*, first printed at Seville in 1482, continued to be issued in the mid-sixteenth century without a mention of the discovery of the Americas in its section dealing with world geography. Eventually, printing led to changes in the presentation of reading matter as printed books ceased to be modeled on manuscripts. The numerous scribal abbreviations that had made reading so slow were gradually abandoned by printers who found them impractical to reproduce; cumbersome manuscript glosses were streamlined; a range of sizes of types allowed different elements of a page to be distinguished at a glance; layout was simplified; the need to economize on paper resulted in cramped typesetting; and the addition of more systematic indexes permitted easy reference. This, in turn, led to different ways of reading and consulting books.

Columbus certainly had access to printed books, some of which he possessed and annotated; several of his own copies are still conserved in the Biblioteca Colombina in Seville. It is known that he read printed versions of Ptolemy's *Geography*, Pierre d'Ailly's *Imago mundi*, Enea Silvio Piccolomini's *Historia rerum ubique gestarum* (Universal history), Pliny's *Natural History*, Plutarch's *Lives*, and the *Book of Marco Polo* (Italian title, *Il milione*). It was probably from the printed tables of Johann Müller (Regiomontanus) that Columbus attempted his calculations of longitude on his second and fourth voyages.

In their turn, Columbus's discoveries were rapidly broadcast by the presses: his *Epistola de insulis nuper inventis* (Letter on the newly discovered islands) was printed at Barcelona, Rome, Basel, and Paris in 1493, and at least nine separate editions in Spanish, German, and Latin appeared before 1500. It is questionable, however, how wide interest in the New World was outside Spain and Portugal until the mid-1550s. Throughout Europe in the fifteenth century the largely fabulous *Travels* of Sir John Mandeville had been more widely read than the more trustworthy narrative of Marco Polo's journeys to the Far East. A parallel development was seen in the following century when, even at Seville, the very hub of administration and commerce with the new Spanish colonies in the Americas, more books were printed providing semifictional descriptions of journeys to Turkey and the Holy Land than reliable accounts of the New World.

Later in the sixteenth century, well after Columbus's death, printing was to have a marked effect upon the standardization of the vernacular languages and upon literacy. It was also instrumental in the rapidity with which some new intellectual or ideological movements, notably the Reformation (embodied in writings in the vernacular languages), swept across Europe.

In 1539 the first press arrived in the lands discovered by Columbus. It was founded in Mexico City as a branch office of the Seville press owned by the Cromberger family.

[See also *Library of Columbus* for further discussion of works owned by Christopher Columbus and his son, Fernando Colón. For further discussion of works related to contemporary knowledge of exploration and discovery, see *Travel Literature* and biographies of writers mentioned herein.]

BIBLIOGRAPHY

Bühler, Curt F. *The Fifteenth-Century Book: The Scribes, the Printers, the Decorators.* Philadelphia, 1960.

Carter, John, and Percy H. Muir, eds. *Printing and the Mind of Man.* 2d ed. Munich, 1983.

Catalogue of Books Printed in the XVth Century Now in the British Museum. 12 vols. London, 1908–1971.

Eisenstein, Elizabeth L. *The Printing Press as an Agent of Change:*

Communications and Cultural Transformations in Early-Modern Europe. 2 vols. Cambridge, 1979.

Escolar, Hipólito. *Historia del libro*. 2d ed. Madrid, 1988.

Febvre, Lucien, and Henri-Jean Martin. *The Coming of the Book*. Translated by David Gerard. London, 1976.

Lowry, Martin. *The World of Aldus Manutius: Business and Scholarship in Renaissance Venice*. Oxford, 1979.

Martin, Henri-Jean. *Histoire et pouvoirs de l'écrit*. Paris, 1988.

Martin, Henri-Jean, and Roger Chartier, eds. *Histoire de l'édition française*. 4 vols. Paris, 1983–1986.

Scholderer, Victor. *Johann Gutenberg: Inventor of Printing*. 2d ed. London, 1970.

CLIVE GRIFFIN

PTOLEMY (fl. around A.D. 127–148), Greek scientist who worked in Alexandria, Egypt. The works of Ptolemy (Greek, Klaudios Ptolemaios) cover astronomy, geography, optics, astrology, music, and other fields. While his astronomical work *Almagest* outlined *klimata* (latitude belts), his *Geography* (*Geographike hyphegesis*, Manual of geography) particularly interested explorers.

Book 1 of the *Geography* outlines Ptolemy's aims: to give coordinates of numerous places and geographical features and to make recommendations for creating a world map and regional maps. He criticizes Marinus of Tyre for lack of consistency, for exaggerating the dimensions of the known world, and for using a projection suited mainly to the latitude of Rhodes. Books 2 and 3 cover Europe; Book 4, Africa; Books 5 through 8, Asia and a summary. Rejecting orthogonal (cylindrical) world mapping, Ptolemy describes three alternative projections. For regional maps he accepts orthogonal projection, but with proportions for each region based on its mean latitude. He considers Thule (Shetland to him) as the farthest point north at 63° N and Agysimba and Prasum promontory, east Africa, as the farthest south at 16°25′S. He considers the due north-south distance of the *oikumene* (known world) to be about 40,000 stades, which, with a stade equal to 184.81 meters (the commonest equivalent under the Roman Empire), gives 7,392 kilometers (4,580 miles). He estimated the east-west distance from the Canaries to Sera, the supposed capital of China, and Cattigara (possibly Hanoi) to be 180 degrees, against Marinus's estimate of 225 degrees. This gave the east-west extent of the *oikumene* on the parallel of Rhodes as 72,000 stades (13,306 kilometers, or 8,250 miles).

At several points in Books 1 and 2, Ptolemy mentions maps that accompanied the *Geography*, using phrases such as "we shall draw maps." But in Book 8 he writes, "we have had maps drawn." He mentions ten maps of Europe, four of Africa, and twelve of Asia, and a world map. Some manuscripts contain the note, "I, Agathos Daimon, a technician of Alexandria, drew a map from the *Geography* of Ptolemy," which must refer to a world map from between the second and the sixth century. The Arabic writer al-Mas'udi (d. ca. 956) mentions a colored map of the *Geography* containing, he says, 4,530 cities and over 200 mountains.

The Byzantine monk Maximus Planudes (c. 1260–1310) discovered a copy of the *Geography* in 1295. Since it had no maps, he reconstructed them from Ptolemy's textual coordinates. The Florentine Jacobus Angelus made the first Latin translation (perversely called *Cosmographia*) in 1406. Place-names were transliterated from a Greek manuscript (Vaticanus Urbinas graecus 82) to a Latin manuscript (Vaticanus latinus 5698) in 1415.

The first Latin printed editions were published in Bologna, Rome, and Ulm between 1477 and 1482, which led to an enormous expansion of readership. Regional maps made on the cartographer Donnus Nicolaus's (fl. 1460s–1470s) trapezoidal projection appeared in the Ulm editions, which were printed in black-and-white; the maps could be colored by hand. Christopher Columbus had a copy of the Vicenza first edition of 1475, without maps. Now in Madrid, his copy bears a common version of his signature, *Christo ferens*, and annotations in his hand. It is obvious that he took account of Ptolemy's as well as Marinus's distances. His brother Bartolomé also had access to printed Ptolemaic maps.

As the results of Portuguese discoveries sponsored by Prince Henry the Navigator emerged, it became apparent that Ptolemaic maps must be amended. Much earlier their depiction of north Britain had been recognized as incorrect. The shapes of Africa and much of Southern Asia—implying an enclosed Indian Ocean—were known to contradict facts. One method of coping with these errors was to include *tabulae modernae* (updated maps); thus Scandinavia, hardly known to Ptolemy, appeared in Claudius Clavus's version (1427).

Columbus's discoveries did not destroy Ptolemy's reputation or remove his name from updated atlases; instead, the *tabulae modernae* system was extended to the New World. The name "America," from Amerigo Vespucci, first appeared in 1507 in a work preparatory to an edition of Ptolemy by Martin Waldseemüller and Matthias Ringmann. In this work the name is applied to South America, but is clearly intended to apply to the whole hemisphere. Among many Ptolemaic world maps that show the American continents is that of Johan Ruysch (1508). The distinction between ancient Ptolemaic maps and contemporary atlases was foreshadowed in Waldseemüller's 1513 edition and was finally effected by Gerardus Mercator, who edited the ancient Ptolemaic maps in 1578 and modern maps at various other periods as independent volumes.

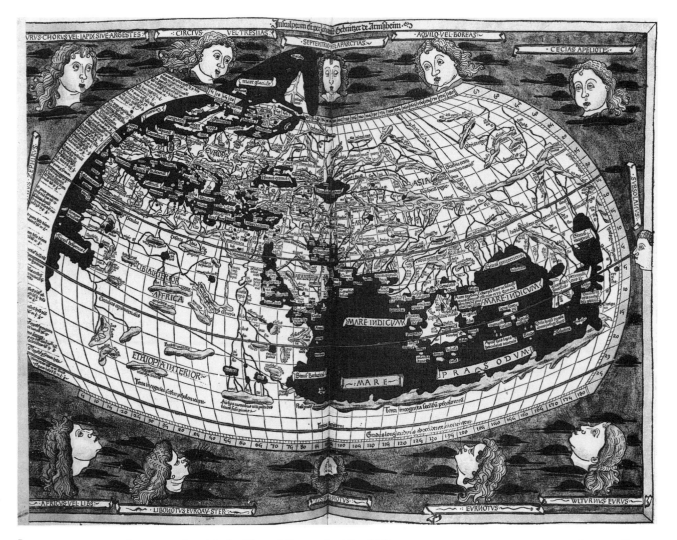

PTOLEMAIC WORLD MAP. From an early printed edition of *Geography.* Ulm, 1482.   LIBRARY OF CONGRESS

BIBLIOGRAPHY

Campbell, Tony. *The Earliest Printed Maps: 1472–1500.* London, 1987.

Davies, Arthur. "Origins of Columbian Cosmography." *Studi Colombiani* 2 (1952): 59–67.

Dilke, O. A. W. *Greek and Roman Maps.* Ithaca, N.Y., 1985.

Harley, J. Brian, and David Woodward, eds. *The History of Cartography.* Vol. 1, *Cartography in Prehistoric, Ancient, and Medieval Europe and the Mediterranean.* Chicago, 1987.

Ptolemy. *The Geography of Ptolemy.* Translated by E. L. Stevenson. New York, 1932.

O. A. W. DILKE

PUERTO RICO. The smallest of the Greater Antilles (after Cuba, Hispaniola, and Jamaica), Puerto Rico is also the most easterly. Its topography is similar to that of the other large islands, with central mountains giving way to plains along the shore. During the fifteenth century it was the frontier of the Taíno people, for the smaller islands to the east were held by the Caribs.

The Taínos of Puerto Rico, or Boriquén as they called it, resembled their cousins to the west. They too lived in villages under caciques (chiefs) and sustained themselves with fish and cassava bread. They built swift canoes, wove hammocks, and worked the gold that was relatively abundant on their island. They seem to have been notable particularly for their addiction to a ball game somewhat resembling pelota; their courts for this game can still be seen on the island.

Columbus reached Boriquén in November 1493 and was well received by the inhabitants. Spanish occupation began in 1508, under the direction of Juan Ponce de León, and relations with the Taínos were at first amicable.

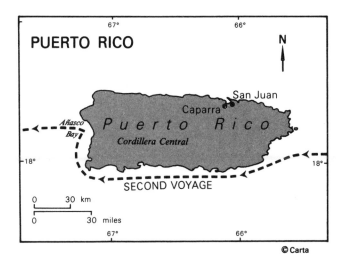

native population, partly through brutal treatment but more, no doubt, through the ravages of European diseases.

In 1510 a capital was founded at Caparra, but this site was soon abandoned for the adjacent one at Puerto Rico, on its magnificent bay. Eventually the island took the name of this town, and the town took the name of San Juan, which had been given the island by Columbus. Like the other islands, Puerto Rico became a backwater once Spanish attention was diverted to the gold-rich mainland. Some sugar cultivation was practiced, using slaves imported from Africa, and there were vast cattle ranches. But the island's chief value to Spain lay in its port of San Juan, which over the years was heavily fortified and which became one of the main stopovers for the yearly *flota*, which maintained communications between Spain and her colonies.

[See also *Indian America*, articles on *Island Caribs* and *Taínos*.]

Perhaps the Spaniards were seen as a counterweight to the Caribs, whose perpetual attacks had made the Taínos abandon eastern areas of the island. However, the conquerors' usual cruelties in their quest for gold eventually incited resistance, and in 1511 the Taínos broke into formal revolt. This was soon put down, however, and then began the usual pattern of a catastrophic decline in the

BIBLIOGRAPHY

Alegria, Ricardo. *Descubrimiento, conquista y colonización de Puerto Rico 1493–1599.* San Juan, 1975.

DAVID BUISSERET

Q

QUADRANT. Three types of quadrant (Latin, *quadrans;* Spanish, *cuadrante;* Portuguese, *quadrante)* have been distinguished in the literature: (1) the *quadrans vetustissimus* (the most ancient quadrant; this term is recent), (2) the *quadrans vetus* (the old quadrant), and (3) the *quadrans novus* (the new quadrant), which is the astrolabe-quadrant. Essentially, a quadrant is a flat plate of wood or metal in the form of a circle, with a plumb line and bob suspended from a hole close to the apex and with a scale of ninety degrees engraved along the circumferential arc; a pair of sight vanes attached to one of the radial edges enabled the instrument to be used for measuring angular elevations. A form of sundial, known as a horary quadrant, was engraved above the degree scale with lines for unequal (planetary) hours and a solar declination scale, and served for use in a particular latitude (the *quadrans vetustissimus*). Such quadrants, known in Islam and medieval Europe, were improved during the twelfth century by the addition of a sliding cursor, enabling the quadrant to be used in any latitude (the *quadrans vetus*). Horary quadrants had a sliding bead on the plumb line, which was held taut either against the solar declination or the date on the declination scale or against the appropriate point on the declination scale on the cursor, which had previously been adjusted for the latitude, while the bead was moved to the declination on the day of use (in the first case) or to the six-o'clock-hour line (in the second case). The plumb line was then allowed to hang freely, and the quadrant was directed toward the sun until the shadow of the foresight fell squarely on the backsight. The position of the bead in relation to the hour lines indicated the time.

When Columbus referred to a quadrant, he would have meant either an instrument of the simplest type (merely an angle-measuring device with a plumb bob and a scale of degrees) or perhaps a *quadrans vetus*. The earliest known representation of a quadrant intended for nautical use does not occur until the 1563 (posthumous) edition of Valentim Fernandes's *Reportório dos tempos* (1st ed., Lisbon, 1518) at the beginning of a chapter entitled "the Regiment [that is, rule] in order that one may be guided, with the quadrant or the astrolabe, by the Pole Star." Compared with the earliest surviving medieval quadrant (c. 1300), Fernandes's quadrant had a much smaller area devoted to the hour lines, no sliding cursor for latitude adjustment (but what were probably declination scales for two different latitudes), and the scale of ninety degrees along the arc was emphasized by lengthening the five-degree and ten-degree intervals, to make it easier to determine the altitude of a celestial body (e.g., the polestar), using the sight vanes and the plumb line. Fernandes explains how to navigate with the quadrant, but his method was already superseded by 1563. The navigator, on leaving Lisbon, is instructed to mark, on the quadrant, where the plumb line falls while observing the polestar with the Guards of the Little Dipper (Ursa Minor) lying east-west relative to that star. When, later, at sea, he wanted to know his north-south distance from Lisbon, he should determine the difference in degrees between the position of the plumb line at his original observation and that of a new observation; then he should convert to distance with one degree equal to 16⅔ leagues. Such a quadrant could have been used in this way at sea for several centuries previously, but its use in navigation is associated with the development of the technique of "running down the latitude."

In the thirteenth century, Prophatius Judaeus of Montpellier reduced the essential circles of the planispheric astrolabe to a quarter of a circle, thereby enabling them to be drawn on a quadrant (for use in a single latitude). This

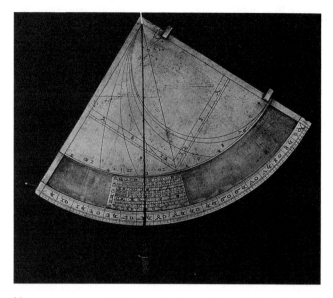

HORARY QUADRANT. This example, from about 1300, is the only surviving *quadrans vetus*.

astrolabe-quadrant was known as the *quadrans novus*. Medieval examples, European or Islamic, are very rare; however, many examples from the Ottoman Empire survive. From the late seventeenth century until the early years of the present century, the astrolabe-quadrant (typically with the astrolabe lines on one side, and a sine/cosine quadrant on the other) was very popular, probably because it provided the *muwaqqit* (time-keeper) in a mosque with a conveniently cheap instrument for determining prayer times.

BIBLIOGRAPHY

Maddison, Francis. *Medieval Scientific Instruments and the Development of Navigational Instruments in the XVth and XVIth Centuries.* Agrupamento de estudos de cartografia antiga, vol. 30. Coimbra, 1969.
Millás Vallicrosa, J. M. "La introducción del cuadrante con cursor en Europa." *ISIS* 18 (1932): 218–258. Reprinted in *Estudios sobre historia de la ciencia española*, by J. M. Millás Vallicrosa. Pp. 61–78. Barcelona, 1960.
Poulle, Emmanuel. *Les instruments astronomiques du moyen âge.* Astrolabica, vol. 3. Paris, 1983.
Schmalzl, Peter. *Zur Geschichte der Quadranten bei den Araben.* Munich, 1929.
Turner, Anthony. *Early Scientific Instruments: Europe 1400–1800.* London, 1987.

FRANCIS MADDISON

QUINCENTENARY. [This entry includes three articles concerning various historical perspectives on the epochal events of 1492:

Caribbean Perspectives
American Indian Perspectives
Hispanic Perspectives
For discussion of how Columbus is remembered in social and artistic media, see *Celebrations; Columbianism; Columbian Societies; Iconography; Literature; Monuments and Memorials.*]

Caribbean Perspectives

Columbus and his crew landed on an island in the Caribbean in October 1492. What was it about this event that would lead it to radically change the world? Why should that date more than any other (according to Tzvetan Todorov, 1984) have marked "the beginning of the modern era"? Why is it that, as contemporary people, it is with Columbus that our intellectual genealogy begins? Most urgently of all, how are "we"—who are inhabitants of the part of the world where Columbus landed and consequently of both European and non-European civilizational and racial origins—to look back on and interpret that event?

Spain, and Europe in general, are preparing to celebrate this event and have chosen to call it "the First Encounters." But the view from the Americas and the Caribbean, unlike that from Europe, must confront the fact that a non-European and indigenous collective historical memory also exists. This memory, in marked contrast to the triumphalist schoolbook stereotype that "in 1492, Columbus sailed the ocean blue" and "discovered America," is scarred. As Wendy Rose (1990) reminds us, for some people this epochal event "is a time of mourning."

Consider that within one generation of 1492, Columbus, the Spanish settlers, and the new diseases that they brought to the Caribbean had virtually "destroyed all the native human life" on the islands (Rose, 1990). Thus, José Marti of Cuba mourned that "a page had been torn from the Book of the Universe!" Moreover, the linkage of that event to the forcible capture and Middle Passage travail of the peoples of Africa to serve as substitute slave labor for the former native population is also historical reality.

So, how are "we"—as descendants of both the invaders and the invaded, the enslavers and the enslaved, whose process of conflictual interaction laid the foundation of the culture of the Americas—to look back on, interpret, and mark that event of 1492? Indeed, how are all later immigrants of non-European (and therefore of nonwhite) origin to do so, if to do so enforces and legitimizes the relations of a sociracial hierarchy between Euro-whites (blancos) and whiter nonwhites (morenos), on the one hand, and between morenos and the Afro-blacks, on the other? If the displacement and defeat of the indigenous people who first domesticated this hemisphere is celebrated on the day when "Columbus discovered America," then so also are the "five centuries of humiliation" (Van Sertima, 1976) undergone by the peoples of Africa and their Diaspora descendants.

Hans Koning, writing about groups who are organizing a countermovement to the official celebrations of the five-hundredth anniversary of Columbus's landing in the Americas, narrated the story of a visitor to a 1492 exhibition in the Southwest entitled "First Encounters." An American Indian was demonstrating in protest outside the exhibition, and the woman called out angrily, vehemently, to him, "You are spoiling the pleasure of our children!"

This incident of the "Protest-ant" and the "Woman Celebrant" brings out the feature that is "new" with respect to how the contemporary Americas and the Caribbean are to view, interpret, and commemorate the event that lies at our origin. It sharply separates the European view of 1492 from the view whose conflictual nature the peoples of the Americas and the Caribbean are now called upon to confront and resolve.

From the historical perspective of Europe, 1492 marks the initial step in the linkage of Europe, Africa, and the Americas, as well as of its eventual rise in the nineteenth century to become a civilization of global hegemony. So without being confronted by a descendant of America's indigenous inhabitants to challenge them, as was Koning's Woman Celebrant in the Southwest, Europeans can without contradiction rephrase the earlier "vulgate" interpretation of "Columbus discovered America" into the euphemistic terms of "First Encounters."

But for us, the immediacy of the Celebrant versus Protest-ant contradiction impels us to a new question that is specific to the "New World": that is, "What are the rules that shape and govern human perception? What are the rules that allow the Woman Celebrant to live existentially in the Americas and yet continue to accept the purely triumphalist, Europe-centered terms of the displacers rather than the dualistic and conflictual terms of the Americas and the Caribbean?"

Western Thinkers. An understanding of this problem is revealed by the historian T. M. Roberts (1985), who explains that for the Americas and all the rest of the world, all that has happened is the "echo" of Western thinkers and a reflection of the "way of life" that their modes of thought have prescribed. The thinkers and actors of Western Europe continue to "transform the world in their image"—that is, in terms of their industrial-technological way of life. Moreover, the entire world has now come to see and know reality through the mediation of the conceptual frameworks generated from the varying images of the human put in place by Western European thinkers from the Renaissance onward.

So completely has this been the case that the struggles directed against this dominance (whether the formidable one of Marxism or more recently of feminism, Afrocentrism, and multiculturalism) have been couched in theoretical terms that are themselves generated from the thought patterns invented by Western European thinkers. Because of these patterns and their underlying conceptions of the human being, as Roberts points out, all humans today live in a "world radically reshaped by the West"—and, therefore, within the "world of rules" by which this reshaping has been effected (Hubner, 1983).

Returning to the example of Koning's Woman Celebrant, it is clear that she interprets the event of 1492 in terms of the United States as a generically white and Euro-American nation-state, a notion that derives from the American history she was taught in school. That history continues to perceive the event of 1492 from the perspective of Western Europe, to whose peoples the Woman Celebrant continues to be linked by the triumphalist terms of the vulgate interpretation and its "unitary system of meanings" (Castoriadis, 1981).

This perspective of the Woman Celebrant puts her in sharp opposition to the Protest-ant American Indian. For although they are of the same nation-state, they do not share a common historical consciousness. Nevertheless, paradoxically, Western thought has also entrapped the Protest-ant, making him continue to see the event of 1492 only in terms of the triumphalism of the upper-dogs. In view of this paradox, we ask why we must remain caught in the conflict described by Gregory Bateson (1969), where "we just go round and round in terms of the old premises," unable to call those premises into question.

A "Root Expansion of Thought." In his *Zen and the Art of Motorcycle Maintenance* (1972), Robert Persig challenged the schoolbook stereotype that Columbus has been made into. Rather than accepting a territorial or technological interpretation of Columbus's achievement, Persig argues that in crossing an ocean that was believed at that time to be nonnavigable, Columbus's actual feat involved a "root expansion of thought."

The point here is that Columbus's voyage, and the chain of reasoning that led to it, challenged the belief structure sustaining both the image of the earth and the rigid noble-nonnoble caste hierarchy of the feudal Christian order of that time. In the symbolic geography of the image of the earth, then, the *orbis* (world) of Christian Redemption was a Jerusalem-centered, tripartite world of Europe, Asia, and Africa. Concomitantly, the Western Hemisphere, as antipodal lands to the *orbis* (that is, as the *orbis alter*, or Other World/Earth), should have been submerged under the infinite expanse of water of the encircling Ocean Sea (of which the Atlantic was considered a part) and, as such, uninhabitable and unreachable.

Despite this theocentric Christian version of Aristotle's physics, Columbus jotted down in the margin of a page of Pierre d'Ailly's *Imago mundi*, "Between the edge of Spain and the beginning of India, the sea is short and can be crossed in a matter of a few days." Thus, Columbus's challenge to the prevailing knowledge of his age was, in his words, "Mare totum navigabile"—"All seas are navigable."

Carrying his thought further, Persig argues that our present space exploration can be effected within the context of a mode of reason that is "adequate to handle it." Thus, it does not involve a true expansion of thought. Any "really new exploration" that would look to us today the way the world looked to Columbus, according to Persig, "would have to be in an entirely new direction," since it would have to move into "realms beyond [present-day] reason."

An analogous call for a "really new exploration" has also been made by the African scholar Theophile Obenga (1987). He argues that Europe's five centuries of triumph and dominance cannot be understood without taking note of the central role played by the new type of lay intellectual who emerged in Europe during the Renaissance. It was the synergistic interaction of "this new type of intellectual" (such as printers, editors, merchants, jurists, and writers) that would lead to the profound "intellectual mutation" that gave rise to a Europe new in "social, economic, cultural, and scientific terms."

Central to this process, Obenga continues, was the Renaissance intellectuals' reconceptualization of their past through a valorization of Europe's Greco-Roman intellectual legacy. That legacy had been reinterpreted and stigmatized in Christian terms during the feudal era; but in the Renaissance it was rediscovered and enriched by astronomers, cartographers, and geographers. Among these were "men of the sea, such as Columbus and Magellan," who not only enlarged the world but also created "a new image of the earth and another conception of the cosmos."

Obenga concludes that African intellectuals, if they are to deal with the vast dimensions of the problems plaguing their continent and their peoples worldwide, have no alternative but to effect a second such "intellectual mutation." This, too, would have to be done through a reconceptualization of the history of Africa, as one reaching back to the very emergence of the phenomenon of the human "from within the animal kingdom," to the rock paintings of the Grotto-Apollo in Namibia (dating back to 28,000 B.C.), and then to the flowering of this hominization in an ancient Egypt. Thus, ancient Egypt would serve Africa in the same way the Greco-Roman world has served Europe.

Toward a New World View of 1492. In this context, the dispute over the interpretation of 1492 opens the possibility of going beyond the limits of our present nation-state system of symbolic representations and attendant modes of cognition and perception. We need to move beyond "conventional reason" in a way that parallels Columbus's "root expansion of thought." Like Obenga's new type of intellectual, we must break out of our present culture-specific mode of thought, its related perceptual matrix, and co-related socioracial and other hierarchies. Indeed, the Janus-faced character of 1492 and its aftermath (evident in its dual effects of human emancipation and enslavement) can now be seen as the result of the partial and incomplete nature of that first intellectual mutation. It effectively led to the natural sciences but left us all in the dark regarding the rules that govern our modes of thought and the perceptions that orient our collective behavior.

A New World view of 1492 therefore has to move beyond our present system of knowledge and the rules that govern its modes of self, other, and societal perceptions. It should challenge symbolic representations, such as "Columbus discovered America," which render invisible America's indigenous peoples. It should also include a radical change from the image of the human as a natural organism that preexists culture to an image of humans emerging out of the animal kingdom and only coming into being simultaneously with culture, that is, with representations and discourse.

A New World view of the event of 1492 should seek to reconceptualize the past in terms of the reality specific to the Western hemisphere. It must recognize, as Cuban novelist Alejo Carpentier points out, that all the major and hitherto separated races of the world have been brought together in the New World to work out a common destiny. This destiny would entail the transformation of an original dominant/subordinate social structure into new ones founded on reciprocal relations.

In conclusion, we must come to terms with the tragic paradox of 1492 that is reflected in Koning's incident of the Woman Celebrant and the American Indian Protest-ant. The fundamental opposition between the two is unique to the New World situation. To resolve it, we must now replicate Columbus's creation of a "new image of the earth" by creating a new "image of the human," based on a transracial mode of inclusive altruism beyond the limits of the national subject and the nation-state.

BIBLIOGRAPHY

Bateson, Gregory. "Conscious Purpose vs. Nature." In *The Dialectics of Liberation*, edited by D. Cooper. Harmondsworth, England, 1969.

Castoriadis, C. "The Imaginary: Creation in the Socio-Historical Domain." In *Disorder and Order: Proceedings of the Stanford International Symposium*, edited by Paisley Livingston. Stanford Literature Studies 1. *Anma Libri* (September 1981): 14–18.

Gonzalez, Alicia. "The New World Will Discuss Process." *The New World* 1, no. 1 (Spring 1990): 3.

Hubner, Kurt. *Critique of Scientific Reason.* Chicago, 1983.

Koning, Hans. "Don't Celebrate 1492, Mourn." *New York Times* (August 14, 1990).

Obenga, Theophile. "Sous-thème: La pensée africaine et la philosophie dans une perspective de renouvellement." Paper presented at a symposium organized by FESPAC, Dakar, December 15–19, 1987.

Persig, Robert. *Zen and the Art of Motorcycle Maintenance.* New York, 1972.

Roberts, T. M. *The Triumph of the West.* Boston, 1985.

Rose, Wendy. "For Some It's a Time of Mourning." *The New World* 1, no. 1 (Spring 1990): 4.

Thorndike, Lynn. *A History of Magic and Experimental Science.* Vol. 4. New York, 1934.

Todorov, Tzvetan. *The Conquest of America: The Question of the Other.* New York, 1982.

Van Sertima, I. *They Came before Columbus.* New York, 1976.

Wynter, Sylvia. "1492: A New World View." *The New World* 1, no. 2 (Spring/Summer 1991): 4–5. This article in *The New World* and the foregoing encyclopedia entry are based on a paper prepared for the conference " 'Race,' Discourse and the Origins of the Americas: A New World View of 1492" (The Smithsonian Institution, October 31 to November 1, 1991).

SYLVIA WYNTER

American Indian Perspectives

Out of the dark, very early one morning, a large object appeared far out in the ocean. The coming of daylight finally allowed the people on the beach to see a ship and men unlike any they had ever seen, strange in appearance and behavior. The generally accepted version of history would record that the leader of these men was called Christopher Columbus, discoverer of the New World. But in actuality he was an arrogant intruder on Guanahani, as the people called their island. It is their version of history—history as perceived by native Americans—that is presented here.

Contemporary books fail to relate how these people viewed Columbus; thus, how American Indians in general have perceived the American experience is unknown to most people. To see history through the eyes of another person is difficult, especially if the individual is from another culture, another world. And the greater the difference between cultures, the more difficult it is to overcome prejudice and recognize another's world. To begin to understand the perspective of the American Indian, consider a coin and then turn it over. It is the same coin, but it presents one image from one side; a totally different, but equal image from the other.

From the "other side" of the events of 1492, the original inhabitants of the Western Hemisphere viewed Columbus as a stranger to their land. From out of the water as far as the eye could see, he came with his people, riding a huge

vessel unknown to them. How could it be that a race of "white" people existed? Why had they come here? What did they want? Why were they different? Was he an intruder or a visitor? And where did he and his men come from? These questions may very well have run through the minds of America's inhabitants as they witnessed the arrival of Columbus that October day.

The dress and behavior of the white stranger and his crew were totally foreign. There was no existing knowledge that would enable the people to address them and learn the answers to their questions. Even the wisest elders could not say who these people were. Columbus and his men had upset the balance of reality of the known world. In such circumstances, only time provides answers to such questions, and people must be patient, for what appears at first to be an answer is not always the truth.

For the American Indians, dreams and visions had produced assumptions that there were other beings who spoke foreign languages; thus, when Columbus did not fit into the realm of existing knowledge, the people presumed him to be a foreigner. Because he did not look or dress like those of their own society, it was assumed he knew no better; therefore, he must not be as intelligent. Certainly he did not speak the language, and what was more, he did not seem to want to learn. And he was obviously lost!

Time revealed that Columbus was a trespasser, not a friend. The unusual-looking stranger had his own agenda and motives, and his plan did not include sharing or helping people. He had come with a single purpose, and it did not involve trying to make their lives better. Later, the people learned that Columbus had a culture of his own, a nation, a world of other people.

Two very different worlds with separate histories now began to form a new history of "Indian" and "white" relations. In such a case, the amount of difference exemplifies the distance between ideas, values, concerns, religions, cultures, and worldviews. On a daily basis, social contact did not lessen the distance; only time brought the two sides closer together. Unfortunately, two diametrically opposed worlds will end in conflict unless each respects the other and agrees on a course of positive relations. Their incongruence continues until one dominates the other, and the result alters the evolutionary course of both peoples.

Columbus's bold entrance into the native world was construed by some to mean that he might be a messenger or the provider of new knowledge, perhaps a prophet. The material items he possessed (his huge sailing vessel was an example) and the ones he gave to the people indicated that he had more knowledge than the wisest elders of Guanahani. The material culture of the stranger was a major difference, and it had a grave effect on the native Americans. First, the foreign goods impressed them and fed their curiosity. The people were seduced by their bright colors and charm, and naturally they wanted them. Among the native Americans, gift giving underscored generosity—a cherished value—and hospitality established a friendly rapport. As Columbus and later Europeans continued to give gifts of trinkets, beads, and whiskey, native Americans responded with their own generous hospitality.

Such gift giving brought the Europeans and native Americans of different nations together on a positive basis. Or at least, so the native Americans thought, until they realized the imperialistic nature of Europeans and learned that all Europeans were not alike. During the sixteenth and seventeenth centuries, the French followed the Spanish, and then the Dutch, English, Swedes, and Russians arrived, desiring land and its bullion of gold and silver or pelts of fur to enrich their motherlands. But wanton greed had no place in the world of native Americans where the abundance of flora and fauna provided the requirements of life.

The native Americans were not as competitive as the Europeans at the same intense, individual level at which one views oneself as the philosophical center of the universe. Rather, the native people stressed sharing, generosity, and hospitality as virtues to bond their communities together, placing solidarity above the values of a single individual. In the Americas, a person alone did not survive very long; chances for a long life increased when one had a family and community to help provide food, shelter, and protection.

Through the succeeding years, every ship brought more people with the same individualistic attitude. Their sheer numbers were beyond belief. At various times, native groups described the white race as being as numerous as the "leaves on the trees" or the "stars at night." How could such a race of people multiply so? The native Americans viewed themselves as separate nations, so they did not realize they, too, were numerous. They did not see themselves as one race called "Indians," nor did any of the tribes have such a generic word in their languages, compelling many groups to invent a phrase that translated as "red man" or "red people." All together, when Columbus arrived, approximately 15 to 20 million people lived in North America (including Mexico and Central America) and an even larger number lived in South America.

The final difference between the native Americans and the Europeans was the advanced level of technology the latter possessed, especially in the eighteenth and nineteenth centuries. As the British dominance over the French and Spanish gave way to the white Americans in the Revolution, the white Americans' superior military weaponry won the final victories over the native nations. The gunpowder, cannon, pistols, and rifles of the white Americans prevailed over the superior knowledge of the land and the ways of nature of the native Americans. The end of the 1800s marked the ultimate defeat of the native Americans and witnessed the emergence of their conquerors as a leading power in the world. This stage of events in the Americas enabled the whites to write their own ethnocentric version of history that has become the accepted perspective of the non-Indian mainstream in the United States.

A history written by conquerors dismisses the perspective of those who were suppressed and attempts to negate the history of others who are not dominant in the culture. American history has failed to include accounts of other minorities and of women, and has stressed the strength of the victorious culture. As a result, politics and economics have been seen as the driving emphases of American civilization; other important aspects of the culture, such as its social, cultural, and religious elements, have been neglected.

An "Indian" version of the American experience should present multiple versions from the many native nations. But, lacking these, a categorical "Indian" version does exist, and it needs to be widely acknowledged for a correction of the historical record. More than five hundred tribal nations existed, and their collective view would present the Indian perspective of the history of the Americas. Because of ethnocentrism on the part of scholars of history and anthropology and other experts who study the American experience, the record of Indian-white relations is incomplete. This prejudice has produced a one-sided view, that of Anglo-America; the other side, Indian America, needs to be heard.

The encounter between Columbus and the American Indians on the shores of Guanahani on that early Friday morning, October 12, 1492, should be reexamined so that the history of their meeting and the events that followed it will be balanced and accurate.

BIBLIOGRAPHY

Berkhofer, Robert F., Jr. *The White Man's Indian: Images of the American Indian from Columbus to the Present.* New York, 1978.

Horsman, Reginald. *Race and Manifest Destiny: The Origins of American Racial Anglo-Saxonism.* Cambridge, Mass., 1981.

Martin, Calvin, ed. *The American Indian and the Problem of History.* New York, 1987.

McNickle, D'Arcy. *They Came Here First: The Epic of the American Indian.* Philadelphia, 1949.

Washburn, Wilcomb E. *The Indian in America.* New York, 1975.

DONALD L. FIXICO

Hispanic Perspectives

When Christopher Columbus returned to Spain after his first voyage to the Western Hemisphere, he took with him news of territories previously unknown. Across ensuing centuries, these lands and the peoples inhabiting them would be incorporated into the European worldview and its economic and political activities. Inclusion of the Americas in the accumulated knowledge and understanding of the Old World was a much slower task than its incorporation into the European political system or its rapidly evolving mercantile-capitalist economic system. A variety of landscapes, plant and animal species, ethnic groups, and social and thought systems were suddenly to be included within a worldview that Europe had taken centuries to elaborate and that encompassed the familiar neighboring lands, people, and cultures. In this view, there was no ready fit for the New World.

Assimilating the Discoveries. A first intellectual undertaking was establishing the contours of the land masses and locating their place on the earth. Spanish navigators and foot soldiers relentlessly explored the islands and the mainland, mapped the shorelines, and described the physical and ecological features they encountered. The information they sent back, leaking out from Seville, allowed Europeans to piece together a reasonably accurate picture of the area within four decades. The New World was recognized as an independent landmass lying between the Western and Eastern parts of the Old World. Geographical curiosity eventually led navigators to discover the spherical shape of the planet and its rotation.

Plants and animals unknown in Europe were acknowledged; others that looked familiar were treated by analogy and given European names, in spite of being native species. Fads for exotic items led to some plants being acclimated in Spanish gardens, although their use as staples was postponed for a few centuries. These new lands and new species shattered many European assumptions about the world. They stunned people but were easy to absorb; they were simply added to the old panoply of known objects.

The New World's peoples and societies raised more philosophical issues and led to elevated debates. Were the beings with whom relations were to be established human, at the same level as Africans, Asians, and Europeans? In practical terms, there was little hesitation: Spanish sailors and soldiers met native females. But on a higher level, did the natives deserve respect as human beings, were they entitled to freedom, and could they be expected to behave morally and comprehend the Gospel, the supreme value in European culture? Natives were brought back to Spain as slaves by Columbus, but it was immediately ordered that they be returned and freed. A debate raged for decades among jurists and theologians of the court to ascertain whether the Crown could legitimately subjugate alien Americans, impose upon them the obligations of vassals, such as paying tribute, and make them participate in Christendom. Emperor Charles V even considered the idea of relinquishing control of the Indies and bringing the settlers home.

Practical reasons prevailed and the Conquest of the New World went on. Indians were thereafter regarded as fully rational people, vassals and Christians, although this did not prevent their maltreatment or exploitation. They were free and entitled to self-government under the suzerainty and guidance of the Crown. A paternalistic attitude prevailed, and Indians were treated as minors.

New World Peoples and Resources in Europe's Hands. Native Americans were thus reckoned as members of the wider world, but they still needed to be accepted on their own ground. Uncovering their self-identity and putting their creations on an equal footing with other world experiences required a longer intellectual process. Recognition of the Indian self began early, amid an attempt to suppress them. Missionaries, intending to understand Indian customs and minds in order to instill the Gospel more effectively, described pre-Columbian usages, institutions, and creeds. There is a fascinating contradiction between the denial of Indians' ways and the information about them that was rescued for future generations. Modern ethnography arose from these detailed accounts of remote cultures. Understanding these peoples often led to empathy. The notion of an openminded and good-natured person—the "noble savage" of the eighteenth-century Enlightenment to come—began to emerge from the early contacts between Spaniards and natives. As Europeans strove to come to grips with the Americas, humankind came to be seen as not inescapably tarnished by original sin: there could still be humans living in a state of innocence; maybe it was civilization that had blemished humans; history could extend back beyond the biblical past; perhaps even paradise could be found on earth. A sense of cultural relativism, dear to our time, emerged.

Among the products of the New World that were shipped back were precious metals. Silver mined in Potosí and Mexico was the most important during the sixteenth and seventeenth centuries. By the eighteenth century, Brazilian gold production took the lead, and silver mining was later revived in Mexico. Both public and private remittances of precious metals reached Spain and Portugal and were spent on luxury goods or hoarded, but most silver and gold coins entered into circulation.

The money supply exploded, increasing the purchasing power for goods and the spread of credit. Consumption rose in Spain, encouraging production and imports. Inflation, however, soon came to harm the Spanish economy. Money drained away toward the rest of Europe, paying for imports and services or defraying the expenses incurred in Spain's expanding involvement in European affairs and wars. In the end, all the European nations, especially the most industrialized, shared in the tide of precious metals flowing from the New World. Europe also obtained the means of payment used in its import trade with the Orient. The global expansion that capitalist exchange acquired in early modern times was largely based on opportunities created by the monetary flow from the New World. Economic conditions changed, but so did economic thinking and behavior. Economic realities were hard to explain within the old moral framework. Theories such as the inflationary effect of increasing monetary supply were then formulated and policy conclusions were drawn. Modern monetarism can be traced back to the arrival of the "American treasure."

Emergence of the Hispanic New World. The union of Castile and Aragón, under Isabel and Fernando, created a powerful state led by a dominant monarchy. It was helped by a professional government bureaucracy checking both the nobility and feudal corporate rights. In the vast Americas, where the vice-kingdoms of New Spain and Peru were quickly established, the Crown had the opportunity to impose its vision of government for secondary kingdoms. The establishment of a semifeudal "nobility" was checked; as in Spain, the church was curbed through the *Patronato Real,* which gave the Crown control over all aspects of Roman Catholic practice. Control rested with Crown bureaucrats whose loyalty was to Spain. Justice was administered in local courts with the right of appeal to the audiencia or to the Council of the Indies in Spain; treasury officials collected taxes and remitted the portion not needed for American expenses back to Seville; public order was maintained. Only as American-born Spaniards with regional vested interests infiltrated the administrative structure, during the Habsburg decline, did colonial interests compete significantly with Crown aims. In Spain itself, the flow of silver from the Americas enabled the Crown to depend less on the goodwill (and contributions) of the estates, stemming the growth of their role in any kind of parliamentary system. The autocrat could afford to act independently.

By 1600 over 243,000 Spanish people had migrated, and during the next fifty years another 195,000 legal passages were noted. These migrants included government bureaucrats, priests and friars, merchants, craftsmen, soldiers of fortune, and ne'er-do-wells. The Americas served as an escape valve for ambitious men. Many came to improve their fortunes, and even when the éclat of the conquest era was over, the lure of the mines and the opportunities

to obtain land or establish themselves in the growing cities were known throughout the Iberian Peninsula and beyond. The Crown encouraged male migrants to take female members of their families to the colonies, but the migration of women was always less than that of men. In addition, by the end of the sixteenth century, the forced migration of African slaves was becoming regionally significant.

Unlike previous mercantile expansion along the coasts of Africa and Asia, where trading enclaves were established, in the Americas, conquerors became settlers in cities. The city was seen as the site of civilization; cities became centers from which novelties and modern ideas, fashions, and practices radiated. Although the Americas had been home to some highly developed urban peoples, they became a laboratory in which Spanish urban ideals were imposed. Cities were established where the Spanish wanted or needed them. They quickly took on the classic grid pattern that still characterizes them, with the church, the cabildo (council hall), the jail, and the homes of prominent citizens clustered around a central square. Within little more than a century, definitive networks of cities were established in the areas of active colonization—Mesoamerica and the Andean region. Through these networks, settlers were connected to the far-off metropolis, and rural hinterlands to the cities.

The catastrophic decline of the native American population, which was overwhelmingly due to Old World diseases, freed up space into which many Iberians moved. Contact between the two societies and tribute exigencies, paid in European plants and animals, modified indigenous production and led to some European products being integrated into indigenous life. Miscegenation led to a mestizo population that became Hispanicized in urban areas and maintained an indigenous cultural identification in rural areas. In some regions of Brazil and the Caribbean, African slaves contributed indelibly to another social and cultural hybrid. Iberian and African migration increasingly opened up the New World and was followed in later centuries by massive European migration, as well as indentured labor from areas as far away as India and China.

In those regions whose indigenous population maintained a critical mass, the encounter unleashed a centuries-long struggle between the attempt to impose Iberian structures and the determination to maintain indigenous ways. This ever-evolving dialectic produced a new society in which, in spite of differences in power and access to resources, all sides were modified.

The New World, which had evolved independently for thousands of years, abruptly entered the human, biotic, economic, and political exchanges of the Old World. Sooner or later this had been bound to occur; there was simply no place on a shrinking globe for an isolated continent to hide. For Europeans, the inclusion of this new reality was difficult intellectually; in the Americas, the process was painful and destructive for the people and the environment in which they lived. On both sides of the Atlantic, exchanges of people, species, and goods expanded consumption and contributed to the economic evolution. Indeed, the encounter forced the opening up of our collective understanding of nature, humanity, and society; it was the underpinning of the rise of modern times.

BIBLIOGRAPHY

Crosby, Alfred. *The Columbian Exchange: Biological and Cultural Consequences of 1492.* Westport, Conn., 1972.

Elliott, John H. *Imperial Spain, 1469–1716.* New York, 1964.

Hamilton, Earl J. *American Treasure and the Price Revolution in Spain, 1501–1650.* New York, 1934.

Pagden, Anthony. *The Fall of Natural Man: The American Indian and the Origins of Comparative Ethnology.* New York, 1982.

Parry, John H. *The Spanish Seaborne Empire.* New York, 1966.

NICOLÁS SÁNCHEZ-ALBORNOZ and DEBORAH L. TRUHAN

QUINTERO DE ALGRUTA, JUAN (b. 1466), boatswain. Quintero was boatswain aboard *Pinta* on Columbus's first voyage of discovery and shared with the Admiral and Pedro de Terreros the distinction of participating in all four voyages. As boatswain, he was in charge of all gear having to do with the efficient and safe operation of the ship. Prior to departure, he directed the proper stowage of all cargo and when underway checked that its lashing remained secure. At sea it was also his duty to check the condition of all spars, sails, rigging, and pumps; to lead the seamen and ship's boys in effecting necessary repairs and carrying out sail-handling and ship-maneuvering orders of the master or pilot; to keep the ship's boats fitted out and ready for use; and to ensure that the wood fire in the stove was extinguished every night.

Quintero was twenty-six years old in 1492. Like Martín Alonso Pinzón, his captain, he was from the seaport town of Palos and no doubt had been recruited by Pinzón to be boatswain of *Pinta.* Columbus had encountered strong resistance to his efforts to recruit experienced seamen to undertake his planned voyage to the west across the Mar Tenebrosa (Dark Sea) to reach Cipangu (Japan), Cathay (China), and the many islands of the Indies. He was a stranger to the seafaring men of the Huelva, Moguer, and Palos region, and they were extremely dubious of the venture's prospects of success. Only when the Pinzón and Niño families of Palos and Moguer, respectively, gave their support to Columbus did it become possible to convince any of these men to become a part of the enterprise. In later years, Quintero, a staunch supporter of the captain of *Pinta,* testified in the Pleitos as to the vital role of Martín Alonso Pinzón in convincing the reluctant seamen to join him and his brother Vicente Yáñez Pinzón, captain of *Niña,* in making the voyage. He also spoke of Martín Alonso's role in calming the seamen on October 10, 1492, when they wished to turn back toward Spain. Land would be sighted in a few days, he told them, and, of course, it was.

Although Quintero participated in all four voyages of discovery, he never sailed on the same ship as Columbus. Perhaps because of this, no mention of his name is found in any of the several accounts of the voyages. But his selection by Martín Alonso Pinzón to the important position of boatswain of *Pinta* and his eventual rise to the position of master of *Gallega* on the fourth voyage attest to his competence in seamanship.

BIBLIOGRAPHY

Gould, Alicia B. *Nueva lista documentada de los tripulantes de Colón en 1492.* Madrid, 1984.

Irving, Washington. *The Life and Voyages of Christopher Columbus and His Companions.* 3 vols. New York, 1849.

WILLIAM LEMOS

R

RÁBIDA, LA. When Columbus's ships sailed from Palos through the narrow estuary to the Atlantic on August 3, 1492, they passed the coastal promontory of La Rábida. From this headland rose a Franciscan monastery, Santa María de La Rábida, that had played an important part in financing the voyage.

The headland took its name from a Muslim fortified monastery (*rabat*) that once stood on the site. Franciscans founded the monastery of Santa María there in 1412. During the fifteenth century, the number of friars grew to twenty-six, and the monastery gained the reputation of sending missionaries to convert the natives of the Canary Islands.

A Spanish historian, Antonio Rumeu de Armas, has finally swept away centuries of exaggerated claims about when Columbus arrived at La Rábida and what kind of help he received there. Rumeu researched the Franciscan archives, the royal treasury accounts, and court records. He discovered that Christopher Columbus stayed at the monastery of Santa María de La Rábida on three occasions.

Columbus first came to La Rábida in 1491, when he arrived with his twelve-year-old son Diego. No one in the region had ever seen him before, and he spoke with a foreign accent. The head of the monastery (whose identity is unknown) provided the travelers with the hospitality of the house. One of the brothers, Juan Pérez, who had worked in the royal accounting office when he was a boy and later became confessor to Queen Isabel, engaged Columbus in conversation about the royal court.

Juan Pérez sent a letter to the queen, asking that she give Columbus's scheme another hearing, and received a favorable reply two weeks later. Riding a mule rented from a citizen of the town of Moguer (Juan Rodríguez Cabezudo), Pérez went to the court in Santa Fe, where he told the queen that Columbus and his son were ragged, without connections, and without funds. The monarchs sent generous assistance, twenty thousand maravedis in florins, to Columbus.

While Juan Pérez negotiated on his behalf at court, Columbus put his stay in the monastery to good use. He visited the towns of Palos, Moguer, and Huelva to talk with pilots and publicize his plans. When Pérez and the royal secretary Juan de Coloma reached an agreement—which came to be known as the Santa Fe Capitulations—Columbus left Diego behind at La Rábida and arrived at court in time to see the Castilian banners raised in Granada on January 2, 1492.

Columbus and Juan Pérez returned to the monastery on the night of May 22—Columbus's second stay at La Rábida. For the next two months, Columbus worked to equip and man his little fleet in Palos, all the time residing in the monastery. He sent Diego to live with Beatriz de Arana before the fleet departed on August 3, 1492.

Columbus's final stay at La Rábida occurred when he brought *Niña* back to Palos after the first voyage, on March 15. He spent the next two weeks in the port, probably visiting his Franciscan friends at the monastery. He departed for Seville on March 29 and never returned to La Rábida.

La Rábida Monastery.   Museo Naval, Madrid

BIBLIOGRAPHY

Rumeu de Armas, Antonio. *La Rábida y el descubrimiento de América: Colón, Marchena y fray Juan Pérez.* Madrid, 1968.
Sale, Kirkpatrick. *The Conquest of Paradise: Christopher Columbus and the Columbian Legacy.* New York, 1990.

HELEN NADER

RATIONS. See *Equipment, Clothing, and Rations.*

RECONQUISTA. The reconquest is the central theme of medieval Spanish history. Generations of the Spanish people were taught that for seven hundred years their ancestors almost singlehandedly held back the Muslims threatening to engulf Christian Europe. In spite of this romantic view, the reconquest is not an artificial concept created by modern historians to render the history of medieval Spain intelligible; rather, it is an idea that developed in the ninth-century Kingdom of Asturias.

The origins of the reconquest go back to the collapse of Visigothic Spain as Muslim forces invaded from North Africa in 711. In later history and literature this event was described as *la pérdida de España* (the loss of Spain). As the Muslims overran Spain, some hardy survivors held out in the mountains of Asturias. Their leader, Pelayo, the first king of Asturias (r. 718–737), declared that he would

achieve the *salus Spanie* (salvation of Spain), and the restoration of the Gothic people. His victory over the Muslims at Covadonga in 722 traditionally is taken to mark the beginning of the reconquest. The inexorability of the struggle was stressed by a ninth-century chronicler who stated that the Christians would wage war against the enemy by day and night "until divine predestination commands that they be driven cruelly thence. Amen!" That hope proved to be illusory, but the ideal of the expulsion of the Muslims and the restoration of the Visigothic monarchy was embedded thereafter in the consciousness of Spanish Christians and recurs again and again in medieval history and literature.

For nearly three hundred years following the initial Muslim invasion, the Christians remained on the defensive, so that one could hardly speak of reconquest. Nevertheless, the breakup of the caliphate of Córdoba in the eleventh century enabled the Christian rulers to make significant progress in the reconquest. The fall of Toledo in 1085, Zaragoza in 1118, and Lisbon in 1147 moved the frontier to the Ebro and the Tagus rivers. Invasions by the Almoravids and Almohads from Morocco in the late eleventh and twelfth centuries halted expansion temporarily, but the Castilian victory at Las Navas de Tolosa in 1212 opened Andalusia to conquest. In the first half of the thirteenth century the kings of Portugal occupied the Alemtejo and the Algarve, as Jaime I of Aragón (r. 1213–1276) subjugated the Balearic Islands and Valencia.

Meanwhile Fernando III of Castile-León (r. 1217–1252) conquered Córdoba and Seville and reduced the Kingdom of Granada to tributary status. In the late thirteenth and fourteenth centuries the kings of Castile tried to gain control of the Straits of Gibraltar so as to seal off the classic invasion route from Morocco. The final Moroccan invasion by the Benimerines was halted by Alfonso XI's triumph at Salado in 1340, but for nearly a century and a half thereafter the Christians failed to press the reconquest.

The reconquest originated as a war to recover territory, but it also assumed the character of a holy war between two mutually exclusive societies. Religious beliefs regulated every aspect of life in both Christian and Muslim Spain, so much so that there was no possibility of full integration. The reconquest was a war not to propagate Christianity or to convert the Muslims but rather to expel them as intruders whose entire way of life was alien to that of the Christians. The reconquest was transformed into a crusade in the twelfth century, as the popes assured those who fought the Moors in Spain they would receive the same indulgences given to those who went off to liberate the Holy Land. From the thirteenth century onward the principal campaigns against the Spanish Muslims had the canonical status of crusades. The bull of crusade remained a characteristic feature of religious practice well into modern times both in Spain and in the Spanish colonies.

The reconquest was accompanied by repopulation or colonization. As the Muslims withdrew before the Christian advance into the Duero River valley and into Extremadura, the newly occupied lands had to be settled. Fortified urban settlements were established that were directly dependent upon the king, and royal charters ensuring personal freedom and other liberties were issued to attract settlers. The military orders founded in the twelfth century received lordships in the frontier region stretching from below the Tagus to the borders of Andalusia. When Andalusia, Valencia, Murcia, and the Algarve were taken, a substantial Muslim population was incorporated into Christian territory. The Mudéjars, as they were called, were expelled from Andalusia following an uprising in 1264, but they remained in Valencia until the seventeenth century.

Fernando of Aragón (r. 1479–1516) and Isabel of Castile (r. 1474–1504) brought the reconquest to completion. Appealing to the pope for crusading indulgences in 1485, they expressed the hope that "these infidels . . . will be ejected and expelled from Spain." In 1492 they informed the pope that "this kingdom of Granada, which was occupied for over seven hundred and eight years by the infidels . . . has been conquered." Some publicists argued that the reconquest would be complete only when Morocco, thought to have once been part of the Visigothic kingdom, was conquered, but the attraction of the

New World soon diverted the Spanish monarchs from North Africa.

The territorial integrity of Christian Spain was now restored, but the problem of creating one people remained. Whereas religious minorities previously enjoyed a measure of religious tolerance and juridical autonomy in Spain, the new idea of the nation-state made that difficult to sustain. For that reason the Jews in 1492 and the Muslims of Granada in 1502 were given the option of accepting Christianity or of being expelled from the realm. Thus the ideal of political, juridical, and religious unity was achieved, at least in theory.

The reconquest helped develop among medieval Spanish Christians a pioneer psychology. A people always living on a frontier, they were ever-ready to give up the security of a settled and peaceful place to seek something better, even though the risks might be great. The long centuries of reconquest and repopulation prepared the people of Spain for the task of overseas exploration and colonization.

[See also *Muslims in Spain*.]

BIBLIOGRAPHY

Collins, Roger. *Early Medieval Spain: Unity in Diversity, 400–1000.* New York, 1983.

Lomax, Derek W. *The Reconquest of Spain.* New York, 1978.

MacKay, Angus. *Spain in the Middle Ages: From Frontier to Empire, 1000–1500.* New York, 1977.

O'Callaghan, Joseph F. *A History of Medieval Spain.* Ithaca, N.Y., 1975.

JOSEPH F. O'CALLAGHAN

RELIGION. [This entry includes two overviews of religion at the time of European overseas exploration: one on European religious traditions and one on the religious systems of indigenous American peoples first encountered by Europeans. See also *Inquisition; Jews; Missionary Movement; Muslims in Spain; Papacy; Reconquista; Spirituality of Columbus*.]

European Traditions

The religious world of Europe in the fifteenth and sixteenth centuries was marked by contention and dissidence. Communities of Jews lived in scattered urban centers throughout Europe, and in the Iberian Peninsula there was a persistent, if often fragile, tradition of *convivencia* (coexistence) among Jews, Muslims, and Christians. Historians of the period, however, habitually assume that most Europeans were at least nominally Christian and had been so for centuries. But what being a Christian—even in a nominal sense—actually meant in terms of belief and practice is another matter. The urgent resurfacing of this ancient issue, as old as Christianity itself, was prompted by external circumstances as well; western Christendom was threatened from without by the persistent incursions of the Muslim Turks into the territories of Byzantium and the Holy Land. This concatenation of religious tensions reshaped both the sacred and the secular worlds in which Europeans lived and thought in fundamental ways.

The origins and dynamics of the spectrum of reform movements that emerged in sixteenth-century Europe remain controversial, but both Protestant and Catholic reformations manifested certain common patterns. When considered within the larger scope of the later medieval and Renaissance periods, they appear to have had a number of important, interrelated historical precedents. These included earlier endemic forms of religious dissent and independent lay pieties that had established themselves in various parts of Europe. Another precedent of a different sort was the development of humanist philology and hermeneutics in Renaissance Italy. These interpretive techniques and the readings they produced would exercise considerable influence on Biblical exegesis in the sixteenth century. In the social and political arenas, the Great Schism of the late fourteenth century and the reconsolidation of papal power in the course of the fifteenth and sixteenth centuries engendered new permutations in the ongoing conflicts with secular rulers.

The best-known heresies of pre-Reformation Europe were those of the Waldensians, the Lollards, and the Hussites. The Waldensians, who traced their origins back to the twelfth century, at one time or another claimed followers in various parts of the continent. The Lollards were concentrated in England and the Hussites in Bohemia and Moravia. There were certainly essential differences among them, but they all shared a resistance to the absolute authority of the pope and ecclesiastical law. To varying degrees they developed alternative doctrines and liturgies in seeking to establish themselves as separate Christian churches. In so doing they can be said to have anticipated the Lutherans and other Protestant sects; some of Luther's early followers were drawn from the Hussite movement.

Other important spiritual traditions, though remaining peripheral to Roman Catholic orthodoxy, were never declared heresies. In the German Rhineland, a lineage of popular preachers inspired by the great Meister Eckhart promised direct union of the aspiring soul with God. Their sermons bypassed the conventional confessional structures of the church and other avenues proffered by the system of indulgences and the intercession of saints, intertwining the messages of mysticism, dissent, and salvation.

In Italy, and then in transalpine Europe, the legend and

MARTIN LUTHER.   Gold medal, 1521.

teachings of Saint Francis guided an assortment of groups both within and without the mendicant order that bore his name. Within the order, first the Spirituals and later the Observants espoused shifting blends of radical poverty and apocalyptic expectations derived from Francis's contemporary Joachim of Fiore and other influential sources. Outside the order, the Beguines, the Fraticelli, and other lesser-known sects adopted associated views.

Accompanying such heresies and heterodoxies were curious local and regional admixtures of Christian and non-Christian doctrine, and residual beliefs and practices of pre-Christian Europe. Probably the most famous infiltration of non-Christian ideas occurred among the Cathars of southern France. Its doctrines, Persian in origin, activated the Albigensian Crusade and a Dominican inquisition sponsored by the papacy that did not altogether succeed in eradicating them. Recent scholarship has demonstrated that other nameless syncretisms, often idiosyncratic and usually very restricted in their influence, prevailed well into the early modern period. They continued to attract the attention and energies of inquisitors and evangelists from the mendicant and Jesuit orders.

These vibrations in the religious life of later medieval and Renaissance Europe resonated in its intellectual world as well. In the course of the fifteenth century, the Italian humanists' recovery and study of antique texts previously unknown in western Europe led to more nuanced understandings of the religion and philosophy of the pagans, Jews, and early Christians of the Greco-Roman world. In seeking to identify and date these texts and to discover their proper cultural contexts, the humanists became versatile in historical and comparative linguistics. Scholars such as Lorenzo Valla and Desiderius Erasmus applied these philological techniques to the text of the Bible itself.

Their work demonstrated that it, like all other texts, was the complex product of accruements and emendations made over a period of time. Scripture was, then, the word of human beings as much as it was the Word of God.

The emergent awareness of the historicity of scripture stimulated important new editions of the two Biblical testaments. Among these were the versions published by Erasmus at Basel in the early decades of the sixteenth century and the great Complutensian Polyglot Bible produced by a team of Jewish and Christian scholars at the University of Alcalá de Henares and printed in 1514–1517 under the patronage of the Franciscan reformer, Cardinal Francisco Jiménez de Cisneros.

This revivification of Holy Writ through the arcana of scholarship and the medium of print both fed and was fed by the rise in literacy and the demand for more widespread dissemination of the Bible through vernacular translations. Such translations would play an important role in the promulgation of sixteenth-century reforms. Martin Luther rendered the New Testament into German in 1522 and completed his version of the entire Bible in 1534.

The traditions of religious dissent and the culture of humanism also influenced the ongoing contest among secular rulers, the papacy, and the episcopate for temporal as well as spiritual control of Christendom. A lineage of political theorists traceable back to Marsilius of Padua in the fourteenth century had argued that the church should be governed by a representative council rather than a centralized papal bureaucracy in Rome. The conciliar movements of the late fourteenth and early fifteenth centuries enjoyed the support of secular rulers since the movements were tied more to local and regional power bases and so gave the rulers more influence in ecclesiastical affairs. Further ammunition was provided in the early fifteenth century when Lorenzo Valla demonstrated that the Donation of Constantine, a key document used by popes in making their claims for temporal authority, was in fact a forgery.

In England and France, where political bases were relatively consolidated, the rulers enjoyed greater autonomy with regard to the papacy and exercised considerable control over ecclesiastical appointments and institutions. In Germany and Italy power was fragmented and conflicts between sacred and secular claims were chronic. The religious world of Spain was subject to circumstances that differed from the mixes that prevailed in other parts of Europe. These circumstances played a not insignificant role in Spain's emergence as a colonial power subsequent to Columbus's voyages of discovery.

In January of 1492, the combined forces of Fernando of Aragón and Isabel of Castile conquered the Kingdom of Granada, the only territory on the Iberian Peninsula still controlled by the Muslims. On March 31, 1492, the Spanish regents issued an edict ordering the Jews resident in their domains either to convert to Catholicism or to submit to permanent exile. These events marked the end of the previous tradition of *convivencia* among Iberian Christians, Jews, and Muslims. They also signaled a revival of the crusading ideal of the Reconquista—the divinely sanctioned conversion of the non-Christian through conquest.

The Reconquista, coming as it did in the final decade of the fifteenth century, activated a complex of apocalyptic fears and expectations as well as reform movements. It permeated the ecclesiastical structures of the Spanish Catholic church and the political ideology of the court of Fernando and Isabel as well as the more fluid forms of monastic and public religious life. To more than a few observers, Fernando and Isabel's actions augured the final conversion of all infidels that would presage the end of time. Together they appeared to be the legendary "Last World Emperor" who, ancient prophecies decreed, would appear on the eve of the end of time to take Jerusalem for the Christians. A number of Christopher Columbus's letters to his monarchs indicate that he was seeking to place his discoveries within this larger apocalyptic framework.

Columbus believed that by sailing west to reach the Far East he had discovered a route that would give his regents efficient access to the wealth of the Orient and, particularly, to the lost mines of King Solomon. This wealth would provide Fernando and Isabel with the necessary means to mount a final crusade against the Turks in the Holy Land. In his letter describing the fourth voyage, Columbus pledged his services to that final crusade, promising to conduct the Christian forces to Jerusalem, presumably by sailing west across the Atlantic. He died in 1506 convinced that the end of the world was at hand. According to several contemporary accounts he was buried in the robes of a Franciscan tertiary, that branch of the order composed of laymen.

The regular members of that order, particularly the Observant Franciscans, would play a leading part in the "spiritual conquest" of Mexico in the course of the sixteenth century. Their actions and motivations were grounded in the European contexts of reconquest and reform as well. The Observant Franciscans' missionary work began with the arrival of twelve friars at Tenochtitlán (Mexico City) in 1524, shortly after Hernando Cortés's conquest of the Aztec empire. These events in the New World were contemporaneous with a cluster of important ones in the Old. In 1519, the Spanish king, Charles I, grandson of Fernando and Isabel, was elected Holy Roman emperor. The following year, Luther published his three incendiary treatises, *To the Christian Nobility of the*

German Nation (August), *On the Babylonian Captivity of the Church* (October), and *On the Freedom of the Christian Man* (November). He was excommunicated on January 3, 1521.

As had Columbus before them, a number of the early missionary chroniclers believed that events in Europe and America were interrelated in the larger plan of providential history. Works such as Diego Valadés's *Rhetorica christiana* (1579) and Gerónimo de Mendieta's *Historia eclesiástica indiana* (1596) linked the evangelization of the indigenous peoples of the New World to Protestant and Counterreformation movements in Germany and Spain. The new souls gathered into the Christian fold by the "pious" Martin of Valencia, the leader of the twelve Franciscans at Tenochtitlán would more than offset the losses suffered to the "cursed arch-heretic" Martin Luther.

In Europe, influential Catholic reformers such as Giles of Viterbo also cast the discovery of the Americas into an apocalyptic framework. In a sermon delivered before Pope Julius II in 1507, Giles argued that the many previously unknown souls revealed by the Portuguese and Spanish voyages surely presaged the age of *unus pastor, unum ovilem* prophesied in *John* 10:16. This was the age in which all infidels would finally be converted to Christianity, the Antichrist Luther would be defeated, and Jerusalem reconquered from the Turks. The discovery of a new world was somehow inseparable from visions of the end of the world, the subsumption of history in the final triumph of Christian universalism.

BIBLIOGRAPHY

Bataillon, Marcel. *Erasmo y España: Estudios sobre la historia espiritual del siglo XVI.* Mexico City, 1950.

Delumeau, Jean. *Catholicism between Luther and Voltaire: A New View of the Counter-Reformation.* London, 1977.

Ginzburg, Carlo. *The Cheese and the Worms: The Cosmos of a Sixteenth-Century Miller.* Baltimore, 1980.

Milhou, Alain. *Colón y su mentalidad mesianica en el ambiente franciscanista español.* Valladolid, 1983.

Phelan, John Leddy. *The Millennial Kingdom of the Franciscans in the New World.* Berkeley, 1970.

Ricard, Robert. *The Spiritual Conquest of Mexico: An Essay on the Apostolate and the Evangelizing Methods of the Mendicant Orders in New Spain, 1523–1572.* Berkeley, 1966.

Spitz, Lewis W. *The Renaissance and Reformation Movements.* Chicago, 1971.

PAULINE MOFFIT WATTS

Amerindian Traditions

In 1492 Columbus came upon a New World of unknown, unexpected, and astonishing religious diversity and intensity. By way of comparison, the diversity of New World religions rivaled that of Europe prior to the introduction of Christianity. North and South America—a vast continent with societies of varying degrees of social, cultural, and political complexity—contained hundreds of languages and thousands of ethnic groups. Religions approaching full-scale state religions, like those of the Incas and the Aztecs, existed alongside simpler tribal religions; all had little in common. For example, in North America alone the hunting religions of the Naskapi Indians of Labrador contrast sharply with the horticultural religions of the Pueblo peoples of New Mexico, and the religions of California Indians bear little resemblance to the religion of sacred kinship of the Natchez people on the Lower Mississippi.

Columbus's initial statements on New World religions indicate that he did not think the natives to be religious at all. In his diary of the first voyage, he mentions native religions three times. In the first instance, he suggests that the natives of San Salvador will become Christians easily because "it would seem to me that they had no religion." Of the natives of La Española, he asserts that it should be easy to convert them to Christianity, too, since they "have no religion of their own and are not idolators."

Columbus's initial statements concerning the lack of religion among Amerindians are echoed in writings from the sixteenth and seventeenth centuries. But contemporary interpreters contend to the contrary that Amerindian peoples were among the most religious peoples in the world and that the most striking similarity underpinning all New World societies was their overwhelming devotion to religion. The Indian world made religion its fundamental business. From the simplest hunting and gathering society to the high civilizations of the Aztecs and the Incas, religion was the one great behavioral force that provided social unity.

Another measure of religious intensity is the comparatively low rate of conversion to Christianity. Spanish and and later French missionaries experienced little immediate success with the native peoples and complained that they rapidly reverted to pagan ways whenever the opportunity presented itself. Conversion was rarely complete, even down to the seventeenth century.

On the other hand, Amerindian religions appear to have had considerable appeal to Europeans. There are numerous accounts of European captives who, after having been taken against their wills, chose to remain with the Indians when repatriation became available. In the history of the transatlantic encounter there are more accounts of Europeans who "went native" than Indians who "went European." Of course, few Amerindians were offered the option of full acceptance within white society, whereas European captives were frequently accorded this opportunity among Amerindians.

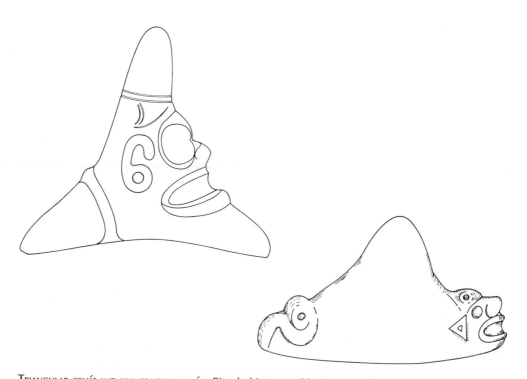

TRIANGULAR *CEMÍE* AND HUMPBACKED *CEMÍE*. Ritual objects used by Taíno Indians in the sixteenth century.

DRAWINGS BY STEPHEN D. GLAZIER

What we think of as Taíno religion is not one religion but the product of waves of migration into the Caribbean from the South American mainland. The first Amerindian group to be contacted by Columbus on San Salvador seems to have been part of a wider religious sphere that had reached an advanced level of development on La Española. The people of San Salvador traded with the Taínos, and linguistic affiliations are evidenced by the fact that Columbus successfully used Indians from San Salvador as translators. In terms of mythology, the Taínos shared much in common with the mythologies of South American peoples, especially the tribes of the Upper Orinoco and Amazon. There is also strong material evidence for connections with Mesoamerica (the Yucatán Peninsula).

From a religious standpoint, the first intense and protracted contact between Europeans and Amerindians took place on La Española. On his third voyage in 1495, Columbus commissioned a humble, poorly educated Hieronymite priest, Ramón Pané, to live with the Taínos for two years and compile a description of their religious beliefs and practices. It is unclear why Columbus chose Pané for this task. He had six priests in his command, including two better educated than Pané. It may have been that Columbus did not consider this a very important or difficult assignment or that Pané was the only priest with experience in the native language. Columbus was motivated not only by his desire for knowledge but by his political and military needs as well. The Taínos had proved themselves earlier to be worthy adversaries in battle, and Columbus hoped to understand them better so he could more easily bring them into submission.

Little is known concerning Pané and the fate of his report to Columbus, which he completed in 1496 or 1497. The original report was lost, but it was reconstructed in 1968 by José Arrom from a 1571 Italian translation. Pané has received recognition for his accomplishments as the first ethnographer of a New World people and baptizer of the first Amerindian to become a Christian, Guaticabanú. His missionary success was short-lived, however, as Guaticabanú was killed shortly after Pané's departure from the Taíno village.

Taíno religion might be best described as animistic, emphasizing a close connection with nature. Although Columbus repeatedly professed that he found no evidence of idolatry among these peoples, Catholic priests, when they began work among the Taínos in the early sixteenth century, found that religious objects known as *cemíes* were revered. *Cemíes* were made from natural materials such as stone, wood, ceramic, seashells, and cotton. Of these, stone *cemíes* have survived in greater number. *Cemíes* were associated with fertility, funerals, divination, and healing. Much to the priests' dismay, natives treated statues of Catholic saints as if they too were *cemíes*. They buried them in the yucca fields and urinated on them to promote the fertility of their crops.

Shamans—variously known as *behiques, behutios,* and *piaïes* among the Taínos and *boyés* among the Caribs— occupied a central position in all known Amerindian societies. Their functions included healing, divining the future, and making offerings to the gods. Healing techniques varied across cultures, but a shaman from any ethnic group could easily have recognized and appreciated the practices of his counterparts elsewhere in the New World, even if separated by vast distances. Among the majority of New World peoples, the role of the shaman appears to have been distinct from that of the political leader. The distinction between political and religious authority, however, does not seem to have been as rigid in all societies. The Taínos, for example, allowed for a close relationship between religious power (the *behutio*) and political power (the *cacique*). Similar close relationships have been noted between religious and political leaders among the Incas and Aztecs as well as in a number of other groups in North and South America.

Early explorers saw Amerindian mythology almost exclusively in terms of Western mythology. The subtlety of Taíno religious thought was lost entirely on Europeans who took Taíno religious statements literally. For example, when the Taínos spoke of a land inhabited entirely by women, Spaniards saw in this a corroboration of the Greek myth of the Amazons. When told of a city of gold, they assumed that the Taínos were substantiating a myth concerning seven Portuguese bishops who fled with their church ornaments to an Atlantic island in order to escape from the Moors (the Seven Cities of Cíbola). Columbus himself was a man of faith who believed not only in Christian dogma but also in cyclopes, mermaids, Amazons, men with tails, and men with dogs' heads. And as is true of others, his beliefs influenced his interpretations of what he found in his new world.

Within forty years of contact, the Taínos and their religion were nearly extinct—victims of Spanish brutality and the introduction of European diseases. Of the groups encountered by Columbus himself, all have been extinct for over 350 years. The Carib Indians to the south fared better than most. They were able to maintain aspects of their religion and culture well into the eighteenth century, because they were a mobile people and Europeans had little interest in settling the smaller islands where they lived.

The religious system of the Aztecs in the valley of Mexico approached European conceptions of religion. In the strictest sense, Aztec society was not a full-scale state system, but it possessed distinguishable ritual, elaborate

NORTH AMERICAN SHAMAN. Drawing by John White, of the Virginia colony, circa 1585. Original in the British Museum.

LIBRARY OF CONGRESS

processions, a hierarchy of religious specialists, and other characteristics with which the Spaniards could identify.

By 1524, the first Franciscans had arrived to begin the work of converting the Aztecs to Christianity, and Bernardino de Sahagún left a revealing record of the debates between European and Aztec religious specialists. The Aztec priests consistently argue from tradition: "This is the religion of our fathers." When one reads these dialogues, it becomes apparent that a major difference between Christianity and the religion of the Aztecs was that the latter emphasized tolerance and pluralism. The Amerindians were looking for a way to put the Christian God alongside their own gods.

Religious tolerance and pluralism in Amerindian traditions are also noticeable in the detailed accounts of Spanish contact with the Incas of Peru, whose religious system most nearly approximated sixteenth-century European Christianity. Franciscan efforts to eliminate idolatry and syncretism revealed a great deal about New World religion. These efforts also spurred exceptionally vivid indigenous accounts such as that of Guaman Pomo, who unsuccessfully attempted to explicate and defend his native culture to the king of Spain.

Encounters between Christianity and the religions of Amerindians are excellent examples of what Cuban anthropologist Fernando Ortiz termed "transculturation." Both Christianity and native religions were inexorably changed by the process. It is easy to overestimate the effects of Christianity on native religions, and at the same time to underestimate the effects of Amerindian religions on European Christianity. This would be inaccurate. Numerically, descendants of Amerindian peoples constitute a sizable proportion of world Catholics and have enjoyed considerable influence in Rome. On the local level syncretism continues unabated, and the resiliency and intensity of Amerindian traditions is notable. Also notable is the persistence of shamans who continue to practice their trade. While much else has changed, shamanism, which has been noted frequently as a unifying factor within the diversity of Amerindian groups, is immediately identifiable and has been little altered over the past five hundred years.

BIBLIOGRAPHY

Dunn, Oliver, and James A. Kelley, Jr., trans. *The Diario of Christopher Columbus's First Voyage to America. 1492–1493.* Norman, Okla., 1988.

Hultkrantz, Åke. *The Religions of the American Indians.* Translated by Monica Setterwall. Berkeley, 1979.

Krickeberg, Walter, Herman Trimborn, Werner Muller, and Otto Zerries, eds. *Pre-Columbian American Religions.* Translated by Stanley Davis. New York, 1968.

Pané, Ramón. *Relación acerca de las antiquedades de los indios.* Translated by José Juan Arrom. Mexico City, 1974.

Stevens-Arroyo, Antonio M. *Cave of the Jagua: The Mythological World of the Tainos.* Albuquerque, 1988.

Sullivan, Lawrence E. *Icanchu's Drum: An Orientation to Meaning in South American Religions.* New York, 1988.

Todorov, Tzvetan. *The Conquest of America: The Question of the Other.* Translated by Richard Howard. New York, 1987.

Wilbert, Johannes. *Tobacco and Shamanism in South America.* New Haven, 1987.

STEPHEN D. GLAZIER

ROME. In the Renaissance period, this former capital of the ancient Roman Empire was important as the seat of the papacy, place of pilgrimage, and capital of the Papal States (one of the five major Italian states). Although the ancient Aurelian walls survived, the inhabited part of the city was restricted, because of the need for water, to the bend in the Tiber River (Campo Marzio and Regula regions) opposite the Vatican complex (the Leonine Borgo) and the Trastevere section on the right bank. Access by land to the city was along the ancient Roman highways (e.g., Aurelian, Flaminian, and Cassian from the north and Appian from the south), through the Roman Campagna where bandits flourished amid large estates given over to grain, wine, cattle, and sheep production. Larger ships docked at Civitavecchia, some thirty-eight miles from the city on the Aurelian Way, and smaller ones used Ostia at the mouth of the Tiber and ferried goods fifteen miles upstream to the city's large landing area (the Ripa Grande) in Trastevere or to the smaller facilities (the Ripetta) in Campo Marzio. Although there were various attempts from 1434 to 1511 to set up an independent Roman republic, the popes retained political control of the city but granted it significant local autonomy with its own constitution in 1469.

In the fifteenth and sixteenth centuries Rome experienced a remarkable revival. During the time of the Great Western Schism, (1378–1417), control of the city shifted among the Roman and Pisan popes, the kings of Naples, condottieri (leaders of mercenary troops) and local feudal barons (notably the rival Colonna and Orsini families). Rome was then a regional market town with a population of about seventeen thousand. What distinguished it from other such towns was the steady stream of pilgrims (about 100,000 annually) who came to pray at the tombs of the apostles Peter and Paul and the martyrs. Serving these pilgrims' needs were various religious confraternities and almost five hundred establishments providing lodgings and food. Jubilee years every quarter century could see a fourfold increase in the number of pilgrims. With the end of the Great Western Schism a unified papacy under Martin V (r. 1417–1431) took up residency in Rome in 1420. Apart from some notable periods of absence during the pontificates of Eugenius IV (1431–1447) and Pius II (1458–1464), the growing central bureaucracy of the Roman Catholic Church was permanently established in the city, attracting numerous prelates, bureaucrats, lawyers, bankers, and petitioners from throughout Christendom. Perhaps only a quarter of the city's population was native; the rest was very mobile and cosmopolitan. The Curia needed people familiar with conditions in various countries, cardinals' households often contained connationals, and relatives and countrymen frequently sought favors from the popes: for example, Venetians from Eugenius IV and Paul II (1464–1471); Spaniards from Calixtus III (1455–1458) and Alexander VI (1492–1503); Ligurians from Sixtus IV (1471–1484), Innocent VIII (1484–1492), and Julius II

(1503–1513); and Tuscans from Leo X (1513–1521), Clement VII (1523–1534), and Julius III (1550–1555). Despite repeated disasters of floods, malaria, epidemics, and famine, the city had grown to about forty thousand by the end of the fifteenth century.

Popes contributed in various ways to this growth. Martin V began the work of renovation by improving the streets, public buildings, and churches. His successor Eugenius IV restored sections of the city walls, bridges, and churches. With the help of Leon Battista Alberti, Nicholas V drew up plans to make Rome a grand monumental city and cultural center. Abandoning the Lateran palace, he moved the papacy permanently to the Vatican, restoring its palace and founding the Vatican Library. He recognized that the ancient basilica of Saint Peter's was beyond repair and envisioned a new one. Although he helped restore forty churches, his grander plans remained unrealized for a lack of time and money. Sixtus IV significantly altered the face of Rome by opening up new roads, prohibiting porches and overhangs that abutted onto existing roadways, and building the Ponte Sisto that joined Trastevere to the rest of the city. He encouraged the construction of palaces and homes by changing church law; clerics could now bequeath to others, rather than having confiscated at death, the buildings they constructed with revenues from ecclesiastical benefices. Among the many palaces built at this time, the most famous was the Cancelleria (1485–1511) of Raffaello Riario. Sixtus IV gained lasting fame for building and decorating at the Vatican the Sistine Chapel for papal ceremonies, consistories, and conclaves. Innocent VIII is remembered for having built the Belvedere villa in the papal gardens. The heart of papal Rome, known as Leonine Borgo, commanded the attention of Alexander VI who restored Castel Sant' Angelo as the papal fortress and

facilitated access to it from the Vatican. He is said to have used some of the first gold from America to decorate the ornate ceiling of Santa Maria Maggiore.

The popes of the sixteenth century further transformed Rome into a center of art and culture. Julius II concentrated on the Vatican complex, significantly enlarging the palace. Above the apartments that had been inhabited by Alexander VI he raised a new series of rooms *(stanze)* whose walls and ceiling he commissioned Raphael to decorate with a series of frescoes depicting historical events and theological themes. Michelangelo was entrusted with decorating the ceiling of the Sistine Chapel with scenes from the book of *Genesis*. In 1506 Julius laid the foundations for a new Saint Peter's basilica to be built on a Greek-cross plan designed by Bramante. Along the left bank of the Tiber he laid out the Via Giulia where he hoped in vain to locate the judicial functions of the Curia.

Under Leo X work continued on decorating the papal apartments, and when Raphael replaced Bramante as architect of Saint Peter's, a Latin-cross plan replaced the Greek. (The indulgence preached to help finance this construction occasioned Luther's Ninety-five Theses and the beginnings of the Protestant Reformation.) Leo X also welcomed to Rome many leading writers and artists and strengthened the local university, Sapienza, founded in 1303, with new faculty, a large student body, and a Greek college. The city experienced phenomenal growth (some ten thousand new homes were constructed), and Leo systematized the three streets radiating from the Piazza del Popolo and developed the Via di Ripetta that led to the smaller river harbor. The three principal commercial centers were also beautified: Piazza del Ponte (banking), Piazza Navona (general merchandise), and Campo dei Fiori (foodstuffs).

Under Clement VII a new art style developed to replace the idealized and harmonious compositions of the High Renaissance. This elongated, off-balance, strangely colored, and overly refined art is known as Clementine Mannerism. Many of its proponents left Rome at the time of the Sack (1527) and thus spread its style. Just prior to the Sack of Rome a census counted at least 53,689 inhabitants. The devastations caused by the unruly army sent by Emperor Charles V and later by a flood in 1530 reduced this number to about 32,000. But the city rapidly recovered, especially under Paul III who repaired its walls and fortifications and laid out streets to encourage development. The medieval-style center of municipal government (the Campidoglio) he transformed into a splendid Renaissance piazza according to the design of Michelangelo with the ancient bronze equestrian statue of Marcus Aurelius as its centerpiece.

Thereafter, baroque rapidly became the typical art style of the city. Pius IV (r. 1559–1565) was able to develop the

St. Peter's Square.   Elsevier Publishing Projects, Amsterdam

area atop the Quirinal along the Via Pia leading to the Porta Pia because of the restoration of the Vergine aqueduct. Tapping into this water supply, Gregory XIII (r. 1572–1585) created many fountains. He embellished the Campidoglio with the palaces of the senator and conservators and laid out connecting thoroughfares between the basilicas of Santa Maria Maggiore and San Croce and San Giovanni in Laterano. The cult of the ancient martyrs was advanced both by Saint Filippo Neri, whose Congregation of the Oratory the pope approved in 1575, and by the accidental discovery three years later of a subterranean cemetery on the Via Salaria. The discovery aroused great interest and led in 1593 to the systematic exploration by Antonio Bosio of numerous other catacombs. With the support of Cardinal Alessandro Farnese and Pope Gregory XIII, the Jesuits built their mother church, the Gesù, and the Roman College with its satellite national colleges.

Under the brief but remarkable pontificate of Sixtus V (1585–1590), Rome became definitively "the sacred city." The new aqueduct (Aqua Felice) he built to allow for the development of the hilly regions of Rome terminated in a fountain with sculpted scenes from the Old Testament. A network of straight streets centering on Santa Maria Maggiore and ending at major churches in an obelisk crowned with a cross proclaiming the victory of Christ over paganism facilitated the processions of pilgrims visiting the shrines of Christendom. The secular character and grandeur of the Belvedere garden, with its collection of ancient statuary despoiled of many of its marble items by the austere Pius V in 1566, was forever tempered by the construction of the Vatican Library wing across its inner courtyard. Work on the massive dome of Saint Peter's was completed just three months before Sixtus died in 1590. By then, Rome with a population of more than ninety thousand had a clearly religious dimension and had become a fitting capital of Catholic Christendom.

BIBLIOGRAPHY

D'Amico, John F. *Renaissance Humanism in Papal Rome: Humanists and Churchmen on the Eve of the Reformation.* Johns Hopkins University Studies in Historical and Political Science, 101st ser., no. 1. Baltimore, 1983.

Delumeau, Jean. *Vie économique et sociale de Rome dans la seconde moitié du XVIe siècle.* 2 Vols. Bibliothèque des Écoles Françaises d'Athènes et de Rome, fasc. 184. Paris, 1959.

Partner, Peter. *The Lands of St. Peter: The Papal States in the Middle Ages and the Early Renaissance.* Berkeley, 1972.

Partner, Peter. *The Papal State under Martin V: The Administration and Government of the Temporal Power in the Early Fifteenth Century.* London, 1958.

Partner, Peter. *Renaissance Rome, 1500–1559: A Portrait of a Society.* Berkeley, 1976.

Paschini, Pio. *Roma nel Rinascimento.* Storia di Roma, vol. 12. Bologna, 1940.

Pecchiai, Pio. *Roma nel cinquecento.* Storia di Roma, vol. 13. Bologna, 1948.

Stinger, Charles L. *The Renaissance in Rome.* Bloomington, Ind., 1985.

Nelson H. Minnich

RUTTER. See *Sailing Directions.*

RUYSCH, JOHAN (d. 1533), Dutch geographer, explorer, and cartographer. Because Johan Ruysch is said to have worked first at Utrecht and then at Cologne, he is called Germanus by Beneventanus in the 1507–1508 Rome edition of Ptolemy's *Geography.* Beneventanus reports (chapter 3) that Ruysch said (*dixit*) that he had sailed from the south of England to fifty-three degrees north latitude and then stayed on that latitude until he arrived at the shores of the east *per angulum noctis* (by the angle [corner] of the night) and visited many islands. Later in the same chapter Beneventanus writes that Ruysch calls the Northern Sea (Mare Aquilonium) part of the Mare Sugenum, a huge area of sea stretching from about seventy degrees north latitude to the North Pole.

Although Beneventanus calls Ruysch a most experienced geographer and a most careful cartographer, nothing of his other work is known. Internal evidence shows clear but not perfect latinity, good draftsmanship, and depictions of coastlines ranging from near perfection to wild surmise. It has naturally been conjectured that Ruysch accompanied John Cabot on his 1497 voyage from Bristol, but he never mentions Cabot in the captions to his map; and Cape Race, Newfoundland, which on Juan de la Cosa's map is called "cauo de Ynglaterra" (Cape England), is in Ruysch's map called "C. de Portogesi."

This map, *Universalior cogniti orbis tabula,* must have been engraved shortly before the 1507–1508 Rome Ptolemy, because it records the fact that Portuguese mariners sailed to Taprobana (to him, Sumatra) in 1507. Whereas he records Portuguese discoveries around the coast of Africa accurately, he illustrates Columbus's view of the New World by combining the eastern coasts of Asia and North America to form one coast. Between Iceland and Greenland he notes that an island was completely burned in 1456. Near Greenland are remarks about magnetism upsetting compasses, with reference to a work on the fortunate discovery by Nicholas of Lynn (1355). Greenland and Terra Nova (Newfoundland) have only a shallow bay between them. Not far west of Terra Nova he places a long shore heading roughly west-northwest toward Gog Magog (cf. *Ezekiel* 38–39) and Cathaya (China). These coasts form a bay called Plisacus Sinus, near the south end of which is Zaito(n), whose caption starts (in translation): "M. Polo says that fifteen hundred miles east is a very large island called Sipa[n]g[us] [Japan]"; Ruysch says, among other things, that it has such a good climate that its inhabitants live to the age of 150.

The West Indies include a large island (Cuba?) or peninsula west of Spagnola (La Española), with a caption saying that the ships of King Fernando of Spain reached the west of it. South America is labeled "Terra sancte crucis sive Mundus novus" (Land of the Holy Cross, or New World), and Ruysch provides a long caption about its inhabitants, who are said to eat their prisoners. He credits the Spanish with naming it Mundus Novus (compare the Pesaro world map of c. 1505). On the east he records some predecessor of Ferdinand Magellan: "Portuguese sailors observed this part of this land and reached latitude fifty degrees south latitude, but did not reach the southern extremity." His fan-shaped map reaches only to thirty-eight degrees south latitude, but this enables him to include the whole of southern Africa.

It has long been known that there are notable variations in different drafts of the map. Recently a systematic catalog of these differences has been attempted, and what may be called a palimpsest has been discovered. It consists of text referring to Arctic islands and their inhabitants that has been replaced by stippling for sea.

BIBLIOGRAPHY

Dilke, Margaret S., and Antonio Brancati. "The New World in the Pesaro Map." *Imago Mundi* 31 (1979): 78–83.

Dilke, O. A. W. "Note on the Ruysch Palimpsest." *Imago Mundi* 42 (1990): 132.

Fite, Emerson D., and Archibald Freeman. *A Book of Old Maps Delineating American History.* Cambridge, Mass., 1926.

McGuirk, Donald L., Jr. "Ruysch World Map: Census and Commentary." *Imago Mundi* 41 (1989): 133–141.

Nordenskiöld, A. E. *Facsimile-Atlas to the Early History of Cartography.* Translated by J. A. Ekelöf and C. R. Markham. Reprint, New York, 1973.

Ptolemy. *Cosmographia (Geography).* Rome, 1507–1508. Facsimile with introduction by R. A. Skelton in *Theatrum orbis terrarum,* 2d ser., vol. 6. Amsterdam, 1966.

Shirley, Rodney W. *The Mapping of the World.* London, 1983.

Swan, Bradford. "The Ruysch Map of the World (1507–1508)." *Papers of the Bibliographical Society of America* 45 (1951): 219–236.

Woodward, David, ed. *Five Centuries of Map Printing.* Chicago, 1975.

O. A. W. Dilke

S

SAILING DIRECTIONS. In the time of Columbus, sailing directions were contained in portolanos (derived from the Latin *portus,* port) and rutters (from the French *route*). Portolanos are medieval Italian books containing a description of the coasts and ports of the Mediterranean and Black seas giving shipmasters all the aids they required for coasting and pilotage. The term has been used in this sense from at least 1295. The earliest surviving manuscript is *Lo compasso da navigare* (Hamilton Manuscript 396, State Library, Berlin) dated 1296, a compilation based on several earlier versions that may date back to 1232.

The contents of *Lo compasso* recall the collections of nautical directions of Greek antiquity of which, according to Strabo, there were two types: *peripli (periploi),* which gave general directions for voyages, and *limenes* (portbooks), which contained details about individual ports such as how to enter and leave them and where to anchor. The anonymous *Stadiasmos of the Great Sea* (A.D. 250–300), the only ancient Greek true sea book to have survived, lists only brief pieces of information on the functions and port facilities of the towns mentioned; it gives only the distance between towns, expressed in stades. *Lo compasso,* which describes the Mediterranean and Black sea coasts, starting at Cape St. Vincent (the southwest extremity of Portugal) to the straits of Gibraltar, in a counterclockwise direction, and then from Gibraltar to Safi on the Atlantic coast of Morocco, supplies information similar to that in *Stadiasmos,* but adds two new items: the depth of anchorages expressed in *passi,* with indications of watering places, and the course to steer between the named ports. These courses are given by the names of the Mediterranean eight-rayed compass: *Tramontana* (north), *Greco* (northeast), *Levante* (east), *Sirocco* (southeast), *Ostro* (south), *Africo* or *Libeccio* (south-west), *Ponente* (west), and *Maestro* (northwest). Distances are given in Italian miles, one mile being equal to 1,230 meters. Usually distances are rounded off to the nearest 10 miles and are somewhat understated. These developments, contemporary with the production of a reliable sea compass and with the first known nautical chart constructed by geometrical methods, the *Carte Pisane* (c. 1275; Bibliothèque Nationale, Paris, Res. Ge. B. 1118), mark a turning point in the history of navigation.

Nineteenth-century writers used the word *portolano* to describe either a book of sailing directions—the generally accepted meaning—or a nautical chart constructed according to bearing and distance, which is now known as a portolan chart. There is no doubt of a close relationship between charts and sailing directions, but the exact relationship is still uncertain. R. B. Motzo, the first editor of *Lo compasso,* believed that it and the early portolan chart belonged to the same work, produced by a single author and based on the same data. A comparative analysis of place-names, however, shows that at least 30 percent of those found in the *Carte Pisane* come from another source. Further, whereas *Lo compasso* is written in Italian, the *Carte Pisane* contains a wide range of dialectical variations. Moreover, a map using data from the portolano can be constructed only by making certain adjustments to overcome the shortcomings of the text; such a map shows grossly simplified coastlines when compared to the sophisticated coastal delineation found on the earliest surviving charts. It may well be that a number of descriptions found in the portolano have their origins in an examination of contemporary charts. Thirteenth-century navigators were not content routinely to hug the shore, and several of the routes described in *Lo compasso* are quite long cross-sea passages of about 500 Italian miles (a little under 650 kilometers, or 400 miles) and even up to 700 Italian miles (roughly 900 kilometers, or 550 miles). It may well be that the drawing up of the chart made a visualization of the crossing possible—perhaps that was their intention—and that their description in the portolano is no more than a verbal translation of the chart. One thing, however, cannot be overemphasized: in the final stages of these crossings, irrespective of whether the hoped-for landfall was a headland, a small island, or a port of call, the portolan chart, because of its small scale, was no longer useful to the sailor, who now had to refer to the more detailed information in the portolano.

Only half a dozen manuscript collections of sailing directions survive from before the last quarter of the fifteenth century. Their titles differ according to the language used. In northern Europe, the oldest is called *Seebuch* (Low German), which covers coasts from Sweden to Gibraltar. Part of the text goes back to the fourteenth century and contains traces of its Italian origin. The *Leeskart* (Flemish) from the same period refers to the same shores. The French title is *routier* (literally route-book). The oldest *routier* is *Le routier de la mer*, an anonymous work, but attributed to the Vendean Pierre Garcie (end of the fifteenth century). The work covers Atlantic waters from the Scheldt to Gibraltar. It is essentially an original work, notably in including detailed descriptions of the physical features of the shore illustrated by the elevation of important points of the hinterland and coast as they would appear to an approaching sailor. Nevertheless, it too incorporated much older material, and in its turn served as a prototype for the first rutter printed in English (1528). The same word (route) turns up again in the sixteenth-century Portuguese term *roteiro* and the Spanish *derrotero*. All these books, following the example of the Italian portolano, focus on the information necessary for coastal navigation and landfall. All derive from the same sources and draw on each other.

If we attempt to identify sea books that Christopher Columbus might have used or to which he might have contributed, we must distinguish three different traditions. The first is the Mediterranean portolano, which Columbus, by origin Genoese, clearly used on his voyages to Chios and England. By the end of the fifteenth century, such works had been changed and enlarged when compared to the *Compasso*, since they now contained data about the Atlantic and the northern European seas taken respectively from either the *Seebuch* or Pierre Garcie's *routier*, or from sources identical to theirs. Although Mediterranean distances continued to be given in Italian miles (1,230 meters), in the ocean Portuguese leagues (5,500 meters) were used; for Atlantic ports, headlands, and channels, there are indications concerning the direction of flow of tidal streams and a definition of their

"establishment," that is, a record of the moon's position on the horizon at high water on days of new or full moons, which gives the pilot the most propitious time for entering and leaving port and place. In the first published portolano, *Questa e una opera necessaria a tutte li naviganti chi vano in diverse parte del mondo* (Bernardo Rizo, Venice, November 1490), about one-fifth of the instructions refer to non-Mediterranean seaboards. The manuscript is anonymous, but can be attributed to the Venetian Alvise Cadamosto, who in the mid fifteenth century had explored the coasts of Senegal and Gambia in the service of Prince Henry the Navigator.

The second tradition was developed in Portugal at the same time. In the final quarter of the fifteenth century the first original *roteiros*—dealing with the African coast and the Madeira, Azores, Canary, and Cape Verde archipelagoes—were being put together. Christopher Columbus followed some of these routes in the period from 1477 to 1482–1483: the route from Lisbon to Madeira regularly and the route from Lisbon to São Jorge da Mina at least once. The oldest Portuguese-produced route book, *Roteiro das ilhas e da Guiné* (available only in a codex of 1506 to 1508, known as the manuscript of Valentim Fernandes) took shape as part of the process of exploration and discloses evidence of its earlier composition. São Tiago Island, in the Cape Verde Islands, for example, is referred to under two names, the second of which, Ilha de Antonio, clearly alludes to Antonio da Noli, who accompanied Cadamosto's expedition in 1455–1456. Another clue to its real age is its layout; it is divided into geographical sections, starting with the coast of Senegal (*tytolo de çenaga*) and then São Jorge da Mina (*Ho livro das rotas do castello de Sam Jorge*), before going from the Niger delta to São Tomé Island (*A qui falla de rota do Cabo Fremoso pera ylha de Samtamtoneo*); that is, it follows the order of exploration and discovery. The route book for Flanders (*Roteiro da Flandres*, found in a much later manuscript, *Lo livro de marinharia de João de Lisboa*), very probably an original Portuguese work of the fifteenth century, covers a familiar and long-known area, and offers various categories of information, for example, distinguishing among indications of distance only (*leguas*), indications of rhumbs and distances for points along the same coast (*rotas* and *derrotas*), indications of rhumbs and distances for points on different sections of the coastline opposite each other (*travessas*), and instructions about how to enter the ports (*pousos*). *Roteiro das ilhas e da Guiné* indicates *travessas* between points of the Iberian and Moroccan coasts on the one hand, and archipelagoes in the Atlantic on the other hand, including the imaginary islands of contemporary nautical cartography (such as the Island of the Seven Cities and Saint Brendan's Isle), clearly showing that at least a few sections of the sea books are indebted to the descriptions in the charts. The African *roteiro* ends with information concerning the establishment of the ports of Sierra Leone and São Jorge da Mina. Therefore, in its conception and contents, it is strictly comparable to the *Portolano Rizo*, though for different shores.

The main achievements of the Portuguese in the field, which cannot be accurately dated, probably did not appear before the early sixteenth century. Two should be given special attention. First, and more important, for each of the points described by the rutter, latitude was mentioned, first in preliminary tables and then integrated in the text itself. Second, the coastal data of the region described were supplemented with information about the safest or the more direct route to sail across the ocean.

The third tradition is Spanish. Both innovations of the Portuguese sea books appear in the first methodical Spanish rutter of the sea areas discovered by Columbus in America. This *derrotero* is a later manuscript (c. 1530), never published in the sixteenth century, which is the fourth part of a general book dealing with nautical science, the *Quatri partitu en cosmografia practica, y por otro nombre espejo de navegantes*. The author, Alonso Cháves, was a well-known pilot and cosmographer to Charles V; in the opening lines of the rutter, he acknowledges his debt to the many pilots who navigated in the region. This version is a compilation of previous works by at least two copyists; despite a number of geographic discrepancies, it was a pioneering book, since it was the first general rutter of navigation to the Indies. It is divided into twenty-five chapters. The first describes the voyage from Spain to the Indies, and the last the return. Chapters 2 to 7 concern the islands, from the West Indies to the Bahamas; chapters 8 to 24 are devoted to continental shorelines. There are two successive clockwise descriptions of the coasts, one around the Caribbean and the Gulf of Mexico from Venezuela to Florida, the second around South and Central America, along the Pacific coast, from Peru to Nicaragua, and again along the Caribbean and the Atlantic Ocean south to the Straits of Magellan.

Like the Portuguese of the same period, Cháves introduced latitude data in his *derrotero*. A thorough study of these latitudes shows that they are consistent with a westerly magnetic variation of about fourteen degrees, something that Columbus observed as early as his first voyage, and that was to generate important secondary effects in contemporary nautical charts. Several indications in the text, such as false orientations of the Bahamas islands that wrench them into appropriate latitudes exactly as they appear on contemporary charts, or the dominance of cardinal bearings (52 percent of the bearings are north, south, east, or west; 27 percent are the intermediate

winds) suggest once again that a part of the *derrotero* was a verbal map. Cháves makes an interesting methodological improvement: a table of place names classified in alphabetical order referring to the corresponding chapter and paragraph, for example. "*Guanahani, isla de Lucayos*, ch. 7, 16." The text explains that this island was the first landfall reached when the Indies were discovered. There are other Columbian reminiscences, such as the description of Tierra Firme from the Gulf of Paria to the Gulf of Uraba, through the Boca del Dragon (Dragon's Mouth, the northern entrance of the Gulf of Paria), which is close to Gonzalo Fernández de Oviedo's description. The route from Spain, starting from Sanlúcar or Cádiz Bay, southwest to Tenerife and Gomera, then sailing directly from Fierro in the Canaries to the Caribbean, corresponds to Columbus's route to the Indies on his second voyage. These details are not surprising since Cháves worked in close collaboration with Fernando Colón from 1526 to 1539. They also indicate that Columbus was a link in an international tradition of sailing directions of which he was both an heir and a creator.

BIBLIOGRAPHY

Castañeda, Paulino, Cuesta Mariano, and Hernandez Pilar. *Alonzo de Chaves y el libro IV de su "Espejo de Navegantes."* Madrid, 1977.

Campbell, Tony. "Portolan Charts from the Late Thirteenth Century to 1500." In *The History of Cartography*, vol. 1, *Cartography in Prehistoric, Ancient and Medieval Europe and the Mediterranean*, edited by J. B. Harley and David Woodward. Chicago and London, 1987.

Conti, Simoneta. "Portolano e carta nautica: confronto toponomastico." *Imago et mensura mundi. Atti del IX Congresso internazionale di storia della cartografia*. Rome, 1985.

Kelley, James E., Jr. "The Map of the Bahamas Implied by Chaves's Derrotero. What Is Its Relevance to the First Landfall Question?" *Imago Mundi* 42 (1990).

Kretschmer, Konrad. *Die italienischen Portolane des Mittelalters*. Berlin, 1909. Reprint, Hildesheim, 1962.

Lamb, Ursula. "The 'Quatri Partitu en Cosmographia' by Alonso de Chaves. An Interpretation." *Agrupamento de estudos de cartografia antiga*, vol. 28. Coimbra, 1969.

Teixeira da Mota, Avelino. "Evolução dos roteiros portugueses durante o seculo XVI." *Agrupamento de estudos de cartografia antiga*, vol. 33. Coimbra, 1969.

Waters, David W. *The Rutters of the Sea*. New Haven and London, 1967.

ISABELLE RAYNAUD-NGUYEN
Translated from French by Anthony Turner

SANTA FE CAPITULATIONS. The capitulations constitute the agreement between Christopher Columbus and the Spanish monarchs concerning the conditions under which Columbus would be permitted to lead an expedition west, into the Atlantic, over which they claimed sovereignty. The two parts of the agreement were signed in the city of Santa Fe de Granada. The first, dated April 17, 1492, spelled out Columbus's privileges and obligations, and the second, dated April 30, defined his titles. The three basic questions concerning these instruments concern their precedents, their nature, and their consequences.

The evident demand for high status, extensive powers, and financial gain by a foreign trader is what makes the agreement unique. Late-medieval precedents, such as contracts between a sovereign and a private party dealing with exploration within a given jurisdiction, are plentiful. The case of Columbus is extraordinary in the speculative, not to say chimerical, goals he presented. Columbus must have felt there was nothing to lose at this stage, when the queen was ready to support the venture on the basis of the argument that the risk was very small, practically, financially, and politically.

How the first five articles of the capitulations were spelled out in detail is revealed in the Pleitos Colombinos, the ensuing litigation. Assuming the most extensive and liberal interpretation in Columbus's favor of the financial privileges and those of office, the obstacles to full implementation can be easily imagined. The unfolding of the Pleitos reveals a larger context of medieval traditions in government (the conferring of titles) combined with the ambitions of a rising entrepreneurial class and sponsorship by a monarchy with antifeudal tendencies. The capitulations became in form, if never in substance, the basis for all subsequent agreements with explorers of the Indies. Contemporary and subsequent interpretations of the good or bad faith shown by both parties to the capitulations have tended to reflect assessments of the outcome of Columbus's venture. Such questions are yet alive today.

Columbus took the original document containing the capitulations of Santa Fe de Granada with him on his first voyage. It is known to have been on deposit with Columbus's papers in the archive of the Carthusian Monastery (La Cartuja) in Seville as late as 1520 to 1526 but has not been found in modern times. Although the original is not preserved, the text survives in the register and file kept in the archive of the Crown of Aragón in Barcelona. Columbus was quite naturally afraid of a mishap or loss of that text, so he had a copy made, witnessed, and registered on December 16, 1495, in Santo Domingo. Columbus wanted to have an authenticated copy in his possession, because of the arrival in October of that year of Juan Aguado, an investigative judge who surely needed to consult the document. This made the Admiral consider the need for an authorized duplicate,

and it was this copy he submitted in Burgos on April 23, 1497, when he requested the confirmation of his privileges. It is now in the collection of the Archive of the Indies in Seville. Of four more copies, dated 1502, referred to as the Privilegios de Veragua, two were sent to Genoa.

The variations in spelling among the copies are judged trivial by the experts. One remarkable exception is a brief clause that refers to "Christopher Columbus, in some satisfaction for *what he has discovered.*" This phrase was changed in the Navarrete Collection, the nineteenth-century edition of the document copy of Burgos (1497), to "what he shall discover."

[See also *Book of Privileges; Lawsuits.*]

BIBLIOGRAPHY

García Martínez, Bernardo. "Ojeada a las capitulaciones para la conquista de América." *Revista de Historia de America* 69 (1970): 1–41.

Schoenrich, Otto, *The Legacy of Columbus: The Historic Litigation Involving His Discoveries, His Will, His Family and His Descendants.* 2 vols. Glendale, Calif., 1949.

Thacher, John Boyd. *Christopher Columbus.* 2 vols. 1902. Reprint, New York, 1967. Spanish and English texts of the capitulations.

Ursula Lamb

SANTA MARÍA. Almost without exception, maritime historians and Columbus scholars have acclaimed *Santa María,* Columbus's flagship on his first voyage of discovery, as the most famous ship in the world. What reader of Samuel Eliot Morison's *Admiral of the Ocean Sea* could feel otherwise? Despite his extensive research, however, not even Morison was able to provide an authentic picture of *Santa María.* He reluctantly reported that "there are no data from which it honestly can be done." Ongoing research, however, has given us some details.

Columbus himself provided important information in the journal of his first voyage. He identified *Santa María* as a nao, a bulky merchant ship with substantial cargo-carrying capacity. He also provided specific information as to the number and type of her sails, listing them as "the main course with two bonnets, the fore course, spritsail, mizzen and topsail." The two bonnets, upper and lower, were horizontal strips of sail laced one above the other to the foot of the mainsail, or main course as it was then called, in light to moderate winds. As wind strengths increased, first the lower and then the upper bonnet would be removed as a substitute for reefing the mainsail. This sail plan was an early development in the transition from one mast with a single large mainsail to three masts with a variety of sails. It was a time of rapid change in rig development with the large mainsail remaining as the major driving force. The much smaller foresail, mizzen, and spritsail, while obviously providing some additional propulsive force, served more to help in directional control and maneuverability, particularly when tacking. The tiny main topsail was still an early tentative addition to the rig. This journal entry about the sails was, regrettably, the only specific reference Columbus made about his ships.

Another reason there is little specific information about ships of the period is that until the seventeenth century there were no naval architects in the modern sense of that profession. There were only shipwrights who built boats and ships the way their fathers and forefathers had built them for centuries. They drew no plans either for use in the building process or for recording their achievements.

To construct a replica or even paint an accurate picture of *Santa María*, the best one can do is to make use of as much data as possible about ships of her type from contemporary paintings and sketches, models, books, and documents of pertinent maritime history and ship construction as well as recent findings developed by nautical archaeologists from their excavations of discovery-era ships.

Most paintings and sketches of fifteenth-century merchant naos, which were commonly referred to as "round" ships, had certain features that were indeed round. The shapes of the stem and frames that governed the shape of the hull, for example, almost invariably were arcs of circles. The radii of these arcs were related to the ship's breadth or beam by simple ratios used by shipwrights of the period. Other identifying features, well illustrated by

MODEL OF *SANTA MARÍA*. The Martinez-Hidalgo model in the National Museum of American History.   THE SMITHSONIAN INSTITUTION

Vittore Carpaccio's painting *The Legend of Saint Ursula* (1495), were the forecastle overhanging the bow, the half deck with a poop deck rising above it in the stern, the graceful arch visually tying the forecastle deck to the bulwark rails port and starboard, the heavy bitt beam protruding through the bulwark planking just forward of the arch, and the distinctive round tuck stern with wales and planking sweeping gracefully upward at about a 45-degree angle to a heavy transom beam mounted atop the sternpost at the main deck level.

Several maritime museums display models of *Santa María* that show many of these features. The Naval Museum in Madrid, the Maritime Museum in Barcelona, and the National Museum of American History in Washington, D.C., have such a model based on a full-size replica designed in 1963 by Capt. José María Martinez-Hidalgo, Spain's foremost authority on Columbus's ships. His plans are reported to be the basis of the 1989 Spanish reconstruction of *Santa María*. Philips Academy in Andover, Massachusetts, has an older well-regarded model by noted English historian R. C. Anderson. Maritime museums in Newport News, Virginia; Savannah, Georgia; and Pegli, Italy, also have excellent models.

From books and documents one finds that there is consensus among maritime historians that *Santa María* was of about one hundred tons burden. In the Columbus era the burden, or cargo-carrying capacity, of a ship was measured in terms of the number of wine tuns (barrels) she could carry. Since a tun of wine weighed very close to a ton, the change from tuns to tons required no change in numerical value. From the value of one hundred tons burden and from commonly used rules of thumb for hull proportions it was possible to arrive at reasonable assumptions of hull dimensions and shape. For a late fifteenth century nao, the accepted proportions of breadth, length of keel, and length of main deck were in the simple ratios of 1:2:3. The master shipwright builder of *Santa María* would have known from his own long experience and from knowledge inherited from his forefathers that if she were to be of one hundred tons burden, her hull dimensions, using those ratios, should be roughly twenty-seven feet for breadth or beam, fifty-four feet for length of keel, and eighty-one feet for length of main deck.

Discoveries and excavations in the 1980s of three shipwrecks of the discovery period have provided particularly valuable and previously unavailable details of hull construction and shape. Two of the shipwreck sites were in the Caribbean and the third was in Red Bay, Labrador. The latter was the remarkably well-preserved 1565 wreck of a Spanish Basque galleon, the immediate successor of the nao with many similar features. Since *Santa María* is believed to have been built in the Basque region of Spain, and since hull construction methods of a particular region were very slow to change, there is good reason to believe that the hull of the Basque galleon was built using much the same methods that would have been used to build Columbus's famous flagship.

The staff of the Institute of Nautical Archaeology and the marine archaeologists of the Canadian Park Service deserve great credit for their important accomplishments in the Caribbean and Labrador, respectively. New hard evidence of hull form and construction details, when combined with documented rules of thumb used by shipwrights of the Age of Discovery, now makes it possible to construct a more authentic replica of *Santa María* than could be done in the past.

BIBLIOGRAPHY

"Marine Excavation of the Basque Whaling Vessel San Juan." Research Bulletins 123, 163, 194, 206, 240, 248, 258. Canadian Park Service. Ottawa, 1980–1987.

Martinez-Hidalgo, José María. *Columbus' Ships*. Barre, Mass., 1966.

WILLIAM LEMOS

SANTÁNGEL, LUIS DE (d. 1505), Aragonese converso and chief financial adviser to Fernando the Catholic. Santángel's personal intervention in 1492, literally at the last moment, was the decisive factor that persuaded Queen Isabel to advance the nearly five million maravedis for Columbus's first voyage.

Columbus knew of the wealthy Santángel family—merchants and lawyers who had served the Aragonese royal family for generations—through their mercantile interests in Genoa. He approached Luis de Santángel in Córdoba as early as 1486 seeking financial support for his proposal to sail westward to India. Even as he sought financial assistance from other European monarchs, particularly King João II of Portugal, Columbus maintained contact with Santángel. By 1492 the Castilians had defeated the Muslim kings of Granada and were finally able to sponsor Columbus. The Granada wars had brought the Castilian treasury close to bankruptcy, however, and to finance Columbus, Santángel had to obtain the funds from a variety of sources including the Aragonese treasury and his own personal fortune. So great was Columbus's gratitude for Santángel's support that the first news of the voyage to reach Isabel and Fernando was through the now famous letter to Santángel in which Columbus described the voyage.

Santángel's faithful service to Fernando spared his family from the persecution of Jews and conversos during the Inquisition. Fernando's personal grant of May 30, 1497, exempted Santángel and his sons from the Inquisition and guaranteed his heirs their personal and financial property.

BIBLIOGRAPHY

Columbus, Christopher. *The Authentic Letters of Columbus.* Edited and translated by William Eleroy Curtis. Chicago, 1895.

Kayserling, M. *Christopher Columbus and the Participation of the Jews in the Spanish and Portuguese Discoveries.* Translated by Charles Gross. 4th ed. New York, 1968.

Mir, Miguel. *Influencia de los Aragoneses en el descubrimiento de América.* Palma de Mallorca, 1892.

THERESA EARENFIGHT

SANTO DOMINGO. See *Settlements,* article on *Santo Domingo.*

SCIENCE. [This entry includes two articles:

Science in the Late Fifteenth Century

Science and Technology in the Age of Discovery

For further discussion of the innovations in European science and technology that supported overseas expansion, see also *Cartography; Medicine and Health; Navigation; Printing; Shipbuilding; Timetelling.*]

Science in the Late Fifteenth Century

With a few notable exceptions, science at the time of Christopher Columbus's voyage in 1492 was largely a continuation of medieval medicine, science, and natural philosophy. Scientists accepted the geocentric representation of the cosmos as firmly in the fifteenth century as in the thirteenth and fourteenth. In some fields, especially physics, logic, mathematics, and natural philosophy, actual achievements in the fifteenth century were inferior to those of the preceding two centuries. Fifteenth-century scientists stood in the tradition of late medieval science and the Greco-Arabic inheritance it received in Latin translation during the twelfth and thirteenth centuries. At the core of this large body of scientific literature, which encompassed the physical and life sciences, were the physical and philosophical works of Aristotle, which formed the basis of the curriculum of the medieval universities, and the medical works of the second-century Greek physician Galen and the early eleventh-century Persian scientist Ibn Sina (Avicenna). During the thirteenth and fourteenth centuries, scholastic natural philosophers and scientists not only absorbed Greco-Arabic science, but added their own achievements in a variety of fields. Their successors in the fifteenth century seemed content to repeat and elaborate the ideas and interpretations of their medieval predecessors.

Few scientists made important original contributions in this century. The great polymath of the period, Leonardo da Vinci (1452–1519), despite his innovations in mechanics, geology, and technology, exercised no influence on the history of science. His massive notebooks were not published until long after his death. Many scientists born in the fifteenth century, such as Nicolaus Copernicus, did not become important until after 1500.

The most notable scientists of the period were Georg von Peuerbach, Regiomontanus, Luca Pacioli, and Nicholas of Cusa. The astronomer Georg von Peuerbach (1423–1461) and his student Regiomontanus (1436–1476; born Johann Müller) produced an abridged translation from Greek into Latin of the *Almagest* of the second-century Greek astronomer Ptolemy. Peuerbach translated the first six books and Regiomontanus completed the project, although the work, entitled *Epitome of the Almagest,* was not published until 1496, twenty years after the death of Regiomontanus. Peuerbach also wrote the *New Theories of the Planets,* which Regiomontanus published around 1474 and which became the basic astronomical text up to the seventeenth century. Peuerbach's *Tables of Eclipses,* completed around 1459 but printed only in 1514, was also a standard treatise in use until the seventeenth century. Although neither made dramatic departures from traditional astronomy, Peuerbach and Regiomontanus together revised and upgraded astronomy while also defining numerous technical terms.

The famous *Summa de arithmetica, geometria, proportioni et proportionalita* (Venice, 1494) of Luca Pacioli (c. 1445–c. 1514) was an encyclopedic mathematical treatise written in Italian that included sections on arithmetic (both practical and theoretical), algebra, tables of moneys and weights, double-entry bookkeeping, and geometry. Comprehensive and useful though it was, Pacioli's work was not an original contribution to the history of mathematics.

The most original thinker among fifteenth-century scientists may have been Nicholas of Cusa (c. 1401–1464), who concluded, contrary to the generally accepted opinion of Aristotle, that the celestial motions had no center. Indeed, the entire universe had no fixed center and no circumference. Consequently, the earth could not be the center of the cosmos nor could it be an immobile body, but it was in motion in space along with the other celestial bodies. In a daring speculation, Nicholas conjectured that life may not be confined to the earth but may also exist on other celestial bodies. Bold and spectacular as they were, Nicholas's cosmological conclusions were highly idiosyncratic conclusions drawn from his own metaphysical theory, which he called the "coincidence of opposites" (*coincidentia oppositorum*), a theory that failed to win adherents and had little impact in the physical sciences.

Although theoretical medicine was largely taught and studied from the texts of Galen, Ibn-Sina, and Razi (Rhazes) as well as medieval texts based on these fundamental works, fifteenth-century surgeons—especially Heinrich von Pfolspeundt (fl. 1460) and the Sicilian surgeons of the Branca family—developed plastic surgery to the face, replacing mutilated noses and lips and providing detailed descriptions of their procedures.

Notwithstanding the century's mediocre achievements in science proper, two major activities in the second half of the fifteenth century—a wave of translations from Greek to Latin and the invention of printing around 1460—made the period important for the history of science. The new translations and the printing press marked the definite beginnings of a challenge to traditional science and natural philosophy, beginnings that would deepen in the sixteenth century and come to fruition in the seventeenth.

The New Translations. Before Greek scientific treatises could be translated, manuscripts of them had to be obtained. This was a significant preoccupation of many fifteenth-century humanists, who were aided by the fact that numerous Greek manuscripts were brought to Italy by Byzantine Greeks, many of whom fled the Turkish siege and then the capture of Constantinople. Manuscripts of works that would be neither printed nor translated during the fifteenth century were salvaged from possible destruction and preserved in European library collections, either papal, royal, or private, to become available in the sixteenth and even seventeenth centuries.

The translations were largely associated with the Italian humanist movement of the fifteenth century, which was characterized by an intense interest in classical Greek and Roman culture and literature. Unlike their medieval scholastic predecessors and contemporaries, who devoted themselves to commentaries on the works of Aristotle that had largely been translated into Latin from earlier Arabic versions, the Italian humanists were interested in the original Latin and Greek texts, not only of Aristotle, but of all Greeks and Romans. Literary style, correct grammar, and philology, which were of little concern in scholastic discourse, were of paramount interest to humanists. In their study of philosophy, Italian humanists were interested in themes of love, friendship, beauty and good citizenship, and much less concerned with natural philosophy, science, and logic than the more analytically oriented scholastic natural philosophers. Not surprisingly, humanists made few, if any, significant contributions to science.

And yet, by their translating activities, fifteenth-century humanists played a significant role in the history of science. By locating and translating Greek texts, they made available new and usually improved Latin translations of Greek authors whose works were already well known, achieving this sometimes by the discovery of better manuscripts of the Greek original. More important, however, were their translations of Greek authors whose works were previously unknown or known only in a fragmentary way during the Middle Ages.

It was in Florence that Cosimo de' Medici (1389–1464) institutionalized this interest by founding the famous Platonic Academy in 1462 or 1463. At the request of Cosimo, Marsilio Ficino (1433–1499) translated the works of Plato into Latin, thus making Plato's philosophy and cosmology available to a wide audience. His translation of Plato's works brought a weighty addition to Western philosophical and scientific literature because few of Plato's works had been available in Latin during the Middle Ages (only two-thirds of the *Timaeus*, along with the *Meno* and the *Phaedo*). At the very least, Plato's works would complement Aristotle's and to some they would offer a significant alternative. Even before his translation of Plato, however, Ficino, in April 1463, completed a translation of the *Corpus Hermeticum*, fourteen Greek works on magic that were thought to have been written by Thoth, the Egyptian god of wisdom—also known as Hermes Trismegistus—who was assumed to have lived long before Plato and Aristotle, but slightly after Moses. With their emphasis on natural magic, the Hermetic treatises, only a few of which had been known during the Middle Ages, would assume a large and significant role in shaping the world view of the late fifteenth and sixteenth centuries.

Other previously unknown works by ancient Greek authors were also translated from Greek to Latin in the fifteenth century. Among them were a two-part handbook on astronomy (*Contemplation of the Highest Orbs*) by Cleomedes (c. first century A.D.); the first book of Alexander of Aphrodisias's (fl. second to third centuries A.D.) *On the Soul* (*De anima*); Aristarchus of Samos's (c. 320–230 B.C.) *On the Sizes and Distances of the Sun and Moon; The Lives of the Eminent Philosophers* of Sextus Empiricus (third century A.D.); the *Cosmographia* (*Geography*) of Ptolemy (second century A.D.); the *Geographia* of Strabo (c. 64 B.C. – after A.D. 23); *On the History of Plants* and *On the Causes of Plants* by Theophrastus (c. 372–c. 287 B.C.), the student of Aristotle; and *The Paraphrase of Aristotle* by Themistius (around A.D. 317–c. 388).

Another category of previously unknown Greek scientific works were those that were neither translated nor printed in the fifteenth century, but which found their way into Europe, usually into Italy, from Byzantine sources and contacts. Most of these works would be translated and printed in the sixteenth or subsequent centuries. In this group, we find Proclus's (around A.D. 410–485) *Commentary on the First Book of Euclid's Elements* and his *Commentary on Plato's Timaeus;* Hero of Alexandria's (first century A.D.) *Pneumatica;* the *Arithmetica* of Nicomachus of Gerasa (fl. around A.D. 100); and the *Moralia* of Plutarch (around A.D. 46–after 119).

Humanists were also interested in traditional Greek authors whose works were well known in the Middle Ages, either from translations from Arabic, or, less often, from the Greek. During the fifteenth century, new translations were made from Greek manuscripts of the works of Aristotle, Galen, and Hippocrates.

The Impact of Printing. Although humanist interest in Greek and Latin texts was instrumental in uncovering a relatively large number of previously unknown, or little known, scientific works by ancient Greek and Roman authors and in translating many of them into Latin, often for the first time, the introduction of printing around 1450 significantly altered the way in which new and old scientific texts were presented and disseminated. In this regard, the fifteenth century marks a milestone in the history of science. Printing from fixed type largely guaranteed that an edition of, say Ptolemy's *Almagest,* would be uniform: readers in London would confront the same text and diagrams as readers in Rome. Such was never the case with manuscripts, where virtually every manuscript was a unique and idiosyncratic version of a given text.

During the second half of the fifteenth century, some 35,000 editions were printed, of which perhaps two or three thousand belonged to science broadly conceived. Most of the scientific texts that printers and publishers chose to print were drawn from the enormous array of contemporary manuscript versions of medieval treatises, with special emphasis on the works of Greek and Arabic authors such as Aristotle, Galen, Hippocrates, Ibn-Sina, and Ibn Rushd (Averröes) as well as texts of the works of Aristotle, Diogenes Laertius (third century A.D.), Theophrastus, and Philo Judaeus (c. 13 B.C. –between A.D. 45 and 50), which Aldus Manutius published between 1495 and 1498.

By their great emphasis on traditional medieval texts, fifteenth-century printers solidified and perpetuated the medieval worldview. Many of their products were commentaries on the physical works of Aristotle. In addition to the popularization of the medieval perception of the physical operation of the universe that was embodied in Aristotelian commentaries, one of the most popular and noteworthy treatises printed was the *Imago mundi* of Pierre d'Ailly (1350–1420), written in 1410 and printed in Louvain in 1483. It provided a general description of the structure of the world, both celestial and terrestrial. D'Ailly included estimates of the size of the earth and attributed to Aristotle the opinion that only a small sea intervened between western Spain and eastern India. Columbus, who owned a copy of the *Imago mundi,* annotated this passage in the margin, presumably because it favored his conviction that the distance between Spain and India was relatively small and that the ocean voyage

was feasible. Also noteworthy is a splendid version of Euclid's *Elements,* which appeared in 1482 and included clear diagrams essential for following the proofs. Numerous medical works also appeared.

But if the overwhelming number of printed scientific works were medieval in origin, significant "new" works were also printed in the fifteenth century and belong to one of two categories: ancient treatises that had been previously unknown or newly written works.

In the first category were Latin translations of Greek works, among which were Ficino's translations of the works of Plato (1484/1485) and the *Pimander,* or *Corpus Hermeticum* (1471, plus six more times in the fifteenth century); Ptolemy's *Geography* (1475); Strabo's *Geography* (1469, plus six more editions in the fifteenth century); Theophrastus's *History of Plants* and *On the Causes of Plants* (1483; the Greek text was printed in 1499); Cleomedes's *On the Contemplation of the Heavenly Orbs* (1497); and Aristarchus of Samos's *On the Magnitudes and Distances of the Sun and Moon* (1498).

Contributions by ancient Roman authors also played a role in expanding the scientific horizons of the fifteenth century. Among Latin works that were virtually unknown during the Middle Ages but were effectively rediscovered and printed in the fifteenth century were *On Medicine* (1478, plus three later printings in the fifteenth century) by A. Cornelius Celsus; *On Aqueducts* (c. 1485) by Sextus Julius Frontinus (around A.D. 35–103); *On the Nature of Things* (1473) by Lucretius (c. 100 to 90–c. 55 to 53 B.C.); *Cosmography* by Pomponius Mela (first century A.D.); and *On Architecture* (1483–1490) by Vitruvius (first century B.C.).

Of new scientific treatises composed and published after the advent of printing, the most significant were those already mentioned: *New Theory of the Planets* (around 1474) and *Epitome of the Almagest* (1496) by Regiomontanus and *Summa de arithmetica* (1494) of Luca Pacioli. Thus printing not only preserved traditional knowledge during the first forty or fifty years of its existence, but it became the vehicle for the addition of new scientific knowledge.

During the voyages of Columbus in the last decade of the fifteenth century, science was still traditionally medieval but, because of the humanist quest for original classical treatises and the introduction of printing, the groundwork had been laid for the great changes in science that would occur in the next two centuries.

BIBLIOGRAPHY

Eisenstein, Elizabeth L. *The Printing Press as an Agent of Change.* 2 vols. Cambridge, 1979.

Grant, Edward. *Physical Science in the Middle Ages.* New York, 1971. Reprint, 1977.

Hall, A. R. *The Scientific Revolution 1500–1800. The Formation of the Modern Scientific Attitude.* London, 1954.

Klebs, Arnold C. "Incunabula Scientifica et Medica: Short Title List." *Osiris* 4 (1938): 1–359.

Lindberg, David C., ed. *Science in the Middle Ages.* Chicago, 1978.

Yates, Frances A. *Giordano Bruno and the Hermetic Tradition.* New York, 1969.

EDWARD GRANT

Science and Technology in the Age of Discovery

In the middle of the fifteenth century, around the time of the birth of Columbus, Europe embarked on a tremendous period of intellectual, scientific, and technological upheaval on a scale that had not been seen before. It was arguably more fundamental and disrupting than even the Industrial Revolution or the electronics revolution of later eras.

From the time of the Crusades (1096–1291), Europe had begun to assimilate a tremendous storehouse of knowledge from the Islamic kingdoms of Spain, Africa, and the Middle East. The Muslims had not only carefully preserved the legacy of classical Greece and Rome; through the centuries, great Muslim thinkers had passed on and added to the ancient wisdom.

Mathematicians had developed the number system that we call Arabic, but that is actually from India. This was a remarkable intellectual achievement, particularly the introduction of zero, which made modern mathematics possible. By the fifteenth century, European merchants and traders had begun to adopt the new style of notation that was especially convenient for bookkeeping and accounting. The new system would later facilitate the development of higher mathematics.

The greatness of African, Asian, and Middle Eastern thinkers, and the intellectual and scientific debt Europe owed them, is not fully appreciated by most Europeans and Americans. But even the great scholars of Islam like Ibn Sina (980–1037) and Ibn Rushd (1126–1198) would have acknowledged that they could have done little on their own without the philosophers, poets, and playwrights of the ancient Mediterranean world. It was the Greeks who served as guides and models for philosophy, geometry, astronomy, and drama as we know them today. It was primarily the Greeks who secularized learning, taking it out of the hands of the temple priests and giving it to ordinary citizens. They established medicine as a branch of science, not of religion.

It is important to stress, however, that the scholars of Columbus's time and for some centuries after did not think of themselves as scientists in the way we use and understand that term. For the educated elite, natural philosophy was the study of subjects we classify as physics, biology, medicine, or chemistry. The overwhelming majority of Europeans had little access to or need for theoretical knowledge. Even the more specialized tradesmen and artisans—mechanics, miners, smiths—learned practical knowledge as apprentices or by trial and error.

Arguably the single most important classical author was Aristotle. Not only was he one of the greatest and most original thinkers of all time, but the range of his interests and the topics on which he wrote were truly encyclopedic: biology and naturalism, physics, astronomy, ethics, logic, poetics, politics, rhetoric, metaphysics, geography, and much else besides. Although initially the universities of Europe were antagonistic to Aristotle because he was a pagan, gradually a group of Christian thinkers called the Scholastics were able to synthesize the teaching of Aristotle with the teaching of the church. These schoolmen, as they were called, dominated university life at the time of Columbus.

The centers of the Scholastic influence were the great universities of Europe like Oxford and the universities of Paris, Padua, and Verona, which date from the time of the Crusades and after. It was here that Aristotle was held up as the final authority on all questions, and here that scholars, trained in the Aristotelian techniques of logic and rhetoric, refuted any challenges to Aristotle's system of the world. In addition to Aristotle himself, classical authors who followed his beliefs, like Galen in medicine or Ptolemy in astronomy, were also venerated.

In the fifteenth and early sixteenth centuries, most Europeans accepted Plato's and Aristotle's belief that everything in the world was made up of a combination of four pristine elements—earth, air, fire, and water—each of which had its own aspects and elements. Earth and water were naturally cold and dense and tended to go down; air and fire were rarified and hot and tended to go up. This system of elements explained why smoke rose and rain fell; why the ground was cold; why fire needed air to burn but was extinguished by water. There was a fifth element, ether, which was what the stars and planets were made of, an eternal, incorporeal essence that traveled in perfect circles along the nine spheres of the heavens around the central and stationary earth. Most people believed that the celestial spheres emanated rays that influenced people, elements, and events on earth, linking all creation into a vast unity. It was for this reason that astrology was an important aspect of university study, especially in medicine.

Additionally, the body contained four fluids, or humors, which were ruled by the elements and responded to the influence of certain planets. This theory explained both medicine and psychology. Each person had a humor based on the type of fluid that dominated the individual's personality; we still use the words that named the humors to describe emotional states, like *melancholy, sanguine, phlegmatic,* and *choleric.* In this period, it was not unusual for doctors to consult their patients' astrological charts before treating them or to prescribe the elimination of bodily fluids to restore the balance of humors necessary for health. Many people regularly allowed themselves to be bled by doctors to treat even simple ailments like colds.

One of the major events of the fourteenth century that recurred periodically until the eighteenth century was the bubonic plague, or Black Death, as it was known. This disease began in Asia and reached the Black Sea around 1334. Ships plying the trading ports of Europe spread it throughout the continent. Rats carried one form of the plague, but another could be transmitted by human contact. The Black Death caused fever, delirium, and swelling and was usually fatal within three or four days. In some parts of Europe, as much as three-fourths of the population died, although some towns escaped lightly or were spared. University doctors were powerless to understand or fight the plague. Some doctors ran away or hid whenever the disease appeared. Such behavior undermined confidence in the universities and indirectly in the wisdom of ancient authorities.

Another fifteenth-century event that contributed to the new critical spirit was the development of printing. Men like Johann Gutenberg and Johann Fust in Germany, William Caxton in England, and Josse Bade in France made accurate, standard versions of texts available in quantity. As a result, more people had greater access to information than ever before. The flood of books spread the spirit of the Renaissance all over Europe.

As people read books like the Bible for the first time, they began to question traditional ideas. Sometimes ancient authorities disagreed. Many lost works of Plato and his followers—especially the so-called Hermetic writings—became available after the fall of Constantinople in 1453. Neoplatonism was more mystical than Aristotelianism, and it suggested that hidden correspondences exist among the heavens, nature, and people. The only way to discover these correspondences was by study, and the Neoplatonic authors like Pico della Mirandola, Marsilio Ficino, and Johannes Reuchlin urged their followers to delve into subjects that the church and the Scholastics condemned as forbidden and heretical. At the time of Columbus the influence of Neoplatonism had not yet made the impact it would in the sixteenth and seventeenth centuries, when men like Paracelsus, Johannes Kepler, Giordano Bruno, and even Galileo Galilei made the study of nature and the rejection of Scholastic authority the basis for the rise of experimental science. For Paracelsus and Galileo, this also meant combining the knowledge of practical arts like mechanics and herbalism

with the more abstract philosophical knowledge of the university.

In another respect, the new spirit of inquiry can be seen in men like Filippo Brunelleschi, who combined studies of the ancients with innovations using improved manufacturing techniques to build such masterpieces as the cathedral of Florence. Prince Henry the Navigator of Portugal is also illustrative of this spirit. It was Henry who brought together the naval and manufacturing arts at Sagres. Henry built an observatory and a naval arsenal; his *marinheiros* (mariners) studied the wind cycle and made charts of the declination of the sun. This was a systematic combination of scholarship and investigation on a scale that had not been seen before in Europe.

Less formal but equally important experimentation was going on in fields like mining, milling, and manufacture, where skilled artisans and craftspeople devised innovative techniques and materials, often without understanding that they were violating the philosophical principles laid down by the ancient Greeks. The importation of the secret of gunpowder from China proved that combinations of substances existed that the Greeks had not considered; this reinforced the need for more practical investigations. Other important technological innovations from the East like the horsecollar and horseshoe helped the average farmer immensely; agricultural output increased as much as fivefold in this period. As the expansion of agriculture depleted the forests, the need for metals to replace items that had formerly been made of wood led to the development of new alloys; tin, for example, became the basis for the movable type used in the new printing presses.

Technological advancement in one area, like milling, for which meshed gears were perfected, was often applied to other fields, like clock making. In the time of Columbus, the clock was quickly becoming the central metaphor of town life; the precise mechanical regularity of clocks reinforced the need for accuracy and standardization.

When Columbus embarked on his voyage in 1492, he carried with him a mixture of attitudes representative of his time. Like many educated, prosperous men, he embraced both the sureties of the medieval world, which was passing away, and the uncertainties of the new era, which he would do much to create. Part of his faith that the Atlantic Ocean could be crossed and would lead to the western coast of India came from Aristotle, who believed that the world was seven parts land and one part water, exactly the relationship between the head and the body of a well-proportioned person. But Columbus had also spent time studying the Atlantic winds, a topic unknown to the ancients. His ship carried the new technology in the form of compass and cross staff; his sails combined the European square sails with the Arabian lateen sails.

Although Columbus was not a scientist in any way, he

helped bring about major economic and social changes. His inadvertent discovery of a continent wholly unknown in ancient authors created another new metaphor of sixteenth-century life: the New World. It was not only that the Americas offered seemingly endless gold and lands to be conquered. The existence of America itself forced a reevaluation of Scholastic authority. The discovery of new animals like the turkey and new plants like potatoes, tobacco, and corn, effectively demonstrated to Europeans that they now stood on the frontiers of new knowledge.

When Columbus was engaged in his voyages of discovery, the two men who embodied the revolutions to come in the next century were embarking on their careers. In 1500, Nicholas Copernicus lectured on astronomy in Rome, digesting the *Epitome of the Almagest,* one of the new texts made available by the printing revolution. Out of his studies came the heliocentric hypothesis, which would, as much as any other single event, stimulate the scientific revolution.

In 1505, near the end of Columbus's life, young Martin Luther experienced conversion during a thunderstorm. He became a monk, trained in the philosophy of William of Ockham, and chose a career as a doctor of theology at the University of Wittenberg. Luther's rejection of Catholic authority culminated in the Reformation, a movement that freed mainly northern Europe to explore questions of conscience in new ways. Although Luther himself personally condemned Copernicus, in general, northern European countries were much more tolerant of the Copernican hypothesis. This was due in part to Protestant interest in challenging traditional Catholic interpretations of the Bible and the new spirit of inquiry and debate over the meaning of scripture. The new freedom of inquiry, combined with wealth from the New World, helped shift the balance of political and intellectual power from the Mediterranean to the Atlantic in the sixteenth century.

BIBLIOGRAPHY

Barfield, Owen. *Saving the Appearances.* Hanover, N.H., 1988.

Jacob, Margaret. *The Cultural Meaning of the Scientific Revolution.* New York, 1987.

Rice, Eugene F. *The Foundations of Early Modern Europe.* Vol. 1 of *The History of Modern Europe.* New York, 1981.

Siraisi, Nancy G. *Medieval and Early Renaissance Medicine: An Introduction to Knowledge and Practice.* Chicago, 1990.

SCOTT MCPARTLAND

SECOND VOYAGE. See *Voyages of Columbus.*

SETTLEMENTS. [This entry surveys six settlements dating from the early days of European presence in the Western Hemisphere. The article on Sevilla la Nueva demonstrates in detail what can be known about such settlements through historical and archaeological research:

La Navidad
La Isabela
Nueva Cádiz
Sevilla la Nueva
Santo Domingo
Concepción de la Vega

For further discussion of the early phases of European settlement of the New World, see *Colonization; Exploration and Discovery,* article on exploration and discovery after 1492. See *Archaeology* for discussion of research techniques that advance understanding of this period. Other places in the New World are discussed in *Bahamas; Canada; Cuba; Cuzco; Española, La; Jamaica; Puerto Rico; West Indies.* See *Vinland* for discussion of Viking exploration and settlement of the New World prior to Columbus's voyages.]

La Navidad

La Navidad was the name given to the first settlement established by Christopher Columbus in the Americas. It is located on the north coast of present-day Haiti, near the small fishing villages of En Bas Saline and Borde de Mer Limonade.

It was near the site of La Navidad, on Christmas Eve, 1492, that Columbus's flagship, *Santa María,* ran aground and settled on a coral reef and could not be saved. On Christmas Day Columbus's men unloaded the cargo and supplies of *Santa María* with the assistance of the Taíno Indian cacique, Guacanagarí, who governed a large Taíno town. Columbus reported that the town was about one kilometer (six-tenths of a mile) from the wreck site. They placed all of the goods in two large houses belonging to the cacique, which he then gave to the Spaniards.

Because it was impossible to accommodate the crew of *Santa María* on *Niña* and *Pinta,* thirty-nine men were chosen to remain at La Navidad until Columbus could return for them. They were given food and supplies for a year, the ship's boat, and instructions to find the source of the Indians' gold in the meantime. The men of La Navidad included a physician, a gunner, a carpenter, a boat builder, a barrel maker, a caulker, and a tailor in addition to the sailors. To make fortifications, they dismantled much of *Santa María* above the water table and used the planks and timbers to fortify an area that may have incorporated the houses given by the cacique.

There are no eyewitness accounts of La Navidad's appearance. Columbus and the remaining Spaniards left La Navidad on January 4, 1493, before the fort was built. By the time they returned, it was destroyed. Columbus alleged, however, in his 1493 letter to Fernando and Isabel, that a moat, tower, and palisade were under

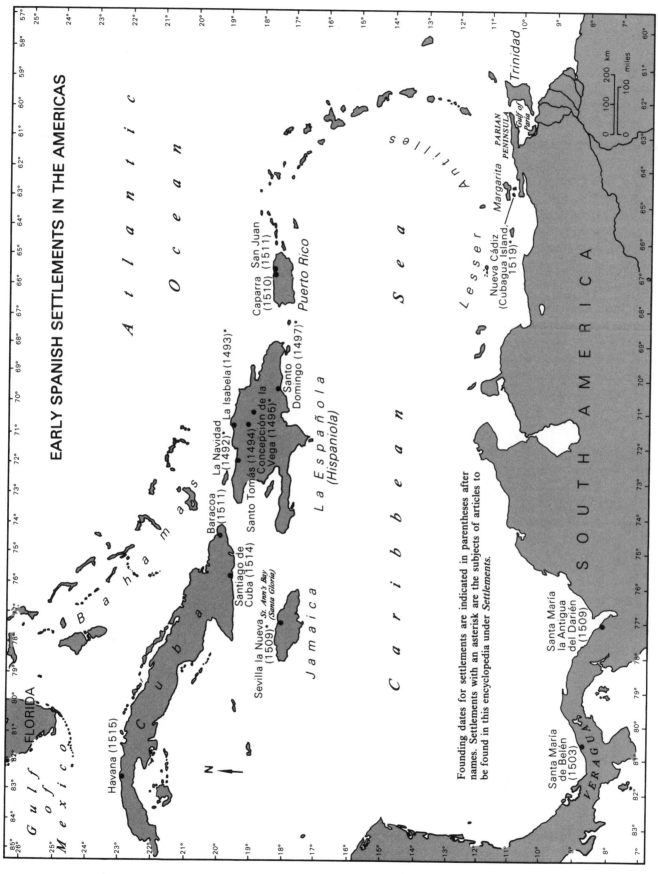

EARLY SPANISH SETTLEMENTS IN THE AMERICAS

Atlantic Ocean

Bahamas

FLORIDA

Gulf of Mexico

Havana (1515)

Cuba

Santiago de Cuba (1514)

Sevilla la Nueva (1509)* *St. Ann's Bay (Santa Gloria)*

Baracoa (1511)

Santo Tomás (1494)

La Navidad (1492)* La Isabela (1493)*

Concepción de la Vega (1495)*

Santo Domingo (1497)*

Jamaica

La Española (Hispaniola)

Caparra (1510) San Juan (1511)

Puerto Rico

Lesser Antilles

Caribbean Sea

Margarita

Nueva Cádiz (Cubagua Island, 1519)*

PARIAN PENINSULA

Gulf of Paria

Trinidad

SOUTH AMERICA

Santa María la Antigua del Darién (1509)

Santa María de Belén (1503)

VERAGUA

Founding dates for settlements are indicated in parentheses after names. Settlements with an asterisk are the subjects of articles to be found in this encyclopedia under *Settlements*.

0   100   200 km
0   100   miles

©Carta

607

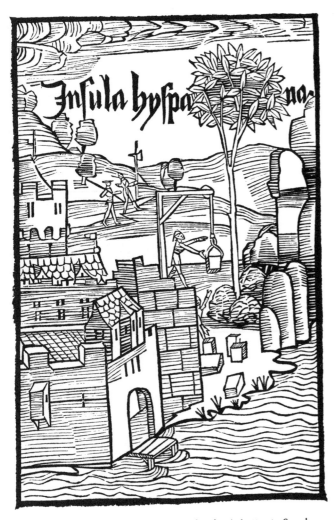

FORT LA NAVIDAD. Engraving from Columbus's Letter to Sanchez, as published in Basel, 1493.   NEW YORK PUBLIC LIBRARY

The location and fate of La Navidad have captured the imaginations of many scholars over the years. Early research by Samuel Eliot Morison concluded that the site of La Navidad should be within a kilometer of the tiny Haitian fishing village of Borde de Mer Limonade. Excavations commissioned by Morison were conducted at that village in 1939 but revealed only remains from an eighteenth-century French blockhouse.

William Hodges, a medical missionary and lifelong student of Columbus, searched for La Navidad for more than twenty years. In 1975, Hodges located the site of a large Indian village at En Bas Saline, about half a kilometer (a third of a mile) inland from Borde de Mer Limonade. Aerial photographs indicate that a tributary of the region's major river, the Grande Rivière du Nord, connected the site to the shore in 1492. Excavations demonstrating that this was probably the town of Guacanagarí have been conducted there by Hodges and by the University of Florida. European artifacts, animal bone, and a series of radiocarbon dates confirmed the occupation of the town shortly after 1492.

Excavations searching for La Navidad were also conducted by Hodges from 1988 to 1990 at Borde de Mer Limonade. None of the excavations undertaken to date at any of the potential sites has unequivocally uncovered the remains of the fort itself.

BIBLIOGRAPHY

Columbus, Christopher. *The Journal of Christopher Columbus.* Translated by Cecil Jane. New York, 1989.

Deagan, Kathleen. "Columbus's Lost Colony." *National Geographic* (November 1987): 672–675.

Deagan, Kathleen. "The Search for La Navidad, Columbus's 1492 Settlement." In *First Encounters,* edited by J. T. Milanich and S. Milbrath. Gainesville, Fla., 1989.

Hodges, William H. "La Fortaleza de la Navidad: Reflections at the End of 1988." Limbé, Haiti, 1988.

Jane, Cecil. *The Four Voyages of Columbus.* New York, 1988.

Morison, Samuel Eliot. "The Route of Columbus along the North Coast of Haiti and the Site of La Navidad." *Transactions of the American Philosophical Society* 31, part 4 (1940): 239–285.

KATHLEEN DEAGAN

construction. Accounts from the second voyage suggest that a well for water and a palisade may have been constructed.

Columbus returned to La Navidad eleven months later to find the settlement and surrounding Indian town burned, all the men dead, and the supplies dispersed among the Indians over a distance of several kilometers. Various accounts indicate that his men had left to trade elsewhere or had died as a result of disease or internal fighting, having antagonized their hosts by their desire for women and gold, and finally by an attack from Indians of the interior regions. Columbus investigated the circumstances of the colony's destruction and searched for the gold he believed his men had acquired, but was unsuccessful in both efforts. He soon left La Navidad and continued westward along the north coast of La Española to found La Isabela, his first intentional settlement.

La Isabela

La Isabela was the first town intentionally established by Columbus in the Americas and the first place at which Europeans established a settled colony. It was founded late in 1493 about 45 kilometers (28 miles) west of present-day Puerto Plata on the north coast of the Dominican Republic. Columbus established La Isabela after he returned to La Española (Hispaniola) on his

HURRICANE ON LA ISABELA, 1485. Engraving from Théodor de Bry's *Americae*. Frankfurt, 1594.

second voyage and discovered that his earlier and inadvertent settlement of La Navidad—built the previous year in what is today Haiti—was burned to the ground.

The second voyage of Columbus was intended as a voyage of settlement. The expedition included seventeen ships, carrying 1,700 men, along with pigs, horses, cattle and other livestock, seeds and plants for crops, and the tools and equipment necessary to start a colony. The site of La Isabela was apparently chosen because of its accessibility to the Bajabonico River and proximity to a good source of stone, fertile ground for cultivation, and native trading routes into the allegedly gold-rich interior. Among the all-male settlers were craftsmen, builders, Franciscan friars, farmers, practitioners of other occupations, and representatives of social classes necessary to implement a Spanish way of life. A cabildo, or town council, was also established.

The town had a plaza at the waterfront, with several buildings constructed of limestone from a nearby quarry. These included a house occupied by Columbus, a stone church, and a fortified storehouse and barracks. Some two hundred palm-thatch huts provided housing for most of the town's inhabitants. The men at La Isabela began to suffer from disease, overwork, and food shortages almost immediately. Indian hostility also developed quickly as the native peoples of the area were pressed into service for labor at the same time that they were fast succumbing to European diseases. Mutinies developed among the men of the colony, leading at one point to Columbus's recall to Spain.

Through all these difficulties, the population of La Isabela declined steadily, dropping to 630 people in 1495, and no more than 300 people in 1496. In 1498 a new capital of La Española was established at present-day Santo Domingo. This marked the effective end of the colony at La Isabela, which was soon depopulated.

La Isabela remained in ruins after its abandonment, occupied occasionally by smugglers and fishermen. In 1526 Bartolomé de las Casas carried stones from La Isabela to be used in the Convento de San Pedro Martir in Puerto Plata. Today the site is occupied by the small Dominican fishing village of El Castillo. The government of the Dominican Republic has set aside the plaza area of La

COLUMBUS'S HOUSE. Excavated and reconstructed ruins of what is believed to have been his dwelling in the central plaza area of La Isabela.

FLORIDA STATE MUSEUM, GAINESVILLE

Isabela—fronting directly upon the bay—as a national park.

La Isabela has been the subject of numerous studies over the past century, including at least fourteen archaeological excavations. It was first tested and mapped in 1892, when the site was visited by members of the North American Commission for the four hundredth anniversary of Columbus's first voyage. The most recent and extensive excavations at the site have been carried out by José Cruxent, working through the Dirección de Parques Nacionales de la Republica Dominicana. Cruxent's extensive excavations in the central plaza area have uncovered the foundations of the barracks and storehouse, the house believed to have been that of Columbus, and other unidentified structures. He also concludes that La Isabela may have had two contemporary settlement locations about ten kilometers (six miles) apart, serving different functions. Cruxent was joined by a University of Florida team in 1989, working outside the park boundaries. That work suggested that the town was originally some 200 meters (650 feet) square.

Earlier projects by the Museo del Hombre Dominicano and others have uncovered the church foundations and excavated a number of burials from the cemetery of La Isabela. The architectural and material remains from research at La Isabela—both in the past and ongoing—have helped to reveal the details of the first and last essentially medieval community in the Americas.

BIBLIOGRAPHY

Cruxent, José. "The Origins of La Isabela." In *Columbian Consequences*. Edited by D. H. Thomas. Washington, D.C., 1990.

D'Anghiera, Peter Martyr. *De Orbo Novo*. Translated by F. A. MacNutt. 2 vols. New York, 1970.

Floyd, Troy. *The Columbus Dynasty in the Caribbean 1492–1526*. Albuquerque, N. Mex., 1973.

Cecil, Jane. *The Four Voyages of Columbus*. New York, 1988.

Major, R. H. *Letters of Christopher Columbus with Other Original Documents Relating to his Four Voyages to the New World*. 1857. Reprint, New York, 1961.

KATHLEEN DEAGAN

Nueva Cádiz

The barren, low, now uninhabited island of Cubagua is located on the eastern Venezuelan continental shelf, between Margarita Island and the Araya Peninsula. Cubagua was discovered by Columbus on his third voyage, while taking colonists to Santo Domingo, on August 15, 1498. He had divided his fleet in the Canary Islands, sending three ships to La Española and taking the remaining three south on an unscheduled exploratory voyage that reached the island of Trinidad and the Gulf of Paria on the mainland. While exploring the area along the eastern coast of Venezuela, he encountered Indians who wore strings of fine pearls that they traded for trinkets. Columbus heard that the pearls came from the present-day Cubagua waters, but apparently did not set foot on the island because his eyes bothered him and, in any case, because he was eager to reach Santo Domingo. The news of the pearls caused a sensation in Santo Domingo as well as in Spain, and a series of official and unofficial exploratory voyages were carried out between 1499 and 1502 by Alonso de Ojeda, Peralonso Niño (Pedro Alonso Niño), Cristóbal and Luis Guerra, Rodrigo de Bastidas, and others. These voyages confirmed the presence of pearls near Cubagua and Margarita and resulted in the exploration of the coast of South America from Suriname to Panama.

The original European settlers came to Cubagua from Santo Domingo shortly after the beginning of the sixteenth century to trade for pearls. In 1519 it was decided that in order to take control of the pearl fisheries, the Indians were to be enslaved; many were brought from all over the Caribbean to toil alongside slaves from Africa on the pearl banks. Simple aboriginal huts (*bohíos*) were built. In response to the predation by Spanish ships along the Cumaná coast, the mainland Indians rebelled in 1520, killing eighty Spaniards and forcing the abandonment of the three-hundred-strong Spanish settlement on Cubagua, which totally depended on supplies from the mainland. Construction of a fortress at Cumaná by Jácome de Castellón in 1523 brought the Indians under control and led to highly profitable pearl production and spectacular masonry constructions. By 1526, the settlement on Cubagua was known as Villa Santiago and in 1528 it received the official name of Nueva Cádiz; it was the first Spanish city founded in South America. The climax of Nueva Cádiz occurred between 1530 and 1535 when its fisheries supported a total population of fifteen hundred people and shipped an average value of 800,000 pesos in pearls annually to Europe. But overexploitation caused the destruction of the pearl beds, leading to the desertion of the island. In 1541 Nueva Cádiz was destroyed by a hurricane. In 1544 French pirates burned what was left of the city and by 1545 the site had been completely abandoned, although sporadic activity in the pearl fisheries persisted throughout the sixteenth century. In recent times the highest production of 1,300 kilograms (about 2,850 pounds) was recorded for 1943.

Archaeological excavations were started by José M. Cruxent and John Goggin in 1954 and systematically continued by Cruxent between 1955 and 1961. Excavations revealed masonry structures arranged in a regular rectangular grid as well as less spectacular structures. The most

NUEVA CÁDIZ. The archaeological site, 1958–1960.

UNIDAD DE FOTOGRAFIA CIENTÍFICA, I.V.I.C.

elaborate building was a Franciscan friary, with carved stone gargoyles imported either from the mainland or Spain. Some houses also had masonry stairways that led to second stories. Rouse and Cruxent reported excavations yielding large amounts of majolica, various kinds of glazed ware, olive jars, china porcelain, stamps, tiles, glass, metals, local Indian pottery as well as pottery from other parts of the Caribbean, human burial sites, remains of animal bones, and other organic refuse that reveal information on diet and pearl exploitation. By the late 1980s the ruins of Nueva Cádiz had been almost totally destroyed and looted. Plans exist to restore the site and convert it into a tourist attraction.

BIBLIOGRAPHY

Otte, E. *Las Perlas del Caribe: Nueva Cádiz de Cubagua.* Caracas, 1977.
Rouse, I. and José M. Cruxent. *Venezuelan Archaeology.* New Haven and London, 1963.
Sauer, C. O. *The Early Spanish Main.* Berkeley and Los Angeles, 1966.
Vila, P. *Visiones geohistóricas de Venezuela.* Caracas, 1969.

Willis, R. "Nueva Cádiz." In *Spanish Colonial Frontier Research,* edited by H. Dobyns. Albuquerque, N.Mex., 1982.

ERIKA WAGNER

Sevilla la Nueva

In 1509, Diego Colón, Columbus's son and heir who had been appointed viceroy of the Indies the year before, sent Juan de Esquivel from Santo Domingo, the capital city of La Española, to found the town of Sevilla la Nueva (New Seville) on the north coast of the island of Jamaica. Esquivel took with him some sixty men in order to pacify and subdue the indigenous Arawak inhabitants as well as to settle the island.

This was one of the first moves of the Columbus heirs to enforce the terms of the contract that Columbus had drawn up with the Spanish Crown as the basis of his 1492 voyage, terms on which the Crown was now reneging. The founding of the town of Sevilla la Nueva was therefore part of a preemptive bid by Diego Colón to forestall the Crown's imposition of its own de facto absolute sovereignty over the island of Jamaica as its officials in La Española had just done in the case of Puerto Rico.

The Siting of the Town. The site of Sevilla la Nueva was selected in the context of the same imperative. Diego ordered it to be built as the capital city on the north coast of the island next to the bay of Santa Gloria where his father and his crew had been shipwrecked for a little over a year (June 25, 1503, to June 29, 1504) at the end of his fourth voyage. Diego thus was asserting the claim of the Columbus family to an island that "all the world knew" his father had "discovered."

Diego's half brother, Fernando, who had been shipwrecked with his father during that year, later wrote that it was on the site of the nearby Arawak settlement of Maima that "the Christians later founded a city named Seville." Contemporary archaeological opinion, however, is that the town was founded near to rather than on the site of Maima, which is the present-day Windsor.

Sevilla la Nueva and its environs had clearly been part of a major settlement of the Taínan-Arawak fishing and cassava complex, one that had supplied the shipwrecked Spaniards with food during Columbus and his crew's enforced stay there. With the Spaniards' arrival in 1509–1510 and their discovery that there was little gold to be had, the Crown ordered that the island be converted into a food-growing, livestock and horse-rearing complex to supply expeditions devoted to slave raiding and exploration, conquest, settlement, and evangelization of the mainland. The town of Sevilla la Nueva therefore served Spain's expansion in the Americas and the Caribbean.

History of the Town. The town's brief history as a capital consisted of three phases—the Esquivel years (1509–1512), the era of Francisco de Garay (1515–1523), and the era of Pedro de Mazuelo (1524–1534).

Esquivel, before his death in 1512, laid the foundations of the town, including erecting a Franciscan monastery staffed by a Belgian lay friar, Father Deule. The Crown had ordered Diego Colón in 1511 to see that Esquivel set in motion the evangelization and conversion of the Indians, since this was the "principal basis" on which the Crown founded its "conquest of these parts." Esquivel would later be accused of having accelerated the processes of Arawak extinction by his harsh treatment of the indigenous inhabitants.

The second phase began with the arrival in Sevilla la Nueva in May 1515 of the new governor appointed by the Crown, Francisco de Garay. This phase would see the town realize its "brilliant beginning" (Chaunu, 1959) in the context of the overall network of the state-organized mercantile system called Seville's (Spain) Atlantic I by Huguette Chaunu and Pierre Chaunu. Under Garay's leadership, the institutional bases for the town's role were established. These included the following:

1. The establishment of a Crown-Garay company and the development of hinterland estates to supply food to the mainland settlers in exchange for Indian slaves captured in slave-raiding expeditions. Skilled supervisory personnel under contract to the company were brought out to oversee and further the island's food provisioning role.

2. The establishment of Sevilla la Nueva as an Indian slave-trading entrepôt from which captured Indians from the mainland, exchanged for food provisions grown on the island by Arawak forced labor on the Crown-Garay estates, were transshipped for sale in Santo Domingo.

3. The relocation of the town from the site where it had been laid down by Esquivel to a new site, probably leading to the shift from the original name El Pueblo de Sevilla to that of Sevilla la Nueva.

4. The construction of a new fortified governor's mansion, which seems to have been of considerable Renaissance splendor. The Crown referred to it as being "as excellent as you say it is," and the Spanish art historian Angulo Iniguez described the plateresque facade, which was discovered in a well in 1937, as being "the finest decorative work to be found in the Caribbean."

5. The building of two sugar mills, which initiated a demographic shift, with the gradual replacement of encomienda and enslaved indigenous labor by that of transported African slave labor.

In 1522, Garay resigned as governor of Jamaica. He had obtained a royal patent that entitled him to conquer and settle a region on the mainland that he intended to call Garayana. He sailed from Sevilla la Nueva in 1523. Defeated in battle by the indigenous inhabitants of the mainland and foiled by Hernando Cortés, he died on the mainland without returning to Sevilla la Nueva. Given the magnitude of the expedition he had outfitted—six ships, forty-four horsemen, seven hundred foot soldiers—he had drained the town of men and resources and dealt it a blow from which it would never really recover.

The third era was presided over by the island's treasurer, Pedro de Mazuelo. He acted in conjunction with another royal official, the comptroller Juan de Torralba, to oversee the dismantling and resale of the Crown-Garay estate. In the process, they diverted much of its assets to their own purposes, as the guardian of the young Garay heir later complained to the Crown.

In 1524, the year of Garay's death on the mainland, Pietro Martire d'Anghiera (Peter Martyr), the Italian humanist-priest and first historian of the New World, was appointed mitred abbot of Jamaica with his seat in Sevilla la Nueva. D'Anghiera used the titles due him to begin the building of a stone church in the town. The church was never to be completed, however. Among the complaints made to the Crown against Mazuelo was that he diverted the Arawaks allotted to building the church to work on his own personal projects and for his private profit.

On the basis of these complaints, the Crown ordered a judicial inquiry, a residencia, into the tenure of Mazuelo and into those of the other royal officials of Sevilla la Nueva, including Torralba. The judge of inquiry, Gil Gonzales Dávila, initiated proceedings soon after his arrival in September 1533. But he died the following year with the residencia incomplete.

Through the influence of his friends at the court in Spain, Mazuelo obtained a royal letter of July 28 that formally granted him the right to shift the capital from the north coast and to a site on the south coast. The decree also gave him permission to found the new town on a site adjacent to his recently built sugar mill. This new town and capital (later to be called Santiago de la Vega, today's Spanish Town) was referred to at first also as "Sevilla," but with the qualifier, "on the bank of the River Caguaya."

Although Diego Colón had died in 1526, the revenues due him from the island had continued to be paid to his heirs. And in August 1536, the original intention that had led to Diego's founding of Sevilla la Nueva on the site where Columbus had been stranded after his shipwreck was finally validated. Judgment was passed on the lawsuit brought by the Columbus family to keep the Crown to the original terms of its agreement. As part of the settlement, sovereignty over the island of Jamaica was conceded to the Columbus family, with the Crown retaining only supreme overall jurisdiction. As Mazuelo presciently warned, this delegation of sovereignty, which took the matter of the island's fortifications out of the direct control of the Crown, made Jamaica the weak link in the Spanish chain. This led to its relatively easy capture by the English in 1655, a century and a quarter later.

Sevilla la Nueva had lapsed into oblivion when the capital was shifted to the south coast. With the capture of the island by the English, the site was allotted to a Captain Hemmings as part of his private estate. Developed as a sugar estate and worked by enslaved African labor, it would continue as such, even after slavery was abolished and slave labor replaced by wage labor.

In the early 1960s, the estate's four hundred acres were purchased by the first government of a postcolonial and independent Jamaica and turned over to the Jamaican National Trust Commission to be developed as a historical site. Since 1981, major archaeological excavations intended to map the two sites of the town have been carried out by a team of Spanish archaeologists funded by the government of Spain and led by Lorenzo Eladio Lopez y Sebastian.

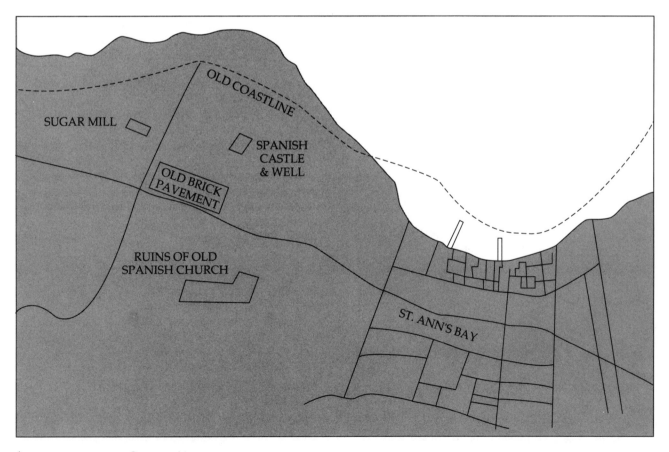

ARCHAEOLOGICAL SITES AT SEVILLA LA NUEVA.

AFTER G. A. AARONS, 1983, P. 45.

The Town's Archaeological and Historical Significance.
There are other reasons, in addition to its intimate link
with the fortress of the Columbus heirs, that make Sevilla
la Nueva significant in American-Caribbean history.

1. It is the site of Columbus's shipwrecked stay as well
as of his writing of his *Lettera rarissima* to the Spanish
sovereigns on July 7, 1503.

2. It includes the site next to the bay where two of
Columbus's caravels were abandoned. G. A. Aarons has
pointed out that although the caravel was the ship type
that opened up the New World to the Old and facilitated
the circumnavigation of Africa that proved to be a gateway
to the East, nowhere in the world does there remain a
trace of any fifteenth- or sixteenth-century caravel, nor
does any model or reproduction exist from the fifteenth or
sixteenth centuries.

The two caravels, *Santiago* and *La Capitana*, have
therefore been sought by several teams of marine archaeologists. Although begun earlier, the search was renewed
in 1981 on the basis of the collaborative efforts of the
Institute of Nautical Archaeology of Texas A&M University
and the government of Jamaica. Roger C. Smith, a
research associate, spearheaded "a site survey in order to
map the data available regarding the possible locating of
the shoreline. . . . Based on these surveys, some indication of where the coastline was located in the fifteenth and
sixteenth centuries has begun to emerge" and "possible
locations for the caravels identified" (Aarons, 1984).

3. The conversion experience of Pedro de la Renteria,
the business partner of Bartolomé de las Casas, took place
in the monastery at Sevilla in June 1514, at the very
moment that Las Casas also had a parallel conversion
experience at Sancti Spíritus, Cuba. Both men, from then
on, would dedicate their lives to the struggle for the
abolition both of the forced-labor encomienda system and
of the slave-trading system, which had been one of the
mainstays of the mercantile system of Seville's Atlantic I,
that moved Indians around the Caribbean and from the
Caribbean to the mainland.

As part of the struggle, Las Casas proposed the introduction of slaves from Africa in order to substitute for
indigenous forced and slave labor. The proposal then took
on a dynamic of its own with the first license granted in
1518, going far beyond its original limited intention.
Although Las Casas later regretted his proposal when he
discovered the unjust and coercive methods by which the
Africans had also been enslaved, his proposal would give
impetus to the process by which the transatlantic slave
trade was set in motion and the culture complex of
Africans, the indigenous peoples of the Americas, and
Europeans merged into the new civilization of the Americas and the Caribbean.

4. The town was connected, as an abbacy seat, with
d'Anghiera, whose *Decades of the New World* initiated
the narrated history of the post-Columbus New World.

5. The town is the site of architectural remains of the
facade of what seems to have been Garay's mansion
fortress. The Spanish art historian Angulo Iniguez described the plateresque complex of carvings on these
pilasters "as belonging to a quite early date going back to
the beginnings of the Renaissance style in Spain" and,
therefore, "as being of the greatest significance, not only
for the history of architecture in America, but for that of
the Iberian Peninsula itself."

As he concludes, no one "could have imagined that the
Spaniards in the first thirty years of their presence in the
island could have had built, at a time when many buildings
were still being built in the Gothic style on the [Iberian]
Peninsula, a beautiful facade according to the latest style
being diffused from Italy."

Although no map or plan of Sevilla la Nueva has been
found, the layout of the original sites has been mapped by
the Spanish archaeological team whose services were
contributed by the Spanish government. This team, which
began exploration in 1981 under the direction of Lorenzo
Eladio Lopez y Sebastian, has made some exciting discoveries, assisted by an interesting new method—the use of
subsurface interface radar to map remaining underground
structures. This method was used for the first time by the
Donohue firm of engineers and architects of Wisconsin
that specializes in techniques of remote sensing.

BIBLIOGRAPHY

Aarons, G. A. "Sevilla La Nueva: Microcosm of Spain in Jamaica."
Parts 1 and 2. *Jamaica Journal* 16, no. 4 (1983); 17, no. 7 (1984).

Accounts for the island of Santiago from the time it was settled to
the year 1536. Contaduria section, no. 1174. Archives of Seville,
Spain.

Anghiera, Pietro Martire d'. *De Orbe Novo: The Eight Decades of
Peter Martyr D'Anghiera.* Translated from the Latin with notes
and introduction by Francis A. MacNutt. New York, 1912.
Reprint, 1970.

Angulo Iniguez. *El Gótico y el Renacimiento en las Antillas.*
Seville, 1947.

Arrenz Marquez, Luis. *Don Diego Colón, Almirante, Virrey, y
Gobernador de Las Indias.* Vol. 1. Madrid, 1982.

Chaunu, Huguette, and Pierre Chaunu. *Seville et l'Atlantique,
1504–1650.* 8 vols. Paris, 1955–1959.

Columbus, Ferdinand. *The Life of the Admiral Christopher
Columbus by His Son, Ferdinand.* Translated and edited by
Benjamin Keen. New Brunswick, N.J., 1959.

Cotter, C. S. "The Discovery of the Spanish Carving at Seville."
Jamaican Historical Review 1, no. 3 (December 1948): 227–234.

Documents relating to early Spanish Jamaica in the Archivo
General de Indias. Transcribed by Irene Wright. National
Library of Jamaica.

Herskovits, M. J. *The New World Negro: Selected Papers in*

Afro-American Studies. Edited by F. S. Herskovits. Bloomington, Ind., 1966.

Jane, Cecil, ed. *Select Documents Illustrating the Four Voyages of Columbus.* 2 vols. London, 1932, 1933.

Landstrom, Bjorn. *Columbus: The Story of Don Cristobol Colon.* New York, 1967.

Las Casas, Bartolomé de. *The History of the Indies.* Translated by Andree M. Collard. New York, 1971.

Morales Padron, Francisco. *Jamaica Española.* Seville, 1952.

Pleitos de Colón (Lawsuits). *Colleción de documentos inéditos para la historia de España.* Madrid, 1875.

Wagner, H. R., with H. Parish. *The Life and Writings of Bartolomé de las Casas.* Albuquerque, N.Mex., 1967.

Wynter, Sylvia. *Major Dates: 1509–1536: With an Aftermath 1537–1655.* Kingston, Jamaica, 1984.

Wynter, Sylvia. *New Seville: Major Facts, Major Questions.* Kingston, Jamaica, 1984.

Wynter, Sylvia. "New Seville and the Conversion Experience of Bartolomé de las Casas." *Jamaica Journal* 17, no. 182 (1984).

SYLVIA WYNTER

Santo Domingo

The oldest European city in the Western Hemisphere, Santo Domingo was founded by Bartolomé Colón in 1497 on the left bank of the Ozama River. Five years later it was relocated across the river to its present site by Governor Nicolás de Ovando. According to early chronicles, this move occurred because of an ant plague, but the present location on the right bank had from the onset many advantages over the original site. Potable water was readily available, and the gold mines at Haina and Cotuí were more easily accessible.

Nicolás de Ovando designed the city "with a ruler and a compass," thereby establishing a quadrilateral pattern that was widely imitated in future urban foundations in Spanish America. The streets were laid in straight angles, calculated from the four cardinal points, and the church was constructed in front of a central square around which public buildings were located.

Though the city's wide streets and the abundance of stone and mortar buildings impressed early travelers, Santo Domingo never became a great city. It never surpassed fifty blocks, twelve of which were occupied by religious institutions.

Santo Domingo was surrounded by a mortar and stone wall reinforced with ramparts built after the mid-sixteenth century to defend it from attacks by corsairs and fugitive slaves. The city became the main exporting harbor for sugar, hides, and ginger, and its inhabitants experienced prosperity until the end of the sixteenth century. With the development of Mexico and Peru, Santo Domingo lost its importance. Portobelo, Veracruz, and Havana became the principal ports of call for the galleon fleets. The city's commercial activities gradually decreased and eventually stagnated; most of its inhabitants emigrated from the island.

In 1586, Santo Domingo fell into the hands of the English corsair Francis Drake. He burned the archives and many houses, took all the available jewels, gold, and silver as ransom, and stole the bells from the churches. For the next 150 years, the city ceased growing. Its inhabitants abandoned their houses and were replaced by professional soldiers brought from other parts of the Caribbean or Portugal. During the Thirty Years' War, Santo Domingo

PALACE OF DIEGO COLÓN, SANTO DOMINGO.

DOMINICAN REPUBLIC MINISTRY OF TOURISM

was converted into a simple military outpost on the fringes of the Spanish Empire. Its walls were rebuilt, and the fortresses and ramparts were refurbished to consolidate the network of fortified towns of San Juan, Cartagena, Portobelo, Veracruz, and La Habana (Havana), which defended the Caribbean Basin.

By becoming a military outpost, the city lost its original commercial character and its role as a communications center. The remaining population became extremely poor. Trade with Spain completely disappeared. Buildings were abandoned, and earthquakes, hurricanes, termites, rains, fungi, and vegetation eroded the sixteenth-century constructions. In the mid-seventeenth century, the development of the French colony of Saint-Domingue on the western side of the island briefly interrupted the city's decline. As the French filled their sugar plantations with African slaves, there was an increased demand for meat, which the Spaniards of Santo Domingo supplied in exchange for European merchandise. In the eighteenth century this active trade helped Santo Domingo to regain some of its lost prosperity.

BIBLIOGRAPHY

Castillo, Guillermo Céspedes del. *Latin America: The Early Years.* New York, 1974.

Floyd, Troy. *The Columbus Dynasty in the Caribbean, 1492–1526.* Albuquerque, N.Mex., 1973.

Lamb, Ursula. *Frey Nicolás de Ovando, Gobernador de las Indias (1501–1509).* Santo Domingo, 1977.

Moya Pons, Frank. *Historia colonial de Santo Domingo.* Santiago de los Caballeros, 1973.

Palm, Erwin Walter. *Los monumentos arquitectónicos de la Española.* Santo Domingo, 1984.

Ugarte, María. *Monumentos coloniales.* Santo Domingo, 1977.

FRANK MOYA PONS

Concepción de la Vega

The town of La Concepción de la Vega was founded by Christopher Columbus in 1495 during his second voyage to the New World. The discovery of gold in the Cordillera Central of La Española attracted settlers from other parts of the island, especially La Isabela, and made Concepción a center for mining. The area also produced sugar cane. The historian Bartolomé de las Casas lived and studied in Concepción.

Concepción was laid out in a checkerboard pattern, with a parade ground at the center and the city's major buildings—the cathedral, the government palace, and a fortress—around it. A Franciscan convent and a mint were also located there. An earthquake in 1562 led to the abandonment of the original site and the establishment of the town of La Vega (in the present-day Dominican Republic) nearby.

In the twentieth century, archaeological excavations of La Vega Vieja have yielded ceramic and metal household objects and numerous coins and have uncovered cemeteries, fortresses, roads, irrigation ditches, aqueducts, and the foundations of religious and secular buildings.

BIBLIOGRAPHY

Moya Pons, Frank. *Historia colonial de Santo Domingo.* Barcelona, 1974.

Pérez Montás, Eugenio. *República Dominicana monumentos históricos y arqueologicos.* Mexico, 1984.

EUGENIO PÉREZ MONTÁS
Translated from Spanish by Paola Carù

SEVILLA LA NUEVA. See *Settlements*, article on *Sevilla la Nueva.*

SEVILLE. Spanning the Guadalquivir River in southwestern Spain, Seville thrived as a commercial and industrial center during the fifteenth and sixteenth centuries. The river's broad alluvial plain surrounded Seville with fertile vineyards, fields, and orchards that provided both food and employment for inhabitants whose numbers increased to more than 100,000 in 1600. Soap manufacturing consumed quantities of oil produced from olive groves, and a ceramics industry developed, using clay from the river's banks. Artisans made casks for shipping these products as well as fish, wheat, oil, and wine to distant ports.

After Isabel directed Seville to outfit the small ships in which Columbus would attempt to discover a western route to the Indies in 1492, this protected inland seaport became the commercial capital of the Spanish Habsburg Empire. The royal government decreed in 1503 that all ships sailing between Europe and the lands claimed for Spain in the New World should pass through the port of Seville, where officials could more carefully control them. The city erected a new mint, a customs house near the river, and, at one side of the cathedral, the beautiful Lonja (the commercial exchange) designed by Juan de Herrera for the Casa de la Contratación, the royal agency supervising colonization in and commerce with the New World.

The seat of an archbishop and site of the third largest cathedral in the Christian world, Seville became the location for the first permanent tribunal of the Inquisition. Dominicans sent to this city in 1480 quickly found evidence of a network of conversos, or Christianized Jews, whom they accused of secretly practicing Jewish rites and plotting to resist attempts to purify the church. Later, in the sixteenth century, inquisitors uncovered in Seville one of the few groups of Protestants on the Iberian Peninsula.

Since 1248, Seville had been ruled as an oligarchy by

nobles loyal to the Christian monarchy that had defeated its Muslim rulers; but it also continued as the home of many moriscos, those Muslims who chose baptism over expulsion after the fall of Granada in 1492. Always suspect as false Christians, this group became identified as politically disloyal. When Philip II ordered the dispersal of moriscos throughout his kingdom following their rebellion in the mountains near Granada in 1568, more than four thousand were sent to Seville, where they were forbidden to live together, to speak Arabic, or to teach it to their children. Inquisitors prosecuted many for apostasy and blasphemy before Philip III finally ordered their expulsion in the early seventeenth century.

The dazzling wealth of some of its citizens, which often masked the city's cruel poverty, supported art, architecture, literature, and learning. Numerous printers published books in this city, where writers such as Lope de Vega, Mateo Alemán, and Miguel de Cervantes lived and worked for a time. Although Muslim influences could be seen in the buildings and fountains of an earlier period, Renaissance architecture and a developing baroque style contributed many impressive structures to the city, most notably the city hall and the Hospital de las Cinco Llagas, which was built to shelter poor women.

[See also *Casa de la Contratación; Inquisition; Jews; Muslims*.]

BIBLIOGRAPHY

Chaunu, Pierre, and Huguette Chaunu. *Seville et l'Atlantique, 1504–1650.* 8 vols. Paris, 1955–1959.

Domínguez Ortiz, Antonio. *Orto y ocaso de Sevilla: Estudio sobre la prosperidad y decadencia de la ciudad durante los siglos XVI y XVII.* Seville, 1946.

Montoto, Santiago. *Sevilla en el Imperio (siglo XVI).* Seville, 1937.

Perry, Mary Elizabeth. *Crime and Society in Early Modern Seville.* Hanover and London, 1980.

Pike, Ruth. *Aristocrats and Traders: Sevillian Society in the Sixteenth Century.* Ithaca and London, 1972.

Mary Elizabeth Perry

SHIPBUILDING. [The following entry surveys the history of shipbuilding in Europe and northern Africa, focusing on technical information about discovery-era ships and how such information has been gained through underwater archaeology. For related discussions, see *Arms, Armor, and Armament; Archaeology,* article on *Underwater Archaeology.* See also *Niña; Pinta; Santa María.*]

Shipbuilding in the Age of Discovery is best viewed as but one stage in an evolutionary process. As with any such process, a better understanding of any particular stage is afforded by at least a brief overview of some of the more significant preceding stages.

Archaeological discoveries of prehistoric dugout log canoes have been unearthed in many regions of the world. As crude as many of them were, they represented an advance from sitting "on" a rough log to sitting "in" a hand-hewn log canoe produced by intelligent beings using tools they had fashioned. As the need for waterborne transportation increased, the dugout canoe was made more seaworthy by fastening first one, then two or more planks to each side and bringing these planks together at each of its ends to keep water out. The log remained as a principal structural member, but its shape and function gradually changed until it evolved into what came to be known as the keel. The resulting vessel in which the shaped log had become a submerged keel was capable of carrying a number of people and a sizable cargo. It was becoming a ship.

Southern and Northern Shipbuilding Traditions

In Europe and the northern regions of Africa, this evolutionary process had two main branches, Southern and Northern. As early as 3000 B.C. waterborne transportation in Egypt had developed to a point that permitted the Egyptians to send ships as far as Crete and Phoenicia. Thus stimulated, the Cretans and Phoenicians soon had fleets of their own. As these were overtaken by Greek and Roman warships and merchantmen, a definite Mediterranean, or Southern, style developed, and the number of ships grew to include Turkish, Spanish, and Portuguese fleets. By 200 B.C. a distinct Scandinavian, or Northern, style began to evolve. Because there was little sea traffic between north and south until the time of the Crusades, these two evolutionary branches of development maintained uniquely regional characteristics.

Although there were obvious similarities between the two styles, there were also significant differences. In the older Southern methods of construction, adjacent planks were fitted together edge to edge, so that the resulting "carvel-planked" hull had a relatively smooth surface. Deck beams protruded through the planking and were supported at each deck level by thicker planks called wales. The earliest sails in both the north and the south were square or rectangular and were set on a horizontal spar or yard on a single mast mounted approximately amidships. Ships so rigged could sail only with the wind coming from abaft the beam and thus were required to wait for favorable winds when trying to sail in a particular direction. In the more populous south with its greater reliance on sea commerce, such a restriction could not be tolerated. To minimize this drawback, the lateen sail of triangular shape set on a long diagonal yard was adopted from the Arabs in about the eighth century A.D. This permitted Southern ships to make progress to windward, particularly when the two-masted rig was developed in the twelfth century A.D., freeing the ships from dependence on the direction of the wind.

LATEEN RIG. Shown on a model of a typical Southern vessel of the fifteenth to sixteenth century. Note also the carvel planking and the wales.   COMISSÃO NACIONAL PARA AS COMEMORAÇÕES DOS DESCOBRIMENTOS PORTUGUESES, LISBON

In the north, "lapstrake," or "clinker" planking methods were used. The first plank, or garboard strake, overlapped a T-shaped lip on the keel and each adjacent plank overlapped the next lower plank, as with clapboards on a wooden house, all the way up to the uppermost plank or sheer strake. Deck beams did not protrude through the planking but instead were supported by an inner shelf that extended from stem to stern. Use of the single square or rectangular sail persisted. But as population increased in the north and seagoing commerce to and from the south began to develop, Northern and Southern shipbuilding traditions melded into a common Atlantic tradition. The single square or rectangular sail had become inadequate. Additional masts and sails were added, and by the end of the fifteenth century, a true oceangoing ship rig had been developed that, in its basic configuration, persisted well into the eighteenth century.

Thus, the sail plan of a ship such as *Santa María*, Columbus's flagship on his first voyage, consisted of a foremast and mainmast carrying square or rectangular sails (referred to as "square-rigged") and a mizzenmast carrying a triangular-shaped lateen sail. In addition, a rectangular spritsail was rigged under the upswept bowsprit and a small square topsail was rigged on a slender unstayed topmast mounted as an extension of the mainmast. Beginning early in the sixteenth century, a similar small topsail was rigged on the foremast. In smaller

vessels, some regional traditions persisted. For example, many small vessels in the north continued to be built with lapstrake planking, a tradition that still survives. Larger oceangoing ships of the new Atlantic tradition, however, were all carvel-planked and square-rigged on mainmast and foremast. In addition, deck beams no longer protruded through the planking. The more watertight system of supporting the beams on an interior shelf had been adopted.

Individual sketches or paintings of ships of the discovery period by some contemporary artists cannot be relied upon to provide authentic information on many details of either the hulls or their rigging. When certain specific features are found in a number of sketches or paintings by different contemporary artists, however, one is justified in assuming that those features are reasonably authentic. Features typical of merchant ships of the period, well illustrated in Vittore Carpaccio's painting *The Legend of Saint Ursula* (1495), are the round tuck stern and general roundness of the hull, the forecastle and the aft castle, the forecastle arch, the heavy bitt beam protruding through the forward part of the bulwarks, and the lapstrake planking filling the triangular space between the bulwark rails and the forecastle deck. The profile shape of the bow almost invariably was made up of arcs of circles with radii related by a simple ratio to the maximum breadth of the ship. The cross-sectional shape of the hull was also normally made up of arcs of circles. At this transitional stage in rig development from one mast to three, the large mainsail remained as the major driving force, with the much smaller foresail, spritsail, and mizzen, although providing some propulsive force, aiding greatly in directional control and maneuverability. A tiny main topsail was still an early tentative addition to the sail plan.

Although it is possible to trace the development of ships up to the age of discovery, it is important to understand that there are no extant original plans of any fifteenth-century ship. The profession of naval architecture as we know it today did not exist at that time. The first reasonably complete construction plans were not produced until the seventeenth century, and not until late in the next century were full sets of detailed working plans generally available. Shipwrights of the period who built ships without benefit of plans had little or no formal education, as was the case with most artisans. They did, however, have a strong background of experience. They started to work as apprentices at a young age and learned to build boats and ships the way their fathers and forefathers had built them for centuries. They learned to use various simple rules of thumb formed by years of trial and error. For example, the generally accepted proportions for the principal hull dimensions of maximum breadth or beam, length of keel, and length of the main

VITTORE CARPACCIO'S *THE LEGEND OF SAINT URSULA*, 1495. Detail, showing typical merchant ships of the period in the harbor of Venice.

ALINARI/ART RESOURCE

deck for a late fifteenth-century merchant ship, called a nao in Spain and a carrack in Italy, were in the simple ratio of 1:2:3. Thus, for a ship capable of carrying a cargo of one hundred tons, such as Columbus's flagship *Santa María,* a master shipwright would know from long experience that he should choose approximate dimensions of twenty-seven feet for the beam, fifty-four feet for the keel length, and eighty-one feet for the main deck length. For caravels like *Niña* and *Pinta,* which were lighter, faster, less bulky ships, the proportions were less precise; the average ratios were 1 for beam, 2.4 for length of keel, and 3.33 for length of hull.

In addition to these ratios for principal hull dimensions, there were other rules of thumb used by master shipwrights of the fifteenth and sixteenth centuries. It should be noted that the ship's maximum beam was the key dimension to which all these rules of thumb were directly

related. For example, the master frame, a major structural assemblage that determined the cross-sectional shape of the hull at its widest point, was made up of components whose size and shape were governed by the dimension of the ship's maximum beam. The master frame consisted of a flat central bottom section called a floor timber and two or three curved sections called futtocks, which extended upward to the main deck. By rule of thumb the floor timber of the master frame was usually given a length of approximately one-third the ship's maximum beam and was made flat except for slightly upturned ends where it was fastened to overlapping first futtocks, usually by means of both iron nails and wooden pegs called treenails. Depending on the height of the main deck above the keel, second and third futtocks were added.

These ancient rules of thumb usually were viewed as a way of doing things that was practical and simple. They were based on experience and practice rather than on scientific knowledge. Master shipwrights used them as convenient approximations, not as rigid requirements. The rules often were adjusted to accommodate the opinions of ship captains and sailing masters on the good and bad points of previous ships. Thus, without benefit of detailed drawings or even any specifications other than the anticipated use of the ship and its desired cargo-carrying capacity, shipwrights regularly built wooden ships by applying these rules of thumb to a simple yet effective method of construction known as the master frame and batten system.

That system consisted of setting up and fastening together a keel, stem, and sternpost. The master frame then was constructed and mounted on the keel at the point of desired maximum breadth, normally slightly aft of amidships. In order to control the shape of the hull both forward and aft, two intermediate frames usually were required, one between the master frame and the stem and another between the master frame and the sternpost. If the ship was to be a nao such as the Spanish *Santa María*, a transom beam would be mounted horizontally atop the sternpost at main deck level. In conformity with the simple 1:2:3 rule of thumb for hull proportions of a nao or carrack, the length of the keel would be about two times the breadth of the master frame. The combined rake or overhang of the stem and sternpost would be made such that the length of the main deck would be equal to about three times the breadth. If the ship was to be a caravel, a flat transom extending from just below the waterline to the main deck would be mounted on the sternpost. For either type hull, temporary straight flexible battens, suitably spaced, would then be bent around the master and intermediate frames from stem to stern, producing a hull form inside of which additional required frames, each consisting of a floor timber and associated futtocks, were then fashioned to fit. When all the frames were in place, the temporary battens would be replaced one at a time by permanent exterior planking, fastened to the interior frames with both treenails and iron nails.

The experience and personal practice of individual master shipwrights governed the location of the master and intermediate frames. The underbody of one English ship was designed to be similar to the shape of a fish on the theory that God had given fish an ideal shape for moving through the water. This located the master frame, and hence maximum breadth and fullness, somewhat forward of amidships. This had the advantage of providing a very fine or slender afterbody that would greatly increase the effectiveness of the rudder but would also result in a very full forebody with some undesirable characteristics. Southern shipwrights opted for a master frame location slightly aft of amidships, which (though it

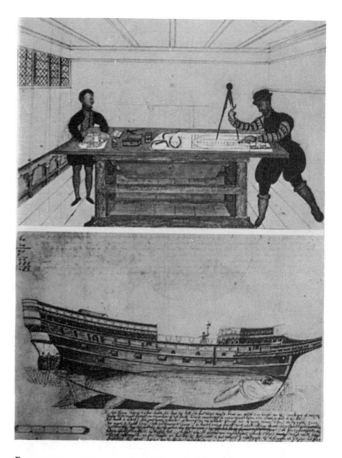

FISH-SHAPED UNDERBODY. And (above) shipwrights at work. English drawings of the sixteenth century.

ELSEVIER PUBLISHING PROJECTS, AMSTERDAM

conforms with modern practice) demanded careful shaping of the afterbody to ensure adequate rudder effectiveness.

Evidence from Nautical Archaeology

The examination of contemporary paintings and the study of the use of certain rules of thumb have provided useful but severely limited information on the construction of discovery-period ships. Fortunately, recent findings of nautical archaeologists have made it possible to develop hard evidence of specific construction details used during the Columbus era. The Institute of Nautical Archaeology in College Station, Texas, deserves great credit for important work in this field. Its reports of on-site study of a number of ancient shipwrecks as well as the construction of authentic scale models by noted ship reconstructor J. Richard Steffy of the institute's staff, have contributed significantly to our knowledge of the evolution of wooden ships up through the Age of Discovery.

In 1982 a group headed by Donald Keith was formed to

locate, survey, and excavate the wrecks of discovery-period ships in the Caribbean. Two shipwrecks that have been surveyed and excavated are thought to be of the discovery era. One is located on Molasses Reef near the Turks and Caicos Islands and the other just off the north shore of Highborn Cay in the northern Bahamas. The size and shape of the reasonably intact mound of stone ballast at the Molasses Reef site indicates that the ship was of the approximate tonnage of *Pinta,* a common size for caravels of that period. A Florida-based treasure-hunting company, Caribbean Ventures, which located the wreck, claimed that it is the *Pinta,* one of Columbus's three original ships of discovery and possibly one of four caravels in a fleet commanded by Vicente Yáñez Pinzón on a voyage of exploration in 1499–1500. It is known that shortly after departing La Española on the return voyage to Spain, the fleet encountered a severe storm and two of the caravels were lost. Many maritime historians, however, believe that there is insufficient evidence to support the claim that it is, in fact, the *Pinta.*

Under the mounds of stone ballast at both the Molasses Reef and the Highborn Cay shipwreck sites the team found sections of wooden hulls, which provided valuable construction details. Substantial portions of the hand-hewn keels, keelsons, floor timbers, and attached first futtocks provided information on shape, dimensions, and methods of attachment. Among recovered artifacts were authenticated fifteenth-century wrought-iron, breech-loading lombards with breech chambers and wedges, smaller breech-loading as well as muzzle-loading swivel guns, various types of shot, and several large anchors. Numerous wrought-iron hull fastenings and other fittings were found scattered about the sites. Iron gudgeons and pintles used to fasten the rudder to the sternpost provided information on the thickness of the sternposts and rudders. Several sets of iron rigging components provided indications of how the ships' standing rigging had been fastened to the hulls. With this sort of detailed information, our knowledge of Columbus-era ships was greatly expanded.

Marine archaeologists of the Canadian Park Service, headed by Robert Grenier, discovered and excavated the wreck of a Spanish Basque whaling ship believed to be *San Juan,* documented as having sunk in Red Bay, Labrador, in 1565. Major components of her flattened hull, not revealed until after extensive excavation, had been remarkably well preserved by the icy water and mud. She was a merchant galleon, successor to the nao and thus of great interest because of her comparability to discovery-era ships. Grenier and his team of marine archaeologists recovered nearly all the major heavy structural members and most of the framing, planking, hull stringers, clamps, hanging knees, skids (or fenders), deck beams, and

SHIP'S ANCHOR AND ANCHOR OF A SMALL BOAT FROM THE MOLASSES REEF WRECK. On display in conservation lab of the Institute of Nautical Archaeology.

INSTITUTE OF NAUTICAL ARCHAEOLOGY, COLLEGE STATION, TEXAS

supports as well as portions of the rigging. All significant pieces were measured and drawn at one-tenth scale to provide a permanent record of all components and make possible the construction of an accurate scale model.

The massive hand-hewn keel and keelson were recovered intact. At its midpoint, the keel was roughly T-shaped in cross section. Toward the bow and stern it became more Y-shaped and near its ends more U-shaped, bringing to mind its gradual evolution from the dugout canoe. The arms of the T, Y, and U cross sections seem to have been designed to take the place of the more usual garboard strakes fastened in place on each side of the keel in later ships. The maximum width and thickness of the keelson were near its expanded midpoint where it was mortised to take the foot of the mainmast, thus accurately locating the position of that major spar. Both forward and aft of this mast step, the keelson was tapered to about eight inches square at each end. The bottom face was notched to a depth of about three inches to fit tightly over the floor timbers, through which the keelson was fastened to the keel by long iron bolts.

Another key structural component, the lower portion of which was recovered virtually intact, was the master frame. This was of particular importance because it confirmed the use of ancient rules of thumb in forming the hull cross section and provided hard evidence of its shape. The floor timber was approximately one-third of the ship's maximum breadth and was flat except for a slight upward curvature at its ends where it overlapped with and was fastened to the first futtocks precisely as prescribed by one of the ancient rules of thumb. An interesting detail not found in any historical text was the manner in which the first futtocks were joined to the floor timbers using carefully fashioned mortises and tenons. The same construction technique was found in the Molasses Reef and Highborn Cay discovery-era wrecks. Here was hard evidence of shipbuilding methods in the Age of Discovery as opposed to conjecture.

Early in the recovery effort it was determined that the flattened remains of the hull could not be raised as a whole and that its individual pieces probably could not be reassembled. Recognizing the importance of providing visual evidence of sixteenth-century Spanish shipbuilding methods, the Canadian marine archaeologists wisely decided to construct a 1:10 scale model of the ship at their headquarters in Ottawa. A complete reconstruction was not attempted, but enough work was completed to permit development of hull lines, to identify important structural details visually, and to show how significant assemblages of individual pieces fit together. The result is a treasure trove of invaluable information for maritime historians.

The efforts of the Canadian Park Service marine archaeologists in excavating and analyzing the remains of this ship have been immensely valuable. The Canadian information on a post-Columbus ship, the information developed by the Institute of Nautical Archaeology on Columbus-era ships, and the evidence provided by Steffy's models of pre-Columbian ships constitute an important sequence of findings that greatly increases our understanding of ship hull form and construction during an important period of history.

BIBLIOGRAPHY

Anderson, R. C. "Italian Naval Architecture about 1445." In *Mariner's Mirror* 11. London, 1925.

Anderson, Romola, and R. C. Anderson. *The Sailing-Ship: Six Thousand Years of History.* New York, 1963.

Bradford, Ernle. *Christopher Columbus.* New York, 1973.

Culver, Henry B., and Gordon Grant. *The Book of Old Ships.* Garden City, N.Y., 1935.

Gibson, Charles E. *The Story of the Ship.* New York, 1958.

Greenhill, Basil. *Archaeology of the Boat.* Middletown, Conn., 1976.

Greenhill, Basil. *The Evolution of the Wooden Ship.* New York, 1988.

Howard, Frank. *Sailing Ships of War, 1400–1860.* New York, 1979.

Keith, Donald. *The Molasses Reef Wreck.* Institute of Nautical Archaeology. College Station, Tex., 1987.

Landstrom, Bjorn. *The Ship.* Garden City, N.Y., 1961.

Lane, Frederick Chapin. *Venetian Ships and Shipbuilders of the Renaissance.* Baltimore, 1934.

Oertling, Thomas J. *Highborn Key Wreck.* Institute of Nautical Archaeology. College Station, Tex., 1988.

WILLIAM LEMOS

SHIPS AND CREWS. [This entry gathers the names of the crew members for Columbus's four voyages to the Western Hemisphere. For further discussion of the three ships of the first voyage, see *Niña, Pinta,* and *Santa María.* For further discussion of the events of these voyages, see *Voyages of Columbus.*]

First Voyage

The following roster of the crews of the ships of the first voyage has been rigorously researched by Alicia Bache Gould and published by the Real Academia de la Historia in Madrid. Roman numerals refer to later voyages. An asterisk indicates that this crew member was left behind in La Navidad and died there.

Santa María

Christopher Columbus, captain

Juan de la Cosa, from Santona, master and owner (there is conflicting opinion about whether this Juan de la Cosa is the same as the Juan de la Cosa of the second voyage)

Peralonso Niño, from Moguer, pilot

*Diego de Arana, from Córdoba, master-at-arms of the fleet

*Rodrigo de Escobedo, from Segovia, secretary of the fleet

*Pedro Gutiérrez, baker of the royal house

Rodrigo Sánchez, from Segovia, comptroller of the fleet

*Luis de Torres, interpreter

*Maestre Juan, surgeon

*Chachu, boatswain

*Domingo de Lequeitio, boatswain's mate

*Antonio de Cuéllar, carpenter

*Domingo Vizcaíno, able seaman and cooper

*Lope, able seaman and caulker

*Juan de Medina, able seaman and tailor

*Diego Pérez, able seaman and painter

Bartolomé Bives, from Palos, able seaman
Alonso Clavijo, from Vejer, able seaman
*Gonzalo Franco, able seaman
Juan Martínez de Azoque, from Denia, able seaman
Juan de Moguer, from Palos, able seaman; also II
Juan de la Placa, from Palos, able seaman
Juan Ruiz de la Peña, from Basque Provinces, able
  seaman
Bartolomé de Torres, from Palos, able seaman; also II
Juan de Jerez, from Moguer, able seaman; also II
Rodrigo de Jerez, from Ayamonte, able seaman
Pero Yzquierdo, from Lepe, able seaman
Cristóbal Caro, silversmith and ship's boy; also II
Diego Bermúdez, from Palos, ship's boy; also III
Alonso Chocero, ship's boy
Rodrigo Gallego, ship's boy
Diego Leal, ship's boy; also II
*Pedro de Lepe, ship's boy
*Jácome el Rico, from Genoa, ship's boy
*Martín de Urtubia, ship's boy
Andrés de Yévenes, ship's boy
Juan, ship's boy
Pedro de Terreros, Columbus's steward; also II, III, IV
Pedro de Salcedo, Columbus's valet; also II, III

Pinta
Martín Alonso Pinzón, from Palos, captain
Francisco Martín Pinzón, from Palos, master
Cristóbal García Sarmiento, pilot; also II
Juan Reynal, master-at-arms; also II
Maestre Diego, surgeon
Juan Quintero de Algruta, from Palos, boatswain; also
  II, III, IV
Cristóbal Quintero, from Palos, owner and able sea-
  man; also III
Antón Calabrés, from Calabria, Italy, able seaman; also
  II
Francisco García Vallejos, from Moguer, able seaman
Alvaro Pérez, able seaman
Gil Pérez, able seaman
Diego Martín Pinzón, from Palos, able seaman; also III
Sancho de Rama, able seaman
Gómez Rascón, from Palos, able seaman
Rodrigo de Triano (also known as Juan Rodríguez
  Bermejo), able seaman
Juan Verde de Triana, able seaman; also II
Juan Vezano, from Venice, able seaman
Pedro de Arcos, from Palos, ship's boy
Juan Arias, from Tavira, Portugal, ship's boy
Fernando Medel, from Huelva, ship's boy
Francisco Medel, from Huelva, ship's boy
Alonso de Palos, ship's boy; also II
Juan Quadrado, ship's boy
Pedro Tegero, ship's boy

Bernal, ship's boy and captain's servant
García Fernández, from Palos, steward
Niña
Vicente Yáñez Pinzón, from Palos, captain
Juan Niño, from Moguer, master and owner
Sancho Ruíz de Gama, pilot
*Maestre Alonso, surgeon
*Diego Lorenzo, master-at-arms
Bartolomé García, from Palos, boatswain; also II, IV
*Alonso de Morales, carpenter
Juan Arráez, able seaman; also II
Pedro Arráez, able seaman
Rui García, from Santona, able seaman
Rodrigo Monge, able seaman
Bartolomé Roldán, from Palos, able seaman and appren-
  tice pilot; also III
Juan Romero, able seaman
Pedro Sánchez, from Montilla, able seaman
Pedro de Villa, from Santona, able seaman
García Alonso, from Palos, ship's boy; also II
*Andrés de Huelva, ship's boy
*Francisco de Huelva, ship's boy
Francisco Niño, from Moguer, ship's boy; also II
Pedro de Soria, ship's boy
Fernando de Triana, ship's boy
Miguel de Soria, ship's boy and captain's servant

Second Voyage

Following his triumphant appearance before the sovereigns in Barcelona upon his return from the first voyage,
Columbus remained with the court making plans for the
second voyage. By the end of May 1493 he had been
designated captain general of the fleet and, together with
Juan de Fonseca, archdeacon of Seville, was made jointly
responsible for all aspects of the preparations. Fonseca, a
good businessman and organizer, within five months
assembled, manned, and outfitted a fleet of seventeen
vessels for a six-month round-trip voyage and provided
food, arms, supplies, tools, and equipment for some
twelve hundred artisans and workmen who were to
establish a self-sustaining colony.

Among the seventeen vessels of the fleet were three
naos, ships of the same type as the original *Santa María*,
which was wrecked on a reef off the north coast of La
Española during the first voyage. Once again the Admiral
named his flagship *Santa María*, but as usual she was
normally referred to by her nickname *Mariagalante*. The
other two naos were named *Colina* and *Gallega*. The
remaining fourteen ships were all caravels and included
gallant *Niña*, which had safely carried Columbus home to
Spain on the first voyage. Twelve of these were *carabelas
redondas* like *Niña*, square-rigged on foremast and mainmast, lateen on the mizzen. The two remaining ships, *San*

Juan and *Cardera,* the smallest in the fleet and chosen by Columbus specifically for exploring shoal rivers and inlets, were lateen-rigged throughout.

Columbus's log of the second voyage has never been found. Fortunately, the biography of the Admiral by his son Fernando and narrative accounts by Michele da Cuneo and Guillermo Coma, gentleman volunteers who participated in the voyage, have provided substantial information. The only official crew lists that have survived are contained in declarations by crew members of the three caravels *Niña, San Juan,* and *Cardera* stating their belief that Cuba was part of the mainland they had been seeking. These depositions, ordered by the Admiral, were taken under oath and recorded by Fernando Pérez de Luna, chief scribe and notary of the fleet. A dagger indicates participation in the first voyage also.

Niña

†Christopher Columbus, captain of the flagship and fleet commander

Alonso Medel, from Palos, master to Cuba and remainder of voyage

Francisco Niño, from Moguer, pilot

†Pedro de Terreros, boatswain

Fernando Pérez de Luna, royal notary

Diego Tristán, from Seville, gentleman volunteer

Francisco de Morales, from Seville, gentleman volunteer

Juan de la Cosa, chart maker (there is conflicting opinion about whether this Juan de la Cosa is the same as the Juan de la Cosa of the first voyage)

Iñigo López de Zúñiga, the Admiral's steward

Johan del Barco, from Palos, able seaman

Morón, from Moguer, able seaman

Francisco de Lepe, from Moguer, able seaman

Diego Beltrán, from Moguer, able seaman

Domingo, from Genoa, able seaman

Estefano, from Venice, able seaman

Juan de España, from Basque Provinces, able seaman

Gómez Calafar, from Palos, able seaman

Ramiro Pérez, from Lepe, able seaman

Mateo de Morales, from San Juan del Puerto, able seaman

Gonzalo, from Basque Provinces, ship's boy

Francisco Ginovés, from Córdoba, ship's boy

Rodrigo Molinero, from Moguer, ship's boy

Rodrigo Calafar, from Caraya, ship's boy

Alonso Niño, from Moguer, ship's boy

Juan, from Basque Provinces, ship's boy

San Juan

Alonso Pérez Roldán, from Málaga, master

Bartolomé Pérez, from Rota, pilot

Alfonso Rodríguez, from Cartaya, boatswain

Johan Rodríguez, from Ciudad Rodrigo, able seaman

Sebastián de Ayamonte, from Ciudad Rodrigo, able seaman

Diego del Monte, from Moguer, able seaman

Francisco Calvo, from Moguer, able seaman

Juan Domínguez, from Palos, able seaman

Juan Albarracín, from Puerto de Santa María, able seaman

Nicolás Estefano, from Mallorca, cooper

Cristóbal Vivas, from Moguer, ship's boy

Rodrigo de Santander, from Moguer, ship's boy

Johan Garcés, from Beas, ship's boy

Pedro de Salas, from Lisbon, ship's boy

Hernando López, from Huelva, ship's boy

Fernando Pérez de Luna, royal notary

Cardera

Cristóbal Pérez Niño, from Moguer, master

Fenerin Ginovés, boatswain

Gonzalo Alonso Galeote, boatswain's mate

†Juan de Jerez, from Moguer, able seaman

Francisco Carral, from Palos, able seaman

Gorjón, from Palos, able seaman

Juan Griego, from Genoa, able seaman

Alonso Pérez, from Huelva, able seaman

Juan Vizcaíno, from Cartaya, able seaman

Cristóbal Lorenzo, from Palos, ship's boy

Francisco de Medina, from Moguer, ship's boy

†Diego Leal, from Moguer, ship's boy

†Francisco Niño, from Moguer, ship's boy

Tristán, from Valduerna, ship's boy

Our only information on the following participants in the voyage comes from occasional mention of certain individuals in the various narrative accounts.

Antonio de Torres, master and owner of flagship *Mariagalante*

†Juan Niño, from Moguer, master from Spain to La Española only

Bartolomé Colín, captain of *India* on return voyage

Juan Aguado, ship's captain

Alonso Sánchez de Carvajal, judge of Baeza and ship's captain

Pedro Fernández Coronel, ship's captain

Ginés de Gorbalán, ship's captain

Alonso de Ojeda, ship's captain and leader of troops ashore

†Peralonso Niño, chief pilot from Spain to La Española only

†Cristóbal García Sarmiento, pilot

†Juan Quintero de Algruta, boatswain

†Bartolomé García, boatswain

Diego de Alvarado, later active in Peru

Francisco de Garay, an associate of Cortés

Juan Ponce de León, future discoverer of Florida

Juan de Luján, from Madrid, gentleman volunteer

Pedro Margarit, commander of fort in interior La Española

Melchior Maldonado, gentleman volunteer

Diego Alvarez Chanca, from Seville, fleet physician and writer of voyage narrative

Michele da Cuneo, from Genoa, writer of voyage narrative

Guillermo Coma, gentleman volunteer, writer of voyage narrative

Bernardo Buyl (or Buil), Benedictine monk

Ramón Pané, Hieronymite friar

Diego Márquez, from Seville, inspector of the colony

Francisco Morales, able seaman

†Juan de Moguer, able seaman

†Bartolomé de Torres, able seaman

†Cristóbal Caro, silversmith and ship's boy

†Juan Reynal, master-at-arms

†Antón Calabrés, able seaman

†Juan Verde de Triana, able seaman

†Alonso de Palos, ship's boy

†Juan Arráez, able seaman

†García Alonso, ship's boy

†Pedro de Salcedo, ship's boy

Diego Colón, the Admiral's youngest brother

In June 1495, a severe hurricane sank three of the four caravels at La Isabela. The hardy *Niña* once again survived. Among the ships' crews were a few shipwrights who, with the assistance of carpenters from the colony, salvaged as much as they could of the wrecked ships' timbers and equipment to build a sister ship of *Niña*. This new caravel, the first European ship to be built in the New World, was officially named *Santa Cruz* but was always called *India*. *Niña* and *India* were dangerously overloaded, carrying 255 passengers, of whom 30 were Indians, back to Spain.

Third Voyage

Columbus requested eight ships for the third voyage, two of which would depart as soon as possible with supplies for La Española. The sovereigns gave approval for this number of ships, but money for the enterprise was slow in reaching the fitting-out port of Seville. Reliable *Niña* and her sister ship *India*, sixty-ton caravels in both of which Columbus owned a half interest, were the first ships to be readied. They sailed from Sanlúcar at the mouth of the Guadalquivir River on January 23, 1498. Not until four months later, May 30, did the next six ships depart: One nao, the *Santa María de Guía*, Columbus's flagship, and five caravels, *Vaqueños*, *El Correo*, *Garza*, *La Gorda*, and *La Rábida*. The latter three, loaded with men and supplies for the colony on La Española, headed directly for their assigned destination from the Canary Islands while the first three ships, under the Admiral's command, took a more southerly course in hopes of discovering the rumored mainland south of the Antilles.

The following roster of the third voyage has been compiled from sources discovered at different times, some in the sixteenth century and some not until late in the twentieth. Ship assignments for most of the crewmen are not available.

Christopher Columbus, Admiral of the Ocean Sea

Pero Fernández Coronel, captain general of *Niña* and *India*

Pedro Francés, captain of *Niña*

Juan Bermúdez, captain of *India*

Pedro de Terreros, captain of *El Correo*

Hernán Pérez, captain of *Vaqueños*

Alonso Sánchez de Carvajal, captain of *Garza*

Pedro de Arana, captain of *La Gorda*

Giovanni Antonio Colombo, the Admiral's Genoese cousin, captain of *La Rábida*

Cristóbal Quintero, owner and master of *Santa María de Guía*

Andrés García Galdín, from Palos, master of *La Castilla*

Francisco García, from Palos, owner and master of *Garza*

Alfón Benítez, from Palos, master of *La Gorda*

García Alfón Cansino, from Palos, master of *La Rábida*

Juan Quintero de Algruta, from Palos, pilot

Juan Quintero Principe, from Palos, pilot

Bartolomé Roldán, able seaman

Diego Martín Pinzón, able seaman

Alfonso Pérez Mateos, from Huelva, able seaman

Alonso Pérez, able seaman

Fernando Pérez de Palos, able seaman

Domingo de Bermeo, able seaman

Juan Griego, able seaman

Diego Galindo, able seaman

Pedro de Valmaseda, able seaman

García de Vedia, able seaman

Juan de Echevarría, able seaman

Diamedes Quaralte, able seaman

Juan de Purcheta, able seaman

Luis de Area, of Palos, able seaman

Diego Ortiz, of Palos, able seaman

Ortuño, of Baracaldo, able seaman

Cristóbal Durán, from Palos, able seaman

Diego Bermúdez, ship's boy

Juan de Amezaga, from Baracalda, ship's boy

Jácome, ship's boy

Pedro de la Maza, ship's boy

Bartolomé de Sanlúcar de Barrameda, ship's boy

Juan Farfán, ship's boy

Ochoa de Etorribalzago, ship's boy

Juan Antonio, the Admiral's head steward

Pedro del Arroyal, the Admiral's steward

Pedro de Salcedo, the Admiral's servant

Andrés de Corral, the Admiral's page

The following individuals could have been either crew members or colonists:

Juan Domínguez, priest
Juan de Caizedo, priest
Juan de Castuera, priest
Maestre Diego, from Palencia, surgeon
Juan Picardo, gunner
Rodrigo Yáñez, from Lepe, cooper
Francisco Sánchez, from Lepe, cooper
Gonzalo, of Fregenal, barber
Juan Rodríguez, from Triana, tailor
Fernando Pacheco, from Seville
Pedro de Arana, from Córdoba
Juan de Amezaga, from Baracalda
Domingo de Alburquerque
Juan de Bolonia
Simón de Piamonte
Gonzalo Moreno
Juan Guillén, from Jerez de Badajoz
Juan de Vera, from Canary Islands
Andrés de Vera, from Canary Islands
Juan Portugués, from Canary Islands
Andrés del Hierro, from Canary Islands

Also without ship assignments or designated occupations were ten pardoned criminals.

The following sixteen *escuderos* (gentlemen volunteers) probably were aboard the three ships headed for La Española, but a few may have been with the explorers in the three ships commanded by Columbus:

Francisco de Alarcón
Francisco de Atienza
Francisco de Barrasa
Pero Carrillo
Luis de Castrejón
Gil Delgadillo, from Jerez de Badajoz
Diego de Escobar, from Seville
Diego de Luna
Antonio Marino
Diego Mexía, from Jerez
Lope de Ribera
Fernando de San Miguel, from Seville
Bartolomé de Torres
Gonzalo de Valdenebro
Alfonso de Vallejo
García de Villanueva, from Jerez de la Frontera
Cristóbal Sánchez de la Cida, from Jerez, in charge of the following labor force destined for the colony:
    Lázaro Ruíz, from Córdoba, locksmith
    Lope Alfonso, from Portugal, blacksmith
    Pedro López, blacksmith
    Cristóbal de Paz, from Seville, mason
    Bartolomé Sánchez, from Seville, mason

    Antón Gutiérrez, from Seville, mason
    Pedro de Requena, from Baena, mason
    Alfonso Rodríguez, from Carmona, mason
    Juan Gascón, mason
    Juan Martínez, from Seville, tile maker
    Navidad Bretón, sawyer
    Benito Sánchez, sawyer
    Juan Rodríguez, copper worker
    Pedro Sánchez, from Baeza, gold worker
    Antonio Maldonado, sword maker
    Juan de Guadalajara, drummer

Twenty-eight *labradores* and *hortelanos* (farmers and vegetable gardeners) and fifty peons (unskilled laborers) were also aboard. Also destined for the colony were sixty-six *ballesteros* (crossbowmen), for a total of about 245 participants in the third voyage.

Fourth Voyage

On September 3, 1501, Nicolás de Ovando was named by the sovereigns as governor and chief justice of the Indies except for those portions of the mainland under the jurisdiction of Vicente Yáñez Pinzón and Alonso de Ojeda. On February 13, 1502, Ovando sailed from Cádiz with a magnificent fleet of thirty ships carrying twenty-five hundred crewmen, colonists, and soldiers.

At this juncture, Columbus, who had been stripped of nearly all his titles and privileges but still retained his designation as Admiral of the Ocean Sea, proposed to the sovereigns an additional voyage of discovery in the as-yet-unexplored western Caribbean in another attempt to find the long-sought strait to the Indian Ocean. The sovereigns, who particularly wanted to have such a strait discovered, were quick to approve his proposal. Four caravels were provided for this voyage, including *La Capitana*, the flagship.

La Capitana
    Christopher Columbus, Admiral of the Ocean Sea
    Diego Tristán, captain (died at Veragua and replaced by Diego Méndez)
    Ambrosio Sánchez, master
    Juan Sánchez, chief pilot
    Antón Donato, boatswain
    Bartolomé Colón, the Admiral's elder brother
    Fernando Colón, the Admiral's son and biographer
    Pedro Fernández Coronel, gentleman volunteer
    Francisco Ruíz, gentleman volunteer
    Alonso de Camora, gentleman volunteer
    Guillermo Ginovés, from Genoa, gentleman volunteer
    Maestre Bernal, physician and gentleman volunteer
    Martín de Arriera, cooper
    Domingo Viscaíno, caulker (died April 6, 1503)
    Diego Francés, carpenter

Juan Barba, gunner (died May 20, 1504)
Mateo, gunner (died April 6, 1503)
Juan de Cuéllar, trumpeter
Gonzalo de Salazar, trumpeter
Martín Dati, able seaman (remained in La Española)
Bartolomé García, able seaman (died May 28, 1503)
Pedro Rodríguez, able seaman (died April 6, 1503)
Juan Rodríguez, able seaman (remained in La Española)
Alonso de Almagro, able seaman (remained in La Española)
Pedro de Toledo, able seaman
Pedro de Mayo, able seaman
Juan Gómez, able seaman
Diego Roldán, able seaman
Juan Gallego, able seaman
Juan de Valencia, able seaman (died January 15, 1504)
Gonzalo Rodríguez, able seaman (died April 4, 1503)
Tristán Pérez Chinchorrero, able seaman
Rodrigo Vergayo, able seaman (remained in La Española)
Diego Portogalete, ship's boy (died January 4, 1503)
Martín Juan, ship's boy (remained in La Española)
Donís de Galve, ship's boy
Juan de Zumados, ship's boy (died April 28, 1503)
Francisco de Estrada, ship's boy
Antón Chavarín, ship's boy
Alonso, ship's boy (died April 6, 1503)
Grigorio Sollo, ship's boy (died June 27, 1504)
Diego el Negro, ship's boy
Pedro Sánchez, ship's boy
Francisco Sánchez, ship's boy
Francisco de Morón, ship's boy
Juan de Murcia, ship's boy
Grigorio Ginovés, ship's boy
Ferrando Dávila, ship's boy
Alonso de León, ship's boy
Juan de Miranda, ship's boy
Juan Garrido, ship's boy (died February 27, 1504)
Baltasar Daragón, ship's boy

Santiago de Palos
Francisco de Porras, captain and chief mutineer
Diego de Porras, chief auditor of the fleet and mutineer
Francisco Bermúdez, master
Pedro Gómez, boatswain
Francisco de Farias, gentleman volunteer
Diego Méndez, gentleman volunteer and hero of rescue mission
Pedro Gentil, gentleman volunteer
Andrea Ginovés, gentleman volunteer
Juan Jácome, gentleman volunteer
Batista Ginovés, gentleman volunteer
Bartolomé de Milán, gunner
Juan de Noya, cooper

Domingo de Arana, caulker (died April 6, 1503)
Machín, carpenter
Rodrigo Ximón, able seaman
Francisco Domingo, able seaman (died February 4, 1503)
Juan de Quijo, able seaman
Juan Rodríguez, able seaman (died April 6, 1503)
Juan de la Feria, able seaman
Juan Camacho, able seaman
Juan Grande, able seaman
Juan Reynaltes, able seaman (died April 6, 1503)
Diego Gómez, able seaman
Diego Martín, able seaman
Alonso Martín, able seaman
Gonzalo Ramírez, ship's boy
Juan Baudrojín, ship's boy (died October 23, 1503)
Diego Ximón, ship's boy
Apricio, ship's boy
Donís, ship's boy (died June 1, 1503)
Alonso Escarramán, ship's boy (died January 23, 1504)
Francisco Márquez, ship's boy
Juan de Moguer, ship's boy
Alonso de Cea, ship's boy
Pedro de Villatoro, ship's boy
Ramiro Ramírez, ship's boy
Francisco Dávila, ship's boy
Diego de Mendoza, ship's boy
Diego Cataño, ship's boy

Gallego
Pedro de Terreros, captain (died May 29, 1504)
Juan Quintero de Algruta, master
Alonso Ramón, boatswain
Gonzalo Camacho, gentleman volunteer
Rui Ferrandes, able seaman
Luis Ferrandes, able seaman
Gonzalo García, able seaman
Pedro Mateos, able seaman
Julián Martín, able seaman (died April 6, 1503)
Diego Cabezudo, able seaman
Diego Barranco, able seaman
Diego Delgado, able seaman
Rodrigo Álvares, able seaman
Pedro de Flandes, ship's boy
Bartolomé Ramírez, ship's boy (died April 6, 1503)
Antón Quintero, ship's boy
Bartolomé Dalza, ship's boy
Gonzalo Flamenco, ship's boy
Pedro Barranco, ship's boy
Juan Galdil, ship's boy (died September 9, 1504)
Alonso Penac, ship's boy
Esteban Mateos, cabin boy
Diego de Santander, ship's boy
García Polanco, ship's boy
Juan García, ship's boy

Francisco de Medina, ship's boy (jumped ship in La
Española)

Juan de San Martín, ship's boy

Vizcaíno

Bartolomeo Fieschi, from Genoa, captain

Juan Pérez, master (died October 7, 1503)

Martín de Fuenterrabía, boatswain (died September 17,
1502)

Alejandre, friar, missionary

Juan Pasan, Genoese, gentleman volunteer

Francisco de Córdoba, gentleman volunteer

Marco Surjano, from Genoa, gentleman volunteer (died
September 11, 1504)

Pedro de Ledesma, able seaman and mutineer

Juan Ferro, able seaman

Juan Moreno, able seaman

San Juan, able seaman

Gonzalo Díaz, able seaman

Gonzalo Gallego, able seaman (jumped ship in La
Española)

Alonso de la Calle, able seaman (died May 23, 1503)

Lope de Pego, able seaman

Miguel de Lariaga, ship's boy (died September 17, 1502)

Andrés de Sevilla, ship's boy

Luis de Vargas, ship's boy

Batista Ginovés, ship's boy

Francisco de Levante, ship's boy

Pedro de Montesel, ship's boy

Rodrigo de Escobar, ship's boy

Domingo Narbasta, ship's boy (died March 26, 1504)

Pasqual de Ausurraga, ship's boy

Cheneco, cabin boy

WILLIAM LEMOS

SIGNATURE. The curious form Columbus adopted for signing his name after his return from his first voyage to the New World has been the subject of considerable conjecture among scholars. The earliest surviving example of Columbus's signature appears in a letter of April 1493 addressed to the Catholic monarchs, and it is found thereafter in almost all his surviving autograph documents. Between forty-five and fifty of these signatures have been preserved, each having the same pyramid of letters arranged in exactly the same way. The signature appears as follows:

.S.
.S. A .S.
X M Y
Xpo FERENS

The letters above the signature are considered to be a pious ejaculation, and it has been suggested that it can be

read beginning with the uppermost letter, "I am the servant of the Most Exalted Savior Xhristus Maria Yosephus."

The final line of the signature, *Xpo Ferens*, is simply a Greek-Latin form of "Christopher." The first half of the signature, *Xpo* (for "Christo"), is derived from the Greek and the second half, *Ferens*, is Latin. Instead of the Latin "Christophorus" or the Italian "Cristoforo" for his given name, Columbus adopted the Greek-Latin form "Christoferens," assumed to signify his role as the bearer of the Christian religion to the pagan peoples in the lands he discovered. It is to be noted that in his map of the West Indies in 1500 Juan de la Cosa portrayed Columbus under the symbol of Saint Christopher bearing Christ over the waters.

This form of signature reflects to some degree the religious and social atmosphere of Roman Catholic countries during the fifteenth century and is an example of a practice not unusual in Spain. It was customary to

SIGNATURE OF COLUMBUS. On a letter to his son Diego in which he mentions a meeting with Amerigo Vespucci.

ARCHIVO GENERAL DE INDIAS, SEVILLE

accompany one's signature with some words of religious purport, often to identify the writer as a Christian in a country in which Jews and Muslims were proscribed and persecuted.

In his biography of his father, Fernando Colón stated that when his father "had to write anything, he would not try the pen without first writing these words, *Jesus cum Maria sit nobis in via.*" Columbus begins his Book of Prophecies with the same words.

At the time that Columbus first began using the device, he had achieved the height of his power and fame, and he undoubtedly wished to embody his seal with the importance of his newly acquired nobility. He was determined, furthermore, to extend the range of his discoveries and privileges to acquire the right to create a viceregal dynasty with virtually sovereign power over a part of the earth that promised potentially great wealth.

In the act of primogeniture Columbus prepared five years later on February 22, 1498, he established that *las armas*—his seal—should be adopted as the standard family coat of arms and that his heirs should have the right to seal documents with his arms and to sign with the monogram he himself had devised, although only after the right of primogeniture had been acquired. The monogram was to be followed by the signature "El Almirante," suggesting that he considered that the device and signature represented dignity, position, and inheritance handed down by himself as the founder of the house to his legitimate successors.

Columbus attached great importance to his signature, and in his entail he instructed his heirs to continue "to sign with my signature which I now employ which is an X with an S over it and an M with a Roman A over it and over that an S and then a Greek Y with an S over it, preserving the relation of the lines and points." These instructions were not followed by the heirs, however. Columbus never revealed their meaning, which is why they have aroused so much speculation.

The signature reveals much of Columbus's peculiar character. He considered himself mysteriously elected and set apart to achieve certain great purposes, as strongly reflected in the formality and solemnity with which he approached all his concerns. Historians attempting to solve the puzzle of the monogram have worked on the assumption that Columbus was deeply religious, accustomed to beginning his writings with *Jesus cum Maria sit nobis in via*, as his son reported, and that he intended the monogram to convey a strictly religious meaning. The puzzle becomes of particular interest in relation to the various claims that Columbus was a Jew, a Spaniard, or a Freemason.

At least eight possible meanings of the initials have been proposed. The third line is probably an invocation to Christ, Mary, and Joseph (*Christe, Maria, Yoseph*). Columbus sometimes confused the Greek Y with the Greek I that begins the names of Jesus and Joseph. The letters have therefore been variously interpreted as *Xhristus, Maria, Yosephus* or *Yesus, Maria, Yosephus.*

The four letters in the first two lines lend themselves to many combinations of which the simplest and most reasonable appears to be:

Servus
Sum Altissimi Salvatoris
(Servant I am
of the Most Exalted Savior)

It has also been suggested that Columbus may have intended the combination of letters to have a mystical meaning, in which case the significance could be established by interpreting it thus:

Yesu, Maria, Yoseph
Sanctus, Sanctus, Sanctus
(Jesus, Mary, Joseph
Holy, Holy, Holy)

Two other interpretations that have been considered are the following:

Sit Sibi Semper Antecedente
Christus Maria Yosephus
(May they always go before him
Christ, Mary, Joseph)

Supplex Servus Altissimi Salvatoris
Iesu Maria Yosephus
(Suppliant servant of the Most High Savior
Jesus, Mary, Joseph)

In the Castilian dialect in that period the letters *I, J,* and *Y* were interchangeable, and the name of the queen was often spelled "Ysabel." Some have substituted "Ysabel" for "Yosephus," thus:

Servidor (de) Sus Altezas Sacras
Jesu Maria Jsabel
(Servant of Their Sacred Highnesses
Jesus, Mary, Isabel)

Some historians claim to have detected in Columbus's signature a potential reference to his long-held plan to mount crusades against the Muslims and to achieve the liberation of the Holy Sepulcher, which can be rendered in either one of two forms as follows:

Sarraceno Subjuget Avertat Submovent
Christus Maria Iosephus
(May the Saracens be subjugated,
turned away and removed by
Christ, Mary, and Joseph)

Salva Sanctum Altissimum Sepulcrum
Christus Maria Iosephus
(Save the most high Holy Sepulcher
Christ, Mary, and Joseph)

Still others have concluded that the signature has no mystical import at all but in an abbreviated form constitutes merely the solemn subscription of Columbus. The signature would be divided into two groups of letters, the first group of letters in the top two lines

A
X M Y

have been interpreted to signify

Christóbal Almirante Mayor [de las] Indias
Christus Maria Yosephus [or Ysabel]
(Christopher First Admiral of the Indies
Jesus, Mary, Joseph [or Isabel])

and it has been suggested that the remaining three letters

.S.
.S. .S.

may have been intended to mean

Sub. Scrip. Si.
(I have signed my name below this.)

In other of Columbus's writings, the last line of the signature sometimes varied, occasionally reading *el Almirante* ("the Admiral"), and on a few documents he used the word *Virey* ("the Viceroy"). To one *Virey* signature in the Veragua manuscripts in the Archivo General de Indias, Columbus added in lowercase letters the words *general a las yndias* above a long tail of the final letter *Y*. Another signature without this addition, which is reproduced in the duchess of Berwick y Alba's *Autógrafos de Colón*, is accompanied by a unique impression of Columbus's seal that appears to have the same monogram featured over a globe.

[See also *Coat of Arms*.]

BIBLIOGRAPHY

Colón, Fernando. *Historie di Cristoforo Colombo*. 2 vols. Milan, 1930, 2:373–378.
Streicher, F. "Die Kolumbus-Originale. Eine paläographische Studie." In vol. 1 of *Spanische Forschungen der Görresgesellschaft*. Münster, 1928.
Streicher, F. "El monogramma de las cartas de Colón." *Investigacion y progreso* (Madrid) 3, no. 6 (1929).
Thacher, J. B. *Christopher Columbus: His Life, His Work, His Remains*. 3 vols. New York, 1903, 3: 455–457.

SILVIO A. BEDINI

SLAVERY. The incidence of slavery in Europe declined after the fall of the Roman Empire and its character changed, but the institution was never threatened with extinction. In rural areas it was transformed into serfdom or at least a dependent peasantry, but in the cities slaves continued in domestic and personal service. Slavery became vital in agriculture once more only with the development of sugar plantations in the eastern Mediterranean in the aftermath of the early Crusades. Throughout the Middle Ages many parts of Europe were a ready source of slaves for the more prosperous non-Christian societies of the Mediterranean. For centuries, indeed, the Germanic peoples and Slavs were to the Middle East and North Africa what Africans would become to the Americas. Primary products and slaves were the only commodities in which Europe could interest its more sophisticated southern and eastern trading partners.

Iberia was both a battleground and a trading nexus for this north-west/south-east dichotomy. Almost all the invaders and external institutional influences that affected the Iberian Peninsula in the centuries before the Columbian expansion practiced or countenanced slavery. Romans, Visigoths, and Arabs, as well as the Christian and Muslim faiths, regarded enslavement as a normal part of any social system. Slavery thus existed continuously in Spain, and indeed in most of the rest of the world, from pre-Christian to early modern times.

Slaves always composed a minority in pre-Columbian Iberia; they made up probably less than 10 percent of the population. As elsewhere in the Mediterranean basin, slavery in both Christian and Islamic Spain was primarily an urban and domestic phenomenon, and recognition of the institution was embedded in Iberian law. The Christian advance in Iberia coincided with a burgeoning interest in and application of Roman law throughout western Europe, and Roman law provided the code for the operation of a slave system. The Castilian code from the mid-thirteenth century, known as the *Siete partidas*, is an example of this influence. The only religious constraint on the institution—not always effective before the late Middle Ages—was that Christians and Muslims not enslave people of their own faith. The political constraint was that rulers did not countenance enslavement of their own subjects.

The Muslim presence and subsequent reconquest reinforced slavery in the Iberian Peninsula. In the early Middle Ages Spain was a major point of exchange in the trade of European slaves and primary products for manufactured and luxury products from the Far East. In addition, during the long wars of reconquest, enslavement of captives reinforced the institution of slavery on both sides of the religious divide. Slaves were often captured as hostages, and organizations such as the Mercedarian Order were dedicated to the redemption of captives held by non-Christians.

The prevalence of war and raids as a source of slaves obscures the fact that the Christian kingdoms in medieval

Spain—Portugal, Castile, and Aragón —could not usually afford to buy slaves through international commercial channels. It was Islamic Iberia that was more likely to purchase slaves from outside the peninsula. Slavery was associated with prosperity and commercial exchange rather than poverty and backwardness. Indeed, as David B. Davis has pointed out, the institution has flourished most in societies recognized as being at the forefront of social, cultural, and economic advance. The shrinking of the slaving frontier within the Iberian Peninsula (with the reconquest of the Muslim south) coincided with expansion of the European economy and the victories of the Ottoman Turks in the eastern Mediterranean—the latter closing off a major source of slaves in the late Middle Ages. It also coincided with the development of the technical expertise needed to conduct long-distance overseas exploration, commerce, and military forays. Hence, just as the Iberian ability to purchase slaves increased, Africa replaced the Black Sea regions as the major source of slaves. The long Iberian historical experience of slavery, an accommodating legal system, and the preexistence of a small trans-Saharan trade ensured a smooth transition from one provenance zone to another.

In the century and a half after 1441 the Portuguese carried perhaps over fifty thousand African slaves to Europe. Several thousand more of the Guanche peoples of the Canary Islands and some aboriginal Americans in the early days of the Spanish conquest of the New World experienced a similar fate. The vast majority went to Portugal and Spain. In both countries two systems of slavery existed side by side: Muslims were the victims in one and Africans in the other, with treatment of the Muslims probably the more severe of the two. In no regions in either country did slaves form a majority, and the pattern of holdings, as before, was predominantly urban. African slaves made up 10 percent of the population of Lisbon in the mid-sixteenth century, for example. In Seville—the largest city in the peninsula—slaves composed a slightly smaller proportion overall, with about half of them of African origin. In Valencia, closer to the Mediterranean and more recently Muslim, there were fewer slaves overall and a smaller proportion of them were Africans. Muslims were enslaved from within the kingdom through judicial procedure as well as from without through raids, even after the long war of reconquest had finished.

By the early sixteenth century, not only were more slaves African, but they also worked in a wider range of occupations than had been usual in medieval times. The Portuguese, in a pattern that anticipated that of Brazil down to the mid-nineteenth century, used slaves in all activities, including some that required skills. They also used more slaves in agriculture than in earlier times, particularly south of the Tagus, but not on the type of plantation that was to become the norm in the Americas. In Spain, or at least in the cities of Seville and Valencia (for which we have the best records), domestic service continued to predominate.

It is probable that the Portuguese used some slaves in sugar production in the Algarve of southern Portugal. In the late Middle Ages, sugar cultivation spread to other parts of the peninsula from Islamic Spain, where it had long been cultivated (in Córdoba and Toledo in particular). By the early fifteenth century, a major expansion in sugar production was underway in Valencia and the Algarve just as production in the eastern Mediterranean—the major source of sugar in medieval Europe — began to decline. Spain and Portugal had thus become steps in the westward march of sugar cultivation that began in Southeast Asia in the pre-Christian era and was to reach the Pacific coastal regions of the New World some two millennia later. A rising European demand for sugar, German finance, Genoese entrepreneurship, and Iberian land (though not at this stage extensive use of African labor) composed a mix, albeit on a small scale, that was to be repeated in first the Atlantic islands and then the Americas. In the broader context it should be noted that Iberian expansion was part of a general European colonization movement to the east and northwest as well as to the Caribbean and South America, and that an element of coercion—whether indentured labor, serfdom (in eastern Europe), or slavery—was common to all.

As the two Iberian states expanded, slavery increasingly assumed much greater importance as a source of labor. Apart from the links between slavery and empire alluded to above, the regions into which the Portuguese and Spanish moved had high land-to-labor ratios, a condition historically associated with coerced labor. Given the long experience of Iberians with slavery, it is not surprising that the new settlements and conquests that were part of Iberian expansion generated genuine slave societies in that they relied on slave labor for the production of the commodities that sustained them.

Despite the continuities, however, the slavery that developed in the Iberian Atlantic settlements was fundamentally different from the institution that went under the same name in medieval Europe, Islamic states, and indigenous societies in Africa and the Americas. In these older societies the slave class lacked racial distinctiveness, and more important, slaves were usually migrants or the immediate descendants of migrants whose status might be regarded as a step toward fuller social integration over a generation or two. In the New World, slavery was no longer an institution for the minority. Eunuchs may have been much less common, but manumission or social integration of any kind was an extremely remote possibility for slaves or their descendants. In the New World the bundle of rights over others was redefined in such a way as to give much more unrestricted power to the master. Slavery may have already existed in Africa and the Americas before Europeans arrived, but the rights that the African slave owner sold to the European trader were altogether less absolute than what the latter in turn sold to the plantation owner in the Americas.

The initial Iberian movement into the Atlantic was to the offshore islands of the Canaries, Madeira, Cape Verde, the Azores, and São Tomé and Princípe in the Bight of Biafra. Only the first of these was inhabited and, after a dispute with Portugal settled in the Treaty of Alcáçovas in 1479, it was taken over by Castilians. The rest were uninhabited before being settled by the Portuguese. First European contact with the islands dates from the mid-fourteenth century, but settlement of Madeira began only in the second quarter of the following century. Significantly, the clearing and irrigation of the largest and most mountainous of the Madeiran islands was carried out by slaves captured in the Canary Islands. Although the early crops were cereals rather than sugar, large initial land grants and an aggressive group of elite settlers ensured that sugar would be introduced well before the mid-fifteenth century. By the end of the century, perhaps a fifth of the population of fifteen thousand was slave. Initially the slaves were Guanches and Muslims from Iberia, but increasingly they were of African origin. For a short time the island was the largest single source of cane sugar consumed in Europe. Sugar also did well in the Canaries, the extinction of whose indigenous peoples led to further reliance on African labor. Similar efforts in the drier Azores and Cape Verde islands were less successful. The last port of call in the Old World in the westward march of sugar was São Tomé in the Bight of Biafra. Prevailing winds and currents made the island relatively easy for sailing ships to reach and, more important, leave, and the soil, precipitation, and ready access to African labor ensured an important sugar sector until Brazilian competition buried the Old World industry in the second half of the sixteenth century. The Portuguese sold perhaps twenty-five thousand African slaves to the Atlantic islands—most to Madeira and the Canaries—and almost four times as many to São Tomé.

Unlike most of the Atlantic islands, the Americas to which the Portuguese and Spanish sailed were not empty lands. The widespread adoption and modification of slavery in the New World was shaped not just by the drive to produce an exportable staple and by the cultural baggage that the Iberians brought with them. It was also influenced by the fact that slavery had long existed in the pre-Columbian Americas. A wide range of aboriginal societies, from the complex Aztec to the less developed Tupinambá in what became Brazil, held slaves. These were often war captives spared from immediate death, though

the risk of eventually being killed and eaten in the case of the Tupinambás or used for live sacrifice in the Aztec empire was very high. Female war captives became wives who rarely lost their slave status but whose children could become full members of the host society, as, for example, among the Caribs. Most slaves in the more complex societies of Central America were nevertheless generated internally through judicial process, indebtedness, or deprivation and the resulting voluntary assumption of slave status. It is likely that the slave class of the Aztec empire was growing at the time of the first Spanish contact.

Nevertheless, no Indian peoples can be said to have created a slave society in the sense of that in ancient Rome or in the Caribbean in the eighteenth century. The economic rationale for slavery among Indian groups was probably less important than motives of prestige, religion (the requirements of ritual), or sexual gratification. Most slaves were domestics, although among the Aztecs, transportation, in the absence of vehicles and horses, absorbed many of them. Slaves were also employed in the tilling of crops, including cacao in an anticipation of the post-Columbian situation, but this activity was neither labor-intensive nor dominant in the catalog of slave uses. Among the Aztecs, slave status, at least for slaves of internal origin, was likely to be temporary. Redemption by self or family, manumission on the death of the slave-owner, and the rendition of a valuable service provided routes to full integration into the community. Internal markets in slaves were not well developed. As in the medieval Mediterranean region, racial distinctiveness was not coterminous with slavery, although Europeans and Africans served as slaves to aboriginal groups in the post-Columbus era. Slaves could marry nonslaves, own property, and exercise other legal rights. In its largely noneconomic, nonracial, and temporary nature, aboriginal slavery differed sharply from the post-Columbian institution that replaced it, especially in the Dutch, English, and French colonies. Yet the Spanish in particular did take over existing aboriginal structures for the exploitation of labor. Among these were tribute labor and slavery. Indeed, the Spanish were most successful at extracting labor from native Americans where such structures were most highly developed in pre-Columbian societies.

Epidemiology was crucial to the creation of the European version of New World slavery. The Americas were a relatively isolated part of the globe compared to the Eurasian and African continents in the sense that flora, fauna, and microorganisms, as well as human societies, had evolved separately for millennia by the time the Iberians arrived. Their coming initiated a merging of two distinct epidemiological zones in the process of which the native population of the Americas was decimated and in some cases—for example, the Arawaks—exterminated. Labor shortages, owing as much to smallpox and measles as to European exploitation, developed within a few years of the initial contact. Even without the epidemiological factor Spanish and Portuguese restrictions on enslavement of native Americans in response to the advocacy of Bartolomé de las Casas, among others, slowed the enslavement and vigorous slave trade of aboriginals in the first phase of Iberian settlement. Moreover, plantation and mine owners in Spanish America and Brazil regarded Indian labor as far less productive than African and European. African slaves throughout the Iberian Americas sold for three or more times as much as their aboriginal counterparts. Systems for exploiting the forced labor of Indians, such as encomienda and repartimiento (and mita labor in Peru), were not as successful as African slavery or even wage labor in those sectors producing commodities for world markets.

If Iberians preferred Africans to Indians, the question remains, why Africans rather than Europeans, either slave or free? One explanation is that as Europeans spread they used settlement methods that had already proved useful closer to home. In northern Europe new lands typically were settled with villages and peasant labor drawn from the home society, whereas in the Mediterranean region colonizers tended to meet labor needs in new areas with alien slaves. Northern Europe had more surplus population than any of the Iberian regions in the later Middle Ages. Thus Barbados in its pre-sugar phase and the Chesapeake plantation colonies originally used white labor, albeit indentured rather than free. The Portuguese and Spanish, following the Mediterranean tradition, used slave labor from the start. A far greater proportion of the English population immigrated to the New World in the first century of English settlement than set out across the Atlantic from Spain in the sixteenth century. Epidemiology had some role in the process. Mortality in the Americas was very high for both Europeans and Africans in the early days of settlement. Whites and blacks died at similar rates on both slave ships and plantations before the nineteenth century. On the other hand, Africans had no choice, whereas Europeans, even indentured servants, could

AFRICAN SLAVES IN THE AMERICAS. Nicolás de Ovando, governor of La Española, imported Africans to work the gold mines. Engraving from Théodor de Bry's *Americae*. Frankfurt, 1594.

NATIONAL MARITIME MUSEUM, GREENWICH

usually choose not to go to a nonplantation region. The basic fact governing nearly four centuries of the slave trade to the New World was that everyone who had a choice avoided gang labor on sugar plantations and in mines.

As we might expect from the discussion so far, the early Iberian slave trade was multilateral and diffuse compared to the massive regularity of the east-west population shift of the eighteenth and nineteenth centuries. The Spanish carried American aborigines in the opposite direction, to Seville before 1500, and shortly thereafter they brought Africans from Spain to the Americas. Indeed, for a quarter of a century, all black slaves in Spanish America came from Spain, not from Africa, partly because the Treaty of Tordesillas excluded the Spanish from the African coast. The Portuguese, as we have seen, took Guanches from the Canaries to Madeira. Before initiating the transatlantic business, they shipped large numbers of Africans from Upper Guinea and what became Angola to yet another part of Africa, the Gold Coast, and exchanged them for a range of African commodities desired in Europe. On the other side of the Atlantic, over a quarter of a million aborigines from southern Brazil endured an ocean voyage up the coast as long and as miserable as any trip across the southern Atlantic before reaching the early sugar plantations in Pernambuco in northeast Brazil. The intra-Caribbean trade in Caribs also preceded the substantial shipment of slaves directly from Africa. Iberians thus organized a massive reshuffling of peoples within the New World prior to 1575 before concentrating on the traffic from Africa to the Americas.

<small>INDIANS BEING TRANSPORTED TO SPAIN AS SLAVES.   Engraving from Théodor de Bry's *Americae*, Frankfurt, 1594.</small>

By the last quarter of the sixteenth century, the pattern for the next three centuries was in place. By far the largest stream of peoples moving to the New World were African until the mid-nineteenth century. Down to 1625, the "New World" for this group meant Spanish America and Brazil. The major carrier—indeed, the only carrier direct from Africa at this stage—was Portugal, in whose ships over 400,000 people left the continent for the Americas. Those who reached continental Spanish America, usually Panama, Veracruz, or Cartagena in present-day Colombia, faced further long land or sea journeys before being set to work. The mainland areas of New Spain and New Granada received more Africans than did the Caribbean islands at this stage. The common impulse behind all this movement—on both sides of the Atlantic as well as across it—was the drive to obtain the labor necessary to the production of a commodity for world markets. As in pre-Columbian days, slavery continued to be associated with conventional concepts of progress, including economic prosperity, but now for the first time it was tied to the production of an export staple.

This does not mean that all slaves or even a majority in all regions were employed in sugar production and mining. The concentration of slaves in urban and domestic environments in both Portugal and Spain was repeated in the Americas. This pattern, however, was supplemented and eventually overwhelmed by the Mediterranean and Atlantic islands pattern of slaves being employed in agriculture and mining. They were rather more dominant in sugar production than in mining, where slavery was used in conjunction with various forms of commandeered aboriginal labor. Slaves were also to be found in cacao production and later the small Peruvian textile industry. Much of the output was exported. Small-scale sugar production began on La Española within twenty years of the Columbian landfall. It spread to other Caribbean islands, such as Puerto Rico, Cuba, and Jamaica, and to Mexico and Peru before the end of the sixteenth century. But the industry did not at this point make a sustained impact on the world market; rather, it concentrated on production for local consumption once the massive sugar complex of northeastern Brazil was established in the last quarter of the sixteenth century. It was this region, closest to Africa and with the lowest transportation costs for labor, that became in many ways the most thoroughgoing slave society in the New World. Although slaves dominated the export sector, there was scarcely an occupation in the economy that did not have a slave component.

Slavery as enforced by Iberians and then imitated by the French and English in the Americas was thus radically different from the institution that had existed before in Europe, Africa, or the Americas. It had become more racially exclusive, less a transitional status in the intergenerational sense, and very much oriented to a world commodity market, especially later under the French and the English. This easy transformation, however, could not have taken place without the institutional foundations in Iberia, the rest of Europe, and to a lesser extent among the aboriginal peoples of the Americas.

[See also Encomienda; Pacification, Conquest, and Genocide.]

BIBLIOGRAPHY

Davis, David B. Slavery and Human Progress. New York, 1984.

Garcia, Carlos Bosch. La esclavitud prehispanica entre los Aztecas. Mexico City, 1944.

Greenfield, Sidney M. "Plantations, Sugar Cane and Slavery." Historical Reflections 6 (1979): 85–119.

Phillips, William D. Slavery from Roman Times to the Early Transatlantic Trade. Minneapolis, 1985.

Russell-Wood, A. J. R. "Iberian Expansion and the Issue of Black Slavery: Changing Portuguese Attitudes, 1440–1770." American Historical Review 83 (1978): 1–28.

Saunders, A. C. de C. M. A Social History of Black Slaves and Freedmen in Portugal, 1441–1555. Cambridge, 1982.

Silva, Alfonso Franco. La esclavitud en Sevilla y su tierra a fines de la edad media. Seville, 1979.

Steward, Julian H., ed. Handbook of South American Indians. 3 vols. Washington, D.C., 1948.

Verlinden, Charles. Péninsule ibérique–France. Vol. 1 of L'esclavage dans l'Europe médiévale. Bruges, 1955.

Vogt, John L. "The Lisbon Slave House and the African Trade, 1486–1521." Proceedings of the American Philosophical Society 117 (1973): 1–16.

DAVID ELTIS

SOCIAL AND ECONOMIC INSTITUTIONS. The social and economic institutions of late medieval Europe grew out of the confluence of agricultural productivity, burgeoning towns, and long-distance trade. Agricultural production still consumed as much as 90 percent of human labor, and all social and economic organization depended upon control of the primary sector of food production. As medieval towns became overlords of the agrarian domain, agricultural surpluses sustained the urban division of labor that provided the catalyst for change. The increasing number of those communes newly founded after the year 1000 in Italy and northern Europe fueled their growth by exchanging goods in two long-distance economic systems. Both a southern and a northern trading circuit maintained a core of numerous and relatively large towns in Italy and Flanders through domination of distant hinterlands. Columbus's discovery of America in 1492 and Vasco da Gama's circumnavigation of Africa to establish a sea route to Asia in 1498 fit into the continuous pattern of trade, exploration, and exploitation that late medieval social and economic institutions had fostered.

The Mediterranean Sea delimited a medieval trading network first focused in the Islamic Middle East by the eighth century. In the ninth and tenth centuries, four Italian maritime communes without substantial agricultural hinterlands—Genoa, Pisa, Amalfi, and Venice—entered the system. In the course of the thirteenth century, a northern Italian commercial, banking, and industrial complex centered in Genoa, Milan, Florence, and Venice took over the system. The Italian cities reaped the profits from price differentials in the long-distance trade from the Near East home to Italy and inland to France and Germany. They also drew raw material goods from around the Mediterranean for industrial transformation and reexport. Luxury goods such as spices, silk, fine woolen cloth, leather, furs, and glass were the most important products, but ordinary bulky cargoes of salt, wine, fish, cheese, butter, oil, cotton, flax, raw wool, common dyes, nonprecious metals, and timber bolstered the carrying trade. Venice emerged as the victor in the eastern Mediterranean with an overseas empire that stretched from the Italian mainland, the Dalmatian coast, and Corfu to Crete, Cyprus, and Constantinople. Genoa pioneered westward into the Atlantic, and in 1293 a joint Castilian-Genoese fleet decisively defeated a Muslim navy to open the way to regular ties with England and Flanders. Two Genoese brothers, Ugolino and Vadino Vivaldi, even attempted an unsuccessful Atlantic voyage to the Indies in 1291.

The Germans themselves spearheaded the somewhat later development of the northern trading network, the Hanseatic League. Lübeck merchants took the lead from the mid-twelfth century, and in 1356 the Hansa became a formal association of towns rather than one only of merchants. As many as one hundred towns subscribed to the Hansa at its height as it oversaw trade in northwest Europe, the North and Baltic seas from Bruges, London, Hamburg, and Lübeck to Bergen and Novgorod. Flanders in the Low Countries, with access to the rich Rhineland, became its urbanized center of industrial production and transshipment.

A long wave of rising and declining economic activity had begun in Europe with the reestablishment of towns in the eleventh and twelfth centuries and crashed in the catastrophic outbreak of bubonic plague in 1348. Europe's internal restructuring as it came out of the century-long social and economic crisis between 1350 and 1450 set the tone for the next economic cycle that began in the third quarter of the fifteenth century. During that century of reorganization after the plague, external changes in international trade also challenged the Italian monopoly of key markets. The fourteenth-century decline of the Mongol Empire in Central Asia, which closed the land routes to Asia, adversely affected Genoese trade through her Black Sea ports. The growing power of the Ottoman Turks, who conquered Constantinople in 1453, further threatened eastern Mediterranean trade, although the Ottomans did not cut off the Venetian access to the southern route to Asia through the Red Sea until 1527. Spurred by the desire to exploit new agricultural hinterlands, to circumvent the Italian city-states' Levant trade monopoly, and to find another route to the Indies to outflank hostile Islamic middlemen, newly amalgamated European monarchical states competed among themselves to sponsor exploratory economic ventures. Fifteenth-century European expansion to Africa, Asia, and America thus capped a medieval urban and commercial revolution and stimulated the development of a single Atlantic Ocean–focused economy conflated from the two earlier trading systems.

Population Size. An important variable that affects both the structure of demand and the supply of labor, population size is a baseline indicator to begin an examination of structure and change in late medieval and early modern European social and economic institutions. Although the Black Death that devastated Europe in 1348 hit a social and economic environment already weakened from overpopulation and strained resources, the immediate three-year death toll of twenty-five million out of Europe's eighty million inhabitants was staggering. Depending on the region and whether a rural or urban setting, between one-fourth to two-thirds of the population died during the pandemic. Further, the immediate crisis was compounded by the fact that the plague bacillus, which is transmitted by infected fleas on host rats, took endemic form and ravaged various places at various times for the next three centuries. In England, plague struck in thirty of the years between 1351 and 1485; in Florence, in twenty-two years between 1348 and 1500; in Paris, in twenty-two years between 1348 and 1596; in Barcelona, in seventeen years between 1457 and 1590. By 1500 with its population ranging between sixty to seventy million, Europe had not yet recovered even one-half of its 1348 plague losses.

Population recovery depended upon a net increase of births over deaths, but this was a society in which birth and death rates closely approximated each other at thirty to forty per thousand. Because of the high mortality that especially affected children (one out of four died in the first year, and one-half never saw twenty), high fertility was necessary to maintain even stable population levels. Consequently, preindustrial Europe's population structure reflected a young age distribution with one-third or more of the population under fifteen years of age.

Ironically, because the significant measure of economic growth is product per capita, not total product, Europe's high mortality worked to long-term economic advantage. Thus, the economic effects of the devastating population losses from the plague—deserted villages and abandoned marginal land, declining agricultural prices and production, the rising price of manufactured goods, an influx of rural populations to the towns, the loosening of the power of merchant guilds, the incorporation of unskilled workers, and the weakening of the traditional landed nobility vis-à-vis the towns and the new monarchical states—led to a strengthening and rebuilding of social and economic institutions. Although rural debt and sharecropping increased, rural mobility was high as the disparity between legal contracts and enforcement weakened because of the labor shortage. Similarly, in the towns, as a result of labor scarcity and the contraction of wealth into fewer hands, salaries were high, unemployment was low, and both the demand for goods and the standard of living increased. European population decline allowed for the restarting of the economy from a stronger per capita product profile.

Late medieval economic, political, and legal constraints led Europeans to adopt unique marriage patterns and reproduction strategies to control fertility and limit family size to about 4.5 to 5 individuals per household. In northern Europe, delayed age at first marriage for both men (twenty-seven to twenty-nine years) and women (twenty-five to twenty-six years), as well as a relatively high percentage of people who never married, characterized family structure in both town and countryside. The household was the chief unit of economic production with women sharing both labor responsibilities and ownership rights. In urban Italy, in contrast, women tended to marry eight to ten years younger, could expect to bear three more children, and did not share the inheritance rights or management expectations of northern European women. Italian families, even when typically maintaining separate residence, were more closely clan-linked, and these lineages played a dominant role in political, social, and economic activity. In both models, however, patriarchal family organization largely determined women and children's work, the family/household economy, and its place in the structure of market production.

The Division of Labor and Wealth. The division of labor in society extended beyond both gender and the family. In the fifteenth century, urban workers who were engaged in activities relating to food, clothing, and shelter—that is, those activities that commanded about 98 percent of private expenditures—accounted for between 55 and 65 percent of the labor force. Specialized crafts such as metalwork, woodwork, and leatherwork comprised between 15 and 20 percent of the labor market, and miscellaneous workers as much as another 20 percent. Larger towns would boast a significant number of professionals (bankers, lawyers, doctors, notaries) who might reduce the miscellaneous total by 10 percent. All in all, the structure of demand for food, textiles, and construction determined the quantity and quality of production and the need for a diversified labor force.

Merchants, who were specialists in organizing the transport and financial arrangements concomitant with both long-distance trade and the round of innumerable internal fairs and markets, acted as middlemen between producer and consumer. An important development growing out of the merchants' capital accumulation and the immediate cash needs of craftsmen-producers encouraged merchants to advance payment to producers who often fell into indebtedness and dependence upon the merchants. Such economic leverage gradually led to a kind of employer-employee relationship. Craftsmen became wage earners while merchants made managerial decisions and enjoyed the profits. These merchant-capitalists expanded their control over production by circumventing entrenched craftsmen guilds in the towns and seeking employee-producers among seasonally underemployed peasants and agricultural laborers, especially women, in what is called the "domestic," or "putting-out" system. Overseers would provide raw materials, typically fibers for spinning and weaving in textile production, to wage earners working in their own homes. The rise of a wage-earning work force along with the division of labor in society and the emergence of the strong centralized states of the new monarchies were the key fifteenth-century developments fostering the rise of capitalism.

Wealth and income distribution followed occupation. Professionals along with members of the larger textile and merchant guilds stood at the top of the urban social and economic hierarchy. Wealth was concentrated into the hands of the few: the richest 10 percent of the population controlled one-half of the wealth, the next 30 percent about one-quarter of the wealth, and the bottom 60 percent as little as 5 to 20 percent. Typically, 10 to 20 percent of the population could be classified as poor or "beggars." The extreme concentration of the wealthy at the top and the poor at the bottom of the scale emphasizes the incipient nature of middle-class society. At the same time, the sharp distinction in this fifteenth-century urban profile from that of medieval feudal society's rigidified orders (those who prayed, those who fought, and those who worked) makes it clear that the diversification of urban occupations, the immigration from the countryside, and the raising or lowering of families and individuals by fortune or disease contributed to extraordinary social mobility and economic dynamism.

The uncertainty and antagonisms wrought in the transition to the nascent capitalist economies of the late medieval towns, especially by the post-plague social and economic dislocations, often found expression in social conflict. In the town, revolts of craftsmen and skilled workers spread throughout Italy and the Low Countries. In the countryside, social and economic discontent erupted into peasant revolts in Flanders, around Paris, and in England, Bohemia, and Catalonia. Often, as in the eleven major peasant uprisings in Germany in the century before the peasant revolt of 1525, social justice identified with Christianity in a call to traditional values and simple virtues.

Christianity also pricked individual consciences. Christianity denounced the unjust profits of usury, encouraged charitable works, and called for a renunciation of worldly goods. In his 1304–1308 *Convivio*, Dante allied Christianity with stoicism in articulating the belief that the vagaries of wealth undermined philosophic and spiritual imperatives: true nobility is founded on the principle that all wealth is valueless because it fills humankind inescapably with a never-satisfied lust for new treasures and at the same time with the sad fear of losing that which has been acquired. Thomas More's satiric indictment of European society's greed in his 1516 *Utopia* called for the abolition of private property based upon the example of native American society gleaned from Amerigo Vespucci's pirated letter describing the "natural man" of the New World. At the same time, countless contrary incantations of the positive connection between civic wealth and virtue filled the air. Leonardo Bruni, the noted early fifteenth-century humanist chancellor of Florence, proclaimed the proud belief that the possessions of the rich were a precondition for the full development of the moral life. Francesco di Marco Datini, the great merchant of Prato who was purported to be the richest man in the world at his death in 1410, linked Christianity and money in his account books, which inscribed a religious formula like "In the name of God and of profit" on the first page of each volume. The uneasy tension in mercantile consciousness between rich and poor or virtue and vice, and the capitalist spirit of worldly asceticism that Max Weber associated with the so-called Protestant ethic of Calvinist culture, long preceded the Reformation; one finds its roots in the conflict between medieval Christianity and the medieval urban revolution.

Such ambivalent mentalities came with the Europeans to the New World as explorers became exploiters seeking gold and souls or slave traders buying and selling native Africans and Americans. In practice, most good intentions of Christian moralists or the reasoned judgments of the neoscholastics of the School of Salamanca were subverted by the extractive greed and paternalistic intransigence of military commanders and missionaries. The intolerant religious zeal of anti-Muslim crusades in the Reconquista and of anti-Jewish bigotry, both exemplified in 1492 by Fernando and Isabel's conquest of Granada and expulsion of the Jews, tied Spanish secular and religious jurisdictions more closely together and carried over to confrontations with native peoples in the overseas expansion.

Despite religious scruples, capital drawn from trade and finance nevertheless continued to fuel the ever-expanding medieval urban revolution. The accumulation of fixed capital that formed the infrastructure of economic life in the city and the countryside had been on the rise from the eleventh century. All fixed capital goods—water mills, windmills, and agricultural buildings such as barns; tools such as shovels, plows, and barrels; livestock for transport, labor, textiles, and meat; and ships, carts, and bridges—remained impervious to the population losses from the plague and again illustrate the importance of per capita measurement.

Organizational and Technological Innovations. Organizational know-how, likewise, facilitated market exchange. Newly developed business techniques were employed—accounting innovations such as modern dating, the introduction of Arabic numerals and double-entry bookkeeping, the check, the endorsement, insurance, commerce manuals, partnership contracts, joint stock companies, the stock exchange, and the central bank. New forms of credit and new forms of partnerships infused money and diffused the expertise of mathematics, literacy, and business entrepreneurship into social and economic institutions.

Technological innovations also contributed to the slow maturation of the medieval economy. Agricultural improvements from the seventh-century diffusion of the heavy plow, eighth-century diffusion of the three-field system, and ninth-century diffusion of the horseshoe and harness for draft animals had contributed to the increasing surpluses to precipitate the urban revolution. Distinctions in northern and southern European agriculture—southern soils limited the range of expansion of the more effective moldboard plow and sparse southern grasslands prevented the substitution of horses for oxen—had a marked effect in creating a long-term productive disadvantage in the primary sector for Mediterranean lands. In the towns, mechanical clocks, developed at the beginning of the fourteenth century, ushered in a worldview distinguishing work hours and merchant time from the seasonal and diurnal rhythms of agricultural labor and the church's agrarian calendar.

From the thirteenth through the fifteenth centuries, technological changes in shipping, navigation, and armaments made water transport more viable, economical, and dominant. Instrumental or mathematical reckoning, facilitated by the development of the magnetic compass, water clock, astrolabe, portolan or naval charts, trigonometric tables, and the sternpost rudder, allowed for greater accuracy in determining position and speed plus the reduction of idle time in winter. Improvements in hull design and shipyard division of labor like that of the Venetian Arsenal, the greatest "factory" system in preindustrial Europe, reduced shipbuilding costs and time. After 1440, the Portuguese lateen-rigged caravel, a ship with triangular sails and a narrower hull, had the ability to utilize both following and contrary winds and to maneuver safely in the open seas and in coastal waters. Finally, the "full-rigged" ship combined the Atlantic and Mediterranean technologies: nautical instruments and the carvel-built hull with a new sail configuration of three masts with a large square sail on the mainmast, a smaller square sail on the foremast, and a lateen (triangular) sail on the mizzen (aft) mast. With the adaptation of artillery, which had been developed along with gunpowder in China and transmitted across the Eurasian steppes, the revolution in military technology that had already affected land warfare and was beginning to undermine the social hierarchy of knight-dominated armies completed the powerful naval tool necessary for long-distance trade and expansion.

A similar confluence of innovations led to the printed book. Paper came to Europe in the thirteenth century from China. Water mills provided the energy to power machines to pulp rags for paper production. Printing also made its way to Europe, again from China; and the application of movable type by the mid-fifteenth century revolutionized the dissemination of information. Between 1450 and 1500, presses in twelve countries had printed millions of books in forty thousand editions. Renaissance ideas, religious reform, and scientific knowledge all spread widely and penetrated deeply into society because of printing.

Wars, Conquests, and Colonization. Not by chance, over two-thirds of fifteenth-century book production came from Italy and Germany. Not only were these two regions cornerstones of the southern and northern trading systems, but the size of their polities, government economic policy, and the devastating wars occupying England, France, and Iberia worked to German and Italian advantage in the late fifteenth century. Since capitalist enterprise arose piecemeal, the economies of scale offered by city-states and small principalities in Italy and Germany nurtured the development of the requisite commerce and industry because mercantile elites were able to play such an important role in decision making. At the same time, war disrupted France and England during the Hundred Years' War (1337–1453) and then afterward tore them apart internally in civil wars during the English War of the Roses (1455–1485) and, especially during the Burgundian wars, in the reconstruction of a French kingdom under Louis XI (1461–1483). In Iberia, similarly, twenty years of civil wars devastated Castile and Catalonia from the 1460s through the disputed succession (1475–1479) of Enrique

IV of Castile. Like famine and disease, war and politics had an important effect upon social and economic structures.

During the Italian peace between 1454 and 1494, established as a defensive alliance after the Ottoman conquest of Constantinople, the wealth of the Italian cities increased, but Italy became a tempting prize for conquest. The 1494 Italian invasions initiated a long struggle for Italy between the new monarchies of France and Spain not settled until the Battle of Pavia in 1525. South German bankers like the Fuggers of Augsburg, who based their wealth on mercantile ties to the core of the two trading systems at Venice and Antwerp and on central European mining, exerted their greatest influence between 1490 and 1525, during the Italian wars and before the Reformation. Reformation wars in Germany, religious wars in France, and the revolt of the Netherlands not only cost lives but also consumed the finances of the new Valois and Habsburg monarchies in the sixteenth century.

The political clout of the new monarchies had been built on their own manpower and resource needs. Portugal's poverty, its small population of one million, and its Atlantic-facing position pushed it first to seek agricultural resources in North Africa, the Atlantic islands, and along the West African coast. Madeira (1420), the Azores (1425), and the Cape Verde Islands (1455) were stepping-stones of conquest and colonization on the way to an African, Brazilian, and South Asian empire. Royal monopolies on gold, slaves (some 150,000 Africans between 1450 and 1500), spices, ivory, and the rights of export and reexport bolstered the strength of the Aviz dynasty, which had come to power in opposition to the old nobility in 1385. Genoese capital helped finance sugar plantations and the slave trade and promoted the sale of African pepper to compete with Asian pepper imported by the Venetians. The Portuguese traded this sugar and pepper first at Bruges and after 1488 at Antwerp.

Spain's success resulted from the marriage between the Aragonese commercial empire plied by Catalan merchants in the western Mediterranean and Castilian population, fiscal, and agricultural resources. The Catholic monarchs, Fernando and Isabel, continued previous government policy in an impoverished kingdom with eight million inhabitants unable to provision a city large enough to sustain the royal court full time for the entire year. In Castile, agricultural production was subordinated to pastoral interests because of the profits to be made from the wool trade to Flanders and Italy and the taxes to be garnered from sheep owners. The large pastoral investors drawn from the nobility and religious institutions thus allied with the Crown to inhibit native textile industries and local town growth. Spanish social organization remained rigidly hierarchical and disproportionately stratified with 2 to 3 percent of the population owning 97

percent of the land. In Aragón, the 1462–1472 civil war revealed the weakness of a kingdom in decline from erosion of its trading empire by the Genoese, from peasant uprisings against the feudal nobility, and from town cleavage between the urban patriciate and small-scale merchants and artisans. The Union of the Crowns, nevertheless, allowed Aragonese economic institutions and bureaucratic expertise to channel Castilian dynamism. Spanish merchants operated in the Medina del Campo fair, the Burgos wool monopoly, and the iron and shipping industries of Bilbao on the north coast. In the South, the Genoese maintained their dominance in New World shipping and finance from Seville through a relationship forged long before the discoveries. Despite the booming sixteenth-century Spanish economy based on New World wealth, Spanish social and economic institutions enjoyed only a transitory success. State expenditures on military ventures, price inflation, and weakening agricultural and industrial production undermined their viability. Real economic dynamism flowed to the Spanish possessions in the Low Countries.

There, Antwerp benefited from products of the old Hansa network, from the English wool staple, from both Bavarian and Genoese financial backing, and from the decline of its neighbor, Bruges. It was able to attract the products from Portuguese and Spanish expansion and become sixteenth-century Europe's most important entrepôt, growing spectacularly from 17,000 inhabitants in 1437 to 50,000 in 1500 and 100,000 in 1555. Antwerp declined only during the revolt of the Netherlands between 1572 and 1585 and gave way to Amsterdam in the seventeenth century.

Europe in 1500, at first contact with the Americas and direct maritime contact with Asia, then, was in the midst of a significant demographic and economic recovery from the previous downturn. For about the first century of the new economic cycle, growth was self-generated and self-sustained. By 1560 when New World products had begun to exert substantial impact upon the Old World, Europe had surpassed fourteenth-century population levels and growth continued until the economic slide after 1620. The period of European expansion thus ran parallel with the two-hundred-year economic cycle of 1450 to 1650. That economic cycle owed its origins to the reorganization of social and economic institutions after the dislocations of the fourteenth-century crisis. It maintained itself through the early seventeenth century on overseas extraction and exploitation, especially African gold and American silver. It faltered in the seventeenth-century collapse of financial markets, in the stalling of commerce and industry, in the political crisis of the Spanish imperial system, and in the dissolutions of the Thirty Years' War (1619–1648) that led to Dutch and English ascendance.

The economic cycle of 1450 to 1650 witnessed the ever-increasing drive of capitalist enterprise and a reorientation of the northern and southern medieval trading networks into a single world economic system with a core in northwestern Europe. The earlier progression of agricultural productivity, urban growth, labor differentiation, and long-distance trade continued to make modern Europe. European social and economic institutions, part and parcel of the new centralized states, added newly transformed technologies unknowingly derived from China (the compass, gunpowder, and printing) to their arsenal. Europeans thus imposed their social and economic institutions, as much as their mentalities, on populations and landscapes in Africa, America, and Asia as they took over old networks, established new ones, and took off toward capitalism, industrialization, and world hegemony.

[For further discussion of innovation in European culture at the time of Columbus, see *Navigation; Political Institutions; Printing; Religion,* article on *European Traditions; Science; Shipbuilding; Timetelling; Trade.* For discussion of American cultures and societies of the period, see *Agriculture; Indian America; Religion,* article on *Amerindian Traditions.*]

BIBLIOGRAPHY

General

Abu-Lughod, Janet L. *Before European Hegemony: The World System A.D. 1250–1350.* New York and Oxford, 1989.

Braudel, Fernand. *Civilization and Capitalism 15th–18th Century.* Translated by Siân Reynolds. 3 vols. New York, 1981–1984.

Braudel, Fernand. *The Mediterranean and the Mediterranean World in the Age of Philip II.* Translated by Siân Reynolds. 2 vols. 2d ed. New York, 1972–1973.

Cipolla, Carlo M. *Before the Industrial Revolution: European Society and Economy, 1000–1700.* 2d ed. New York and London, 1980.

Cipolla, Carlo M., ed. *The Fontana Economic History of Europe.* 6 vols. Vol. 1, *The Middle Ages.* Glasgow, 1972. Vol. 2, *The Sixteenth and Seventeenth Centuries.* Glasgow, 1974.

Davis, Ralph. *The Rise of the Atlantic Economies.* Ithaca, 1973.

Goldthwaite, Richard A., ed. "Recent Trends in Renaissance Studies: Economic History." *Renaissance Quarterly* 42 (Winter 1989): 760–825.

Howell, Martha C. *Women, Production, and Patriarchy in Late Medieval Cities.* Chicago, 1986.

Jones, E. L. *The European Miracle: Environments, Economies and Geopolitics in the History of Europe and Asia.* 2d ed. Cambridge, 1987.

Miskimin, Harry A. *The Economy of Early Renaissance Europe, 1300–1460.* Cambridge, 1975.

Miskimin, Harry A. *The Economy of Later Renaissance Europe, 1460–1600.* Cambridge, 1977.

Wallerstein, Immanuel. *Capitalist Agriculture and the Origins of the European World-Economy in the Sixteenth Century.* Vol. 1 of *The Modern World-System.* New York, 1974.

Wolf, Eric R. *Europe and the People without History.* Berkeley and Los Angeles, 1982.

Spain

MacKay, Angus. "Recent Literature on Spanish Economic History." *Economic History Review* 31, no. 1 (1978): 129–145.

Phillips, Carla Rahn. "Time and Duration: A Model for the Economy of Early Modern Spain." *American Historical Review* 92, no. 3 (1987): 531–562.

JOHN A. MARINO

SOLAR PHENOMENA. The sun was still considered a planet when Christopher Columbus began his voyages in the hope of reaching India by following the apparent course of the sun. The two solar phenomena important in Columbus's lifetime were the apparent circular movement of the sun and, less important, solar eclipses.

The circular movement of the sun was essential to determining latitude. Astronomers drew up tables that gave the solar declinations for each day of one year. Observers saw the position of the sun in the ecliptic and observed its meridian height. If they knew the declination, using the information in the tables, and by means of simple arithmetical calculations, they ascertained their latitude. Quadrants and astrolabes were used for these observations; cross-staffs were introduced later.

The traditional solar tables, such as Abraham Zacuto's *Almanach perpetuum coelestium motium* (Perpetual almanac of the heavenly bodies, 1496), however, did not give declinations directly or did not give them at all. In the former case, users of Zacuto's work first consulted a table that offered the "position" of the sun—in degrees, minutes, and seconds—in a given zodiacal sign; this position corresponded to its celestial longitude. Finally, observers used a table of declinations to calculate this celestial coordinate. This procedure required more complicated arithmetical calculations (multiplication and division) that were often difficult for observers in the fifteenth century.

Tables with this structure were used by some pilots. Francisco Rodrigues mentions them in a short guide to navigation appended to the *Suma oriental* (Oriental summa) by Tomé Pires (c. 1515). We know that the cosmographer Pedro Nunes recommended that navigators use this type of table, but in practice a good arithmetician who knew how to do the necessary operations worked out simpler tables of declinations for all the days in one or four years on which navigators could read directly the solar coordinates relative to their position.

A table of the first type can be found in the *Guia náutico de munique* (Nautical guide of Munique) and was reproduced by Francisco Rodrigues. There are also fragments of quadrennial tables for the late fifteenth and the sixteenth centuries. One for the four years between 1497 and 1500 could have been used by Vasco da Gama's pilot. One of the most widespread tables was that for 1517 to 1520, the work of Gaspar Nicolas, the author of the first arithmetical book published in Portugal (1519).

Tables were worked out for four-year periods. They could be corrected at the end of the year or of the quadrennium, but this did not always happen. Thus, many quadrennial tables continued to be used well beyond the limits of their validity, requiring that observers perform further calculations to correct them. Using out-of-date tables compromised the exactness of the latitudes calculated from them.

Christopher Columbus must have known how to obtain geographical latitude by observing the sun. In one of the books that may have belonged to him, there is a handwritten note referring to the procedure, though there is doubt that the handwriting is Columbus's. Columbus was, however, familiar with Portuguese pilots and sailed in Portuguese ships to Guinea. In sailing from Europe to the Antilles, he tried to navigate at a constant latitude, using observations of the polestar to determine latitude.

Solar eclipses, like lunar eclipses, could be observed to determine geographical longitude by noting the local time of the beginning of the eclipse in the place of the observation and comparing it with the time reported in a reference table. Although Petrus Apianus (Peter Bennewitz, 1501–1552) refers to solar eclipses in his *Cosmographia* (Cosmography, 1524) as the best means to determine longitude, the method was prone to error and even Columbus made a major error when he attempted to use it.

REPORT OF THE EXPLORATIONS OF DE SOTO. Published in Evora, Portugal, 1557. This title page reads: "A truthful report of the work that the Governor Hernando de Soto and certain Portuguese gentlemen performed in the discovery of the province of Florida."

COURTESY OF THE JOHN CARTER BROWN LIBRARY, BROWN UNIVERSITY

BIBLIOGRAPHY

Albuquerque, Luís de. *Astronomical Navigation.* Lisbon, 1988.
Cotter, Charles A. *A History of Nautical Astronomy.* London, 1968.
Taylor, E. G. R. *The Haven-Finding Art: A History of Navigation from Odysseus to Captain Cook.* Rev. ed. London, 1971.
Waters, David W. *The Art of Navigation in England in Elizabethan and Early Stuart Times.* London, 1958.

LUÍS DE ALBUQUERQUE
Translated from Portuguese by Paola Carù

SOTO, HERNANDO DE

SOTO, HERNANDO DE (1497?–1542), Spanish explorer. De Soto, born in Extremadura, went with the expedition of Pedro Arias de Ávila (Pedrárias Dávila) to Costa Rica in 1513–1514. Schooled under this infamous soldier, De Soto spent his late teens mastering horsemanship, weaponry, and the art of conquering Indians. By his early twenties, he exhibited the traits for which he would be famous: he was independent, headstrong, a superb horseman, a good commander, and fearless in battle.

Following Columbus's voyages, Spain sought to penetrate the interior of the newly discovered continents. De Soto played a role in conquering and exploring more territory than any of his contemporaries. He participated as a very young man in the conquest of Costa Rica and later, in 1524, in the conquest of Nicaragua. From 1531 to 1535 he was one of the principal players in the conquest of the Incas. He is best known, however, for his exploration of the present-day southern United States in 1539 to 1542.

In 1536, after the conquest of the Incas, De Soto returned to Spain an exceedingly wealthy man and married Isabel de Bobadilla, daughter of Governor Pedrárias. But De Soto was not content to remain in Spain. He wanted a governorship of his own and the honor that would come from commanding a major expedition of exploration and conquest.

In 1537 De Soto was granted the right to conquer La Florida—an indefinite area of North America that at this time had been explored only along the Gulf and Atlantic coasts. Appointed governor of Cuba and adelantado of La Florida, De Soto landed with more than six hundred persons at Tampa Bay in May 1539. The expedition proceeded to the chiefdom of Apalachee in present-day Tallahassee, where it wintered. In the spring of 1540 the expedition proceeded northeastward through Georgia to the chiefdom of Cofitachequi in South Carolina; from there they turned northward, crossed the Appalachian Mountains, and then circled back through northwestern Georgia and central Alabama before continuing on to the chiefdom of Chicaca, west of Columbus, Mississippi, where they spent the winter of 1540–1541. In the spring they traveled northwestward, discovered and crossed the Mississippi River a few miles south of present-day Memphis, explored northern Arkansas, and then turned southwestward, skirting the Ozark Mountains. They ascended the Arkansas River before looping southward through the Ouachita Mountains and again returned to the Arkansas River, where they spent the winter of 1541–1542.

In the spring of 1542 they traveled to Guachoya, just below the junction of the Arkansas and Mississippi rivers. Here De Soto realized that there was no society comparable to that of the Aztecs or Incas in La Florida, and therefore his expedition was a hopeless failure and he was ruined. At this point he caught a fever, it is said, and died. The survivors of the expedition then attempted to reach New Spain (Mexico) by traveling overland through Texas. But midway they realized they would starve if they continued, so they returned to the Mississippi River where they spent the winter of 1542–1543 building boats. The next summer they sailed down the river and reached New Spain. Only about half of the original force had survived.

[See also *Indian America*, article on *Indians of La Florida*.]

BIBLIOGRAPHY

Albornoz, Miguel. *Hernando de Soto: Knight of the Americas.* New York, 1986.

Hudson, Charles. "A Synopsis of the Hernando de Soto Expedition, 1539–1543." In *De Soto Trail.* National Park Service, 1990.

Lockhart, James. *The Men of Cajamarca.* Austin, Texas, 1972.

Rubio, Rocio Sanchez. *Hernando de Soto.* Cuadernos Populares, no. 25. Mérida (Badajoz), 1988.

Swanton, John R. *Final Report of the United States De Soto Expedition Commission.* Washington, D.C., 1985.

CHARLES HUDSON

SOUTHERN CROSS. The constellation of the Southern Cross was generally unknown in Europe until the fifteenth century, when exploration along the African coast brought European sailors to relatively low latitudes in the Northern Hemisphere. The first navigator to mention it was the Venetian Alvise Cadamosto, who traveled to the coast of Guinea twice in the 1450s, under the sponsorship of Prince Henry the Navigator. The drawing of the constellation that appears in his report does not represent the Southern Cross accurately (though the only surviving copy dates from the late fifteenth century). He calls it the Southern Chariot because it was used in navigation in a way similar to the Northern Chariot (one of the names of Ursa Minor).

The Southern Cross was next represented more than forty years later in a letter sent to King Manuel I from Pôrto Seguro (Brazil) by Mestre José, the king's astrologist and doctor, who had sailed with Pedro Álvares Cabral. In this letter, written in an unrefined Castilian, Mestre José (perhaps a converted Castilian Jew) includes a representation of the southern stars, among them the Southern Cross. His main preoccupation was to designate a star (probably a star in either Octans or Hydrus, which are closer to the South Pole than the Southern Cross is) that could serve as a polestar for navigators in the Southern Hemisphere and to provide a *regimento* (set of rules) similar to the northern *regimento*. Later *regimentos*, such as *Guia náutico de Munique* (Nautical guide of Munique) and *Guia náutico de Evora* (Nautical guide of Evora) omit all mention of the Southern Cross.

The oldest reference to the Southern Cross is found in the *Tratado da agulha de marear* (Treatise on the nautical pointers), a short but significant text (despite its errors) summarized by the famous pilot João de Lisboa, probably before 1508. He knew the "body of rules" and represented the constellation in two engravings (one of which contains numerical errors.) He refers to how the rules can be used, not only to determine latitudes at night, but also to define the local meridian line, and therefore to know the value of the declination of the compass.

Andrea Cosali drew the Southern Cross in a letter (1515) addressed to Duke Giuliano de' Medici that was reproduced by Battista Ramusio in *Navigationi et viaggi* (Navigations and voyages; first edition, 1551). Cosali's sketch of the stars is evidence of the fascination that the Cross held for voyagers of the time. The drawing was reproduced in 1600 by Francisco da Costa in *Arte de navegar* (Art of navigation).

The text of this set of rules never filtered into cosmographers' works during the sixteenth century, but it frequently appeared in the *livros de marinharia* (books of navigation) attributed to various pilots. These works can be found as well in a large number of atlases, in which astronomical data that could be of interest to pilots were included. They are usually referred to as the "body of rules of the sun," the "body of rules of the polestar," and as the "body of rules of the Cross."

BIBLIOGRAPHY

Albuquerque, Luís de. *Astronomical Navigation*. Lisbon, 1988.

Costa, A. Fontoura da. *A marinharia dos descobrimentos*. 2d ed. Lisbon, 1939.

Cotter, Charles A. *A History of Nautical Astronomy*. London, 1968.

Randles, W. G. L. *Portuguese and Spanish Attempts to Measure Longitude in the 16th Century*. Coimbra, 1985.

Taylor, E. G. R. *The Haven-Finding Art: A History of Navigation from Odysseus to Captain Cook*. Rev. ed. London, 1971.

LUÍS DE ALBUQUERQUE
Translated from Portuguese by Paola Carù

SPAIN. In the fourteenth century, the Iberian Peninsula experienced the same catastrophes as the rest of Europe: epidemics of bubonic plague, crop failures, depopulated towns, civil wars, and business bankruptcies. The medieval society organized for war crumbled under the impact of these disasters. Out of the ruins, Spaniards during the fifteenth century created a new society organized for peace. The innovation and stability that enabled Spain to explore and settle the Americas grew out of its experience as a society that reconstructed itself during the Renaissance.

Six separate medieval monarchies coalesced during the

THE IBERIAN PENINSULA IN 1304

fifteenth century to form Spain. They were bonded together by a single ruling family, the Trastámara, an illegitimate branch of the Castilian royal family that had seized the throne of Castile during a brutal civil war between 1366 and 1369. In 1412, a brother of the Trastámara king of Castile was elected king of Aragón, Catalonia, and Valencia, and his descendants inherited the Kingdom of Navarre. When Isabel, crown princess of Castile, married Fernando, crown prince of Aragón, in 1469, they reunited the Trastámara dynasty, and went on to conquer a sixth monarchy, the Muslim Kingdom of Granada, in 1492. The individual monarchies in the union retained separate laws, customs, and languages, while their combined strengths enabled the Trastámara monarchs to pursue a single-minded policy of expansion. Aragonese commerce expanded east into the Mediterranean, and Castilian commerce turned west into the Atlantic.

The part of Spain that refashioned itself most successfully was the Kingdom of Castile, which became one of the largest, most populous, and dynamic countries of Europe. By 1530, Castile's population numbered six million, while all the other Spanish kingdoms together counted one and a half million inhabitants. The most important impetus to Castile's growth was a legal fact: Castilians were free men and women. Serfdom never developed in Castile, and King Fernando extended this freedom to the serfs of Aragón in 1485. The Spanish monarchs never allowed their subjects to be enslaved and, by royal decree in 1500, guaranteed this legal freedom to their American Indian subjects. Royal policy toward nonsubjects, however, was the opposite: non-Christians captured in war and subjects who rebelled against the royal sovereignty could be enslaved. And the monarchs permitted the purchase of African slaves from the Portuguese, who held a monopoly on slaving in sub-Saharan Africa.

Whether noble or freemen, clergy or farmers, Spaniards lived in cities, towns, and villages. Nearly all the land of Spain was incorporated in municipalities—more than 32,000 of them. The isolated farmhouse in the countryside was the rare exception. Those few people whose occupations required them to live outside of towns were regarded as outside the norms of society. Roadside innkeepers, millers, and shepherds were often depicted in popular and high literature as lecherous, venal, and violent. The fictional Don Quixote's bizarre adventures could have taken place only outside the norm of municipal life.

Spaniards were free citizens of their home cities, towns, and villages. Virtually every notarial document of the period began "I, John Doe, citizen of the town of X, and I, Jane Smith, his wife and citizen of the town of X, do hereby . . . ." These citizens governed themselves through

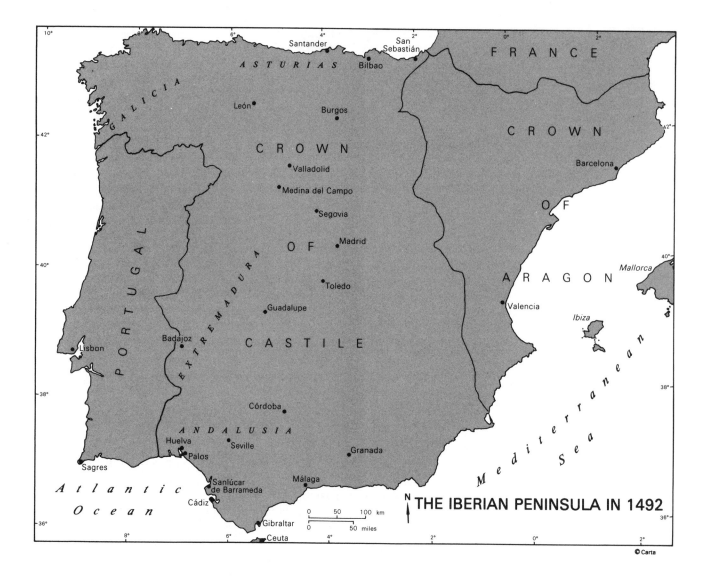

THE IBERIAN PENINSULA IN 1492

democratic town meetings and elected town councils and judges. Each citizen's household possessed a vote, but only married men had the right to cast the vote in town meetings and to hold municipal office. Women could speak in town meetings but could not hold office or vote. Widows possessed the vote of their household but had to ask a male proxy—usually a son or the town judge—to cast their vote. Unmarried males could not vote or hold office.

The economic consequence of this free population living in self-administering municipalities was that Spanish farmers and workers were not subject to forced labor service. Farmers, who comprised over 90 percent of the population, owned their own land, lived in town, and walked out to their fields to plow, plant, and harvest. Their farming produced the staples of the Spanish diet: wheat for bread, olive oil for cooking, grapes for wine, and pork for hams and sausages. Women provided most of the variety in the diet: they made cheese and raised the chickens and eggs that supplied most of the animal protein and cultivated gardens of legumes, green vegetables, and seasonings. During slack seasons, farmers worked as textile manufacturers, fishermen, teamsters, building contractors, livestock breeders, tanners, cabinetmakers, and soldiers, while day in and day out women spun raw wool, flax, and silk into thread.

The town council provided for the common welfare by inspecting weights and measures in the marketplace (plaza), hiring the town schoolteacher, and building hospitals, schools, fountains, laundries, and churches. The council managed and developed the economic infrastructure of the town's farmland by constructing dams, roads, bridges, mills, and irrigation systems. The town sheriff arrested suspects and brought them before the town judge, who heard cases, pronounced sentence, and imposed fines and punishments.

There were no regional governments (provinces were not created until the nineteenth century), so the monarchy depended on municipal governments to carry out royal policy at the local level. City and town councils wrote directly to the kings when they were carrying out their administrative duties, creating a vast treasure of testimony about everyday life witnessed by ordinary citizens. Trastámara monarchs encouraged towns and cities to form cooperative law courts (hermandades) for judging cases involving fugitives and livestock that crossed municipal boundaries. In the sixteenth century, the Habsburg kings depended on city and town councils to collect the royal taxes.

Every city and town had its own constitution (fuero) that defined its relationship with the king or lord and contained the municipal ordinances governing elections, commerce, contracts, and inheritance. Despite the number and diversity of law codes, an ideal of equality prevailed in the inheritance laws throughout the Spanish kingdoms. In general, all the children of a marriage, both male and female, had the right to inherit equitable portions of their parents' property. Parents could not favor one child over another nor could they exclude a child, except in extreme cases such as a child who attempted to murder a parent. Because these laws of partible inheritance were mandatory and enforced by the town judge, parents had no need to draw up wills, which were extremely rare in the fifteenth century.

These institutions and customs that were most effective in rebuilding Castile shaped Spanish settlement in America. Because town life was the norm for Spaniards, they could not conceive of a civilization without municipalities and, when they did not find towns in the Caribbean, they proceeded to build them. Spaniards founded twenty-seven towns and cities on the islands of La Española, Cuba, Puerto Rico, and Jamaica between 1496 and 1515. In between the hundreds of Indian cities and towns that already existed in central Mexico, they established another fifteen Spanish towns and cities between 1519 and 1531. Spanish America came to be, like Spain itself, a few large cities surrounded by hundreds of smaller, autonomous towns.

Enjoying legal freedom and engaging in wide-flung business enterprises, Spaniards were notorious travelers. They went as pilgrims to the Holy Land, pirates to Africa, sailors to the North Atlantic fishing banks, university students to France and Italy, churchmen to Rome and Avignon, ambassadors to Denmark, Bohemia, England, and Florence, and merchants to the trading centers of Bruges, London, and Bordeaux. At home in Spain, farmers traveled to other towns to buy and sell, to shrines for pilgrimages, to the mountains for summer pasture, to less populous regions to start new lives.

SPAIN AS THE HEAD OF EUROPE. Engraving from Sebastian Münster's *Cosmographia*, 1527.   ELSEVIER PUBLISHING PROJECTS, AMSTERDAM

With travel came infections. Spain suffered the same diseases as the rest of Europe during the Renaissance, an age of unprecedented epidemics. The Black Death epidemic of bubonic plague in 1348–1350 caused up to 40 percent overall mortality in large cities, and as much as 60 percent mortality in smaller towns and villages. After that first epidemic, bubonic plague appeared in Europe at least once every generation between 1350 and 1720. Castile suffered huge population losses from plague epidemics in 1575–1577, 1596, 1601–1602, and 1630. Other infectious diseases had equally disastrous effects. An influenza pandemic in 1580 resembled the devastating influenza of 1918, in that morbidity and mortality were high among young adults, leaving a reduced number of adults of child-bearing age to replace the population lost in the bubonic plague epidemics over the next fifty years. One of the new infectious diseases was typhus, believed to have been brought to Spain and Italy in the late fifteenth century through warfare against the Turks in the Mediterranean. The chronicler Andrés Bernáldez and most of his parishioners were afflicted by this new disease in 1507, during an epidemic that swept through Castile killing about 40 percent of the population in the cities and towns it reached. The record of epidemics of smallpox in Europe and Spain is negligible before the 1560s; a milder strain of smallpox probably prevailed. Virulent smallpox entered Spain in the early seventeenth century, and held a prominent place among diseases of the seventeenth and eighteenth centuries.

No segment of the population escaped the ravages of disease. The early Trastámara monarchs were afflicted with tuberculosis, which carried them off at an average age of thirty-seven. Their successors, the Habsburg monarchs, suffered agonies with tubercular joints and respiratory crises, and more than a dozen royal children died before reaching adulthood. Whole families of aristocratic children died of smallpox during the seventeenth century, leaving a handful of lucky distant cousins to inherit multiple noble titles and vast fortunes. The flower of Castilian manhood died of influenza without ever seeing battle in the invasion of Portugal in 1580. The great city of Barcelona never recovered the population, manufacturing, and commercial losses it suffered as a result of bubonic plague deaths in the fourteenth century. In the Extremadura farm town of Cabeza de Vaca, so few citizens survived the epidemic of 1507 that they decided the place was unhealthful; they tore down the houses, salted the ground, and moved to other towns.

These demographic losses opened the way for new economic leaders. Some of Spain's most spectacular fortunes in wool, international trade, and landed estates started from modest beginnings in the early fifteenth century when Castile regained its pre–Black Death population levels and embarked on nearly a century of domestic growth. With rising fortunes came upward social mobility. Successful farmers became wealthy businessmen; they used their plow mules and oxen to transport their produce to the cities, sold it, used the profits to buy city goods, and sold these back in their home towns.

Some Spaniards did not need to be citizens of municipalities. They were the tax-exempt (hidalgo) upper classes: officers and officials who administered the royal household and court, nobles who gave military and diplomatic service to the king, and clergy. Yet like other Spaniards they resided in cities and towns. They also participated in the social mobility of the age. Soldiers rose to become knights, knights rose to become well-rewarded commanders, and victorious commanders became nobles.

Just as Spain was a monarchy of cities and towns, a

Top Grandees of Castile in 1520

Title	Date	Family	Annual Income in ducats
Constable of Castile	1492	Velasco	50,000
Admiral of Castile	1405	Enríquez	32,000
Dukes			
Alba	1465	Toledo	30,000
Infantado	1475	Mendoza	30,000
Medina Sidonia	1445	Guzmán	50,000
Béjar	1485	Zúñiga	24,000
Medinaceli	1479	La Cerda	16,000
Alburquerque	1464	La Cueva	24,000
Arcos	1493	Ponce de León	30,000
Escalona	1472	Pacheco	24,000

noble estate was a cluster of towns. Trastámara monarchs gave away the government of royal towns as hereditary property to the military leaders who helped them gain the throne in the civil war. To ensure that these new seignorial towns would remain in loyal hands, the Trastámara monarchs required that they be placed in perpetual trusts (*mayorazgos*), of which the monarchs were the trustees and the new lords were the beneficiaries.

After 1400, the monarchs introduced another innovation, giving hereditary noble titles to lords of seignorial towns. The first hereditary title was count of Alba, granted in 1439 by King Juan II and elevated to duke of Alba in 1465 by King Enrique IV. In 1400 Castile had fewer than a dozen titled nobles; by the end of the century, the kingdom boasted more than one hundred. In 1520, Charles V ranked the titled nobles and designated the wealthiest as grandees. The dates when those hereditary noble titles were created, and the size of their annual incomes by 1520, shown in the accompanying table, indicate how quickly social status and financial fortunes were changing in fifteenth-century Castile.

The grandees of Castile were a new nobility, and thus Columbus's ambition to achieve noble status was a realistic and attainable goal. Although Fernando and Isabel refused to give hereditary lordship in the Americas to anyone, Spaniard or Indian, they did give the conquerors lifetime lordship (encomienda) over Indian towns. And their grandson, Charles V, gave two hereditary lordships in the Americas: in 1529 he gave the conqueror of Mexico, Hernando Cortés, hereditary lordship over the valley of Oaxaca, with the title "marquis of the Valley," and in 1537 he named Columbus's grandson duke of Veragua (modern Panama) and marquis of Jamaica.

The Castilian language in the fifteenth century displayed this same dynamism and, like the municipal tradition, gave cultural unity to both Spain and Spanish America. The vernacular had been the language of government and law since the thirteenth century, when the king decreed the dialect of Toledo to be the standard by which contracts and laws would be interpreted in litigation. Latin continued as the language of church, university, and foreign diplomacy, but it became a dying language, replaced by the Castilian vernacular in literature, government, and law courts.

Portugal and Aragón also abandoned Latin as an official language in the thirteenth century, but sheer numbers of population gave Castilian vernacular dominance in the peninsula. At the end of the fifteenth century, four-fifths of the inhabitants of Spain spoke Castilian. Castilian served as the most common language for intrapeninsular transactions, by its very prestige and ubiquity inspiring bilingualism even in the Portuguese authors of the period. By the beginning of the fifteenth century, Castilians developed their own Renaissance in literature, launching a "golden century" of poetry, chronicles, novels, and plays. In 1492, the Spanish humanist Antonio de Nebrija published a grammar of the Castilian language—the first grammar of a European vernacular—and dedicated it to Queen Isabel with the reminder that Castilian would be to Spain's empire as Latin had been to Rome's.

By virtue of its diffusion within the peninsula and its status as a literary and official language, Castilian in the fifteenth century had already developed into the modern language of nearly all Spaniards. Speakers of the modern language find little difficulty in reading Renaissance Castilian, in contrast to the vernaculars of the other countries of western Europe, which continued to use Latin in legal proceedings until well into the seventeenth century. The mobility of the Castilian people imparted a remarkable uniformity to the language despite the many political differences that separated one region from another. Even the minor dialects that persisted into the fifteenth century were mutually intelligible. Genoese and Venetians might have had difficulty finding a common comprehensible dialect of Italian; Florentine poets might have had to choose between writing in Latin, which could be read throughout Italy, or their local dialect, which was easily understood only in Tuscany. Castilian authors did not have to make such choices. And even a Genoese merchant long resident in Portugal might easily have found himself most comfortable writing in Castilian.

Along with these traditional social and cultural bonds, Spaniards shared a lively curiosity for the new and exotic. Spanish merchants traveled the markets of Europe to satisfy an almost compulsive taste for novelty among Spanish consumers. They sent back cloth and hats in the Burgundian fashion, spices and aromatics from Venetian warehouses in the eastern Mediterranean, novels of chivalry from France, and Renaissance poetry from Italy.

THE ESCORIAL. Palace and monastery intended to serve as the court of the kings of Spain. Built by Philip II between 1563 and 1584, it was one of the most ambitious architectural undertakings of the Renaissance.

ELSEVIER PUBLISHING PROJECTS, AMSTERDAM

International artists found ready markets in Spain for their skills. Musicians, painters, and architects from the Netherlands, England, and Germany were the rage in the reign of Fernando and Isabel. Moral conservatives who fought against luxurious dress found no fault with foreign styles, as long as they were not extravagant.

Spain had long been one of the great seafaring nations of Europe; by the end of the fifteenth century, it had become a leader in the new enterprise of exploring the Atlantic. Through its Renaissance transformation into a society organized for peace, Spain went beyond exploration to take the lead in colonizing the Americas.

[See also *Barcelona; Columbus, Christopher,* articles on *Columbus in Spain, The Final Years, Illness and Death; Colonization,* article on *Spanish Colonization; Córdoba; Granada; Isabel and Fernando; Jews,* article on *Expulsion from Spain; Madrid; Muslims in Spain; Reconquista; Seville; Toledo; Valencia; Valladolid.*]

BIBLIOGRAPHY

Carmichael, Ann G., and Arthur M. Silverstein. "Smallpox in Europe before the Seventeenth Century: Virulent Killer or Benign Disease?" *Journal of the History of Medicine and Allied Sciences* 42 (1987): 147–168.

Ladero Quesada, Miguel Angel. *Spain in 1492.* Bloomington, Ind., forthcoming.

McAlister, Lyle N. *Spain and Portugal in the New World, 1492–1700.* Minneapolis, 1984.

Nader, Helen. *Liberty in Absolutist Spain: The Habsburg Sale of Towns, 1516–1700.* Baltimore, 1990.

Nader, Helen. *The Mendoza Family in the Spanish Renaissance, 1350 to 1550.* New Brunswick, N. J., 1979.

Pérez Moreda, Vicente. *Las crisis de mortalidad en la España interior, siglos XVI–XIX.* Madrid, 1980.

Phillips, William D., Jr. *Slavery from Roman Times to the Early Transatlantic Trade.* Minneapolis, 1985.

Vassberg, David. *Land and Society in Golden Age Castile.* Cambridge, 1984.

HELEN NADER

SPICES. Throughout history, spices have been used as drugs, foods, preservatives, and cosmetics. From prehistory to the Age of Exploration in the sixteenth century, the demand for spices contributed to the development of intercontinental trade and even influenced the rise and fall of nations. The terms for spices in English and many other languages have a broader application than the modern meanings. A number of products were called spices that are today called aromatics, condiments, perfumes, cosmetics, preservatives, and, above all, drugs. Pharmaceutical uses were primary in accounting for their value. Because the spice products are often derived from plants that are grown only in specific locations, the trade in spices was a significant part of the international and intercontinental trade prior to the Industrial Revolution. Columbus's voyages and others that immediately followed were largely motivated by interests in shipping pharmaceuticals (spices) from the Pacific rim to Europe by the least expensive means.

Primarily, the traffic in spices came to Europe from the south in East Africa and from the east (India, China, Southeast Asia), Persia (Iran), and Arabia, with the latter often serving as a depot and controller of the Incense Road. The principal spices imported from China and Southeast Asia were aloewood (*Aquilaria malacensis*), benzoin (a resin derived from *Styrax*), camphor, cinnamon, cloves, galingale, ginger, nutmeg, sandalwood, and turmeric. From India came amomum, bdellium (which included myrrh and balm), cardamom, cinnamon (some species different from Southeast Asian cinnamon), cyperus, pepper, putchuk or costus, sandalwood, sesame, spikenard, sweet flag or calamus, sweet rush or ginger grass, and turmeric. From Persia came a number of products from saracocolla, various species of *Ferula* (giant fennel), including asafetida and panax (all-heal). Arabia produced balsam, frankincense, and myrrh. From East Africa came two different kinds of frankincense, cultivated ginger, cassia, balsam, aloes, myrrh, and ambergris (an animal product).

From classical antiquity to the sixteenth-century European explorations, there were several trade routes along which goods were transported to Europe. One route, the so-called Silk Road, went from China across Asia to the Black Sea. Another was more direct from India through Syria and Persia. Two sea routes went from India to Arabia (so-called Arabia Felix, now Yemen) and directly from the Pacific Islands of Malaysia, Indonesia, and Guinea (among others) across the Indian Ocean to the east coast of Africa and Madagascar (the so-called Spice Route). Pliny the Elder (died A.D. 79) described the trade carried in ocean-going double-outrigger canoes (which he called rafts). An important depot on the African mainland was Rhapta, located somewhere opposite Zanzibar, where African products were added to the trade. The *Periplus of the Erythraean Sea,* an anonymous sailor's and trader's guide to the trade in the Red Sea area written in Greek around the first century A.D., provides a detailed account of the spice items found in each port of call. Almost always the trade went from east and south to the north and west. One of the exceptions is saffron (crocus), which was grown in the Mediterranean area and exported to East Asia, where it was a valued drug. The Chinese developed uses for saffron as a condiment or food and learned to cultivate the plant, thereby ending their dependence on the Western export.

As demand for spices grew, new products were developed and added to the trade. Camphor was discovered in Asia, possibly Korea, and was mentioned in Arabic sources in the seventh century; by the ninth century, camphor was known by a Latin version *(camphora)* of its Asian name *(kapur)*. Cassia was first a species or kind of cinnamon produced in the Malay peninsula; at some time during the early Middle Ages, a new product was substituted for it, derived from the true *Cassia* plant, which grew in East Africa. Cassia was confused with cinnamon for many centuries thereafter, although it was an important and common laxative. In classical antiquity, a spice drug from a species of *Ferula,* called *silphium,* was so highly valued as an oral contraceptive that it was hunted out of existence. The plant grew only in a narrow band along a mountain range in Libya and resisted all attempts at cultivation. As it became extinct, an inferior substitute was employed from the *Ferula assafoetida* plant, grown in Syria and Persia, which is now used as a condiment in making Worcestershire sauce. Pepper, oranges, lemons (known as the "medical apple"), sugar, tea, coffee, tobacco, and chocolate are examples of "spice" drugs that were imported into Europe as pharmaceuticals and later were used as foods, condiments, and other categories.

As early as the New Kingdom in Egypt the importance of the spice trade was seen by the pharaohs Sahure (c. 2400 B.C.) and Hatshepsut (Hashepsowe, c. 1490–1468 B.C.), who attempted to extend their power to the land of Punt, roughly modern Somalia and Yemen, which was a central producer and trader in spices. A Roman document preserved in Justinian's *Digest* lists some fifty-four spices and a few other trade items, such as ivory and purple cloth, and the import duty on each item imposed in the port of Alexandria. The resulting unfavorable balance of trade between the Mediterranean world and spice pro-ducers is considered a factor in the decline and fall of the Roman Empire.

During the early Middle Ages, spices were often a substitute for money. The early monks often used spices as exchange gifts when moving between monastic communities. So important were spices that approximately one-third of the drugs given in pharmaceutical prescriptions between the seventh and tenth centuries were from products produced in Asia or Africa. The Byzantine Greek term for "warehouse" or "trade depot" is *apoteca*, which came to mean "drug store" or "pharmacist" in European languages. The trade in drugs and spices increased during and after the Crusades. The disruptions in trade caused by the Crusades were a stimulant to find alternative routes, as can be seen by the voyage of Marco Polo. Because of a population increase in Europe between about 1000 and 1320, there was a sharp rise in the demand for spice drugs. Also, a general increase in prosperity enlarged the demand for spices as condiments, preservatives, perfumes, and cosmetics.

One of the best sources for information on the subject is found in *Coloquios dos simples e drogas he cousas medicinais da India* (1563), by Garcia d'Orta (c. 1500–c. 1568). For over thirty years d'Orta, a Portuguese physician in Goa, wrote an account of the spices that he saw. He corrected much of the information about the flora of South Asia because, heretofore, much of the rest of the world knew the items only by their derived products, for example, ginger only as a root, cinnamon as a bark, and pepper as a pod. D'Orta's primary interest was medicinal uses but, because of his broad curiosity, he explored regions for new plants, cultivated them in his garden, and introduced to Europe new food items, such as mangoes, mangosteens, durians, and jackfruit.

A prominent use of spice drugs, especially those with aromatic qualities, was as an ingredient in salves and unguents for flesh wounds, sores, and ulcers. A symptom of festering wounds and sore was an unpleasant smell and the fragrance was thought to be beneficial. Since most of these spice drugs were resins and resins have a mild antiseptic quality, early peoples observed a pharmaceutically active effect. One of the most prized was balsam from *Commiphora opobalsamum,* a tree that grew in a royal garden in Jerusalem and Jericho, where local kings controlled its production as a monopoly. In the first century a pint of balsam sold for one thousand denarii, a considerable sum. Spice drugs had many other uses. Indian nard was good for digestion and jaundice when taken internally, and for sores on the eyelids in ointments. Cinnamon was a menstrual regulator when drunk with myrrh, an antidote against deadly poisons, a diuretic, and, in a salve, good for sunburn. Costus stimulated the libido, expelled intestinal parasites, and, in an ointment, was good for sunburn. Sweet flag was good for the kidneys,

SUGAR PROCESSING IN THE NEW WORLD. Engraving by Théodor de Bry.

coughs, and hernias. Saffron stopped watering of the eyes, acted as an aphrodisiac, and mitigated inflammations resulting from erysipelas. Frankincense taken internally helped the arteries and bowels, but drunk in too great a quantity was thought to produce madness. Finally, the juice of the narcissus bulb was thought to be effective against cancer, a use that modern chemotherapy of cancer has confirmed.

Spice or aromatic drugs were an essential feature in making perfumes and cosmetics. In antiquity and the medieval period, until the formulation of increasingly specialized guilds, the sellers of spices were often the same as druggists, cosmeticians, and perfumers. From the early Sumerian epic legend (as early as c. 3000 B.C.), a distinguishing characteristic of a civilized person, male or female, was smell. Most spice plants have aromatic qualities. Although a few, such as iris roots, were indigenous to the West, a sizable number were trade items. The Syrians in antiquity gained a reputation as specialists in perfumes and cosmetics. A massage with aromatic oils and a wearing of perfume were a routine part of many people's lives.

Various spices' chemical actions to preserve food were known but, because of their high costs, were not often used. Pepper and, later, sugar, in particular, were seen as preventing decay of meat (the action is known to the modern world as enzyme retardation). Whereas the cost was high for sufficiently high quantities to have these results, it was possible to mask the unpleasant smells and tastes of overripe meat by adding these and other spices and condiments. Spices were added to foods for medicinal, preservative, and taste reasons. Detailed recipes using spices as condiments are prominently found in the works of Apicius (fl. early first century A.D.; *De re coquinaria*) and Platina (Bartolomeo Sacchi, 1421–1481; *De honesta voluptate et valitudine*).

Myrrh and frankincense are the spices most used in various religious rituals. Good spirits or gods were thought to enjoy pleasant, uncorrupted air, and the burning of these aromatics improved the environment for spiritual ceremony. The Christian church maintained a great demand for myrrh and frankincense in its rituals throughout the Middle Ages. Myrrh was also used to cause abortions.

BIBLIOGRAPHY

Burkill, I. H. *A Dictionary of the Economic Products of the Malay Peninsula.* 2 vols. Reprint, Kuala Lumpur, 1966.

Greene, Edward Lee. *Landmarks of Botanical History.* 2 parts. Edited by Frank N. Egerton. Stanford, Calif., 1983.

Miller, J. Innes. *The Spice Trade of the Roman Empire, 29 B.C. to A.D. 641.* Oxford, 1969.

Orta, Garcia d'. *Aromatum, et simplicium aliquot medicamento-*

rum apud indos nascentium historia. Antwerp, 1567. Facsimile reprint, Nieuwpook, 1963.

Riddle, John M. "The Introduction and Use of Eastern Drugs in the Early Middle Ages." *Sudhoffs Archiv* 49 (1965): 185–198.

JOHN M. RIDDLE

SPIRITUALITY OF COLUMBUS. In popular biographies and textbooks, Columbus has frequently been depicted as the intrepid "Admiral of the Ocean Sea." In these accounts, Columbus, champion of the spirit of rational, scientific inquiry, struggled against the religious prejudices and superstitions of his day in seeking to gain acceptance for his "Enterprise of the Indies." This enterprise—Columbus's proposal that the Far East could be reached by sailing west across the Atlantic—was based upon the idea that the earth was round and that the distance separating the Atlantic coastlines of Europe from the archipelagos that lay on the outskirts of Cathay was navigable. It was the innovative nature of his beliefs regarding the size and shape of the earth that supposedly accounted for the difficulties he encountered first in Portugal and then in Spain, especially from influential ecclesiastics within the court of Fernando and Isabel.

Contemporary sources such as Bartolomé de las Casas's *History of the Indies* and Fernando Colón's biography of his father, *The Life of the Admiral Christopher Columbus*, do indeed recognize the importance of the title "Admiral of the Ocean Sea" to Columbus. In fact, both suggest that ultimately it was not the novelty of Columbus's geography and cartography (for which there were well-known ancient and medieval precedents) that impeded royal funding for his enterprise. Instead it seems that it was his persistent demand for a substantial package of titles, offices, and revenues from any lands he might discover that almost cost him the support of Fernando and Isabel.

But Columbus held dear another self-image, one that has been less frequently acknowledged in the vast literature regarding his actions and motivations. This second self-image reflects Columbus's spiritual side. It is encoded in a title, *Christoferens*, or "Christ-bearer," bestowed upon him, Columbus believed, not by any earthly ruler but by God.

The earliest known document Columbus signed with *Christoferens* is a memorandum to Fernando and Isabel dated 1493. Thereafter it appears on almost everything he signed until his death in 1506. The signature was accompanied by this curious acronym, which has not yet been definitively deciphered:

.S.

.S. A .S.

X M Y

Xpo FERENS

In his biography, Fernando Colón provides some pertinent information regarding the mystical etymology of his father's name. Columbus's given name, Fernando explains, signified that God had designated him as a second Saint Christopher. Just as the converted pagan giant had once carried the Christ Child across a treacherous river, "so the Admiral Christophorus Colonus, asking Christ's aid and protection in that perilous pass, crossed over with his company that the Indian nations might become dwellers in the triumphant Church of Heaven."

Columbus's surname, which means "dove," also held a higher meaning, according to Fernando. God had sent the "dove" Columbus to carry the message of Christianity to the New World, just as he had previously sent a dove to mark the baptism of Christ and a dove to signal the end of the Flood to Noah: "over the waters of the ocean, like the dove of Noah's ark, he [Columbus] bore the olive branch and oil of baptism, to signify that those people who had been shut up in the ark of darkness and confusion were to enjoy peace and union with the Church." And, in a letter written shortly before his death, Columbus described himself as a divinely sent messenger: "God made me the messenger of the new heaven and new earth of which He spoke in the Apocalypse of Saint John after having spoken of it through the mouth of Isaiah: and He showed me the spot where to find it."

This second self-image has proved discomfiting to Columbus scholars. It is more often than not treated as the product of his unhappy, waning years, an unfortunate but inevitable surfacing of the deposits of medieval religious sentiment in an otherwise modern prototype. But to deprive Columbus of his spiritual identity misrepresents him and his culture. There was an important religious dimension to Columbus's understanding of the genesis and historical significance of his enterprise. And his spirituality in this regard was not especially anomalous or eccentric. It was derived from and responded to a variety of contexts and environments encountered by Columbus in the books he read and in the world in which he lived.

In his *History of the Indies,* Las Casas describes Columbus as "a most observant Christian" and a man of intense personal piety. According to Las Casas, Columbus frequently confessed, took communion, and prayed at the appointed canonical hours as would members of the regular clergy. He was particularly devoted to Saint Francis and the Virgin Mary. Both his writing and speaking were laced with homilies. In addition to the signature described above, he was accustomed to insert the phrase "Jesus with Mary be with us on the journey" *(Iesus cum Maria sit nobis in via)* in his letters. He was openly angered by and intolerant of blasphemy.

Columbus seems to have had particularly close connec-

tions with the Franciscan order. When he arrived in Castile from Portugal in 1485, he first stayed at the Franciscan monastery of Santa María de La Rábida, located near the port of Palos where he had disembarked. During this five-month sojourn and a second one in 1491, he was apparently instructed and succored by several of the resident monks. His cause was supported within the royal court by Antonio de Marchena, an influential Franciscan cosmographer and by Juan Pérez, a member of the community of La Rábida, who was the confessor of Isabel. There is some reason to believe that later in life Columbus joined the Third Order of Saint Francis, which consisted of laypersons. Las Casas reported that after his second voyage to the Americas, Columbus was observed walking in the streets of Seville dressed in the sackcloth of a Franciscan penitent; Columbus's son Diego said that his father was buried in the robes of a Franciscan tertiary.

Columbus apparently developed the self-image of *Christoferens* over a period of time encompassing his stay in Spain, his four voyages to the Americas, and his unhappy last years. It can be traced through his annotations to certain books, in passages he collected for an unfinished work he named the Book of Prophecies, and in a number of letters.

Among the books Columbus read and annotated were Pliny the Elder's *Natural History,* Plutarch's *Lives,* Marco Polo's *Travels (Il milione),* a popular history written by the humanist Enea Silvio Piccolomini (Pope Pius II), and a collection of works compiled by the early-fifteenth-century philosopher and theologian Pierre d'Ailly. These works all enjoyed a relatively wide circulation in both manuscript and printed editions. They acquainted Columbus with a variety of ancient and medieval authorities and provided him with a traditional body of knowledge regarding cosmography, geography, and history. The works of d'Ailly appear to have been particularly important in the development of both the "Enterprise of the Indies" and the self-image of *Christoferens.*

Columbus's copy of d'Ailly's works was published between 1480 and 1483, but it is difficult to determine when he read it. In a note to the best-known piece in the collection, a work titled *Imago mundi,* Columbus refers to a voyage made down the west coast of Africa by Bartolomeu Dias in 1488. And in the margins to another piece, *De correctione kalendarii,* Columbus calculated the date of the vernal equinox for "this year 1491." These annotations suggest that he was actively using d'Ailly's book in the late 1480s and early 1490s—that is, prior to the first voyage of discovery.

In addition to these two titles, Columbus annotated a group of short works in which d'Ailly discussed the interrelationships among astrology, prophecy, and history. D'Ailly believed that there were divinely ordained concurrences among the unfolding of significant historical events, the fulfillments of ancient prophecies, and the appearance of certain celestial phenomena. Columbus adopted the framework of providential history and eschatology that d'Ailly set forth and sought to place his role as *Christoferens* within it.

According to one of d'Ailly's works, *Tractatus de legibus et sectis contra supersticiosos astronomos,* the world had already passed through ages marked by the ascendancy of the Hebrews, the Chaldeans, the Egyptians, and the Saracens. In each of these ages the patron planet of the dominant group had entered into conjunction with the planet Jupiter. In the present age of the Christians, Jupiter was conjoined with Mercury and the final age of Antichrist would be signed by the conjunction of Jupiter and the Moon. Columbus followed d'Ailly's theory of planetary conjunctions closely, sometimes summarizing the salient points in phrases or sentences, sometimes copying passages directly from d'Ailly's text.

D'Ailly and Columbus, though separated by several generations, shared the conviction that the world was rapidly nearing the end of the age of the Christians. They were therefore especially interested in identifying the preordained events that would mark the imminent advent of Antichrist. In seeking to do so both made use of a number of late antique prophetic texts that enjoyed considerable currency throughout the medieval period. One such prophecy, which foretold the unleashing of "a race which has been shut up within the Caspian gates," a race that would supply Antichrist with his armies, was taken by d'Ailly from Roger Bacon's influential thirteenth-century work *Opus maius.* D'Ailly and Columbus supposed that it referred to different episodes of the endemic conflicts between Christian and Muslim forces in the Holy Land and Byzantium. A second prophetic passage that attracted the attention of d'Ailly and Columbus originally derived from the seventh-century Byzantine apocalypse of Pseudo-Methodius. It outlined eight events that would augur the appearance of Antichrist. Columbus copied this passage from d'Ailly and designated it for inclusion in the Book of Prophecies.

Other prophecies guided Columbus in placing his achievements and those of Fernando and Isabel within the eschatological framework adopted from d'Ailly's works. These too were gathered by Columbus and his collaborator, the Carthusian monk Gaspar Gorricio for inclusion in the Book of Prophecies. Columbus's role as *Christoferens* is evoked in two prophecies in particular. The first is the famous passage from *John* 10:16 that predicts the penultimate conversion of all the peoples of the world to Christianity: "And I have other sheep, that are not of this fold; I must bring them also, and they will heed my voice. So there shall be one flock, one shepherd." The second

prophecy is from the Stoic Seneca's tragedy *Medea:* "The years will come, in the succession of the ages, when the Ocean will loose the bonds by which we have been confined, when an immense land shall lie revealed, and Tethys shall disclose new worlds, and Thule will no longer be the most remote of countries." In the manuscript of the Book of Prophecies Fernando Colón wrote next to this excerpt, "My father, the Admiral Christopher Columbus, fulfilled this prophecy in the year 1492." In breaking the bonds of the Ocean Sea, *Christoferens* revealed the existence of previously unknown souls; the promise of their conversion indicated that the end of postlapsarian time and space must be at hand.

Corroboration lay in another prophecy applicable to Fernando and Isabel. Attributable to a prominent medieval Iberian diplomat and apocalyptist, Arnau de Villanova (c. 1250–1312), it prophesied that "he who will restore the ark of Zion will come from Spain." That Columbus believed it was the historical destiny of his king and queen to lead the Christian forces in the final recovery of Jerusalem from the infidel is evident in the prefatory letter to the Book of Prophecies.

After reviewing his training as a navigator and mapmaker and his many years of experience at sea, Columbus declares that these skills "were of no use to me in the execution of the enterprise of the Indies." Instead, he argues, it is divine providence that guided him and that will guide Fernando and Isabel to the reconquest of Jerusalem: "Who would doubt that this light, which comforted me with its rays of marvelous clarity . . . and urged me on with great haste continuously without a moment's pause, came to you in a most deep manner, as it did to me? In this voyage to the Indies Our Lord wished to perform a very evident miracle in order to console me and the others in the matter of this other voyage to the Holy Sepulcher."

Columbus's views that Fernando and Isabel were destined to play important roles in providential history were not unique. Rather they need to be understood within the apocalyptic and prophetic contexts of medieval and early modern political imagery and ideology. In seeing his regents as emperor-messiahs, Columbus was but investing in a tradition traceable back at least to the court of Charlemagne. As his letter prefacing the first voyage suggests, he was casting his achievements not within an eccentric framework but within one that would have been familiar and operative at the royal court. If Columbus represents his regents correctly, they elected to send him on his voyage for purposes that were in significant part evangelical:

> Your Highnesses, as Catholic Christians and as princes devoted to the holy Christian faith and propagators thereof, and

enemies of the sect of Mahomet and of all idolatries and heresies, took thought to send me, Christopher Columbus, to the said parts of India, to see those princes and peoples and lands and the character of them and of all else, and the manner which should be used to bring about their conversion to our holy faith.

And even if (as was likely the case) the monarchs' motives were not so single-minded as Columbus suggested, there can be little doubt that he became increasingly focused upon the recovery of the Holy Land. In the letter describing the fourth voyage, Columbus offered to guide such an expedition via his new westward sea route: "Jerusalem and Mount Zion are to be rebuilt by the hands of the Christians as God has declared by the mouth of his prophet in the fourteenth Psalm. . . . Who will offer himself for this work? Should anyone do so, I pledge myself, in the name of God, to convey him safely thither, provided the Lord permits me to return to Spain."

Columbus's own readings and writings thus consistently reveal that *Christoferens* was not a peripheral part of his self-image. This spiritual self was as essential to his understanding of history and his place in it as was the Admiral of the Ocean Sea. *Christoferens* was as grounded in the religious culture of his world as was the Admiral of the Ocean Sea in the jurisdictional and seignorial cultures. The two faces of Columbus need to be understood as complementary if he and his age are not to be misrepresented in the light of contemporary bifurcations of the sacred and the secular.

[See also *Library of Columbus; La Rábida; Signature; Writings,* article on *Book of Prophecies;* and biographies of figures mentioned herein.]

BIBLIOGRAPHY

Columbus, Ferdinand. *The Life of Christopher Columbus by His Son Ferdinand.* Translated by Benjamin Keen. New Brunswick, N. J., 1959.

Milhou, Alain. *Colón y su mentalidad mesianica en el ambiente franciscanista español.* Valladolid, 1983.

Reeves, Marjorie. *The Influence of Prophecy in the Later Middle Ages: A Study in Joachimism.* Oxford, 1969.

Watts, Pauline Moffitt. "Prophecy and Discovery: On the Spiritual Origins of Christopher Columbus's 'Enterprise of the Indies.' " *American Historical Review* 90 (1985): 73–102.

PAULINE MOFFITT WATTS

STAMPS. See *Iconography,* article on *Philately.*

STRABO (64/63 B.C.–A.D. 24 or later), geographer and historian. Strabo was born in Amasia, Pontus, to a noble Greek family of partly Asiatic descent. He studied rhetoric at Nysa, Caria, and in about 44 B.C. went to Rome to study geography and philosophy, eventually becoming a Stoic. He spent several years in Alexandria, traveling south to Syene (Aswan) and the Ethiopian frontier with the Roman governor Aelius Gallus and his entourage. Although not a great traveler, he knew Asia Minor and other parts of the eastern and central Mediterranean quite well.

Strabo wrote the lost work *Historical Sketches,* in forty-seven books, and *Geography,* in seventeen books, which is extant except for parts of Book 7. The latter work describes Spain, Gaul, Britain, Italy, northern and eastern Europe, Greece, Asia Minor and the surrounding areas, the Middle East, India, and the parts of Africa known to the Romans. It is likely that Renaissance explorers made only limited use of Strabo's *Geography.* The work is discursive, and much of the text concerns areas that were relatively well known by the fifteenth century. Strabo was convinced that the inhabited world could be circumnavigated and that the North and South Atlantic were not separated by an appreciable body of land. He was obviously interested in exploring the Atlantic, writing, "We [humans] are in a way amphibious, not more landlubbers than seafarers."

In addition to recounting events such as the ancient circumnavigation of Africa commissioned by the Egyptian pharaoh Necho, Strabo stresses the importance of geometrical and astronomical contributions to geography and cartography. He discusses, though without details, Eratosthenes's measurement of the circumference of the earth and gives some details of Eratosthenes's world map. In Book 1 of *Geography* Strabo writes, "Eratosthenes says that . . . if the size of the Atlantic did not prevent it, we could even sail from Iberia to Indike [India/China] along the same parallel over more than a third of the total distance, assuming that the circle through Athens, on which we have made our calculation of the distance from India to Spain, is less than 200,000 stades in circumference." Eratosthenes reckoned the circumference of the earth at the equator to be 252,000 stades, or between 37,292 and 46,620 km (that is, between 23,120 and 28,900 miles; a stade in his day was variously reckoned at 185 meters, 148 to 158 meters, or other equivalents). By examining Strabo's text, it is clear how Ptolemy came later to make Taprobane (Sri Lanka) too large: Strabo, who orientates it wrongly, gives its length as over 5,000 stades.

The manuscript tradition of Strabo's *Geography* is tenuous. The work was evidently little read in ancient times. All extant manuscripts are derived from one source (around A.D. 850). The earliest surviving manuscript, apart from palimpsest fragments, is in the Bibliothèque Nationale, Paris (Greek manuscript no. 1397) and dates from the late tenth century. A Latin translation (Rome, 1472) by Guarinus Veronensis and Gregorius Tifernas was later revised by J. Andreas (1480) and edited by A. Mancellinus (1494). The first Greek edition did not appear until 1516. There is no evidence that Strabo included maps in the *Geography,* and none were included in the early editions; those printed in later editions were constructed from his text and from Renaissance maps.

BIBLIOGRAPHY

Aujac, Germaine. *Strabon et la science de son temps.* Paris, 1966.
Strabo. *Geography.* 8 vols. Translated by Horace Leonard Jones. 1917. Reprint, Cambridge, Mass., 1969.

O. A. W. Dilke

SYPHILIS. An infectious disease, syphilis is usually transmitted by sexual contact (venereal syphilis), but it can also be transmitted to a newborn infant by an infected mother (congenital syphilis). Its origin has long been a matter of scholarly debate. Some have maintained that it originated in the Old World and, like so many other infectious diseases, was carried to the New World by explorers in the Age of Discovery. Others, however, have argued that it existed in the New World prior to 1492 and was introduced into Europe by the returning explorers. In order to understand the terms of this debate, one must first understand how the disease affects the human body.

After an incubation period of ten to ninety days, the primary lesion, or chancre, of venereal syphilis appears in the anogenital region. Secondary lesions develop later on the skin and mucous membranes of other regions of the body. In more advanced stages (tertiary), the disease can affect bones as well as other organs.

Syphilis is one of several treponemal diseases—venereal syphilis, endemic syphilis, yaws, and pinta—that have similar symptoms. All are thought to be caused by a species of the bacterium *Treponema,* and in their more advanced stages, all but pinta affect bone in similar ways. In fact, some have argued that all these diseases are really different expressions of a single disease caused by *Treponema pallidum.* Endemic syphilis is best known from Syria and areas of Africa. Yaws primarily affects children in rural populations of the tropics. Pinta, which also occurs in the tropics, ranging from Mexico to Ecuador, primarily affects the skin and does not involve internal organs.

Venereal syphilis usually affects the skeleton in the area of the cranial vault, the bones of the nasal area, and the tibia of the lower leg. In the cranial vault, venereal syphilis typically produces a "worm-eaten" scarred pattern of lesions on the outer table of the frontal bone termed "caries sicca." This condition frequently is accompanied by extensive destruction of the bone around the nose area and the upper jaw. In the remainder of the skeleton, the disease causes inflammation of the periosteum, a tissue adjoining the bone's exterior surface that has the capability to form new bone. The inflamed periosteum produces characteristic bony lesions that range from small striated extensions to large lesions with rough surfaces. Yaws produces very similar skeletal effects. In congenital syphilis, the teeth are frequently deformed, a condition termed "mulberry molars" or "Hutchinson's teeth."

Syphilis now is controlled by the antibiotic penicillin. Prior to the discovery of its effectiveness in treating the disease in about 1910, syphilis infected as many as 5 percent of people throughout the world living in urban areas. It is estimated that between 10 and 20 percent of those infected with the disease had skeletal involvement.

Those who argue that the disease originated in the Old World cite numerous passages from the Bible, as well as early literature from Greece, Italy, Spain, India, and China, that describe conditions similar to those known for syphilis. Frequently, these accounts correlate the disease with sexual encounters, further bolstering the interpretation of venereal syphilis. These advocates also argue that, in the early literature, syphilis was confused with leprosy and that the hospitals and colonies set up to isolate lepers from the rest of society actually contained many individuals suffering from syphilis. This argument is supported by early accounts mentioning the effective use of ointments containing mercury, a substance of little use in treating leprosy but widely employed in treating syphilis.

Critics of the Old World origin of syphilis point out the uncertain diagnoses of the disease and its likely confusion with a multitude of other diseases having similar symptoms. The mercury-based ointments may have been aimed not at leprosy but at related diseases other than syphilis. Recent studies of human remains from leper cemeteries have failed to find any skeletal evidence of syphilis. And an analysis of large samples of human remains from Europe, including over ten thousand from Czechoslovakia alone, turned up no examples of the disease. On the other hand, several skeletons from Southeast Asia (Borneo, Australia, and the Mariana Islands) that predate 1492 seem to have skeletal lesions matching those expected with syphilis or a related treponemal disease.

Evidence for the other side of the debate—that syphilis existed in the New World prior to 1492—now seems overwhelming. Many skeletons have been found from a variety of pre-Columbian archaeological sites that show all the features of both venereal and congenital syphilis. Given the high frequency of affected individuals at some sites, the highly diagnostic nature of the lesions, and the geographical distribution of the disease throughout the Western Hemisphere, there seems little doubt that syphilis, or a closely related treponemal disease, was in the Americas prior to 1492.

Those who argue for a New World origin also cite an apparent epidemic of syphilis that struck Europe in about A.D. 1500. The rapid spread of the disease throughout Europe at that time indicates to them that it must have been a "new" disease among populations having no prior immunity. Alternative explanations are that epidemics of syphilis had struck before but were not recognized as such or that the epidemic was stimulated by the unprecedented population movements that occurred throughout Europe at that time.

Collectively, however, the evidence suggests that treponemal disease, including syphilis, was present in the New World long before 1492. The disease may also have been present in the Old World prior to that year, but the evidence for that is concentrated mostly in Southeast Asia. It seems very likely that, whereas many diseases crossed the Atlantic with Columbus and subsequent European voyagers and caused great mortality among the native New World populations, syphilis and related treponemal diseases may have traveled in the opposite direction.

[See also *Disease and Demography*.]

BIBLIOGRAPHY

Baker, Brenda J., and George J. Armelagos. "The Origin and Antiquity of Syphilis: Paleopathological Diagnosis and Interpretation." *Current Anthropology* 29 (1988): 703–737.

Crosby, Alfred W., Jr. "The Early History of Syphilis: A Reappraisal." *American Anthropologist* 17 (1969): 218–227.

Ortner, Donald J., and Walter G. J. Putschar. *Identification of Pathological Conditions in Human Skeletal Remains*. Washington, D.C., 1985.

Quétel, Claude. *History of Syphilis*. Translated by Judith Braddock and Brian Pike. Baltimore, 1990.

Steinbock, R. Ted. *Paleopathological Diagnosis and Interpretation*. Springfield, Ill., 1976.

DOUGLAS H. UBELAKER

T

TAÍNOS. See *Indian America*, article on *Taínos*.

TALAVERA, HERNANDO DE (1428–1507), bishop of Ávila (1485); archbishop of Granada (1492). Hernando de Talavera was one of the main characters in the making of the legend of Columbus. He has often been depicted as the stalwart foe of Columbus's plans, rejecting the enterprise of the Indies and showing his ignorance and resistance to progress. The evidence, however, shows otherwise.

A member of a hidalgo family of modest means from the area of Sigüenza, Talavera was educated at the University of Salamanca, thanks to the financial support of one of his relatives. He studied moral philosophy and theology in what was then the usual curriculum for those not interested in the law. A man of great austerity and simple piety, he joined the Hieronymite Order at age thirty-five. He rose to prominence swiftly, being named prior of the monastery of the Prado in Valladolid and, soon after, confessor to the Castilian queen, Isabel.

As an ecclesiastic in the inner circle of the Castilian court, he played a central role in the diplomatic negotiations with Portugal after the conclusion of the civil war between the followers of Juana de Castilla (La Beltraneja) and Isabel. He was also instrumental in negotiating the agreements by which the Crown recovered income and lands alienated to the nobility during the reign of Enrique IV.

His service to the queen and the realm was rewarded by his appointment as bishop of Ávila and then as archbishop of the newly established see of Granada after the conquest of the city in 1492. As archbishop he instituted a benevolent policy of gentle persuasion toward the Muslims, avoiding any attempts at forced conversion. This attitude and his opposition to the establishment of an inquisitional tribunal in Granada drew the ire of the Inquisition. Because he enjoyed the favor of the queen, he was spared, and the Inquisition limited its displeasure to charging some of his relatives with heresy. Soon after Isabel's death in 1506, however, Talavera was imprisoned and accused of befriending Moors and conversos, of hindering the work of the Inquisition, and, finally, of being of Jewish descent. The archbishop remained in prison until an appeal to Pope Julius II brought a dismissal of the charges as fictitious and slanderous. His exoneration, however, was of little solace, for Talavera died soon afterward in 1507.

As confessor to the queen, Talavera presided over the so-called Junta de Salamanca, which through most of 1486–1487, received, assessed, and rejected Columbus's proposal for a westerly voyage to the Indies. The consensus of most historians is that Talavera's opposition to the project rested on two legitimate considerations: First, that the voyage might be considered an incursion into Portugal's Atlantic possessions, and second, that Columbus's demands and expected rewards were excessive. On both counts Talavera's objections were valid. Peace with Portugal, after the defeat of efforts to secure the Castilian throne for Juana de Castilla, had been obtained at great cost, and the security of Castile's western frontier was a prerequisite before the final push against Granada. Columbus's conditions and demands were indeed exorbitant.

Thus, Talavera's decision was not based on animosity toward Columbus or on ignorance. By not rejecting Columbus's proposal outright and by granting Columbus a small pension, Talavera guaranteed that the proposal would be resubmitted after the conclusion of the Granada campaign and that the future Admiral of the Ocean Sea would remain in the service of Castile.

BIBLIOGRAPHY

Nader, Helen. *The Mendoza Family in the Spanish Renaissance, 1350–1550.* New Brunswick, N.J., 1979.
Mariéjol, J. H. *The Spain of Ferdinand and Isabella.* Translated and edited by Benjamin Keen. New Brunswick, N.J., 1961.

TEOFILO F. RUIZ

TECHNOLOGY. See *Science.*

TENOCHTITLAN. See *Indian American,* article on *Aztecs and Their Neighbors.*

TERRESTRIAL PARADISE. Within the Judeo-Christian tradition, the terrestrial paradise is a garden created by God that was the abode of Adam and Eve before the Fall. The principal description of the terrestrial paradise in scripture occurs in *Genesis.* According to *Genesis* 2:8, the garden of Eden was situated in the East. Its verdant flora were watered by a river that flowed forth from the garden in four branches: Pison, Gihon, Hiddekel, and Euphrates. From these branches the whole earth was watered. After the expulsion of Adam and Eve from the garden, God surrounded it with cherubim and a "flaming sword which turned every way" to prevent humankind from reentering (*Genesis* 3:24).

A second description of the terrestrial paradise is found in *Ezekiel* 28:13–19, which relates that the "garden of God" was located at the top of a holy mountain and was rich in precious stones of many kinds. From it God cast out the "son of man." Neither the *Genesis* nor the *Ezekiel* account indicates that God destroyed the terrestrial paradise after exiling humankind from it. Therefore, it was widely presumed still to exist and was incorporated into the geography, cartography, and travel literature of the medieval Latin West.

Medieval geographies are characterized by their fusions of Greco-Roman and Judeo-Christian sources. Works such as Aristotle's *On the Heavens* (fourth century B.C.), Pliny the Elder's *Natural History* (first century A.D.), Martianus Capella's *The Marriage of Philology and Mercury* (late fourth to early fifth century A.D.), and Macrobius's *Commentary on the Dream of Scipio* (fifth century A.D.) were among the most important antique pagan sources for medieval cosmographers and geographers.

These works conceived of the earth as round and encased in three layers of concentric spheres consisting of the elements of water, air, and fire. The inhabitable part of the world, called the *oikumene* by the Greeks, extended from the coastlines of Britain, France, Spain, and North Africa in the west to the Ganges River in the East. Its northern and southern limits were somewhat vaguer, but generally were extended to the Baltic Sea and to the mouth of the Arabian Gulf. The *oikumene* was completely surrounded by the Ocean Sea.

In a lineage of authoritative medieval texts that can be traced from Isidore of Seville's *Etymologiae* (seventh century) to Pierre d'Ailly's *Imago mundi* (fifteenth century), this ancient image of the world was embellished with peoples and places derived from scripture and popular legends. In these accounts, Jerusalem was usually located at the center of the world in accordance with *Ezekiel* 5:5 ("This is Jerusalem: I have set it in the midst of the nations and countries that are round about her"), and the terrestrial paradise was placed in the east beyond India, in accordance with *Genesis* 2:8. Some writers, notably the tenth-century Syrian Moses Bar-Cepha in his *On Paradise,* make the terrestrial paradise an island separated from the *oikumene* by the band of Ocean Sea. It is often described as being elevated in height because it remained untouched by the inundations of the Flood described in *Genesis* 6–7.

Such combinations of real and imagined geographies are manifest in medieval *mappaemundi* (world maps). A series of well-known *mappaemundi* that includes the family of maps named for the eighth-century Iberian monk Beatus of Liebana, the thirteenth-century Psalter and Ebstorf world maps, and the mid-fifteenth-century maps of Giovanni Leardo share certain elements. They are all oriented with the east at the top, where they locate the terrestrial paradise. Usually depicted in some detail, the terrestrial paradise includes the figures of Adam and Eve bracketing the tree of wisdom entwined by a snake. Sometimes the garden is surrounded by tongues of flame; sometimes it is an island in the Ocean Sea, as in the famous Fra Mauro map (1459). From the garden the four streams flow, visibly feeding all the waters delineated on the map.

The terrestrial paradise is also mentioned in a widely circulated sequence of tales of legendary journeys. The sixth-century Irish monk, Saint Brendan, purportedly found it in the North Atlantic. In the twelfth century, the mythical Christian king of the Far East, Prester John, supposedly sent a letter to the Byzantine emperor in which he remarked that his kingdom was but three days journey from paradise. During the same century there also proliferated a genre of stories concerning the travels and exploits of Alexander the Great. In one of these popular romances of Alexander, the *Iter ad paradisum,* Alexander is said to have reached the gates of paradise during his eastern campaigns.

The terrestrial paradise is also an important locus in the great cosmic journey of Dante's *Divine Comedy.* Echoing *Ezekiel,* Dante places it at the top of the mountain of Purgatory. And, as had Moses bar-Cepha and others, he also made Purgatory and its paradisal summit an island, located in the waters of the southern hemisphere, directly opposite Jerusalem, the navel of the *oikumene* of the northern hemisphere. *Purgatorio* culminates with Dante the pilgrim taking a purificatory bath in the rivers of the terrestrial paradise in preparation for his ascent to the celestial spheres.

John Mandeville's fictitious *Travels,* originally composed in French in 1366, proved to be an especially attractive example of the genre of imaginary journeys. In it, he recorded his travels to Jerusalem and thence to the kingdom of Prester John and mentioned being in the vicinity of paradise, though he never actually saw it. Mandeville's *Travels* was rapidly translated into several vernaculars and circulated widely in both manuscript and printed versions.

Christopher Columbus read and annotated a copy of Mandeville's *Travels.* It supplied him, as did a number of other works, with the geographical and literary frameworks for the terrestrial paradise. There seems little doubt that he believed that it actually existed and expected to find it in the course of his voyages of exploration. Columbus's letter to Fernando and Isabel describing the third voyage contains a lengthy passage in which he considers the question of the location of the terrestrial paradise, reviewing a variety of standard theories. He concludes that he has just passed close to it, citing as evidence the fresh water he found pouring into the sea at a point that he called the Dragon's Mouth (Boca del Dragón). He was actually in the Gulf of Paria between Trinidad and Venezuela. The fresh water Columbus took to be the four rivers of the terrestrial paradise was streaming from the mouth of the Orinoco River.

BIBLIOGRAPHY

Boas, George. *Essays on Primitivism and Related Ideas in the Middle Ages.* New York, 1978.

Graf, Arturo. *Miti, leggende e superstizioni del medio evo.* Milan, 1984.

Kimble, George H. T. *Geography in the Middle Ages.* New York, 1968.

Major, R. H., ed. and trans. *Christopher Columbus: Four Voyages to the New World.* Gloucester, Mass., 1978.

Wright, John Kirkland. *Geographical Lore of the Time of the Crusades.* New York, 1925.

PAULINE MOFFITT WATTS

THIRD VOYAGE. See *Voyages of Columbus.*

TIDES AND CURRENTS. Early explorers quickly learned from Columbus to sail westward from the Canary Islands in the northeast trade winds and north equatorial current. Returning from the Caribbean they sailed northward into the region of eastward currents and westerly winds. Both wind and current were very important in providing propulsion for the ships and affecting their course and speed. As they approached land, explorers were concerned about tides: swift tidal currents could carry them helplessly onto rocks or shoals, and large variations of sea level could play havoc with anchoring.

Tides. In mid-ocean, where it is a matter of no concern to mariners, the mean range of the tide is only a few feet and tidal currents are generally not strong. Near shore, tides and their associated currents are usually amplified, sometimes severely. Northwestern France and southwestern England have tides reaching forty feet as does the Bay of Fundy between Maine and Nova Scotia. More typical along the coasts of North America and Africa are tides of about five feet, although in two regions—the mouth of the Amazon River and off Guinea Bissau in West Africa—they reach fifteen feet and are accompanied by swift currents. Despite the Caribbean's low tides, which are usually less than two feet, tidal currents there reach several knots around islands and through passages. Although tidal height variations are well known and predictions are routinely prepared for the world's harbors, tidal currents—which can have complicated patterns around shoals, islands, and headlands—are not nearly so well known even today. Safely sailing through dangerous reefs in the presence of these swift currents requires considerable expertise and some luck. It was probably a tidal current that carried Columbus's becalmed *Santa María* onto a reef north of La Española where she was lost. Columbus was forced to switch to *Niña,* on which he successfully returned home, narrowly surviving several winter gales.

Tides are caused by the gravitational attraction of the moon and sun with the moon's influence being more than twice that of the sun. The tide at any given place consists of a number of partial tides each of which is related to the complicated motion of the earth relative to the moon and sun. Most regions have semidiurnal tides, or two high tides each day 12.4 hours apart caused by the moon. Some regions such as the Gulf of Mexico have a diurnal tide, that is, only one high tide each day. Mixed tides, consisting of two markedly unequal high tides each day, occur in the Gulf of St. Lawrence and in the Caribbean. Significant variations in sea level and associated currents can also be generated by the wind and atmospheric pressure changes.

Although these changes are not tidal, they can augment tides and tidal currents, modify their timing, and make them much more hazardous.

Currents. Since the winds are the primary driving force of surface ocean currents, their patterns are strongly linked. Large-scale ocean currents and winds generally flow clockwise around the mean mid-latitude high-pressure region in the North Atlantic. Currents, however, tend to be skewed to the west and are much narrower and swifter on the western sides of ocean basins. Thus, in the west, wind and current patterns do not necessarily match.

The most comprehensive data of surface currents are historical ship drifts measured over the past hundred years by both merchant and navy ships. Ship drift measurements of surface current are determined from the difference between shipboard navigational fixes and the estimated velocity of the ship through the water. Most current atlases and pilot charts are based on these data, which show the general currents. The Gulf Stream begins in the Straits of Florida and flowing at a speed of four to five knots follows along the coast northeastward to Cape Hatteras. Its speed must have been difficult for southward-sailing explorers to stem, especially around Cape Hatteras with its dangerous shoals and through the Florida Straits where the stream is bounded on both sides by shoals. Sailors probably hugged the shore where there is a weaker current and sometimes even a counterflow. A short time after Columbus's voyages Spanish mariners learned to sail northeastward in the stream and then eastward to Spain with favorable winds and currents.

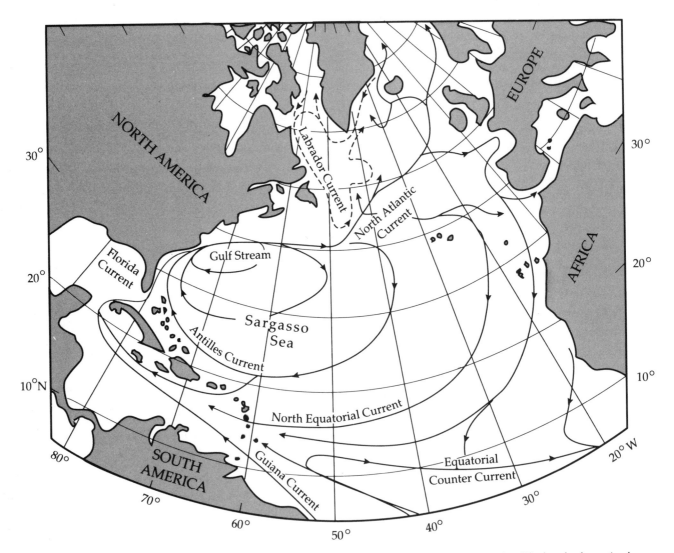

NORTH ATLANTIC CURRENTS. Chart showing main features of the upper layer circulation. Currents are simplified and schematized.

AFTER SVERDRUP, JOHNSON, AND FLEMING, 1942

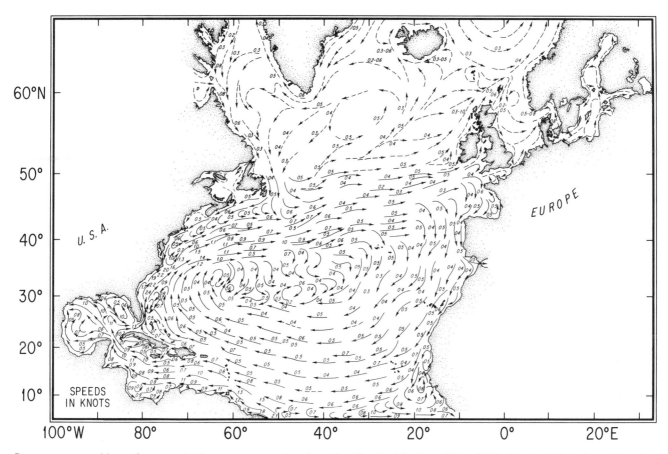

PILOT CHART OF THE NORTH ATLANTIC. Surface currents as taken from the pilot chart for June 1978 published by the U.S. Defense Mapping Agency. Along the Canary Islands–to–Caribbean route, velocity values are typically 0.5 knots, although the technique used to obtain these values tends to inflate speeds. WOODS HOLE OCEANOGRAPHIC INSTITUTION, WOODS HOLE, MASSACHUSETTS

Downstream from Cape Hatteras the Gulf Stream leaves the coast, meanders widely, and sheds intense eddies or current rings, which populate both sides of the stream. In this region the instantaneous stream is approximately a hundred kilometers wide, but the meanders cause its time-averaged width to be much wider. Downstream of the Grand Banks of Newfoundland the stream breaks down into numerous current filaments and eddies, and the main currents become difficult to follow. The most energetic eddies are located in the stream south of New England; the strength of these eddies decreases as one moves away from the mean axis of the stream.

Roughly half of the volume of water transported by the Gulf Stream through the Straits of Florida originates in the South Atlantic and flows northward as a warm current across the equator into the Caribbean and Gulf of Mexico. A deep cold compensating current flows southward across the equator at depths of from one thousand to four thousand meters. This large-scale circulation—northward in the upper thousand meters and southward in deeper water—is responsible for the northward heat flux in the Atlantic and is an important factor in climate. The other half of the transport in the Straits of Florida is return flow from the stream that has recirculated and entered the Caribbean through numerous passages. The stream increases in transport to the north, reaching its maximum south of Nova Scotia. The major part of this flow recirculates westward on both sides of the stream as countercurrents, but some continues eastward across the Atlantic, splitting southeast of Newfoundland into northward and southward branches. Because of strong eddies and swift current filaments, the mean flow is difficult to map even today. The northward branch mixes with other waters, is cooled, and eventually turns into deeper colder water during winter, forming the beginning of the southward flow that much later crosses the equator. The southward branch flows clockwise around the Atlantic and into the Caribbean. The north equatorial current part of this branch is some of the steadiest flow of the ocean—both winds and currents flow southwestward with very little

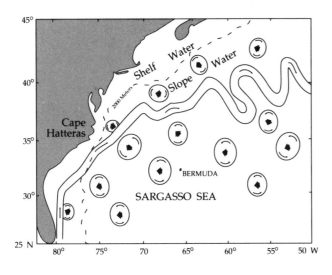

THE GULF STREAM. A schematic, synoptic representation of the path of the Gulf Stream and the distribution and movement of rings. The width of the Stream is typically around 100 km and the diameter of rings, 200 km. The rings usually move westward but can also interact with the Stream and drift downstream. The general fate of rings is coalescence with the Stream after a few months to a few years. Swirl speeds in young rings are similar to speeds in the Stream.

WOODS HOLE OCEANOGRAPHIC INSTITUTION, WOODS HOLE, MASSACHUSETTS

variation in time. There are even eddies here, however, and currents are not always southwestward despite the average pattern. Sailing to the Caribbean is usually a delight, but returning directly to Europe is not easy. The only option is to sail northward into the westerlies as Columbus discovered on his first voyage.

Farther to the south are located very swift equatorial currents, which have enormous seasonal variations. The south equatorial current flows westward in the vicinity of the equator, splitting near the eastern tip of Brazil. Most of the current flows northwestward along the coast of South America as the swift (up to three to four knots) north Brazil current, then Guiana current, and then Caribbean current. During the latter half of each year most of the near surface north Brazil current turns offshore at five to ten degrees north, forming the origin of the eastward-flowing north equatorial countercurrent, which has speeds of three knots in the west and meanders with a two hundred-mile north-south displacement and five hundred-mile wavelength, the distance between successive meander crests. During the first half of the year the countercurrent is replaced by a generally westward current. At this time the north Brazil current continues up the coast. This seasonal variation of currents modulates the northward heat flux in the Atlantic. Amazon River water

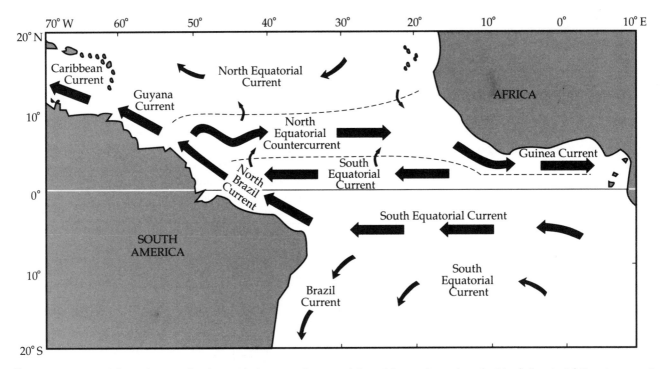

TROPICAL CURRENTS. Schematic map of major tropical currents between July and September, when the North Equatorial Countercurrent flows swiftly eastward across the Atlantic into the Guinea Current. From January through June the countercurrent disappears and westward velocities are seen in this area. Heavier arrows show swiftest currents, generally greater than 0.5 knots.

AFTER RICHARDSON AND WALSH, 1986

enters the Atlantic near the equator forming large pools and filaments of fresh water, which are carried northwestward up the coast of South America and eastward into the countercurrent. These swift equatorial currents and their strong seasonality could have been difficult for early explorers to navigate. Those heading south along the coast toward the eastern tip of Brazil would have found very strong currents against them and, during the second half of the year, the southeast trades against them, too. Sailing northwestward along the coast would have been much easier. South of the eastern tip of Brazil the currents and winds are much more favorable for sailing southward. Early mariners soon learned to pass well clear of the eastern tip of Brazil when sailing from Europe to the South Atlantic.

The strong current seasonality observed in the equatorial region from ten degrees north to ten degrees south is caused by the seasonal shifting of trade winds: the northeast and southeast trades converge toward the intertropical convergence zone, or doldrums, which lie near the equator. In the latter half of the year the wind pattern shifts northward and the doldrums generally lie between five and ten degrees north coinciding with the countercurrent and largely responsible for it; during the first half of the year the doldrums lie close to the equator. Often in spring the easterly trades along the equator are replaced by westerly winds. The result is a swift eastward current jet within a few degrees of the equator. The doldrums are known for their very light breezes, so before the days of engine power, sailing vessels often lay becalmed there for weeks drifting unknowingly large distances sometimes eastward in the countercurrent or the jet along the equator and sometimes westward in the south equatorial current. On his third voyage, Columbus sailed southwestward from the Cape Verde Islands reaching the doldrums in the middle of July 1498, where he was becalmed for eight miserable days in terrible tropical heat. At this time Columbus probably drifted eastward in the countercurrent, which is usually well developed during July. Finally, the cool trade winds reappeared, filled Columbus's sails, and drove him toward Trinidad where he made landfall nine days later.

The currents through passages into the Caribbean can be very swift and are difficult to describe in the general sense because they vary with the large-scale currents as well as with local winds, eddies, and tides. One can imagine that each passage has its own complicated and different flow pattern, depending on the direction of wind and the configuration of islands and sea floor. Eddies can be generated in the lee of islands, some stationary, some carried downstream. The numerous shoals and low islands in the Bahamas plus the time-varying currents there must have been particularly tricky for early navigators.

Numerous recent wrecks attest to the difficulty of sailing in these waters even today. More detailed information of these waters can be found in the Coast Pilots, Sailing Directions, and Tide and Tidal Current Tables.

BIBLIOGRAPHY

Richardson, P. L. "Gulf Stream Rings." *Oceanus* 19, no. 3 (1976): 65–68.

Richardson, P. L., and D. Walsh. "Mapping Climatological Seasonal Variations of Surface Currents in the Tropical Atlantic Using Ship Drifts." *Journal of Geophysical Research* 91 (1986): 537–550.

Robinson, Allan R., ed. *Eddies in Marine Science.* Berlin, 1983.

Stommel, Henry. *The Gulf Stream.* London, 1958.

Sverdrup, H. U., M. W. Johnson, and R. H. Fleming. *The Oceans.* New York, 1942.

U.S. Naval Oceanographic Office. *Oceanographic Atlas of the North Atlantic Ocean, Section 1, Tides and Currents.* Bay St. Louis, Miss., 1965.

Warren, Bruce A., and Carl Wunsch, ed. *Evolution of Physical Oceanography, Scientific Surveys in Honor of Henry Stommel.* Cambridge, Mass., 1981.

PHILIP L. RICHARDSON

TIMEGLASS. A timeglass (also called sandglass, hourglass, or running glass) consists of two conical phials joined at the apexes and held in a symmetrical frame that can be placed either end up. A fine material, sometimes sand but more commonly finely ground eggshell or other material is sealed into the phials and can trickle in a known amount of time from the upper phial to the lower; the time depends upon the quantity and nature of the material and upon the diameter of the aperture at the junction of the two phials. In other languages, the timeglass was called *horologium* (Latin); *horloge de mer* or *sablier* (French); *orologio, ampoletta,* or *clessidra* (Italian); *ampulheta* (Portuguese); *ampolleta* (Spanish); and possibly also *dyoll* (English), which presents linguistic problems (perhaps a misreading of *fyoll*), but seems confirmed by the mention of "smale diale sonde" in a tract (after 1534) on the circumnavigation of England.

The construction of any timeglass clearly presupposes a certain skill in glassblowing (known in Syria from the first century B.C.), but the earliest timeglasses consisted of two independently blown phials joined by wax and binding, with a small brass plate pierced by an aperture between them. Later, in the eighteenth century, timeglasses were blown in one piece, the narrow aperture being created by drawing out the softened glass. Timeglasses could be made to run for periods from a few minutes up to several hours and measured equal intervals of time. Thus, they were used at sea with the log for determining speed and distance sailed (dead reckoning) and for dividing the day

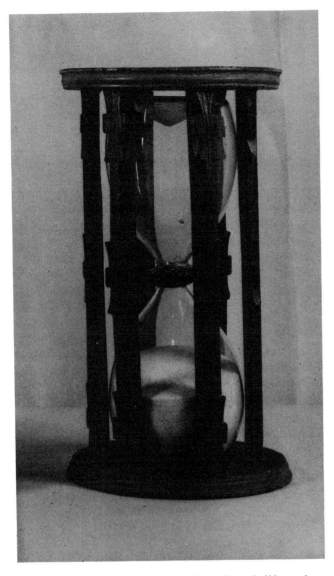

TIMEGLASS. A fifteenth-century *ampoletta* of one-half-hour duration.   NATIONAL MARITIME MUSEUM, GREENWICH

sand was substituted for water, as also, probably, was al-Khazini, writing in A.D. 1121/1122. In Europe, references are ambiguous until the fourteenth century, when the clerk of the English king's ship *La George* recorded in 1345/1346 the sums he paid in Flanders for twelve glass horloges and another four of the same sort. There are several subsequent references in the fourteenth century: in France in 1380, to a large *orloge de mer* comprising *deux grans fiolles plains de sablon* (two large phials full of sand); in Catalonia in 1380 as a wedding-present; in France in 1392 to 1394 in a recipe for filling domestic timeglasses; and in Switzerland, where the tolling of a town bell was to be regulated by a timeglass. A fresco by Ambrosio Lorenzetti in the Palazzo Publico in Siena uses a timeglass to symbolize temperance; it is uncertain whether the painting, as now seen, dates from 1338/1339 or nearly twenty years later. The next known illustration of a timeglass is found in a German-Hebrew Pentateuch of 1395, in which the timeglass, hanging by a becket from a hook on a wall, is timing a lesson. Only the first of these fourteenth-century references comes from a nautical context, but they show that, by the beginning of the fifteenth century, the timeglass was well known and not uncommon. No medieval timeglasses have survived intact; only a few fragments have been found.

Columbus refers to the *ampolleta* in his account of his first voyage. By extension of meaning, he uses this word to mean "the time the timeglass measures," by which he means always half an hour.

BIBLIOGRAPHY

Balmer, R. T. "The Operation of Sand Clocks and Their Medieval Development." *Technology & Culture* 19 (1978): 615–632.

Drover, C. B., P. A. Sabine, C. Tyler, and P. G. Coole. "Sand-Glass 'Sand,' Historical, Analytical, Practical." *Antiquarian Horology* 3 (1960): 62–72.

Junger, Ernest. *Das Sanduhr Buch.* Frankfurt am Main, 1957. French translation, *Le traité du sablier.* Paris, 1981.

Naish, G. P. B. "The Dyoll and the Bearing-Dial." *Journal of the Institute of Navigation* 7 (1954): 205–8.

Turner, A. J. "'The Accomplishment of Many Years': Three Notes towards a History of the Sand-glass." *Annals of Science* 39 (1982): 161–172.

Turner, A. J. "Water-clocks, Sand-glasses, Fire-clocks." Part 3 of vol. 1 of *The Time Museum: Catalogue of the Collection.* Rockford, Ill., 1984.

Varela, Consuelo, ed. *Cristóbal Colón. Textos y documentos completos. Relaciones de viajes, cartas y memoriales.* Madrid, 1982.

Waters, David W. *The Art of Navigation in Elizabethan and Early Stuart Times.* London, 1958.

Waters, David W. "Early Time and Distance Measurement at Sea." *Journal of the Institute of Navigation* 8 (1955): 153–173.

FRANCIS MADDISON

and night into watches. However, continuous periods of time measurement achieved by reversing the timeglass as quickly as possible each time it had run (or starting another at that moment) were likely to be inaccurate, and the pitching and rolling of a ship were not conducive to constant interval measurement.

The history of the timeglass is obscure. The timeglass was apparently not known in antiquity, nor is the first definite Muslim evidence, in sixteenth-century Turkey, earlier than medieval European evidence. About the year A.D. 1000, al-Biruni, in Ghazni, Afghanistan, preferred sand to water in time measurers, but there is no reason to suppose that he was referring to a glass-phial device, rather than to an open clepsydra (water clock) in which

TIMETELLING. Although the measurement of time has preoccupied humankind from the earliest periods of civilization, it was at best still only approximate during the Age of Discovery and in fact until a relatively modern period. The most common timekeeping devices prevalent in the fifteenth century in both the West and in the East were the sundial and the water clock (clepsydra), neither of which was capable of the precise measurement required for astronomical observations or navigation.

Water and Sand Clocks. Like the sundial, the water clock was commonly used in the Middle East and Far East as well as in the Western world from a very early period. Knowledge of Islamic forms of both sundials and water clocks was transmitted to the West by translations of Arabic texts. Notable among these were five books of the *Libros del saber de astronomia* (Books of knowledge of astronomy) compiled in about 1277 for King Alfonso X of Castile (Alfonso the Wise) and containing descriptions of a water clock, mercury clock, candle clock, and two sundials.

It is not known with certainty whether the water clock of the European medieval period was derived entirely from the Islamic water clock or was a continuation of the Roman anaphoric clock tradition. Basically, an anaphoric clock was a form of celestial calculator consisting of a constant-flow clepsydra and a disk on which were painted the signs of the zodiac and a number of stars behind a fixed grill, which represented the hours and the observer's local coordinates. It was already in use in European monastic houses in the twelfth century and possibly earlier. The earliest known description is found in a tenth- or eleventh-century manuscript in the Benedictine monastery of Santa María de Ripoli in the Pyrenees. The device's primary purpose was not to measure time in hours but to strike an alarm to awaken the bell ringer who would then strike the monastery bell to announce the canonical hours or offices that governed the daily life of the community. Several of the regulations of the early twelfth-century Cistercian rule confirm the widespread use of clepsydrae in monastic houses, including one rule that specified that the sacristan was to be instructed to set the "clock" and cause it to strike before lauds on winter weekends unless it was daylight. In the eleventh century similar instructions were issued by Abbot William of Hirsau to his sacristan.

In addition to its monastic functions, the water clock was used in rural areas in medieval Spain to control water distribution for irrigation. The sinking-bowl form as well as the *gadus* (a bucket of the noria or waterwheel, punctured in such a manner as to function as a makeshift outflow clepsydra) served this purpose, as did the sand clock, in which fine sand performed the same function as water. The sand clock was especially popular with astrol-ogers and mariners. (Later, in the late fifteenth century, the mechanical clock was also adapted for regulating water rights. Such a timekeeper was installed by the local lord, Père Bon, at his castle in the village of Collosa near Alicante. Constructed by a Valencian clockmaker, Micer Rubi, it was welcomed by the villagers because for the first time "the water of irrigation is divided into hours." A clock installed at Granada in the 1490s governed water flow for irrigation by the striking of "the Irrigation Bell.")

Until the late fourteenth century, large sand clocks, constructed in some of the larger cities by Mallorcan artisans identified as "cartographers," were installed in the towers of the communities' tallest public buildings. Keepers were employed to maintain them and to strike a bell each hour as indicated by the flow of sand. Such a timekeeper was ordered for the city of Barcelona by King Juan I of Aragón, and others were recorded in use in Tortosa and Zaragoza.

Mechanical Clocks. Late in the fourteenth century sand clocks were replaced by mechanical clocks installed in cathedrals and some monasteries in the major cities of Aragón and Castile. The earliest were in Tortosa and Burgos. The records indicate that for the most part the late fourteenth-century clock makers working in Spain were Jews, in addition to a few Catalans and Mallorcans.

The origin of the mechanical clock in the Western world has never been satisfactorily explained. Horological scholars have long debated the conflicting traditions relating to its introduction. One proposes that it was brought from China by seafarers to a major Italian port—Livorno, Amalfi, or Venice—at the beginning of the fourteenth century and from there proliferated through Italy and then the rest of Europe. Another tradition suggests that it evolved from an alarm developed for timing roasting spits in monastic kitchens or for awakening the bell ringer in time to toll the bell marking the divisions of the day.

In any event, by the early fourteenth century, the mechanical clock had revolutionized time measurement in Western society. The earliest public clock of record was installed in 1309 in the bell tower of the Church of San Eustorgio in Milan, and others soon followed. The cathedral at Beauvais had "a clock with bell" before 1324, and by 1335 the Church of San Gottardo in Milan had a clock with a bell that struck the twenty-four hours, the number of each hour indicated by the number of strokes. Many of the earliest public clocks were water-powered but were subsequently replaced with mechanical movements designed to strike bells at periodic intervals, making it possible at last for the populace to regulate their day.

Evidence indicates that these pioneering clocks only struck the hours—a dial for visual timekeeping was a later addition. By the mid-fourteenth century, public clocks were equipped with bells and simple dials as well as complicated astronomical dials and automatons. And at the end of the century clocks not only struck the hours and quarters but indicated them visually along with the day of the week, the month, the lunar phases, and conjunctions of the heavenly bodies. Mechanical clocks like these had now made their appearance on church and monastery buildings in a number of the larger Spanish cities, including the cathedrals of Barcelona, Tarragona (in Aragón), Valencia, Burgos, Seville, and Lérida.

It was not until the early sixteenth century that clock making evolved as a professional craft in its own right, brought about primarily by the demand for timepieces from the European royal courts and the rising class of bourgeois and wealthy merchants. Portable clocks and watches for domestic use evolved principally as possessions of the privileged, the princes, and the prelates. Generally they were products of great artistry involving the skills of the goldsmith and engraver as well as the mechanician. The time measurement function of these "toys of the wealthy" remained during this period of secondary importance to their interest as curiosities or as symbols of affluence and status. (They were often featured in portraits of individuals of power to denote position and wealth.)

The early clocks were weight-driven, having a crown wheel and verge escapement regulated by a foliot, which was subsequently replaced by the more accurate balance wheel. In time the spring drive replaced the falling weight as a power source, making it possible for the timepiece to assume various portable forms including the neck watch, the table clock, and the traveling clock.

Timekeeping at Sea. The early mechanical timekeepers usually lost or gained a great deal during the course of twenty-four hours, and it was not until much later even that a minute hand was added. Because of their lack of accuracy, they served no purpose for the astronomer or navigator. To measure time at sea, sailors consulted the stars at night or used a time glass or sand glass (reloj de arena or ampoletta). These glasses were produced in Venice, and because of their extreme fragility, a ship would carry as many as one or two dozen on a voyage. The flowing sand of the form used on fifteenth-century vessels measured thirty minutes. On shipboard the time glasses were maintained by a ship's boy (grummet) whose responsibility was to turn it immediately when the sand ran out. Consequently, the accuracy of time measurement depended on the degree of the grummet's diligence.

According to Columbus's journal, the ship's crew was divided into two watches, called cuartos or guardias. Each watch was of four hours' duration, and each was supervised by one of the ship's officers. Whether a standard procedure existed for changing the hours of watches on early Portuguese and Spanish ships is not known, but Columbus noted that on his ships, watches were changed at 3:00, 7:00, and 11:00. Columbus may have selected 7:00 for his first watch because it was approximately the time of sunset, and he developed the rest of his schedule from there at four-hour intervals. (It is to be noted that in Italian timekeeping the first hour began at half an hour after sunset, a practice that continued until the seventeenth century.)

The timing of the time glasses was corrected at noon and at night. Utilizing the card of the ship's compass as a sundial, the shipmaster or seaman would insert a pin at the center of the card, which would throw its shadow upon the center of the north point at exactly noon; at this moment the glass would be turned, establishing the correct time. For timing events Columbus used, in addition to the time glasses and the changing of the watch, the canonical hours or offices of prayer, which he undoubtedly learned during his stay at the monastery at La Rábida.

Columbus and other navigators of his time were probably also equipped with an early form of an instrument called the nocturnal, possibly hand drawn on paper. Through an opening at the center of this instrument or card, the polestar could be sighted at night and a movable arm representing the Little Dipper turned until it reached Kochab, one of the Dipper's two brightest stars. In this manner the precise position and the time were indicated.

Timetelling's importance in navigation was related to the need to determine longitude at sea. But until the late sixteenth century the accuracy of the timepieces used at sea—the sort used by Columbus—was at best only approximate within a quarter of an hour. In 1530 Rainer Gemma Frisius proposed the use of mechanical clocks on shipboard for determining longitude, but this was not yet possible because mechanical clocks were not sufficiently accurate. English voyagers, too, proposed using clocks at sea in the late sixteenth century, but the problem was not to be satisfactorily resolved until the last quarter of the eighteenth century when the English clockmaker John Harrison invented the chronometer. In the interim many sought a solution by devising specialized timepieces capable of being used on shipboard, but none was successful.

It was not until the scientific revolution of the seventeenth century when the clock became an important tool in the new sciences that it achieved precision. The growing preoccupation with astronomy, navigation, microscopy, and mechanics in particular brought about a closer relationship between the scientist and the craftsman who designed and constructed the tools of science. The greatest need was for tools of measurement of increasing precision, and although it was realized that in principle the clock could serve a multitude of scientific needs, it first had to be improved, particularly in its regulation.

Following the invention of the pendulum regulator,

conceived by Galileo in 1642 and first patented by Christian Huygens in 1657, improvements in the clock followed in rapid succession, including the English inventions of the anchor escapement, the compensated pendulum, the dead-beat escapement, and the balance spring. The establishment of the Royal Astronomical Observatory at Greenwich, England, in 1675 provided even greater impetus for developing clocks and watches of increasing accuracy.

[See also *Hourglass; Navigation,* article on *Instruments of Navigation.*]

BIBLIOGRAPHY

Bedini, Silvio A. *The Pulse of Time: Galileo Galilei, the Determination of Longitude, and the Pendulum Clock.* Florence, 1990.

Drover, C. B. "A Medieval Monastic Water-Clock." *Antiquarian Horology* 1, no. 5 (December 1954): 54–58, 63.

Glick, Thomas F. *Irrigation and Society in Medieval Valencia.* Cambridge, Mass., 1970.

Glick, Thomas F. "Medieval Irrigation Clocks." *Technology and Culture* 10, no. 3 (July 1969): 424–428.

Herrero García, Miguel. *El reloj en la vida española.* Madrid, 1955.

North, John D. "Monasticism and the First Mechanical Clocks." In *The Study of Time II: Proceedings of the Second Conference of the International Society for the Study of Time.* Edited by J. T. Fraser and John Lawrence. New York, 1975.

Vielliard, Jeanne. "Horloges et horlogers Catalans à la fin du moyen âge." *Bulletin Hispanique* 63 (1961): 161–168.

Whitrow, G. J. *Time in History.* New York, 1988.

SILVIO A. BEDINI

TOBACCO. See *Flora,* article on *Tobacco.*

TOLEDO. At the time of Columbus's voyages, the city of Toledo was one of the most important of Spain. It was a center of commerce and trade, a meeting site for the itinerant Castilian Crown and Cortes, and the see of the most powerful Castilian prelate, the archbishop of Toledo.

Toledo's prominence owed much to its central location. It straddled the major trade routes with Lisbon to the west, and with the southern and northern cities of the Crown of Castile. As the largest city of New Castile, Toledo was the center of a flourishing local and regional economy.

The city's population in 1492 is unknown, but Fernando Colón, writing in the early 1500s, estimated that it was between 18,000 and 20,000 souls. In the first recorded census of 1528, the population was about 29,490 inhabitants and rose to a high point of 62,060 in 1571.

The Toledo political scene was dominated by two rival factions: the Ayalas, the counts of Fuensalida; and the Silvas, the counts of Cifuentes. When these factions were not involved in open warfare, Toledo was governed by a city council presided over by a Crown-appointed corregidor, whose business it was, among other things, to steer the city council along paths favored by the Crown. After the comunero revolt of 1520–1521, the clans' bloody street battles subsided, although rivalry continued in other spheres.

A powerful figure in the city was the archbishop of Toledo, who presided over an enormous archdiocese, an impressive income, and vast opportunities for patronage. The Toledo prelates frequently occupied other high offices, as presidents of royal councils, close royal advisers, or inquisitor-generals of Castile. Men of prodigious influence, they played an important role in local politics and society. As church revival took on more urgency under the leadership of Cardinal-Archbishop Francisco Jiménez de Cisneros, Toledo experienced a proliferation of new religious, charitable, and educational foundations, confraternities, and lay groups devoted to religion. The patrimony of Toledo owes much to the munificence of its prelates.

Below these powerful figures were the more numerous and lesser-known citizens, among them a sizable population of Jews. By 1485, when the Inquisition arrived in the city, many Jews had converted to Christianity. Known as conversos, in 1486 they accounted for about 20 percent of the population. The political, social, and financial success of many conversos engendered tensions throughout the fifteenth and sixteenth centuries.

Despite setbacks from the Inquisition, the Toledo merchant and financial community, dominated by conversos, remained dynamic. After the conquest of Granada, several Toledo conversos established themselves as collectors of the royal tax levied on Granada silk. This connection was probably instrumental in the development of Toledo's silk industry, which came to dominate the city's manufacturing activities in the sixteenth century.

Toledo citizens were active in exploring new regions of the ever-expanding empire. Some families made their fortune by participating in the conquest of the Canary Islands, and many formed commercial companies to trade with the New World. Some people dedicated themselves to evangelization in remote parts of the empire, including the Philippines and Japan, others filled posts in the imperial bureaucracy, and some emigrated in search of a better life.

From the 1580s onward the Toledo economy experienced a decline, and the city lost much of its regional monopoly to the new capital, Madrid. What had been a dynamic, varied, and intellectually curious society of merchants, clerics, artisans, professionals, and local elites slowly faded to a frail, provincial society, living in a city that retained little of its former glory except for the importance of the church.

BIBLIOGRAPHY

Benito Ruano, Eloy. *Toledo en el siglo XV: Vida política.* Madrid, 1961.

Martz, Linda. "Converso Families in Toledo: The Importance of Lineage." *Sefarad* 48 (1988): 117–196.

Martz, Linda. *Poverty and Welfare in Habsburg Spain: The Example of Toledo.* Cambridge, 1983.

Phillips, Carla Rahn. "Time and Duration: A Model for the Economy of Early Modern Spain." *American Historical Review* 92 (1987): 531–562.

LINDA MARTZ

TOLEDO Y ROJAS, MARÍA DE (d. 1549), wife of Diego Colón, second Admiral of the Indies; daughter-in-law of Christopher Columbus; vicereine of the Indies. María Toledo y Rojas was the daughter of María de Rojas and Fernando de Toledo, lord of Villorias, grand falconer, *comendador mayor* of León, and member of the order of Santiago. Her father's brother was the second duke of Alba. She was married to Diego Colón in 1508 with a promised dowry of one million maravedis (2,667 ducats) drawn from her mother's property. In addition, she stood eventually to inherit a portion of her parent's joint property. Diego Colón offered her a marriage settlement of two thousand ducats. During the decades that followed, she and her kinsmen in the house of Alba were strong advocates for Colón's claims as heir to the Santa Fe Capitulations.

Accompanying her husband to Santo Domingo in 1509, she quickly established a miniature court and just as quickly began to bear children in a succession interrupted primarily by Diego's absences in Spain in 1511, 1513, and 1515 to 1517. In preparation for the latter journey, Diego named her cogovernor of La Española, with Gerónimo de Agüero, his former tutor. She had no real power; the audiencia and various royal agents had taken command of the government. Indeed, she was unable to prevent them from taking encomiendas and offices from Diego's friends and appointees. In 1518 she (and perhaps Diego) took her children, Felipa, María, Juana, and Isabel, to Spain to join her husband in seeking satisfaction of his claims under Christopher Columbus's agreements with the Catholic monarchs.

It is not known whether she traveled with him as he followed Charles V's court during 1518 and 1519. But she did return to Santo Domingo with him in 1520. Their first son, Luís, was born in 1521. During the next three years she bore two more sons, Cristóbal and Diego. The latter had not been born when his father was again summoned to Spain in the fall of 1523. She remained at Santo Domingo until 1529, seeing to the probating of her husband's will in May 1526 (he died in February).

Confirmed as tutor for her son Luís and thus empowered to exercise his rights, she soon came into conflict with the audiencia of Santo Domingo, royal appointees, and some municipal councils. When challenged by a royal official, she is said to have made the telling reply that a particular action followed the custom in the domains of the duke of Alba; the official rejoined that they were in the domains of the king. Because no resolution of the different visions of the admiral's power was possible at Santo Domingo, in 1529 she journeyed to Spain in order to preserve her son's rights as she understood them. Historians differ as to whether Luís and the other children accompanied her at this time.

Another reason for her journey was that her late husband's appeal of the decisions of 1520 (regarding the second lawsuit in the Pleitos Colombinos) was consolidated in 1527 into an entirely new lawsuit. María's father represented the family in 1527 and 1528; her presence was necessary because the royal attorney objected that even he could not speak for Luís. The lawsuit was concluded in 1534 with a settlement that left unanswered the important questions of whether Luís should be put in possession of the viceroyalty and governorship and what revenues he was to enjoy as admiral. A new lawsuit resulted, from which came the settlement of 1536–1537. During the years these cases were being heard, María continued to appoint officials and claim revenues according to her interpretation of her son's privileges.

Under the terms of the settlement of 1536–1537, Luís received a fixed income in place of the percentage of royal revenues and certain admiralty fees he had received, Jamaica and a land grant in Veragua (Panama), and new titles, but had to give up the title of viceroy of the Indies. His unmarried sisters and youngest brother, Diego, received lifetime pensions. María was awarded four thousand ducats over a four-year period to repay her costs in pursuing the litigation since 1526 and a lifetime pension of one thousand ducats a year. She later assigned this to her daughter María, probably as part of her dowry.

Adding to María's achievements in providing for her family were the marriages of her daughters María, Juana, and Isabel, although she did not live to see all of them. María married Sancho de Cardona, admiral of Aragón. Juana married Luís de la Cueva, brother of the third duke of Albuquerque, in 1536. Isabel married Jorge de Portugal, count of Gelves, in 1531. The oldest daughter, Felipa, became a nun.

Having thus provided for the financial security of her family, María joined her son in lobbying for his appointment as captain general of La Española, a title he was given in 1540. She apparently accompanied him back to Santo Domingo that year and remained there for the rest of her life, exercising such influence as she could over Luís.

The last years of her life were marked by her success in breaking up Luís's marriage in 1542 to María de Orozco and by the disastrous effort in 1546 to colonize Luís's land grant in Veragua. She undoubtedly had a hand in Luís's marriage in 1547 to María de Mosquera. The Mosquera marriage probably brought new financial resources to the family as well as strengthened ties to an important, wealthy local family, whose founder, Juan de Mosquera, had been a poor immigrant in the earliest days of the colony. Ties to another important and wealthy family resulted from the marriage of María's second son, Cristóbal, to Leonor Zuazo, daughter of Alonso Zuazo, once Diego Colón's antagonist and then his supporter in the struggle over power in 1517 and 1518. María de Toledo died at Santo Domingo on May 11, 1549.

BIBLIOGRAPHY

Colección de documentos inéditos relativos al descubrimiento, conquista, y organización de las antiguas posesiones españoles de América y Oceanía, sacados de los archivos del reino, y muy especialmente del de Indias. Edited by Joaquín F. Pacheco et al. 42 vols. Madrid, 1864–1884. Vols. 37, pp. 436, and 40, pp. 373–397.

Floyd, Troy S. *The Columbus Dynasty in the Caribbean.* Albuquerque, N.Mex., 1973.

Thacher, John Boyd. *Christopher Columbus, His Life, His Work, His Remains.* 3 vols. 1903–1904. Reprint, New York, 1967.

PAUL E. HOFFMAN

TOMB OF COLUMBUS. See *Burial Places.*

TORDESILLAS, TREATY OF. See *Treaty of Tordesillas.*

TORQUEMADA, TOMÁS DE (1420–1498), first inquisitor general. Tomás de Torquemada was the son of Pedro Fernández de Torquemada, of Jewish lineage, and nephew of the Dominican theologian Cardinal Juan de Torquemada (1388–1468), who in 1450 defended the conversos in Rome in his famous *Treatise against Midianites and Ishmaelites.* Torquemada entered the Dominican convent of San Pablo, Valladolid, founded by his uncle, and soon became the prior of Santa Cruz in Segovia, a position that he held for twenty-two years. He knew Isabel, then living as a princess in Segovia, who made him her confessor, whereby he gained special authority over her as well as over Fernando. Contrary to the common understanding, Torquemada did not request that the Inquisition be established, although he was associated with it from its beginning in 1478. In 1482 his order asked him to oversee the foundation of the convent of Santo

Tomás in Ávila, to which he retired in 1496, and where he died. Also in 1482, the sovereigns named him as one of several inquisitors in Castile and León, kingdoms without any inquisitorial tradition. Feeling the need to organize a tribunal with unified jurisdiction and knowing Torquemada's abilities, in 1483 they asked Pope Sixtus IV to appoint him inquisitor general of Spain, including Aragón, thus superseding the medieval Aragonese (papal, or so-called French) inquisition. Helped by fellow inquisitors, Torquemada wrote in 1486 the *Instrucciones*, the basic by-laws of the Spanish Inquisition for its entire duration. He then organized its Supreme Council as an ecclesiastical branch of the government, divided Spain into districts, and supervised inquisitorial activities until Pope Alexander VI appointed four bishops both to help and restrain him. In 1492 he not only supported but actively promoted the expulsion of the Jews, although neither his title nor his name appear in the text of the decree of expulsion. Torquemada, rightly or wrongly, became the symbol of religious—and even general—intolerance. In 1808 French troops desecrated his remains. His life and activities continue to be reevaluated by contemporary scholarship.

BIBLIOGRAPHY

Huerga Criado, Pilar. *El inquisidor general Torquemada.* Madrid, 1984.

Meseguer Fernández, Juan. "Tomás de Torquemada, inquisidor general." In vol. 1 of *Historia de la Inquisición en España y América*, edited by J. Pérez Villanueva and B. Escandell. Madrid, 1984.

Wood, Clement. *Torquemada: Rack of the Inquisition.* New York, 1930.

ANGEL ALCALÁ

TORRES, ANTONIO DE (fl. late 1500s), ship's captain and fleet commander. Torres was owner and master of Columbus's flagship on his second voyage. The principal purpose of the voyage was to establish a self-sustaining colony on La Española, and to that end a grand fleet of seventeen vessels was manned and outfitted in Cádiz with food, arms, supplies, and equipment for more than twelve hundred seamen, officials, ecclesiastics, artisans, workmen, and men-at-arms. The fleet sailed from Cádiz on September 25, 1493, for an intended six-month round-trip voyage.

Twelve of the vessels, under the overall command of Torres, then sailed from La Isabela, the newly established colony on La Española, on February 2, 1494, to return to Spain for additional supplies. Following the example set by Columbus on the return to Spain from the first voyage, Torres proceeded along the north shore of the island to its eastern end and then headed to the northeast until he caught the favorable westerly winds, arriving in Cádiz on March 7, 1494, after a swift passage.

Torres returned to La Española that fall with four caravels laden with supplies requested by Columbus and with a message of approval from the sovereigns, dated August 16, 1494. Torres again set sail from La Isabela on February 24, 1495, with the four caravels laden with about five hundred male and female Indian slaves. For some reason he chose a more southerly route than he had used previously and wasted a month beating to windward along the northern coasts of La Española and Puerto Rico. Running low on food and water, he finally changed course to the north to find the westerlies. These favorable winds sped him on to the island of Madeira where he was able to reprovision before resuming his voyage to Cádiz. The suffering of the Indians, confined below decks, can only be imagined. About two hundred of them died and were cast overboard. The remainder, many of whom were sick, were disembarked in Cádiz about May 1, 1495, and put up for sale in Seville by Bishop Juan Rodríguez de Fonseca.

There followed an interval in which there is no record of Torres. He reappears in 1502 as captain of the flagship of a magnificent fleet of thirty ships carrying twenty-five hundred mariners, colonists, and soldiers. Aboard the flagship was Nicolás de Ovando, newly appointed governor of the Indies (except those portions under the jurisdiction of Vicente Yáñez Pinzón and Alonso de Ojeda). The fleet sailed from Cádiz on February 13, 1502, and arrived in Santo Domingo, the new capital of La Española, in early April.

The fleet remained anchored until July in the mouth of the Ozama River, the site of Santo Domingo, and was making preparations to return to Spain when Columbus arrived at the mouth of the river, seeking refuge for his four caravels from an approaching hurricane. The Admiral, having gained experience from two previous hurricanes in the Caribbean, urged that the fleet not leave port until the storm had passed. Ovando refused Columbus access to the harbor and scoffed at the hurricane warning. The fleet sailed and had just entered the Mona Passage between La Española and Puerto Rico when the hurricane struck. Several ships capsized at sea, and most of those that survived the first winds were driven ashore and destroyed. Only five of the thirty ships survived, and over five hundred men were lost, among them the fleet commander, Antonio de Torres.

BIBLIOGRAPHY

Gould, Alicia B. *Nueva lista documentada de los tripulantes de Colón en 1492.* Madrid, 1984.

Irving, Washington. *The Life and Voyages of Christopher Columbus and His Companions.* 3 vols. New York, 1849.

WILLIAM LEMOS

TOSCANELLI, PAOLO DAL POZZO (1397–1482), Florentine mathematician, astronomer, astrologer, and geographer. Toscanelli (Latin, Paulus de Puteo Toscanello; also Paulus medicus, physicus, astronomus, etc.) was born and died in Florence, where he spent most of his long life. He studied medicine and other subjects at the University of Padua, gaining his doctorate in 1424. His most important extant work is a treatise on comets, *Immensi labores et graves vigilie Pauli de Puteo Toscanello super mensura comete* (Immense toils and serious lucubrations of Paolo dal Pozzo Toscanelli on the measurement of comets), which contains celestial maps showing the successive positions of each comet at its appearance. His fame as a geographer rests on his knowledge and appreciation of the voyages of Marco Polo, his interviews with travelers visiting Florence from distant lands (such as Tatars from the Don and clerics from Ethiopia), and his connection, whether direct or not, with Columbus's plans for exploration.

While in Padua he became a close friend of Nicholas of Cusa, with whom he shared an interest in geography. In 1425, he met the Florentine architect Filippo Brunelleschi, who designed the dome and lantern of the cathedral of Florence. When the city was hit by an earthquake in 1453, the Signoria consulted Toscanelli as an astrologer. In 1468 he constructed an astronomical gnomon in Brunelleschi's lantern, where an opening let the sun's rays shine on the gnomon (later replaced), so that the timing of solstices, eclipses, and other astronomical data could be established. The opening also allowed the sun to shine on a stone set in the floor of the cathedral at noon on the summer solstice. Both these astronomical devices helped establish latitude and longitude.

According to Bartolomé de las Casas's *Historia de las Indias,* Afonso V of Portugal asked Canon Fernão Martins to write to Toscanelli about the possibilities of sailing west to Asia. On June 25, 1474, Toscanelli replied with a detailed letter and a map. The originals of both are lost, but a presumed copy of the letter attached to Columbus's copy of Enea Silvio Piccolomini's geographical work was made public after Columbus's death. J. Henry Vignaud's attempts to prove that this letter was spurious are no longer accepted by most scholars.

In his letter, Toscanelli says that he is very glad that the king is seeking a shorter sea route to the spice-producing areas than by way of Guinea. He includes a map or chart, made with his own hands, "in which are drawn your shores and the islands from which you may begin to sail continuously west, and the lands which you must reach, and how far you must deviate from the pole or the equator, and for what distance, that is, for how many miles you should sail to reach most fertile lands producing all spices and gems." He claims that, as the land distance from Lisbon east to the coast of the Far East covers 230 degrees, only 130 degrees of sea separate Lisbon from the east coast of Asia (at 100 kilometers [62½ miles] to the degree, this distance would be 13,000 kilometers [8,125 miles]). Toscanelli claimed that only 116 degrees separated Cape Verde from the coast of Asia and that both the legendary island of Antilia and Cipangu (Japan) lie on the route, there being only 50 degrees between the two.

In contrast to Ptolemy's implication that the unknown world was 180 degrees across from east to west, and Marinus of Tyre's implication that it was 135 degrees across, the actual distance at the latitudes involved is nearly 250 degrees. If there had been no intervening land, this stretch of open ocean would have proved an insuperable obstacle. Toscanelli's estimate of 62½ miles to a degree was the middle of three estimates (56⅔, 62½, and 66⅔ miles) given by Fra Mauro in his 1459 world map. Columbus, following Pierre d'Ailly, who in turn was indebted to Alfraganus (al-Farghani), preferred the smallest figure, 56⅔ miles.

Toscanelli's map may have resembled the 1894 reconstruction by Hermann Wagner, with cylindrical projection similar to that of Marinus and with the west coast of Cipangu placed about 1,000 miles from the nearest point of China (Marco Polo had placed Cipangu 1,500 miles from China, and Toscanelli may have done likewise or modified the distance from his interviews). The map may have had

a directional line past Antilia, wherever that was thought to be, and from Cipangu to Quinsay (Hangchow, China). According to W. G. L. Randles, the extant map corresponding most closely to Wagner's reconstruction of Toscanelli's is the world map (c. 1490) by Henricus Martellus Germanus (Yale University Library).

Toscanelli's letter and map had no immediate effect. Columbus's plans were rejected by a Portuguese royal committee of cosmographers appointed in 1483–1484 and by similar committees in Spain in 1486–1487 and 1491. During that period, learned men in both countries were arguing for or against the plans, with both sides appealing to Aristotle and even to *Genesis*. To explain the emergence of dry land from water, the Spanish *converso* Paul de Burgos (c. 1350–1435) had maintained that on the third day of creation, when God said "Let the waters under the heaven be gathered together unto one place, and let the dry land appear," God moved the sphere of water so that the spheres of earth, water, air, and fire were no longer concentric. Ptolemy writes in his *Geography*, "From mathematical calculations it may be assumed that the collective surface of land and sea is in all its parts spherical"; he knew of no land in Asia beyond islands near its east coast. Arguments from such authorities were likely to be sterile, whereas Toscanelli, by combining the statistics of a mathematical geographer with an economic

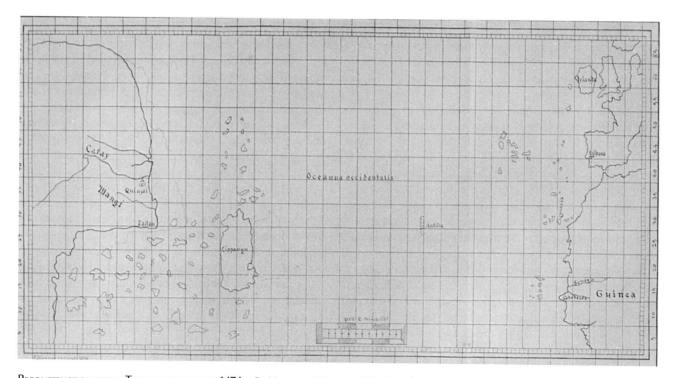

RECONSTRUCTION OF THE TOSCANELLI CHART OF 1474.   By Hermann Wagner, 1894. Based on presumed copy of the Toscanelli letter to Canon Martins that is copied into Columbus's copy of Enea Silvio Piccolomini's *Historia rerum.*

FROM *NACHRICHTEN DER K. GESELLSCHAFT DER WISSENSCHAFTEN ZU GÖTTINGEN* (1894), P. 313.

factor (the search for spices and jewels), may well have helped to influence the new committee and the Royal Council of Castile in 1491, some years after his death. The *mappamundi* that Columbus exhibited at that time may have been Toscanelli's map with the distance shortened.

BIBLIOGRAPHY

Morison, Samuel Eliot. *Admiral of the Ocean Sea: A Life of Christopher Columbus.* 2 vols. Boston, 1942.

Randles, W. G. L. "The Evaluation of Columbus' 'India' Project by Cosmographers in the Light of the Geographical Science of the Period." *Imago Mundi* 42 (1990): 50–64.

Uzielli, Gustavo. *La vita e i tempi di Paolo dal Pozzo Toscanelli.* Rome, 1983.

Vignaud, J. Henry. *The Columbian Tradition on the Discovery of America and of the Part Played Therein by the Astronomer Toscanelli.* Oxford, 1920.

Vignaud, J. Henry. *Toscanelli and Columbus.* London, 1902.

O. A. W. DILKE

TRADE. [The following entry includes two articles on trade in the Age of European Exploration:

Mediterranean Trade

Caribbean Trade

For further discussion of the importance and impact of trading, see *Atlantic Rivalry*.]

Mediterranean Trade

By about 1460 the Western world had begun to recover from the demographic devastation wrought by the Black Death of the mid-fourteenth century. Although scholars argue about the nature and extent of the revitalization, it seems clear that populations were beginning to rise, labor wages remained relatively high, and demand for both domestic and imported goods increased as the century wore on. The augmented output of raw materials, such as metals, wool, and wood, and industrial products, such as cloth, glass, arms, and soap, satisfied much domestic demand and also provided valuable commodities for exchange with other Christian countries, both Mediterranean and northern, and with Muslim countries and lands farther east.

The Mediterranean economy of the second half of the fifteenth century was, however, still largely agrarian and localized. Although only about one in ten Europeans lived in cities, these urban centers needed to import large amounts of foodstuffs. Some food came from the countryside controlled by the cities, from estates often owned by rich burghers, but in times of shortfall, and often on a regular basis, more had to be imported. Civic governments were adamant about ensuring food supplies since

shortages could easily lead to social disruption—something civic officials everywhere wanted to avoid. Thus, cities usually allowed unrestricted importation of necessaries, with the only predictable tariffs being levied on wine in Spain and southern Italy. Cities like Genoa or Naples that were poor in local agricultural production had to import vast amounts of grain, salt, oil, fish, and sometimes wine. Fernand Braudel has estimated that the average European consumed annually about 440 pounds of grain, and given frequent disruptions in local supply, it could prove profitable to import grain even from enormous distances. Sicilian and Apulian grain could be found in Flanders, and German wheat in Egypt, while Crimean grain was routinely sold as Genoese bread.

As the European economy began to grow after 1460 or so, industry also picked up momentum. The development of printing in the 1450s created new markets for both expensive volumes and cheap pocketbooks, tracts, and broadsheets; it also stimulated the paper and ink industries. The Venetians started a new woolens industry in 1458, although it had stagnated by the early sixteenth century. Venice also made substantial additions to its arsenal shipyards in 1473, and the manufacture of soap and glass increased over the years. Production of cloth—including woolens, silks, linens, and cottons, and fancy velvets, damasks, and brocades—also expanded. Flemish and English cloth sold regularly in Mediterranean ports, and cheaper grades of light woolens from Florence had a ready market at Levantine fairs. Richer grades were always in demand, increasingly so in the Levantine markets where domestic production had fallen off. This high rate of production stimulated demand for raw material, usually imported into production centers like Florence; alum, needed in the cleaning and dying process of wool and extracted at only a few places in Europe; and dyestuffs, the best quality and variety of which came from Asia. Milanese arms and armor and firearms still commanded a steady market, although competition from Spain and southern Germany was growing.

Short-haul trade provided the bulk of Mediterranean traffic, but the real profits were to be made in luxury trade with Asia. Traditionally, oriental products reached the West by caravan to the Black Sea ports like Tana, or up the Persian Gulf and through Mesopotamia to Syria, or up the Red Sea to Egypt's ports, especially Alexandria. When the Turks captured Constantinople in 1453, they effectively blocked European trade with the Black Sea ports, restricting already diminishing trade with the northern caravan routes and producers in the Black Sea region. The silks, drugs, aromatics, and spices that had traveled overland from India and China now filtered through Turkish hands if they came through at all. This area had provided wheat and slaves, which were now at the mercy of the "infidel," as were the valuable alum mines of Focea, captured from the Genoese in 1455.

Farther south in Syria and Egypt, an area ruled by the Mamluks and threatened by further Turkish advances, the situation was one of social decline and general impoverishment. Although Beirut, Damascus, Tripoli, and Alexandria remained important transit ports between east and west, their native economies based on fancy cloth, glass, and even grain and cotton disintegrated, as high taxation for defense and recurring epidemics hammered the population. This forced the Mamluk authorities to raise tariffs, force the purchase by western merchants of certain surplus goods, especially pepper, and otherwise raise the revenues from the transit trade. Glass and silks, once major export items, were now imported by the Venetians.

Venice, long the most vital and powerful maritime nation in the Mediterranean, dominated Western trade with the Levant. Venetians brought to that region cheap cloth from England and northern Italy, oil, honey, nuts, and sometimes wheat, copper, and tin from northern Europe, and soap, glass, and coral from Venetian lands. The Venetian galley fleets returned with cotton, precious stones, dyes, aromatics, and spices from Malaysia, Burma, India, Ceylon, and China. As European economic production rose, less specie was needed to pay for these goods. In addition, the prices of spices, especially pepper and ginger, fell dramatically after mid-century because of economic conditions in the East, which sweetened the appeal of the spice trade for Europeans.

Venice handled much of this in large, regularly sailing fleets of galleys sponsored and controlled by the state. Upon their arrival at Alexandria or Beirut, huge fairs (*mudda*) were held, which facilitated exchange between the East and West. According to the foremost authority on the Levant trade, Eliyahu Ashtor, during the second half of the fifteenth century, "the spice trade flourished more than in any time before." Venetian merchants were responsible for about 60 percent of this trade, with a gross annual average around the end of the century of 650,000 ducats out of some 1.1 million ducats.

Until the Turkish conquest of the northeast Mediterranean, the Italian city-state of Genoa controlled trade in this region through a number of important trading colonies. The chief entrepôt was the Aegean island of Chios, which remained the key to eastern Genoese trade even after the surrender of Pera (1453) and the losses of Focea and Lesbos (1462). Genoa accounted for about 140,000 ducats per annum in trade with Egypt and Syria in the late 1400s, but whereas the Levant trade was vital for Venice, it represented only about 25 percent of Genoa's trade volume. Because of its location in the western Mediterranean, Genoa traditionally looked both east and west. Like Venice, Genoa served as a transit point for Mediterranean

goods going north, especially to Milan, Switzerland, and the fairs of France, but Genoa also came to dominate trade between the eastern Mediterranean and Iberia, England, and Flanders.

The Genoese used a variety of ships, each specializing in a certain type of cargo. Some carried high-bulk goods such as alum, wheat, or lumber; smaller, faster ships would transport higher-priced, lower-bulk items. Although the Genoese used galley fleets, in general their trade was not under state control, as the Venetians' was; rather it was guided by individual initiative on the part of merchants and shipowners. This lent a good deal of flexibility to Genoese practices, although it also exposed merchants to greater risks. Indeed, as the Turks gobbled up Genoa's eastern colonies, the metropolis did practically nothing. On the other hand, Genoese ships did not have to make mandatory stops, often sailing directly from Chios to Flanders or from England to Chios. In addition, the Genoese could ship foreign goods, thus serving the interests of foreign individuals and states, as they did in transporting alum from Tolfa in the Papal States.

The stability, continuity, and experience of Genoese traders and their practices contrast favorably with those of their rivals. Although all Mediterranean countries carried out coastal trade in commodities like wine, wheat, and salt (wheat, in fact, was a very important item in Genoese trade), few could carry on sustained trade with the East like Venice or even Genoa, at least not before 1500. Catalan trade declined as political and economic conditions in the region were disrupted, especially during the war between Aragón and France in the 1460s. French overseas trade was also upset by this war, as it had been by the long war with England that had only recently ended. The French monarch Louis XI, however, had a lively interest in Levant trade, and he established regular galley voyages from Marseilles to Alexandria in the 1470s and 1480s. The Italian cloth and banking center of Florence dealt most heavily with the old Byzantine, now Turkish, centers, which tended to alienate the rival Mamluks and resulted in only a small traffic in Levantine spices. Florence's attempt at establishing a galley fleet at this time is evidence of Italian merchant vitality, despite the fact that the effort failed. Naples was a great center for the exchange of goods, but owing to a policy of free trade its own goods were frequently handled by foreign traders.

The profits from longer-distance luxury trade were substantial. European demand for oriental products increased over the second half of the century, which tended to raise their value. In general, the costs of delivering these items to European markets fell at least slightly. These two factors augmented the profit margin. Freight charges, commissions, and duties at home and abroad added about 25 percent to the price paid in the Levant, but profits still lay in the range of 20 to 25 percent for spices and 45 to 50 percent for cotton from the East. Freight charges tended to drop as ships got larger, and other dues could fluctuate according to local conditions. Duties paid in the Levant amounted to about 40 percent of transport costs, but the uncertainty created by the Turkish threat kept this an unstable figure. Since the Mamluks counted on Western support against the potential threat of the Turks, however, they tried to tread lightly (though on several occasions they sequestered Western merchants for the misdeeds of other Europeans). All the same, the profits were high, compared with the 9 to 10 percent gained from trade with central Europe (whose overland freight charges were very high). Trade with the East would continue to grow, but in what direction?

There must have been those who, like the brothers Ugolino and Vadino Vivaldi in the 1290s, dreamed of making direct commercial contact with the producers themselves in the East. Such direct contact would eliminate the costs of coastal voyages in the waters of the Indian Ocean, Red Sea, and Persian Gulf, and of caravan transport from southern ports. The often corrupt and unpredictable Mamluks and their charges could be avoided, and if the Turks were to capture the Mamluk ports, then a continued supply would be ensured. Cutting out these middlemen could more than compensate for the costs of increased sailing time.

Although the Venetians were generally contented with their Levant trade and saw its volume and profits increase over the latter half of the fifteenth century, the Genoese and Portuguese, who were already trading in the Atlantic, were far more likely to seek alternative routes to the East. The Genoese were well established in the North African coastal trade and, along with the Portuguese, probed down the Atlantic coast. Many Genoese served with or for the Portuguese and other Iberian rulers or were independent merchants trading out of Cádiz or Lisbon. The independent-mindedness of the Genoese well served the Iberian monarchs who were already attempting early forms of mercantilism, especially the Portuguese in the Madeiras and the Canaries. The colonial practices of the Genoese and to a lesser extent the Venetians, honed in the Aegean and Cyprus, proved apt models for later Iberian expansion. The tightly organized Venetian state galley fleets were as well direct precursors of the East Indian fleets of Spain and Portugal.

In many ways economic conditions in the Mediterranean during the latter half of the fifteenth century made European expansion into and beyond the Atlantic almost inevitable. Venetian domination of the trade with Mamluk ports, and the Turkish threat to those ports, made alternative routes to the East very appealing to such western powers as Genoa, Spain, and Portugal. Falling

prices of spices, dyes, and aromatics in the East seemed to ensure continued high profits, as did generally improving demographic and economic conditions in the West. The Genoese had proven that long continuous voyages, such as that from Chios to Flanders, were practical and profitable. The Genoese and Venetians had also established models for both extractive and trading colonies, such as the alum mines of Focea and highly successful *fondouks*, or trading headquarters, in Alexandria, Damascus, and Beirut. The Genoese and Iberians, seeking to tap into African gold, ivory, slaves, and some spices, had long traded with North Africa, and during the fifteenth century they expanded commercial contacts well down the African Atlantic coast. By the time the westward-looking Genoese Christopher Columbus approached the Spanish monarchs and convinced them to support his venture, any economic arguments he made must have sounded self-evident.

[See also *Florence; Genoa; Spices; Venetian Republic.*]

BIBLIOGRAPHY

Ashtor, Eliyahu. *Levant Trade in the Later Middle Ages*. Princeton, 1983.

Heers, Jacques. *Gènes au XVe siècle: Activité économique et problèmes sociaux*. Paris, 1961.

Kedar, Benjamin. *Merchants in Crisis: Genoese and Venetian Men of Affairs and the Fourteenth-Century Depression*. New Haven, 1976.

Lane, Frederic C. *Venice and History: The Collected Papers of Frederic C. Lane*. Baltimore, 1966.

Lopez, Robert S. "Venice and Genoa: Two Styles, One Success." *Diogenes* 71 (1970).

Pike, Ruth. *Enterprise and Adventure: The Genoese in Seville and the Opening of the New World*. Ithaca, N.Y., 1966.

Tracy, James D. *The Rise of Merchant Empires (1350–1750)*. New York, 1990.

Verlinden, Charles. *The Beginnings of Modern Colonization*. Ithaca, N.Y., 1970.

JOSEPH P. BYRNE

Caribbean Trade

Once Columbus had discovered America, the Spanish monarchy wanted to monopolize all production in the new lands as well as all the mercantile transactions between Spain and the Indies. To achieve this goal, the Crown established a system whereby the production of the colonies was regimented according to a complicated system of royal rights, licenses, and grants that regulated the cultivation or exploitation of specific products. This system of trading colonies followed the model of the *factorías* set up by the Portuguese in Africa.

A *factoría* was a commercial outpost owned by two or more partners who divided the profits derived from trading with the natives; labor was provided by white artisans and craftsmen employed under a rigid wage system. Columbus used this experience in Africa to set up the first *factoría* at La Isabela in the island of La Española. Given the harsh working conditions imposed by Columbus on the Spanish laborers, a rebellion soon broke out and the *factoría* collapsed, thus forcing the Spanish Crown to reconsider its colonization scheme in the New World.

Within the new colonial framework initiated in 1502, the Spanish monarchs set up a fiscal policy that guaranteed a steady revenue for the royal exchequer. A tax of one-fifth was placed on all gold found in the Indies; another, the *alcabala*, put a 10 percent surcharge on all operations of buying and selling carried out in the colonies; and yet another, the *almojarifazgo*, imposed a 7.5 percent duty on all merchandise imported by the colonists. Thus, what the monarchs could not obtain by directly controlling colonial commerce and production they could get by taxing all the economic activities in the New World.

These activities were supervised by the Casa de la Contratación, which started its operations in Seville in 1503. Without its permission, no voyages or commercial transactions could be undertaken between Spain and the Indies. In each port of the New World the Casa maintained officials to supervise the production of gold, silver, precious stones, and many agricultural products. Other functionaries collected taxes, kept the account books of the royal exchequer, and gave permission to navigate and trade between the different regions. These officials included factors, inspectors, accountants, and treasurers, and their counterparts in Seville.

Spain's monopolistic policies put heavy restrictions on colonial trade. According to a policy established in 1503, there could be no commerce with foreigners. Therefore, foreigners could not go to the Indies to trade without the risk of severe punishment. Ships could leave for the Indies only from the port of Seville. Colonial products could not be sent to any port other than Seville or Cádiz, thus leaving all the other ports of the Iberian Peninsula outside the great stream of trade generated by colonization.

Such control had its most noticeable effects on prices, since the Casa de la Contratación responded generally to the interests of Seville's merchants rather than to the needs of the colonists. Thus, throughout the sixteenth century, it was almost impossible for the colonists legally to obtain merchandise directly from other parts of Spain or Europe; items they needed had first to be imported into Spain from other European countries. After paying maritime insurance, freight rates, and other duties, such merchandise cost up to six times its original price when it arrived at the colonies. On the other hand, the merchants of Seville often paid the lowest possible prices for colonial products in order to maximize their profits, a practice resented by the colonists.

The Spanish monopoly on the colonial market was also resented by the European merchants who were seeking means to expand their external markets. To circumvent the trade controls, many non-Spanish merchants maintained agents in Seville and various colonial cities operating through third parties. These foreign merchants acted as shipowners, exporters, and importers or as moneylenders and financiers for the many Spanish businessmen in Seville who were always in need of money. Even Charles V became deeply indebted to foreign merchants. As the sixteenth century advanced, Seville's economic life became more dependent upon foreign investors who anxiously awaited the return of ships from the New World to receive their payments, rents, and commissions. There were entire years during which the shipments of gold coming from Mexico and other colonies were mortgaged even before embarking to Spain. Because of this foreign domination over Spanish trade and finances, almost all the gold, silver, and other products that arrived in Seville were finally handed over to the very nations Spain wanted to keep away from its colonies. By 1589, Seville had some fifteen thousand foreign residents out of a total population of only ninety thousand.

Other responses elicited by the European opposition to Spain's monopoly in the New World were piracy and contraband. As early as 1513, for example, French pirates waited around the Canaries for Spanish ships coming from the Indies. In 1522, a French pirate named Jean Fleury attacked a ship sailing from Santo Domingo to Seville with a cargo of sugar, which Fleury stole and took to France. Soon, these pirates moved into the Caribbean. Piracy had a drastic effect on prices in the Indies as freight and insurance rates rose several times, and it presented a grave problem to the Spanish monopoly. In 1543, the Crown decided to protect its trade between Seville and the New World by ordering its ships to make their trips together in well-guarded fleets. These fleets were to leave twice a year from Seville and return through the ports of Veracruz in Mexico and Nombre de Dios on the Isthmus of Panama. The system of fleets, however, did not function regularly until 1566 when the use of galleons was inaugurated.

The fleets notably altered the rhythm and flow of navigation in the Caribbean and eventually completed the isolation of Santo Domingo, Puerto Rico, Jamaica, and the eastern part of Cuba as Mexico and Peru gained in importance within the Spanish Empire. Ships bound from Seville to the Caribbean islands could sail from Spain only with the fleet. But upon arriving in the Caribbean, they would have to proceed without protection through pirate-infested waters as the fleet continued on to other ports. Thus, navigation and trade to these islands became more expensive as freight rates rose in proportion with maritime insurance. Havana became the most important port in the Caribbean, and Santo Domingo, Puerto Rico, and Jamaica were left on the sidelines. Havana was on the gulf route, and its port was a much more convenient spot for the fleets to stop and take on provisions of food and water for the return voyage.

The inhabitants of the Caribbean islands were always in great need of wheat, wine, flour, cloth, soap, perfume, cloves, shoes, medicine, paper, dried fruit, iron, steel, knives, nails, and many other articles. Since Spain could not provide them except at high prices and under monopolistic conditions, the colonists increasingly turned to smugglers. Evidence of contraband appeared as early as 1527, when an English ship appeared in the harbor of Santo Domingo and asked to be admitted to rest its crew and take on fresh water on the pretext that it had been thrown off its course to North America. Although the authorities permitted it to anchor, they soon discovered that the English were seeking to establish trade with the city's residents. Moreover, the colonial authorities realized that despite existing prohibitions, there were abundant signs that African slaves were being introduced as contraband by the Portuguese and Germans who brought these blacks from the coasts of Guinea and Senegal.

As the sixteenth century progressed, the contraband trade became the norm in the Caribbean. In the early years, the colonists in the islands had patiently awaited Spanish ships to buy their products. But as the arrival of ships became more and more infrequent, the people gradually turned to French, English, and Portuguese smugglers. Indeed, contraband offered the inhabitants of these islands distinct advantages over the official Spanish trade. The smugglers sold their goods at cheaper prices and offered higher prices for the colonists' sugar, hides, and other products, and the colonists avoided paying export taxes to the Spanish government.

At first the colonists preferred trading with the Portuguese smugglers since the latter spoke a similar language and offered the merchandise most desired by the Spaniards—African slaves. But because Portugal, like Spain, possessed little industry, most of the manufactured goods needed by the residents were produced in other countries, particularly England and France, and were cheaper when obtained directly from French, English, and Dutch intermediaries. The willingness of the colonists to trade with the smugglers was intolerable to the Consulado of Seville and the Casa de la Contratación, even though their system of fleets was placing the islands on the sidelines of the official trade routes.

Dozens of cedulas, royal orders, and laws were sent from Seville to the colonial authorities commanding an end to the contraband that reduced the fiscal revenues, and the merchants of Seville continually sent representa-tives to apply pressure on the islands' governments. But in only a few cases was this pressure successful. Contraband continued to flow into the islands without hindrance throughout the sixteenth century, for the lack of European manufactured goods affected all the population, and everyone, authorities and commoners alike, were equally involved in a business necessary to their subsistence.

[See also *Casa de la Contratación*.]

BIBLIOGRAPHY

Céspedes del Castillo, Guillermo. *Latin America: The Early Years.* New York, 1974.

Haring, Clarence H. *Trade and Navigation between Spain and the Indies in the Time of the Habsburgs.* Gloucester, Mass., 1964.

Moya Pons, Frank. *Historia colonial de Santo Domingo.* Santiago de los Caballeros, 1973.

Parry, John H. *The Spanish Seaborne Empire.* London, 1967.

Pike, Ruth. *Enterprise and Adventure: The Genoese in Seville and the Opening of the New World.* Ithaca, N.Y., 1966.

FRANK MOYA PONS

TRAVEL LITERATURE. Columbus's claim that he could reach the East by sailing west from Spain across the ocean was inspired as much by his reading of travel and geographical writers—most of them medieval, but some classical and contemporary—as by his varied experiences at sea. Before 1492, most likely during the time he lived in Portugal and Spain, Columbus began the eclectic perusal of such authorities; his reading is reflected in his own subsequent writings and attested by his son Fernando, Andrés Bernáldez, and other contemporaries. He continued his bookish investigations throughout the decade of his four voyages, less, it seems, to entertain new ideas than to find confirmation of his conviction that he had indeed reached Asia. Some of the works Columbus (perhaps with his brother Bartolomé) read and annotated for their information about the earth have survived, although they probably constitute only a fraction of the "books of cosmography, history, chronicle, and philosophy" that Columbus in 1501 said that he had studied for years (*Cristóbal Colón: Textos y documentos completos, relaciones de viajes, cartas y memoriales,* ed. Consuelo Varela [Madrid, 1982]). A few of these annotated volumes and certain other travel and geographical works known to Columbus made important contributions to the argument that he presented to his sponsors about the feasibility of a westward voyage of discovery.

Crucial to this argument was his belief in the greatest possible eastward extension of Asia and in a correspondingly narrow Ocean Sea. In Ptolemy's *Geography* (compiled in the second century A.D. but discovered by western Europeans only in the fifteenth century), Columbus found authority for the notion that the continuous Eurasian landmass covered half of the earth's circumference. He relied, in addition, on the learned opinion of the contemporary Florentine geographer Paolo dal Pozzo Toscanelli that Asia extended thirty degrees farther east than even Ptolemy had estimated. These views were strongly corroborated by Pierre d'Ailly's *Imago mundi* (1410), a standard handbook of geographical lore for the later Middle Ages. The annotations in Columbus's copy of this book reveal his close attention to d'Ailly's verdict that Asia stretched farther into the ocean than Ptolemy had figured and that the sea between Spain and China was narrow. D'Ailly discussed but did not take a position on the age-old question of whether a fourth continent existed and was inhabited; Columbus also encountered uncertainty and skepticism about the existence of the antipodes in Aeneas Sylvius's (Enea Silvio Piccolomini, later Pius II) *Historia rerum ubique gestarum* (1477), a copy of which survives from the Admiral's library.

While these old and new geographers strengthened Columbus's faith in the possibility of a short ocean voyage to the Indies, several medieval travel narratives shaped his expectations about the places and peoples he eventually found there. Columbus borrowed what he needed from the scholarly experts to bolster his ideas—and he occasionally disputed their authority; but the *Travels of Marco Polo* (*Il milione*, Italian title), a copy of which he owned; John Mandeville's *Travels*, which Bernáldez, Las Casas, and his son Fernando Colón affirmed he read; and a few other accounts of Atlantic exploration he may have known, impressed him because they seemed to reflect the results of actual traveling.

Polo's narrative offered the fullest description of the Orient available in the West, and his merchant-traveler's focus on its wealth resonated with Columbus's own mercantile motives. What Columbus remarked on in his copy of Polo was the prevalence of gold, the signs of the far-flung Chinese trading network, the rich centers of civilization, and the vastness of Asia. Polo also taught Columbus about Cipangu (Japan), which supposedly lay fifteen hundred miles from Cathay; indeed, Polo's estimate of that distance was what convinced Toscanelli (and Columbus in turn) that westward ocean voyage could be relieved by a stop at Japan or at any of the thousands of islands beyond the mainland that Polo reported.

Mandeville's *Travels*, the most popular European travel account of the Middle Ages, would have affected both practical and visionary dimensions of Columbus's enterprise. Mandeville argued that the earth was circumnavigable, that it was inhabited everywhere, and that an anonymous northern European had already sailed around the globe. His portrayal of Asian peoples as ethically superior to Europeans helped define Columbus's assumptions about the Caribbean natives he met. And Mandeville's emphasis on the ultimate centrality of Jerusalem coincided with Columbus's crusading desire to help rescue the Holy Land for Christianity.

An important letter written to Columbus in 1497 by an English businessman, John Day, refers to narratives or news of two late medieval English voyages into the Atlantic that Columbus either knew of or wished to know of. Columbus seems to have requested from Day a copy of *Inventio fortunata*, a now-lost Latin narrative allegedly composed by Nicholas of Lynn, following travels in the North Atlantic during the mid-fourteenth century, and generally known to various geographers and mapmakers in Europe in Columbus's time. In the same letter, Day promised the Admiral a copy of the chart drawn by John Cabot while coasting along his unidentified North American landfall.

Day's letter is a sobering reminder of how much is not known about Columbus's sources of information and access to books. In his Genoese youth he may have heard or read about the centuries-long exploits of Genoese traders in distant Asia and about voyages like those of the Vivaldi brothers in 1291 into the Atlantic. He sailed with the Portuguese to Africa and must have been familiar with the record of their exploration south into the Atlantic; the time he spent in the Atlantic islands and his apparent visits to Ireland and Iceland would have made him knowledgeable about accounts of assorted European ventures in the Atlantic toward the end of the Middle Ages. It is clear, however, that he read widely and frequently, and his own writings show that he habitually blended his reading with his maritime experience.

[See also *Library of Columbus* and biographies of figures mentioned herein.]

BIBLIOGRAPHY

Andrews, K. R., N. P. Canny, and P. E. H. Hair, eds. *The Westward Enterprise: English Activities in Ireland, the Atlantic, and America, 1480–1650.* Liverpool, 1978.

Campbell, Mary B. *The Witness and the Other World: Exotic European Travel Writing, 400–1600.* Ithaca, N.Y., and London, 1988.

Gil, Juan, ed. *El Libro de Marco Polo.* Madrid, 1986.

Keever, Edwin F., trans. *Imago Mundi by Petrus Ailliacus.* Wilmington, N.C., 1948.

Morison, Samuel Eliot. *Admiral of the Ocean Sea: A Life of Christopher Columbus.* 2 vols. Boston, 1942.

Phillips, J. R. S. *The Medieval Expansion of Europe.* New York, 1988.

Taviani, Paolo Emilio. *Christopher Columbus: The Grand Design.* London, 1985.

Vigneras, L. A. "The Cape Breton Landfall: 1494 or 1497; Note on a Letter from John Day." *Canadian Historical Review* 38 (1957): 219–228.

CHRISTIAN K. ZACHER

TREATY OF ALCÁÇOVAS. The Treaty of Alcáçovas was concluded by Fernando and Isabel of Spain and Afonso V of Portugal on September 4, 1479. The treaty was ratified by the Spanish rulers at Toledo on March 6, 1480, and by Afonso V at Évora on September 8, 1480; Pope Sixtus IV confirmed it in his bull *Aeterni Regis* on June 21, 1481.

The treaty resolved several outstanding issues. The most pressing was the controversy over the succession to the kingdom of Castile. Afonso V abandoned his efforts to uphold the rights to the Castilian throne of Juana de Castilla (La Beltraneja), the daughter of King Enrique IV. Given the option of retiring to a convent or marrying the son and heir of Fernando and Isabel, Juana chose the former, entering the monastery of Santa Clara de Coimbra in 1480. As a guarantee of permanent peace between the two realms, Isabel, the daughter of Fernando and Isabel, was betrothed to Afonso, a grandson of Afonso V.

The eighth article of the treaty was the most important from the point of view of overseas expansion because it established spheres of influence in the Atlantic Ocean. The treaty confirmed Portugal in possession of "all the trade, lands, and traffic in Guinea, with its gold mines, and whatever other islands, coasts, and lands" that might be discovered, as well as Madeira, the Azores, the Cape Verde Islands, and any other islands that might be found and conquered below the Canaries and opposite Guinea. The Canary Islands were explicitly reserved to Castile. Fernando and Isabel also promised not to allow any of their subjects or foreigners living in their dominions to travel to or to conduct business in the islands and lands of Guinea already discovered or to be discovered, without the permission of the king of Portugal.

Portugal derived the greatest benefit from the treaty in that Castile was now effectively limited to the Canary Islands and the sea routes leading to them. The treaty said nothing about navigation westward across the Atlantic, but it did reserve to Portugal complete and sole control of navigation along the Guinea coast. While Castilians might travel to the Canaries, they were prohibited from intruding in those ocean spaces reserved to Portugal. Fernando and Isabel strictly upheld these restrictions on navigation in the Atlantic, but when Columbus presented his proposals to them, their horizons were expanded. That may explain why in the Santa Fe Capitulations, their agreement with Columbus, Fernando and Isabel entitled themselves "lords of the ocean seas." When Columbus returned from his epic voyage to the New World, João II of Portugal cited the Treaty of Alcáçovas to lay claim to whatever lands Columbus had discovered. As a consequence, Fernando and Isabel appealed to Pope Alexander VI to set down the Line of Demarcation between the Portuguese and Spanish areas of discovery. The conclusion of the Treaty of

Tordesillas between Spain and Portugal in 1494 eventually resolved these issues.

[See also *Line of Demarcation; Treaty of Tordesillas.*]

BIBLIOGRAPHY

Davenport, Florence Gardiner. *European Treaties Bearing on the History of the United States and Its Dependencies to 1648.* 4 vols. Washington, D.C., 1917–1937.

Diffie, Bailey W., and George D. Winius. *Foundations of the Portuguese Empire, 1415–1580.* Minneapolis, 1977.

Pérez Embid, Florentino. *Los descubrimientos en el Atlántico y la rivalidad castellano-portuguesa hasta el tratado de Tordesillas.* Seville, 1948.

Joseph F. O'Callaghan

TREATY OF TORDESILLAS. The Treaty of Tordesillas was signed on June 7, 1494, by Spain and Portugal. The purpose of the treaty was to establish the Line of Demarcation in the Atlantic Ocean, assigning the lands west of the line to Spanish exploration and colonization and those east of the line to Portugal. The treaty was the consequence of a long debate between the two kingdoms that reached a critical stage when Columbus landed in the New World in 1492. Inasmuch as João II (r. 1481–1495) of Portugal challenged Spain's rights to the newly discovered lands, Fernando of Aragón (r. 1479–1516) and Isabel of Castile (r. 1474–1504) appealed to Pope Alexander VI, who upheld Spanish pretensions. In the papal bull *Inter caetera*, the pope, on May 3, 1493, confirmed Spain's rights. Nevertheless, as the wording was vague, he issued another bull, also called *Inter caetera*, dated May 4, in which he drew the Line of Demarcation from the North to the South Poles, assigning the lands one hundred leagues west and south of the Azores and the Cape Verde Islands to Spain, provided they were not subject to any other Christian ruler. Still later, on September 26, in response to Spanish requests for further clarification, he declared in the bull *Dudum siquidem* that Spain was entitled to all lands discovered by sailing westward or southward toward the Orient and India.

João II was dissatisfied by these papal decisions and proposed negotiations with Fernando and Isabel. Their representatives concluded the Treaty of Tordesillas on June 7, 1494. The Spanish sovereigns ratified it at Arévalo on July 2 and João II did so on September 5 at Setúbal. Although both sides agreed not to submit the treaty to the papacy for approval, Pope Julius II, at the request of King Manuel I of Portugal (r. 1495–1521), confirmed it in 1506.

The treaty consisted of four clauses. As the king of Portugal suggested, the first clause drew "a stripe or straight line from pole to pole, from the Arctic pole to the Antarctic pole, that is, from north to south," 370 leagues

allowed an exception: if Columbus before June 20 should discover any lands beyond the first 250 leagues, they would belong to Castile. Any others east of that point would be reserved to Portugal.

In practical terms the most important consequence of the Treaty of Tordesillas was that it gave Portugal undisputed title to Brazil. Even so, the difficulty of determining exactly where the Line of Demarcation ought to run provided the basis for continuing disputes over the extent of Brazil and also over claims to islands in the Pacific Ocean. For example, although the Portuguese had reached the Moluccas Islands in 1512, Spain claimed them after Ferdinand Magellan's ships landed there in 1521. The Treaty of Zaragoza, signed in 1529, finally recognized the Portuguese title to the islands. A similar dispute arose concerning the Philippines, which the Spaniards had occupied, even though the Portuguese claimed that those islands also fell within their zone. The Treaty of San Ildefonso, concluded in 1777, brought these controversies to a close by establishing the western limits of Brazil and confirming Spanish rights to the Philippine Islands.

[See also *Line of Demarcation; Treaty of Alcáçovas*.]

BIBLIOGRAPHY

Davenport, Frances. *European Treaties Bearing on the History of the United States and Its Dependencies to 1648.* 4 vols. Washington, D. C., 1917–1937. Vol. 1, no. 9, pp. 84–100.

Diffie, Bailey W., and George D. Winius. *Foundations of the Portuguese Empire, 1415–1580.* Minneapolis, 1977.

El Tratado de Tordesillas y su proyección. 2 vols. Valladolid, 1973.

Morison, Samuel Eliot. *Admiral of the Ocean Sea: A Life of Christopher Columbus.* Boston, 1942.

Nowell, Charles E. "The Treaty of Tordesillas and the Diplomatic Background of American History." In *Greater America: Essays in Honor of Herbert E. Bolton.* Berkeley, 1945.

Pérez Embid, Florentino. *Los descubrimientos en el Atlántico y la rivalidad castellano-portuguesa hasta el tratado de Tordesillas.* Seville, 1948.

JOSEPH F. O'CALLAGHAN

THE TREATY OF TORDESILLAS. The first attempt to define global spheres of influence. Signed by representatives of João II of Portugal and Isabel and Fernando of Spain, June 7, 1494; ratified July 2, 1494. ARQUIVO NACIONAL DA TORRE DO TOMBO

west of the Cape Verde Islands. Everything east of the line, to the north and south, would belong to Portugal, and everything west would pertain to Spain. As a consequence, the Western Hemisphere fell to Spain and the Eastern to Portugal. In the second clause each party pledged not to explore in the regions reserved to the other and to yield lands that they might by chance discover in the other's region. The third clause provided for a period of ten months in which to establish the meridian marking the zones. Each party agreed to send one or two ships, with pilots, astronomers, and mariners to the Island of Grand Canary, from which they would sail directly to the Cape Verde Islands and then westward to determine the point where the line should be fixed. As this was eventually seen to be impractical, it was not carried out. In 1495 the two kingdoms agreed to abandon that idea but to inform one another of new discoveries. The fourth clause granted permission to Castilian subjects to cross the Portuguese zone on the way west, but without stopping to explore. This was important for Columbus who had already started on his second voyage and of necessity had to cross the Portuguese zone. The treaty

TRISTÃO, NUNO

TRISTÃO, NUNO (d. 1446), navigator and knight. Knowledge of the life of Nuno Tristão stems from narratives that are described by the chronicler Eanes Gomes de Azurara in his *Crónica dos feitos da Guiné* (Chronicle of the events in Guinea). During the reign of Prince Henry the Navigator, the navigator Tristão was also a merchant and a warrior. When he began his trips to the western coast of Africa, he often attacked practically defenseless coastal populations with the goal of capturing Africans to be sold as slaves. Besides capturing slaves, he also hunted seals, which were profitable for their oil and skins. He sometimes traded with the natives, who sought peaceful contacts with the navigators, a practice that was still common between 1440 and 1450. Further, his trips contributed to expanded exploration of the coast.

Chroniclers report that Prince Henry gave Tristão a caravel for his first expedition and explicitly recommended that he go beyond the "Pedra da Galé, over there, as far as possible" and that he should capture native Africans in any possible way. Tristão's voyage in 1422 set him in competition with another warrior-navigator, Antão Gonçalves, who was likewise engaged in sorties and slaving raids. Tristão was thus prompted to follow Gonçalves's route and to accomplish his goals with Gonçalves as an occasional companion.

Tristão reconnoitered farther to the south than he had been ordered, reaching Cape Blanc. The following year, still in a caravel, he continued his mission, but did not travel farther than the island of Adegete, some 40 kilometers (25 miles) from the point he had previously reached. The island was later called Arguim, the site of a farm-fortress built by the Portuguese. Tristão's penultimate voyage took place in 1445. He left Lagos in his caravel and traveled toward the island of Garças, not far from Arguim. After realizing that it would be impossible to take prisoners in that place, he kept sailing south and explored the coast to a place called Palmar on a fifteenth-century Italian map. Since he could not engage in trade with the local population, he landed with the intention of taking prisoners, but this venture was not very successful. In 1446 he intended to explore the coast south of Cape Vert. However, upon reaching the coast of Guinea, he arrived at the mouth of a large river (historians are still divided as to this river's identity) that he and his crew entered in search of a village. There, they were attacked by Guinean warriors, who killed twenty of the twenty-two Portuguese, Nuno Tristão among them.

BIBLIOGRAPHY

De Lery, Jean. *History of a Voyage to the Land of Brazil Otherwise Called America*. Translated by Janet Whatley. Berkeley, 1990.

Diffey, Bailey W. *Prelude to Empire: Portugal Overseas before Henry the Navigator*. Lincoln, Neb., 1960.

Diffey, Bailey W., and George D. Winius. *Foundations of the Portuguese Empire, 1414–1850*. Edited by Boyd C. Shafer. Minneapolis, 1977.

Morison, Samuel Eliot. *Portuguese Voyages to America in the Fifteenth Century*. New York, 1965.

LUÍS DE ALBUQUERQUE
Translated from Portuguese by Paola Carù

TUPINAMBÁS. See *Indian America*, article on *Tupinambás*.

V

VALENCIA. The capital of a former Muslim kingdom on the east coast of the Iberian peninsula that fell to the Aragonese in 1238, Valencia in the fifteenth century experienced profound tensions as the economic and social monopolies of the urban medieval craft guilds were challenged by peasants and foreigners.

The greater participation of the peasantry in the crafts throughout the century was opposed by the artisans, who tried to retain their monopoly of markets and protect themselves from rural competition. The development of shipyards in the first half of the fifteenth century brought expansion of crafts linked to the arsenals and shipyards; metalworking was revived by the manufacture of armor, weapons, and artillery for the armies of Alfonso V. The rural textile industry, which depended on contracts and raw material from native and foreign merchants based in the city, unsettled the old order and brought about modifications to the production system. New construction, including renovation and refurbishment of existing structures, sought to impose a Christian order on the old Muslim town and upgraded the building crafts—masonry and carpentry—and the profession of master builder.

Increase of foreign goods competed with local production, which was too weak to resist the products of other cities and states. Artisans and a section of the bourgeoisie who favored a protectionist trade policy were pitted against nobles who favored a liberal trade policy because they exported the majority of their agricultural production through foreign intermediaries. The Crown was pulled in both directions, wishing to protect local industry but grateful for the revenue produced by foreign trade.

Of the groups of foreigners, Italians—Florentines, Sienese, Romans, and Genoese—were the best integrated and most prosperous, especially as silk makers and papermakers. The Sienese specialized in banking. In the final quarter of the century, Valencia was one of the great printing centers of Europe, with seven German printers operating in the city. Valencia's commercial community included merchants from the Empire (Germans and Swiss), France, Portugal, and the other Spanish kingdoms.

Christians were a majority of the population by the fifteenth century, although the Muslim minority continued to play an important role in the economy and life of the city because of the links it retained with the Berbers and the Kingdom of Granada. Despite the warfare of the Reconquista, contacts between Christians and Muslims were maintained, under royal protection. The tiny Jewish community disappeared in 1492.

BIBLIOGRAPHY

Berger, Philippe. *Libro y lectura en la Valencia del renacimiento.* Valencia, 1987.

Bisson, Thomas N. *The Medieval Crown of Aragon.* New York, 1991.

Hadjiiossif, Jacqueline Guiral. *Valencia, puerto mediterraneo en el siglo XV.* Valencia, 1989.

JACQUELINE GUIRAL HADJIIOSSIF

VALLADOLID. Center of the most important demographic and urban region of Castile, Valladolid underwent a great overall development during the fourteenth and fifteenth centuries. Situated in the center of the basin of Castile and close to the River Duero, Valladolid is an easy gateway to the north and a natural link with both the eastern and western regions.

The starting point of this expansion was the increasing importance of Valladolid's political function. Even though the Castilian-Leonese monarchy did not have a fixed capital, the frequent presence of the court in Valladolid made it the de facto capital of the kingdom. It was also one of the favorite spots at which to hold the Cortes, the parliamentary assembly. The political importance of Valladolid is also attested to by the fact that it was the place where Isabel, princess of Castile, and Fernando, heir to the throne of Aragón and king of Sicily, were married on October 19, 1469.

Another factor that greatly contributed to the development of Valladolid was the establishment of the Audiencia Real, or Chancillería—highest appellate court for civil suits and criminal cases. In 1442 King Juan II of Castile designated Valladolid as the seat of the Chancillería, but his ordinance was not effective until Isabel established it as such in 1485.

Political progress in the fourteenth and fifteenth centuries was not paralleled by the development of the urban nucleus. The city's territory was still defined by the wall erected in the first decades of the fourteenth century, although the area outside expanded owing to the increasing importance of Valladolid.

The economy of the city was characterized by three elements: agriculture and cattle raising, luxurious crafts, and commerce. The chief crops of the area, wheat and barley, were enough to satisfy the more immediate necessities of the villagers. There was also a good provision of wine produced in the valleys of the Duero and the Pisuerga rivers. Livestock was abundant with a predominance of sheep, although cows, goats, and pigs were also raised.

Even though the most important industrial activity was the weaving of wool into cloth of ordinary quality, in the fourteenth and fifteenth centuries Valladolid saw an enormous growth of luxurious crafts: silversmithing, jewelry, furriery, painting, enameling, armors' craft, and tailoring. This growth was related to the presence of nobles and their retinues in the village.

From a very early date Valladolid held annual fairs, which were attended by an important number of foreign merchants, mostly Italians and Flemish. These fairs lost their importance in 1491, however, when the sovereigns made those of Medina del Campo the general fairs of the whole kingdom.

From an ecclesiastical point of view, Valladolid was dependent on the bishopric of Palencia. The highest position in the clergy was that of the collegiate chapter of Santa María la Mayor. In Valladolid there were other numerous monasteries and convents, the most important being that of San Benito. Established by King Juan I of Castile in 1390, San Benito had become the head of the majority of the Benedictine monasteries of Castile and León by the end of the fourteenth century.

The University of Valladolid, created in the thirteenth century, had four schools at the beginning of the fifteenth century: law, arts, theology, and medicine. It was world famous for its highly specialized surgical work. In addition to the university, other centers of study known as *colegios* were established in the last third of the fifteenth century by illustrious ecclesiastical patrons with the idea of providing the monarchy and the clergy with a new generation of more educated public servants and priests. The two most important *colegios* were Santa Cruz, established by Cardinal Pedro González de Mendoza, and San Gregorio, established by Alonso de Burgos.

In May of 1505, a few months after returning from his fourth journey to America, Christopher Columbus, following the court, moved to Segovia. There he presented his claims to King Fernando about his titles of admiral, viceroy, and governor, and all the rights and privileges associated with them. Without having reached a solution Columbus moved to Valladolid in April 1506 where his family had a modest house. There he spent his last days enduring the pain of gout and arthritis. He died on May 21, 1506; his body was deposited in the convent of San Francisco, and his obsequies were celebrated in the parochial church of Santa María la Antigua. A few years later his remains were transported to Seville. The house where he is supposed to have lived and died, known today as Casa de Colón, serves as a museum and houses the Department of the History of America.

BIBLIOGRAPHY

Highfield, Roger, ed. *Spain in the Fifteenth Century, 1369–1516.* New York, 1972.
Mariéjol, Jean H. *The Spain of Ferdinand and Isabella.* New Brunswick, N.J., 1961.
Ribot García, Luis A., et al. *Valladolid, corazón del mundo hispánico: Siglo XVI.* Valladolid, 1981.
Ruiz Asencio, Manuel, and Julio Valdeón Baruque. *Historia de Valladolid: Valladolid medieval.* Valladolid, 1980.
Trevor Davies, R. *The Golden Centuries of Spain, 1501–1621.* New York, 1967.

FRANCISCO GAGO JOVER

VÁZQUEZ DE AYLLÓN, LUCAS. See two entries under *Ayllón, Lucas Vázquez de.*

VENETIAN REPUBLIC. Poised in a lagoon near the northern end of the Adriatic Sea, medieval Venice turned away from the Italian mainland from which its first settlers had migrated, fleeing the poverty, disorganization, and warfare that accompanied the fall of ancient Rome. Offering nothing at first but fish and salt, its merchants traveled eastward, extending their realm from nearby ports to the cities of the Balkan coast, Greece, Crete, Cyprus, the whole of the Levant, and Egypt, until their chosen leader, called doge, could claim domination by Venice and its gold ducats of *quartum et dimidium* (one-quarter plus one-eighth) of the world that Rome had once ruled. But in the centuries that encompassed the birth and death of Columbus, who sought a route to the east that avoided the routes that Venice dominated, the city turned westward. From 1404–1406, when it seized neighboring Padua, Vicenza, and Verona, until 1571, when at the battle of Lepanto it reached the zenith of its Mediterranean career, Venice claimed one-half of northern Italy, thanks to its well-run standing army, one of the first in Europe, and the unyielding policies forged by black-robed councilors in the halls of the ducal palace—the seat of one of Europe's first republican governments.

Venetian greatness was built on trade. A prerogative of the city's elite of noblemen and citizens was the license to trade under the Venetian standard, which gave access to Mediterranean ports and participation in the state fleets, escorted by armed galleys, that sailed to the Black Sea, the Levant, Alexandria, and Flanders. Meanwhile, merchandise from Asia, Africa, and northern Europe was purveyed by foreign merchants at the Rialto, the single bridge across the city's serpentine Grand Canal, and its commercial center. Organized merchant communities kept their representatives there, housed in office blocks such as those named for the Germans—the Fondaco dei Tedeschi—and the Turks—the Fondaco dei Turchi. The numerous foreigners in Venice seemed almost to overwhelm the indigenous population, who were daily exposed to conflicting faiths and customs and a symphony of languages. Meanwhile, native craftsmen organized in guilds produced glass, lace, and ships of great renown. After 1500, Venice continued to flourish but at a slackening pace: its appetite for commercial activity was curbed by Turkish encroachment in the eastern Mediterranean and by the lure of mainland territories, which the city's noblemen sought as a haven from the risks of maritime trade. Thus the seafaring merchant princes of Venice turned landlord following the conquest of the hinterland.

The transformation of the nobility that occurred during the age of exploration was a crucial social and political series of events, since Venice's distinctive political institutions were designed to foster the interests of that class. During the fourteenth century, participation in the government of Venice was limited to a set of noble families

VENICE IN 1486. Woodcut, from Breydenbach's *Journey to the Holy Land*.

and their legitimate heirs; this limitation was called the *serrata* (locking) of the Great Council, the largest of the city's deliberative bodies. Thenceforth, Venice's republican machinery expanded, always powered by birth and driven by privilege. The fifteenth century brought the rise in influence of the Senate, which stood behind the strategy of expansion, and the elevation of the Collegio, an advisory circle around the doge that included sets of counselors, "sages" expert in naval, military, and diplomatic affairs, and members of the Council of Ten, the secretive body created to guard against treachery. Coincidental with this governmental elaboration, the ancient custom by which the whole assembled people approved the election of the doge was ended. The sixteenth century saw the further extension of the influence of the distinctly undemocratic Ten and the creation of councils of censors, reformers, and inquisitors. Although the aristocratic government of Venice departed steadily from the more democratic practices of the traditional commune, its processes of discussion and decision making, as well as its handling of foreign affairs, were a legacy to later nation states. Sent as ambassadors to courts and cities on three continents, Venetian nobles pioneered modern diplomacy,. and their achievement was witnessed by their famous *relazioni* (reports), minutely describing foreign customs, courts, and personalities.

Venetian government was run by nobles dedicated to their own self-interest as much as to the common welfare. An increase in the numbers of aristocrats in the fifteenth century dating from the downturn that began with the Black Death of 1348 occasioned bitter competition for positions, both among those seeking honorable office without pay and those seeking lesser positions for high salaries. As the nobles competed with one another for office, for villas in the country, and for the perpetuation of lineage and reputation, their posts in the commercial (and even the cultural) world were taken by members of the "citizen" class. Made up of *cittadini originari* (citizens by birth) and citizens by privilege, who had acquired Venetian trading rights, the citizenry was a kind of lesser patriciate, quite as restricted as the nobility. Each of the two groups comprised about 5 percent of a population that fluctuated around 100,000. Among them were merchants, state secretaries, teachers, and physicians, leaders in the *scuole* (social organizations for religious and charitable purposes), and, like the noblemen they imitated, patrons of art and ideas. Lower in the social hierarchy were artisans and common laborers, servants and prostitutes, and that uniquely Venetian shipyard proletariat, the *arsenalotti* (workers in the Arsenal).

Workers, citizens, and nobles alike joined in a distinctively Venetian piety, scrupulously correct yet wary of Rome. The whole populace engaged in ritual observances that were both religious and civic, such as the procession of doge, councilors, senators, secretaries, and citizens, and the *Scuole grandi* in tableaux vivants, in celebration of Corpus Christi. Venetian neighborhoods were tightly organized around the parish church standing in each *campo* (square), where business and culture was also centered. Armed with saints' relics from around the world, more than a hundred churches brooded over Venice, and half as many monasteries and convents hugged the periphery or sat on the encircling islands. These monasteries engendered reform movements that rose again and again in these centuries, led by charismatic nobles or citizen ascetics. From the upper ranks of the Venetian secular clergy, headed by their own patriarch after 1451, reformers of international stature emerged. Their activity was eventually halted as the Roman Inquisition (after 1542) and the Council of Trent (1545–1563) moved to suppress all heterodoxy. Thereafter, Venetians conformed, but they resisted orders from Rome about censorship, prosecution of heresy, and papal authority.

In this city that looked simultaneously outward and inward, east and west, there developed, as in Florence, a culture that was unique in the history of European civilization. Patrician and citizen intellectuals studied philosophy and law, collected libraries, wrote histories, learned Greek, and mastered the humanist curriculum, while the Venetian press became the most active in Europe. Poets and painters, architects and sculptors, mathematicians and philosophers gravitated to this cosmopolis that offered, in its patrician courtyards, its schools and printshops, and its narrow and thronged *calli* (streets), unmatched opportunity for the exchange of image and idea. From this matrix emerged some of the greatest artists of the age—Giovanni Bellini, Titian, Tintoretto, Paolo Veronese—who memorialized the special light, power, and spectacle of Venice.

BIBLIOGRAPHY

Bouwsma, William J. *Venice and the Defense of Republican Liberty: Renaissance Values in the Age of the Counter-Reformation.* Berkeley and Los Angeles, 1968.

Cozzi, Gaetano, and Michael Knapton. *La repubblica di Venezia nell' età moderna: dalla guerra di Chioggia al 1517.* Turin, 1986.

Finlay, Robert. *Politics in Renaissance Venice.* New Brunswick, N.J., 1980.

Grendler, Paul F. *The Roman Inquisition and the Venetian Press, 1540–1605.* Princeton, 1977.

Hale, John R., ed. *Renaissance Venice.* London and Totowa, N.J., 1973.

King, Margaret L. *Venetian Humanism in an Age of Patrician Dominance.* Princeton, 1986.

Lane, Frederic C. *Venice: A Maritime Republic.* Baltimore, 1973.

Logan, Oliver. *Culture and Society in Venice, 1470–1790: The Renaissance and Its Heritage.* London and New York, 1972.

Mallett, Michael E., and J. R. Hale. *The Military Organization of a Renaissance State: Venice c. 1400–1617.* Cambridge and New York, 1984.

Muir, Edward. *Civic Ritual in Renaissance Venice.* Princeton, 1981.

Queller, Donald E. *The Venetian Patriciate: Reality versus Myth.* Champaign-Urbana, Ill., 1986.

Romano, Dennis. *Patricians and Popolani: The Social Foundations of the Venetian Renaissance State.* Baltimore and London, 1987.

MARGARET L. KING

VERRAZANO, GIOVANNI DA (1485?–1528), Italian navigator and explorer for France. There have been several controversies concerning the life of Giovanni da Verrazano (also spelled Verrazzano), not the least of which is the question of his birth. Was he truly a Florentine, born in Greve in Tuscany, part of the Florentine dominion, or was he the son of Alessandro di Bartolommeo da Verrazano and his wife, Giovanna, of Lyons, France? Even if he was born in Lyons (where there were several Florentine merchants), he would have and, in fact, did, consider himself a Florentine. No documentation concerning his birth or that of his brother, Gerolamo, into the Tuscan family has survived; but neither is there any real evidence of his connection to the Lyons branch of the Verrazano family, aside from the latter's investing in Verrazano's 1524 voyage to the New World.

Almost nothing is known about Verrazano's life before the preparations for his 1524 voyage under the auspices of King Francis I of France. There is a possibility that he sailed as a member of Thomas Aubert of Dieppe's 1508 voyage to Newfoundland and the Gulf of St. Lawrence. It was this mission that brought back to France the first North American natives in 1509. Participation in that voyage would explain why Verrazano is supposed to have said to Henry VIII of England in 1525 or 1526 that he had already been three times to New World shores, although he had probably been only twice by 1525.

In the period between 1509 and 1523, when the outfitting for the 1524 voyage to America began, there are several isolated mentions of Verrazano. A responsible Portuguese official recorded that in 1517 Verrazano had been in Portugal and Spain in the company of Ferdinand Magellan. Bernardo Carli, a Florentine merchant in Lyons, later wrote to his father in Florence about Verrazano, informing him that Verrazano had been in Egypt and Syria, indeed, throughout the known world, before 1524 and was esteemed as another Amerigo Vespucci or Ferdinand Magellan. It is unclear from the surviving evidence whether Verrazano was a land-based factor in the Levant or one who traveled with goods shipped to that region.

Additional evidence of Verrazano's stature in 1523 can be found in a report to King João III of Portugal from Portuguese merchants in France who were concerned about a voyage to Brazil being planned by Verrazano and the French court. By the late spring of 1523 negotiations for the expedition were under way. Although the actual royal commission by Francis I to Verrazano has not survived, several extant letters make clear the French king's involvement in Verrazano's 1524 voyage to North America.

Like Christopher Columbus and John Cabot, Verrazano hoped to find an all-water route to the Far East. Instead his six-month voyage served the purpose of charting the eastern coastline of America from Cape Fear, South Carolina, to Cape Breton in Nova Scotia. Although the original plans of the expedition called for four ships, Verrazano set out on January 1, 1524, with only one, the royal *Dauphine*. Much of the financial support for the voyage came from the group of Florentine merchants and bankers in Lyons. The Cèllere Codex in the Pierpont Morgan Library is the record of the voyage in the form of a letter to King Francis I, and it includes a description of the land, its vegetation, its people, and the prominent geographical features seen from *Dauphine* and the ship's small boats launched to explore the new territory. Early in this letter Verrazano states,

> So we anchored off the coast and sent the small boat in to land. We had seen many people coming to the seashore, but they fled when they saw us approaching; several times they stopped and turned around to look at us in great wonderment. We reassured them with various signs, and some of them came up, showing great delight in seeing us and marveling at our clothes, appearance, and our whiteness; they showed us by various signs where we could most easily secure the boat, and offered us some of their food. We were on land, and I shall now tell Your Majesty briefly what we were able to learn of their life and customs.

Bearing in mind his royal patron, Verrazano named various discoveries after Francis I's mother and sister and the king himself as well as other members of the French court. Those areas explored by Verrazano include the coasts of present-day Virginia and Maryland; New York harbor; Narragansett Bay and the harbor of Newport, Rhode Island; Nantucket; Cape Cod; Maine; Nova Scotia; and Newfoundland.

When Verrazano returned to France on July 8, 1524, he wanted to embark on another voyage right away in order to find the elusive passage to Cathay that he and others had sought for so long. When that plan fell through, he spent some time in both England and Portugal seeking support for another voyage. Later he became involved with a project under the leadership of Philippe Chabot, which led to a voyage in 1526–1527 to look for a passage to the Spice Islands. A syndicate was formed under Chabot to compete with the 1526 voyage of Sebastian Cabot under the flag of Spain. The main purpose of Verrazano's expedition was to bring back spices to be used for food and pharmaceutical applications. This trip, Verrazano's third to the New World, was full of problems and mysteries. He appears to have sailed along the eastern coast of South America, failed to navigate the Straits of Magellan, and crossed the Atlantic to try to round the Cape of Good Hope. When most of his ships failed to make it around the Cape, he went back to South America, sailed along the coast of Brazil, loaded his ships with products there, and returned to France in September 1527.

Although several historians in the eighteenth and nineteenth centuries mistakenly identified Verrazano with Jean Florin, who was executed for piracy by the Spaniards in November 1527, we now know this is incorrect, since it is certain that Verrazano conducted another expedition to America in 1528. This final voyage was to fulfill the aims of the Chabot expedition of 1526. Three groups were involved: the officers and crew of *Flamengue;* investors in Fécamp, France, who chartered the ship; and Verrazano's friends and associates who supplied trade goods and some of the crew's wages. Once again Verrazano was seeking a passage from the Atlantic to the Indies. Although no maps of this voyage have survived, he apparently explored Florida, the Bahamas, Panama, and other islands in the Caribbean. It is commonly believed that Verrazano died during this voyage and fell victim to cannibals on an island in the Caribbean. In any event, *Flamengue* returned to France without its captain but with a cargo of dyewood from the Caribbean or South America in March of 1529.

Giovanni da Verrazano was among the great navigators and explorers of the sixteenth century whose efforts directed the attention of European merchants to the riches of the New World. It is certainly fitting that the Verrazano Narrows Bridge in New York is named for the navigator who did so much to explore the eastern coastline of the United States.

BIBLIOGRAPHY

Murphy, Henry C. *The Voyage of Verrazzano.* New York, 1875.

Thrower, Norman J. "New Light on the 1524 Voyage of Verrazzano." *Terrae Incognitae* 11 (1979): 59–65.

Wroth, Lawrence C. *The Voyages of Giovanni da Verrazzano, 1524–1528.* New Haven, 1970.

MARGERY A. GANZ

VESPUCCI, AMERIGO (1454–1512), Italian navigator and cosmographer. According to a long-held tradition, Vespucci made four voyages to America: two (1497–1498 and 1499–1500) in the service of Spain and two (1501–1502

AMERIGO VESPUCCI. Detail from a sixteeth-century painting in the Uffizi Gallery, Florence.   LIBRARY OF CONGRESS

and 1503–1504) in the service of Portugal. During the first voyage, it was said, he reached Paria, thus discovering the South American continent before Columbus. This tradition was based on the so-called Letter to Soderini, which was attributed to Vespucci. Printed for the first time in Florence in 1505–1506, it was distributed in a Latin version contained in the *Cosmographiae introductio* published at Saint-Dié in 1507. Attached to it was a large planisphere by Martin Waldseemüller, who, thinking Vespucci had discovered the southern part of the New World, inscribed it with the name *America.* This is the first appearance of the name. Another work, the *Mundus novus,* also consists of letters attributed to Vespucci. It recounts his voyage of 1501–1502 and was widely read in the first years of the sixteenth century.

But during the last half of the eighteenth century, three handwritten letters by Vespucci were found in archives in Florence. All were addressed to Lorenzo Pier Francesco de' Medici, cousin of Lorenzo de' Medici (known as Lorenzo the Magnificent). The first, from Seville, July 8, 1500, tells of the 1499–1500 voyage; the second and third, from Cape Verde in June 1501 and Lisbon in 1502, recount the 1501–1502 voyage. Because of discrepancies between these letters and the ones known earlier, scholars have concluded that the traditional ones are apocryphal and probably not truthful. Vespucci, they think, made only two of the four voyages attributed to him—the ones in 1499–1500 and 1501–1502.

Amerigo Vespucci, born the son of a noble merchant family in Florence, was the third child of Nastagio di Amerigo and Lisa di Andrea Mini. In 1483, after the death of his father, he entered into the service of Lorenzo Pier Francesco de' Medici and sometime between October 1489 and March 1492 went to Seville. There he worked with two other Florentines, Donato Nicolini and Giannotto Berardi. The latter at that time also looked after the interests of Columbus, and through him Vespucci came to know the Genoese, perhaps immediately after the discovery of the New World.

Vespucci's activities in Seville are well documented until February 1496. He worked with Berardi even after Berardi ceased his association with the Medicis in 1493. After Berardi's death on December 2, 1495, he continued preparations for an expedition of four caravels Berardi had planned. They were to have been the first of eighteen ships to be sent to Haiti at a very low price to avoid Columbus's interests being damaged by other competition. The caravels sailed on February 3, 1496, but they were destroyed in a storm. Nothing is known of Vespucci's activities after this date until May 1499. Thus, there is no proof that he made the 1497–1498 voyage attributed to him in the Letter to Soderini.

It is certain, however, that on May 18, 1499, he embarked with Alonso de Ojeda and Juan de la Cosa on the first expedition to explore the coasts of the New World after that of Columbus's (1498–1499). Sources disagree on the number of ships involved (two or four) and their itinerary. According to Vespucci's letter of July 8, 1500, he reached the South American coast in twenty-four days. The expedition headed south as far as 6°30' S and then turning north sailed as far as Trinidad and followed the coast westward to the Venezuelan littoral. After visiting Aruba and Curaçao and following the coast for three hundred leagues (to beyond the Rio Magdalena), Vespucci decided to turn back.

But we know from other sources that Ojeda was already in Haiti on September 5, 1499, and since the itinerary Vespucci describes is too long for only three and a half months' sailing, some authors have asserted that Vespucci did not push farther south than the Suriname River (six degrees north). Others have hypothesized that he had separated from Ojeda and thus continued by himself the exploration he recounts in his letter. Both explanations are open to argument.

We do not know what tasks Vespucci carried out on this expedition, for his name is not on the list of members of the crew. Perhaps he represented the Seville merchants who had contributed to the costs of the voyage. We know he made astronomical observations and tried to measure longitude by a new method, using the conjunction of the moon with Mars on August 23, 1499, as his reference.

After his return to Spain in June 1500, he was summoned to Lisbon by King Manuel. On May 13 of the following year he sailed with a fleet of ships in the service of Portugal. Again we do not know what his tasks were. It is probable, however, that the king, having learned that Vespucci had found a new system for measuring longitude, had ordered him to fix the position of the land discovered the year before by Pedro Álvares Cabral with respect to the Line of Demarcation to see whether it was east or west of the line. If it was west, it would belong not to Portugal but to Spain.

After a stay at Cape Verde (on the western coast of Africa), Vespucci headed south-southwest, reaching the South American coast at Cape Saint Augustine (8°64' S). The exact place and date of arrival are still debated, as is the itinerary for the rest of the voyage. Again, the sources disagree. According to the most authoritative, Vespucci reached latitude forty-six degrees south, always sailing along the coast. During this expedition Vespucci, being much interested in the Indians he encountered, made long stays in their villages. He returned to Lisbon in July 1502.

After his letter of 1502 there is another documentary gap until February 5, 1505, the date of a letter from Columbus to his son Diego Colón. It is clear from Columbus's words that there was a deep friendship between the two Italian navigators. The letter proves that no rivalry existed between them.

In the following years, Vespucci, now living in Spain, busied himself with preparations for a new expedition, which, however, never sailed. On August 6, 1506, by decree of Queen Juana, he was appointed first *piloto mayor* of Spain with the task of instructing pilots bound for the Indies. He also elaborated and updated the official nautical chart, or *padron real*. He kept this position until his death at Seville on February 22, 1512.

Among his contemporaries Amerigo Vespucci was esteemed as a cosmographer. What distinguished him from the other great navigators of his time was his interest in the scientific problems connected with the discovery of the New World, whose existence, as a continent in itself separate from Asia, he was certainly one of the first—if not the first—to explain.

[See also *America, Naming of.*]

BIBLIOGRAPHY

Arciniegas, Germán. *Amerigo and the New World: The Life and Times of Amerigo Vespucci.* Translated by Harriet de Onís. New York, 1955.

Caraci, Giuseppe. *Problemi vespucciani.* Rome, 1987.

Laguarda Trias, Rolando. *El hallazgo del Rio de la Plata por Amerigo Vespucci en 1502*. Montevideo, 1982.

Pohl, Frederick Julius. *Amerigo Vespucci, Pilot Mayor*. New York, 1944.

Magnaghi, Alberto. *Amerigo Vespucci*. 2 vols. Rome, 1926.

ILARIA LUZZANA CARACI
Translated from Italian by Arthur Lomas

VINLAND. Two of the Icelandic sagas, *Eiríks saga rauða* (The saga of Eric the Red) and *Grœnlendingasaga* (The saga of the Greenlanders), tell of a land called Vinland discovered by Leif Ericsson. The texts make it clear that this must be somewhere in America, but the location of Vinland had been discussed in a large body of literature for centuries without being solved until the 1960s. Scientific assessment has shown that the Kensington Stone in Minnesota and other rune stones found in North America were not genuine Norse artifacts.

As the two sagas differ radically, it is important to ascertain which of them is the more reliable. In the past, most scholars, including Gustav Storm in 1889 and Finnur Jónsson in 1912, accepted *Eiríks saga* as being mainly historically correct. This saga relates that in about A.D. 1000 Leif Ericsson sailed from Greenland to Nidaros (Trondheim) in Norway, where the Norwegian king commissioned him to preach Christianity in Greenland. On his return to Greenland, Leif lost his way at sea and came to an unknown land, where he found vines and fields of wild wheat. He sailed to Greenland that same year.

This passage can hardly be accepted as historically accurate. For one thing, it is permeated with Christian reflections alien to the Viking age. In addition, the voyage described here—nearly 5,000 nautical miles as the crow flies—would have been nearly impossible. The distance from Trondheim to one of the northernmost areas of coastal eastern North America where grapes grow is about 3,000 nautical miles. If Leif really came to North America, his situation must have been desperate. He did not know where he was, he was sailing an open boat with square sails, and he had no instrument to determine his latitude. His only chance was to follow the coast northward for another 2,000 nautical miles or more, braving autumn storms and driftice. Presumably the provisions for his crew (probably of thirty) were intended only for the direct journey to Greenland. A voyage such as that described here would have meant starvation.

The subsequent text, about Thorfinn Karlsefni's search for Vinland, seems more than dubious. According to *Eiríks saga*, Karlsefni, who should have sailed south, sails north, following Leif's route as given in the *Grœnlendingasaga*. The author furthermore credits Karlsefni with having discovered Helluland and Markland, which, in the other saga, Leif had discovered and named. In *Eiríks saga*,

Karlsefni then makes his headquarters at a place called Straumfjord, which seems to be a substitute name for Vinland, the next land mentioned in the *Grœnlendingasaga*. Here the author is forced to stop his borrowing of names from the other saga, since the use of the name Vinland in this location would be in conflict with the story in *Eiríks saga* about Leif's discovery of Vinland during a voyage from Norway. Instead, he invented the name Straumfjord.

He then sails south and makes his camp at a place called Hop, which is accorded an effusive description of all the blessings found there, vines and self-sown wheat, game and fish, almost like a fairy tale. Again the author makes use of the *Grœnlendingasaga*, for this description is almost identical with that saga's description of Vinland. Helge Ingstad (1985) offers a detailed analysis to show that the *Grœnlendingasaga* must have been used throughout this passage, but in such a way that nothing would conflict with Leif's discovering Vinland during a voyage from Norway to a land with vines. Indeed, so many essential

NORSE LONGSHIP. About 1000 years old. Excavated in 1904 and now on display in the Viking Ship Museum, Oslo.

NORWEGIAN NATIONAL TOURIST OFFICE

elements are unreliable that *Eiríks saga* must be judged as being largely fiction.

The Icelandic scholar Jón Jóhannesson pointed out in 1956 that the author of *Eiríks saga* must have known and made use of the *Grœnlendingasaga*, probably the earlier of the two, and he concluded, "Leif did not discover Vinland on his way from Norway to Greenland, and there remains no reason to doubt that the saga of the Greenlanders preserves the original and correct account of the discovery of the new lands in the Western Hemisphere."

According to the *Grœnlendingasaga*, Bjarni Herjulfsson makes an accidental discovery of a strange coast, and then Leif Ericsson carries out a planned expedition to find this coast. Next, Leif's brother Thorvald explores the land, finding it excellent, and finally, Thorfinn Karlsefni sails to the new land with women and livestock on board in order to settle there.

Leif followed Bjarni's route in the opposite direction, sailing first northward along the coast of Greenland, probably to Disko Island, and then crossing Davis Strait, which is only about 250 nautical miles wide. He probably came to Cape Aston in Baffin Island, a flat, barren land with glaciers, that is called Helluland (Flatstone land), and then sailed south, along the coast of Labrador, which he called Markland (Land of forests). There was forest here and extensive, impressive beaches, which can hardly be anything other than the long beaches north and south of Cape Porcupine. From there Leif sailed two days and nights and came to a third land, which must be the northern coast of Newfoundland. There he landed and built "large houses." It was at this coast that the Norse settlement was discovered.

Maps by Sigurdur Stefánsson (1590) and Hans Paulsen Resen (1605) indicate a northerly Vinland. Moreover, it is important to note that Leif would have to start late, perhaps in early August, because of the ice, and that he had to settle as soon as possible, in order to have time to make the necessary preparation for winter, building houses and securing provisions by hunting and fishing. The northern part of Newfoundland lies about nine degrees south of Leif's home in Greenland, and the route indicated by the sagas, along the coasts, from his Greenland home, Brattahlid, to the north coast of Newfoundland, covers about 1,800 nautical miles. Newfoundland offered forest for timber, fish, seal, and game; there were meadows for pasture if a permanent settlement was contemplated. It was a more favorable land than Greenland, a northern land where the Greenlanders would feel at home. There was no reason for them to continue south; on the contrary, sailing on would have been a hazardous venture.

For nearly three hundred years, it has generally been held that the sagas' information about wine and grapes is historically correct. As a consequence, it has been sug-gested that Vinland was located far to the south, in Massachusetts, Rhode Island, or Virginia. But the sagas' mention of grapes is probably because of Adam of Bremen (c. 1070), who, as a German, probably did not know that in Old Norse the syllable *vin* meant "meadows" when the *i* was short and "wine" when the *i* was long, and therefore associated the word with wine and grapes. His mistake is also made very clear by his statement that "Beyond this island [Vinland] no habitable land is found in the ocean, but all that is beyond is full of intolerable ice and immense mist"—no place for vines and grapes, but an accurate description of conditions in the ocean north of the Norse settlement at L'Anse aux Meadows at the northern coast of Newfoundland (51°35' N). Since the sagas were popular stories mainly intended for entertainment, the author or the scribe must have been delighted to borrow the detail of wine and grapes from the classic work by Adam of Bremen.

Taking most of the above arguments into consideration, Helge Ingstad (1966) came to the conclusion that Vinland must be located somewhere in Newfoundland and that it might be possible to find the remains of Leif's "large houses" by a systematic investigation of the coasts from sea and air. He carried out such an investigation in 1960, and with the assistance of George Decker, a fisherman, he found a number of indistinct overgrown elevations on an ancient marine terrace in an area called L'Anse aux Meadows.

From 1961 to 1968, Helge Ingstad and a team of international scholars, including Anne Stine Ingstad (1977) as archaeological leader, carried out seven expeditions to the area. A small river, Black Duck Brook, runs through the marine terrace and flows out into a very shallow bay. Eight houses, made of turf, were found, some of which were up to 24 meters (78 feet) long. They are of Norse type, and related to Icelandic and Greenlandic houses of the Viking period. The same also applies to the form and position of the hearths. There may have been room for almost a hundred people in these houses. The middens were fairly small, which indicates that the houses cannot have been occupied for long.

Of particular interest was the smithy, a small house dug into the terrace. In the middle of the room there was a big, flat, earthfast stone anvil. On the floor lay fragments of iron, slag, and bog-ore, the smith's raw material. Large quantities of bog-ore were found under the turf in a nearby bog. Close to the smithy there was a kiln where charcoal for work in the smithy had been produced. In other words, the old Norse method of producing iron had been transferred to America.

There were a number of other interesting finds: iron nails, a piece of copper that had been melted down, a stone lamp, a needle-hone, and fragments of what are apparently pig bone. A soapstone spindle-whorl of Norse type and a bronze ring-headed pin of Viking Age type indicate the presence of women, of which the sagas speak. Artifacts deriving from Indians and Dorset Eskimos were also found; according to the sagas, the Norse traded and fought with the natives, known to the Europeans as Skraelings.

A series of radiocarbon analyses have yielded an approximate date of A.D. 1000 for the settlement, about the time that, according to the sagas, Leif Ericsson discovered Vinland.

It is now internationally acknowledged that the settlement at L'Anse aux Meadows is Norse. The Canadian government has made the area into a national park, built a Viking museum there, and made the place into a tourist attraction. UNESCO has included the settlement in its World Heritage List as one of the most valuable historical monuments in the world.

It seems reasonable to assume that, once the route to the favorable areas in North America had been discovered, other groups of Greenlanders should have sailed to the new lands during the five hundred years their community existed. An important reason for crossing to America must have been the need for timber; Greenland had none, and timber for shipbuilding was of vital importance. A few sources may indicate such traffic. The *Icelandic Annals* for 1120 note that "Eric Upsi, bishop of Greenland, sailed in search of Vinland"; nothing more is known about him. The *Skálholt Annals* for 1342 note that the inhabitants of Greenland (probably in the Western Settlement) forsook the true faith and religion and turned to the people of America. The same annals for 1347 note that a ship with eighteen men arrived in Iceland, having sailed from Markland (Labrador).

What, if anything, did Leif Ericsson's discovery mean to Columbus? It seems likely that he did not know about it, and if he did know, it is doubtful that it would have been of any importance to him. According to a biography written by his son Fernando Colón, Columbus journeyed to an island in the north, probably Iceland, in 1477. He mentions the city of Bristol; a number of Bristol ships participated in the fishery off Iceland and it is reasonable to suppose that Columbus took part in one of these voyages. It has been claimed that the young Columbus, though he did not know the language, was informed by the Icelanders about the Vinland voyages, but this is conjecture.

[See also *Icelandic Sagas* and the biography of Leif Ericsson.]

BIBLIOGRAPHY

Adam of Bremen. *History of the Archbishops of Hamburg-Bremen.* Translated with an introduction and notes by Francis J. Tschan. New York, 1959.

Columbus, Ferdinand. *The Life of the Admiral Christopher Columbus.* Translated by Benjamin Keen. New Brunswick, N.J., 1959.

Ingstad, Anne Stine. *The Norse Discovery of America.* Vol. 1. Oslo, 1977. Reprint, Oslo, 1985.

Ingstad, Helge. *Land under the Pole Star.* London and New York, 1966. English translation of *Landet under Leidarstjernen,* Oslo, 1959.

Ingstad, Helge. *The Norse Discovery of America.* Vol. 2. Oslo, 1985.

Ingstad, Helge. *Westward to Vinland.* London and New York, 1969.

Storm, Gustav. *Studies on the Vineland Voyages.* Extraits des Mémoires de la Société royale des antiquaires du nord 1888. Copenhagen, 1889.

Wahlgren, Erik. *The Kensington Stone: A Mystery Solved.* Madison, Wis., 1958.

HELGE INGSTAD

VINLAND MAP. A world map seemingly produced in the second quarter of the fifteenth century, the Vinland Map was found bound with two medieval manuscripts, one of which included an account of European travels to the land of the Tatars at the eastern edge of Asia. The map, on its western edge, included a large island described as "Vinlanda Insula" west of Greenland and Iceland. Although no known map of this period included such a place, it was nevertheless known through the Icelandic saga narratives that recounted the voyages of Norsemen Thorfinn Karlsefni Thordarson and Leif Ericsson to a land west of Greenland at the end of the tenth century A.D. and the beginning of the eleventh. The Vinland Map continues to puzzle scholars and the lay public. Is it a forgery or authentic? That is still an open question, although partisans on both sides continue vociferously to argue their points of view.

The map (and accompanying manuscripts), which came from a still undisclosed seller and location in Europe (the seller anxious to avoid tax and customs problems that might otherwise have impeded the sale), was examined and rejected by skeptical authorities in the British Museum in the 1950s. It was later purchased by a rare-book dealer from New Haven, Connecticut, Laurence Witten, who was convinced of its authenticity and importance. Thus began the long trip toward apparent respectability, which culminated in the publication of *The Vinland Map and Tartar Relation* by Yale University Press in 1965. But the publicity associated with its publication, because it coincided with the celebration of Columbus Day, created a public outcry as those unfamiliar with the unquestioned noncartographic evidence for the Norse discovery of America assailed Yale University for insensitivity and callous disregard of Italian and Spanish pride. On a

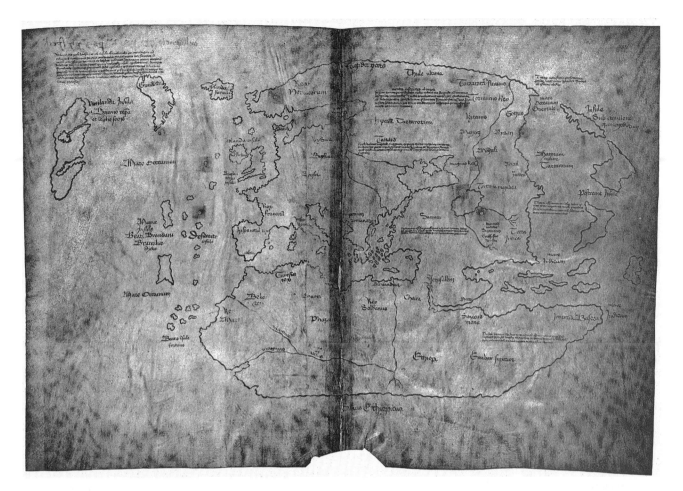

THE VINLAND MAP.

scholarly level, the fact that the work had been completed in secret by scholars associated with Yale's library (working with a library scholar from the British Museum) rather than with Yale's history department generated skepticism and hostility on the part of those excluded from the discovery. The air of secrecy with which the Vinland Map was shrouded was, in fact, simply the desire of a generous donor to Yale to avoid the irritating publicity to which he felt he would be subjected if his name were attached to the publication of the book.

In the controversy that ensued, scholarly courtesy and sometimes objectivity were often absent, and arguments concerning the motives and competence of those associated with the map were hurled by those who remained skeptical of its authenticity. A conference to bring the warring participants together was held at the Smithsonian Institution in 1966, the results of which were published in *The Proceedings of the Vinland Map Conference* in 1971. The participants, who were leading scholars in the field of the history of cartography, debated the character and

significance of the map. In considering the question of authenticity, no one was able to demonstrate through paleographic, cartographic, linguistic, or historical evidence that the map was not what it purported to be. No one, however, could dispel the serious doubts of many of the participants. It was concluded that technical analyses of the paper, ink, and binding of the document might help determine whether the map was authentic or a clever forgery. Yale University thereupon asked Walter C. McCrone, director of an independent laboratory, to take samples of the ink from the map and analyze them. The results were dismaying to those who believed that no one had either the skill or the motive to forge such an exceptional document. The McCrone analysis concluded that anatase, a preparation of titanium invented only in 1920 and subsequently used in the manufacture of ink, was present on the map in significant quantities.

Yale University accepted the judgment of the McCrone laboratory, but others remained skeptical of that work, and the question of the authenticity of the map did not die. Through the agency of individuals who believed the map to be authentic, additional tests were carried on in other laboratories, most notably at the University of California, Davis, by a group led by Thomas Cahill. The Davis study asserted that the elements the McCrone laboratories had concluded derived from a substance not manufactured before 1920 was in fact present in numerous medieval manuscripts analyzed along with the Vinland Map. The Davis study thus left open the question of the map's authenticity. McCrone responded aggressively to the Davis report, reasserting the validity of his original research. As of 1990 the issue was still clouded, with further tests being undertaken by both McCrone and others in an attempt to clarify the discrepancies.

The relevance of both the Vinland Map and its accompanying documents to the Columbus story is patent. Columbus, whose careful assembling of data concerning the Ocean Sea separating Europe from Asia benefited from his own voyages north as far as Iceland and south to the Portuguese trading depots in sub-Saharan Africa, may have been aware of the reports of Norse voyages to lands beyond Iceland and Greenland in the Far North. The Vinland Map, assuming it is authentic, provides cartographic confirmation of fifteenth-century knowledge of the existence of land in what we now know to be North America. Later explorers in the sixteenth and subsequent centuries sought unsuccessfully to find the route to the riches of Asia through the northern seas, but Columbus, whether or not he knew of the existence of Vinland, chose to try to find his way to the fabled Orient through more southern seas. Nevertheless, the Vinland Map remains a tantalizing and important piece of evidence—even with its authenticity questioned—to explain European conceptions of the globe on the eve of the Age of Discovery.

[See also Icelandic Sagas; Vinland.]

BIBLIOGRAPHY

Cahill, Thomas A., et al. "The Vinland Map Revisited: New Compositional Evidence on Its Inks and Parchments." Analytical Chemistry 59 (1987): 829–833.

McCrone, Walter C. Chemical Analytical Study of the Vinland Map; Report to Yale University. New Haven, Conn., 1974.

McCrone, Walter C. "The Vinland Map." Analytical Chemistry 60 (1988): 1009–1018.

Skelton, Raleigh A., Thomas E. Marston, and George D. Painter. The Vinland Map and the Tartar Relation. New Haven, Conn., 1965.

Towe, Kenneth M. "The Vinland Map: Still a Forgery." Accounts of Chemical Research 23 (1990): 84–87.

Washburn, Wilcomb E., ed. The Proceedings of the Vinland Map Conference. Chicago, 1971.

Witten, Laurence C., II. "Vinland's Saga Recalled." Yale University Library Gazette 64 (1989): 10–37.

WILCOMB E. WASHBURN

VIVALDI, UGOLINO, AND VADINO VIVALDI

(d. 1291?), Genoese merchants and explorers. The Vivaldi brothers are often credited with the earliest European attempt to reach "the Indies" by sailing from the west coast of Africa. Sultan al-Ashraf's capture of the last crusader outposts and Pope Nicholas IV's embargo on trade with the "infidel" blocked Western access to merchandise from the Orient. The Vivaldi family had been active in tapping into the valuable overland trade from India, so the brothers now sought a way to bypass the Muslim middlemen, much as Columbus would do two hundred years later.

In the spring of 1291 the Vivaldi brothers outfitted two galleys for a long voyage. According to the Genoese annalist Iacopo Doria, whose chronicle covers the period 1280–1294, they were going "per mare Oceanum ad partes Indiae," a statement ambiguous as to both route and ultimate destination. It is known, however, that they sailed through the Straits of Gibraltar and coasted south at least as far as Cape Juby, near the Canaries. Their expedition was never heard from again. They may have intended any of three routes: circumnavigate Africa, sail up one of Africa's western rivers (believed to be branches of the Nile), or cross the Atlantic Ocean, anticipating Columbus's later voyage. No contemporary evidence is clear, and later statements about their intent are flawed by such ambiguities as Doria's.

Nevertheless, knowledge of the Vivaldis' attempt was widespread, and there are many references to the expedition in both books and maps dating from the fourteenth through sixteenth centuries. Ugolino's son Sorleone is said to have searched the east coast of Africa for his father on tips from travelers, and as late as the 1450s, Antoniotto Usodimare, a Genoese merchant, claimed to have met a descendant of a member of the ill-starred party on the west coast. The glory of the goal, the audacity of the leaders, and the mysterious conclusion of the enterprise continued to excite interest, and after Columbus's successful voyages, his fellow Genoese depicted the Vivaldis as the great discoverer's precursors with patriotic certainty. After all, the Vivaldis were not working for the Spanish. In good Genoese fashion they were working for themselves.

BIBLIOGRAPHY

Caddeo, Rinaldo. Le navigazioni atlantiche di Alvise da Cadamosto, Antoniotto Usodimare e Niccoloso da Recco. Milan, 1928.

Magnaghi, A. Precursori di Colombo? Il tentativo di viaggio transoceanico dei genovese fratelli Vivaldi nel 1291. Rome, 1935.

Moore, Gilliam. "Le spedizione dei fratelli Vivaldi e nuovi

documenti d'Archivio." *Atti della Società Ligure di Storia Patria* 82 (1972): 387–402.

Rogers, Francis M. "The Vivaldi Expedition." In *Seventy-Third Annual Report of the Dante Society*. Cambridge, Mass., 1955; 31–54.

JOSEPH P. BYRNE

VIZINHO, JOSÉ (c. 1450–c. 1520), Jewish astrologer and physician. Some scholars claim that José Vizinho was born in Portugal and some specify Viseu as his birthplace. It is thought that he was of Castilian origin since, when appointed to translate from Latin or Hebrew, he did so into Castilian, not Portuguese. In any case, he was fairly well rooted in Portugal before 1485. Because pilots on transatlantic voyages needed to know standard measurements of astronomical coordinates related to the stars or the sun, King João II of Portugal asked Vizinho to provide the necessary information.

The first and most elementary solution to the problem of maritime expeditions that lacked known coastal markers apparently began with a very simple comparison of altitudes taken at one of the meridian passages of the polestar. This was probably a widely accepted procedure. It is explained, with a slightly different purpose, in the *Tractatus de sphaera* (Treatise on the sphere) by Johannes de Sacrobosco. However, the need to proceed further and determine latitudes at sea required knowledge of books in which such problems were explained, and those who had access to these books were astrologers such as Vizinho.

Vizinho was undoubtedly familiar with the treatises on the astrolabe and the quadrant and related issues. Of special importance were works on the determination of latitudes by starting from the solar meridian altitude and its declination on the date of the observation. Many books taught how to make the determination, including the ninth-century treatise on the use of the astrolabe by Messahalla and the *Libros del saber de astronomia* (Books of astronomical knowledge) compiled by a group of scholars for Afonso X of Castile in the thirteenth century. The rules examined in these books were not complete because they did not include all possible cases.

It is very possible that Vizinho was appointed to study and complete these rules. Yet, once a *regimento* (a body of rules) was established to suit all predictable situations, it had to be verified in practice. Vizinho was assigned this task as well. Christopher Columbus notes, "In 1485 the king of Portugal sent to Guinea *magister Josepius* [José Vizinho], his physician and astrologer, to summarize the altitude of the sun in all Guinea . . . ." The experiment gave positive results and as a consequence, in 1487 and 1488, Bartolomeu Dias was able to use the *regimento* in his voyage when he rounded the southern tip of Africa.

Tables needed to calculate solar declination in using the *regimento* were included in the *Almanach perpetuum* (Perpetual almanac) by another Jewish astrologer, Abraham Zacuto. They were also published in Leiria in 1494 in parallel editions with "canons," that is, explanatory introductions, in Latin and Castilian. The Castilian version was written by Vizinho, who states that he is a disciple of Zacuto.

BIBLIOGRAPHY

De Lery, Jean. *History of a Voyage to the Land of Brazil Otherwise Called America*. Translated by Janet Whatley. Berkeley, 1990.

Diffey, Bailey W. *Prelude to Empire: Portugal Overseas before Henry the Navigator*. Lincoln, Neb., 1960.

Diffey, Bailey W., and George D. Winius. *Foundations of the Portuguese Empire, 1414–1850*. Edited by Boyd C. Shafer. Minneapolis, 1977.

Morison, Samuel Eliot. *Portuguese Voyages to America in the Fifteenth Century*. New York, 1965.

LUÍS DE ALBUQUERQUE
Translated from Portuguese by Paola Carù

VOYAGES OF COLUMBUS. [This article focuses on the details of Columbus's four voyages to America. For further discussion of Columbus's life and works, including reference to his efforts to win support for his voyages of discovery, see the various articles under *Columbus, Christopher*.]

Christopher Columbus made four voyages across the Atlantic Ocean. Clearly, the first was most important. His landfall on a tiny island in the Bahamas in 1492 changed the world dramatically and fundamentally. Although more than ten years would pass before Europe realized that Columbus had discovered, literally, a New World, not lands on the fringes of Asia, the knowledge that vast territories, new peoples, and potential riches lay within reach captured people's imaginations and stimulated efforts in every field. The age of European exploration, discovery, and colonization followed immediately; the Renaissance spread across the Old World, and people attained new heights of creativity and accomplishment. Columbus never found what he sought but the prize was far greater than he realized.

In itself, the first voyage was unremarkable: after an easy thirty-three day sail from the Canary Islands, Columbus landed on an island in the Caribbean. Given his careful but incorrect calculations, he was sure he was on the outskirts of India. Sailing southwest from San Salvador, he explored the coast of Cuba, searching for gold and spices. *Santa María* ran aground on Christmas Eve, forcing Columbus to stop exploring. He built a fortress on La Española (Hispaniola) and left a group of men there to gather the gold that the Indians said was nearby. Returning to Spain with a cargo of exotic birds, plants, gold nuggets and masks, and ten Indians, Columbus made a triumphant journey across Spain to Barcelona where King Fernando and Queen Isabel greeted him as an equal.

Columbus's second voyage followed within months. He guided seventeen ships loaded with fifteen hundred men, livestock, trees, and seeds back to La Española to establish a settlement. But this successful seaman was less adept as an administrator. His nationality and low birth reduced his authority in the eyes of many of the gentlemen adventurers who had signed on for the voyage. The hot and humid climate, difficult work, and inadequate food hampered efforts to create a viable colony. The expectations of the hidalgos for abundant, easily acquired gold were never fulfilled. Columbus spent most of the two years of this voyage trying to bring order to La Española and was able to explore only the southern coast of Cuba.

The signal event of Columbus's third voyage—his discovery of South America—was completely overshadowed at the time by strife on La Española. In fact, Columbus and his two brothers were sent home in chains by the administrator assigned by the Crown to bring order to the area. Even after this ignominious return, however, Columbus managed to regain the respect of the sovereigns and their permission for a fourth voyage of exploration. However, the powers originally promised to Columbus as Admiral of the Ocean Sea and Viceroy and Governor of the Islands were never restored, an injustice that rankled Columbus for the rest of his life.

On his fourth voyage, Columbus hoped to discover a passage to India at the western end of the Caribbean, but the strait was not there to discover. He tried to establish another tiny settlement on the Central American coast, where he found more gold than in La Española, but hostile Indians made it impossible. In his two remaining ships, so worm-eaten they looked like honeycomb, Columbus sailed as far as Jamaica where he had to beach them. He and his men were marooned for twelve months. When Columbus finally returned to Spain, Isabel was dying and Fernando had little time for the ill and aged navigator.

The First Voyage

It would be impossible to overstate the importance of Christopher Columbus's first voyage of discovery. His endeavor to reach the riches of the Orient by sailing across the Atlantic Ocean changed the face of the world as it was then known. Suddenly, the Mar Tenebrosa, the Dark Sea, was no longer dark or trackless. It could be crossed in a month, and more important, it could be recrossed back to Europe. Even though Columbus thought he had discovered the eastern extremity of Asia, the fact that people, plants, animals, and riches existed

where nothing was thought to exist before galvanized Europe. The Old World was fired with enthusiasm and the energy to learn and gain from this New World even before the size and nature of the American continents became clear.

It took Columbus twelve years to win support for his endeavor. King João of Portugal turned him down twice on the advice of court scientists and mathematicians who said his theory about a western route to the Indies was nonsense. Fernando and Isabel of Spain put him off for seven years, being more occupied with fighting the Muslim Kingdom of Granada than with sponsoring dubious sailing expeditions. But in 1492 Granada was conquered. Perhaps more important to Columbus's fortunes was the expulsion from Spain of all Jews who refused to convert to Christianity. Jewish lands, money, and other valuables were seized by the Catholic sovereigns, and this confiscated wealth helped to underwrite Columbus. So this stubborn, courageous, deeply religious Genoese mapmaker, seaman, and navigational genius was given his chance.

Christopher Columbus set out to "discover and acquire islands and mainland in the Ocean Sea" one-half hour before sunrise on August 3, 1492, just over four months after the Spanish sovereigns Fernando and Isabel had finally agreed to sponsor and help finance the venture. Efforts to obtain, outfit, and man the three ships needed for the voyage had been hampered by a number of difficulties. Columbus's notion that a western route to the Indies could be crossed before supplies ran out was ridiculed. Seamen were afraid to risk their lives in such a dangerous endeavor. Even royal commands failed to produce movement. Eager to save money, Fernando ordered the town of Palos to furnish two fully equipped and manned caravels for the voyage in penalty for earlier pirate activity against Spanish ships. Palos refused. Royal orders directed local officials to provide supplies and assistance to Columbus, but officials ignored the orders. Even the dispatch to Andalusia of Juan de Peñalosa, an officer of the royal household, could not force compliance with the sovereigns' decree. Finally, an influential Palos shipowner named Martín Alonso Pinzón announced that he and his brothers, Vicente Yáñez and Francisco Martín, would sail with Columbus. With this support, magistrates of the town were able to press a caravel, *Pinta*, into service despite the complaints of her owner, Cristóbal Quintero. Martín Alonso Pinzón agreed to sail as captain of *Pinta* with his brother Francisco Martín as her master. Vicente Yáñez Pinzón agreed to sail as captain of the caravel *Niña*, furnished by the equally influential Niño family of Moguer; her owner, Juan Niño, sailed as master of his caravel. Columbus was able to charter a third, larger vessel named *Santa María* from Juan de la Cosa and to persuade him and some of his crew to join in the venture. By the end of July, a total of eighty-seven crewmen had been recruited.

After bidding anguished farewells to family and friends, for few expected success in their venture, the crew of the tiny fleet waited for the tide and then crossed the bar of the Saltes at the mouth of the Tinto and Odiel rivers at 8:00 A.M. and sailed out into the Atlantic Ocean. Columbus set course for the Canary Islands, his point of departure for the fabled Orient. He began his log immediately. In its prologue, written for the king and queen, Columbus promised to record "very diligently" everything he saw and did each day, and to "make a new sailing chart" locating "all of the sea and the lands of the Ocean Sea in their proper places." "Above all," Columbus wrote, "it is very important that I forget sleep and pay much attention to navigation in order thus to carry out these purposes, which will be great labor." Although the original log was lost centuries ago, an excellent transcription of excerpts from it was made by Bartolomé de las Casas in his invaluable *Historia de las Indias*.

The voyage began inauspiciously: *Pinta's* rudder broke loose three days out (Columbus suspected deliberate sabotage by her owner, Cristóbal Quintero, who accompanied him but continued to oppose the voyage), and *Niña*, with her lateen rig, had difficulty keeping up with *Pinta* and *Santa María*, both square-rigged and better able to take advantage of the favorable winds from astern. Martín Alonso Pinzón was able to effect temporary repairs to the rudder, and the ship limped into Grand Canary on August 9. Columbus sailed on to Gomera to try to find a replacement for the damaged ship.

Three weeks of frustration followed, with Columbus waiting for a suitable ship to arrive (it never did) and for word from Pinzón that he had repaired the rudder (which he never sent). Columbus finally returned to Grand Canary, ordered Pinzón to make a new rudder, and directed that *Niña* be rerigged, changing her triangular lateen sails to square sails. Columbus knew the Atlantic winds blow steadily from the east or northeast in these latitudes. A square-rigged ship would have better maneuverability. He planned to return from the Indies with the westerly winds he had observed personally in the winter along the coast of Portugal and Galicia. Also, Columbus had sailed to England with the Portuguese in the past and had learned that the westerlies blew year-round in the higher latitudes. Obviously, Columbus knew how he would return to Spain. Nevertheless, the fear of being stranded somewhere at the end of the world dogged many in his crew throughout this first voyage.

When the two caravels were ready, the fleet returned to Gomera to pick up enough fresh supplies for twenty-eight days and a detachment of men left there earlier by Columbus. It then sailed west on September 6, more than a month after leaving Palos. A three-day calm kept them within sight of land, and there was some concern that a Portuguese squadron reported to be in the area might try to prevent Columbus from sailing west. Fortunately, no squadron appeared and a brisk northeast wind finally came up to move the ships on their way. Crewmen wept on September 9 when Hierro (Ferro), the westernmost of the Canaries, disappeared from view, but Columbus comforted them with promises of land and riches. He also decided to keep two accounts of distances traveled: an accurate reckoning for himself, and another for the crew that would report fewer leagues sailed "so in case the voyage were long the men would not be frightened and lose courage."

The next thirty-three days were marked by sunny skies, fair winds, and calm seas. Columbus picked up the northern fringe of the northeast trade belt, and it carried him smoothly to the outer cays of the Bahama Islands. Were the crew as convinced of ultimate success as Columbus, it would have been a peaceful voyage. Instead, according to Columbus, the days were filled with emotional highs and lows. As a number of log entries record, every imaginable sign of land was taken as real. Martín Alonso Pinzón first thought he spied land on September 18, only nine days out from Hierro. Every bird, every patch of sargasso weed, even a crab in a clump of weed ("a sure sign of land, for crabs are not found even 240 miles from shore"), was recounted in the log. Columbus knew the voyage would take some weeks, but the nervous crew wanted it to end as soon as possible. By September 24, the crew was so uneasy that, according to later testimony, some apparently planned to throw Columbus into the sea if he refused to turn back. The Admiral would calm some fears only to have new grumbling arise from another quarter. Still the fleet held together and kept on its westerly course. On October 1 Columbus's phony log showed they had sailed 1,734 miles from Hierro. His private reckoning showed 2,121 miles. On they went. Columbus had long since grown weary of the constant cries of "Land!" and had told the men that anyone making a false claim would forfeit the ten thousand maravedis reward (about eight hundred dollars) promised by the sovereigns to the first to sight the Indies. Despite this, *Niña* claimed to sight land on October 7, but by evening, it was clear the "land" was yet another cloudbank.

On October 11, birds, fresh reeds, and an apparently hand-hewn staff were sighted in the sea. Some of the crew's apprehensions were soothed, and at evening vespers, special thanks were given for the many signs of land. Columbus ordered extra lookouts and urged everyone to be especially vigilant. At about 10:00 P.M. he reported seeing a light to the west, bobbing up and down

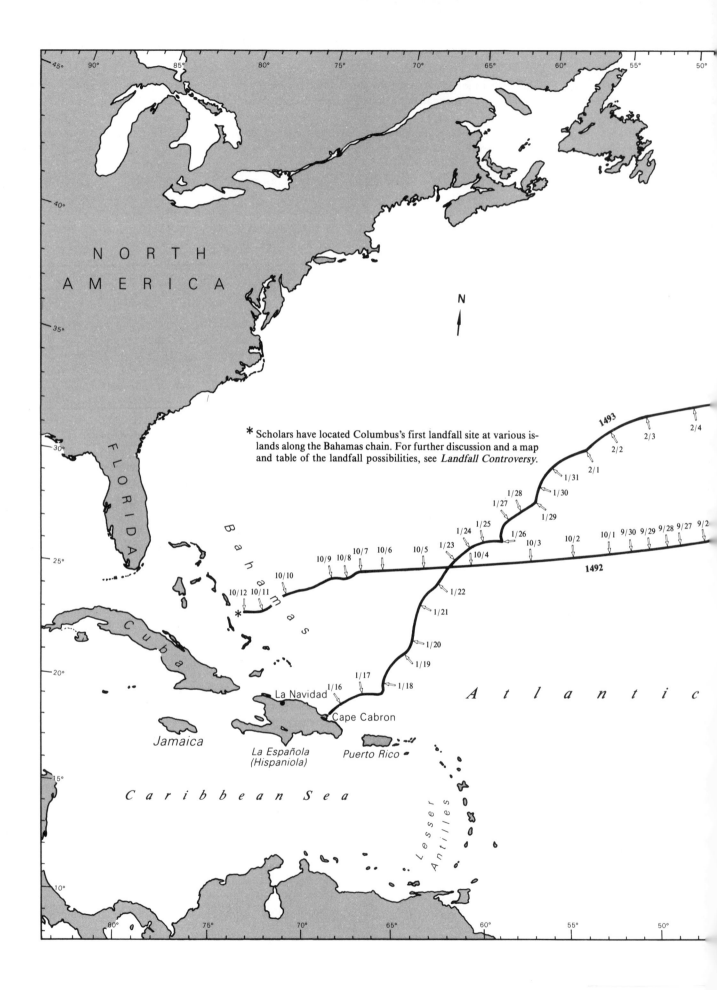

* Scholars have located Columbus's first landfall site at various islands along the Bahamas chain. For further discussion and a map and table of the landfall possibilities, see *Landfall Controversy*.

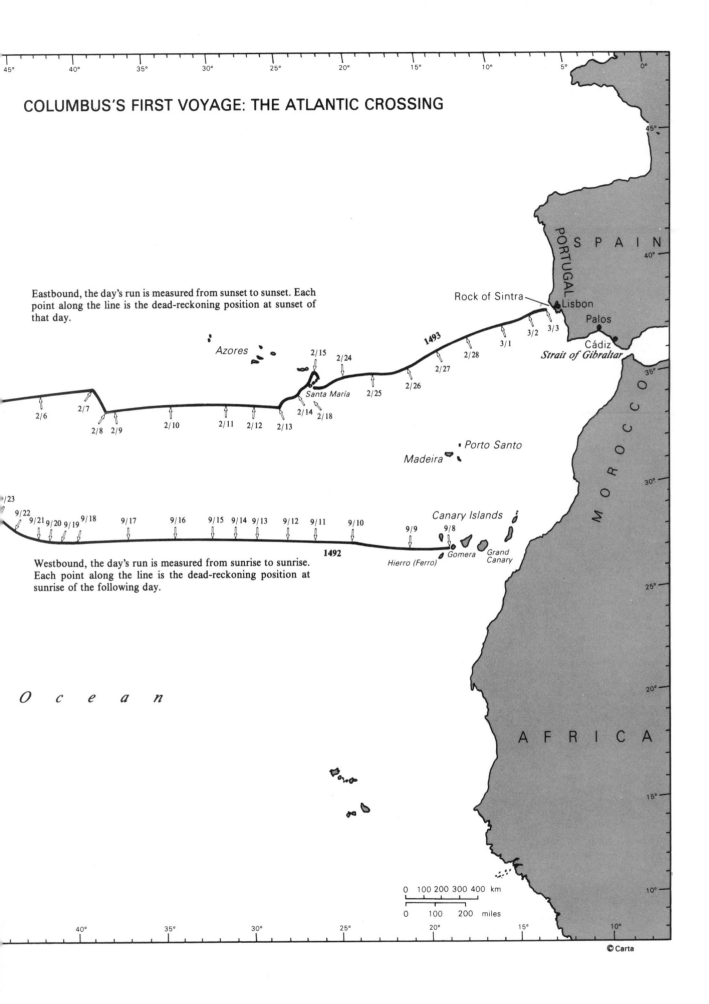

COLUMBUS'S FIRST VOYAGE: THE ATLANTIC CROSSING

Eastbound, the day's run is measured from sunset to sunset. Each
point along the line is the dead-reckoning position at sunset of
that day.

Westbound, the day's run is measured from sunrise to sunrise.
Each point along the line is the dead-reckoning position at
sunrise of the following day.

Azores

Santa María

1493

Rock of Sintra

PORTUGAL

S P A I N

Lisbon

Palos

Cádiz
Strait of Gibraltar

2/15 2/24

2/14 2/18 2/25 2/26 2/27 2/28 3/1 3/2 3/3

2/6 2/7 2/8 2/9 2/10 2/11 2/12 2/13

Madeira • *Porto Santo*

M O R O C C O

9/23
9/22 9/21 9/20 9/19 9/18 9/17 9/16 9/15 9/14 9/13 9/12 9/11 9/10 9/9 9/8

Canary Islands

Hierro (Ferro) • Gomera Grand Canary

1492

O c e a n

A F R I C A

0 100 200 300 400 km

0   100   200 miles

© Carta

as if being carried on a boat or by hand over rough terrain. Pedro Gutiérrez, a representative of the king's household, also saw it. A few minutes later, though, it had disappeared, and "it was something so faint that [I] did not wish to affirm that it was land," wrote Columbus.

At 2:00 A.M. on October 12, *Pinta* fired her cannon in the prearranged signal for landfall. Seaman Rodrigo de Triana had spotted a sandy beach in the moonlight. (Columbus himself was later awarded the prize for being the first to see land, based on his report of the bobbing light.) The fleet, in uncharted waters and bearing down on a lee shore before a strong following wind, was wisely ordered by Columbus to shorten sail and lay-to until dawn. At daybreak, the fleet rounded the island and found a suitable anchorage on the leeward side. Then Columbus, the Pinzón captains, secretary of the fleet Rodrigo de Escobedo, comptroller Rodrigo Sánchez, and others landed on the island called Guanahani by its natives. Making the declarations that were required, the Spanish took formal possession of the island for Fernando and Isabel. Columbus named the island San Salvador.

Columbus was sure this level, tree-covered island lay at the extremity of India. When the natives rushed to the shore, he called them *Indians*, a term subsequently applied to all aboriginals of the New World. In a scene that was to be repeated almost without change during the remainder of the first voyage, natives crowded around the richly dressed and armed strangers. The Indians were "as naked as their mothers bore them," well built with brown skin and straight, coarse, black hair. Faces and bodies were painted in black, red, white, and other colors; some carried small spears made of wood. They were curious, friendly, docile, and trusting. Eager to please the demigods they thought had descended from heaven, the Indians offered food, water, balls of cotton thread, parrots, and "a kind of dry leaf that they hold in great esteem." Columbus ordered his men to take nothing without offering something in exchange, and the Indians were thrilled with the beads, hawkbells, pieces of colored glass, and other baubles presented by the Spaniards.

Where did Columbus actually first set foot in the New World? The question has been debated for hundreds of years. The three favorite choices today are Watlings Island (now officially named San Salvador), Samana Cay, and Grand Turk Island. (Cat Island, East Caicos, and Concepción [Conception Island] have been vigorously promoted in the past, but their support among experts has faded.) Watlings Island was legally named San Salvador in 1926; among those who have supported it as the landfall in recent years are the respected Columbus scholars J. B. Thacher, Samuel Eliot Morison, and Mauricio Obregon. In 1985, when debate was renewed, the Society for the History of Discoveries spearheaded a new research effort, aided by the National Geographic Society. A large team of specialists (mathematicians, computer experts, archaeologists, cartographers, navigators, and translators) combined efforts and concluded that Samana Cay, first proposed as the landfall by Capt. Gustavus V. Fox in 1894, was the correct site. The debate continues.

Columbus left San Salvador on October 14. Seven Indians were taken along as guides and interpreters. Santa María de la Concepción (Crooked Island) was claimed for the Crown on October 16 and La Fernandina (Long Island) two days later. It was on Fernandina that Columbus first saw a hammock. At La Isabela (Southern Crooked Island) Columbus was told by the Indians that a great king "who wears much gold" lived in an inland village. A search party failed to find him, however, and on the twenty-fourth Columbus left in search of Cuba, described by the Indians as "very large and of great commerce . . . [with] gold and spices and great ships and merchants. And in the spheres that I saw and in world maps it [Japan] is in this region."

This reference to "spheres" may refer to the terrestrial globe produced in 1492 by Martin Behaim of Germany, which displayed the accepted view of the world at this time. While scholars debated the size of the globe, no one imagined any land mass lying between Europe and Asia. (For example, Viking discoveries were mapped as part of Asia.) Not until 1510 did some Europeans suggest a new continent had been found and many maps made in the late sixteenth century still appended the Americas to Asia. Balboa did not discover the Pacific Ocean until 1513. Additionally, Columbus based his calculations on a glaring mistake: he underestimated the length of degrees of longitude. And so did everyone else until 1670. Columbus believed a degree equaled 56.666 miles. In fact, as was learned much later, a degree of longitude at the equator measures 69 miles. Using the shorter estimate, Columbus believed Asia lay 1,100 leagues west of Europe. He sailed 1,111 leagues from the Canary Islands and found land. Where else could he be but Asia? As he wrote in the log on October 21, he planned to go to "another very large island that I believe must be Cipango [Marco Polo's name for Japan] according to the indications that these Indians that I have give me, and which they call Colba [Cuba]. In it they say there are many and very large ships and many traders. And from this island (I intend to go to) another that they call Bohío . . . I have already decided to go to the mainland and to the city of Quinsay [Hangzhou, China] and to give Your Highnesses' letters to the Grand Khan and to ask for, and to come with, a reply."

On October 28 Columbus made landfall on the north coast of Cuba and named it Juana, after Prince Juan. He coasted the northern shore for several days and then anchored in the Río de Mares (Bahía de Gibara) to make needed repairs on the ships. On November 2, believing that land of such a size must be the continent, Columbus sent Rodrigo de Jerez and Luis de Torres, who spoke Hebrew, Chaldean, and Arabic, plus two Indians, to find the Grand Khan, giving them strings of beads to trade and instructions from the sovereigns asking the khan's help in learning about his land. The delegation returned two days later, reporting they had found a large native village and had been warmly received by the inhabitants. They had seen cultivated fields of sweet potatoes, maize, and beans. The men reported "in one house alone, 12,000 pounds" of cotton and "dogs that do not bark," but they did not find the Grand Khan.

On November 12, Columbus decided to retrace his path to the east southeast in search of another island, called Bohío by the Indians, said to contain great riches. Actually, there are two islands to the southeast of Cuba, Babeque (Great Inagua) and Bohío (La Isla Española, also known as Hispaniola). The Indians told Columbus both were sources of gold, spices, and pearls. Heading east by south, two days later Columbus saw "so many islands [he] could not count them all, of good size and very high lands full of trees of a thousand kinds." Columbus believed these islands "are those innumerable ones that in maps of the world are put at the eastern end." He believed there were great riches and precious stones and spices there. He was in Tanamo Bay and decided to explore among the islands in the ship's boat, planting a cross wherever he stopped.

Departing from the bay on November 19, Columbus tried to reach Babeque, but adverse winds drove him north, not east. On November 21, while Columbus was heading back toward Cuba, Martín Alonso Pinzón "because of greed and without the permission and will of the Admiral, departed with the caravel *Pinta*, thinking that an Indian whom the Admiral had ordered put on that caravel was going to give him much gold. And so he went away without waiting and not by reason of bad weather, but because he wanted to.... he has done and said to me many other things." *Pinta* carried on to the east and Babeque; *Niña* and *Santa María* returned to Cuba and continued along the coast. The loyalty to Columbus of Martín Alonso's brother, Vicente Yáñez Pinzón, captain of *Niña*, is notable.

On December 5 *Santa María* and *Niña* reached the eastern end of Cuba. Believing it to be the eastern extremity of the Eurasian continent, Columbus named it Alpha and Omega (present-day Cape Maisi). From this vantage point he could see a high, mountainous land to the southeast, which the Indians called Bohío, a name Columbus believed meant "abounding in gold." Sailing there, over the objections of the Indians who said the natives living there were cannibals, Columbus named it La Isla Española, or the Spanish Island, because it reminded

him of the beauties of Castile. The Latin form, "Hispaniola," was first used by the historian Pietro Martire d'Anghiera (Peter Martyr) in a letter of October 20, 1494, and became the familiar name for the island.

Kept in place by adverse northerly winds for several days, Columbus and his men explored close to the harbor of Port Conception (today the Bay of Moustique) and on December 12, with marked solemnity, erected a great cross at the entrance to the harbor, formally claiming the island for Fernando and Isabel. By the fourteenth, Columbus was able to visit a small island opposite the harbor, which he named Tortuga. On December 16 he returned to La Española, and on December 20 the two ships anchored in what is now Acul Bay, a place that is "extremely beautiful and would hold all the ships in Christendom." As before, natives crowded the shore or rowed out to *Santa María* and *Niña* in canoes, offered food, water, small golden ornaments, in short, anything they had. Neighboring caciques (chiefs) invited the Spaniards to their villages and cried when they departed. The grand cacique Guacanagarí who ruled over the region invited Columbus to anchor closer to his village, and early in the morning of December 24, Columbus left Acul Bay and headed east with light winds.

At 11:00 P.M., the change of the watch, Columbus decided to retire to his cabin. Seas were calm and the ship almost motionless. His men had visited the coast the previous day and reported no rocks or shoals, and the Admiral had had no sleep for the past forty-eight hours because of the hundreds of Indians visiting his ships. When Columbus retired, however, so too did the rest of the crew, including the officer of the watch, Juan de la Cosa, disobeying a cardinal rule aboard ship. The helm was left to one of the ship's boys. Silently, gently, *Santa María* lodged on a coral reef. The ship's boy didn't notice anything wrong until the rudder stuck fast. Columbus jumped up instantly when the boy cried out; he woke Juan de la Cosa and ordered him to rouse the rest of the crew, launch the small boat, and cast an anchor astern to haul the ship off the reef. De la Cosa and several others leapt into the boat, but instead of doing as they were ordered, they fled to *Niña*. Her captain properly refused to let them board and sent *Niña*'s own boat to try to pull *Santa María* clear; Columbus tried to float her by cutting away the heavy mainmast. Nothing helped. The currents pushed *Santa María* farther onto the reef, and then the seams opened.

Columbus transferred his crew to *Niña* for safety reasons and at daybreak sent Diego de Arana, master-at-arms of the fleet, with a party of men to ask Cacique Guacanagarí for help. The cacique reportedly wept when he heard of the disaster and promptly sent people and large canoes to help unload the ship. Everything was

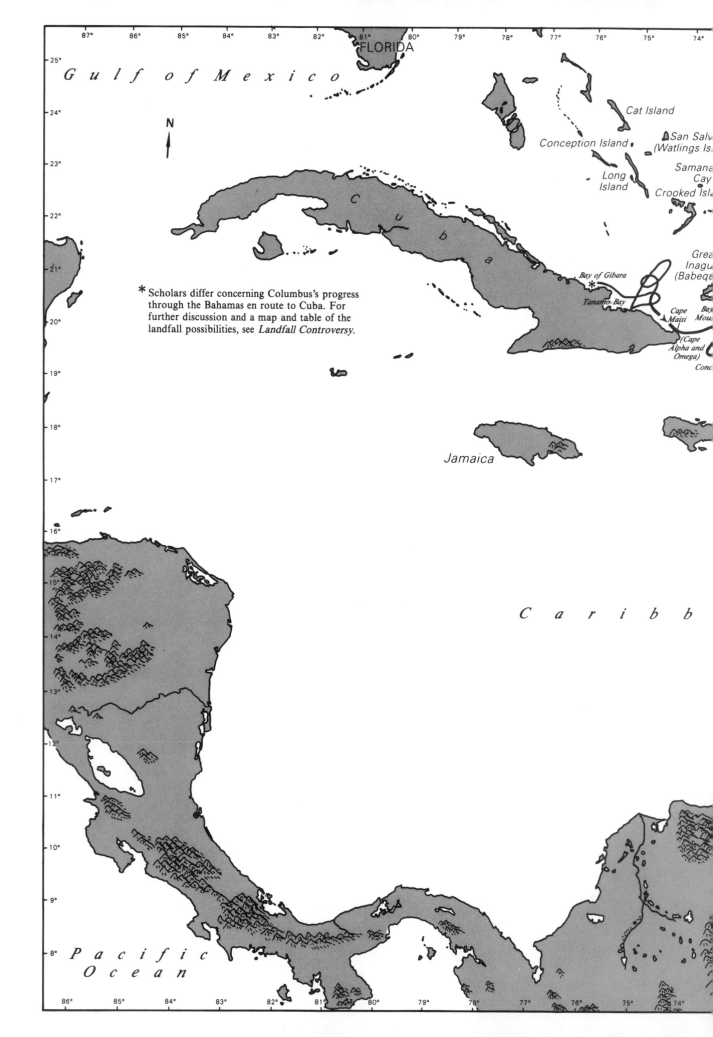

*Scholars differ concerning Columbus's progress through the Bahamas en route to Cuba. For further discussion and a map and table of the landfall possibilities, see *Landfall Controversy*.

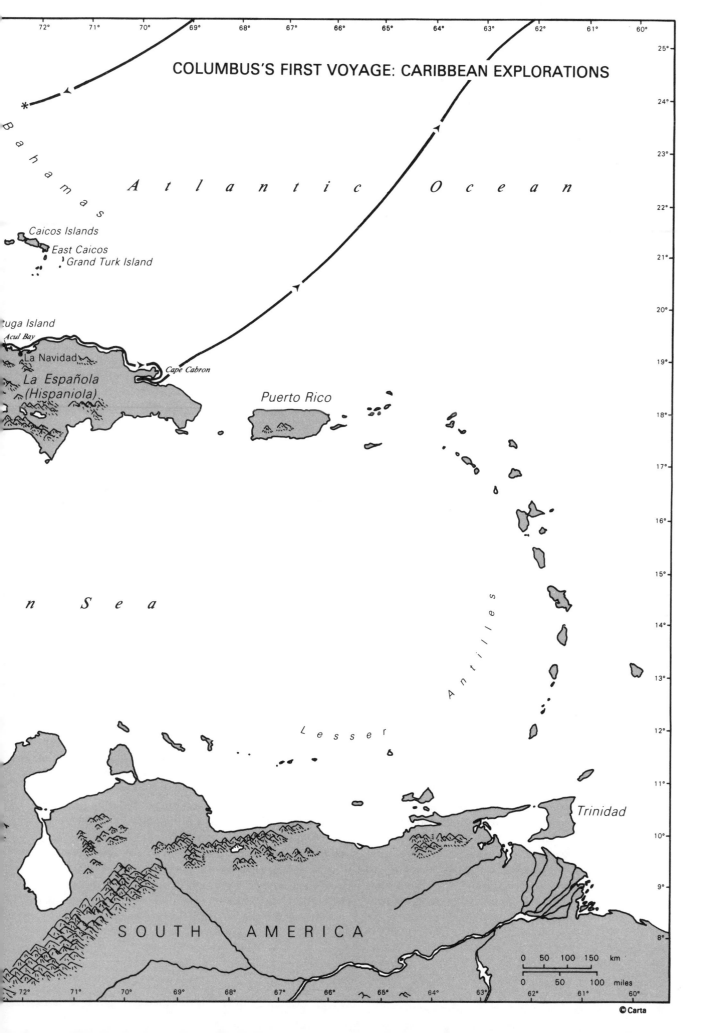

COLUMBUS'S FIRST VOYAGE: CARIBBEAN EXPLORATIONS

Bahamas

Atlantic Ocean

Caicos Islands
East Caicos
Grand Turk Island

...tuga Island
Acul Bay
La Navidad
La Española
(Hispaniola)
Cape Cabron

Puerto Rico

...n S e a

A n t i l l e s

L e s s e r

Trinidad

SOUTH AMERICA

| 0 | 50 | 100 | 150 | km |

| 0 | 50 | | 100 | miles |

©Carta

rescued, stored ashore, and carefully guarded by the Indians. "Not even a shoe string was lost," according to Columbus, who added, "I assure Your Highnesses that I believe that in all the world there are no better people or a better land." Columbus believed the loss of *Santa María* was an omen: "Our Lord had caused the ship to run aground there so that he would found a settlement there." Columbus had not intended to remain long in this area, largely because the cumbersome *Santa María* was "not suited to the work of discovery" close to shore.

During the ensuing days Columbus came to know the Indians, particularly Cacique Guacanagarí, and believed them when they spoke of great riches. Guacanagarí, Columbus wrote, knew where there was much gold nearby and told him that there was gold in Cipango, which they call Cybao." In Columbus's day, Japan was Cipangu (or Cipango), Marco Polo's name for it. Columbus thought Cybao (Cibao) was the Indian version of Cipangu. In fact it referred to the interior region of today's Dominican Republic.

Columbus decided to build a settlement on the coast adjacent to the grounded *Santa María* and named it La Navidad in commemoration of the day of the disaster. He ordered a tower and fortress to be constructed, and chose forty-two men to stay and find the gold mine described by Guacanagarí. As he wrote in the log, he had come to believe that everything that had happened—the gentle grounding of *Santa María* ("so softly that it was not felt, nor was there wave nor wind,") and the "treachery" of the ship's master in refusing to follow orders to cast the anchor astern and thus enable Columbus to save the ship—were signs from God that he was meant to found a settlement on La Española. When forced by these events to move ashore, Columbus saw the lush beauty of the land and, more important, learned of great riches nearby. He said, also, that he hoped "in God that on the return that he would undertake from Castile he would find a barrel of gold that those who were left would have acquired by exchange; and that they would have found the gold mine and the spicery, and those things in such quantity that the sovereigns, before three years [are over] will undertake and prepare to conquer the Holy Sepulcher."

Columbus left La Española on January 4, 1493. The reduction of the fleet to one ship precluded his staying to explore farther, and he was eager to return to Spain and report his findings to Fernando and Isabel. Before he left, he took great care to prepare the small garrison he was leaving behind at La Navidad. His orders were clear: the men were to obey Diego de Arana, Pedro Gutiérrez, and Rodrigo de Escobedo, the officers in charge; they were to show respect, honesty, and friendship toward the natives and under no circumstances injure any of them, particularly the women; they were to stay together within the

territory controlled by Guacanagarí, explore for gold, and locate a good place to build a more permanent village.

Two days later, not far from La Navidad, *Pinta* sailed into view. The two ships backtracked thirty miles to Monte Cristi where they could anchor and Pinzón could board *Niña* to explain himself. He apologized for going off on his own, claiming the weather forced him on to that course. He said when he failed to find gold on Babeque, he headed for Bohío (La Española) because other Indians claimed it was the site of riches. He had come within forty-five miles of La Navidad some twenty days earlier. Columbus privately rejected Pinzón's explanations, believing he had deliberately gone out of greed and arrogance, but decided to ignore his actions for the good of the voyage.

The two ships followed the coast of La Española to the east for six days and then anchored in a broad bay just beyond Cabo del Enamorado (Cape Cabrón) on January 13, 1493. When a contingent went ashore for *ajes*, "sweet potatoes," they encountered natives quite different from the gentle people they had previously met. Columbus suspected these ferocious, heavily painted and armed Indians to be Caribs, spoken of with fear by the Tainos and Arawaks of earlier landfalls. Caribs were cannibals and warriors who raided the settlements of their more peaceful neighbors. In fact, these were Ciguayos, different in name but not in behavior from the Caribs. They seemed friendly during initial trading, but when men were sent ashore to continue the exchange the Ciguayos attacked. The Spanish were able to drive them off and return to their ship.

The homeward leg of the first voyage began on January 16, 1493. The ships were leaking badly, little gold had been found, and the men were uneasy. At one point that morning, Columbus altered course to the southeast to explore an island said to be the home of the Caribs and another said to be inhabited only by women. But when the wind blew favorably for the return trip and Columbus recognized the dismay of his crew at his temporary change of direction, he abandoned plans for further discoveries and set course for Spain. They enjoyed pleasant weather for most of January, but the winds were easterly and hindered fast progress. Also, *Pinta*'s mizzenmast was weak (Columbus was annoyed that Pinzón hadn't relaced it in the Indies), and she couldn't sail close to the wind. Columbus generally followed a course northeastward to the approximate latitude of Bermuda, where he was able to get out of the adverse easterly trade winds and steer more directly toward Spain with favorable westerly winds.

Niña and *Pinta* were separated again on February 12 not by deceit but by a severe storm that forced both captains to shorten sail and run before the wind. *Pinta* was carried northward and out of sight. The two small caravels were caught up in one of the worst storms seen in the Atlantic for years. For a week *Niña* was tossed furiously by huge waves breaking over her. Columbus ordered lots drawn for three pilgrimages to be performed in thanksgiving when and if they were delivered from the storm. Columbus himself twice drew the chick-pea marked with a cross and promised to pay the expenses of the seaman who drew the third. Short of ballast, Columbus ordered empty water and wine casks to be filled with seawater to help stabilize *Niña*. Despite these efforts, both spiritual and temporal, "all were resigned to being lost due to the terrible storm." Columbus was particularly worried that no one would know of his achievement if *Niña* perished. He wrote an account of the voyage on parchment, sealed it in waxed cloth, and placed it in a barrel, which was tossed into the sea. It was never found.

Finally, after sunrise on February 15, they sighted land. Three days later they were able to draw near enough to anchor and send a boat ashore. *Niña* had reached the island of Santa Maria in the Azores. Here, political problems added to Columbus's difficulties. The king of Portugal had sent orders to his officials in distant islands and ports to seize Columbus if he should appear. King João feared Columbus's expedition would interfere with the Portuguese rights to the eastern route to the Indies. When half the crew was sent ashore on Santa María to make a pilgrimage to a shrine in fulfillment of the pledge made at sea, they were captured and jailed by a local official. While Columbus waited anxiously for their return, the official came out to *Niña* with a boatload of armed men to take him prisoner, but the Admiral refused to yield and the Portuguese official feared coming too close. A stand-off ensued during which the local contingent eventually withdrew and the remaining crew of *Niña* was able to repair some of the storm damage to their ship and fill more casks with seawater for ballast.

The harbor in which they were anchored was completely unprotected from winds out of the north, and when yet another gale blew up from that direction *Niña*'s anchor cable parted and Columbus was forced to put to sea again to save the ship. He had only half his crew at this point and only three were sailors. For two days, *Niña* "was in constant danger and difficulty." But he was able to return to the harbor on the evening of February 21, when a notary and two priests, in *Niña*'s boat with five of the captured seamen, requested permission to come aboard and see his orders from Fernando and Isabel. Columbus showed them his royal commission and the emissaries went ashore satisfied, releasing *Niña*'s boat and all the captured Spanish seamen.

On the twenty-second, Columbus weighed anchor and sailed around the island until he found a good anchorage at a place on the south coast where he might take on wood

and some stone ballast. That night, however, the wind shifted to the southwest, which was favorable for setting a course for Spain and unfavorable for sending boats to the beach for wood and stone. The decision to leave Santa Maria on a course for Spain was not difficult to make. For the next few days, Columbus and his storm-weary crew enjoyed favorable weather, but it was only a brief respite. On March 3 a violent squall split all of *Niña*'s sails and the ensuing storm drove her under bare poles throughout the day and into the night. Fortunately, at the start of the first night watch, about 7:00 P.M., the winds subsided somewhat and a full moon broke through the clouds, making it possible for a lookout to sight land ahead. Columbus set a spare mainsail and kept *Niña* offshore during the remainder of the night. At daylight on the fourth, he recognized the Rock of Sintra, a prominent landmark just north of the mouth of the Tagus River. Within a few hours, *Niña* entered the river and anchored at Rastello, later named Belém, the outer port of Lisbon.

Columbus wrote immediately to King João, requesting permission to sail to Lisbon and assuring him he had come from the Indies, not from Guinea or any other Portuguese colony. He also wrote to Fernando and Isabel of his safe return. Word spread of his achievement, and for the next several days the Tagus was thronged with boats and people eager to see the plants, animals, and, above all, the Indians brought back by the Spanish. Columbus traveled overland to Valparaiso to meet King João, who treated him with honor and respect. He also called on the queen and then returned to *Niña* and set sail for Palos on March 13, 1493. Two days later he crossed the bar of the Saltes and anchored in the harbor he had left more than seven months previously. Bells rang, shops closed, and people jammed the streets of Palos when *Niña* dropped anchor. A joyful carnival atmosphere prevailed, as it did in Seville when Columbus arrived there to await orders from the king and queen.

Pinta entered the river only a few hours after *Niña*. Martín Alonso Pinzón waited until Columbus had departed for Seville before he quietly slipped ashore. His ship blown to the north by the Atlantic storm, Pinzón had sought refuge at Bayona in Galicia. From there he wrote to Fernando and Isabel announcing his discoveries and successful return. He had waited in Bayona for their response, expecting praise and congratulations. Instead, the sovereigns replied in reproachful terms and forbade him an appearance at court. His health impaired by the rigors of the journey, Pinzón was further weakened by this rejection. He died within a few days of his return.

The sovereigns replied immediately to Columbus, addressing him as "Don Cristóbal Colón, our Admiral of the Ocean Sea and Viceroy and Governor of the Isles discovered in the Indies." They praised his achievement, invited him to court in Barcelona, and ordered him to begin immediate preparations for a return voyage to the Indies. Columbus responded with a list of ships, men, and munitions he would require, and then set out for Barcelona with six Indians, live parrots, stuffed birds, and the fruits, plants, and other materials he had collected.

In his triumphant trip across Spain, crowds gathered to see their hero and his wondrous companions. The royal reception at Barcelona was an elaborate and joyful occasion. A gold brocade canopy covered an open court, and hundreds of cavaliers and officials crowded in. Fernando and Isabel welcomed Columbus warmly and then broke protocol by inviting him to sit in their presence—something not often done by these proud rulers.

Word of the discovery spread throughout Spain and on to France, Italy, and England; spirits soared at the expansion of the world's horizons and the prospect of wealth and adventure across a sea thought to be trackless. No one fully realized yet the extent of Columbus's discovery, however; all agreed that Cuba was part of the Asian mainland and that the surrounding islands lay in the Indian Sea. The islands were called the West Indies and the New World referred to the unexplored regions of the vast Asian continent described by Marco Polo two hundred years before.

Political maneuvering for control of these lands had begun even before Columbus arrived in Palos. Upon receipt of his letter from Lisbon, Fernando and Isabel moved quickly to secure his discovery for their Crown. They had no doubt of their right to possession of this territory: during the Crusades, the Christian rulers in Europe had developed a doctrine highly favorable to themselves—it permitted their invasion and seizure of infidel territory to save it for Christianity. The pope was accorded the supreme right to dispose of captured heathen lands. Thus, Pope Nicholas V, in 1455, had awarded to Portugal all lands discovered on the African coast, and Pope Sixtus IV had confirmed, in 1481, Portuguese sovereignty as agreed with Spain in the Treaty of Alcáçovas (1479). With the Venetians controlling the overland routes to the east and Portugal jealously guarding the sea route down the western coast of Africa and eventually around the Cape of Good Hope to India, Fernando and Isabel were determined to control this new western route to fabled wealth.

On May 2, 1493, Pope Alexander VI, under pressure from Fernando, issued a papal bull granting Spain the same rights and privileges in the new territories as had been accorded Portugal in 1479. On May 3, the famous Line of Demarcation was promulgated; it ran north and south 100 leagues west of the Azores and the Cape Verde Islands, later adjusted by the Treaty of Tordesillas (June 7, 1494) to 370 leagues west of the Cape Verde Islands. Spain was granted control of everything to the west of this line; Portugal everything to the east. But no papal bull could deter England, France, and Holland from joining in the race for territory in the New World discovered by Columbus.

The Second Voyage

Christopher Columbus's second voyage to the New World, unlike the other three, is not remembered for new discoveries made by the Admiral of the Ocean Sea. Rather, this was the voyage during which he tried and failed to establish a viable colony in what he believed to be the Indies. As viceroy, he was held personally responsible for the failure, but the blame belonged to many.

Preparations for the second voyage began while Columbus was still at the court in Barcelona reporting on the first. Fernando and Isabel were anxious to protect his discoveries for Spain, particularly against any possible Portuguese incursions. The Spanish sovereigns wanted men and arms in place as soon as possible. Formal instructions issued on May 23, 1493, directed Columbus to convert the natives to Christianity and establish a Crown trading colony on La Española. Columbus was granted full powers and control of this expedition, but because the sovereigns wanted a detailed accounting of every expenditure, the archdeacon of Seville (later patriarch of the Indies) Juan de Fonseca was named to watch over royal interests.

On September 25, 1493, crowds lined the streets and quays of Cádiz to cheer the departure of the seventeen-ship fleet. Columbus sailed on *Mariagalante*, one of three medium-sized ships, known as naos, of up to two hundred tons burden; the others were *Colina* and *La Gallega*. Antonio de Torres, owner of *Mariagalante*, was also her master. Fourteen smaller caravels, including hardy *Niña* of the first voyage, were more suitable for coastal exploration. Juan Niño sailed again as owner and master of *Niña*, this time with his brother Francisco as pilot. Cristóbal Perez Niño was master of *Cardera*. Other captains included Juan Aguado, Pedro Fernández Coronel, Alonso Sánchez de Carvajal, Ginés de Gorbalán, and Alonso de Ojeda. Most of the seamen came from Palos, Moguer, Huelva, and Lepe, as on the first voyage, although there were some Genoese and Basques among the crew. Juan de la Cosa signed on as able seaman aboard *Niña*, but he is better remembered for his 1500 chart of the New World.

Despite the gaiety and confident optimism that abounded at the fleet's departure, several facts augured ill for the voyage and, more particularly, for Columbus. His authority rankled Fonseca and his assistants; they tried in subtle ways to undercut his position. Graft and corruption characterized the provisioning of the expedition. The twenty good horses gathered by Columbus, for example, were exchanged at the last minute for inferior steeds. Some three hundred men stowed away, most of whom had been denied passage earlier; thus fifteen hundred men crowded space and drew on food and water planned for twelve hundred. Provisions themselves were substandard. Casks leaked (much of the supply of wine ran into the bilges during the first month), and biscuits and meat were of poor quality. Columbus had been given responsibility for choosing the passengers and had called for humble, hardy workers to till the soil, work mines, and build homes. However, he had been forced to take many recommended by the royal court, men who owed him no allegiance and were ill suited to the purpose of the voyage—to colonize the New World. There were soldiers, bored now that the wars against the Moors were over, adventurers, speculators, cavaliers of noble heritage, most of whom had joined the expedition for quick wealth and glory, not for the hard, mundane work envisioned by Columbus.

Among the presumed settlers on the second voyage were Ponce de León, future discoverer of Florida; Melchior Maldonado, a gentleman adventurer; Diego de Alvarado, who later fought with Pizarro; and Francisco de Garay, an associate of Cortés. Columbus's younger brother Diego accompanied him, as did Diego Alvarez Chanca, a physician from Seville who later wrote about the experience. Friar Buyl, a monk sent with twelve other ecclesiastics to convert the Indians to Christianity, brought complete equipment for the first church in the New World, a gift of Isabel.

The fleet cost some 24 million maravedis, four times the initial estimate. Part of the money to finance it came from royal church tithes and from wealth taken from the Jews expelled from Spain in 1492. Assembling such massive quantities of men, animals, food, and equipment in only five months was a prodigious feat, the first of this scale ever undertaken.

The fleet headed directly for the Canary Islands, steered well clear of Portugal, made landfall at Grand Canary on October 2, went on to Gomera for more supplies (fresh water, fruit and vegetable seeds, fowl, pigs, sheep, hogs, goats, and calves), and set sail again on October 7. They passed Hierro, farthest west of the Canaries, on the thirteenth and headed west by south (about 259 degrees). Columbus gave sealed instructions to his captains, explaining the route to take if the fleet were to become separated, but moderate winds and seas permitted them to remain together. On November 3, 1493, they sighted land.

Columbus's more southerly track on this voyage, which took the fleet to the southern Antilles, or Windward Islands, was deliberate. He wanted to explore the Carib islands he had been unable to visit at the end of his first voyage. As Chanca wrote, "Columbus rectified his course to discover [the Caribee islands] . . . because they were nearer to Spain and the route thence to La Española was direct. [And] to these islands by the goodness of God and the 'buen saber' [good knowledge] of the Admiral, we came as straight as if we had been following a well-known and customary course."

The first island was sighted on a Sunday and named Dominica. Not immediately finding a suitable harbor there, the fleet anchored off a nearby smaller island to the north. Columbus named it Mariagalante (now Marie Galante) and took formal possession for the Crown. On the fourth, he made an exploratory landing on a larger island a short distance to the west and named it Santa María de Guadalupe (now Guadeloupe). The natives fled, and when the Spanish explored their empty huts, they found human bones and skulls in addition to huge parrots, tame geese, and pineapples. Landing at a second harbor, they captured several women and boys who had been taken from their homes by marauding Caribs; the boys had been castrated and the Spanish thought they were being fattened like cattle for later slaughter. The fleet was forced to delay at Guadalupe until November 10 because a boatload of men, sent inland to explore, failed to return. Diego Márquez of Seville had taken a party of ten for purposes of plunder, and because dense foliage had made it impossible to sight the sun or stars to check direction, they became lost. Four search parties failed to find the missing men and came close to getting lost themselves. The original group managed to reach the shore just as Columbus was about to leave without them. Michele da Cuneo, an Italian gentleman on the voyage, wrote, "We thought they had been eaten by the . . . Caribs who are accustomed to do it."

The ships sailed northwest, and as they passed islands en route, Columbus named them Santa María de Monserrate (now Monserrat), Santa María la Redonda (Redonda), Santa María la Antigua (Antigua), San Martin (Nevis), San Jorge (St. Kitts), Santa Anastasia (St. Eustatius), San Cristóbal (Saba), Santa Cruz (St. Croix), Santa Ursula y las Once Mil Vírgines (Virgin Islands), and San Juan Bautista (Puerto Rico). On November 14 they landed on Santa Cruz and looted some of the native huts. A band of Carib men and women armed with poison arrows came toward them in canoes and wounded two of the Spaniards. One later died from the poison and was buried on La Española. The Caribs were captured to send back to Spain, and the fleet continued on to Puerto Rico, where the natives hid while the Spaniards took on fresh provisions.

On November 22 the ships reached the eastern end of La Española and three days later anchored at Monte Cristi. The first sign of disaster was the discovery of four corpses

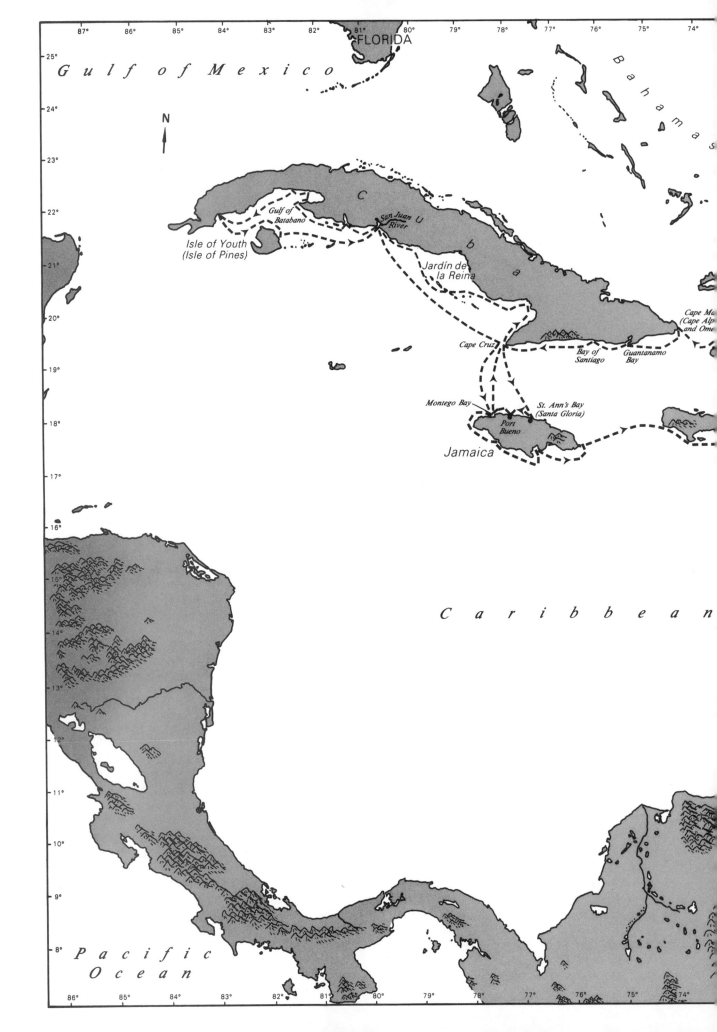

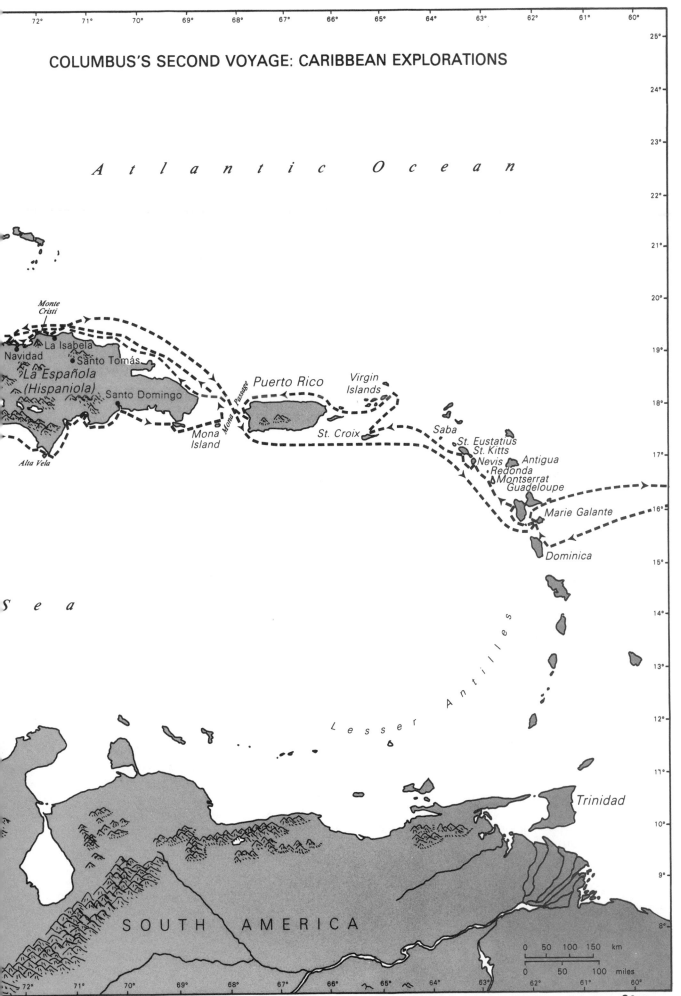

COLUMBUS'S SECOND VOYAGE: CARIBBEAN EXPLORATIONS

Atlantic Ocean

Monte Cristi

La Isabela
Navidad
Santo Tomás
La Española (Hispaniola)
Santo Domingo

Alta Vela

Mona Passage
Mona Island

Puerto Rico

Virgin Islands

St. Croix

Saba
St. Eustatius
St. Kitts
Nevis
Redonda
Montserrat
Guadeloupe

Antigua

Marie Galante

Dominica

Sea

Lesser Antilles

Trinidad

SOUTH AMERICA

| 0 | 50 | 100 | 150 | km |

| 0 | 50 | 100 | miles |

© Carta

on the shore; one was bearded, a clear sign of European ancestry. On the twenty-seventh, the fleet arrived opposite the harbor of La Navidad, site of the first Spanish colony in the Indies. It was night and Columbus dared not enter, but when a few lombard shots drew no response—no shouts, no lights—his fears mounted. At midnight, a canoe of Indians approached his ship, led by a cousin of the chief, Guacanagarí, who had been friendly to Columbus on the first voyage. He explained that the Spaniards had quarreled among themselves, split up, and taken Indian wives in different parts of the island. The Carib chief Caonabó had attacked and wounded Guacanagarí when he had tried to defend the fortress. The following morning, the Spanish landed at the ruin of La Navidad. There was no treasure to be found, only several corpses lying in the open to be buried. Columbus visited Guacanagarí a few days later, and the cacique repeated the story of attack by Caonabó. He spoke of his effort to defend La Navidad and his sadness at the deaths of the Spaniards as well as several of his own people. Guacanagarí showed his own wound from the battle, but Chanca examined it and believed the cacique was feigning the injury. Columbus trusted his old friend, however. Gifts were exchanged, the Spanish receiving gold for worthless trifles.

On December 8 Columbus ordered the fleet out of La Navidad. The low, marshy area was unsuitable for any permanent settlement. They explored along the northern coast to the east and by January 2, 1494, had chosen a site for the first permanent European settlement in the New World. It was not perfect, but livestock were dying on the ship and had to be unloaded. Named La Isabela after the queen, the site lay between two rivers and was not far from the mines of Cibao. A church was constructed and the first mass held on January 6, celebrating Epiphany. Most of the Spaniards fell sick almost immediately; the climate was hot and humid, the work hard and provisions scanty. Columbus had planned to send half his fleet back to Castile laden with gold gathered by the La Navidad garrison. This was impossible now, and he was under pressure to prove to the sovereigns the richness of his discovery. Consequently, early in January, he sent two expeditions of forty men each to find the mines of Cibao that the Indians promised would yield great wealth. Alonso de Ojeda and Ginés de Gorbalán commanded the two contingents and soon returned full of optimism, reporting that large nuggets of gold lay openly in riverbeds.

On February 2, twelve ships left for Castile commanded by Antonio de Torres and carrying specimens of gold, fruits and other plants (cinnamon, pepper, sandalwood), sixty parrots, and twenty-six Indians, three of them Caribs. Columbus wrote to the sovereigns asking for fresh supplies as soon as possible and saying he would be unable to make new discoveries immediately because his first duties were to find gold and secure a settlement. Five ships were left at La Española: the naos *Gallega* and *Mariagalante* and the caravels *Niña*, *San Juan*, and *Cordera*.

By April, a settlement of sorts existed at La Isabela. Crops had been planted and were seen to grow far more rapidly than in Spain. Two hundred small cabins roofed with thatch had been constructed, but provisions were dangerously low, native food unpalatable, and sickness prevalent. The majority of the settlers were loath to take orders from Columbus, who was viewed by them as an upstart foreigner unworthy of his newly acquired rank. They had come expecting quick, easy wealth, not debilitating heat and illness, unpalatable and insufficient food, and hard work tilling fields or mining gold. Factions had formed even before this disparate group reached La Española, and factional strife continued to plague the colony. The royal comptroller, Bernal Díaz de Pisa, and the assayer, Fermín Cedo, plotted to seize the remaining ships and return to Castile. Columbus learned of the plot and confined Díaz de Pisa on the *Mariagalante* until he could be sent back for trial.

With banners flying and trumpets sounding, the first overland march of Spanish conquistadores set forth from La Isabela on March 12, 1494. Columbus led four hundred armed men in search of the fabled mines of Cibao. Mounted cavalry and foot soldiers with swords, arquebuses, or crossbows protected the expedition, which included carpenters, masons, ditch diggers, and miners with equipment for mining gold and building fortresses. Many well-born gentlemen had refused to work at the settlement, but they carved out of the rugged mountain terrain the first road built by Europeans in the New World. Columbus named it El Puerto de los Hidalgos (Pass of the Gentlemen) in their honor, and the name endured for generations.

After making their way through this narrow pass, the Spanish got their first views of the vast fertile valley described by Las Casas as "one of the most admirable things in the world . . . so fresh, so green, so open, of such color and altogether so full of beauty that as soon as they saw it they felt they had arrived in Paradise . . . and the Admiral, who was profoundly moved by all these things, gave great thanks to God and named it Vega Real, the Royal Plain." With the help of Indians, they found a place to ford the Río Yaque del Norte and, after continuing across the valley, stopped at the Río Jánico. Here Columbus decided to establish a fort, Santo Tomás, to be a center of mining in Cibao.

Columbus stayed five days to see that work began properly, during which time Indians from miles around brought food and gold nuggets to trade with the Spaniards. Some two thousand castellanos worth of gold was officially collected, and as Cuneo recorded, "there was also exchanged in secret, against the rules and our agreement, to a value of 1000 castellanos. As you know, the devil makes you do wrong and then lets your wrong be discovered; moreover, as long as Spain is Spain, traitors will never be wanting. One betrayed the other so that almost all of them were exposed, and whoever got caught was well whipped; some had their ears slit and some the nose, which was very pitiful to see." Leaving a fifty-six-man garrison under Pedro Margarit to continue exploration and find more gold, Columbus returned to La Isabela with the bulk of the force.

The Indians had been friendly and helpful to the Spanish during Columbus's expedition inland. When he returned to La Isabela, however, word was sent by Margarit that Caonabó was rumored to be planning an attack. In fact, the Spanish had begun taking gold without trading for it and had abducted native women. Columbus sent only a small force to Santo Tomás. He was less worried about Margarit than about the situation at La Isabela. The heat and humidity, so wonderful for sugar and certain other crops, were harmful to people. Most were ill, and the well-born among them suffered also from wounded pride, being ordered by Columbus to perform hard, menial tasks. They refused, for example, to help build a flour mill, even though they needed bread as much as everyone else. Columbus resorted to strong measures to compel their obedience, thereby creating long-lasting resentment.

Although Columbus was eager to get on with further exploration of Cuba, he could not leave so large a group of discontented people at La Isabela. He decided, therefore, as a means of keeping them occupied, to send everyone able to walk on another expedition to explore the interior. On April 9, Ojeda led a force of 20 officers, 16 horsemen, 250 crossbowmen, and 110 arquebusiers to Santo Tomás to relieve Margarit. En route, Ojeda learned that three Spaniards had been robbed of their clothing by a small group of Indians. He caught one of the thieves and publicly cut off his ears and then captured the local cacique and his son and sent them to La Isabela in chains. Columbus threatened to behead them but rescinded the order when another chieftain pleaded for their lives. Las Casas records that "this was the first injustice, with vain pretension of justice, that was committed in the Indies against the Indians and the beginning of the shedding of blood which has since flowed so copiously in this island."

Columbus believed things were calm enough now to allow him to leave. He appointed a junta to manage affairs in La Isabela, presided over by his brother Diego and including Friar Buyl, Pedro Fernández Coronel, Alonso Sánchez de Carvajal, and Juan de Luján. On April 24 he set out in the three caravels: *Niña*, his flagship, with Alonso Medel as master, Francisco Niño as pilot, and chartmaker Juan de la Cosa as a seaman; *San Juan*, with Alonso Pérez Roldán as master; and *Cordera* with Cristóbal Pérez as master. Convinced as he was that Cuba was part of the Asian mainland, Columbus planned to follow its coast to reach Cathay. When he reached Cape Alpha and Omega (now Cape Maisi) at Cuba's eastern tip, he went ashore, set up a column topped by a cross, and took formal possession again of Juana, as Columbus still called Cuba. He called a council of pilots, officers, and gentlemen adventurers to discuss their route. The unanimous vote was to explore the south coast, the then popular geographical theory being that anything good is more likely to be to the south than to the north.

Landing at Guantánamo Bay on April 30, Columbus found great quantities of fish and two large iguanas roasting on open fires. No Indians were in sight. The Spaniards helped themselves to the fish and then went looking for the cooks. Their interpreter, the Taino Indian captured on the first voyage and baptized Diego Colón, managed to convince the natives that the Spaniards were friendly and offered gifts in exchange for the fish. The natives had been preparing this food for an important feast, but they were grateful the iguanas had been spared: capturing them was hard work and their meat delicious. Forty miles west of Guantánamo, the fleet entered the great Bay of Santiago lined by many Indian villages. These Indians and others who canoed out to the ships as the fleet continued westward along the coast said a great island to the south was the source of their gold. On May 3, having reached Cabo de Cruz and finding that the coastline there doubled back to the northeast, Columbus decided to head south for the promised gold of Jamaica.

On May 6, the Admiral anchored for only one night at Santa Gloria (St. Ann's Bay) and then sailed fifteen miles to the west and put in at Puerto Bueno, a better harbor, to make needed repairs on the ships. The Indians of Jamaica were more warlike than those on Cuba and hurled wooden spears and stones at the Spanish when they first tried to land. Columbus sent a boatload of crossbowmen ahead who "pricked them well and killed a number"; then they set loose a big dog "who bit them and did them great hurt, for a dog is worth ten men against Indians," wrote Cuneo. After this the Indians brought cassava, fruit, and fish to the Spaniards throughout their stay.

Columbus put back to sea and continued west along the Jamaican coast to Montego Bay. Having found no gold, he set sail for Cuba on May 13, returned to Cape Cruz, and headed northwest into a shallow archipelago, which he called El Jardín de la Reina, or Queen's Garden. Largely uninhabited, the area abounded in aromatic, lush vegetation and flamingos and other tropical birds. Some twenty days were spent sailing in and out of the intricate collection of canals and keys before heading for deeper water. After sailing farther west, they returned to the shore to take on provisions and water, encountering large numbers of peaceable Indians, most of whom said there was no end to their country. They said this part of their land was called Ornofay and that Magon lay beyond, where people had tails like beasts. Columbus believed Magon to be Mangi, a southeastern Chinese province mentioned by Marco Polo.

Continuing on, they reached the Gulf of Batabano, the westernmost point of the voyage. Similar to the Queen's Garden, these shallow waters went from milky white to green to black because of the chalk and fine sand churned up from the bottom. Ships were damaged repeatedly from running aground and being hauled off. By early June, the men wanted to go no farther. Columbus pressed on for three or four more days, though he was convinced that any land this large had to be the mainland. Because he wished to forestall accusations that he had returned prematurely (and his word had sometimes been doubted in the past), he asked the men to sign a statement that they believed Cuba to be the mainland of Asia. Punishment for retraction would be severe. Everyone willingly signed the statement. Two or three more days of sailing west would have established Cuba as an island.

Columbus began his return trip to La Española on June 13 and took on water at the Isle of Pines (now the Isle of Youth). Unable to make progress against the strong adverse winds and currents in the deeper water, he was forced to tack against the lighter winds and currents in the shoal waters around the coastal islands. Progress was exceedingly slow. On June 30, *Niña*, largest of the three ships, ran aground and was damaged when she was pulled off. Daily downpours added to the sailors' misery. After twenty-five dispiriting days, they had sailed only two hundred miles to windward. Finally, the three ships anchored in the Río San Juan, which Columbus renamed Río de las Misas because Sunday Mass was celebrated there. Staying outside of the Queen's Garden, the fleet beat to windward for ten days (July 9 to 18) in terrible weather. Las Casas wrote:

> All the winds and waters concerted to fatigue [Columbus] and heap anxiety on anxiety, difficulty on difficulty, and surprise on surprise, for he had neither the time nor the opportunity to take breath; among things that he suffered was a thundersquall so sudden, horrible and perilous that it threw the flagship on her beam ends, and with great difficulty, and it seems only with the help of God, did they strike the sails, and at the same time anchor with the heaviest anchors. Much water worked down below the floor timbers, which increased their danger, and the mariners could hardly pump it out because all were exhausted by continual labor. Provisions went so short that they had

nothing to eat but a pound of putrid biscuit and a pint of wine or its dregs except when they happened to catch some fish. . . . With these dangers and unceasing afflictions he arrived on July 18 at the cape which he had already named Cabo de Cruz, where the Indians received him well and brought him cassava bread, fish, fruits of the earth and everything they had, with great good will and pleasure. There they stayed and rested two or three days.

Because the winds were still wrong for sailing to La Española, Columbus headed for Jamaica again and sailed around the southern coast of the island. Crossing the Windward Passage to the southwestern cape of La Española, Columbus decided to explore the southern coast of that island. The ships became separated; *Niña* reached Alta Vela, an isolated rock marking the southernmost point of La Española, and waited six days for the others to catch up. Although, or perhaps because, Columbus was in bad health, he decided to raid the Carib islands and destroy their canoes so they could not attack the gentle Tainos. The ships headed toward Puerto Rico and Mona Island. Here Columbus became seriously ill with a high fever and alternate periods of coma and delirium. His officers turned around immediately and headed back for La Isabela, arriving there on September 29, 1494.

Columbus awoke to find his older brother, Bartolomé, at his bedside. Named to command three provision ships sent from Castile, Bartolomé had arrived in La Isabela just after Columbus sailed for Cuba. Their reunion was joyous—but this was the only happy note in La Isabela. During Columbus's absence, conditions in the colony had deteriorated drastically. In April, when Ojeda had been sent to Santo Tomás, Margarit had been ordered to tour the island, awing the natives with a display of power but conciliating them and treating them fairly. Columbus was convinced that just treatment of these basically friendly and helpful people would contribute to the success of the Spanish endeavor. But when Margarit marched into the Vega Real, he was anything but conciliatory: he and his men stole food and gold from the Indians, used their women, and pillaged randomly. Diego Colón's warning to change his tactics outraged Margarit, who marched to La Isabela in a fury. He was joined by a group of malcontents including Friar Buyl who, from all accounts, converted not one Indian during his months on La Española. Margarit and Buyl commandeered the ships in which Bartolomé Colón had sailed to La Española and left for Spain.

With their commander gone, bands of soldiers began roving at will and indulging in outrageous excesses against the Indians. It was only a short time before the Indians lost their timidity and retaliated. First, they attacked small groups of Spaniards. Then Caonabó led ten thousand warriors against Santo Tomás, manned by Ojeda and about fifty men. Despite a thirty-day siege by the Indians,

Ojeda held the fort and the threat receded temporarily.

In November 1494, Antonio de Torres arrived in La Isabela with four more supply ships. Along with food, the ships brought the millers, mechanics, fishermen, gardeners, and farmers the colony desperately needed. Torres also returned to Columbus the letter he had written to Fernando and Isabel and dispatched the previous year. On it were written the sovereigns' comments, dated August 16, 1494. They agreed with his plan to search for gold and establish a settlement and asked him to return to help draw the new Line of Demarcation agreed to in June. Columbus was too ill to return and sent his brother Diego in his place.

The sovereigns postponed a decision on Columbus's plan to establish a slave trade to help pay for the colony until the gold mines came into full production. Initially, he planned to send only Caribs who were the enemies of the Taínos. Fernando and Isabel did not look kindly on this proposal. But Columbus had nothing else of value to send back with Torres, apart from some gold specimens and more fruits and vegetables. When this fleet returned to Castile on February 24, 1495, it was loaded with five hundred male and female Indians to be sold at the slave market in Seville. Many of these were Taínos captured during the recent punitive expedition to the Vega Real. He has been roundly criticized for this, but Columbus was practicing a custom of his time, one sanctioned by the church and employed by Fernando in the wars against the Moors. It proved unsuccessful; two hundred died during the long voyage and the rest soon after their arrival in Spain.

After Torres left, the caciques Guatiguana, Mayrionex, and others assembled an impressive force in the Vega Real (Guacanagarí refused to join). Columbus took to the field with two hundred soldiers, twenty horses, and twenty bloodhounds, one of the most savage weapons used against the Indians by the Spaniards. Close to 100,000 natives poured into the central plain. The Spanish split up and attacked from different directions, galloping their horses, firing rifles, and charging with the dogs. The terrified Indians fled.

This left Caonabó to be dealt with, and Ojeda devised a devious plan. Going to Caonabó's headquarters, Ojeda offered him the bell from the steeple of the church in La Isabela as a gift. Caonabó believed the bell was magical, since every time it rang, all the Spanish hurried to the church. He agreed to accompany Ojeda to La Isabela to receive it but insisted a band of warriors attend him. As the story goes, Ojeda showed Caonabó a highly polished set of manacles and told him they were royal ornaments sent from heaven, that the Spanish sovereigns always wore them. He suggested that Caonabó bathe, be decorated with the manacles, and ride a horse into La Isabela like the Spanish king. Caonabó agreed, mounted behind Ojeda, and was "decorated," at which point Ojeda galloped off at full speed. Caonabó was kept in chains in La Isabela until he could be sent to Castile.

Columbus followed his rout of the Indians with a tour of the island designed to reduce them to total submission. He reinforced existing fortresses scattered around the island and built six new ones. Desperate to raise money, he imposed a heavy tribute of gold in Vega, in Cibao, and around the mines, and demanded an equally stiff tribute in cotton from those Indians not living near the mines. Las Casas called the system irrational, burdensome, impossible, intolerable, and abominable. It soon destroyed the Indians. Docile and imprudent largely because there had been no need to be otherwise, they were unable to meet the harsh tributes imposed by the Spaniards. The unrelenting labor killed many. Others fled to the mountains and hid from the pursuing Spaniards in wretched caves or hollow tree trunks; thousands died of famine because they were too terrified of recapture to leave their hiding places to fish or gather fruit. Those forced to return to work in the fields or to search for gold died of exhaustion. Guacanagarí, Columbus's friend among the Indians, was overwhelmed by the tributes. His people reviled him for befriending the Spaniards, who had become such cruel oppressors. Las Casas says Guacanagarí hid in the mountains and died alone in misery. By 1496, the island was pacified. But by 1550, the Indians had disappeared almost completely.

During this time, Columbus's fortunes in Spain began to fall. Margarit and Friar Buyl had presented a long list of grievances to Fernando and Isabel when they returned to Spain in November 1494. The sovereigns' confidence in Columbus was shaken by the allegations; they were also concerned that some harm might have befallen him on his voyage to Cuba. They decided to send someone to investigate the charges lodged by Margarit and Buyl and to report back on conditions in general. Juan de Aguado was chosen for the task. The sovereigns said Aguado "was to be under the Admiral's authority in all things." At the same time he was to take charge in Columbus's absence and "remedy" any wrongs if he were present. Aguado had not yet left Castile when Torres returned there on April 10, 1495, with Diego Colón and the shipload of slaves. Upon hearing Diego's side of the story, the sovereigns were somewhat reassured but did not alter Aguado's conflicting orders.

With a fleet of four caravels loaded with supplies, Aguado departed Cádiz at the end of August and arrived at La Isabela in October 1495. He assumed the functions of viceroy immediately, countermanded Bartolomé's orders (Columbus had named his brother adelantado, or judge), and took depositions from the disaffected colonists.

When Columbus returned to La Isabela from the interior, he treated Aguado with deferential courtesy, assuring him he would follow his sovereigns' directions. Aguado was slightly deflated by Columbus's moderation but continued to act as overlord.

Meanwhile, in June 1495, before Aguado's arrival, the first hurricane experienced by the colonists had struck. The force of the wind and tidal surges sank three ships in the harbor. Only *Niña* survived, and she in a battered state. Columbus organized repairs to *Niña* and directed that a new ship, *Santa Cruz*, be constructed out of the wreckage of the others. While this work was going on, plans were laid to move the settlement to another site. The anchorage at La Isabela offered no protection from north winds, the climate was unhealthy, and the small amounts of gold discovered were beyond easy reach. An exploring party, sent out to find a more suitable site, chose the mouth of the Ozama River because of its fertile land, good harbor, and gold-bearing rivers. Before he sailed for Castile, Columbus directed Bartolomé to abandon La Isabela and build a new settlement, Santo Domingo, at the chosen site.

On March 10, 1496, Columbus and Aguado set out for Spain. Only five hundred men remained at La Isabela. Columbus sailed once again on *Niña*, and Aguado on *Santa Cruz*, appropriately nicknamed *India*, the first European ship built in the New World. Some 225 colonists were crowded aboard, along with thirty Indians, including Caonabó who was being taken back to exhibit to Fernando and Isabel. (The fierce Carib chieftain died of a broken spirit on the voyage.) The return trip was difficult because Columbus failed to sail beyond the reach of the adverse easterly trade winds. His route was ill chosen, in contrast to the more northerly track he had followed home after his first voyage. The ships reached only as far as Guadalupe by April 9; provisions were so low they landed there to take on a supply of native food and water. At the first anchorage, a horde of native women attacked the landing party and then calmed enough to tell the Spaniards they had no bread— their husbands, at the northern end of the island, would furnish what they needed. The two caravels proceeded to this point where the landing party was met with a fusillade of arrows. The Caribs fled when the Spaniards fired on them, but three boys and ten women were captured. Holding them as hostages, the Spaniards persuaded the Indians to teach them how to make bread from cassava roots. The crews remained for nine days, baking a three-week supply of bread and taking on firewood and water. They released all but two of the hostages and left for Spain on April 20.

By May 20, they had made little progress and provisions were so low everyone was put on rations of six ounces of bread and one and one-half pints of water a day. By June, conditions were so bad that someone suggested eating the Indians, an idea Columbus rejected. On the night of June 7–8, he ordered sails taken in, for he was sure they were off Cape St. Vincent. The pilots laughed at him, but once again his remarkable dead-reckoning ability proved accurate. On June 8 they spotted the Portuguese coast, about thirty-five miles north of São Vicente. The ships reached Cádiz on June 11, 1496.

The Third Voyage

Christopher Columbus had discovered the New World on his first voyage across the western sea, but neither he nor anyone else in Europe realized it. He discovered the South American continent on his third voyage, but again failed to comprehend the magnitude of his accomplishment. His discovery of Trinidad and the Gulf of Paria and his ceremonial taking possession on the Venezuelan coast of a continental landmass previously unknown to Europeans were overshadowed by a greed-inspired rebellion on La Española, which culminated in the Admiral's being sent home in disgrace, manacled hand and foot.

When Columbus returned from La Española in June 1496 after his second voyage, he stayed with Andrés Bernáldez, curate of Los Palacios and chaplain to the archbishop of Seville. Deeply religious, even mystical, Columbus was more comfortable in the company of ecclesiastics than in that of grandees or cavaliers. He gave Bernáldez his journals of the second voyage and other documents, which the priest used in compiling his *Historia de los Reyes Catolicos* (History of the Catholic Kings). Columbus adopted monastic garb at this time; the coarse brown habit of a Franciscan monk became his usual costume when in Spain. Fernando and Isabel wrote on July 12, 1496, expressing pleasure in his safe return and inviting him to court. Columbus set out with two Indians—Caonabó's young nephew and a brother who had been christened "Don Diego" by Bernáldez—caged parrots, jewelry, masks, winged crowns, woven cotton articles, and other Taíno artifacts. Don Diego wore a golden collar and chain that weighed six hundred castellanos. At the court, Columbus was reunited with his sons, Diego and Fernando, pages to Prince Juan. The sovereigns received him gracefully and were presented with a substantial quantity of gold, including some large nuggets. Columbus reported on his voyage to Cuba and the discovery of gold mines at Haina, which he believed might be the mines of Ophir mentioned in the Bible. Then he proposed a third voyage for which he requested eight ships. Two would sail immediately with provisions for the colony; he would lead the other six on another voyage of discovery. Fernando and Isabel were interested in everything he told them and, being satisfied with his report, readily agreed to a third voyage. But it was nearly two years before Columbus set sail.

King Fernando's political machinations were the principal cause of delay. He was preoccupied with the French invasion of Italy and its aftereffects, and he was determined to solidify and expand Spain's power through advantageous marriage alliances. The latter demanded huge sums of money and great numbers of ships and men. For example, a fleet of 130 ships was assembled to escort Fernando and Isabel's daughter Juana to Flanders for her marriage to Archduke Philip of Hapsburg and to return Philip's sister, Princess Margaret of Austria, to Spain for her marriage to Prince Juan, the heir apparent to the Spanish throne. Moreover, popular opinion held that there was little wealth in La Española, and in fact, relative to expectations, little had been returned to Castile. The benefit to royal coffers of another voyage to the Indies seemed dubious.

But finally, on April 23, 1497, orders were issued for the third voyage. Columbus was to take three hundred settlers at royal expense, including farmers, artisans, gold miners, and laborers, plus thirty women who were to pay their own way. Columbus was relieved of having to pay an eighth of the cost, as he had before, and the sovereigns appropriated a sum of 2,824,336 maravedis for the voyage. Fernando and Isabel reaffirmed Columbus's original titles, rights, and privileges and confirmed Bartolomé's appointment as adelantado. Also, the orders included a provision offering pardon to criminals (except those convicted of major crimes such as murder, treason, heresy, or sodomy) who would accompany Columbus and stay in La Española for one or two years, depending on the nature of their crime. Earlier enthusiasm for the Enterprise of the Indies had long passed; recruitment of settlers had become increasingly difficult.

Unfortunately, the promise of financial support was one thing, but actually prying money from the treasury, controlled by Juan de Fonseca, bishop of Badajoz, was something else altogether. Of the 2,824,336 maravedis appropriated in April 1497, Columbus had received only 350,094 by February 1498. Fonseca and one of his accountants, Jimeno Breviesca, threw up countless obstacles to delay the outfitting of the fleet. Before he finally was able to sail, Columbus in exasperation came to blows with Breviesca.

First to set sail, taking provisions to the colony on January 23, 1498, were sturdy *Niña* and *India,* the popular name for *Santa Cruz,* the ship built in La Isabela after the hurricane of 1495. Juan Bermúdez was captain of *India,* Pedro Francés of *Niña.* Pedro Fernández Coronel was captain general of the expedition. Four months later, the other six ships requested by Columbus were ready at last. Three caravels, *Garza, La Gorda,* and *La Rábida* captained by Alonso Sánchez de Carbajal, Pedro de Arana, and Giovanni Colombo, a Genoese cousin of the Admiral, were to take provisions to La Española. The other three ships, two caravels and a nao, Columbus's flagship, would

undertake the voyage of discovery. Pedro de Terreros and Hernán Pérez commanded the caravels *El Correo* and *Vaqueños,* Columbus the nao *Santa María de Guía.*

Columbus knew his chances of continuing in royal favor and holding on to the honors and titles already bestowed upon him depended on his finding major sources of gold. As Las Casas wrote, "He saw that his signal services were held of slight value, and that suddenly the reputation that these Indies at first had enjoyed was sinking and declining, by reason of those who had the ear of the Sovereigns." Fearing that Fernando and Isabel would abandon the project altogether and he himself would end in poverty, Columbus designed his route to take him to the most likely source of wealth.

His plan reflected Aristotle's doctrine that similar products existed in the same latitudes. The Portuguese had discovered gold in Guinea. If land could be found across the ocean at the same latitude, then it should be far richer than La Española. The route reflected also the prevalent belief that valuable things such as gold, spices, gems, and drugs came from hot regions, where dark-skinned people lived. Columbus planned to sail southwest until he reached the latitude of Sierra Leone and Cape St. Ann in Guinea, and then he would sail west to the meridian of La Española. If at that meridian he had not yet sighted land, he would sail south again.

Columbus's goal also was to ascertain the truth of King João of Portugal's contention that a great landmass existed west of La Española. Wishing to ensure Portugal's claim to that landmass, João had insisted that the Line of Demarcation established by papal bull be moved to 370 leagues west of the Cape Verde Islands. If land were found east of the line, it would belong to Portugal; if west, Spain would reap the benefits. Fernando, obviously preferring the second eventuality, had covered the first by arranging for his daughter, Princess Isabel, to marry João's son and heir, Manuel.

The six ships sailed from Sanlúcar de Barrameda, at the mouth of the Guadalquivir River, on May 30, 1498 and headed for Madeira, where Columbus had lived as a young man and where he was given a warm welcome. He stayed there six days replenishing water and wood and then proceeded to Gomera in the Canary Islands. On June 21 the fleet sailed from Gomera for Hierro and then split up. Columbus gave exact instructions to the captains of the three provisioning ships for the course to Dominica and thence to Santo Domingo, the new settlement on La Española. The three ships whose mission was discovery set a course for the Cape Verde Islands. Columbus had not been there before and found the name misleading: there was nothing green there; everything was dry and sterile. They stocked up on salted goat meat and water and, on July 4, headed southwest.

Columbus wrote in his journal on July 13 that "the wind

stopped so suddenly and unexpectedly and the supervening heat was so excessive and immoderate that there was no one who dared go below to look after the casks of wine and water, which burst, snapping the hoops of the pipes [wine casks]; the wheat burned like fire, the bacon and salt meat roasted and putrefied. This heat lasted eight days." Had it not been cloudy, he wrote, "many people must have perished." (One hopes the Spanish sailors removed their heavy woolen clothing, but as Morison notes, there is no evidence of these early explorers ever getting a suntan.) On July 20 the wind picked up, and they had ten days of good sailing. Water was running dangerously low, however, and Columbus had decided to head north toward Dominica to resupply when the lookout in the crow's nest, Alonso Perez, saw three rocks or mountains to the west. Columbus had planned to give the name Trinidad to the first landfall as a thankful tribute to the Trinity of his religion. That the landfall turned out to be a trinity of mountains seemed to him to be a miracle, a sign that he had been destined to discover this land. The three ships headed toward the island "and all the people glorified the divine bounty ... singing the Salve Regina according to the custom of ... our mariners of Spain."

On August 1 the Spaniards landed on Trinidad behind Punta de la Playa (Erin Point) to take on water. They saw signs of people, farms, and villages, but the natives kept in hiding. Columbus saw "toward the south, another island more than 20 leagues long," which was in fact Bombeador Point, part of Venezuela, his first sight of the South American continent, although he failed to recognize it as such. Keeping to the southern coast of Trinidad, the three ships sailed on to Point Arenal and on August 2 passed through the Boca de Sierpe (Serpent's Mouth), a dangerous spot where the fresh waters of the Orinoco River pour swiftly into the ocean through four channels separated by reefs. The fleet passed safely, however, and anchored on the southwest cape of Trinidad.

Soon after weighing anchor to sail north on August 4, Columbus and his men had a great fright, which he described in a letter to the sovereigns: "Standing on the ship's deck, I heard a terrible roaring which came from the southward toward the ship. And I stood by to watch, and I saw the sea lifting from west to east in the shape of a swell as high as the ship, and yet it came toward me little by little, and it was topped by a crest of white water which came roaring along with a very great noise ... and sounded to me like the rote of surf on rocky ledges, so that even today I feel that fear in my body lest the ship be swamped when she came beneath it." Happily, no damage was done, for the great wave passed under the flagship, raising her to an immense height and then dropping her to what seemed the bottom of the ocean. Las Casas and others believed this was a tidal bore, but

later experts have suggested the massive wave was probably caused by volcanic eruption.

Columbus left the Boca de Sierpe (still known as the Serpent's Mouth), headed north through the Gulf of Paria and anchored near the eastern extremity of the Parian Peninsula of the Venezuelan mainland, probably at Bahía Celeste. On August 5 he sailed south and west along the succession of mountains and headlands that constitute the peninsula. He sent boats ashore on this date, probably at Ensenada Yacera, the first positive landing of Europeans on the American mainland. They found "fish and fire and signs of people and a great house," and fruit "some like apples and others like oranges with the inside like figs"; the mountains "were covered with monkeys." The Indians fled, however, so Columbus delayed taking formal possession until the next day when the natives were on hand to witness the event.

Columbus himself may not have gone ashore for the ceremony because he was suffering from an eye infection. He was in poor health throughout this voyage, from arthritis and other maladies. Evidence is contradictory. Capt. Hernán Pérez testified later concerning the lawsuits known as the Pleitos that he was the first ashore but that Columbus, with fifty men, followed with banners and swords to perform the ceremony. On the other hand, the Admiral's page, Andrés de Corral, testified that Columbus remained on board because of his inflamed eyes and sent Capt. Pedro de Terreros to take possession. Unfortunately, Captain Terreros died on the fourth voyage and was not available to testify at the trials. In any case, although Columbus's personal presence ashore is uncertain, there is no question that men under his command landed on the South American continent in 1498. (Amerigo Vespucci sailed to Paria in 1499 with Ojeda, but changed the date to 1497 when he wrote about the voyage, unfairly claiming to have discovered the continent that bears his name.)

Over the next five days, the ships continued along the northern shore of the gulf, trading with the natives who offered food and a fermented drink made from maize and embroidered cotton kerchiefs similar to those worn by natives in Guinea. On August 6 a great cross was raised at the Rio Guiria, where "many people came out and told me that they called this land Paria." These Indians were taller than those in the Indies, with long brown hair. They wore polished gold disks like mirrors suspended around their necks. They traded these and a copper and gold alloy called "guanin," which was common to this area and was later found in Central America. The natives valued copper more than gold and sniffed all the articles offered by the Spanish to detect it. The women wore beautiful pearls, which they said they gathered in the gulf and on the Caribbean side of Paria. These Indians seemed to have a somewhat more advanced culture than that found in the Caribbean islands discovered on the first two voyages. They were more proficient in metallurgy and in weaving cotton. Some of their canoes, used to carry quantities of freight, were very large and often had a cabin built amidships.

Columbus was eager to explore this rich area, but provisions were spoiling and he had to get them to La Española. Seeking an outlet from the gulf at its western extremity, he sent *El Corréo*, the smallest of the three ships, to explore in waters too shallow for the others and discovered another vast basin fed by four large rivers. These were the four mouths of the Río Grande, the northern branch of the Orinoco. Columbus named this the Gulf of Pearls but, because of the need to deliver the provisions, decided he could not spare the time to explore it himself.

Writing to Fernando and Isabel, Columbus praised them for their sponsorship of his voyages and reminded them it took five years for Portugal to reap any benefits from Guinea. He added, "no prince of Castile is to be found . . . who has ever gained more land outside of Spain, and Your Highnesses have won these vast lands, which are an Other World where Christianity will have so much enjoyment and our faith so great an increase."

On August 13 the fleet took a dangerous departure from the Gulf of Paria through the Boca del Dragón (Dragon's Mouth) at its northeastern end where fresh water pours out and the sea rushes in. When the wind died in midcrossing, Columbus feared disaster, but fresh water overcame the salt and swept them out of the Mouth of the Dragon into the Caribbean. He sailed west along the northern coast of Paria (which he believed to be an island) seeking a back entrance to the Gulf of Pearls. He meant to keep close to the shore, but when he was forced to retire because his eyes troubled him, his pilots edged off shore. On August 15 he decided to head for La Española, "leaving the Cabo de Conches to the south and Margarita [Island] to the west." Had he explored for a day or so he would have found the rich pearl fisheries behind Margarita, but as he wrote to the sovereigns, "I omitted to prove this because of the provisions and the soreness of my eyes and because a great ship that I had was not suitable."

He did change his mind about the nature of his discovery, however, realizing that South America was a continent, not an island. He wrote in his journal, "I have come to believe that this is a mighty continent which was hitherto unknown . . . and if this is a continent, it is a matter for great wonderment and that it is such will be considered among all learned men since from it issues a river so immense that it fills a fresh sea 48 leagues long." In a letter to the sovereigns, Columbus propounded his belief that the world is not a sphere but pear-shaped with

a bulge below the equator something like a woman's breast. The land he had discovered, he wrote, was the Garden of Eden, the Terrestrial Paradise, "because all men say that it is at the end of the Orient, and that is where we are." Did not Paria have a temperate climate and delicious fruit such as were found in the Garden of Eden? And what about *Genesis* 2:10? "A river flowed out of Eden to water the garden, and there it divided and became four rivers." Had not his men in Correo discovered four rivers at the western end of the Gulf of Paria? He described in some detail the many wonders he had seen—copper, lapis, amber, cotton, pepper, cinnamon, aromatic gum, ginger, gold, pearls—and drew a detailed map of the location of the gulf, including star sights, currents, and tides. But because he was ill, his men tired, and the provisions spoiling, he would return to La Española and send his brother Bartolomé back to continue the exploration of the mainland.

Columbus's amazing dead reckoning took the fleet to La Española on August 20. In *Admiral of the Ocean Sea*, historian Samuel Eliot Morison wrote of this accomplishment: "Columbus was approaching Hispaniola by a new angle, from a newly discovered continent. He had left Isabella in March 1496 and had never visited the site of Santo Domingo." At sea since May 30, Columbus had not been able to check his position against known land since July 4. He had taken a new route across the Atlantic and ended up far to the south and west of his previous Caribbean landfalls. "Yet all this time he had kept such accurate dead-reckoning that he knew the correct course for Hispaniola." Columbus was annoyed that his landfall was to leeward of Santo Domingo rather than seventy-five miles to windward as he had planned, but correctly decided that strong currents had been the cause. By any account, this was a remarkable feat of navigation.

Columbus must have been surprised when his brother Bartolomé sailed to Beata Island to meet him. Someone in Santo Domingo had spotted three caravels sailing to leeward and Bartolomé, assuming they carried Columbus, had set out to meet him. In fact, those ships has been the three provision ships Columbus had last seen in the Canary Islands. They had sailed off course and become hopelessly lost, finally fetching up at Jaraguá at the far western end of La Española. This was a clear indication that the Atlantic crossing and navigating among the Caribbean islands demanded a level of navigational expertise not all pilots possessed.

When Columbus reached Santo Domingo on August 31, 1498, he found the colony in a disastrous state. Illness—both fever and syphilis—plagued the colonists (some 160 of them, or 20 to 30 percent, probably had syphilis). The Indians had stopped paying the harsh tribute demanded by the Spaniards, mines were not being worked, farms

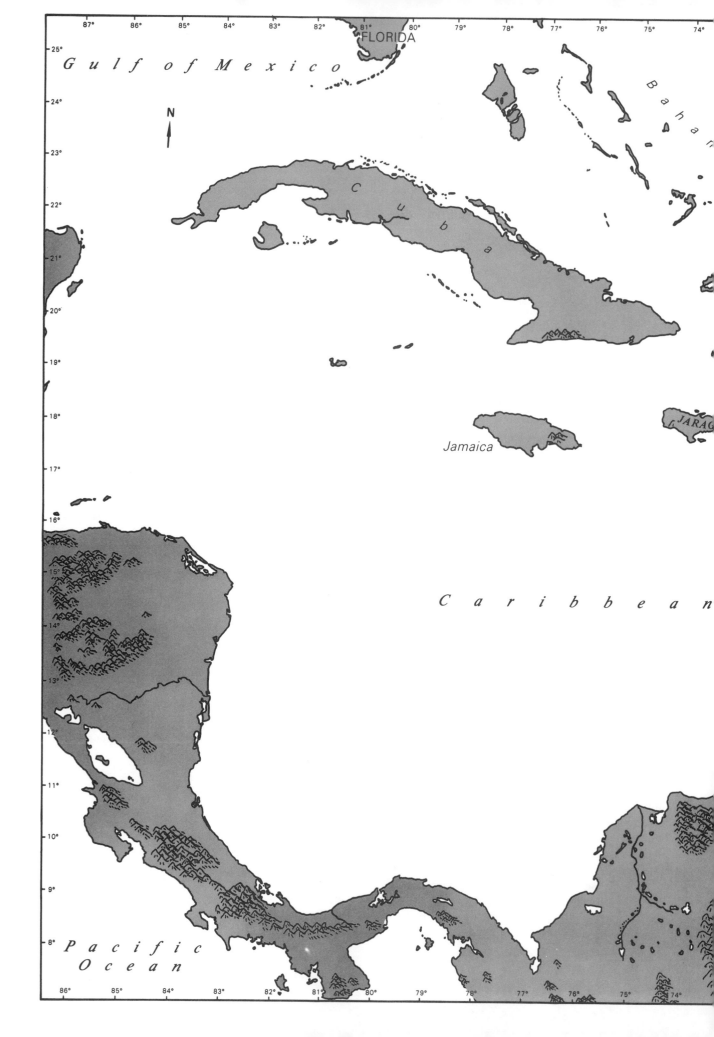

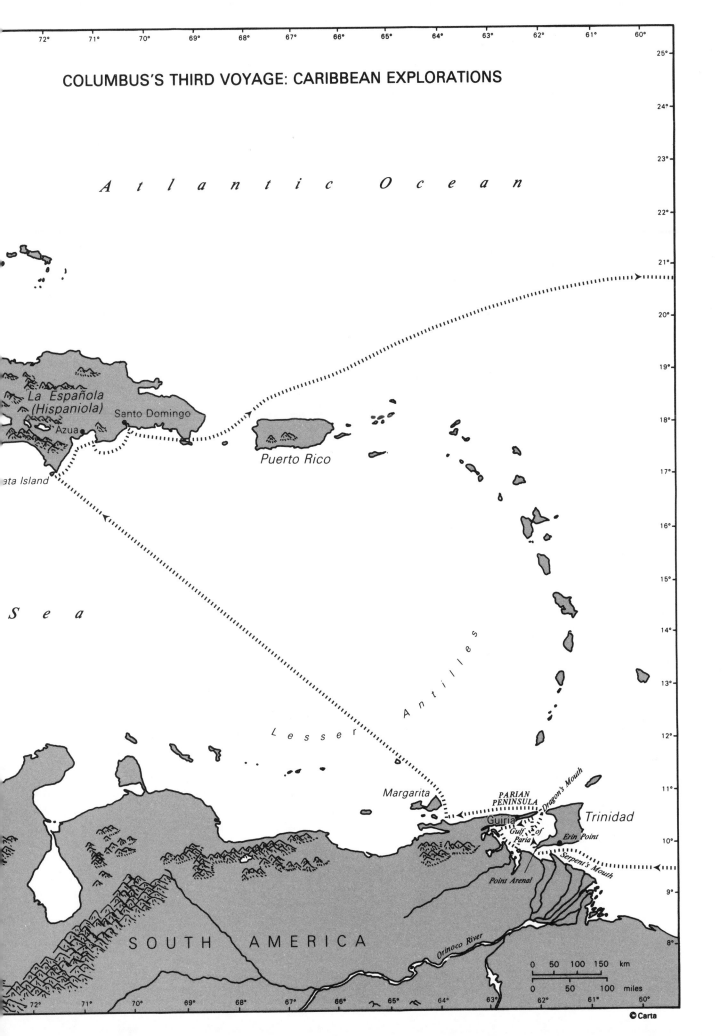

COLUMBUS'S THIRD VOYAGE: CARIBBEAN EXPLORATIONS

Atlantic Ocean

La Española (Hispaniola)

Santo Domingo

Azua

...ata Island

Puerto Rico

Lesser   Antilles

Sea

Margarita

PARIAN PENINSULA

Dragon's Mouth

Guiria

Gulf of Paria

Trinidad

Erin Point

Serpent's Mouth

Point Arenal

Orinoco River

SOUTH   AMERICA

| 0 | 50 | 100 | 150 | km |

| 0 | 50 | 100 | miles |

© Carta

were neglected. Most serious was a rebellion that had split the colony apart. The Spaniards hated the stern rule of that "foreigner" Bartolomé and were discontented with the climate and the chronically inadequate supply of food; above all, they were greedy for gold.

While Bartolomé had been away from La Isabela on his expedition to found the new settlement of Santo Domingo, the chief justice appointed by Columbus, Francisco Roldán, joined by a large group of malcontents, raided the armory and fanned out into the countryside, seeking gold and exploiting the Indians. Roldán abducted the wife of the then friendly cacique Guarionex, and his men were responsible for many other outrages against the natives. Bartolomé, although preoccupied with moving the colony from La Isabela to Santo Domingo on the banks of the Ozama River on the southern coast and building the new city and ships suitable for coastal trading, was nevertheless able to hold Roldán at bay at Fort Concepción, on the mule track between the two cities. When *Niña* and *India,* the advance ships of the Third Voyage, arrived with much needed provisions, the flotilla commander, Pedro Fernández Coronel, also brought royal confirmation of Bartolomé's appointment as adelantado and of Columbus's rank and privileges. Roldán had hoped the anti-Columbus faction in Spain had been able to secure the removal of the two brothers. When he learned this had not happened, he and about seventy followers moved to Jaraguá, at the western tip of the island, where Cacique Behechio permitted them to stay. Bartolomé then marched against the caciques Guarionex and Mayobanex who had joined with Roldán, captured them, burned their villages, and subdued that part of La Española temporarily. Meanwhile, however, Roldán was still at large in Jaraguá.

When the three provision ships got lost, overshot Santo Domingo, and landed at Jaraguá, many of the sailors who had signed on to mitigate criminal punishment in Spain were suborned by Roldán. Carvajal, one of the three captains, tried to reason with the rebel and then returned overland to Santo Domingo to report that he might give up his rebellion if granted amnesty. The other two captains, Arana and Giovanni Colombo, sailed back to Santo Domingo with all three ships. Roldán, joined by Pedro Requelme and Adrián de Moxica, two of the leading malcontents, moved into the Bonao Valley and planned to attack Fort Concepción. The commander, Miguel Ballester, offered Roldán pardon as directed by Columbus, but Roldán rejected it. He refused to deal with Ballester and insisted that Carbajal be sent to mediate.

On October 18, 1498, Columbus sent five ships back to Spain, loaded with brazilwood and other produce, many discontented colonists who wished to return home, and a large contingent of Indians for the slave market. He also sent two letters to Fernando and Isabel. In one he described how Roldán and others had rebelled against his

and their authority, pillaged the island, prevented the Indians from paying tribute, and stolen gold and women, including the daughters of several caciques. He requested that Roldán be summoned to Spain for judgment and complained that Fonseca's neglect of the colony, particularly the failure to provide adequate supplies of food and medicine, had been the principal cause of the settlers' discontent. He reported that he was sending home as many worthless, lazy settlers as possible and urged that industrious men be sent in their place so the natural wealth of La Española might be returned to Castile. He asked for a number of priests to help reform the dissolute Spaniards and convert the natives, and requested a man learned in the law to act as judge. He also asked that the colonists be permitted to keep Indians as slaves for two more years, using only those captured in wars or insurrections.

The second letter, written earlier, discussed his views on the shape of the earth and his discovery of Paria and the Garden of Eden; he enclosed the chart he had drawn detailing its location. He reiterated his promise to send his brother Bartolomé to continue explorations of Paria and added his intention to establish a colony there as soon as he could leave La Española. Obviously, this was not the time.

After dispatching the ships, Columbus sent Carvajal as his emissary to Roldán and his principal assistants, Adrián de Moxica, Pedro de Gámez, and Diego de Escobar. His letter to the rebels was conciliatory; he expressed concern for their feud with Bartolomé and promised them safe conduct. Terms were proposed back and forth until November, when the rebels agreed to leave for Spain in two ships provided by Columbus within fifty days. Columbus granted a number of concessions here—safe conduct, pay, slaves for their personal use or permission to take native wives in place of slaves. Two ships left Santo Domingo for Jaraguá in February 1499 but ran into violent weather and were delayed until March; one was so damaged it had to return to Santo Domingo. When Carvajal, in the replacement vessel, finally got to Jaraguá, the rebels refused to leave, claiming the ships had been deliberately delayed and were unseaworthy and ill supplied.

In another attempt to straighten things out, Columbus sailed to Azua, west of Santo Domingo, and met aboard ship with Roldán, Moxica, and others. In September Columbus agreed to the rebels' outrageous demands that all charges against them be dropped, that Roldán be reinstated as alcalde (chief judge) that fifteen rebels be allowed to return to Spain, and that the rest be given land grants, including natives living on the land, in lieu of pay. The land grant scheme, or repartimiento, was to become a cornerstone of Spanish colonial policy in the New World.

Columbus wanted to return to Spain in two caravels dispatched in October to make a personal explanation of these sorry events, but he dared not leave La Española in such an unsettled state. Instead, he wrote another letter to the sovereigns explaining that the perilous state of affairs on the island had compelled him to go along with the rebels' demands and urging them not to ratify the agreement. He repeated his request that a learned judge be sent to administer the laws of the island.

Another reason Columbus delayed his departure was the clandestine arrival of Alonso de Ojeda, whose four ships anchored off the western end of La Española. Ojeda was a favorite of Bishop Fonseca. When Columbus's letter describing Paria arrived in Castile, complete with detailed charts, Fonseca had shown them to Ojeda and then issued to him a private license to explore the area. Similar licenses were issued to Peralonso Niño and Vicente Yáñez Pinzón, undermining the authority of Columbus. Ojeda left immediately for the Gulf of Paria, accompanied by Amerigo Vespucci, a Florentine merchant, and Juan de la Cosa, the mapmaker who had sailed as a seaman on *Niña*. Ojeda departed in May 1499. Although trying to adhere to Columbus's course, he made his landfall on the southern continent some six hundred miles southeast of Trinidad but eventually passed through the Gulf of Paria into the Caribbean and proceeded along the coast to the west. He too neglected to avail himself of a treasure in beautiful pearls along the shores of the island of Margarita just off the north coast of Venezuela. Instead, he sailed on to the west finally reaching the northern tip of what is now Colombia. Having failed to find any of the Oriental splendors he had sought, he headed toward La Española for provisions. Arriving at Jaraguá, he met with Roldán's former cohorts. These men believed Roldán had deserted them by his agreement with Columbus; they wanted back pay and urged Ojeda to lead them to Santo Domingo to confront Columbus. Learning of Ojeda's arrival at Jaraguá, Columbus sent Roldán to establish order. The two crafty adventurers maneuvered for control, with Roldán finally emerging victorious. Ojeda sailed for Castile, stopping first in the Bahamas to take aboard captives for the slave market in Seville.

The turmoil in La Española continued. Roldán was now determined to enforce the laws he had so recently opposed. He imprisoned a young cavalier named Guevara, a cousin of his former lieutenant Adrián de Moxica. Moxica recruited many of his old friends to help free Guevara and kill both Roldán and Columbus. Learning of the plot, Columbus surprised and captured the ringleaders, hung Moxica, and imprisoned his accomplices. The rebels fled to Jaraguá, but Roldán followed and captured them.

La Española now began to settle down; fields were cultivated and the Indians were peaceful. Unfortunately for Columbus, events in Spain were about to culminate in his downfall. Columbus had few supporters at the court and many enemies, including Roldán's followers who spread tales of the Admiral's misrule. More important to King Fernando, gold—needed to support both his political ambitions in Europe and the colony itself—was not arriving in Castile. When more followers of Roldán returned to Spain with more tales of Columbus's tyranny and when more slaves arrived, further offending Isabel's sensibilities, the sovereigns decided to appoint someone to investigate affairs in La Española.

They appointed Francisco de Bobadilla as interim judge with powers to arrest rebels, seize their effects, and take over all royal property from Columbus, who was commanded to obey his orders. Bobadilla arrived in Santo Domingo on August 23, 1500, just at the time that Columbus had put down the rebellion led by Adrián de Moxica. As Bobadilla landed he saw seven corpses swinging from a gallows, proof to him of Columbus's cruelty. High-handedly, he seized the fortress where five other prisoners were held, released them, and took over Columbus's private quarters and possessions. (Columbus himself was at Fort Concepción at the time.) Diego was in charge in Santo Domingo, and Bobadilla jailed him. He interrogated several unhappy settlers and then issued a general license to search for gold and pay only a tenth of that found to the Crown instead of the third previously levied. When Columbus returned to Santo Domingo to meet with Bobadilla, he too was imprisoned and chained hand and foot. Later, Bartolomé joined his brothers in captivity.

The three Columbus brothers were sent home to Spain in chains. They left La Española in October 1500 aboard *La Gorda* and arrived in Cádiz at the end of the month. Alonso de Villejo, appointed to take charge of the prisoners, and Andreas Martín, master of *La Gorda*, offered to remove the manacles but Columbus refused, preferring that the sovereigns order them removed. On the sad voyage home, Columbus wrote a letter to Juana, sister of his friend Antonio de Torres and nurse to the Infante Juan, reviewing these events. Dignity intact, he made clear his outrage:

> It is now seventeen years since I came to serve these princes with the Enterprise of the Indies; they made me pass eight of them in discussion, and at the end rejected it as a thing of jest. Nonetheless, I persisted therein ... and have placed under their sovereignty more land than there is in Africa and Europe, more than one thousand seven hundred islands, without counting Hispaniola.... In seven years I, by the divine will, made that conquest. At a time when I was entitled to expect rewards and retirement, I was incontinently arrested and sent home loaded with chains, to my great dishonor and with slight service to their Highnesses.

The accusation was brought out of malice on the basis of

charges made by civilians who had revolted and wished to take possession of the land.... In this endeavor I have lost my youth, my proper share in things, and my honor.... I was judged as a governor who had been sent to take charge of a well-regulated city or town under the dominion of well-established laws, where there was no danger of everything turning to disorder and ruin; but I ought to be judged as a captain sent to the Indies to conquer a numerous and warlike people of manners and religion very different from ours, living not in regular towns but in forests and mountains. It ought to be considered that, by divine will I have brought all of these under the sovereignty of their Majesties, giving them dominion over another world, whereby Spain, heretofore poor, has become the richest of countries.

When this letter was read by Isabela, she became indignant and together with Fernando ordered that Columbus be set free. With gratitude and affection, they invited him to the court.

The Fourth Voyage

The fourth voyage of Christopher Columbus was referred to by him as El Alto Viaje, "High Voyage." He thought it would be his most significant, most profitable expedition, a fitting cap to his illustrious career. Columbus sought to discover a strait to the Indian Ocean, a shorter and more direct route to the opulent East than the route around Africa discovered in 1497 by Vasco da Gama. In fact, El Alto Viaje was the least profitable and most dangerous of all his voyages. He discovered Central America and more gold than in La Española, but he found no passage to India, returned no quantities of gold to Castile, lost many men and all four of his ships, and was marooned on a Jamaican beach for twelve months.

Six weeks after Columbus's ignominious return from La Española in chains in October 1500, the sovereigns ordered his release and invited him to the court. They sent him two thousand ducats to enable him to travel from Seville to Alhambra where they warmly received him on December 17. His brothers, Bartolomé and Diego, accompanied him, and Columbus was reunited with his sons, Diego and Fernando, who were serving as pages at the court. Isabel appears to have been genuinely upset over the harsh treatment of the Admiral by Bobadilla who in less than a year was dismissed from his position in La Española. The sovereigns agreed to restore Columbus's income and rights but turned a deaf ear to his plea that his position as viceroy be restored or that he be given a new position. In 1492, when Fernando conferred power and authority on Columbus, the scope of his discoveries could not have been anticipated. Now, merely six years later, voyages by Ojeda, Niño, Pinzón, Bastides, Lepe, Cabral, and Vespucci pointed to the vast size and richness of the South American continent. Could Fernando permit Co-

lumbus and his heirs to be governors and viceroys forever of this huge new world, with the right to tithe all trade and nominate officials? Furthermore, Columbus had failed in Fernando's eyes as colonial administrator. The job was more important now, for both England and Portugal were by this time encroaching on Spain's territories in the New World. The king planned to secure his possessions there by establishing local governmental commands at strategic places, under central control from Santo Domingo. Columbus was not the man for this vital position.

The sovereigns told Columbus that time was needed to settle things in La Española, that bad feelings still existed toward him and his brothers and it would be dangerous for them personally if they returned too soon. Bobadilla would be dismissed, but someone else would be sent to investigate events and remedy the wrongs that existed. Columbus was permitted to send a representative to ensure that his wealth and belongings were returned to him. Carvajal was chosen for this task. The new administrator would hold office for two years, after which time Columbus might return to La Española. Isabel apparently believed Columbus would be restored to his previous status after this period of time, but Fernando's conduct indicates he had no such intention.

On September 3, 1501, Nicolás de Ovando was named governor and supreme justice of the islands and mainland of the Indies. He sailed for the New World on February 13, 1502, with the largest fleet ever assembled. Thirty ships carried twenty-five hundred seamen, colonists (including seventy-three families), artisans, doctors, and soldiers, along with provisions, livestock, and munitions. Ovando had an impressive personal retinue and was allowed to take sumptuous silks and jewels to display the importance of his office. It must have been difficult at best for Columbus to view this demonstration of power and luxury which, by earlier royal decree, belonged to him.

On February 26, 1502, hardly two weeks after Ovando's triumphant departure, Columbus requested a fourth voyage to find a strait in the western Caribbean through which he could sail on to India. He knew from his own voyage to Paria and from others who had sailed there that the South American continent stretched far to the west. He also believed that the south coast of Cuba, which he still thought to be part of the Asian mainland, continued on to the west. And he had observed the strength of the current that ran westward through the Caribbean. Columbus concluded that this current must have an outlet to the west and that a strait through to the Indian Ocean must exist along the unexplored lands in the western Caribbean. In fact, the current south of Cuba does flow west; it then is deflected to the north by the Central American landmass and curves around the Gulf of Mexico to exit the Caribbean basin around the Florida cape.

Isabel may have felt that a few ships were little enough

to give to the discoverer of the New World, particularly in view of the great fleet sent with Ovando. Fernando's greed must have been aroused by the thought of a direct route to the riches of India. Portugal was growing richer with the bounty being returned around Africa along the route discovered by Vasco da Gama. If Columbus could discover a strait—and he certainly had the navigational skills to do it—da Gama's achievement would pale and Spain would gain its share of India's gold, spices, and pearls.

Formal authorization from Fernando and Isabel came on March 14, 1502. It was the last letter Columbus would receive from them. Addressing him as "Don Cristóbal Colón, Admiral of the Islands and Mainlands of the Ocean Sea in the direction of the Indies," the sovereigns said Columbus would receive ten thousand gold pesos for fitting out a fleet and all the arms and munitions he needed. He was to search for islands and continents "in the Indies in the part that belongs to us" (west of the Line of Demarcation). The gold, silver, pearls, precious stones, and spices he found were to be placed under the control of Francisco de Porras, who would sail as official comptroller. Columbus was to take no slaves. An accompanying letter of introduction to Vasco da Gama, then about to undertake a second voyage to India around the southern tip of Africa, said "it may be that you will meet on your course," indicating the sovereigns hoped that Columbus would discover a strait to the Indies and sail home around the world. They promised that his privileges would be preserved intact and confirmed anew if necessary.

Four caravels made this last voyage. Diego Tristán, a loyal servant to the Admiral, was captain of the flagship, *La Capitana*. Columbus, now fifty-one years old and in poor health, chose not to command the vessel himself. Bartolomé Colón sailed on *Santiago de Palos*, whose owner and master was Francisco Bermúdez. Francisco de Porras was titular captain, but Bartolomé, by far the better seaman, was de facto captain. Porras's brother, Diego, was auditor and Crown representative. The sister of the Porras brothers was the mistress of the treasurer of Castile, Alonso de Morales, and Morales forced Columbus to take the brothers along. *El Gallego* was captained by Pedro de Terreros, and *Vizcaíno* by Bartolomeo Fieschi, a Genoese and old family friend of the Columbuses. One hundred and forty men and boys sailed with Columbus, according to his twelve-year-old son, Fernando, who accompanied them.

The four ships set sail on May 9, 1502, heading first to Arzila, a Portuguese fortress on the Moroccan coast, to help repel an invasion of Moors. Apparently King Fernando asked that they make this detour to help maintain good relations with Manuel, king of Portugal and Fernando's son-in-law. Hostilities had ended before their arrival, so the fleet sailed on to the Canary Islands. After reprovisioning, Columbus left Hierro behind on May 26 and set a course west by south. He reached Martinique in only twenty-one days, the fastest crossing of any of his voyages.

They rested, bathed, and repaired the ships and then sailed along the Leeward chain; by the end of June they were off the Ozama River just out from Santo Domingo. Fernando and Isabel's instructions forbade Columbus to land at La Española on this outward leg, but he had pressing reasons to request permission to enter the port. He wanted to trade *Santiago* for a ship more suitable for exploration and to send letters home with a large fleet about to depart for Castile. But his principal reason was to seek shelter from a tropical storm he saw brewing. Columbus knew well the subtle signs of an approaching hurricane—the oily swell from the southeast, an oppressive feeling in the air, cirrus clouds racing across the sky, perhaps twinges in his arthritic joints.

So he sent a note ashore to Ovando, requesting permission to enter and urging him to keep the fleet in port because of the impending storm. Ovando refused the request and ignored the warning. The thirty-ship armada left port and had just entered the Mona Passage when it was shattered by a massive hurricane. Only one of the ships made it to Spain—ironically, the least seaworthy of them all, aboard which Ovando had placed the four thousand pieces of gold belonging to Columbus. All the other ships were lost, either sunk with all hands or battered so heavily as to be useless. The flagship of the armada sank, killing one of Columbus's old friends, Antonio de Torres, as well as Bobadilla, Roldán, and the conquered Cacique Guarionex, and taking with it to the bottom 200,000 castellanos worth of gold. In all, more than five hundred lives were lost at sea and Santo Domingo was flattened.

Columbus and his four ships survived the storm. He had anchored close to land, possibly off the Jaina River, and was protected from winds coming from the north and west. Although the fierce winds tore three ships loose from their moorings (only *Capitana*'s anchor held), all were able to ride out the hurricane safely. Columbus wrote (probably cursing Ovando as he did so), "What man ever born, not excepting Job, who would not have died of despair when in such weather, seeking safety for my son, brother, shipmates and myself, we were forbidden the land and the harbors that I, by God's will and sweating blood, had won for Spain?" His battered ships rendezvoused in Ocoa Bay on July 3, and the rested crews and repaired vessels left La Española on July 15.

Columbus had planned to return to Margarita Island off Venezuela and then sail downwind along the continental coast until he found the strait he sought. His decision to put in at Santo Domingo ruled out that course because he was too far north and west to beat back against both wind

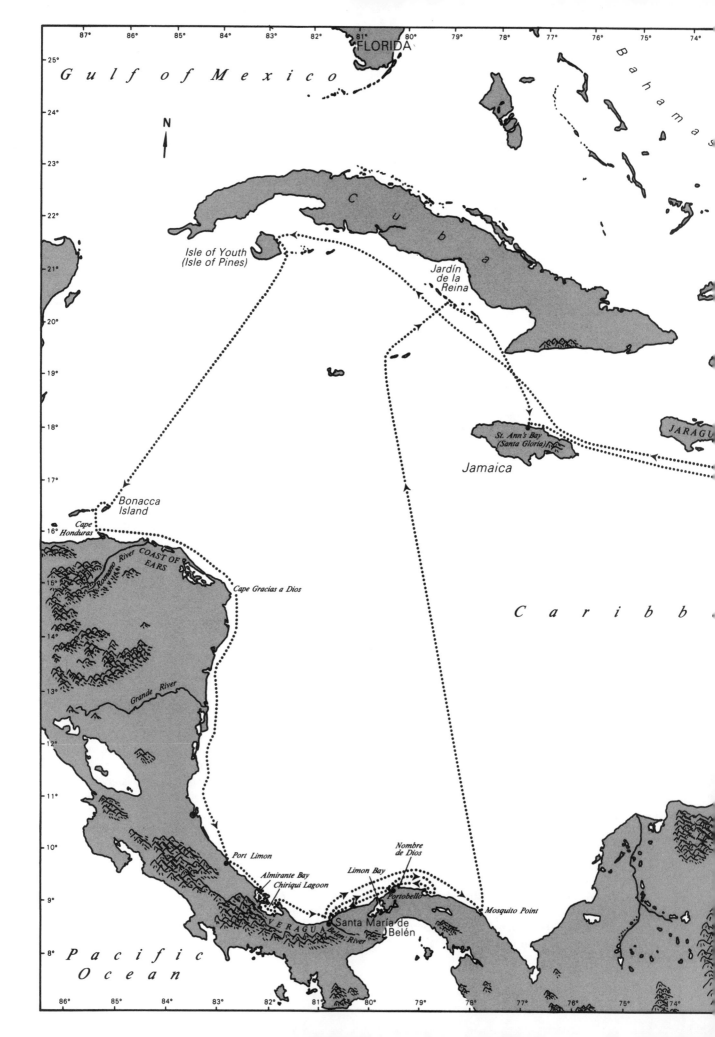

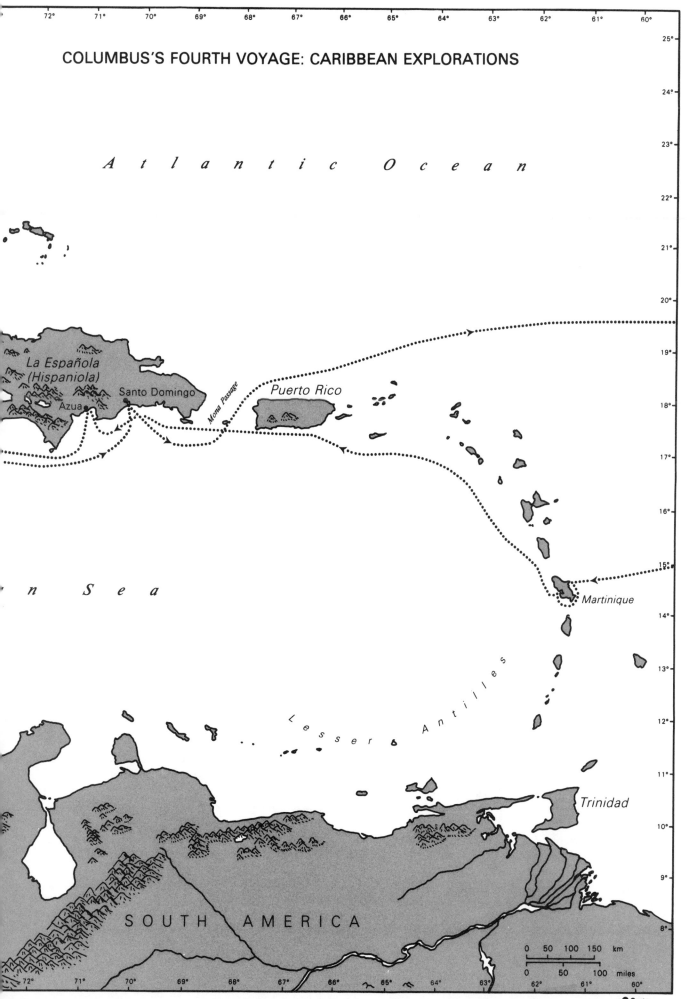

COLUMBUS'S FOURTH VOYAGE: CARIBBEAN EXPLORATIONS

A t l a n t i c   O c e a n

*La Española
(Hispaniola)*

Santo Domingo

Azua

Mona Passage

Puerto Rico

n   S e a

Martinique

L e s s e r   A n t i l l e s

Trinidad

SOUTH AMERICA

0   50   100   150 km

0   50   100 miles

© Carta

and current, so he set off downwind into the western Caribbean. Light winds and strong currents carried them past Jamaica and then northwest toward Cuba. After anchoring off the Isle of Pines for three days, they picked up a stiff northeast wind and sailed 360 miles to the southwest. On the thirtieth, a seaman sighted Bonacca Island, off the Honduran coast.

Bartolomé went ashore, but the Indians had no gold or pearls to trade. A dugout canoe as long as a galley and eight feet broad, with a twenty-five-man crew, approached the ships. Women and children were sheltered by a hutlike structure of palm leaves amidships. The Spaniards captured it and exchanged the usual baubles for clay vessels, sheets of dyed cotton, flint-edged swords, and copper hatchets, all of a quality superior to what they had seen before. Like the Moors, the women covered their faces. The Indians, who were probably trading between Bonacca and the Honduran mainland, may have been part of a high culture akin to the Mayan. The Spanish captured the elderly skipper of the canoe to use him as interpreter, and he proved to be intelligent and helpful. The ships continued on toward the mainland and anchored in the lee of Cape Honduras, where they made the first landing on the mainland of North America.

After a long beat to windward they anchored off Río de la Posesión (now the Romano River), so named because Columbus took formal possession there on August 17. Father Alexander celebrated mass, and hundreds of Indians came to watch the ceremonies. They traded fowl, fish, red and white beans, and other commodities for the hawkbells, beads, and trinkets offered by the Spanish. They were darker than the Indians on La Española and tattooed or painted with designs of animals; they painted their faces "black and red . . . to appear beautiful, but they really look like devils," wrote young Fernando. Columbus called the region the Coast of the Ears because these natives had earlobes with holes as large as eggs.

The explorers then endured twenty-eight days of foul weather along the "Miskito Coast" of Honduras. Headwinds were strong, it rained fiercely, thunder and lightning tore the skies. The men were soaking wet continually, provisions were ruined, and the hard toil of pumping never ended. Still, Columbus was determined to find the strait, so they pressed on, beating off shore each day and anchoring close to shore each night: in strange waters, Columbus dared not sail after dark. Finally, on September 14, the fleet rounded the cape so aptly named Gracias a Dios (Thanks be to God) by Columbus and found favorable winds and currents. Sailing south along the Nicaraguan coast, they anchored on the sixteenth near the mouth of a large river, probably the Río Grande, where the surf was so strong one boat sent ashore for wood and water was swamped and two men drowned. Continuing south for 130 miles, they reached Costa Rica eight days later.

On September 25 the ships anchored off what is now called Puerto Limón. Here they encountered Talamanca Indians, who were curious but superstitious. They refused to accept any gifts from the Spaniards, and when they saw a man writing, they threw powdered herbs into the air to blow the magic away. Columbus sent a boat ashore on October 2, and the men reported seeing "a great palace of wood covered with canes and within some tombs, in one of which was a corpse dried and embalmed . . . with no bad odor, wrapped in cotton cloth; and over each tomb was a tablet carved with figures of beasts, and on some the effigy of the dead person, adorned with beads and guanin, and other things that they most value." (Guanin was a copper and gold alloy.)

Taking two of the Indians as interpreters, Columbus headed southeast. When he found a channel the evening of October 5, he may have thought he had discovered the strait, but it led into Almirante Bay, not the Indian Ocean. Here Columbus "found the first sign of fine gold, which an Indian wore like a large medal on his breast and traded it." The Indians directed Columbus to another narrow strait, which again he may have thought to be the one he sought. But it led only to the landlocked Chiriqui Lagoon, thirty miles long and fifteen miles across. The fleet spent ten days in the lagoon, resting, fishing, and trading. Indians here had pure gold ornaments, not guanin. The two Indian interpreters had learned Castilian quickly. They told Columbus he was on an isthmus between two seas and that the people on the other side, a nine-day march away, had vast quantities of gold and of coral ornaments, wore rich garments, and carried swords. Columbus believed that area, called Ciguare by the natives, was actually Ciamba, Marco Polo's name for Cochin China. From this point on, Columbus concentrated on finding gold and gave up his search for the strait. He may by now have become convinced that no strait existed.

On October 17 the ships left the Chiriqui Lagoon and sailed southeast along the shore but found no harbors. They passed by five villages, one of which was called Veragua, where the Indians said gold was collected. Columbus sailed farther east but found he had passed the gold-trading part of the coast and decided to return to Veragua. Unfortunately, the rainy season began with rough seas and high adverse winds. A storm blew the fleet to Puerto Bello (now Porto Bello), a harbor just past the present Panama Canal entrance. Here they found tilled fields, good-sized villages, and amicable natives who traded spun cotton and food—but no gold. The riches of Central America lay to the west. The ships set out again but were driven back to where Nombre de Dios now is.

There they worked on their ships whose bottoms had been eaten through by *toredos* (shipworms).

Between December 6 and January 6, 1503, winds and currents battered the fleet back and forth between Puerto Bello and the Chagres River. Columbus wrote:

> The tempest arose and wearied me so that I knew not where to turn; my old wound opened up, and for nine days I was as lost without hope of life; eyes never beheld the sea so high, angry and covered with foam. The wind not only prevented our progress but offered no opportunity to run behind any headland for shelter; hence we were forced to keep out in this bloody ocean, seething like a pot on a hot fire. Never did the sky look more terrible; for one whole day and night it blazed like a furnace, and the lightning broke forth with such violence that each time I wondered if it had carried off my spars and sails; the flashes came with such fury and frightfulness that we all thought the ships would be blasted. All this time the water never ceased to fall from the sky; I don't say it rained, because it was like another deluge. The people were so worn out that they longed for death to end their dreadful sufferings.

And Fernando wrote of an occurrence, "one no less dangerous and wonderful, a waterspout which on Tuesday, December 13, passed by the ships ... it raises the water up to the clouds in a column thicker than a water butt, twisting it about like a whirlwind." Columbus helped to exorcise the waterspout, clasping his Bible in one hand and his sword in the other as his sailors recited John's gospel.

The fleet put in twice at Puerto Gordo (Limón Bay, within sight of today's Panama Canal entrance at Cristóbal), once on December 17 and again from December 26 to January 3, after being blown back by storms. Everyone was exhausted, hungry, and sick, but finally on January 3 favorable winds let them put to sea again and on the sixth, they dropped anchor off the Belen (Bethlehem) River in Veragua. After taking soundings at the sandbar across the entrance, they entered a calm basin. Columbus decided to stay and explore inland. Bartolomé took a small group up the Veragua River and encountered the resident cacique, El Quibián, who paid a return visit to Columbus and exchanged gifts with the Admiral. On a second expedition, Bartolomé found more gold in just a few days than in four years in La Española. Columbus decided to build a settlement here and leave Bartolomé in charge while he returned to Spain for reinforcements. During the month of February 1503, the Spanish put up ten or twelve houses on the west bank of the river, the beginning of Santa María de Belén.

Many gifts were given to El Quibián to secure his friendship and keep the Spanish safe from attack. Although most of the European provisions had been exhausted, fish, maize, bananas, coconuts, and pineapples were easily found, so food seemed to be adequate. But just as Columbus was about to leave for Spain, the rains stopped and the water level of the river dropped, trapping the ships inside the sandbar. The Indians' attitude also changed. They had been willing to countenance a temporary visit from these foreigners, but when they saw houses being built they grew uneasy.

Diego Méndez, a trusted aide of the Admiral, was the first to notice suspicious Indian activity. Rowing along the coast, he found a thousand warriors gathered on the riverbank just up from the settlement. He stayed close off shore all night, holding the Indians in place. Columbus wanted more definite information before giving up his plan to establish a colony in this rich area. Méndez offered to get it, and there followed a bizarre incident. Méndez, apparently having mastered the local dialect, talked with some warriors who frankly told him they planned to attack the Spanish in two days. Méndez asked to be taken to El Quibián's village where the warriors were gathering. He claimed he wished to cure an arrow wound incurred by the chief. Although shoved about by one of the chief's sons, Méndez remained calm and staged a scene planned earlier, counting on the Indians' curiosity to make it work. Méndez sat on the ground and his companion, Rodrigo de Escobar, combed and trimmed his hair. The chief watched and then asked for the same treatment. When Escobar had cut his hair, he gave the barber's set to El Quibián. Méndez then asked for food and the two Spaniards ate a friendly dinner with the chief. The hostility of the surrounding Indians was ominous, however, and Méndez returned to warn Columbus that an attack was definitely coming. He suggested a daring plan, which was carried out with great skill by him, Bartolomé, and eighty men. El Quibián, several members of his family, and his principal subordinates were captured, as well as a good deal of gold. Unfortunately, through the laxness of his guards, the clever cacique was able to escape, but the other captives were imprisoned in the hold of one of the ships.

While this was going on, the rains resumed and raised the level of water over the bar, so that three ships could be towed out into the ocean. Bartolomé, Méndez, and seventy men were to stay at the settlement with the worm-eaten *Gallega*. While the two parties were saying good-bye, four hundred Indians armed with bows and arrows, slingshots, and spears attacked, wounding several Spaniards, including Bartolomé, and killing one. Just before the Spaniards drove off the Indians, Diego Tristán of *La Capitana* had rowed ashore in the ship's boat to take on water. Indians attacked his party, smashed the boat, and killed Tristán and all but one of his men who managed to escape and report the disaster. For eight days the situation remained tenuous. El Quibián did not attack again, but the hostages being held on *Santiago*, many of them members of El Quibián's family and thus a restraining influence on him, forced the hatch and some were able to escape. (The rest hanged themselves rather than submit to the Spaniards.)

Remembering the tragic loss of the force left at La Navidad in La Española on the first voyage, Columbus realized that the situation ashore had become untenable, and he reluctantly decided that it was prudent to abandon the settlement. Diego Méndez constructed a raft out of two dugout canoes and cross timbers. In two days he transported to the ships all of the garrison, together with the food and gear that had been stored ashore. When Méndez came aboard with the last load, the Admiral embraced him and promoted him to captain of the flagship *La Capitana* to succeed Diego Tristán. The worm-eaten *Gallega* was abandoned.

On Easter Sunday, April 16, 1503, the three remaining ships, all infested with shipworms, set sail for La Española. Within a week, *Vizcaíno* had to be abandoned at Puerto Bello because her condition was beyond repair. Her crew crowded aboard the two remaining vessels, both of which leaked badly. Columbus planned to call at Santo Domingo to repair the ships and take on provisions, and then continue on to Spain. He worked his way to the east so as to be able to make Santo Domingo on one tack. When he reached a headland, probably Punta de Mosquito, his pilots and captains prevailed on him to strike out for La Española. They thought they were east of the Caribee Islands when actually they were nine hundred miles to the west. With the ships leaking badly, they headed north on May 1. On the twelfth they reached the Jardín de la Reina, Cuba. Fernando wrote: "As we lay here at anchor ten leagues from Cuba, suffering greatly from hunger because we had nothing to eat but hard-tack and a little oil and vinegar, and exhausted by working three pumps day and night to keep the ships afloat, for they were ready to sink from the multitude of holes made by shipworms, there came on at night a great blow." *Santiago's* anchor broke loose and she crashed into *La Capitana*, severely damaging both ships. In the morning after the storm, the Spanish found only one strand of *La Capitana's* anchor cable intact.

On the twentieth of May they headed east, "the ships pierced by borers worse than a honeycomb, the people spiritless and desperate," wrote Fernando. Given the strong adverse wind and currents, they could not reach La Española. Columbus took the most sensible course available: he headed for Jamaica. From there, if the ships were still afloat, they could jump off for La Española. On the night of June 22–23, with the depth of water in the bilge increasing despite continuous pumping, they reached Jamaica. On June 25 they struggled into the reef-enclosed harbor of Santa Gloria (St. Ann's Bay). There was no way to keep the two ships afloat, so Columbus ordered they be run ashore as far as possible and beached close together. The Spanish shored up both sides so the ships could not move and built cabins on the decks and at the fore and stern castles where they could be safe from the weather and any hostile Indians. Here they were marooned from June 25, 1503, until June 29, 1504.

One hundred sixteen men were left: six had died or deserted before Veragua, twelve had been killed at Belen, and six had since died. They had no food and Columbus could not let his men go freely ashore, knowing from past experience what they would do. Even the mild Taino Indians of Jamaica would be upset by their probable actions. Méndez and three others were sent to explore. Méndez struck a deal with a number of caciques: the Indians would provide food in exchange for beads, hawk-bells, red caps, mirrors, and so on. In exchange for a chamber pot, a cloak, and a shirt, a cacique at the eastern end of the island provided Méndez with a large dugout canoe loaded with provisions and six natives to return him by sea to the beached ships.

How could the Spanish get home? They had no tools with which to build new ships. Their only chance was to send a messenger by canoe to La Española. This involved a 180-mile trip against the wind and currents to the western cape of La Española and another 250 miles to Santo Domingo. In July, Méndez volunteered to make the crossing. With one other Spaniard and six Indians, he reached the eastern end of Jamaica but barely escaped from a hostile attack and returned alone. Columbus sent Bartolomé with a force of men to accompany Méndez to the eastern end on a second attempt. This time, Méndez and Bartolomeo Fieschi, the Genoese captain of *Vizcaíno*, each took a dugout canoe, six Spaniards, and ten Indians to paddle. If both canoes made the crossing, Méndez was to go on to Santo Domingo and Fieschi would return to Jamaica with news of their success. After seventy-two hours, during which water ran out and one Indian died of thirst, they reached the island of Navassa, a crossing of seventy-eight miles. Several of the Indians died on the island after drinking too much water too quickly; others were very ill. That night, however, they were able to make the crossing to La Española. No one would accompany Fieschi on the return trip to Jamaica, so the marooned Spaniards had no knowledge of the successful crossing.

Méndez recruited new Indian paddlers and set out for Santo Domingo. At Azua, he learned that Ovando was in Jaraguá on an expedition against the natives and went there on foot. Ovando kept Méndez at his headquarters for seven months while he brutally put down an Indian uprising. He hanged or burned alive eighty caciques including a beautiful *cacica*, Anacoana. It was not until March 1504 that Méndez finally reached Santo Domingo, again on foot. Ovando refused to let him use the small caravel in the harbor to return to Jamaica, so he was forced to wait another two months for ships from Spain.

On Jamaica, the Spanish were fearful, unhappy, and increasingly restive in their close quarters. Sure that they had been abandoned, they blamed Columbus for their troubles. With the onset of winter and bad weather, discontent reached a peak. Francisco and Diego de Porras led a conspiracy against Columbus. They may have felt themselves safe from any subsequent charges of mutiny because of their connection with Alonso de Morales, the treasurer of Castile. On January 2, 1504, Francisco entered Columbus's cabin and accused him of not trying to get back to Spain. Columbus said he wanted to return as much as anyone, but until a ship was sent, he saw no way to do so. Porras then cried, "I'm for Castile with those who will follow me." At this signal, "Castile!" the conspirators (forty-eight men, or about half the company) seized the ships. Columbus might have been murdered if a few of his loyal servants had not kept him safe in his cabin.

The rebels then seized ten dugout canoes tied up to the beached ships and fled ashore, ravaging Indian villages and stealing food and abusing women. Reaching the eastern end of the island, they set out for La Española, but heavy winds forced them to turn back. Frightened as the waves washed over the sides of the canoes, they tried to lighten them by throwing everything but their weapons overboard. Then they forced their Indian paddlers into the sea and when they clung to the sides of the canoes hacked off their hands or stabbed them. Eighteen died, but the mutineers returned safely to shore. They tried the crossing again a month later and again failed. After that, Porras and his band abandoned the canoes and started back to Santa Gloria on foot, living off the Indians and abusing them as they went.

After the rebels deserted the beached ships, the quantity of food provided by the Indians began to decrease. The actions of the Porras mutineers surely contributed to the Indians' unwillingness to help these intruders. Since most of those left with the beached ships were sick, including Columbus, it was difficult for them to gather their own food. By February, as famine loomed, Columbus had a brilliant idea. He remembered noting in his astronomical almanac that an eclipse of the moon was due and summoned all the neighboring caciques to Santa Gloria on February 29, 1504. When they had assembled, he told them his God would punish them for refusing to help him and his men and would send a sign of disapproval by making the moon disappear. The Indians were terrified when the eclipse occurred and begged Columbus to intercede with his God and save them from calamity. Columbus waited in his cabin until the eclipse was about to end and then emerged and said the moon would

reappear only if the Indians continued to bring food. From then on, food was plentiful.

At the end of March, Ovando sent a small caravel to spy on Columbus and his increasingly restive men. The ship stayed out of the harbor while a small boat bearing Diego de Escobar, a former ally of Roldán, came to the shore with some wine and a slab of salt pork for the marooned men. He brought a message from Méndez saying he would come to their rescue as soon as a ship was available. Columbus sent a return message to Ovando describing his plight and begging him to send help. Publicly, Columbus reassured his men that help was coming. Privately, he believed Ovando had deliberately neglected him, fearing Columbus would be reinstated as governor of La Española. Columbus then tried to effect a compromise with the Porrases. He sent part of the pork brought by Escobar and offered them pardon if they would return to Santa Gloria and obey his command. They refused the offer. A fight between loyal and rebellious Spaniards ended in victory for the loyalists. Francisco Porras was captured, and the remaining rebels begged for pardon, which Columbus granted.

Méndez finally was able to charter a caravel commanded by Diego de Salcedo to send to Jamaica. Méndez himself sailed to Spain with Columbus's letters to the sovereigns. The survivors sailed for La Española on June 29. The voyage was long and difficult because of adverse winds and current and because the ship leaked so badly they had trouble keeping her afloat. They arrived in Santo Domingo on August 13. Ovando pretended joy at seeing the Admiral but set the Porras brothers free, a better indication of his feelings. Neither was ever punished for the mutiny. On September 12, Columbus, his son, his brother, and twenty-two others began another long and arduous journey, this time home to Spain. The mainmast broke on October 19, but Columbus and Bartolomé were able to fashion another out of one of the yards. The crossing took fifty-six days but ended safely at Sanlúcar de Barrameda on November 7, 1504.

The ailing Columbus retired to Seville, waiting to be called to the court. He waited in vain. Queen Isabel died on November 26, 1504, and Columbus was not granted permission to see her before her death. Finally, in May 1505, Columbus traveled by mule to the court, but he received nothing from King Fernando. Christopher Columbus, one of the world's greatest navigators and discoverer of the New World, died in Valladolid on May 20, 1506.

[See also *Columbus the Navigator; Equipment, Clothing, and Rations; Dead Reckoning; Grand Khan; Landfall Controversy; Lawsuits; Line of Demarcation; Navigation; Niña; Pinta; Santa María; Settlements; Ships and Crews;* and biographies of numerous figures mentioned herein.]

BIBLIOGRAPHY

Columbus, Ferdinand. *The Life of the Admiral Christopher Columbus.* Translated and annotated by Benjamin Keen. New Brunswick, N.J., 1959.

Dunn, Oliver C. and James E. Kelley, Jr. *The Diario of Christopher Columbus' First Voyage to America, 1492–1493.* Norman, Okla., 1987.

Fuson, Robert H. *The Log of Christopher Columbus.* Camden, Maine, 1987.

Irving, Washington. *The Life and Voyages of Christopher Columbus and his Companions.* 3 vols. New York, 1849.

Jane, Cecil. *The Voyages of Christopher Columbus.* London, 1930.

MacKie, Charles Paul. *The Last Voyages of the Admiral of the Ocean Sea.* Chicago, 1892.

Morison, Samuel Eliot. *Admiral of the Ocean Sea: A Life of Christopher Columbus.* 2 vols. Boston, 1942.

Nunn, George E. *The Geographical Conceptions of Columbus.* New York, 1924.

Parry, J. H. *The Age of Reconnaissance.* 1963. Berkeley, 1981.

Winsor, Justin. *Christopher Columbus.* Boston, 1892.

WILLIAM LEMOS

W, Z

WALDSEEMÜLLER, MARTIN (c. 1470 – 1519), humanist, scholar, Roman Catholic priest, cartographer, and surveyor. The son of a butcher, Waldseemüller was probably born near Freiburg, Germany. On December 7, 1490, Waldseemüller matriculated at the University of Freiburg but soon interrupted his studies to travel to Basel, probably to work in the print shop of his uncle, Jakob Waldseemüller. At Basel it is believed he became associated with members of the printing community. He subsequently returned to the university and pursued his studies in theology; in time he was ordained a priest of the Diocese of Constance.

Nothing more is known of his career until 1506, when he arrived at Saint-Dié in the Vosges Mountains of northeastern France. Waldseemüller was soon asked to join a small intellectual circle called the Gymnase Vosgien organized by Canon Gauthier Lud, chaplain and secretary to Duke René II of Lorraine. Lud had set the Gymnase to work upon the project of producing a new translation and modern version of the *Geography*, the world atlas of Claudius Ptolemy. At the time of Waldseemüller's arrival, the philosophical circle, in addition to Lud, consisted of: Lud's nephew, Nicolas Lud; Jean Basin de Sandaucourt, a colleague and vicar of the church of Notre-Dame; and Canon Mathias Ringmann, a skilled translator of Latin and Greek. Waldseemüller, with his extensive knowledge of geography and ability to design and print maps, provided the additional skills needed for the project.

How Waldseemüller became acquainted with Lud is not known; perhaps Lud learned about him in Strasbourg in the print shop of Johann Grüninger, or it may have been there that Waldseemüller learned of Lud's project for an atlas and obtained an introduction. In any event, Lud presented the young canon to the duke of Lorraine as "a man most knowledgeable about these matters," who was willing to work as a printer in Lud's home on the projected atlas. Following the practice of humanists of the time, Waldseemüller adopted a Greek form of his name, Hylacomylus or Ilacomilus, meaning "the miller of the lake in the forest," which was a literal translation of his name in German.

The scholars had already begun work on the atlas when the duke received from Lorenzo Pier Francesco de' Medici several marine charts depicting the newly discovered lands of the New World in addition to a French translation of the *Mundus novus,* Amerigo Vespucci's letter describing his four voyages. Lud promptly decided not only to incorporate information about the newly discovered lands into the atlas but also to make the discoveries known by other means. Work on the atlas was put aside temporarily, and the Gymnase set to work to produce a world map featuring the new lands. At the same time Basin de Sandaucourt was asked by the duke to translate the Vespucci letter into Latin for publication.

For an introduction to the world map and the atlas, Waldseemüller and Ringmann wrote a small tract on cosmography relating to the geography illustrated by the maps. This work, *Cosmographiae introductio cum quibus dam geometriae ac astronomiae principiis ad eam rem necessariis. Insuper quattuor Amerigo Vespuccii navigationes* (An introduction to cosmography with several elements of geometry and astronomy required for this science, and the four voyages of Amerigo Vespucci), was first published at Saint-Dié in April 1507, and four editions appeared before the end of the year. In his text Waldseemüller suggested that the new lands, which formed the fourth part of the world, should be named "Amerigo" or "America" to honor Amerigo Vespucci, whom he believed had discovered them. The little volume was widely distributed, and as a consequence the name "America" for the New World became generally accepted.

Next Waldseemüller produced a set of twelve gores, or triangular sections, for a terrestrial globe in which the name "America" was also incorporated, and he then designed a sea chart in which the name was again included. Entitled *Orbis typis juxta hydrographorum traditionem* (An image of the world [drawn] after those of sea charts), the chart apparently was not distributed, although it was later included in the atlas produced at Saint-Dié, but with the name "America" deleted.

Waldseemüller then turned to the design for a world map, the *Universalis cosmographia secunda Ptholemei traditionem et Americi Vespuccii aliorum que lustrationes* (A drawing of the whole earth following the tradition of Ptolemy and the travels of Amerigo Vespucci and others). Once more it featured the name "America" in the section that later was identified as South America. The map was produced in twelve large sheets reportedly in an edition of a thousand copies.

Between 1507 and 1516 Waldseemüller designed a great number of maps. In 1511 he tried unsuccessfully to interest Duke Antoine in his cartographical projects and dedicated to him the first printed wall map of central Europe, *Carta itineraria Europae*, for which Ringmann

compiled a descriptive text. A particularly interesting feature of this map is the presence on the lower border of a drawing of a compass showing magnetic declination, attesting to Waldseemüller's familiarity with a scientific phenomenon that until then had been little noted.

When the Saint-Dié edition of the *Geography* was finally published in 1513 it was not with the patronage of the duke, but at the expense of two private citizens of Strasbourg. That Waldseemüller was informed about surveying and the scientific instrumentation of his time is reflected in the detailed maps of Lorraine and the Upper Rhine he produced for the *Geography* and in a surveying instrument it is believed he invented and that was illustrated in a woodcut accompanying his treatise *Architecture et perspective rudimenta*. The significance of this instrument, which Waldseemüller named the polimetrum, lies in the fact that it was the earliest application of the principle of the theodolite to a surveying instrument and that it was the first European prototype of the theodolite, commonly used in surveying for traversing and for the simultaneous measurement of vertical and horizontal angles. It is probable that Leonard Digges learned of this instrument and from it derived his own invention of the theodolitus, which he described in his *First Book of Pantometria* (c. 1550).

In 1514 Waldseemüller was appointed cleric of the

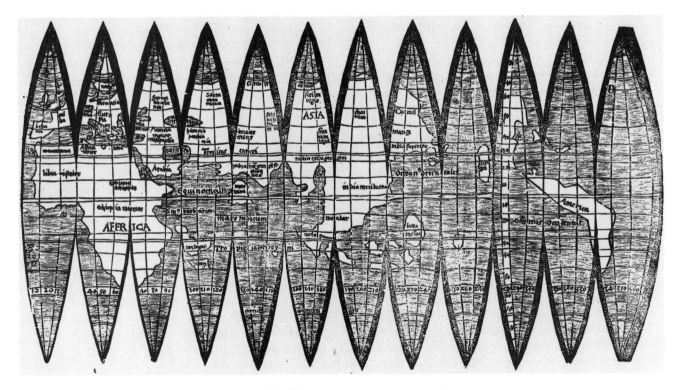

WALDSEEMÜLLER GLOBE GORES. Woodcut, Saint-Dié, 1507. The name *America* appears at right.

Diocese of Constance for the canonry at Saint-Dié, but continued his cartographical work. He produced a map of the world published in Gregor Reisch's *Margarita Philosophica nova* (1515) and in 1516 designed a large marine wall map, *Carta marina navigatoria,* which included important changes from the world map of 1507. Waldseemüller was asked by the Strasbourg printer Johann Grüninger to prepare German inscriptions for the map and to supply it with a full illustrated text in German. But before he was able to complete this task, or a new smaller version of Ptolemy's atlas he had planned, Waldseemüller died in his canon house at Saint-Dié on March 16, 1519.

BIBLIOGRAPHY

Avezac de Castera-Macaya, M. Armand P. d'. *Martin Hylacomylus Waldsemüller: Ses ouvrages et ses collaborateurs voyage d'exploration et de découvertes à travers quelques épitres dédicatoires préfaces et opuscules en prose et en vers du commencement du XVIᵉ siècle. Notes, causeries et digressions bibliographiques et autres par un géographe bibliophile.* Paris, 1867. Reprint, Amsterdam, 1980.

Bagrow, Leo. "*Carta itineraria Europae* Martini Ilacomili, 1511." *Imago Mundi* 11 (1954): 149–150 and plate.

Fischer, Josef, and Franz von Wieser. *The Oldest Map with the Name America of the Year 1507 and the Carta Marina of the Year 1516 by M. Waldseemüller (Ilacomilus).* Innsbruck and London, 1903.

Kish, George. "Waldseemüller, Martin." In vol. 14 of *The Dictionary of Scientific Biography.* Edited by Charles C. Gillispie. New York, 1976.

Stevenson, E. L. "Martin Waldseemüller and the Early Lusitano Germanic Cartography of the New World." *Bulletin of the American Geographical Society* 36 (1904): 193–215.

Taylor, E. G. R. "A Regional Map of the Early Sixteenth Century." *The Geographical Journal* 71 (1928): 475–478.

SILVIO A. BEDINI

WEATHER AND WIND. Wind was the fuel that powered Columbus's voyages of discovery. His ability to take advantage of favorable winds and avoid the worst effects of unfavorable winds and weather contributed to his success as an explorer.

The Trade Winds. In planning his westward route, Columbus made perhaps his most important meteorological decision: to cross the Atlantic Ocean far enough to the south to take advantage of the northeasterly trade winds, with their typical speeds of four to sixteen knots. The northern limit of the trade-wind belt shifts with the season, ranging from about 30° N in January to 35° N in July. The southern limit of the trades shifts from near the equator in January to about 10° N in July. The trades are the world's steadiest wind system. Between 50 and 80 percent of the time the wind direction is within forty-five degrees of the most frequent wind direction. The trade

winds originate over the subtropical region of high surface pressure centered over the North Atlantic at 33° N 25° W in January and 36° N 37° W in July. The exact position of the high-pressure center can vary, and it can even develop two separate centers. When displaced to the east, it is known as the Azores high; when displaced to the west, it is known as the Bermuda high. Surface air flows outward from the center of high pressure toward the doldrums, the region of lower pressure closer to the equator. This equatorward flow in the trade-wind region is deflected to the right as a result of the rotation of the earth; this deflection, called the Coriolis effect, gives the trades their northeasterly direction over the North Atlantic Ocean.

The region occupied by the trade winds, while occasionally traversed by storms, is dominantly an area of fair weather. Skies can be exceptionally clear, though on occasion dust from the Sahara Desert travels across the Atlantic Ocean as a visible haze aloft. Average temperatures range from 68 to 80 degrees Fahrenheit (20 to 27 degrees Celsius), a few degrees lower than the ocean surface. Gentle sinking motions through the depth of the atmosphere in the trade-wind region inhibit the upward air motions needed for the development of storm systems. This sinking extends downward to within 6,000 feet of the surface, providing a lid that caps the growth of cumulus clouds in the trades; this cap is called the trade wind inversion. Overall, the relatively high pressure and sinking air motions make the trade-wind region over the North Atlantic an oceanic desert.

Even though the cumulus clouds that form beneath the trade-wind inversion are comparatively shallow (bases near 2,000 feet and tops usually less than 10,000 feet) the taller clouds poke through the inversion and can produce occasional showers. Trade-wind cumuli have many large cloud droplets that grow by colliding with and collecting smaller droplets until they eventually fall out of the clouds as raindrops. This warm-rain process differs from the typical mid-latitude or cold-rain process, which involves the systematic growth of small ice particles at lower temperatures and greater heights.

Local Wind Systems. Once Columbus reached the New World, his skills as a mariner were tested regularly as he sailed among islands that set up their own local-wind systems. These local winds include the land-sea breeze and, where local topography includes hills and mountains, the mountain-valley wind. Both types of local winds are caused by the daily cycle of heating and cooling over land.

Air temperature changes more during the course of the day over land than over water, as water maintains a more constant temperature than land. By late morning the land has warmed enough to set up a circulation in which air rises over the land, flows seaward aloft, and is replaced at low levels by the cool sea breeze, which blows landward

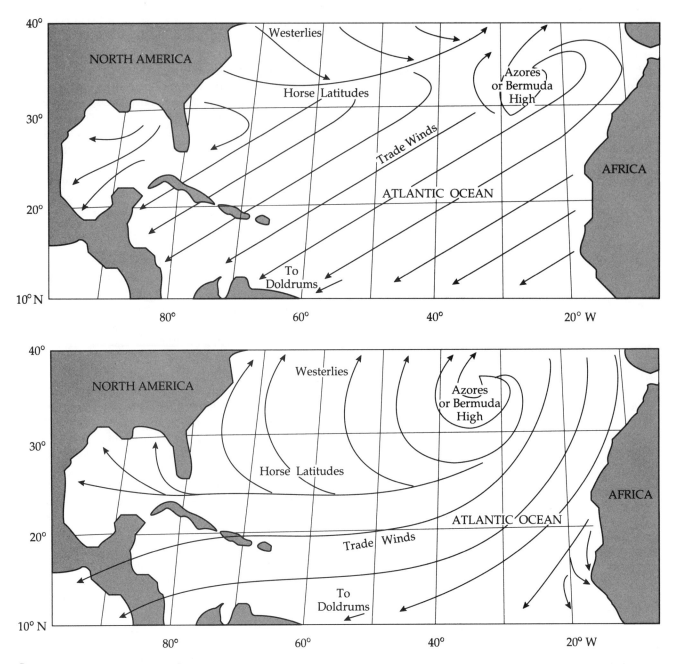

PREVAILING WINDS OVER THE WATERS COLUMBUS SAILED. Arrows show the prevailing wind directions for January *(above)* and July *(below)*. By traveling westward south of latitude 30° N, Columbus was able to take advantage of the northeasterly trade winds and the westward currents they generate. The trade winds originate near latitude 35° N in the clockwise wind flow from a high-pressure center located near longitude 25° W in January and near 35° W in July. On his eastward voyages, sailing north of latitude 30° N, Columbus was able to take advantage of prevailing westerly winds.

from the sea. At night, when the sea is warmer than the land, the direction of the circulation is reversed, and at the surface the land breeze blows seaward. The land breeze assisted Columbus's early-morning departures from islands in the Caribbean Sea. Likewise, he avoided a

dangerous lee shore by not making landings during those daytime hours when the sea breeze was strongest.

The mountain-valley wind system also shifts from day to night. During the daytime, air flows up the slope of the terrain where the mountains and hills are elevated sources

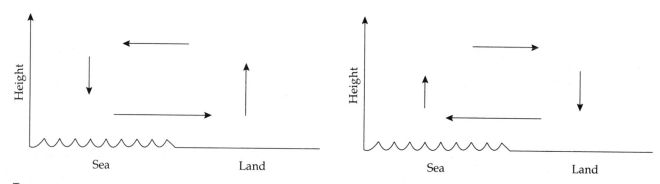

THE LAND AND SEA BREEZES. The daily circulation of air in coastal areas. By late morning the sea breeze *(left)* blows from the water onto the land. The sea breeze is part of a circulation that also includes rising air motion over the land, sinking air motion over the water, and, at higher altitudes, a return flow from land toward the water. At night and in the early morning hours, the circulation is reversed *(right)*, and the land breeze blows from the land toward the water. Columbus avoided the sea breeze and took advantage of the land breeze when he landed at and departed from islands.

of heat. At night, cooling reverses this airflow to downward drainage. The mountain-valley wind system and the land-sea breeze can reinforce each other. When large-scale winds like the trades are weak, local winds predominate. In the presence of the trade winds, local winds can either reinforce or oppose the trades, depending on the orientation of sea and land. Whenever the combination of wind flows sets up convergence of winds from different directions near the surface, showers are more likely.

Records show that Columbus saw a waterspout. This meteorological phenomenon is not especially rare over the Gulf of Mexico and the Caribbean Sea, particularly when water temperatures are relatively warm. Waterspouts occur beneath cumulus clouds, usually those large enough to produce rain. Part of a rotating wind flow within the cloud that extends below cloud base, sucking up sea spray in a visible funnel, a waterspout can overturn small boats and cause damage on the decks of larger vessels. Winds at the center of a waterspout can be as strong as one hundred knots.

Tropical Storms and Hurricanes. Tropical storms (maximum sustained winds of thirty-four to sixty-three knots) and hurricanes (winds of sixty-four knots or more) occur each year in the waters Columbus sailed, and he encountered three during his voyages of discovery. Over the tropical North Atlantic and the Caribbean Sea, tropical storms usually form over warm ocean waters between 7° N and 30° N during the months from June until November. South of 25° N, the average hurricane moves northwestward at a speed of eight to twelve knots, steered by easterly winds aloft. North of 25° N, storms tend to curve back to the east under the influence of westerlies aloft.

These violent storms present special hazards for ships at sea and in port because of the high winds and seas they generate. Although the strongest winds and heaviest rains occur in the wall of the eye just outside the calm central eye of the hurricane, gale force winds may extend hundreds of kilometers outward in spiral bands of thunderstorms. Some portions of the storm are more dangerous than others. In the Northern Hemisphere, the right

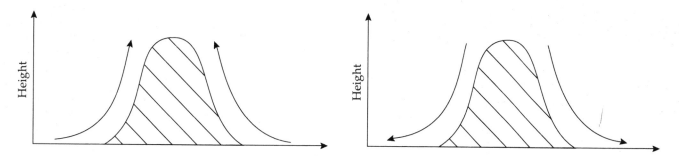

THE MOUNTAIN AND VALLEY BREEZES. The daily circulation of air in mountainous areas. During daytime hours the mountain breeze blows up the slope as the land heats *(left)*. At night, when the land on the slope cools, the valley breeze blows down the slope *(right)*. The mountain and valley breezes can augment the land and sea breezes. Columbus encountered such winds when he sailed into harbors of the Canary Islands, the Cape Verde Islands, and various Caribbean islands.

forward and rear quadrants contain the strongest winds because of the forward speed of the storm and the counterclockwise rotation of the winds around the storm center. The storm surge, a high sea driven shoreward by strong winds, is a particular danger on and just off shore. High tides and strong local currents can augment the storm surge.

Weather and Wind North of the Trades. While the trade winds greatly favored Columbus's journeys, his voyages were not immune to the influences of winds and weather north of the trades. During the winter season, strong cold fronts occasionally move southeastward off the North American continent. Although the arctic air behind these fronts has been considerably warmed by the time it reaches the Caribbean Sea, these northers are sometimes accompanied by showers, sudden wind shifts, and gusty winds from the northeast through northwest, as well as cooler temperatures and clear skies.

Over the open ocean, Columbus skirted the northern edge of the trades on his westward voyages. There he occasionally encountered the horse latitudes, just north of the trades, where winds are light and variable. This region was so named on account of the animals that died there during voyages of discovery and settlement when ships were becalmed in the light winds.

On his return voyages to Europe, Columbus traveled a more northerly route than on the westward voyages. In so doing, he avoided beating to windward against the trade winds and the prevailing ocean currents for part of the journey. At the more northerly latitudes, he encountered the prevailing westerlies. These are not as steady as the trades, but can be disturbed by extratropical weather systems with high winds and seas. Without a barometer, Columbus had only the signs of the clouds and the swell traveling ahead of storms approaching from the west to warn of difficult weather conditions to come.

An extratropical cyclone has a counterclockwise circulation that can be observed over a thousand miles from the center of low pressure. The fronts that extend outward from the low pressure center usually have marked wind shifts and stormy weather, particularly along and just ahead of the cold front. Such fronts stretch far southward and westward from the storm center, to latitudes south of 35°N in winter, and travel from west to east at speeds up to twenty-five knots or more. The rainbands along cold fronts can contain lines of showers with intense rainfall, gale-force winds, and high seas. Columbus encountered one such storm near the end of his first return voyage.

It speaks highly of the skill of Columbus as a mariner that, without modern meteorological and navigational instruments, he accomplished four transatlantic voyages, while encountering nearly the complete range of weather and wind conditions.

BIBLIOGRAPHY

Brooks, Charles F. "Two Winter Storms Encountered by Columbus in 1493 Near the Azores." *Bulletin of the American Meteorological Society* 22, no. 8 (1941): 303–309.

Crutcher, H. L., and R. G. Quayle. *Mariners Worldwide Climatic Guide to Tropical Storms at Sea.* Washington, D.C., 1974.

Fuson, Robert H., ed. and trans. *The Log of Christopher Columbus.* Camden, Me., 1987.

Hastenrath, Stefan, and Peter J. Lamb. *Climatic Atlas of the Tropical Atlantic and Eastern Pacific Oceans.* Madison, Wis., 1977.

Morison, Samuel Eliot. *Admiral of the Ocean Sea: A Life of Christopher Columbus.* 2 vols. Boston, 1942.

Morison, Samuel Eliot, ed. *Journals and Other Documents on the Life and Voyages of Christopher Columbus.* New York, 1963.

Palmén, Erik, and Chester W. Newton. *Atmospheric Circulation Systems: Their Structure and Physical Interpretation.* New York, 1969.

Peterson, Richard E. "Waterspout Statistics for Nassau, Bahamas." *Journal of Applied Meteorology* 17, no. 4 (1978): 444–448.

Riehl, Herbert. *Tropical Meteorology.* New York, 1954.

COLLEEN A. LEARY

WEST INDIES. The name "West Indies" was given by the Europeans in the early sixteenth century to the chain of islands that stretches in a great arc about 3,200 kilometers (2,000 miles) long from Florida to the South American coast. They saw the islands as the counterpart to the "East Indies," which they reached by sailing east from Europe, and did not at first realize that they formed part of a distinct continent; they also made the mistake of calling the inhabitants "Indians," a misnomer that has survived.

The West Indies consist of the four Greater Antilles (Cuba, Jamaica, Hispaniola, and Puerto Rico) in the west and the innumerable Lesser Antilles along the eastern rim. All these islands lie on the line of an ancient range of mountains, and they are still subject to earthquakes. In the Lesser Antilles, there is a sort of double line of islands, the ones on the Atlantic side, like Anguilla and Barbados, being relatively flat, and the ones on the Caribbean side, like Grenada and Dominica, being very mountainous. All the Lesser Antilles are small, with short rivers; some are edged with fertile plains.

The West Indian islands enjoy a moderate climate, for although they lie within the tropics, the surrounding ocean moderates temperatures. However, they are subject to hurricanes, storms of devastating force that generally sweep in from the southeast and can cause very heavy damage. On the rainy sides of the islands great forests once grew, but on Hispaniola and to a lesser extent Jamaica and Cuba, these forests have been largely de-

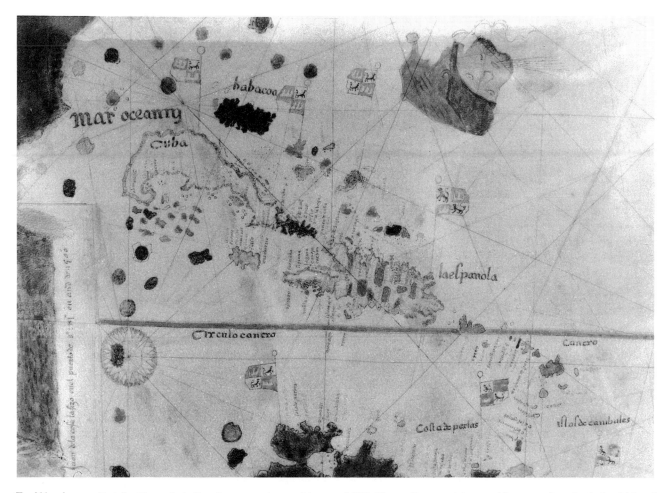

THE WEST INDIES. Detail of Juan de la Cosa's manuscript world map of 1500. The earliest surviving world map to show both the Old and New Worlds.

stroyed, which has produced a heavily eroded and dry landscape.

The West Indies were populated in a process that proceeded from the southeast to the northwest, along the line of the strongly prevailing winds and currents. Out of Venezuela came successive waves of immigrants, descendants of those peoples who originated in Asia and had long before entered the American continent in the northwest. The oldest groups still identifiable in the fifteenth century were the Ciboney and Guanahatabey, by then confined to the western end of Cuba. Throughout the rest of the Greater Antilles were the Taínos, a branch of the Arawak family. The Lesser Antilles were the home of the fierce Caribs, who when Columbus arrived were in the process of harrying the Taínos from their homes in Puerto Rico and slowly driving them westward.

It is extremely difficult to come to any firm conclusions about the populations of these native groups. The ac-

counts written by the Spaniards relied on a fairly superficial acquaintance with island societies, which in any case were rapidly reduced by the European intrusion. Archaeological investigations have given us some idea of the geographical distribution of the indigenous villages, but no very accurate notions as to their populations, since the structures have all perished and numbers have to be assessed largely from the size of kitchen middens, which may have grown in size over many years.

Here and there in the islands and on the mainland there survive groups of people closely related to the indigenous inhabitants; from these, and from the early European accounts, it is possible to have quite a good idea about how they lived. If we remain ignorant about their total numbers—which some authorities have put as high as six million—one thing is certain: the arrival of the Europeans was a demographic disaster that quite soon claimed the lives of virtually all the original inhabitants.

[See also *Cuba; Española, La; Jamaica; Puerto Rico; Indian America*, articles on *Arawaks and Caribs, Island Caribs,* and *Taínos*.]

BIBLIOGRAPHY

Milanich, Jerald T., and Susan Milbrath, eds. *First Encounters: Spanish Explorations in the Caribbean and the United States, 1492–1570*. Gainesville, 1989.
Morison, Samuel Eliot. *The European Discovery of America: The Southern Voyages A.D. 1492–1616*. New York, 1974.
Sauer, Carl Ortwin. *The Early Spanish Main*. Berkeley, 1966.

DAVID BUISSERET

WILL OF COLUMBUS. See *Writings*, article on *Last Will and Testament*.

WIND. See *Weather and Wind*.

WOMEN IN THE AMERICAS. The discovery of America was a process that began in different places at different times. In four transatlantic voyages Columbus made a brave beginning, but finding and laying claim to all that the New World had to offer required that many discoverers embark on voyages or mount up for *entradas*. Promising discoveries were followed by wars of conquest and settlements supported by Indian tribute and labor; disappointing discoveries were redeemed by taking slaves. Like Noah filling the ark, Columbus collected natives to display as curiosities, kidnapping equal numbers of males and females.

Encountering the nakedness of Arawak and Tupinambá women, discoverers in the Caribbean and Brazil thought of marvels, subhuman species such as mermaids, and Eves in new Edens. From a distance, theologians debated the rights of barbarians, but they did not question the self-evident propositions that in the natural order of things an inferior was meant to serve and a woman to be governed.

The first Spaniards to see the wonders of Mesoamerica and the Andes reported approvingly that the women of these advanced cultures were veiled and silent and did not look men in the face. Spanish etiquette, part Moorish, called for women of quality *(de calidad)* to live in near seclusion. They sat on pillows, not chairs. In the street, they donned the black mantle of the *tapada*, covering everything but one eye.

An earlier, Visigothic influence, was apparent in Spanish law. Partible inheritance was the norm. Males and females inherited equally, and unless the estate was entailed no one heir could be favored with more than "a third and a fifth." Marital gains were community property. The wife's dowry and *arras* (bridegift from the husband) remained her own. With the husband's consent, often guaranteed in the marriage contract, the wife could manage property and conduct business as freely as a widow. When her relatives failed to provide her with financial security, a woman of quality turned to her peers. To protect gentlewomen against loss of status, wealthy patrons made bequests for dowries and founded nunneries, and many a resourceful widow, citing the services of her husband and kinsmen, appealed to the king.

Paternalism, however, had its limits. As conquests in the Americas gained momentum, the actions of the conquerors regressed to those of a warrior society, treating women as the prizes of war. From the imperial halls of Mexico and Peru to the council houses of La Florida, women were deemed commodities. It was an insult to call a warrior a woman. Exchanged as pledges, tribute, or slaves, women had little to lose by casting their lot with the conquerors. One who did so was Cortés's translator and mistress, Doña Marina, known as Malinche and now maligned as the epitome of racial treachery.

The vanquishing of native Americans was first military, then sexual; the men defeated in battle were humiliated a second time when the women were ravished. In some cases the sexual conquest was legitimized. A conqueror of common origins could marry an emperor's daughter in Mexico or Peru and lay hands on her estate; in Paraguay, he could practice polygamy and make labor demands on his wives' relatives. More commonly, however, conquerors acquired one or more concubines—the common form of union with a woman of lesser rank in Spain—and sired a generation of mistrusted mestizos.

Consolidation followed discovery and conquest. Once a taxable region was securely held, Crown and Church initiated steps to curb the random violence of men of war and sanction a system of structured inequality. During the first colonial century, 440,000 Spaniards emigrated to the New World, primarily to the silver-producing colonies. Three out of ten of these emigrants were women, in contrast to the one in ten Portuguese who went to Brazil. Only New England would attract a higher proportion of female colonists than did Mexico and Peru.

Transplanted to the American viceroyalties, Iberian societies, accepting deference as natural, acquired a new dimension, namely caste. A white elite presided over tribute-paying Indian peasants and traded in African slaves; it outlawed interracial marriage, for if an *esclavo* married an *india* his children were free. Extending the meaning of *limpieza de sangre* (purity of blood) from its original sense of religious orthodoxy and *hidalgo* status to apply to racial distinctions, the elite further hardened the social boundaries with caste restrictions on the avenues to power: the bureaucracies, the professions, and the religious orders. Consequently, mestizos and mulattoes, male and female, sought the greater freedom of the frontiers.

Marriage had long been regulated under canon law as a sworn contract. In the mid-sixteenth century the Council of Trent reaffirmed matrimony to be a sacrament, and sexual acts outside of marriage to be sins. Confessors made valiant efforts to eradicate polygamy, adultery, fornication, concubinage, onanism, and sexual daydreams, while counseling the married to pay one another the "matrimonial debt." Nonetheless, commoners continued to regard marriage as a privilege of the elite; more than half of the children brought in for baptism were born of consensual unions.

The elite combined a strict sense of public honor with private flexibility. A promise of marriage often initiated sexual relations; a "protected pregnancy" did not affect the bride's reputation. There were also degrees of illegitimacy. For example, an *hijo natural*, born of unmarried parents, could be legitimized postnatally, unlike an *hijo adulterino*, a foundling, or the child of a priest.

Nunneries offered respectable seclusion for abused or erring wives, motherless girls, elderly women, and spinsters. While *Indias, mestizas,* or *mulatas* could be lay sisters, only a member of the white elite could profess as a nun. A convent often housed several women of the same family. Many nuns were socially and economically active, owning slaves, conducting their business out of convent parlors, and entertaining visitors with confections and evenings of music. For a few, such as the poet Juana Inés de la Cruz (the nun Sor Juana), the convent offered an opportunity to pursue an intellectual life.

The easy life of the elite was supported by Indian tribute and labor. The burden of tribute fell with inordinate heaviness on the women, who were the ones who wove the cotton *mantas* and picked the tiny cochineal insects off nopal cacti, and village quotas were seldom adjusted to reflect the decline in native population. The various labor drafts disrupted families: the repartimiento took the men to work in the mines and on public projects, and the semilegal *servicio personal* took the women to cities for domestic service. In order to escape both tribute and compulsory labor, men hired themselves out for wages at the mines, and the women stayed on in the cities, where they opened small stores and taverns, took in laundry and boarders, and acted as healers and midwives.

On the frontiers, the discovery of America continued. Some native societies were matrilineal, with the children belonging to their mother's clan. Some were uxorilocal, with the husband living in the wife's hometown. In some, a gender-based division of labor between hunting and farming led to nomadic husbands and sedentary wives,

with women owning the houses and fields. Other than the people themselves, these frontier areas had few resources, and as Crown and Church were united in opposition to the practice of making war to take slaves, the conquest came to a standstill. Spanish settlements on the edges of empire attempted to establish elites, but they had little revenue to support them. Nonwhite women predominated, and as always, did what they had to to survive.

[See also *Pacification, Conquest, and Genocide.*]

BIBLIOGRAPHY

Altman, Ida. *Emigrants and Society: Extremadura and Spanish America in the Sixteenth Century.* Berkeley, 1989.

Gutiérrez, Ramón A. *When Jesus Came, the Corn Mothers Went Away: Marriage, Sexuality, and Power in New Mexico 1500–1846.* Stanford, 1991.

Lavrin, Asunción, ed. *Latin American Women: Historical Perspectives.* Westport, Conn., 1978.

Lavrin, Asunción, ed. *Sexuality and Marriage in Colonial Latin America.* Lincoln, Neb., 1989.

AMY TURNER BUSHNELL

WRITINGS. [This entry includes five articles on Columbus's literary remains:

An Overview
Journal
Letters
Marginalia
Book of Prophecies
Last Will and Testament

For further discussion of documentary sources concerning Columbus, see *Bibliography; Book of Privileges; Library of Columbus; Museums and Archives.*]

An Overview

Christopher Columbus was a prolific and often eloquent reporter of his voyages and business affairs. About one hundred pieces of Columbus's writings have survived in various forms. When these are published in modern format, they comprise about 320 pages of material. Columbus wrote everything in the Castilian language, with the exception of some Latin notes in the margins of his Latin books. Even when he wrote to Italians, such as his brother Bartolomé and the city councilmen of Genoa, he wrote in Castilian. His Castilian, however, was heavily mixed with other languages: Portuguese, Latin, Italian, and the Mediterranean sailors' pidgin, "Levantisca." The earliest of his writings are some marginal notes (postils) he wrote in books that he owned and that his son Fernando preserved in his own much larger library, known as the

Biblioteca Colombina. None of these books owned by Columbus was published before 1484, although we do not know when Columbus bought the books nor when he wrote the postils. His last writings were dictated to clerks in Valladolid on May 19, 1506, the day before his death.

Forty-two of Columbus's short writings have survived in the original; they are letters and notes in his own handwriting or official documents written by a clerk and signed by Columbus. Despite the fact that Columbus never wrote Castilian or any other language correctly, his holographs are forceful, pungent, and sometimes even eloquent. These short, original writings reveal a great deal about Columbus the loving father of two sons and Columbus the hardheaded businessman. The official documents are written in correct Castilian, because Columbus was dictating to Castilian clerks who were trained to write in language that would be unambiguous and binding in a court of law. These official documents reveal Columbus the administrator of America's first European colonies.

The longest and most important of Columbus's writings are his reports on three of his voyages to America. These are Columbus's diary (Diario) of the first voyage (1492–1493) and a long letter (Primera carta de América) to King Fernando and Queen Isabel written during the return passage. He left no report on his second voyage (1493–1496), so for that voyage we depend on several reports written by passengers. Columbus also wrote a report on his third voyage (1498–1500), and a letter to the monarchs reporting on his fourth voyage (1502–1504).

None of Columbus's writings about his voyages and explorations survives in his own handwriting or in notarized copies. Bartolomé de las Casas included large parts of them in his invaluable history of America. Scholars now believe that Las Casas was a meticulous copyist of what he included, although we do not know how much he left out. Most of Columbus's other writings have come down to us in copies that were not made by clerks and, therefore, raise questions of authenticity, completeness, and accuracy.

The tone of Columbus's writings changed dramatically during his career. Until 1497, he wrote to the monarchs as he would to business partners, expressing optimism in their joint enterprise and gratitude for the confidence the monarchs had in him. During the third voyage, however, his writing fills with complaints about other explorers, the Spanish settlers, the monarchs' loss of confidence in him, and his own poor health. Ironically, these changes occur as his writing becomes more purely Castilian, with fewer and fewer words and spellings from other languages.

BIBLIOGRAPHY

Varela, Consuelo. "Prólogo, edición, y notas." In *Christopher Columbus, Textos y documentos completos: Relaciones de viajes, cartas, y memoriales.* Edited by Consuelo Varela. Madrid, 1984.

HELEN NADER

Journal

Until early in the nineteenth century, students of Columbus's first voyage had few details of the journey at their disposal. Other than the biography of Columbus attributed to his son Fernando Colón, which was published posthumously in Italian in 1571, there were only a few sources. Foremost among these was Columbus's letter to the Spanish court written on the return voyage, which, although rich in rodomontade, was meager on precise details. In addition, there were the brief accounts that opened the relations of Pietro Martire d'Anghiera (Peter Martyr), Gonzalo Fernández de Oviedo, and others.

This state of affairs ended in 1825 when Martín Fernández de Navarrete published a text he had discovered in the archives of the Duke of Infantado around 1790. The new source was sixty-seven folios in length and consisted of a detailed day-by-day account of the first voyage from the time the three ships left Palos in August 1492 until their return more than seven months later.

The new source, however, was not a shipboard log, even though it had that appearance. Rather it was a paraphrase, perhaps abridged, in the handwriting of Bartolomé de las Casas, whose own *Historia de las Indias* (completed by 1560 but not published until 1875) in turn paraphrased this source, which has come to be referred to as the journal, or Diario. About 20 percent of the Diario is not a paraphrase of some original, at least not by Las Casas, who presented it as "the very words" of Columbus. This portion of the text is characterized by being in the first person and the present tense. The degree to which the remaining four-fifths of the Diario departs from any original source is unknown. Nor do we know whether it was Las Casas, an earlier copyist, or both who changed the text.

Navarrete's edition, which introduced the Diario to the scholarly world and continued to be the basis for all transcriptions until 1892 and even later, was not an exact transcription of the holograph manuscript. Instead, Navarrete modernized and normalized the text by adding punctuation, changing the spelling, inserting paragraphing, and "correcting" words and phrases that he thought must be in error. He also attempted to fill in the various brief lacunae that exist in the Diario.

All further editions and translations of the Diario that were based on Navarrete's edition, of course, repeated his departures from the text, and added to them either deliberately or through carelessness. It was not until 1892 that, in honor of the quatercentenary of the discovery, a new and much more exact transcription was prepared under the direction of Cesare de Lollis. This edition, known as the *Raccolta* edition after the series of Columbian texts in which it appeared, came far closer to reproducing the manuscript text and, in addition, provided numerous textual notes as well as passages from the works of Fernando and Las Casas that dealt with the first voyage. This last attribute of the *Raccolta* edition has never been repeated, and so the edition retains value to the present.

Further editions and translations well into the twentieth century relied on Navarrete or on the *Raccolta,* but until 1976 none of them improved on the status quo. In that year Manuel Alvar published a two-volume edition of the Diario. In the first volume he provided a retranscription of the exact text, and in the second, a modernized version along the lines of, but superior to, those of Navarrete and others. To the first volume Alvar added extensive linguistic notes, and to the second, similarly extensive historical and geographical annotations. In the process he created the best ensemble edition then available.

Several further editions of the Diario were published in Spain and Italy during the 1980s, most of them better than any of the pre-1976 editions. Although these were not all equally satisfactory, they demonstrated that at long last the critical textual editing of the Diario according to modern standards had come to be regarded as a necessary prelude to studying the first voyage.

A marked advance in this progression was the diplomatic transcription and English translation prepared by Oliver Dunn and James E. Kelley, Jr. (1989). Although Alvar had for the first time scrupulously indicated all the changes, additions, crossovers, and marginalia in the Diario (about twelve hundred in all), he did so in his notes rather than graphically within the text itself. Dunn and Kelley, on the other hand, displayed the placement of these materials in a way that replicated the manuscript as closely as possible by means of modern typography. This innovation had the advantage of allowing users to see easily how Las Casas wrote out the text he had before him.

In addition, Dunn and Kelley's translation is the most literal yet, in any language, as they abandoned the fluid prose of most translations in favor of fidelity to the original text. These advantages combined with a thorough discussion of the paleographical issues, informative, often provocative, notes, and a detailed subject index together with a concordance (neither provided in any previous edition) to provide a valuable supplement to Alvar's edition.

These two editions rendered obsolete all editions and translations published before 1976 and 1989 respectively. Those preparing interpretations of the first voyage must rely on these editions (as well as on the facsimiles published by Carlos Sanz in 1960 and Alvar and Francisco Morales Padrón in 1984) and consult other editions only in the course of historiographical investigations.

The absence of rigorous editions of the Diario is in part responsible for the lack of authoritative studies of the activities of the first voyage, particularly the quest for Columbus's first landfall, an issue that has dominated study of the Diario from the beginning.

Form and Content. The Diario consists of approximately fifty-five thousand words, and many of these have been the object of scrutiny and controversy. In both format and content the Diario lives up to its name. It begins with an extensive prologue in which Columbus promises to investigate and conquer new lands (in Asia, he thought) for the Spanish Crown. Then follows a daily account of the voyage from Spain to the Canaries, from August 3 to August 9, 1492. Columbus remained in the Canaries until September 6, 1492, but the Diario contains no information on this sojourn, although there is some information in Fernando's biography. There is an entry in the Diario for every day from September 6, 1492, until March 15, 1493, except between November 7 and 11, when Columbus was apparently becalmed in a Cuban harbor. There are a few exceptions to the pattern; for instance, the events of October 11 and 12 are included in a single entry dated October 11.

From the perspective of the Diario Columbus's first voyage divides into five parts: September 6 to October 11, or the outward voyage; October 12 to October 27, the landfall and the cruise through the Bahamas to Cuba; October 28 to December 5, when Columbus sailed, first west and then east, along the northern coast of Cuba; December 6 to January 15, as Columbus sailed slowly along the coast of La Española, making frequent stops to inquire of the Indians after precious metals; and January 16 to March 15, the homeward voyage, which included two unscheduled stops, one of three days at Santa María in the Azores and the other for a period of over a week, when Columbus was the reluctant guest of the Portuguese court near Lisbon.

The level of detail the Diario provides varies greatly and is most dense during Columbus's six-week sojourn in La Española. In general, the detail is greatest whenever the Indians are mentioned, which many take to reflect the input of Las Casas into the extant version, although it is likely that Columbus too was interested in this new race, which he found unable to assimilate to his experience and expectations. There are also many passages in the Diario on the physiography of the New World in which Columbus found himself. Much of this is characterized by a degree of exaggeration and bewilderment that makes it difficult to evaluate in terms of matching it to modern conditions.

Of navigational details there is much, although perhaps not as much as might be expected in a shipboard log.

Some believe that this means that either Las Casas or another copyist, or even Columbus himself, omitted much of this material because it was uninteresting or unnecessary, or because of a desire on Columbus's part to keep to himself the details of the route to the New World. That which remains, however, has proved to be of great interest to most modern students of the voyage.

In addition to an apparent lack of navigational details, the Diario appears to be reticent on the matter of the disaffection of the crews, perhaps amounting to mutiny, that all other early accounts of the voyage mention. In contrast, the Diario tells of only a single incident, a few days before landfall, and even then treats it as a minor episode that Columbus had no difficulty in controlling.

On the morning of October 12, Columbus anchored at an island that the Indians seem to have called Guanahani, and which he christened San Salvador. It is all but certain that Guanahani was one of the Bahamas, but there agreement ends: no fewer than nine Bahamian islands (as well as Grand Turk and Caicos) have been advanced as the site of the landfall. This lack of unanimity is due to the fact that Columbus was uncharacteristically reticent in describing Guanahani's attributes in the Diario. He fails, for instance, even to estimate its size—it is referred to as both an "islet" and "a fairly large" island. Moreover, it is described as low-lying and green, with a lagoon "in the middle" as well as a large harbor, all criteria that many islands in the Bahamas can meet.

The remainder of the Diario's account of Columbus's journey through the Bahamas (which is described throughout as being in the words of Columbus and is by far the longest verbatim section) is similarly vague, contradictory, and intermittent. Sometimes intentions are stated but without any indication that they were carried out. Sometimes the ships seem to be in one place at the end of a daily entry and somewhere else at the beginning of the next. Some natural features are specified, only to be contradicted, and very few distances are included at all. In sum this portion of the Diario is marked by a wealth of apparent information, but only a fraction of it turns out to be testable, consistent, or plausible.

Once Columbus reached Cuba, the Diario becomes more integrated but not always more intelligible. Identifying the point at which he first reached Cuba depends entirely on matching his physical description of that place with various modern-day possibilities. Columbus's firm belief that he was on the periphery of the Far East influenced both his perceptions and the way he expressed them; superlatives became more than ever his normal rhetorical fare. Mountains were higher, rivers deeper, and harbors larger than life, as Columbus (or someone else) effectively turned the Diario into a literary rather than a nautical document.

Columbus cruised along the northern coast of Cuba, constantly inquiring of the Indians as to the whereabouts of "the Grand Khan" and associated riches until he reached the eastern end of the island and then crossed to La Española. Of the various cultures Columbus encountered on the first voyage, none impressed him as much as those on La Española. It seemed to him (if the Diario is correct) that he had at last reached an outpost of civilization. The wealth seemed greater, the political authorities more imposing, the population larger. When *Santa María* was beached and wrecked on Christmas Day, Columbus quickly had a fort erected on the site to shelter the men who would have to be left behind. He was certain both that sources of gold were close at hand and that the local ruler was well-disposed toward the opportunities Columbus believed he was offering him. Columbus continued to sail east along La Española until he reached its end, whereupon, although he was told of other interesting locales to the east, he chose to attempt the return voyage.

This, the last leg of the trip, was more eventful than its outbound counterpart. Columbus was forced to experiment with courses in order to catch the westerly winds, and the reduced fleet was subjected to several storms, one of which separated the ships and caused Columbus to fear for his survival. This storm drove *Niña*, under Columbus's command, into Portuguese territory in the Azores. After some conflict with the authorities there, Columbus renewed his voyage, only to be driven into Lisbon harbor and the clutches of his former patron turned enemy João II.

Eventually Columbus convinced João that he had not trespassed on Portuguese rights granted by the Treaty of Alcáçovas in 1479 and was permitted to sail home. Arriving in Palos on March 15, 1493, he dispatched a message to the Spanish court, then at Barcelona, and awaited their summons, which came about a month later. From Columbus's view, the voyage ended only when he received an audience with Fernando and Isabel and claimed his promised rewards.

Textual Questions. The account of the voyage in the Diario, however, ends abruptly with Columbus debarking at Palos. The most crucial question about the Diario is whether work on the shipboard log ceased at the same time. It has generally been the view of modern scholarship that, though the Diario indisputably contains both obvious and suspected errors, as well as its share of unintended distortion, it also reflects to a very great degree the shipboard log. The belief in this case is that Columbus left each entry as it stood and declined to revise earlier entries when later information came to hand, thereby accounting for most of the discrepancies that exist in the Diario. By this interpretation, the principal task of those studying the first voyage is to strip away later incrustations by Las Casas, and possibly by others, and it is widely accepted that these can be recognized in one way or another.

It is the case, for instance, that Las Casas discloses that certain data in the Diario are not Columbus's. This is most obvious when such data are anachronisms, as when Las Casas mentions the Lucayos, the name given to the Bahamas well after 1492, or when he mentions Florida by name, though it had not yet been discovered. Moreover, many of the numerous statements in the Diario about the Indians are of a nature more akin to Las Casas's frequently expressed beliefs than to any views ever expressed by Columbus. Moreover, Las Casas clearly intended that most of the some two hundred marginal notes serve as his own commentary on the text, and he occasionally interjected his own observations directly into the text. But even when these instances are identified and studied, there remains a host of anomalies that ultimately need to be explained as more than slips of the pen.

Opportunities and motives for tinkering with any documents relating to the first voyage arose long before Las Casas came into contact with the text he copied and edited. By the late summer of 1493, any records Columbus had turned over to the Spanish authorities had become political documents. By then Columbus and the Spanish authorities, on the one hand, and the Spanish and Portuguese monarchs, on the other, were already jockeying for position in the geopolitical situation that had unexpectedly arisen. The question is: how early might the log have come to be regarded as having ends other than faithfully representing things done and places seen during the first voyage? If this occurred during the voyage itself, as Columbus began to speculate on his own future role in the discoveries, then he might already have been overhauling the log even before he returned to Spain, perhaps even before he reached Guanahani.

Moreover, we cannot be certain that Columbus surrendered to the Spanish Crown the very log, whether or not revised, that he maintained during the voyage. His relations with Fernando and Isabel had always been brittle and strained; it had been only with great difficulty that he had prised any funds and concessions from them. As early as February 18, the Diario speaks of Columbus's desire to remain "master of the route of the Indies," and it would have been a guileless Columbus indeed who would have turned in the only copy of the log or, for that matter, an exact copy that could be used to circumvent him.

The trail then leads to the copy of the log that was transcribed by royal scribes and returned to Columbus just before he embarked on his second voyage several months after his return. At the time, the Portuguese emissaries were hovering around the Spanish court preparing to make a case that "the Indies" belonged to the Portuguese Crown by right of treaty. It is reasonable to suspect that the Spanish authorities protected themselves to the extent of preparing a special recension of the log (still not yet the Diario) should they have to share it with the Portuguese.

Finally, it is necessary to consider just which one of all these possible copies (and there may have been others) eventually fell into the hands of Las Casas. Unfortunately, there is no way to know this, nor to know whether that copy had not in turn undergone further changes in the sixty years (1552 is the most widely accepted date for the creation of the Diario) after Columbus returned to Spain.

The only copy of any shipboard log, then, that is known to modern scholarship is at least two transcriptions removed from any original. Moreover, the information in any shipboard log was so valuable to several interested parties that it probably underwent changes on behalf of these parties, each of which had ample opportunity. For the moment it is necessary to defer hopes of reconstructing and interpreting Columbus's voyage in precise detail and search for evidences of revision.

One of the many aspects of the Diario's account that has aroused particular interest is the incomplete set of double numbers that are embedded in most of the daily entries for the outward voyage. There an official reckoning of distance traveled each day is accompanied by a lower figure. The latter resulted, says the Diario, from Columbus's desire to allay the fears of the crews as day after day passed with no land in sight. These so-called double distances have been interpreted in various ways; some have suggested that they show that Columbus was temperamentally inclined to dishonesty, whereas others see them as an indication of his sensitivity to the feelings of the crew or as emphasizing his navigational skills.

Whatever the interpretation, few have doubted that these numbers were part of the original shipboard log that were carried forward accurately through several transmissions until Las Casas entered them into the Diario. But there are several problems with this view. The alleged stratagem was deployed too soon to warrant such an explanation. The first false number appears in the entry for September 9, when the ships were only a few days west of the Canaries and before Columbus could have been aware of any need to minimize the distances traveled. The arithmetic of the lower distances does not match up, either proportionately or cumulatively, with other figures recorded in the Diario. Many of these figures are written in Roman numerals, which are otherwise sparingly used. These constitute serious grounds to suspect that one or another of these sets of numbers was added at some point after the outward trip.

According to the Diario, a crew member on *Pinta* sighted land early in the morning of October 12 (other sources, including Oviedo, date the sighting a day earlier). The Diario then adds that, several hours before this, Columbus had seen a mysterious light that was a sign of land or of its imminence. On the basis of this, Columbus claimed and received the reward promised to the individual who first sighted land. The story as it is told in the Diario is implausible in content and strangely placed as well. It may be that it was a later interpolation, although it is common to use this sighting as an argument for or against particular landfalls.

The description of the banners used as part of the possession-taking ceremony on Guanahani is so detailed that it suggests that it too was added for the benefit of readers other than those for whom Columbus was writing, for officials at court would not have required such information. Under the date October 13 we find another entry peculiar in itself and strangely placed. There it is reported that Guanahani was on a line due west from Hierro, the most southwesterly of the Canaries. By consulting his log, Columbus would have noticed that he had spent the equivalent of several days sailing southwest at various points in the journey. Either he had no log to consult then, he misinterpreted its testimony, or this information was added at a later point, perhaps to allay the fears of João II into whose hands Columbus (and the log?) had fallen. Whatever the case, it is evident that this datum is incomprehensible if it is treated as an integral and original part of any log.

In the combined entry for October 11 and 12, Las Casas writes (claiming to quote Columbus) that Columbus observed wounds on the Guanahani Indians, which he "believed and believe" came from Indians raiding from somewhere to the west. This emphatic juxtaposing of past and present tenses is not without counterparts in the Spanish of the time, but does not occur elsewhere in the Diario. It may be that Columbus interpolated the additional "believe" at a later point in order to emphasize that the Guanahani Indians needed protection—Spanish protection—against existing enemies. The word makes the best sense when thought of in this way, but at the same time its presence underscores that Columbus and others had no particular reasons to treat the text of the log and its successors as sacred, but simply as one of several means to desired ends.

Four times during the return trip, storms so imperiled *Niña* that Columbus ordered that lots be drawn for the purpose of determining who would make pilgrimages of thanksgiving should they survive. One chick-pea for each crew member (a total of twenty to twenty-five) was placed into a hat. One of these was marked with a cross and whoever drew the marked pea was obligated to make the required pilgrimage. In three of the four cases Columbus drew the marked pea. The odds against this happening exactly as depicted in the Diario vary according to the

circumstances of the drawing, about which we know nothing, but are at best only 1 in about 1,250. This indicates that some aspects of the stories must have been added later, probably with the purpose of showing that Columbus was marked by divine providence for special distinction, a view held by Fernando in his biography.

These and other instances suggest that it is not inappropriate to suspect that the Diario written by Las Casas in about 1552 differed in many respects from any shipboard log that Columbus kept. By this view, the Diario was the end product of a dynamic text that both influenced and was influenced by the events that surrounded its genesis, a process that took as many as sixty years to complete. This notion is supported by the fact that many diaries in history—including most famously those of Samuel Pepys and Anne Frank—were routinely and extensively revised by their authors and transmitters before being committed to posterity, yet were eventually published in a quotidian format that served to mask that fact.

In addition to this historical perspective, literary and textual critics have begun to turn their attention to the Diario in hopes of understanding more about the nature of the first documented encounter between Europe and America. In this endeavor they devote greater attention to how the Diario expresses itself than to what it says, or to whether there is a demonstrable relationship between its testimony and independently determined reality. This study is beginning to show that, in recounting his experiences on the first voyage to America, Columbus reflected closely the rhetoric of the travel accounts of the Middle Ages, which were often contrived at the metaphorical rather than the empirical level. This is particularly the case with regard to Columbus's attention to the natural world—the people, the flora, the landforms—as he came into contact with it in the West Indies.

In sum, the Diario is an extraordinarily complex text in its discursive fits and starts, its linguistic eclecticism, its panoply of beguiling, yet often elusive, detail, and its Manichean authorial posture. These elements combine to form a text that resists easy and sure analysis more than most historical documents. The application of literary and textual criticism in combination with traditional historical analysis is likely to yield results that advance the knowledge of the character of this, the primary source for knowledge of Columbus's first voyage.

BIBLIOGRAPHY

Campbell, Mary B. *The Witness and the Other World: Exotic European Travel Writing, 400–1600.* Ithaca, N.Y., 1988.
Cioranescu, Alejandro. *Primera biografía de C. Colón: Fernando Colón y Bartolomé de las Casas.* Tenerife, 1960.
Columbus, Christopher. *Diario del descubrimiento.* Edited by Manuel Alvar. 2 vols. Gran Canaria, 1976.
Columbus, Christopher. *The* Diario *of Christopher Columbus's*

First Voyage to America, 1492–1493. Edited and translated by Oliver Dunn and James E. Kelley, Jr. Norman, Okla., 1989.

Columbus, Christopher. Scritti di Cristoforo Colombo. Edited by Cesare de Lollis. 2 vols. Rome, 1892–1894.

Fuson, Robert H. "The diario de Colón: A Legacy of Poor Transcription, Translation, and Interpretation." Terrae Incognitae 15 (1983): 51–75.

Henige, David. "Edited . . . and not Precipitated; Three Recent Editions of Columbus' diario." Terrae Incognitae. Forthcoming.

Henige, David. "Samuel Eliot Morison as Translator and Interpreter of Columbus' diario de a bordo." Terrae Incognitae 20 (1988): 69–88.

Henige, David, and Margarita Zamora. "Text, Context, Intertext: Columbus's diario as Palimpsest." Americas 46 (1989): 17–40.

Morison, Samuel Eliot. "Texts and Translations of the Journal of Columbus's First Voyage." Hispanic American Historical Review 19 (1939): 235–261.

Parker, John. "The Columbus Landfall Problem: A Historical Perspective." Terrae Incognitae 15 (1983): 1–28.

Ramos Pérez, Demetrio. La primera noticia de América. Valladolid, 1986.

Tanselle, G. Thomas. "The Editing of Historical Documents." Studies in Bibliography 31 (1978): 1–56.

Zamora, Margarita. " 'Todas son palabras formales del Almirante': Las Casas y el diario de Colón." Hispanic Review 57 (1989): 25–41.

DAVID HENIGE

Letters

Leaving aside his marginalia, his Book of Prophecies, and his Book of Privileges, we have today about one hundred documents attributed to Columbus. Forty or forty-two of them are autographs, and the remainder consists of various copies drawn in different periods, receipts in the Archives of Protocol, two printed sheets published during the Admiral's lifetime, and twenty-five handwritten transcriptions by Bartolomé de las Casas. The documents may be classified as follows:

1. *Juridical-administrative documents.* Autograph writings include three orders of payment written in the Indies upon returning from his fourth voyage. Among the copies are: (a) the Capitulations, (b) appointment of Bartolomé Colón as lieutenant governor, (c) institution of rights of primogeniture, (d) two contracts, in part with Fonseca and in part with Antonio Mariño and Pedro Salcedo, to sell soap, (e) empowerments to the tutor of his sons, Ximeno de Briviesca, and to his Florentine brother-in-law Francesco de Bardi, and a safe-conduct to Francisco Roldán, and (f) a land distribution letter to Miguel Ballester.

2. *Reports, memorandum books, and records.* In these Columbus writes about a variety of subjects: from memorandums on the way the Indies became populated to a report on how the navigation from Laredo to Flanders should take place on the occasion of the meeting between Princess Juana and Philip, who were to be married. This report was requested by Queen Isabel, who apparently held the Admiral's nautical knowledge in high esteem. The following documents, or their signatures, are autographic: (a) muster roll of the first voyage, (b) memorandum of Antonio Torres, (c) various memorandums on the populations of the Indies, (d) memorandums of offenses, and (e) a memorandum preceding the fourth voyage. Copies by Las Casas are the records of the first and third voyages.

3. *Official correspondence.* Autograph material includes various letters to the Catholic monarchs and one to the queen, two letters to the ambassador Nicoló Oderico, one letter to the San Giorgio Bank in Genoa, letters to Fernando the Catholic and to Philip I and Juana, and two letters to Nicolás de Ovando, governor of La Española. Columbus's letter to Pope Alexander VI is a copy written perhaps by his son Fernando Colón.

4. *Private correspondence.* Eleven letters to Gaspar Gorricio and twelve letters to Columbus's son Diego are autographs. Copies by Las Casas include a letter to Juana de la Torre and the fragment of a letter to his brother Bartolomé.

These documents are preserved in various archives. The archive of the dukes of Veragua, which today is entrusted to the General Archive of the Indies in Seville (Archivo General de Indias), contains sixteen documents; twenty are stored in the ducal Archive of the Casa de Alba in Madrid; one is in the Library of the Academy of History of Madrid; one is in the General Archive of Simancas; and one is in the National Library of Madrid. The Columbus Library of Seville holds the books that Columbus glossed personally as well as a letter to the monarchs, which he copied at the beginning of his Book of Prophecies. Only three autograph letters are kept in Italy; they are deposited in the City Hall of Genoa.

The majority of Columbus's autographs are, for obvious reasons, in the first two archives mentioned above, since both ducal houses included direct descendants of Columbus and remained united for over a century. When a lawsuit separated the two families, the Albas gave the Veraguas the family archive of Columbus with the exception of one file that was permanently misplaced in their library. The Albas kept and even expanded their bequest through purchases, but the Veraguas sold their documents to the Spanish state in 1929, when they were deposited in the archive at Seville. The documents that are in Genoa are the letters that Columbus sent to Nicoló Oderico, the ambassador of the Republic of Genoa to the Catholic monarchs, which a descendant of the diplomat donated to the city. The letter to the San Giorgio Bank remained stored in the Town Hall until it was discovered in the archives of the defunct bank. Of the remaining autographs, one document is in the Royal Academy of the

History of Madrid, and three autographs, which had once been misplaced from the Royal Chancellery of the Kings of Spain, turned up in their rightful place in the Seville archive (these had not been delivered in time for the original transfer of the materials concerning America to the General Archive of the Indies in Seville in 1786).

Copies of Columbus's writings are also located in the General Archive of the Indies. Among them are Columbus's will, his recently discovered letter book, and the letter to the pope. The City Hall of Genoa as well as the Bibliothèque Nationale, Paris, and the Library of Congress in Washington, D.C., have copies of the Book of Privileges among their manuscripts.

As for the chronology of Columbus's autographs, they cover the period from 1492, date of the Diario (journal) owned by the ducal house of Alba, to December 1505, date of the last known letter by Columbus to his son Diego. We do not know of any other writings by Columbus written before 1492, since today it is certain that all the annotations to his books are later than this date. It is possible to group his autographs into various series. The first consists of the Diario of 1492. The second, a cycle of the year 1498, includes documents written during the preparation for the third voyage: the memorandum to the monarchs on the population of the Indies, various letters to Diego and Gorricio, and the muster roll of the first voyage. The third series, covering the period between the years 1500 and 1502, corresponds to the time Columbus spent in Spain between the third and fourth voyages: reports and memorandums of offenses, a letter to the queen, and some letters to Gorricio. The fourth series relates to the return from the last voyage to the New World: three receipts (the only documents written in the Indies) and letters to Diego, Gorricio, and various Italian friends.

Conveyance and Editing of the Texts. In 1493, upon returning from his first voyage and while still on board his ship, Columbus wrote a letter to Luis de Santángel, clerk of the Catholic monarchs, announcing his discoveries. In that year the letter was published nine times in a translation into Latin addressed to Gabriel Sánchez, treasurer of Aragón. Basically a letter that could be used to correspond with various addressees, it was copied three times in Italian, once in German, and twice in Castilian. It was in effect a best-seller that appeared in various editions in the following years. In this way the news of the discovery spread rapidly throughout Europe.

On March 7, 1505, an Italian version of the fourth voyage report was published in Venice. The rapidity of the copying process is demonstrated by the fact that Columbus had returned to the Iberian Peninsula only four months before. The letter apparently was published in Spanish, but we do not have a copy of it, so that the Italian version is known under the name of lettera rarissima (extremely rare letter), as its new editor, Bartolomeo Morelli, called it in 1810. No other publications are known to have been issued during the Admiral's life.

In 1554 the original Diario of the first voyage was about to be published. Luis Colón, a grandson of the discoverer, obtained the license and the exclusive rights to it for a period of ten years. He was an unscrupulous man and thought he could make more money out of another arrangement he had in mind: as a result the Diario, which was in his archives, was lost forever. To enhance Columbus's prestige during the Pleitos Colombinos (Columbus's lawsuits) the existence of a manuscript on the history of the Admiral was boasted by the circle of family members near to María de Toledo, Diego Colón's widow. In this book an ancestry and honorable past are claimed, and the exclusive rights of the discovery used as evidence. Various hands edited a book in which lies and truth were combined and in which a considerable amount of authentic copies of letters and notes by Columbus's hand were included. Luis decided to negotiate the sale of the manuscript in Genoa, so in 1571 the so-called Historia del Almirante escrita por su hijo Hernando Colón (The Admiral's history written by his son Hernando Colón) appeared on the Genoese market translated into Italian by Alfonso de Ulloa.

No previously unknown text by Columbus appeared during the seventeenth and the eighteenth centuries, for Columbus had fallen out of fashion. More appealing to the public during these years were the stories of great conquerors whose actions were more spectacular. Thus only a few texts by Columbus are known before the nineteenth century, and of these no original is known.

In 1823, G. B. Spotorno's Codice diplomatico Colombo-Americano ossia Raccolta di documenti originali e inediti was published in Genoa. It is a collection of documents that Columbus had gathered and is also known as Libro de los privilegios (The Book of Privileges). Two years later, in 1825, Martín Fernández Navarrete published for the first time the Diarios del primero y el tercer viaje (Logbooks of the first and the third voyages), which were copies by Las Casas that had been previously unknown as well as the autograph letters that were the property of the dukes of Veragua. For the first time autograph writings by Columbus appeared in an edition that was accessible to a wide audience. The Carta a la Banca de San Giorgio (Letter to the San Giorgio Bank) was printed in 1857, and the Historia general de las Indias (General history of the Indies) by Las Casas, which contains copies of many of Columbus's letters, was published in 1879. In 1892 the duchess of Alba published part of the letters from her archive. In that same year the Italian government published the magnificent Raccolta Colombiana (Columbus Collection) on the occa-

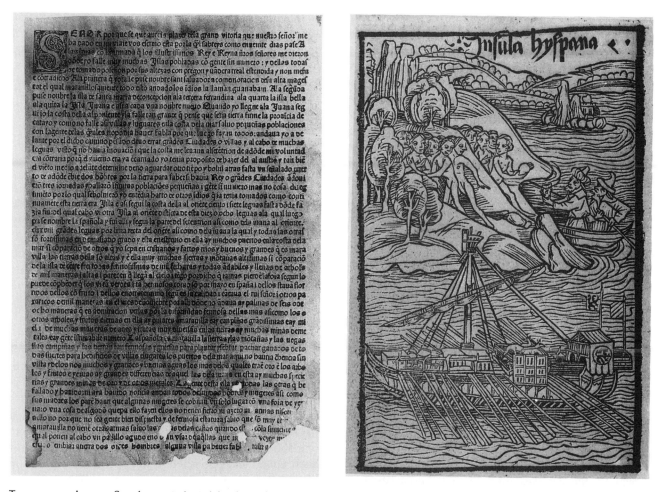

THE LETTER TO LUIS DE SANTÁNGEL. *Left:* A folio from the Barcelona edition of 1493. *Right:* A woodcut illustration, "Trading with the Indians," from the Basel edition of 1493.

NEW YORK PUBLIC LIBRARY, RARE BOOK AND MANUSCRIPTS DIVISION

sion of the celebration of the fourth centennial anniversary; in this splendid edition were collected all the writings by Columbus known to that date.

Columbus became fashionable in the nineteenth century, the period of literary romanticism that glorified picturesque voyages and the sort of hero exemplified by Columbus. Perhaps the enormous amount of previously unknown documentation had an influence on Columbus's popularity. Its impact was such that the government of the United States sent Washington Irving to Madrid with the task of translating the books on the discovery that Navarrete was about to publish. Irving saw that they contained many official documents, and realizing that they might be boring for the American reader, he decided to write the Admiral's biography. He was helped in this work by Navarrete, who gave him access to the new documentation. Irving also had access to important libraries and was therefore able to publish in English for the first time a series of autographs by Columbus that were not known even in Spanish. The generosity of his friend Navarrete was so great that Irving was allowed to translate Navarrete's documents even before Navarrete published them in Spanish.

New documents continued to appear in the twentieth century. In 1902 the duchess of Alba published the famous map that represents the northern coast of La Española and a series of previously unpublished letters from her archives. Finally, in 1942 Columbus's only letter addressed to Isabel was discovered in the Archive of Simancas.

Description of the Autographs. All autographs are written on paper, the material the Admiral used to write his letters, the Book of Prophecies, and the copy of the Book of Privileges he kept in his archive. The only copies made of parchment were those sent to Nicoló Oderico and to Gaspar Gorricio.

State of preservation. The documents are well preserved. All are neat, without erasures and underlinings; marginal words appear rarely. This allows us to suppose that Columbus wrote rough drafts of his letters, a habit possibly not followed only in the incomplete autographs. The handwriting is good; the lines are straight; the left margin is altered only by the initial letters, which extend out of the block.

Heading. Both Las Casas in his *Historia general de las Indias* and Fernando Colón in his *Historie* state that Columbus would not take pen in hand without writing these words first: *Jesus cum Marie sit nobis in via* (Let Jesus and Mary be with us on our path). Nonetheless, this heading appears in only three of the autographs owned by the house of Alba, in the copy of the letter to Miguel Ballester, and in the letter to the monarchs copied at the beginning of the Book of Prophecies. It does not appear in any other autograph or in the numerous copies of the Admiral's letters made by Las Casas. As a consequence, it may be that the heading was used by Columbus on only a few occasions and that Las Casas was exaggerating in order to emphasize the piety of his hero. What Columbus's biographers, on the other hand, do not point out is that in all his writings the text is preceded by a cross, and that in the letter to the queen the heading is the abbreviation *JHS*. If this had been his habit, the Admiral would readily have included the quoted invocation under this cross, which he did not forget to write even in his promissory notes.

Signature. With the exception of the reports that are rough drafts, Columbus signed all his letters. For these he used a curious anagram—never satisfactorily explained—which he himself described when he established the rights of primogeniture in 1498. Columbus used three different types of signatures in his writings. From the beginning of 1502 he always signed with an anagram followed by the words *The Admiral,* with the exception of those authorizations for monopoly in the Indies in which he printed the word *Virrey* (Viceroy) after the anagram. The second form changed and substituted *The Admiral* with the famous and well-known Greek-Latin phrase *XPO FERENS* (Christ bearer) in capital letters. A third signature is used in three payments and in his last letter to his son Diego (wherein he wrote *xpo ferens* in small letters). These four documents were prepared by an amanuensis, and Columbus only signed them. A heading usually appears to the left of the signature, and all documents carry numbering in some of the upper corners. Doubtless, these numbers correspond to the pagination given by Columbus himself when he organized them in his archive.

Orthography and paleography. The accents are finely written and placed high and usually to the right of the letter they stress. The period serves only to indicate certain abbreviations such as *S.M.* or *V.M.* In order to mark a full stop or a semicolon, Columbus inserts vertical lines (single or double), suggesting that to a higher degree

of solemnity corresponds the higher number of vertical lines. Among other details are a series of orthographical norms that Columbus never altered, such as the use of the cedilla for the groups çe and çi, the links between the letters *st, to,* and *tu,* and following *f* and *h.* He always abbreviated *que* as *q* and the toneme *ser* as γ.

[See also *Lawsuits; Library of Columbus; Signature.*]

BIBLIOGRAPHY

Columbus, Ferdinand. *The Life of Admiral Christopher Columbus by His Son Ferdinand.* Translated by Benjamin Keen. New Brunswick, N.J., 1959.
Las Casas, Bartolomé de. *Historia de las Indias.* Mexico City, 1951.
Varela, Consuelo, ed. *Cristóbal Colón: Textos y documentos completos.* 3d ed. Madrid, 1987.

CONSUELO VARELA
Translated from Spanish by Paola Carù

Marginalia

Christopher Columbus was an enthusiastic reader who read for both knowledge and pleasure. It was his habit to keep notebooks (now lost) of data and references and to lard the margins and flyleaves of the books he owned with marginal notes, known as postils. He wrote the postils mostly in Latin or Spanish, with occasional Portuguese and Italian usages. These marginal notes run in length from one abbreviated word to several pages. The postils have been edited and published in full by Césare de Lollis in volume 2 of his *Raccolta di documenti e studi pubblicati dalla R. Commissione Colombiana per quarto centenario dalla scoperta dell'America.*

In the extant books owned by the Admiral, there are between 2,700 and 2,750 postils. The figure varies according to how one counts them (some scholars would merge selected marginal notes, whereas others would count them as two). The following are estimates for each of the books Columbus owned:

1. Pierre d'Ailly, *Imago mundi,* Louvain, 1480–1483; 898 postils.
2. Enea Silvio Piccolomini (Pope Pius II), *Historia rerum ubique gestarum,* Venice, 1477; 861 postils.
3. Marco Polo, *De consuetudanibus et conditionibus orientalium regionum (Il milione),* Antwerp, 1485; 366 postils.
4. Pliny, *Historia naturalis,* Venice, 1489; 24 postils.
5. Plutarch, *Las vidas de los ilustres Varones,* Seville, 1491; 437 postils.
6. Libro de las profecías (Book of Prophecies, a notebook of prophecies collected by Columbus and others at Seville, 1501–1504); 147 postils.

Not all the marginal notations in these texts are in the

hand of Columbus. Some surely are in the hand of his brother Bartolomé, but it is difficult (sometimes impossible) to tell the difference in their handwriting. Other notes are in the hand of Columbus's youngest son, Fernando Colón. All the notes in Plutarch's *Lives*, for example, are in the son's hand. Scholars have made two attempts at a general paleographic analysis of the postils, but they vary greatly in their conclusions about who wrote which notations.

The marginalia remain basically unstudied as a source material. It is through these marginal notations, however, that one can begin to enter the mind of the explorer, develop an idea of his learning, and see the formation and progress of his objectives. The notes vary according to his purposes. Many are simply a marginal index of subjects, composed of one or two words. Others are supplemental to the text with the reader adding his own information. Still others cross-reference to other passages in the same book or to passages in other texts. Occasionally, a marginal note indicates disagreement with the text, in which case the reader almost always offers differing opinions from other authorities. Perhaps the most exciting postils are lengthy summaries of information gleaned from many sources. Usually, this type is located on the flyleaves to the book. For example, in a note to Piccolomini's *Historia rerum ubique gestarum*, where the author discusses the earth's habitable zones, Columbus states in the margin:

> Parmenides held the earth to be divided into five zones, just like the sky. He considered to be uninhabitable the two zones closest the poles because of the cold, a third directly under the course of the sun [uninhabitable] because of the heat. The contrary has been proved in the south by the Portuguese, and in the north by the English and the Swedes, who navigate in those parts.

Columbus made copious notations in the margins of the books he read for the same reason we all make notes. According to the old Chinese proverb, "The palest ink is better than the best memory." Reading is an adaptive process between the demands of the writer and the background of varied experiences occupying the mind of each reader. Through the postils one can see a selective mechanism at work where information is being extracted by a reader with certain intentions. For example, Columbus desired impeccable scholarly support for his conclusion that the world was much smaller than contemporary thinking indicated so he searched the texts for such evidences and noted it in the margins. He frequently cross-referenced such information to other authorities.

Any time a reader interacts with a text, that reader's knowledge about the contents of that text affects the nature of the information stored and retrieved by the

MARGINALIA. A page from *Historia rerum ubique gestarum*, by Enea Silvio Piccolomini (later Pius II). The handwriting here is almost certainly that of Columbus. BIBLIOTECA COLOMBINA, SEVILLE

mind. In the process of understanding a text, information it contains is integrated or rejected according to the reader's existing knowledge about the topic. The reader must select, repress, relate, and organize the data being gathered according to an already set cognitive structure within his or her mind. Thus, through the postils, we can see the Admiral's mind at work. We can judge his education, learning, and style of thinking through his ability to process information on a new occasion and in a new context.

Studying the postils also helps us understand how education and information filtered from elite scientific thinkers of the fifteenth century through the schoolmasters to the public. Columbus represented a growing class of self-taught, middle-class merchants who were inspired by the ideas of cosmology, astronomy, geography, theology, and other sciences being developed in Renaissance centers of learning. He was a complex personality whose expectations were grounded in contemporary scientific theory, in his own experiences, and in legendary, visionary, and allegoric geography. His postils demonstrate the filters through which he imagined the unknown environment of terrae incognitae. In the postils written in the margins of the books he owned, we can see the well-formed, well-thought-out image of the physical world present in the mind of the explorer before he sailed.

BIBLIOGRAPHY

Lollis, Césare de. "Introduction, Ilustrazione alle postille." In *Raccolta di documenti e studi pubblicati dalla R. Commissione Colombiana per quarto centenario dalla scoperta dell'America.* Vol. 2. Rome, 1892–1894.

Raffo, Giuliano. "Sulle postille di Colombo relativo alla storia romana." In *Studi Colombiani.* Genoa, 1952.

Streicher, Fritz. "Las notas marginales de Colón en los libros de Pedro Aliaco, Eneas Silvio, y Marco Polo, estudiadas a la luz de las investigaciones paleográficas." In vol. 3 of *Investigación y progreso.* Madrid, 1929.

Taviani, Paolo E. *Christopher Columbus: The Grand Design.* London, 1985.

DELNO C. WEST

Book of Prophecies

The Book of Prophecies (Libro de las profecías) was the name given by Columbus to a work he never completed. A manuscript of materials apparently gathered in preparation for the book by Columbus and a collaborator, a Carthusian monk named Gaspar Gorricio, survives in the Biblioteca Colombina in Seville, Spain. It consists of passages excerpted from the Bible, the Apocrypha, and various patristic and medieval exegetical works. These are accompanied by a prefatory letter written by Columbus to Fernando and Isabel, some fragments of verse in Spanish, and notes in the hands of Columbus, Gorricio, Columbus's son Fernando, and Columbus's brother Bartolomé.

The dating of the manuscript of the Book of Prophecies is problematic. A note in Columbus's hand at the beginning indicates that he and Gorricio began to gather the excerpts after his third voyage to the Americas, which he completed in 1500. He appears to have composed the prefatory letter to Fernando and Isabel between September of 1501 and March of 1502—that is, between the third and fourth voyages.

It is difficult to determine precisely what Columbus had in mind for the Book of Prophecies, given the fragmentary nature of the materials that remain. Nevertheless, the excerpts do consistently manifest certain configurations and themes, and taken together with the prefatory letter, they reveal the pattern of Columbus's intention. It appears that he wanted the Book of Prophecies to place his achievements and those of his monarchs within the framework of a providential history. He believed that the end of time was near at hand and that a number of

contemporary events including his own discovery of a "new world" were penultimate fulfillments of ancient prophecies.

In preparing the larger framework of providential history, Columbus made use of a number of well-known Biblical commentaries and glosses on Augustine, Isidore of Seville, and Nicholas of Lyra. But his principal source was a collection of short works on the interrelationships among history, astrology, and prophecy written between 1410 and 1414 by the late medieval thinker Pierre d'Ailly (1350–1420). Columbus used an edition of these works printed by John of Westphalia between 1480 and 1483. D'Ailly's works were not original but rather gatherings or cullings of materials drawn from a variety of late antique and medieval sources. Principal among these were Augustine, Pseudo-Methodius, and Roger Bacon. D'Ailly's works thus provided Columbus with a repertoire of established authorities upon which to base his Book of Prophecies.

Columbus's reliance upon d'Ailly's works is evident in the consistent correlations between the passages he annotated and the excerpts he selected from the works for his manuscript. These notes and excerpts are all concerned with modes of periodizing history and in particular with forecasting the advent of Antichrist. This event is presumed by d'Ailly and Columbus to be imminent. It will presage the end of postlapsarian time and space, of the cosmos and of history.

In constructing this framework, Columbus appears to have paid particular attention to d'Ailly's *Tractatus de legibus et sectis contra supersticiosos astronomos*, a treatise involving an ongoing debate among medieval philosophers and scientists regarding the use of astrology to forecast the fulfillment of prophecies and other determinant forces in historical process. In the first four chapters, d'Ailly outlines a theory in which history consists of six ages. In each age a different religion has dominated; its ascendancy was signed in the heavens by the conjunction of its particular planet with Jupiter. Thus, according to d'Ailly, the past conjunctions of Jupiter with Saturn marked the age of the Jews; with Mars, the age of the Chaldeans; with the Sun, the Egyptians; and with Venus, the Saracens. The present age of the Christians coincides with the conjunction of Saturn and Mercury, and the final age, the age of Antichrist, will see the conjoining of Jupiter and the Moon.

This linking of chronology and astronomy was derived from the ninth-century Muslim astronomer Albumazar (Abu Ma'shar) and was known to d'Ailly through Roger Bacon's *Opus maius*. According to d'Ailly's interpretation of these earlier medieval sources, the conjunction of Jupiter with the Moon, which would signal the unleashing of the forces of Antichrist, was not far off. A key passage from the fourth chapter describing the events that would

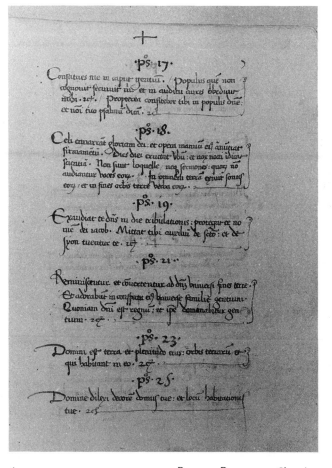

A FOLIO FROM THE MANUSCRIPT OF THE BOOK OF PROPHECIES. Showing excerpts of Biblical psalms. BIBLIOTECA COLOMBINA, SEVILLE

occur in the age of Antichrist was among the excerpts Columbus gathered for the Book of Prophecies. Further evidence was drawn from a second work by d'Ailly on the concordances between celestial phenomena and historical process (*Tractatus de concordia astronomie veritatis et narrationis hystorice*). In this treatise, d'Ailly provides a set of eight events that will augur the advent of Antichrist. They were copied verbatim from a seventh-century Byzantine Apocalypse by a figure known as Pseudo-Methodius, which enjoyed a considerable currency throughout the medieval period. Columbus's annotations indicate that he followed these passages from the works of d'Ailly carefully; both were excerpted for the Book of Prophecies.

When set within the historical context provided by d'Ailly and the other glossarists mentioned above, the selections from the Bible that form the bulk of the Book of Prophecies appear consistently to address two interrelated themes. The first is the anticipated final recovery of Mount Zion, symbol of the Holy Land, from the infidel.

The second is the penultimate conversion of all the peoples of the world to Christianity as prophesied in *John* 10:16: "And I have other sheep, that are not of this fold; I must bring them also, and they will heed my voice. So there shall be one flock, one shepherd."

Other nonscriptural materials contained in the Book of Prophecies appear to have been designed to establish the specific roles of Columbus and his monarchs within this general apocalyptic vision of history. A passage taken from Seneca's tragedy *Medea*—which predicts that "the years will come, in the succession of ages, when the Ocean will loose the bonds by which we have been confined, when an immense land shall lie revealed"—is accompanied by a note in Fernando's hand stating that "my father, the Admiral Christopher Columbus, fulfilled this prophecy in the year 1492." And a diplomatic letter to Fernando and Isabel, applying a thirteenth-century prophecy that claimed that "he who will restore the Ark of Zion will come from Spain," appears as well.

These latent patterns become more explicit in the incomplete and somewhat rambling prefatory letter addressed by Columbus to the Spanish monarchs. He begins by recalling his training and decades of experience in navigating and mapmaking. He goes on to assert, however, that it was not technical expertise but divine providence that determined the success of the Enterprise of the Indies: "In this voyage to the Indies Our Lord wished to perform a very evident miracle in order to console me and the others in the matter of this other voyage to the Holy Sepulcher." Columbus believes that he has been chosen by God to carry Christianity to the infidels of the New World in fulfillment of *John* 10:16 and that Fernando and Isabel have been designated to lead the final conquest of Jerusalem.

According to the prefatory letter, these events will unfold rapidly. Columbus points out to his regents that the calculations of d'Ailly demonstrated that but 155 years remained before the end of the world. Thus, although the Book of Prophecies is difficult to decipher, it is essential to the understanding of Columbus's conception of history and his place in it.

[See also *Antichrist; Spirituality of Columbus;* and biographies of d'Ailly and Bacon.]

BIBLIOGRAPHY

Lollis, Césare de. *Scritti di Colombo.* Vol. 2 of *Raccolta de documenti e studi pubblicata della R. Commissione Colombiana.* Rome, 1894. [Contains the text of the Book of Prophecies.]

Milhou, Alain. *Colón y su mentalidad mesianica en el ambiente franciscanista español.* Vol. 11 of Cuadernos Colombinos. Valladolid, 1983.

Watts, Pauline Moffitt. "Prophecy and Discovery: On the Spiritual Origins of Christopher Columbus's 'Enterprise of the

Indies.' " *American Historical Review* 90 (February 1985): 73–102.

West, Delno, and August Kling. *Vision and Discovery: A Study and Translation of Columbus's Libro de las profecias.* Gainesville, Fla., 1991.

PAULINE MOFFITT WATTS

Last Will and Testament

The last will and testament of Christopher Columbus were as complicated as most of his business affairs in Spain. First, he placed his assets in a perpetual trust for his son Diego. In four later acts he confirmed this trust and gave Diego instructions for the final disposition of his business affairs and charitable and pious donations.

Establishment of a Perpetual Trust (*Mayorazgo*). Christopher Columbus used an extralegal maneuver, a perpetual trust, to provide for his heirs. In Burgos after the second voyage, he petitioned Fernando and Isabel for royal permission to establish a trust, and on April 23, 1497, the monarchs issued a letter patent that gave Columbus "license and authority to make one or more trusts in favor of Sir Diego Colón, your legitimate eldest son, or any of your heirs and children." The patent allowed him to include in this trust any property, goods, and heritable offices that he had received from the monarchy.

Columbus was attempting with this trust to exempt his property from the Spanish laws of inheritance. The laws were very strict, requiring that all legitimate children receive equitable shares of their parent's estate and that the testator set aside no more than 10 percent of the estate for charitable and religious bequests. Parents had so little discretion in the partition of the estate that they rarely made wills, and when they did, it was to specify how they wanted the pious and charitable donations to be distributed.

Wealthy and noble families who wanted to prevent partition of the family fortune generation after generation found a way around the law, by establishing trusts. The Trastámara monarchs allowed parents to remove assets from the partible estate and use them as the principal of a perpetual trust (*mayorazgo*). The parents designated one of the children, usually the eldest son or daughter, as the beneficiary of the trust. After the parents' deaths, their remaining assets and liabilities were partitioned equitably among all the legitimate children of the marriage.

In Seville the next year, Columbus wrote a draft of the perpetual trust, making his son Diego the beneficiary. He finished the draft on February 22, 1498, in the midst of his preparations for the third voyage. First, he listed the offices and revenues he had received as heritable property from the monarchs: the offices of admiral of the Ocean Sea and viceroy and governor of the islands and mainland he had discovered, with their salaries and revenues; 10 percent of all the resources found there, and the right to invest one-eighth of the Indies commerce and receive one-eighth of the profits from it. He stated his desire to place "these offices, tenth, eighth, and salaries and revenues" in a perpetual trust. He placed the usual restrictions on this trust: the beneficiary could not touch the principal but had full use and possession of the income. At no time did Columbus mention how much the principal of the trust might be worth in cash, and that, too, was typical of the founding documents of perpetual trusts; the capital assets were listed, but the income was expected to grow from year to year.

Next, Columbus established the method of selecting the beneficiary of the trust. He named his son Diego as the beneficiary. If Diego should die without a male heir, Columbus's second son, Fernando, should succeed to the trust, then Columbus's brother Bartolomé, and then the youngest Columbus brother, Diego, if the latter should leave holy orders and marry. Throughout the generations, the heir should always be the eldest son of an eldest son, or the male heir most closely related to Christopher Columbus and bearing the surname Colón. He excluded females from inheriting the trust unless no male heir with the name Colón could be located anywhere in the world.

Columbus stated that he was establishing the trust this way in order to perpetuate his family name and the memory of his own attainments. He ordered Diego to display the admiral's coat of arms and to sign all documents with the same rubric that he had used—the as yet undeciphered letters arranged in a triangle—and with the title "The Admiral" no matter what other offices and titles the king might later give him.

Columbus was giving absolutely everything he possessed to Diego, yet he wanted to provide for his other son and for his brothers. So he instructed Diego to use the income from one-quarter of the trust to give an allowance to Bartolomé of up to one million maravedis per annum. Another quarter of the trust's income was to be set aside to provide Diego's half-brother, Fernando, with an annual allowance of one million maravedis. If Fernando's quarter of the principal should grow, Diego could give him up to two million maravedis per year. Columbus's youngest brother, Diego, was to receive an annual allowance sufficient to his station as a clergyman, until he received a church position.

Next, Columbus required the beneficiary of the trust to give one-tenth of the annual income in charitable donations to the poorest relatives of the Columbus family. The tenth was to be calculated by extrapolating from the income produced by the one-quarter of the revenue assigned to Bartolomé. Diego must diligently send people all over the world to seek out these poor relatives and give the money to them, especially to pay the dowries of the poorest young females—a standard type of charitable donation during the Renaissance. Christopher Columbus's two closest male relatives must audit the accounts and make sure that Diego gave 10 percent of the income in charity. Diego must also provide an allowance to a Columbus relative living with his wife and family in Genoa, making sure that they had enough to live with dignity and with enough stature to demand the benefits of Genoese citizenship.

To ensure that the family income would be secure, Columbus ordered Diego to deposit his money in the San Giorgio Bank in Genoa. The profits should be spent on financing a conquest of Jerusalem by Fernando and Isabel, or a similar crusade in Oran. In gratitude for the support that Fernando and Isabel had given him, Columbus ordered Diego and his heirs to always serve the Castilian monarchs. And in recognition of the city where he was born, he instructed Diego to work for the honor, welfare, and growth of Genoa.

Finally, Columbus provided for the disposition of his soul. He instructed Diego to build a church, to be named Santa María de la Concepción, and a hospital on the island of La Española, with a chapel in which masses would be sung for the salvation of his soul and the souls of his ancestors. Diego must also support four professors of theology on the island of La Española to teach and convert the Indians to Christianity. This endowment must be commemorated in the church by a stone plaque engraved with the information.

All of the trust was typical of Castilian trusts of the period, and Columbus appeared satisfied with it. He deposited this and his other valuable documents in the monastery of Las Cuevas in Seville, and he later affirmed the trust on three occasions.

Memorandum of Instruction for Diego. In May 1502, before leaving on his fourth voyage, he wrote a memorandum of instruction for Diego, leaving him in charge of the family's business and legal affairs and instructing him on how to manage these in the event of Columbus's death. He told Diego where the valuable papers were deposited and reminded him to tithe every year, to treat people of all stations in life with dignity, and to continue serving the king and queen. Then he ordered Diego to make specific payments to his closest female relatives. To Beatriz Enríquez de Arana, mother of Columbus's illegitimate son, Fernando, he must give ten thousand maravedis per annum payable from butcher shop leases in the city of Córdoba, and he was to treat her as lovingly as he would his own mother. To Diego's aunt, the sister of Felipa Perestrelo y Moniz, he was to give the same amount, payable quarterly.

The Admiral seems always to have treated his brother Diego with that special care and tenderness that an oldest brother displays toward a youngest. In this memo he instructed his son to provide and care for his uncle, who was living in Cádiz, "because he is my brother and has always been very obedient." He also instructed his son to persuade the king to give his brother Diego a canonry or some other church position, because he was a clergyman—an instruction that was never carried out.

Columbus gave his son good advice on the conduct of his personal affairs; he commanded him to make a monthly balance of his assets and liabilities, to seek the advice of the priest Gaspar de Gorricio, to postpone the royal arrangements for his marriage until Columbus returned, and to depend on the influence of Luis de Soria in political matters. The Admiral had appointed Alonso Sánchez de Carvajal as his business agent to collect his revenues from the Indies, and he instructed Diego to receive the money from Carvajal and pay him a per diem of five hundred maravedis for his time in La Española, as well as fifty thousand maravedis if he took care of Columbus's business in Spain.

With the money that Carvajal would bring, Diego must pay Italian investors who had advanced Columbus the capital to buy merchandise to sell in the Americas—the one-eighth of the total value of cargoes agreed on in the April 17, 1492, partnership agreement—and to pay off the Admiral's other creditors.

While these orders seem clear enough, they were in fact not clear at all. This ambiguity became apparent after Columbus returned from his disastrous fourth voyage and became embroiled in a dispute with the monarchy about just what his offices and revenues included. Until the law courts defined these, there was no way of knowing what capital assets Columbus could include as principal in the trust. The differences dividing the two parties were enormous and would take years of litigation to settle.

Amendments. Meanwhile, Columbus claimed as much as possible and even more. After returning from his fourth voyage, he stopped over in Segovia on his way to Valladolid, headquarters of the royal appeals court (*chancillería*), and wrote another memorandum to Diego on August 25, 1505. Columbus confirmed the trust and memorandum and added details that changed the proportion of donations and allowances. In this memorandum, he wrote as a hardheaded businessman who thought he was being cheated of his fair return on investment. He declared that he was entitled to one-third of all that was found in the Indies, in addition to the tenth and eighth that he claimed earlier. Although no profits had yet been realized from the Indies, he trusted that "through the benevolence of Our Lord the revenue will become very large."

In anticipation of this future revenue and apparently

more appreciative of his younger son's character and affections after their year of being shipwrecked together on Jamaica, Columbus changed his instructions to Diego about partitioning the income from the trust. Instead of dividing it into quarters and giving one of these to Bartolomé, he now ordered Diego to divide the trust's annual income into ten shares. After giving one share to charity, he would keep six shares and divide the remaining shares into thirty-five shares, which he must partition in the following way: to the Admiral's son Fernando Colón, twenty-seven shares; to the Admiral's brother Bartolomé, five shares; and to the Admiral's youngest brother, Diego, three.

As usual in Columbus's writing, this distribution seems straightforward but turns out to be a wish. In the Admiral's next words, he reveals the problem:

My wish would be for my son Sir Fernando to receive annually 1.5 million maravedis, Sir Bartolomé 150,000, and Sir Diego 100,000. But I do not know how this can be possible, because up to now neither the source nor the amount of the income from the trust is known. I say that the procedure I have outlined above should be followed until the two-ninths grow and are sufficiently increased to provide the stated sums to Fernando, Bartolomé, and Diego. When this level of revenue has been achieved, which will be when the two-ninths are producing annual revenues of 1.75 million maravedis, then everything above that amount shall be inherited by my son Sir Diego or his heir. If this revenue should increase a great deal more, I would be pleased if the portions for Sir Fernando and my brothers were also increased.

Columbus then showed the new affection and concern he felt for his son Fernando. "The part that I order given to my son Sir Fernando I am placing in a trust for him, and this will be hereditary in his male descendants forevermore. This trust cannot be sold, traded, given away, or removed from the descendants in any way and must be treated in the same way as the trust I established for my son Sir Diego."

Columbus ordered Diego, when he had enough income from the trust and inheritance, to establish a chapel endowed with three chaplaincies to say three masses every day: one in honor of the Holy Trinity, one dedicated to the Conception of the Virgin Mary, and the other for the souls of all the faithful and for the souls of Columbus's father, mother, and wife. If this chapel could be on the island of La Española, "which God miraculously gave me, I would be very pleased if it could be on the spot where I invoked the Holy Trinity, which is in the part of the Vega that is called La Concepción."

Finally, Columbus gave Diego an intriguing instruction that reveals much about his own conscience. "I order him to be responsible for Beatriz Enríquez, mother of my son Sir Fernando, to provide for her so that she can live decently, because she is a person to whom I owe a great

deal. And this must be done to clear my conscience, because this weighs heavily against my soul. It would not be proper to explain here the reason for this."

Columbus's Final Confirmation of the Trust and Instructions to Diego. Within a year, on May 19, 1506, Columbus lay on his deathbed in Valladolid. A royal judge and notary, Pedro de Hinojedo, and legal witnesses were summoned. Hinojedo testified that in his presence Christopher Columbus, who claimed to be admiral, viceroy, and governor-general of the islands and mainland discovered and to be discovered in the Indies, being ill of body, rectified and approved as valid his earlier trust and memos. Columbus named as executors of his estate his son Diego Colón, his brother Bartolomé Colón, and the treasurer of Vizcaya, Juan de Porras, and gave them his power of attorney.

Finally, Columbus appended instructions in his own handwriting ordering Diego to pay sums anonymously to a number of old friends and creditors, all of them foreigners.

"First, to the heirs of Girolamo del Porto, father of Benito del Porto, chancellor of Genoa: 20 ducats or its equivalent.

"To Antonio Vazo, Genoese merchant who used to live in Lisbon: 2,500 Portuguese reales, which are a little more than 7 ducats at the rate of 375 reales to the ducat.

"To a Jew who lived at the entrance to the Jewish quarter in Lisbon, or to whomever a priest shall designate, the equivalent of one-half mark of silver.

"To the heirs of Luigi Centurione, Genoese merchant: 30,000 Portuguese reales; at the rate of 375 reales to the ducat this is approximately 75 ducats.

"To these same heirs and to the heirs of Paolo di Negro, Genoese, 100 ducats or its equivalent; half to one group of heirs and half to the other.

"To Baptista Spinola or his heirs if he is dead, 20 ducats. This Baptista Spinola is the son-in-law of Luigi Centurione. He was the son of messer Nicolò Spinola de Locoli de Ronco, and, for an address, he was resident in Lisbon in the year 1482."

With this final act, Columbus reconfirmed the earlier dispositions and repaid old debts. By making these legal dispositions, he provided handsomely for his sons, his former mistress, his relatives and creditors in Genoa, Spain, and Portugal, and for the souls of his parents and wife.

[See also *Lawsuits; Signature.*]

BIBLIOGRAPHY

Columbus, Christopher. *Testamento de Cristóbal Colón.* Transcription and introduction by Demetrio Ramos. Valladolid, 1980.

Columbus, Christopher. *Textos y documentos completos: Relaciones de viajes, cartas, y memoriales.* Edited by Consuelo Varela. Madrid, 1984.

HELEN NADER

ZACUTO, ABRAHAM (c. 1450–c. 1515), navigational astronomer. Abraham Zacuto had a great influence on the development of astronomical navigation, which bloomed in the second half of the fifteenth century. His contribution was due mainly to his *Almanach perpetuum coelestium motium* (Perpetual almanac of the heavenly bodies), which was probably known in Portugal in its original version before 1493, when Zacuto took refuge there because of a Castilian law that exiled all Jews who did not convert to Catholicism.

Diogo Ortiz (known in Portugal as Diogo Calzadilha), who had taught astrology at the University of Salamanca, had taken refuge in the Portuguese kingdom after supporting Afonso V of Portugal in the disastrous war that the king had waged in support of his claim to the Crown of Castile. It is probable that he knew Abraham Zacuto before 1475, when Ortiz was forced to leave Salamanca. Knowing Zacuto's value, he apparently recommended him to the Portuguese king, thereby facilitating Zacuto's entrance into the court of Lisbon, where he received the title of royal astronomer. Zacuto offered assistance in the fields in which he was a specialist, particularly navigation. Despite his position, he fled to the Near East in 1496 because of a law of Manuel I expelling Jews.

Zacuto's *Almanach perpetuum*, probably written while he was at Salamanca, has an introduction in Hebrew, written under the name Hajibul Hagadol. This proved to be a highly influential work on navigation. Other works written by Zacuto have been forgotten, with the exception of his *Tratado breve de las influencias del cielo* (Short treatise on the influences in the heavens), an astrological book with some paragraphs on meterological information.

So-called astronomical navigation undoubtedly began much earlier than Zacuto's arrival in Portugal. Shortly after 1460 the navigator Diogo Gomes made references to the navigational use of the quadrant. Moreover, Christopher Columbus notes that in 1485 the astrologer José Vizinho systematically examined the sun in Guinea in order to test a body of rules that enabled one to determine the geographical latitude of a place by starting from the observation of the meridian height of a star. In 1487 and 1488, Bartolomeu Dias used the astrolabe to determine latitudes in his voyage around the south of Africa and into the Indian Ocean. Dias's determinations were witnessed by Columbus, who was with King João II when the king received Dias after his return.

Zacuto's importance lies in the fact that the solar declination tables, essential for the calculation of geographical coordinates, were based on his tables. His *Almanach perpetuum* allowed a competent skipper to do the necessary calculations and to prepare the solar declination tables, using both single tables and, later, quadrennial tables. The tables in the *Livro de marinharia de André Pirese* (André Pirese's book of navigation) were copied for various quadrenniums, all of them based on the *Almanach perpetuum*: for 1493–1496, 1497–1500 (which might have been used by Vasco da Gama), 1501–1504, 1517–1520, 1521–1524, 1529–1532, and 1549–1552. The tables for 1517–1520 appeared in a pamphlet possibly printed in 1516 and known today as the *Guia náutico de Evora* (Nautical guide of Evora).

Four editions of the *Almanach perpetuum* exist: a well-known edition, published in Venice in 1502; a badly defined edition said to have "variations in its tables," one copy of which is reported to be in the library of the Escorial; an edition with comments by Alfonso de Cór-

ASTRONOMICAL TABLES. From Abraham Zacuto's *Almanach perpetuum coelestium motium*. Facsimile, 1915.

doba and reportedly also in the library of the Escorial; and an edition printed in Venice in 1525 by Johannes Michael that follows almost literally the original edition but which is sometimes erroneously dated 1500.

This fundamental book by Abraham Zacuto was both appreciated and useful. His knowledge and his merits, though, were not rightly used to the best advantage in Portugal.

BIBLIOGRAPHY

De Lery, Jean. *History of a Voyage to the Land of Brazil Otherwise Called America.* Translated by Janet Whatley. Berkeley, 1990.

Diffey, Bailey W. *Prelude to Empire: Portugal Overseas before Henry the Navigator.* Lincoln, Neb., 1960.

Diffey, Bailey W., and George D. Winius. *Foundations of the Portuguese Empire, 1414–1850.* Edited by Boyd C. Shafer. Minneapolis, 1977.

Morison, Samuel Eliot. *Portuguese Voyages to America in the Fifteenth Century.* New York, 1965.

Waters, David W. *Reflections upon Some Navigational and Hydrographic Problems of the XVth Century Related to the Voyage of Bartolomeu Dias, 1487–88.* Lisbon, 1988.

LUÍS DE ALBUQUERQUE
Translated from Portuguese by Paola Carù

Index

VOLUME 1: pp. 1–400; VOLUME 2: pp. 401–754.
*Numbers in boldface refer to the main entry on the
subject. Numbers in italic refer to illustrations.*

VOLUME 1: pp. 1–400; VOLUME 2: pp. 401–754.
Numbers in boldface refer to the main entry on the subject. Numbers in italic refer to illustrations.

VOLUME 1: pp. 1–400; VOLUME 2: pp. 401–754.
*Numbers in boldface refer to the main entry on the
subject. Numbers in italic refer to illustrations.*

VOLUME 1: pp. 1–400; VOLUME 2: pp. 401–754.
*Numbers in boldface refer to the main entry on the
subject. Numbers in italic refer to illustrations.*

VOLUME 1: pp. 1–400; VOLUME 2: pp. 401–754.
*Numbers in boldface refer to the main entry on the
subject. Numbers in italic refer to illustrations.*

VOLUME 1: pp. 1–400; VOLUME 2: pp. 401–754.
*Numbers in boldface refer to the main entry on the
subject. Numbers in italic refer to illustrations.*

VOLUME 1: pp. 1–400; VOLUME 2: pp. 401–754.
Numbers in boldface refer to the main entry on the subject. Numbers in italic refer to illustrations.

VOLUME 1: pp. 1–400; VOLUME 2: pp. 401–754.
*Numbers in boldface refer to the main entry on the
subject. Numbers in italic refer to illustrations.*

VOLUME 1: pp. 1–400; VOLUME 2: pp. 401–754.
*Numbers in boldface refer to the main entry on the
subject. Numbers in italic refer to illustrations.*

VOLUME 1: pp. 1–400; VOLUME 2: pp. 401–754.
*Numbers in boldface refer to the main entry on the
subject. Numbers in italic refer to illustrations.*

VOLUME 1: pp. 1–400; VOLUME 2: pp. 401–754.
Numbers in boldface refer to the main entry on the subject. Numbers in italic refer to illustrations.

VOLUME 1: pp. 1–400; VOLUME 2: pp. 401–754.
*Numbers in boldface refer to the main entry on the
subject. Numbers in italic refer to illustrations.*

Nasca culture, 227

Nasrid dynasty, 492

Native American Church, 279

Native Americans. *See* Indians; specific peoples

Natural History (Pliny), 294

Natural History of Carolina, 402

Nautical archaeology, 30

Nautical charts, 221, **501–505**, 512, 514, 542, 729

Nautical instruments, 215, **512–515**
   see *also* specific instruments

Navajos, 368

Navidad, La, 25, 27–28, 34, 37, 194, 195, 196, 248, 532–533, **606–608**, 702, 708

Navigatio, 75–76

Navigatio in Novum Mundum, 73, 95

Navigation, 49, 50, 164, 181, 291, **505–515**, 542, 753
   altura, 16, 508, 542
   art, practice, and theory, **505–512**
   celestial, 62, 246, 512
   of Columbus, **204–205**
   importance of Mercator to, 465
   instruments of, 215, **512–515**
   lead and line, **420**
   sailing directions, **595–597**
   solar phenomena, 640–641
   Southern Cross, **642–643**
   timetelling's importance to, 666
   see *also* Compass; Dead reckoning

Navigationi et viaggi, 150, 642

Nebrija, Antonio de, 377, 383, 647

Neckham, Alexander, 205, 506–507

Negri, Giovanni Maria, 208

Negri, Niccola, 208

Negro, Gian Antonio, 170, 171

Negro, Paoli, 163, 170, 171, 173, 175, 176, 286, 441

Nemquethaba. *See* Bochica

Neoplatonism, 605

Neri, Saint Filippo, 593

Neruda, Pablo, 432

Netherlands, 540

Neuwes Astrolabium, 48

New Andalusia, 524

Newfoundland, 84, 85, 91, 154, 157, 689

New France, *150*, 152–153

New Granada, 395–396

New Laws, 64, 241, 363, 411, 462

New Mexico, 142

New Passage to Cathaia, A, 91

Newport, Christopher, 154, 155

New Seville. *See* Sevilla la Nueva

New Spain. *See* Mexico

New Theories of the Planets, 601, 603

Newton, Isaac, 438

Nezahualcoyotl, 364, 365

Nezahualpilli, 365

Nicaragua, 56, 272, 327

Nicholas IV, 692

Nicholas V, 539, 592, 704

Nicholas of Cusa, 297, 550, 601, 670

Nicholas of Lynn, 593, 677

Nicholas of Lyra, Saint, 297, 748

Nicholson, H.B., *as contributor*, 364–368, 485–486

Nicolas, Gaspar, 641

Nicolasa, La (ship), 33

Nicolaus, Donnus, 569

Nicolini, Donato, 687

Nicotine. *See* Tobacco

Nicuesa, Diego de, 60, 61

Nidaros. *See* Trondheim

Nietzsche, Friedrich Wilhelm, 429

Niña (ship), 25, 38, 184, 185–186, 193, **515–516**, 543, 546, 548, 619, 623, 624, 625, 695, 699, 703, 704, 708, 709, 710, 712, 713

Ninan Cuyuchi, 311, 312

Niño, Francisco, 704, 709

Niño, Juan, 515, **516–517**, 694, 704

Niño, Pedro Alonso. *See* Niño, Peralonso

Niño, Peralonso, 261, 418, **517–518**, 548, 610, 719

Nitaínos, 346

Nixon, C.E., 334

Niza, Marcos de, 210, 472

Noachid maps. *See* T-O maps

Nobunaga, Oda, 121

Noche Triste, 17, 211, 446

Nocturnal, 245, 666

Noli, Antonio, 0, 90, 596

Nombre de Dios, 144

Noort, Oliver de, 264

Noronha, Martim de, 186

Noronha, Pedro de, 177, 178

Norse civilization
   artifacts, 688
   exploration and settlement, 257–258
   longship, *688*

North America
   Cabot's discovery, 85

early English colonies and explorations, 154–158
   see *also* specific colonies and settlements

North Magnetic Pole, 465

North Star, 204, 229, 230, 245, 406, 412, 508, 512

Northwest Passage, 55, 90, 91, 153, 157–158, **518–522**

North-West Passage Company, 157

Novara, battle of, 438

Novinsky, Anita Waingort, *as contributor*, 426–427

Novo cristãos. *See* Conversos

Nowell, Charles E., 183

Nueva Cádiz, 27, **610–611**
   excavations at, *28, 611*

Nueva Isabela, 249

Numismatics, **325–327**

Nunes, Pedro, 51, 208, 426, 437, 510, 511, 514, 640

Núñez, Eleonora, 24

Núñez, Lucía, 209

Núñez Cabeza de Vaca, Alvar. *See* Cabeza de Vaca, Alvar Núñez

Núñez de Balboa, Vasco. *See* Balboa, Vasco Núñez de

Núñez de Vela, Blasco, 552

Núñez Vela, Blanco, 462

Nuns, 737

Nuova Raccolta Colombiana. See Raccolta Colombiana

O

Obenga, Theophile, 576

Ober, Frederick A., 402

Obregon, Mauricio, 405, 698

O'Callaghan, Joseph F., *as contributor*, 12–14, 71, 311, 423–426, 442, 554–556, 584–585, 678, 678–679

Ocute, 370

Oddino, Bartolomeo, 163

Ode to Columbus and Columbia, 159

Oderigo, Lorenzo, 488

Oderigo, Nicolò, 161, 488, 743

Odiel River, 695

Odoric of Pordenone, 372, 564, 565

Oertel, Abraham. *See* Ortelius, Abraham

VOLUME 1: pp. 1–400; VOLUME 2: pp. 401–754.
*Numbers in boldface refer to the main entry on the
subject. Numbers in italic refer to illustrations.*

Pérez, Juan, 191, 192, 193, 536, 583, 651
Pérez, Martín, 454
Pérez de Guzmán, Alvar, 535
Pérez de Luna, Fernando, 624
Pérez de Oliva, Hernán, 490
Pérez de Quesada, Hernán, 357
Pérez Montás, Eugenio, *as contributor*, 616
Pérez Niño, Cristóbal, 704, 709
Pérez Roldán, Alonso, 709
Perfumes, 650
Periplus of the Erythraean Sea, 648
Perna, Petrus, 316
Pernambuco, 147, 148
Perry, Mary Elizabeth, *as contributor*, 616–617
Perry, Matthew C., 122
Persico, Luigi, 478
Persig, Robert, 575–576
Pertussis, 459
Peru, 17, 64, 141, 410, 462, 466, 524, 551
  agriculture, 5
  conquest of, 472, 552
  Mendoza as viceroy, 462–463
  mining in, 469
Perugino, Pietro, 44
Pessagno, Manuel, 508, 560
Petén, 361
Peter of Alexandria, 216
Peter of Ghent, 473
Peter Martyr. *See* Anghiera, Pietro Martire d'
Petrarch, 500
Peuerbach, Georg von, 601
Peyote, 279
Pfolspeundt, Heinrich von, 602
Philately, **327–333**
Philip I, 116, 133, 282, 384, 395, 397, 399, 437, 454, 713, 743
Philip II, 42, 116, 242, 284, 358, *378*, 385, 411, 442, 463, 464, **540–541**, 563, 617
Philip III, 492, 541
Philip the Handsome. *See* Philip I
Philippa of Lancaster, 308, 560
Philippines, 265, 277, 679
Philip of Savoy, 450
Phillips, Carla Rahn, *as contributor*, 52–55, 315–321, 494–497
Phillips, William D., *as contributor*, 209, 249–257
Philology, humanist, 586
Phoenicia, 617
Piccolomini, Enea Silvio. *See* Pius II

"Pictures of Columbus, the Genoese" (Frenau), 433
Pietà, 46
Pigafetta, Antonio, 240, 444
Pigs, 236
Pilgrims, 156–157, 158
Pilot books, 506, 542
Piloting, **542**
Pilóto-mayor, 513
Pina, Rui de, 182, 186, 423
Pinelli, Francesco, 292, **543**
Pinelo, Bernardo, 200
Pinheiro Marques, Alfredo, *as contributor*, 96–97, 146–149, 452–454, 553–554
Pinta (ship), 31, 184, 193, 515, **543–544**, 546, 581, 619, 621, 623, 694, 695, 698
Pinto, Bento Teixeira, 394
Pinto, Fernão Mendes, 120, **545–545**
Pinturicchio, Bernardino, 44
Pinzón, Arias Pérez, 546
Pinzón, Francisco Martín, **545–546**, 694
Pinzón, Martín Alonso, 374, 418, 543, 545, **546–548**, 581, 694, 695, 699, 702, 703
Pinzón, Vicente Yáñez, 146, 186, 224, 261, 418, 544, 546, **548–549**, 581, 621, 626, 694, 699, 719
Pinzón family, 193
Piombo, Sebastiano del, 315–316, 318
Pipino, Francesco, 557
Piracy, 171, 173, 675, 686
Pires, André, 399, 511
Pires, Tomé, 119, 120, 640
Pisuerga River, 682
Pius II, 14, 175, 251, 422, **549–550**, 591, 677
Pius III, 12
Pius IV, 592–593
Pius V, 411, 593
Pivot, 205
Pizarro, Francisca, 552
Pizarro, Francisco, 17, 52, 56, 116, 220, 236, 312, 358, 472, **550–552**
Pizarro, Gonzalo (1512–1548), 220, 469, 524, **552**
Pizarro, Gonzalo (father), 550
Pizarro, Hernando, 143, 220, **552**
Pizarro, Isabel, 553
Pizarro, Juan, 551, **552–553**
Pizzigano, Zuane, 105, 260, 503, 553
Pizzigano chart, 105, *106*, **553**
Plague. *See* Black Death

Plane charts, 501, 504
Planisphaerium, 47
Planispheric astrolabe, *48*
Planking, 617, 618
Plantain. *See* Banana
Plants. *See* Flora
Planudes, Maximus, 569
Plastic surgery, 602
Platen, August, 429
Plateresque, 43
Plato, 259, 602, 604, 605
Platonic Academy, 602
Plautius, Caspar, *76*, *95*
Pleito del Darién, 417–418
Pleitos Colombinos. *See* Lawsuits
Plinean races. *See* Monsters
Pliny the Elder, 14, 123, 294, 648
Plows, 4, 7, 8
Plymouth Company, 154
Plymouth Harbor, 156–157
Pocahontas, 156
Poetae laureati geographia liber unus, 300
Poetry, 158–159
Polaris. *See* North Star
Polaris clock, 245
Polar map, *522*
Polckij, Simeon, 429
Polimetrum, 730
Political institutions, **554–556**
Pollaiuolo, Antonio, 43, 44
Polo, Maffeo, 252, 303, 556
Polo, Marco, 14, 117, 120, 125, 126, 127, 175, 182, 187, 244, 252, 303, 449, **556–558**, 564, 670
Polo, Niccolò, 252, 303, 556
Polyglot Bible. *See* Complutensian Polyglot Bible
Polygyny, 354, 366
Polzer, Charles W., *as contributor*, 490–491
Poma de Ayala, Guamán (Guaman Pomo), 358, 591
Pombo, Rafael, 432
Ponce, Hernando, 272
Ponce de León, Juan, 140, 141, 262, 272, 304, 401, **558–559**, 565, 570, 705
Ponce de León, Rodrigo, 558
Popol Vuh, 362
Population, 636
Porras, Diego de, 721, 727
Porras, Francisco de, 132, 721, 727
Porras, Juan de, 752
Port Conception, 699

VOLUME 1: pp. 1–400; VOLUME 2: pp. 401–754.
*Numbers in boldface refer to the main entry on the
subject. Numbers in italic refer to illustrations.*

VOLUME 1: pp. 1–400; VOLUME 2: pp. 401–754.
Numbers in boldface refer to the main entry on the subject. Numbers in italic refer to illustrations.

VOLUME 1: pp. 1–400; VOLUME 2: pp. 401–754.
Numbers in boldface refer to the main entry on the subject. Numbers in italic refer to illustrations.

W

VOLUME 1: pp. 1–400; VOLUME 2: pp. 401–754.
*Numbers in boldface refer to the main entry on the
subject. Numbers in italic refer to illustrations.*

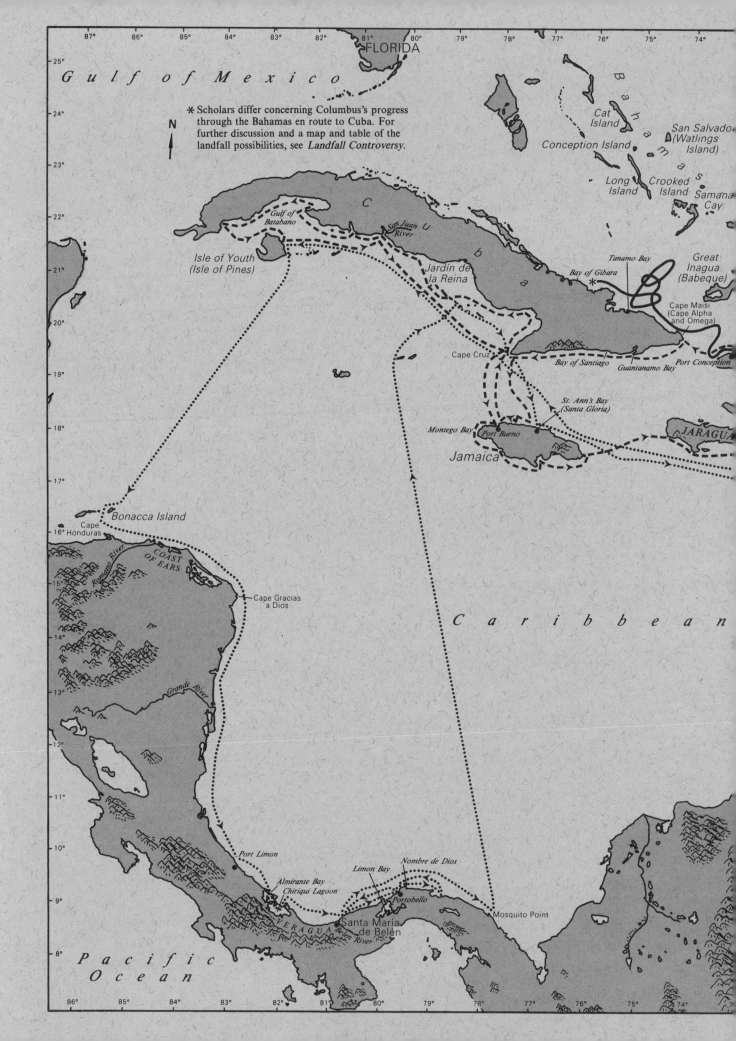

* Scholars differ concerning Columbus's progress through the Bahamas en route to Cuba. For further discussion and a map and table of the landfall possibilities, see *Landfall Controversy*.

Gulf of Mexico

FLORIDA

Bahamas

Cat Island

Conception Island

San Salvador (Watlings Island)

Long Island

Crooked Island

Samana Cay

Gulf of Batabano

C u b a

San Juan River

Jardín de la Reina

Tanamo Bay

Bay of Gibara

*

Great Inagua (Babeque)

Cape Maisi (Cape Alpha and Omega)

Isle of Youth (Isle of Pines)

Cape Cruz

Bay of Santiago

Guantanamo Bay

Port Conception

St. Ann's Bay (Santa Gloria)

Montego Bay

Port Bueno

JARAGUA

Jamaica

Bonacca Island

Cape Honduras

Romano River

COAST OF EARS

Cape Gracias a Dios

Grande River

C a r i b b e a n

Port Limon

Nombre de Dios

Limon Bay

Almirante Bay

Chiriqui Lagoon

Portobello

VERAGUA

Belen River

Santa María de Belén

Mosquito Point

Pacific Ocean